D1571463

FROM LATIN TO SPANISH

Vol. I: Historical Phonology and Morphology of the Spanish Language

By
PAUL M. LLOYD

Professor of Romance Languages,
University of Pennsylvania

Review Copy

MEMOIRS OF THE
AMERICAN PHILOSOPHICAL SOCIETY
Held at Philadelphia
For Promoting Useful Knowledge
Volume 173

Library of Congress Catalog card No.: 86-72883
International Standard Book No.: 0-87169-173-6
US ISSN: 0065-9738

Jacket illustration: Page from Villanova's *Rudimenta Grammaticae* (1500)
in Haebler's *Typographie Ibérique de Quinzième Siècle*

PREFACE

Students of Spanish historical grammar have long felt the need for a new historical grammar of Spanish. Menéndez Pidal's classic *Manual de gramática histórica española* was last revised in 1941, and, although it will never lose its value, can hardly be considered the latest word in the historical grammar of Spanish. V. García de Diego's *Gramática histórica española* of 1951 is only slightly more recent in date of publication.* During the twentieth century, much has been written on Romance and Spanish historical grammar and yet we still lack a synthesis of the research that has illuminated much of the phonetic and morphological development of Spanish. It was to fill this lack that this volume was written. The recent publication of Alvar and Pottier's *Morfología histórica del español* has made the section on inflectional morphology less useful than it might have been, but I believe that I have included in my own sections on inflectional morphology some aspects of study that may still be useful.

This volume was completed, to all intents and purposes, after many years of work and many delays, in 1981. A further year was required for typing the final version, and more than another year passed before the American Philosophical Society accepted it for publication. I have attempted to incorporate in the final version of the text some of the results of more recent research on various problems, but cannot be sure that everything of relevance since 1981 has been included. A second volume will take up problems of word formation and syntactic development.

This book owes much to many people. I can single out only a few who deserve special thanks: to my graduate students who have asked me so many questions over the years; to Curtis Blaylock for supplying material on Latin verbs and Old Spanish past participles which I have incorporated into the text; to Jerry Craddock, for his very useful collection of materials on Old Spanish sound change and morphological change; to Ernst Pul-

---

* Thomas A. Lathrop. *The evolution of Spanish. An introductory historical grammar* (Newark, DE: Juan de la Cuesta, 1980) and Melvyn C. Resnick, *Introducción a la historia de la lengua española* (Washington, DC. Georgetown University Press, 1981) are both intended as introductory texts for undergraduates.

i

gram for a close reading of Chapter One and many suggestions for revisions; to Roger Wright for numerous other suggestions; to the University of Pennsylvania for a summer grant and two sabbatical leaves. The University of Pennsylvania Research Foundation very generously contributed a grant toward the costs of publication. Finally, I must make special mention of my teacher and friend, Yakov Malkiel, who read many sections of this volume in an early form, and whose immense contributions to Romance philology and Spanish historical grammar can hardly be calculated. His influence will be obvious on every page of this book.

Paul M. Lloyd, June 1987

PHONETIC SYMBOLS AND DIACRITICAL MARKS

(Most phonetic symbols in the text are the standard ones of the International Phonetic Alphabet, but in some cases other symbols are utilized.)

[b̄]   voiced bilabial fricative
[č]   voiceless palatal affricate
[đ]   voiced apicodental fricative
[dᶻ]   voiced predorsal affricate
[ə]   shwa, mid central vowel
[g]   voiced dorsovelar fricative
[ḥ]   voiceless pharyngeal fricative
[ļ]   palatal lateral
[ņ]   patatal nasal
[φ]   voiceless bilabial fricative
[ś]   voiceless apicoalveolar sibilant
[š]   voiceless palatal hushing sibilant
[θ]   voiceless interdental fricative
[tˢ]   voiceless predorsal affricate
[x]   voiceless dorsovelar fricative
[ź]   voiced apicoalveolar sibilant
[ž]   voiced palatal hushing sibilant

[̢]   more open (vowels); partially voiced (consonants), e.g. ẹ ọ p̦ ţ
[.]   more closed (vowels), e.g. ẹ ọ
[:]   longer, e.g. a: e:, p: t:

iii

TABLE OF CONTENTS

Chapter 4: From Late Latin to Old Spanish

Chapter 5: From Medieval to Modern Spanish

CHAPTER 1

On The Nature of Linguistic Change

SOUND CHANGE AND SOUND LAWS

One of the great accomplishments of historical linguistics in the nineteenth century was the demonstration of the regularity of sound change, and the establishment of such change as the object of scientific study. Although there has been considerable argument about details, and much disagreement about whether it is valid to regard sound change as essentially regular, in practice all students of historical linguistics have followed this principle. An overwhelming mass of evidence supports it, and no one has thus far been able to show that as a basis for the study of sound change the principle of regularity is not tenable.[1] This principle means that when one examines the same words or morphemes at two stages in the evolution of a language, one finds that in a great number of cases most, if not all, examples of sound A, and certainly all characteristic examples, have become (or been replaced by) sound B. Thus, if a large number of words in Latin containing the consonant spelled with the letter **T**, e.g. (all examples given in the accusative singular form, minus the final -**m**) VĪTA 'life', SITI 'thirst', MŪTU 'mute', PRĀTU 'meadow', ROTA 'wheel', SCŪTU 'shield', STĀTU 'state; position', PATRE 'father', LATUS 'side', and many more, are compared with their modern Spanish reflexes, it will be seen that the T is consistently replaced by a consonant written with the letter **D**: *vida, sed, mudo, prado, rueda, miedo, escudo, estado, padre, lado.* It is not difficult to find a great many examples of this kind of regular replacement in a wide variety of languages.

---

[1] See Pulgram 1955 for a brief but pertinent discussion of the principle of regularity of sound change. Pulgram remarks, "Up to this day, no reputable historical linguist has brought the charge that the 'working hypothesis' of the regularity of sound laws does not work" (61). The reason for this is simple: "If . . . authors did not take this stand [that sound change is regular], they would have no objective, scientific method of describing and classifying the phenomena of phonemic substitution."

1

A closer examination, however, will show that it is not sufficient to write down a simple formula such as "Lat. /t/ > Sp. /d/" in order to sum up in a brief fashion the somewhat longer statement, "The Latin consonant /t/ regularly is replaced by (or changes into) the modern Spanish consonant /d/." Complications appear as soon as one begins to examine a larger sample of Latin words containing /t/, e.g., TRĒS 'three', TABULA 'board', TANTU 'so much', FORTE 'strong', STĀRE 'to stand', AUTUMNU 'autumn', SEPTE 'seven', TECTU 'roof, ceiling', FORTIA 'strength', and others, and compare them with their Spanish descendants. In these cases the Latin /t/ has either remained unchanged or has been replaced by some other consonant: *tres, tabla, tanto, fuerte, estar, otoño, siete, techo, fuerza.*

It is evident, therefore, that even in the case of some very simple sound changes, certain limitations must be put on the statement that sounds change regularly. The amended form of the principle must be, "Sounds change uniformly in the same phonetic environment." In the formula illustrating the fate of Latin /t/, it would be necessary to say that Lat. /t/ becomes Sp. /d/ between vowels or between a vowel and /r/. A short form of this statement would be:

$$\text{Lat. } /t/ > \text{Sp. } /d/ \ /V_____V$$
$$/V_____/r/$$

where V represents any vowel or diphthong (providing that we ignore those diphthongs that prevent voicing, and vowels in hiatus). In order to determine what happened to /t/ in other phonetic conditions, it would be necessary to classify all occurrences of /t/ and their modern Spanish equivalents and then examine the surrounding sounds to see how they have affected the /t/.

If one then sets out to examine another area of vocabulary, it will soon become apparent that further modifications of the basic principle are needed. If we take the Latin words CITĀRE 'to summon, call', EXPLICITU 'straightforward', ROTULA 'little wheel', PATERNU 'paternal', PATRŌNU 'patron, protector', VĪSITĀRE 'to visit', VĪTALE 'vital', and compare them with their Spanish equivalents, we find that the /t/ has been retained: *citar, explícito, rótula* 'kneecap', *paterno, patrón, visitar, vital.* The phonetic environment in which the /t/ appears in these words in no way differs from those cited earlier in which it was replaced by /d/. These examples suffice to show that phonetic conditions alone cannot explain why /t/ has remained in these words. If, however, we attempt to find when these words first appear in written Spanish, it appears that the earliest attestation for any of them is 1220 for *visitar.* The other words have attested first appearances in writing at later dates: *citar* 1490, *explícito* 1737, *rótula* 1727, *paterno* 1343, *patrón* 1450, *vital* 1440 (Corominas 1967). Most of the items in which /t/ becomes /d/, on the other hand, have been part of the vocabulary of Spanish since the beginning. In other words, they have been used continually by speakers since the implantation of spoken Latin in the Iberian peninsula, without any special influence of literary forms. These phonetically aberrant words, on the contrary, which have not participated in this change, are *learned words*. That is, they were taken directly from literary Latin after the adoption of the new system of reading written Latin aloud instituted under the Carolingians as a part of the standardization of religious practice (Wright 1982). Therefore they do not reflect the change of /t/ > /d/ that characterized the popular words. As a result, we must limit the principle of regular sound change further: "Sounds change regularly at the same period of time." Words borrowed from Latin or other languages at a period later than the one in which the /t/ > /d/ replacement occurred will not show that change. Also words that have not been a part of the "popular" vocabulary (i.e. the vernacular stock, which includes items transmitted orally) are not likely to show popular sound changes.[2]

Similarly, on examining the modern equivalents of Latin words in areas outside the Iberian peninsula, we discover that they do not all show the /t/ > /d/ change. The Italian words corresponding to the preceding illustrative examples are *vita, sete, muto, prato, ruota, scudo, padre, lato*. In Rumanian the words are *viaţa, sete, mut, roată, scut, stat* (the missing words having been replaced by words from other sources.) The Italian words are particularly puzzling because two of them show the /t/ > /d/ replacement. Nevertheless, we would be forced to conclude that the change did not occur everywhere in Italy (speaking broadly) or in Rumania. Therefore a further limitation of the principle of regular sound change is required: "Sounds change regularly in the same general geographical area."[3]

Having thus examined briefly a few examples of a particular sound change, we can state in proper form the basic principle of the regularity of sound change: Sounds change regularly when they are found 1) in the same phonetic conditions, 2) at the same period of time, 3) in the same general area (or the same speech community). Some other modifications could also be made for certain special exceptions like the word RETINĒRE, 'to hold back, hold fast', which appears in Spanish as *retener*. In this example, the /t/ was apparently preserved because speakers associated the prefixed verb with the simple verb *tener*, 'to have, hold', and thus did not class it with other words having a /t/ between vowels, but rather as a synchronic derivative of *tener*. In fact, the general principle might be stated as above with the additional proviso: "provided that no other factor

---

[2] This is best explained by medieval diglossia, i.e., the coexistence of spoken Romance vernaculars, much evolved, with more conservative Latin in ecclesiastic/intellectual circles. Bilingual scribes mixed older words, especially those pronounced according to the new system of pronunciation for written Latin adopted with the Carolingian reform, with their own vernacular forms (see Wright 1982).

[3] This limitation can be considered to beg the question because geography is, after all, not an active factor in determining the nature of a speech community. The "same" area is, in reality, the area defined by a single speech community. See note 26 below.

interferes with a sound in any particular word or group of words." Other factors, for example, could be overriding semantic considerations or dialect mixture.[4]

By carefully accounting for all the possible causes of interference with regular sound change, nineteenth-century linguists could conclude that there are no exceptions to sound change. By this statement they meant, of course, not that exceptions to regular change could not be found, but rather that it was necessary to seek and explain all interfering factors. Once every element that could affect the development of a sound and the phonetic conditions in which it appeared was carefully delimited it would turn out that sounds do, in fact, change without exception.[5]

One might ask then whether the basic principle of the regularity of sound change is not so restricted as to make it rather limited.[6] Once again the answer would be that there is a great deal of evidence that sounds do change regularly, but there are numerous factors at work at the same time that may interfere with a sound in one particular word or in a group of words. Although it is risky to compare one science with another, especially when one is a natural science and the other a social science (see below), one might think of Newton's first law of motion. In its simplest formulation it states that an object at rest or in motion will continue in the same state until acted upon by some disturbing force. In practice, it is clear that when one throws an object, it does not continue indefinitely in motion, but soon falls to earth. This effect is produced by the pull of gravity and can thus be explained by the law of gravitation. Air resistance has a further effect on the motion of the object, and the amount of this effect will be determined by the density of the air and the shape of the object. No one would seriously object that Newton's first law does not work simply because we never see any object continue in motion on earth. The laws of motion are postulated on the assumption of motion in a perfect vacuum and in the absence of gravity. The fact that perfect vacuums and the absence of gravity are never found in nature does not invalidate the law. In a similar, although not exactly parallel fashion, the regularity of sound change is not necessarily invalidated because a variety of factors may interfere with its outcome.[7]

---

[4] A variant form of this condition is one presented by Wang: "A sound change is regular *if no other changes compete against it*" (1969, 102; emphasis in original).

[5] It is interesting to note that those who first formulated the principle in its most uncompromising form, i.e., "sound laws know no exception," based themselves on *synchronic* material (Weinreich, Labov, and Herzog 1968, 115, note 23).

[6] One scholar goes so far as to speak of the determination of various sound shifts as the "regularist game": "The whole process of sifting out the data is rather like peeling an onion—we take away layer after layer (analogical changes, sound-substitution changes, borrowing, learned forms, etc.) only to discover, often, that the core of 'regular' forms is minimally small. What, we may wonder, prevents us from advancing further—from peeling away the core too?" (Posner 1966–67, 324–25).

[7] A similar comparison of the principle of regularity and other scientific laws is found in Hall 1968, 118, and Katičić 1970, 52.

A great deal of ink has been spilled over this problem, because scholars have sometimes tended to adopt extreme, dogmatic positions, either affirming complete regularity of all sound changes and condemning those who seek to make the principle more subtle, as believers in chaotic sound change,[8] or asserting that belief in regular sound change is somehow mystical, belied by the evidence of exceptions.[9] There is in reality, however, nothing especially mysterious about such regularity which exists any more than there is in regular changes in other human institutions. Sounds maintain a certain fixed pattern in speech, and if speakers shift a sound in a certain direction, it is not surprising that they should treat all sounds exposed to the same forces in the same way. The problem is whether the principle is worth maintaining unless it can be proved to have no possible exceptions. A more sensible point of view might be that "a sound change *may* be absolutely regular, but then it may not; it is therefore safer to treat 'regular' as a relative term, some sound changes being more regular, others less" (Devine 1970–71, 354).[10]

Such considerations led many influential nineteenth-century linguists to speak of the various regular formulas of sound replacements as "sound laws,"[11] sometimes said to operate blindly. The term is still used in a number of texts, in spite of the fact that the word *law* has frequently been condemned as inadequate and misleading. *Law* tends to suggest a parallel between sound change and the laws of nature, elaborated by scientific theory and confirmed by experimentation. As we saw above, parallels between sound change and natural laws may be drawn, but it is important to note that there are some fundamental differences between them. Natural laws are assumed to operate at all times and places (at least from the human viewpoint), while sound changes are historical events, limited to specific historical periods and well-defined geographical areas. It makes no more sense to speak of a "law of voicing," in reference to the fate of Latin intervocalic /t/ in Ibero-Romance, than it would to speak of a "law of Americanization" to account for the fact that at the end of the American

---

[8] An interesting book on this matter is Vennemann and Wilbur 1972. They quote Schuchardt's very apposite remark: "I would like to know who among pre- and non-neogrammarian linguists, including my own humble self, has ever considered and treated sound change as chaotic"(62).

[9] One radical polemicist even goes so far as to declare: "There is no such thing . . . as a *regular* change (as opposed to the *irregular* change). . . .[T]he whole question of *regular* and *irregular* is absurd in theory and mischievous in practice" (Bonfante 1946, 247–48; emphasis in original). It might be pointed out that this same person found no difficulty in operating with these concepts in his own work.

[10] See Fourquet 1964 and Rodríguez Adrados 1969 for good general discussions of various ideas on "regularity" and "irregularity." A very abstract consideration of the basis of the regularity hypothesis is found in Dyen 1963. Dyen's treatment, however, is based on speculation about "dialect cohesion" rather than on empirical evidence.

[11] Pulgram (1955) remarks that "sound law" is a translation of German *Lautgesetz* in which *Gesetz* might better be translated as 'regularity'. Since *Gesetz* is used in almost all the same contexts as the English word *law*, it seems an appropriate translation. Useful documentation of the original writings on the topic is found in Schneider 1973 and Wilbur 1977.

Revolution all free citizens of the United States ceased to be British subjects and became American citizens. To class historical events as some kind of law may be more likely to obscure than to clarify the problems involved in adequate historical explanations.[12]

Types of Sound Changes

Before attempting to deal with the many and often intricate problems of adequate description and explanation of sound changes and their causes, it is necessary to be clear about the various types of sound changes that can be found.

Assimilation

One of the commonest types of sound change is that in which *a sound or class of sounds adopts a phonetic feature* found in a neighboring sound or sounds. It is then said to have *assimilated* to that sound: in other words, it has become more like it. For example, when the Latin intervocalic /t/ in Ibero-Romance lost the feature of voicelessness and became /d/, speakers stopped turning off the vocal cord vibrations for intervocalic consonants and kept the voicing found in the surrounding vowels. Thus, it can be said that the consonants assimilated to the vowels.

The features adopted in assimilation may be of varying types. In the case of /t/ > /d/, the assimilation was one of *manner of articulation*. Another

---

[12] For a discussion of the problem of historical "laws" in general, see Gardiner 1952, as well as Dray 1964 and McClelland 1975 (especially the first two sections) and the journal *History and Theory*. The problem of regularity is one common to history and the social sciences in general, and is due at least partly to the fact that it does not seem possible to *predict* sound changes, although it could be maintained that if sound change is truly regular it should be possible to make such predictions. A quote from Gallie is especially pertinent:

1) A characteristically genetic explanation seeks to establish, or at least helps to indicate, some kind of continuity, between one or a number of temporally prior conditions and a subsequent result. 2) On the other hand, a characteristically genetic explanation does not pretend to predictive power: the prior event is not, taken in conjunction with certain universal laws, to constitute a sufficient condition of the occurrence of the subsequent event. 3) Moreover, a characteristically genetic explanation emphasizes the one-way passage of time—what came earlier explains, in the genetic sense, what came later, and not *vice versa*. In other words the prior event is not taken, in conjunction with certain universal laws, to constitute both a sufficient and necessary condition of the occurrence of the subsequent event (1955, 161).

Another study (Joynt and Rescher 1959, 368) points out that "explanation in the field of human relations is not wholly reducible to a natural science using truly general laws because both in history and in the social sciences there arises a requirement for generalizations based on time and place-bound particulars. Explanation in history and the social sciences can be furthered by the use of general laws, but cannot be exhausted by the use of such laws." It is even possible to make the claim that "the social studies are not sciences characterized by their own laws, but a heterogeneous collection of inquiries strung together on the common theme of human action" (Louch 1969, 236). Perhaps the same can be said of linguistics, that it is "not so much a field as a field-encompassing field" (Harvey 1966, 55).

type of assimilation often found is to the *place of articulation*. For example, the Old Spanish word *comde* 'count' has become modern Spanish *conde*. The bilabial nasal /m/ has ceased to be bilabial and has adopted the dental articulation of the following /d/. Vowels may also assimilate to the place of articulation of other vowels, a type of assimilation known generally as *vowel harmony* or *metaphony*. For example, the final /i:/ of Lat. POTUĪ 'I was able' was a high vowel. The Spanish reflex *pude* shows that the first vowel has adopted the high articulation of /i:/. (Some scholars prefer to call this last kind of change *umlaut*, its German name.)

If a sound assimilates to another sound found after it in a word, it can be said to be *anticipatory*, as in *comde* > *conde*: that is, the distinctive feature of dentality is anticipated. If, on the other hand, the sound which follows is assimilated to the preceding sound, the assimilation can be called *lag*, as in the English *seven* being pronounced as [sevm], in which the labial quality of /v/ has been held and applied to the nasal. (The traditional terms for these two types of assimilation are "regressive assimilation" for anticipation and "progressive assimilation" for lag. As they are easy to confuse, the terms used above will be employed in this book [Anttila 1972, 73].)

A special type of very common assimilation is *palatalization*, which occurs when a consonant adopts the palatal quality of a neighboring sound and often absorbs it completely. For example, Latin consonants followed by a palatal semivowel (or *yod*) became pronounced as palatals in Late Latin, e.g., Lat. VĪNEA 'vineyard' > Sp. *viña*, Lat. FĪLIU 'son' > It., Port. *fi[l]o* (spelled *gli* in Italian orthography and *lh* in Portuguese, e.g. *figlio*, and *filho*). In these examples, instead of pronouncing in a linear fashion first a consonant and then a palatal, speakers produced both simultaneously.

Dissimilation

This phenomenon is the opposite of assimilation. In dissimilation a sound loses a feature of articulation that it shares with a neighboring sound and thus becomes less like it. For example, the early Ibero-Romance reflex of Lat. HOMINE 'man' > *omne*, underwent a dissimilation of the second nasal in the Castilian dialect. The feature of nasality was lost in this consonant which then became a vibrant /r/ > *hombre* (cf. Lat. FĒMINA 'woman' > *hembra* 'female', *NŌMINE 'name' > *nombre*, etc.) Dissimilation seems to affect liquids and nasals more frequently than other types of sound,[13] e.g., Lat. ARBORE 'tree' > Sp. *árbol*, It. *albero*.

Metathesis

This is the change of the position of a sound in a word. For example, Lat. MĪRĀCULU 'miracle' > OSp. *miraglo*, metathesized the liquids producing

---

[13] For a discussion of the problem of dissimilation, see Posner 1961, and the review by Togeby 1963–64. Further pertinent discussion is found in Malkiel 1967.

the MSp. *milagro.* If two consonants change places as in the preceding example, the process is called *reciprocal metathesis.* If only one sound changes place, it is called *simple metathesis,* e.g., Late Lat. APPECTORĀRE 'to hug', lit. 'to press against the chest' > Sp. *apretar.*

Syncope

This is the loss of an unstressed vowel within a word. For example, almost all Latin posttonic vowels in the penultimate syllable except for /a/ were lost in the development of Castilian, e.g., Lat. COMITE 'companion; count' > OSp. *comde,* MĪRĀCULU > *miraglo.*

Apocope

When it is the final vowel of a word which is lost, the process is called *apocope,* e.g., Lat. SŌLE 'sun' > Sp. *sol, alguno > algún.*

Apheresis

This is the loss of an initial syllable, e.g., Late Lat. APOT(H)ĒCA (<Greek) 'storeroom, wine cellar' > Sp. *bodega.*

Epenthesis

This phenomenon is the addition of a new sound to a word. For example, in the Lat. (H)UMERU 'shoulder', the loss of the posttonic vowel brings into contact the two consonants /m/ and /r/. In this particular combination, the opening of the lips following the pronunciation of the labial nasal produces a sound that gives the acoustic impression of a bilabial occlusive /b/, resulting in the modern form *hombro.* Such epenthetic consonants are sometimes called *intrusive consonants.* For example, Lat. PHASEOLU 'kidney bean' developed an intrusive /r/ in Sp. *frijol.* Intrusive /r/ usually appears after occlusives, especially dentals, e.g., Lat. STĒLLA 'star' > Sp. *estrella,* Sp. *estopajo > estropajo* 'mop.'

When the sound added is a vowel at the beginning of a word, it is termed a *prothetic vowel.* For example, in many areas of the Roman Empire the combination of initial /s/ with another consonant developed a supporting vowel, e.g. Lat. SCHOLA 'school' > Sp. *escuela,* Fr. *école.*

Some other relatively rare types of phonetic change are discussed below, p. 28.

How Do Sounds Change?

Since linguistics is (or aspires to be) an empirical science (as far as it is possible), one might think that historical linguists would have dedicated much time and effort to observing sound change in progress in order to gain some idea of how changes have occurred in the past. In reality, however, very little investigation of current sound change has been undertaken.[14] The majority of historical linguists have been content to rely on elaborate "thought-experiments" in determining how sound change actually happens, rather than on direct investigation of real speech communities (Labov 1970, 202). Much more effort seems to have been expended in explaining away any inconvenient data that fail to fit into preconceived theories than to elaborating theories that accurately fit the data.

An essential preliminary to any discussion of sound change is a careful definition of the terms involved. Too often scholars have tended to use a variety of common words that are so ambiguous that they can be interpreted to mean a number of different things. First, we should ask just what is meant by "sound change." In the preceding sections, the change of Lat. /t/ to Sp. /d/ can be understood primarily by comparing two historical epochs and how the words containing /t/ at one period were pronounced by Latin speakers and how modern Spanish speakers pronounce the same words.[15] The brief formula /t/ > /d/ is a statement of diachronic correspondence and nothing else.[16] It does not "explain" anything in the sense that we are given any information about how, when, or why the change took place. It is not even clear whether we should speak of sound "change" rather than sound "replacement."[17] Nevertheless, unless we are to be content to set up tables of correspondences and do nothing more, some attempt must be made to examine the circumstances that made it possible to formulate such a statement.

How did the feature [−voice] become [+voice] in Late Latin (if we use feature notation)? May we assume that the correspondence formula represents a change that occurred instantaneously in the speech of all speakers of Latin in the area where the change took place? In other words, is it likely that at one moment everyone was saying [patre] and the next day (or the next moment) [padre]? No one has ever observed such an instantaneous change. Nothing that we know about the actual conditions of speech indicates that an abrupt shift of this nature could take place. In fact, the only reason for proposing such an absurdity is to discard it as a hypothesis of how sounds change.

If it is inconceivable that all speakers of Latin in the western Roman Empire should have made a shift of this nature at the same time, is it any

---

[14] Some studies were made at the end of the nineteenth century and the beginning of the twentieth: Rousselot 1892, Passy 1892, Gauchat 1905.

[15] Even a word like "same" may lend itself to misinterpretation. Can we avoid a lurking suspicion that Lat. PATER and Sp. *padre* are not really just the "same" word in two different historical periods?

[16] See Andersen 1972, especially 11–18, for a searching discussion of the difference between "diachronic correspondences" and phonetic change.

[17] For example, Hoenigswald 1960, 8.2–8.3. Lord speaks of sound substitutions rather than change: "It is not even certain that sounds do actually change; it could be said that new pronunciations are substituted sounds spread by imitation or some other process" (1966, 81).

easier to imagine such an abrupt change occurring in the speech of a small group or even of a single speaker? As far as we can tell, people simply do not act in this way.

One assumption is that if sounds cannot be considered to change suddenly and abruptly, they must therefore change gradually and unconsciously. This theory is supported by our experience of some changes in other aspects of life without our being necessarily aware of them because they happen so gradually. One's physical appearance, for example, changes throughout life, and yet from one day to the next we have the impression that we look the same simply because the physical changes are so slight over very short periods of time. It is only when we look at photographs of ourselves taken years apart that we realize that our appearance has changed, often very strikingly.[18] It is possible, then, to conceive of sound change as a very similar type of physical process that proceeds by infinitesimal steps unnoticed by speakers. Sound change in a linguistic community, in this view, is simply a slow shifting of statistical averages. If this assumption is true, it must follow that to observe sound change in progress must be exceedingly difficult, since it would involve making extremely detailed and complex observations over a considerable period of time. One scholar imagines, in an elaborate thought-experiment, what procedures would be necessary, in the following terms:

> Suppose that over a period of fifty years we made, each month, a thousand accurate acoustic records of clearly identifiable initial /t/'s and /d/'s, all from the members of a tight-knit community. At the end of the first five years we could compute and draw the curve representing the sixty thousand observations made up to that time: the resulting graph would be a reasonably accurate portrayal of this portion of the community's expectation distribution. After another year, the first year's observations would be dropped, the sixth year's added, and a new curve drawn. Each subsequent year the same operation would be performed. The resulting series of forty-six curves would show whatever drift had taken place. The drift might well not be in any determinate direction: the maxima might wander a bit further apart, then come closer again, and so on. Nevertheless, the drift thus shown would constitute sound change (Hockett 1958, 444–45).

Although such a vast and complicated experiment is conceivable, in practical terms it would probably not be possible. Therefore, according to this

---

[18] This was the reasoning of Jespersen (1922, 166), quoted approvingly by Hockett (1965, 193): "But no one knows if he pronounces his mother-tongue in every respect in the same manner as he did twenty years ago. May we not suppose that what happens with faces happens here also? One lives with a friend day in and day out, and he appears to be just what he was years ago, but someone who returns home after a long absence is at once struck by the changes which have gradually accumulated in the interval."

theory, we must be satisfied with the conclusion that "no one has yet observed sound change" (Hockett 1958, 439).

This conclusion seems to leave linguists in an untenable position. There is plenty of evidence that sounds have changed in all languages throughout history, and yet the theory that all changes must occur in gradual and practically unobservable steps implies that empirical data for observing these changes are almost unobtainable. If this conclusion is valid and, in fact, it really is impossible to observe sound change in progress, as so many have claimed, then, of course, we must accept it. But we may be left with some doubts. The experiment outlined above was a purely mental one. We may be tempted to ask: has anyone ever tried to conduct any actual experiments on sound change in progress? Is the conclusion that sound change is unobservable based on concrete evidence, or is it simply the result of adopting *a priori* a certain kind of theory about how sounds *must* change? After all, other linguistic changes have been observed in progress, such as changes in morphology, syntax, and vocabulary, even in the life and usage of one person.[19] Why should only sound change seem to be unobservable?

Some critics have attempted to challenge the bases of this theory and to argue that sounds do not necessarily have to change by small, unnoticed steps. One linguist argues that he cannot conceive of any gradual articulatory shift between an alveolar trilled [r] and a uvular trilled [r] (a sound shift that has already occurred in French and Portuguese and is now taking place in certain dialects of modern Spanish) (Hoenigswald 1960, 73).[20] He suggests, therefore, that the theory of phonetic change by gradual, imperceptible steps may be simply "a remnant of prephonemic days." Although such reasoning could hardly constitute proof that all sound changes must be non-gradual, others have followed this lead to come to precisely this conclusion. Thus, from one extreme we are carried to another: if some sound changes are not gradual, then no sound changes can be gradual. One scholar even goes so far as to deny that there is any evidence whatever for gradual sound change: "Subject to counter-evidence yet to be produced, we reject gradualness as a necessary condition for the implementation of any phonological change" (King 1969, 115).[21]

One of the factors favoring a belief in abrupt sound changes is probably the fact that separate phonemes are distinct classes of sounds. Since how-

---

[19] One well known example is the development of Goethe's language throughout his life. See Maurer 1932 and Mattausch 1965. Of course, it is possible that in Goethe's case we are dealing with a much more formal literary dialect rather than natural, spontaneous speech.

[20] This remark should suffice to put us on guard against relying on imagination in the absence of demonstrable facts. A gradual articulatory shift from a trilled alveolar [r] to a uvular pronunciation is not only possible but has been observed and studied in Swedish (*Language* 48, p. 14, note 3) and in certain Spanish dialects (Granda 1973, 456).

[21] Surveys of various theories of graduality versus abruptness are found in Bhat 1968 and Scalise 1976. Sturtevant (1947, chap. 8) showed that not all sound changes can be gradual but did not leap to the conclusion that none of them is.

ever, "classes" are, to some extent at least, abstract categories, they are realized by physical sounds that may be more or less like sounds in other classes without the classes themselves thereby being merged. Thus, any realization of /t/ must still belong to the phoneme /t/ regardless of how close it may be to normal realizations of /d/. In phonetic terms it is possible to conceive of a gradual addition of varying degrees of voicing to realizations of /t/, but phonemically any given sound must be either /t/ or not-/t/. There is no way in which we can classify a sound as partially in the category of /t/ and partially in the class of /d/ (except, of course, in the case of phonological neutralization). Therefore, it is difficult to imagine how one phoneme might gradually merge with another. Phonemic change, for this school of thought, must necessarily be sudden, although there is no way that we could hope to observe this kind of change, any more than, according to the other school, it is possible to observe gradual sound change.[22] A very similar point of view is held by some theorists of generative phonology who maintain that the only consideration is not the actual realization of phonemic systems ("performance") but rather the underlying system that determines that performance ("competence"). Since one of the notational conventions of this school requires that underlying phonological systems be represented by the absence or presence of phonological features, sound change can be imagined to be simply the addition or subtraction of a "rule" in the underlying grammar. A natural conclusion would be that "sounds don't change; grammars do" (King 1969, 109).[23] The adding or deleting of a rule is necessarily abrupt since a rule is either present or not. No halfway position is possible.

It would not do to conclude that the last word has been said. As one linguist remarks regarding the description of sound change as the change of rules of grammar: "What the rule changes always describe then, is the before–after relationship. They give a mechanism for description, not a historical explanation, except in accidental cases. This fact is often forgotten" (Anttila 1972, 129). Another scholar examines some of the arguments in favor of abruptness of change and dismisses them as the result of "lack of knowledge and imagination" and contributing "as little to our understanding of sound change as Zeno's paradox does to our understanding of motion" (Andersen 1972, 14). At this point, one not dogmatically committed to any narrow theory may well wonder whether any theory, or, indeed, any evidence available to us, can cast light on the problem of "graduality" versus "abruptness" of sound change. A careful reading of opposing views on the subject reveals that at least part of the problem lies

---

[22] "Yet there is no reason to believe that we would ever be able to detect this kind of sudden event by direct observation" (Hockett 1957, 456–57).

[23] Postal argues in the same fashion: "sound change [is] *the addition of rules to grammars*" (1968, 270). A more intelligent and realistic comment is: "A grammar is changed by successive generations of speakers; grammars don't change, speakers change grammars" (Maher 1973, 51a).

in the fact that "graduality" has been used indiscriminately to refer to at least four different things: physical graduality, graduality in number of speakers, graduality of lexical diffusion, and graduality of conditioning. Those who claim that change is "abrupt" seem to be referring to the difference or correspondence between synchronic states of a community (often with a distressing lack of precision about just how they conceive sound change to occur), while those who opt for graduality can cite in their favor statistical averages of usage by speakers of different ages.[24] So as one scholar says: "To the question whether phonological change is sudden or gradual, the only possible answer is 'Both' " (Sommerstein 1977, 250).

What is needed then is not new speculation but rather much more hard evidence of what is actually occurring in language today. It is especially important that investigations not be deterred by *a priori* assumptions about the impossibility of observing sound change, or theoretical considerations about how sound change *should* happen. Those who have actually studied sound change in progress have discovered that much of the confusion over its nature has resulted from some basic misconceptions.[25] The first is that the focus of sound change must be on the *idiolect,* the speech of a single individual. Linguists of most theoretical schools seem to have accepted this notion without question: the *Junggrammatiker,* exemplified in the work of Hermann Paul, the schools of European structuralism inspired by Saussure, American descriptivists following Bloomfield, and, most recently the theoreticians of generative phonology headed by Chomsky. Although lip service is frequently paid to the idea that language is a social product, in practice the study of speech has often been limited to the usage of one person, in a written text at that, described as though it represents the language of an entire community. The result of this approach is what Labov calls the "Saussurian paradox": namely, that since that which is common to all members of a community can be found in any one individual, a linguist can therefore analyze his own idiolect and claim that it is the language of the whole community, while the study of individual usage, either that of single individuals or groups of individuals, requires an investigation of many different persons (Labov 1975, 826).

A second misconception is that language must be conceived as homogeneous, i.e., as though there were a single norm of competence that is the same for the individual and all members of his speech community.[26]

---

[24] It should be noted that King does not deny the gradual spread of sound change throughout a linguistic community (1969, 117ff.) which is what Andersen (1972) seems to mean also when he affirms the graduality of sound change. Andersen's strictures are a good illustration of how the vague use of words has confused issues. In fact, nine different meanings for the adjective *gradual* are given in Schourup 1972.

[25] Much of what follows is based on Weinreich, Labov, and Herzog 1968, an absolutely fundamental item for any serious study of historical linguistics.

[26] "Speech community" is a purposely vague term. It may refer to a single small group or all the speakers of a single language. Labov says most appropriately that "[I]t seems plausible to define a speech community as a group of speakers who share a set of social attitudes toward language" (1970, 74, note 38).

Again, all major schools of linguistics seem to have assumed that whatever differences of pronunciation exist among individuals in the same speech community must be due largely to personal differences only, or possibly to the various physical or psychological factors that may interfere with speech production. The norm of the speech community must be, according to this view, a sort of average of the speech of all its members, or the abstract, underlying system, assumed to be the same for all speakers. Those differences that cannot be explained as the result of individual idiosyncrasies can be ascribed to a combination of different standards, usually geographically based, i.e., "dialect mixture." As Labov expresses it:

> There is a kind of folk-myth deeply embedded among linguists that before they themselves arrived on the scene there existed a homogeneous, single-style group who really "spoke the language." Each investigator feels that his own community has been corrupted from this normal model in some way—by contact with other languages, by the effects of education and pressure of the standard language, or by taboos and the admixture of specialized dialects or jargons. But we have come to the realization that this is the *normal* situation—that heterogeneity is not only common, it is the natural result of basic linguistic factors (Labov 1970, 42).

As an example of this type of explanation, we could take the speech of a speaker of Spanish who sometimes pronounces a final aspirate [-h] where at other times he pronounces a final sibilant [-s]. This variation could be said to be the result of a mixture of two separate dialects. Alternatively, one could claim that "free variation" is the only possible explanation, meaning that a person may use either pronunciation with no functional difference.[27]

Thus, if only one individual's pronunciation, which is presumed to be basically uniform, is to be the sole object of study in historical linguistics, the inevitable result must be the insoluble difficulties sketched above. According to the theoretical model adopted, sound change should be impossible, and yet sounds do change. The conclusion that such changes must be unobserved and/or unobservable seems to be the only way out of the dilemma.

Another possible solution would be the assumption that sound change must occur at a period in a speaker's life when his linguistic habits are not yet firmly fixed, as they seem to be for adults. In other words, some have supposed that sound change occurs not throughout one's life, but rather during childhood, when one is still learning his first language. There is an evident discontinuity between one generation and another. What could be more natural, then, than to assume that this "generation gap" is the point

---

[27] As an example of this attitude, several investigators of the English of New York City chose to believe that the presence or absence of postvocalic [-r] was simply massive free variation (Labov 1966, 35–38).

at which changes in pronunciation occur? If children learn their parents' language imperfectly, they can introduce innovations that thereafter become part of their mature language competence. There would be no contradiction between this theory and the theory of gradual, imperceptible change, since it could be argued that if children realized that they were speaking differently from their parents they would naturally notice and try to correct their pronunciation—unless, possibly, the generations are on unfriendly terms. A good statement of this conception of sound change is the following:

> The transmission of pronunciation from one generation to another is discontinuous, in the sense that the child is forced to learn everything over again. During apprenticeship, doubtless, hereditary dispositions play some part, but it is not difficult to realize how many accidents may affect the integrity of pronunciation with each new generation. It rarely happens, indeed, that when its apprenticeship is ended the child's phonetic system is exactly like that of its parents (Vendryes 1925, 1936).

There is, indeed, some evidence that different generations show differences in pronunciation of some sounds,[28] which would seem to confirm the supposition that sound changes occur with each generation, but there is no consistent pattern of regular alteration with every generation as might be expected if change occurred always and only during childhood,[29] nor does the theory account for the direction of change. Likewise the supposition implies that a change is completed in a single generation. Finally, there is evidence that although children learn to speak primarily from their parents, their language usage is modified by their peers and slightly older children (Weinreich, Labov, and Herzog 1968, 145). In short, to the misconceptions regarding the idiolect as the primary object of study and the supposed homogeneity of language and linguistic systems, there must be added the misconception that change can occur only between generations. It would not do, of course, to conclude that there is *no* relation between language change and children's learning of language, but there is no simple one-to-one relationship between the generations of a family and linguistic change. In some instances, for example, certain ways of expression may be adopted by an individual as he becomes older simply because he is accommodating himself to a new role in society: that of "senior citizen."

---

[28] Rousselot gave an example of how his own pronunciation of the palatal liquid [ḽ] differed from that of his sister who was four years younger than he. While he maintained a palatal lateral in all positions, his sister used a palatal fricative [j] in all positions except after velar consonants. Younger people used [j] in all positions (1892, 265).

[29] Sommerfelt emphasizes this point: "L'enfant joue un rôle important dans l'évolution sans que les alternances de générations soient en elles-mêmes la cause de l'évolution. Si elles l'étaient l'évolution aurait un caractère beaucoup plus régulier qu'elle ne l'a. Les facteurs d'importance pour la compréhension des changements sont très divers: évolution matérielle et spirituelle du groupe social, manifeste surtout dans le vocabulaire, mobilité sociale à l'intérieur du groupe, influence d'autres langues et de substrats, etc." (1970, 139).

Sound change, however, may not be affected in the same way as other features of language.

It cannot be claimed that having exposed certain widespread misconceptions about the nature of sound change, we are now in possession of all there is to know about the subject. Nevertheless, any reasonably satisfactory theory of sound change must deal first with the basic fact that languages are *not* homogeneous (including single dialects) and that whatever varieties exist in the speech of individuals or speech communities are not simple peculiarities that can be averaged out, or some vague kind of dialect mixture. The differences that exist in usage are *systematic* because language is a *differentiated system*, composed of a variety of coexisting subsystems: "[I]n most speech communities distinct forms of the same language . . . coexist in roughly the same proportion in all of the geographic subregions of the community" (Weinreich, Labov, and Herzog 1968, 159). Their conclusions, a set of general principles for the study of language change, deserve careful consideration:

1. Linguistic change is not to be identified with random drift proceeding from inherent variation in speech. Linguistic change begins when the generalization of a particular alternation in a given subgroup of the speech community assumes direction and takes on the character of orderly differentiation.

2. The association between structure and homogeneity is an illusion. Linguistic structure includes the orderly differentiation of speakers and styles through rules which govern variation in the speech community; native command of the language includes the control of such heterogeneous structures.

3. Not all variability and heterogeneity in language structure involves change; but all change involves variability and heterogeneity.

4. The generalization of linguistic change throughout linguistic structure is neither uniform nor instantaneous; it involves the covariation of associated changes over substantial periods of time, and is reflected in the diffusion of isoglosses over areas of geographical space.

5. The grammars in which linguistic change occurs are grammars of the speech community. Because the variable structures contained in language are determined by social functions, idiolects do not provide the basis for self-contained or internally consistent grammars.

6. Linguistic change is transmitted within the community as a whole; it is not confined to discrete steps within the family. Whatever discontinuities are found in linguistic change are the products of specific discontinuities within the community, rather than inevitable products of the generational gap between parent and child.

7. Linguistic and social factors are closely interrelated in the development of language change. Explanations which are confined to one or the other aspect, no matter how well constructed, will fail to account for the

rich body of regularities that can be observed in empirical studies of language behavior (Weinreich, Labov, and Herzog 1968, 187–88).[30]

A good illustration of the relation between a sound change and social attitudes and norms is found in Labov's study (1963) of the change in the realizations of the diphthong /au/ on Martha's Vineyard from a low or slightly backed [au] to a centralized [əu] during a period of about thirty years. He discovered that, far from needing massive documentation over a period of many years, all one had to do was interview a number of informants (69, in fact) of different ages over a relatively short period. Relying on the results of the *Linguistic Atlas of New England* (Kurath 1941), Labov found that in 1933, when interviews for the atlas were made on Martha's Vineyard, there was only a slight trace of centralization of /au/. The oldest speaker interviewed in 1961, a man of 92, showed the same pattern of pronunciation as that revealed in the atlas. An examination of the pronunciation of other speakers from decreasing age groups showed that there was an increasing amount of centralization before voiceless obstruents (e.g., in words like *out* [əʊt], *about* [əbəʊt], *mouth* [məʊθ], etc.), paralleling the decrease in age. In other words, the centralized pronunciation has become the norm among the younger inhabitants of the island.

Superficially, it might appear that the correlation between age and the progress of this particular sound change confirms the hypothesis that generational differences are the cause of a sound change. A closer look at the social situation on Martha's Vineyard, however, reveals that the problem cannot be related simply to a difference in generations, but rather to the overall social pattern of the island. Martha's Vineyard was once an independent community, but in the last generation has come to rely increasingly on the summer vacation trade for its economy. Much of the land has been bought by outsiders who do not reside permanently on the island. The reaction of the natives has ranged from "fiercely defensive contempt for outsiders to enthusiastic plans for furthering the tourist economy. A study of the data shows that high centralization of /ai/ and /au/ is closely correlated with expressions of strong resistance to the incursions of the summer people" (Labov 1963, 297).

The centralization began in a particular subgroup on the island, a rural community of Yankee fishermen, descendants of the original settlers. From this nucleus it spread to a group of Indians, and a generation later to the descendants of Portuguese settlers. In another study, Labov concludes:

---

[30] A very similar set of general principles is presented by Vennemann in Vennemann and Wilbur 1972, 171–74, a book which seems to imply that there is some connection between this view of language development and transformational-generative grammar, which is hardly the case (see Anttila 1972, chap. 6). He makes no reference to Weinreich, Labov, and Herzog (1968), although the similarities between Schuchardt's viewpoint and theirs are quite striking.

It appeared that the rise of (au) was correlated with the successive entry into the main stream of island life of groups that had previously been partially excluded. It was concluded that a social value had been [more or less arbitrarily] associated with the centralization of (ay) and (aw), and that the social value could best be expressed as "native status as a Vineyarder." Thus to the extent that an individual felt able to claim and maintain status as a native Vineyarder, he adopted increasing centralization of (ay) and (aw). Sons who had tried to earn a living on the mainland, and afterwards returned to the island, developed an even higher degree of centralization than their fathers had used. But to the extent that a Vineyarder abandoned his claim to stay on the island and earn his living there, he also abandoned centralization and returned to the standard uncentralized forms (Labov 1968, 269).

From this study and from the study of sound changes in New York City, Labov reached certain general conclusions about the manner in which a sound change progresses. A sound change, in his view, begins in a particular subgroup of a linguistic community during a period in which there has been, for some reason, a weakening of its separate identity. The form that begins to change is often a sign of regional status and at first is simply a linguistic *variable*. The variable is then generalized to all members of the subgroup who may not be conscious of its having any special social function. As Ferguson and Gumperz put it: *"Any group of speakers of language X which regards itself as a close social unit will tend to express its group solidarity by favoring those linguistic innovations which set it apart from other speakers who are not part of the group"* [original emphasis] (1960, 9). The variable is now, in Labov's terms, an *indicator,* a function of group membership. As new generations of the group respond to the same social pressures, they adopt the form and exaggerate it beyond the limits of their elders. This is *hypercorrection from below.* The variable is now indicative of age level as well as of group membership. As other subgroups in the speech community adopt the values of the original group, they adopt the variable also and the function of group membership spreads to all those who share "a common set of values in regard to language." The change is now a *marker,* one of the norms of the speech community to which all members react in the same way (although not necessarily in a conscious fashion). The position of the sound in the phonological system has an effect on other related sounds (a topic discussed in detail below) and a readjustment of the system takes place. Any new subgroups that enter the speech community after this will adopt the original variable and any related changes as though they were all on the same level. As Labov terms it, this process constitutes a *recycling stage,* and is a source of "continual origination of new changes."

If the change in question does not originate with the subgroup having the highest status in the community ("status" being defined differently in different types of communities), the members of the high status group may stigmatize the changed form. Such stigmatization will have the effect of *change from above*: that is, those who use the stigmatized form will become conscious of the *prestige model*, the speech norm of the high status group. Speakers who wish to imitate this model will begin to correct themselves sporadically and irregularly in careful speech and the prestige form is the one they will hear themselves using, even when they do not manage to avoid the use of the stigmatized form. The variable now shows "regular stylistic stratification as well as social stratification," with careful speech contrasting with casual speech styles. At this stage there may be further hypercorrection, but this time hypercorrection from above: that is, the careful speech of those who want to avoid the stigmatized form will exaggerate the prestige form in a direction farther away from the condemned form than the limits set by the prestige group. In extreme cases the changed form may become the topic of overt comment, or a *stereotype* which may disappear from actual use although in common opinion it may still be considered to exist as a sign of ignorant, uncultivated speech. If, on the other hand, the changed form originated with the high status group, it will become the prestige model and will be imitated by other groups to the extent that they come into contact with the prestige model and try to imitate it (Labov 1968, 278–80).

Alternatively, a group which formerly was in a position of relative social inferiority in a society may displace a dominant class and reject those linguistic features that do not correspond to its own usage. Norms that were formerly condemned are now accepted as high prestige models. It has often happened that the social estimation of a particular usage becomes reversed and a pronunciation formerly looked down upon is accepted as the norm for all.

Many of the basic implications of the type of research done by Labov had been realized long before by Menéndez Pidal in *Orígenes del español* (first edition 1926) who observed the fluctuations in spelling in Low Latin documents from ninth and tenth century Spain and concluded that these fluctuations did not reflect just anarchic "free variation" or "dialect mixture" but rather the coexistence and competition between varying linguistic norms:

> Cualquier cambio en la actividad colectiva tradicional, lo mismo respecto al lenguaje, que a la canción popular, que a la costumbre jurídica, etc., se funda en el hecho de que muchas generaciones *consecutivas* participan de una misma idea innovadora y la van realizando persistentemente, a pesar de pequeñas variantes en el modo de concebirla; constituyen una tradición nueva, en pugna con otra tradición más antigua. . . . La innovación lingüística individual tiene que vencer la resistencia enormemente mayor que le ofrece la inmensa masa de hablantes apegados a una tradición arraigada. Un cambio fonético no suele ser nunca obra exclusiva de las tres o cuatro generaciones en que de un modo arbitrario se considera dividida la población conviviente, sino que es producto de

una idea o un gusto tradicional que persiste a través de muchas genera-
ciones de hablantes (532–33).[31]

Even earlier one can find similar thoughts, although not usually elaborated
to the extent they are now (see note 28 above).

Implications for Historical Linguistics

There is no reason for assuming that phonetic change in the past operated any differently than it does today. The same general factors, *mutatis
mutandis,* that act to produce sound change today must have been active at
all times in very similar ways. Today, however, we cannot conduct the
type of sociolinguistic research on the past that has been so illuminating for
present-day changes. We often have only a few skimpy data that may hint
at the social factors that influenced the spread of a particular historical
change. Ancient historians were not sociologically oriented and more often
preferred to recount the deeds of illustrious men, rather than the obscure
movements of the lower social classes. Most often we have to utilize
indirect evidence and just speculate about the social forces that may have
been at work.

When it comes to evidence of particular sound changes, once again the
type of evidence we are forced to deal with does not lend itself to easy
interpretation. For one thing, scribes were unlikely to record purely phonetic changes that did not affect the phonemic system or which violated
the established rules of spelling. At the beginning of the voicing of the
intervocalic /t/ in the western Roman Empire, for example, most speakers
may well have been completely unaware that some voicing was being
added to the articulation of the consonant.[32] Even if a scribe happened to
notice some difference in speech, he would not be inclined to write differently, but would rather follow the established traditions of spelling. As
long as the consonant was identified with the phoneme /t/, anyone
wanting to write a word containing it would have used the letter *t,* regardless of whether the the pronunciation was completely voiceless or not.
Even if a phonemic split had occurred and a new phoneme had become
part of the system of speech, the absence of any letter (or any tradition of
inventing new letters) to represent it would have inclined scribes to maintain the older spelling.[33] Only in the case of phonemic mergers are we
likely to find some evidence of phonetic change. In the latter case, less
skilled scribes who are not certain of correct spellings are more inclined to
make spelling mistakes that show us that a sound change has occurred.
Nevertheless, in spite of these difficulties, the recent discoveries of the

---

[31] See Lloyd 1970 for more details.

[32] Many speakers of modern American English are probably unaware that they regularly
pronounce an intervocalic /-t-/ with voicing. See Malécot and Lloyd 1968.

[33] Menéndez Pidal gives a sketch of the problems faced by the early Romance scribes when
trying to represent the new sounds of Romance (*Orígenes,* §§1–11).

close relation between sound change and social change will at the very least alert us to the possibilities of finding some indications in the past of similar relations.[34]

The Spread of a Sound Change

The problems of "graduality" versus "abruptness," discussed briefly above, needs to be reexamined from a different perspective. Now that we have seen how the adoption of a sound change is related to changes in social structure and social attitudes, it is appropriate to consider how particular innovations spread through the language as a whole.

Conditioned and Unconditioned Change

In the example of the change in the pronunciation of vowels on Martha's Vineyard studied by Labov, the change of [aṵ] to [əṵ] was a conditioned sound change. The new pronunciation appears only before voiceless obstruents. As long as this phonetic condition persists, the diphthong /au/ will have two realizations on Martha's Vineyard. If, however, the centralized pronunciation should be extended to other positions and then finally to all positions, the final result would be the pronunciation [əṵ] everywhere. The change would thus become unconditioned, and the historical linguist, when setting up a correspondence formula, would simply write /au/ > /əu/.

It is in relation to the extension of a pronunciation to new conditions that we can see one aspect of sound change that definitely is gradual. If we set up a table representing different conditions for a new sound (abbreviated C_1, C_2, C_3, C_4) and place the older pronunciation A and the newer pronunciation B in relation to different time periods (abbreviated t_1, t_2, t_3, t_4, t_5), we will have a paradigm of a sound change A > B from a conditioned to an unconditioned change:[35]

	t_1	t_2	t_3	t_4	t_5
C_1	A	B	B	B	B
C_2	A	A	B	B	B
C_3	A	A	A	B	B
C_4	A	A	A	A	B

Lexical Diffusion

In addition to an extension of a new pronunciation to new phonetic conditions, it appears that a sound change often spreads from one mor-

---

[34] See particularly Labov 1972 for some illustrations of how the present can illuminate the past.
[35] This table is adapted from Wang 1969, 20. See also Chen and Hsieh 1971.

pheme to another rather than being used at once in all morphemes having the appropriate phonetic conditions in which it might appear. The effects of this type of extension are that at any one time and place some words may be pronounced with the older pronunciation, some with the new, and others with both. As Chen puts it:

> Instead of changing a speaker's entire vocabulary overnight, as it were, sound change begins as an innovative pronunciation of a single word or a group of words, and then progressively spreads to other portions of the lexicon. . . . [E]xceptions . . . can be regarded as residual forms of a sound change which has not yet completed its course, or has come to a premature end, or has been thwarted by a competing sound change overlapping with it along the time dimension (1972, 493).

Varying pronunciations may also be distributed geographically, as can be seen in the map (fig. 1, see p. 69)[36] In the case of NŌS ALTERŌS, the form found in Spain shows a different development: /alC/ > /aC/.[37] In other words, it appears that the pronunciation /au/ is dependent not only on the area, but also on the particular word in which it is found.

In many instances, there may be no geographical distribution of variant pronunciations. Instead, there will be a large number of doublets in the speech of many individuals. The use of one form or another will be dependent on the interaction of a variety of different factors—social, personal, etc. To quote one scholar:

> At any moment, between the initiation and the conclusion of these changes, we have a state characterized by the presence of more or less free variants, so that the speakers have the choice between alternative expressions. In each case the choice will be determined by an interplay of factors, some linguistic, some esthetic and social, an interplay so complex that most often the choice will appear as being due to pure chance (Vogt 1954, 367).

In some cases the syntactic context in which a particular word appears favors the retention of an older pronunciation or a certain paradigm variant may favor the adoption of a newer pronunciation, while in others it may be the meaning of the word that influences a speaker, or the prestige of those who prefer one form over another. Thus, any particular sound change may have a very complex pattern: "Instead of a discrete *Zeitpunkt* on a one-dimensional *Zeitfolge*, a phonological change has a chronological profile of its own, and can incorporate, coincide or overlap with another,

---

[36] This map is adapted from Guiter 1966 with some simplifications for purposes of illustration.
[37] As a matter of fact, the distribution of forms of **talpa** is much more complicated than indicated on the map. Several western areas preserve the [al]: [taḷpa], [taḷpo], [taḷp].

and has intermediate phases during which both conservative and innovative speech forms coexist side by side'' (Chen 1976, 25).

As an example of a modern sound change we may take the disappearance of the intervocalic /-d-/ in modern peninsular Spanish. In ordinary conversational style, all speakers eliminate the /-d-/ completely in the past participial suffix -*ado* [-áo]. Some speakers use an even more evolved form in which the final vowel has been raised to a semivowel: [-aṷ]. When, however, a speaker finds himself in circumstances that require a more polished style, he will normally use a form with a fricative [đ]: [-ađo], (often with the consonant pronounced very weakly). Thus, for the past participle *estado* 'been', one can hear on various occasions and in different social groups everything from [estáđo], [está^do] to [estáo] or [estáṷ]. When the same form is used as a noun, on the other hand, even a person who normally says [estáo] as a past participle, is likely to pronounce the fricative fully, with the meaning 'state'. A number of other words ending in -*ado* are almost always pronounced with the fully articulated fricative: *enfado*, *hado*, *vado*, etc., while *lado* is commonly pronounced [láo] under all circumstances.

In the feminine form of the past participle, however, sharp regional differences appear. In Andalusia the disappearance of the fricative and the consequent reduction of the two syllables to one [á] is very common in all social classes. In the north of the peninsula this reduction is considered extremely low class and is avoided to such an extent that some hypercorrections have become almost standard, e.g., *Venceslada* for *Venceslá*. In the case of other words in which the intervocalic /-d-/ is found, middle class conversational usage is characterized by extreme irregularity. The tendency is to maintain the fricative in the suffixes -*ido*, -*adero*, etc. In southern Spain the disappearance of the /-d-/ is general: [-ío], [-aéro]. It would seem likely that in time the innovation of the elimination of the intervocalic fricative would become general everywhere and that eventually a historical linguist would be able to write the formula /-d-/ > /Ø/.[38] One can never be sure, however, and there are some indications of a reaction against the disappearance of /-d-/ in the past participle among younger people in Madrid (Lorenzo 1966, 24), although it may be that the restoration is a spelling pronunciation.

For some, the contrast between the spread of a sound change through gradual extension to more and more phonetic environments seems to suffice to prove that sound change is indeed a mechanical movement, unrelated to any other linguistic factors. There is, however, sufficient evidence of lexical diffusion to cause us to wonder how it is possible for both

---

[38] See Catalán 1955, 92–97. The irregular distribution of fricative [đ] and Ø illustrates a feature generally characteristic of formal styles. The pronunciation of vowels in *r*-less speech in New York City, for example, is extremely irregular in formal pronunciation. The most spontaneous speech, however, reveals a very regular system (Weinreich, Labov, and Herzog 1968, 134–35).

processes to be valid. Is lexical diffusion truly irregular?[39] For example, the Middle English long /e:/ generally evolved into a long high vowel /i:/, e.g., *bead, read, mead,* etc., but in some words the vowel shortened and did not change in tongue height, e.g. *head, dead, deaf, breath, sweat.* The phonetic conditions for both sets of words seem identical and yet the results are irregular (Labov 1981, 297). Similarly, in the modern English of Philadelphia, a number of words originally containing a short *a* have a very irregular phonetic result: *bad, mad,* and *glad,* for example, are pronounced with a tense in-gliding vowel that tends to rise, e.g., [mæ:d] >[mɛ:ᵊd] > [miˇᵊd], while *sad* and *dad* are pronounced with a low front lax vowel [æ] and show no sign of rising (Labov 1981, 289, 295). How can we account for such irregularity, if sound change is regular? A possible solution for this apparent paradox suggested by Labov is that absolute phonetic regularity is found when we are dealing with allophonic phonetic variation, i.e. phonetic output rules, while lexical diffusion is more likely to occur when more abstract rules or processes are involved such as tensing and laxing, shortening and lengthening, monophthongization and diphthongization, or change of place of articulation of consonants (Labov 1982, 65; Labov 1981).[40] Limitations of space make it impossible to examine this problem in greater detail here, and further research will undoubtedly cast more light on the problem (Janson 1983).

One can visualize the spread of a pronunciation across the lexicon in the same fashion as the spread to phonetic contexts in the table given above. If symbol C is now read as semantic or syntactic "context" rather than phonetic condition, an innovation can be conceived of as spreading in the same gradual way. The table, of course, represents an innovation completing its course and replacing an older pronunciation everywhere, as, for example, when the Latin diphthong /au/ monophthongized to a single /o/ in Castilian, e.g. Lat. CAUSA > *cosa*, AUTUMNU > *otoño*, etc. If, however, at any time during the process of the advance of a new sound through a language one should make a static analysis, one would see not absolutely regular replacement of one sound by another, but rather a

---

[39] In fact, Bailey criticizes Chen and Wang (1975) for their claim that the spread of change through the lexicon is unpatterned. He remarks that "one cannot prove anything about sound change, which is their object, unless one gives evidence from phonological rules. But their evidence comes from morphological rules" (Bailey 1975, 22). Bailey insists that only changes that are phonetically motivated can be called phonological changes. One may wonder if this conclusion is not simply a matter of definition. Thus, Hoenigswald (1976) points out that the *Junggrammatiker* defined as sound change only those changes which were phonetically determined and completely regular, while other kinds of changes were defined as something else.

[40] We could presume that if a sound change should begin in a lexically irregular fashion, it would very shortly be generalized to a specific phonetic environment in order not to place an intolerable burden on the speaker's memory. This point is stressed by Householder (1972, 2a). On the other hand, if different phonemes are involved, lexical irregularity might be more common since variant pronunciations of words showing different phonemes are common enough, e.g. modern English *economics* pronounced either as /iykənamiks/ or /ekənamiks/ or *either* which can be pronounced as /ayðr/ or /iyðr/.

mixture of competing forms, varying widely in different circumstances. The analyst might well conclude that there is no regularity but only massive irregularity, and that the supposed "regularity of sound change" is nothing but an illusion. It all depends on whether one examines a change in progress or after its completion. Menéndez Pidal, in a well-known passage in the *Orígenes del español*, made the following comparison:

> [C]ada palabra que en fonética parezca discordante de sus análogas, puede estar sometida a una tendencia general que la impulsa en unión con las otras. Todas son llevadas por la misma corriente, como multitud de hojas caídas en un río; cada hoja sigue su curso especial, tropieza acaso con obstáculos que la desvían, la retrasan o la detienen, pero todas están sometidas a la misma fuerza, ora las arrastre, ora solamente las empuje, y sería ceguedad empeñarse en observar el curso de cada una sin darse cuenta de la corriente que las domina a todas. La dialectología, mostrándonos una fotografía instantánea de un momento del lenguaje, puede hacernos pensar que cada palabra tiene su historia fonética y que no hay leyes generales que las rijan; pero la protohistoria lingüística, observando el curso de varios siglos, nos dice claramente que cada palabra es un mero episodio en la historia general de cada uno de los elementos que la integran. Cada sonido o grupo habitual de sonidos de una lengua es un elemento constructivo de que dispone el idioma, y como tal tiene una existencia ideal propia; es algo independiente en cierto modo de las palabras de que forma parte (*Orígenes*, 3rd ed., 531).

If it should turn out, for some reason, that there are some words that never take on the new pronunciation and no further changes of the members of a particular category occur, then there will be some exceptions to the general change. In this case, it could be said that the sound change was "terminated" but not "completed" (Hsieh 1972). For example, at the time that the Latin monophthong /au/ was becoming /o/, the combination /al + consonant/ was also beginning to shift to a diphthongal pronunciation /au/ and thus tended to be carried along with the monophthongizing current, e.g. Lat. ALTERU > [autro] > MSp. *otro* 'other'. In a number of words, however, the process did not take place soon enough, or was reacted against by speakers, so that the original form of the combination remained, e.g. Lat. ALTU 'tall' > Sp. *alto*, Lat. CALVU 'bald' > Sp. *calvo,* and some others. In some formations, however, the change to /au/ > /o/ does appear, e.g. the place name *Montoto,* i.e. 'tall mountain'. Thus this particular change can be said to have terminated before going to completion. In the case of a completed sound change, the historical linguist, when comparing the original sound and its eventual result, will be able to set up a simple formula, a "diachronic correspondence,"[41] of the

---

[41] The term "diachronic correspondence" is taken from Andersen 1972, 11–12.

type /A/ > /B/. One can then speak of these correspondences as being "sound laws." A formula, however, simply gives the beginning and the end of the process. It tells nothing at all about how, when, or why the change took place. A simple diachronic correspondence bears less relationship to phonetic change than the inscription of the date of birth and the date of death on a person's tomb does to the story of his life.

Sporadic Sound Change

The preceding discussion of the spread of a sound change through the lexicon of a language illustrates one reason why an examination of vocabulary is likely to reveal exceptions to a general sound change. Although, as Menéndez Pidal pointed out, one can consider sounds as having, in a certain sense, an independent life of their own, it is no less true that individual words, groups of words, and morphemes have independent trajectories. Any one word may be exposed to influences that can cause it to deviate from the path taken by others of a similar phonetic structure. The workings of analogy have long been recognized by linguists of all theoretical persuasions as an important interfering force in the smooth development of many sound changes. Malkiel has suggested that it would be possible to rank sound changes by the degree of final regularity that each one shows (1970, 140). Such "degrees of regularity," being expressed as percentages, would necessarily be connected with the total number of phonemes or phoneme combinations that would be subject to any particular change. Thus, one way of eliminating many apparent exceptions to a sound change is to remove from consideration all words or morphemes that were not a part of the language at the time when the change occurred. As we saw, all learned words in Spanish that were borrowed after the period of voicing had ended were excluded in determining the phonetic conditions for the voicing of the Latin intervocalic /t/.

Having taken up the topic of "exceptions to sound laws," we cannot any longer postpone some discussion of just how a scholar must proceed in establishing those changes that he will consider to be "regular" or normal. First of all, he must choose with great care those items that he will consider to be popular words in continuous use through the period that he is studying, and, as mentioned in the preceding paragraph, exclude from his corpus of evidence any word that may not have been part of the language during the period he is studying or which may have been subject to any kind of analogical influence from other words or groups of words. Once this is done, and utilizing only those words that can be reasonably assumed to have been a constant part of popular vocabulary, in many cases it will probably be reasonable to conclude that if the vast majority of the remaining examples show one particular outcome, then that change can be considered the norm. Still, one may wonder whether it is scientifically valid to assume that the majority must rule in historical linguistics as in democratic society.

Is it possible that the frequency of occurrence of a phoneme or phoneme group (understood as the frequency of appearance in different morphemes, or "incidence," not the frequency of occurrence in the spoken chain) is related to the statistical degree of final regularity of a change? Sounds appearing in many hundreds of words will give at least the impression of greater regularity of change than those that appear infrequently, simply because any exceptions to a change affecting such sounds will form only a small percentage of the total. Sound or combinations of sounds of lesser frequency may show less regularity because a few exceptions can form a higher percentage out of the total number of occurrences. Some combinations of sounds may, in fact, be so rare that it is practically impossible to decide which outcome should be considered "regular," e.g. the Latin initial combination /fl-/ in its development into Castilian (Wright 1982, 11-13) (v. chap. 4). Another possibility is that a very frequently occurring phoneme will, by sheer force of numbers, make it more difficult for exceptions to become established.

In the end, however, we may find a number of difficult cases where it may be that the percentage of words showing one particular outcome, although not the majority, is sufficiently large as to make us think that it is not really possible to declare unhesitatingly that one change is regular, and that all words showing some other change must have been influenced by some other factor which we cannot now perceive. Let us take the example of the change of the Latin short high back vowel /u/. In Italian and French, for example, we would not hesitate to declare that it fell together with the reflexes of the mid back long vowel /o:/ since the greatest number of popular words show just this change. In Ibero-Romance, on the other hand, we find enough examples of words that reveal a merger of /u/ with the long high vowel /u:/ that make us wonder whether we can confidently exclude them from the body of popular words, e.g. DULCE 'sweet' > OSp. *duz/duce* (MSp. *dulce*), DUBITA 'doubt' > Sp. *duda*, Port. *dúvida*, PUNCTU 'point, small hole' > Sp. *punto*, SUMMA 'sum; gist, main point' > Sp. *suma*, *CULMINE 'top, summit, ridge' (C.L. CULMEN, neuter) > Sp. *la cumbre*, CRUCE 'cross' > Sp. *cruz*, VULTU 'face' > Sp. *bulto* 'form, shape; bulk', JUGU 'yoke' > Sp. *yugo*, MUNDU 'world' > Sp. *mundo*, FURTU 'robbery, theft' > Sp. *hurto*, JUNCU 'reed' > Sp. *junco*, PUGNU 'fist' > Sp. *puño*, SURCU 'furrow' > Sp. *surco*, Port. *sulco*, plus some Portuguese words that contrast with their Castilian cognates, CURTU 'shortened' > Port. *curto* 'short', CURVU 'crooked' > Port. *curvo* 'curved, arched', FUNDU 'deep' > Port. *fundo*, URSU 'bear' > OPort. *usso*, SURDU 'deaf' > Port. *surdo*, PLUMBU 'lead' > Port. *chumbo*, etc. (Malkiel 1983a, 207-08). The simplest solution to the problem of accounting for the relatively large number of items showing the /u/ > /u/ change is to declare that all words containing /u/ rather than /o/ are "learned words," i.e., those that reflect the innovative medieval Latin pronunciation instituted with the Carolingian reform (Wright 1982). The only task remaining then is to explain how it is that such humble terms as Sp. *surco, yugo, junco, puño,* and others

could have been subject to such "learned" influence, when speakers of
Italian, for example, had no difficulty with a "popular" pronunciation of
words that might possibly be suspected of having suffered the influence of
church Latin, e.g. It. *croce* 'cross', *mondo* 'world', *dolce* 'sweet', plus many
others. "Learned" pronunciation is certainly an easy way out, and one that
many have chosen, but we cannot avoid many lingering doubts about
whether such a solution is anything other than a declaration that we
actually are not sure what the true popular sound law is (v. chap. 4).

Finally, there are certain types of sound changes that appear to be
somewhat different from others in that they are not necessarily limited in
time and space as those considered so far. These changes can appear at any
time or place and in any language. Variously labelled "fenómenos espe-
ciales," "changements particuliers," "allgemeine Erscheinungen," "acci-
denti generali," "spontaneous" or "sporadic" sound changes (Malkiel
1962), they have long troubled linguists because they cannot be easily
fitted into any general theory of sound change. These *may* include any of
those described in the list of types of sound changes given above, but in
practice they are more often limited to:

1) *metathesis*, e.g. Lat. **FABRICA** 'workshop' > [frábika] > [fraƀga] > Sp.
fragua 'forge'.
2) various types of *epenthesis*
   a. of [r], e.g. It. *bùssola* > Sp. *brújula* 'compass';
      OSp. *hojalde* 'puff pastry' (< Lat. **FOLIATILIS**) > MSp. *hojaldre*;
   b. of [n], e.g. Lat. **MACULA** > Sp. *mancha* 'stain';
3) *dissimilation*, e.g. Lat. **ANIMA** 'spirit' > Sp. *alma*; Eng. *chimney* >
   chimbly.
4) *anaptyxis* (or *svarabhakti*), the opposite of syncope, that is, the addition of a vowel between two consonants in contact, e.g., OSp.
   corónica 'chronicle' < *crónica*; Eng. *athalete* < *athlete*.
5. *paragoge*, the opposite of apocope, or the addition of a vowel at the
   end of a word, e.g., Sp. *cuchara* 'spoon' < OSp. *cuchar*.

A detailed discussion of these changes is out of place here, but it should
be noted that there is nothing in their nature that makes them essentially
different from all other types of change.[42] Thus, although metathesis is
usually irregular, it may assume a certain degree of regularity, e.g., OSp.
miraglo, parabla, periglo > MSp. *milagro, palabra, peligro*. Dissimilation
and epenthesis are perfectly regular in the development of the Latin consonant cluster /m'n/ in Castilian (where ' represents a lost vowel), e.g., Lat.
HOMINE > OSp. *omne* > MSp. *hombre*. It is worth noting, nevertheless,
that these phenomena, when they are truly sporadic, more often than not
involve liquids and nasals rather than other classes of sounds. One may
wonder whether it may not be their phonetic character as sonorants which

---

[42] See Niedermann 1926.

exposes them to more frequent slips of the tongue which may be the ultimate source of such changes.

Is it possible too, as Malkiel (1962) has suggested, that there is some connection between these sporadic changes and other changes with a low degree of regularity (tentatively labelled "weak phonetic change" by Malkiel) and analogy? It may be argued that if sporadic changes come from slips of the tongue, they may be subject to all sorts of interference from other words. The reasons for their acceptance in the standard forms of words would have nothing to do with their sporadic character or phonetic nature, but would have to be sought in the special historical development of each word or word group. No clear-cut solution to the problem of every unusual or apparently inexplicable change can possibly be given, especially if one thinks that a single, general explanation for all possible changes must be given. Only further research can enlighten us.

The Causes of Sound Change

> Cum igitur omnis nostra loquela . . .
> sit a nostro beneplacito reparata post
> confusionem illam . . . et homo sit
> instabilissimum atque variabilissimum
> animal, nec durabilis nec continua
> esse potest, sed sicut alia que nostra
> sunt, puta mores et habitus, per
> locorum temporumque distantias
> variari oportet.
> —*De vulgari eloquentia*, I. 9. 6-7.

One of the most perplexing questions of historical linguistics continues to be the explanation of why sounds change. Traditional historical grammars of the nineteenth-century style are usually limited to the description of most sound changes, with much less emphasis on accounting for their causes. The term "sound law" undoubtedly helped to foster the belief that description was sufficient because it gave the impression that sound changes were more or less like physical laws of nature, blindly and implacably moving through language. Of course, even the most committed descriptivist could not avoid having to explain why, in some cases, certain words or groups of words managed to escape the effects of sound laws. The traditional answer was usually analogy, which is examined in more detail in the next section.

In one sense, to ask the question, "why do sounds change?" is not a linguistic question at all, because it tends to give the impression that language is (or should be) essentially static and that there is something unusual about its constant changes. As Dante observed, human institutions are always subject to change over time and distance, and therefore language could hardly be expected to escape the fate that awaits all other human inventions. A general answer to the general question then would be: "Language changes because humans and their society change."[43] (In fact, one might observe that change is characteristic of everything in nature.) Such a general answer could hardly satisfy anyone who wishes a linguistic answer, any more than a physician could accept as an answer to the question, "Why do people die?" a general answer like: "All living things must die."

Before becoming more specific, it should be pointed out that the definition of the word "cause" and the problem of causation in general is a philosophical rather than a strictly historical or linguistic one. Nevertheless, even those not especially concerned with the philosophy of history must have some conception of what they will accept as a cause of any particular historical event, including sound change. A useful definition is one given by a philosopher: "[I]n its most rigorous form causality denotes the sum of the necessary and sufficient conditions for the occurrence of any event" (Cohen 1942, 19). In determining what the cause of a change may be, it is useful to distinguish between the necessary conditions for a change and the active factors that impelled it. For example, in the explanation of the voicing of the intervocalic Latin /t/, one can speak of the intervocalic position as being a cause of voicing in the sense that this position was a necessary condition of voicing. It could not have been the sufficient cause of voicing, however, because voicing occurred only in part of Romania, indicating that some other factor or factors must have been involved. These other factors are the ones that should be considered the direct or more immediate causes of voicing.

Those who think that some general cause for all sound change can or must be found have often felt baffled in seeking this cause. One answer to the problem, albeit a very unsatisfactory one, is that there is no answer. Bloomfield declared flatly: "[T]he causes of sound-change are unknown" (1933, 385). Even today there are those who feel the same way. A study by an author of the school of "generative phonology" proclaims: "Of course, one still does not know the CAUSE . . . of any linguistic change. In general, explanation of the cause of language change is far beyond the reach of any theory ever advanced" (Harris 1969, 550).[44]

---

[43] Malmberg remarks: "The idea of the unchanged linguistic system as a condition for communication evidently implies that the relations between language and other social conditions—in a word the material to be communicated and the situation in which the communication takes place—remains unaltered. But if the social background changed while language remained identically the same, this would imply a break in the sociolinguistic relations and prevent communication" (1967, 179).

[44] As Coseriu says: "La actitud «prudente» es la que admite que las causas del cambio lingüístico son desconocidas o se desconocen «por ahora». Esta actitud parece razonable y, en efecto, quienes la adoptan se salvan por lo menos del error de indicar causas que no son tales; sin embargo, en el fondo, no es menos errónea que la anterior, pues implica la creencia de que habría causas más o menos misteriosas y que podrían descubrirse; el no haberlas descubierto sería sólo una deficiencia circunstancial de la lingüística" (1973, 190). It is curious how often we find linguists eager to proclaim that we know nothing about why sounds change, as

It may well be that behind such bafflement lies a fundamental misconception of the nature of history and historical explanation. A relevant
quote may make this clear:

> Misled by the ambiguities hidden in the word 'cause,' philosophers have
> believed that somewhere in every historical situation there is present a
> factor of a certain type and that once this factor is pinpointed, everything
> else can be seen to follow from it. But this belief is an illusion. The
> historical process is not like a machine that has to be kept in motion by a
> metaphysical dynamo behind the scenes. And there are no absolute Real
> Causes waiting to be discovered by historians with sufficiently powerful
> magnifying-glasses. What do exist are historians writing upon different
> levels and at different distances, historians writing in different contexts
> and from different points of view (Gardiner 1952, 109).[45]

It is odd too how often historical linguists have been reluctant to consider what is a basic principle of all other historical disciplines, namely that
there may be more than one cause for any event: "[A]n *insistence* on a
single cause—what Jespersen called the all or nothing fallacy—has
been, in the past one of the main drawbacks to progress in diachronic
linguistics. In both pure and applied science, the principle of multiple
conditioning is a commonplace. Yet in the study of linguistic change it has
been treated with suspicion; for long, the linguist who suggested a combination of causes operating in the past was accused of ambivalence" (Samuels 1972, 3).[46]

Closely related to the position that holds that the causes of sound change
are unknown (and possibly unknowable) is the view that sound change

---

though over a hundred years of scholarly work had all been for nothing. Hockett, comment-
ing on another study, says, "as a matter of fact, we know nothing about any other factor in
sound change either" (1967, 320).

[45] Harris' capitalization of "CAUSE" seems to show that he is looking for just this mysterious, metaphysical dynamo that keeps language moving, or at the very least for a vast,
all-encompassing theory that will explain everything forever about language change. A witty
comment on this point of view is offered by Coseriu: "[P]reguntarse cuál es «*la causa*» del
cambio lingüístico es como preguntarse 'qué forma tienen los objetos' y pretender contestar
que la tienen redonda o cuadrada" (1973, 184).

[46] Malkiel (1967) presents a valuable introduction to multiple causation in language
change. The fact that such a study had never been done before is a sign of how little historical
linguistics had been considered to be another branch of historical studies. Most historians
long ago accepted multiple causation:

> Multiple causation is obviously less dramatic than monistic causation. It is always arresting
> to point the finger at one cause and say, "This did it!" Moreover, when a multiplicity of
> causes are admitted, it is often difficult to assign the correct weight to each, and the labors
> of the historian are enhanced. . . . Nevertheless, it will be observed that the more scientific
> the historian is, the more he will lean to a multiple explanation of events: the deeper he
> goes into the subject, the surer he will find such a course imperative (Nevins 1938, 228).

See also Bunge 1959 and Wallace 1972, as well as Conkin 1974.

needs no special explanation. As one writer puts it simply: "At present, it looks as if we must simply say that habits of articulation are subject to changes in fashion, just like habits of dress, eating, and so forth—and, just as these latter vary with no apparent reason, so do habits of pronunciation" (Hall 1964, 298). Another linguist, of the school of generative phonology, agrees wholeheartedly: "It seems clear to the present writer that there is no more reason for languages to change than there is for automobiles to add fins one year and remove them the next, for jackets to have three buttons one year and two the next, etc. That is, it seems evident within the framework of sound change as grammar change that the 'causes' of sound change without language contact lie in the general tendency of human cultural products to undergo 'nonfunctional' stylistic change" (Postal 1968, 283). Underlying this view, of course, is the unstated assumption that changes in fashion have no causes, or, at least, no causes worthy of study. This assumption will certainly be questioned sharply by historians and sociologists.[47]

Other linguists have thought that physical causes can be found for sound changes. According to this view, the slightest shift in the organs of articulation can be the start of a sound change: "In this interplay of complex movements which constitutes the phonetic system, the organ may either exaggerate or inhibit its action to a very slight extent. A muscle may be somewhat weak or slow in executing a movement or it may, on the contrary, be unusually vigorous and rapid. As a result there is a discrepancy between the phonetic systems of successive generations" (Vendryes 1925, 36). The scholar who formulated this view of sound change realized that such physical causes cannot be sufficient to explain sound change because they would account only for variations in the pronunciation of a single individual. One individual's deviation cannot explain those changes that are adopted by an entire social group.[48] Physical explanations also fail to account for the direction that sound changes take, since physical deviations from a norm, in the absence of other factors, would be essentially non-directional, a "drifting of allophones" (Hockett 1965, 202).[49]

---

[47] As a matter of fact, Smelser 1963 attempts to elaborate an explanation of just such behavior. See especially chap. 7, "The Craze." Pp. 207–208 deal with clothing fashions.

[48] "For a long time it was believed that all phonetic changes started from an individual and were only individual changes generalized. This conception is incorrect. No individual could have the power of imposing upon his fellows a pronunciation against which their instinct would rebel. There is no force capable of generalizing a phonetic change. In order that a phonetic change may become general for a social group, all the members of the group must possess a natural tendency to adopt it spontaneously" (Vendryes 1925, 40). This spontaneous, natural tendency is nowhere explicated.

[49] It is interesting to note that Hockett is confident that "this drifting of allophones, and hence of distinctive features, is SOUND CHANGE." In another sense, Hockett seems to claim that sound change has no cause: "Sound change CAN go on because language is redundant. . . . Sound change does go on because of NOISE" (1965, 203–204). Evidently, according to his view, there is no cause for sound change except pure chance, a non-directional, random drift of pronunciation. A contrasting view is that of Labov: "[S]ound change is just this mixed effect of borrowing, analogy, imitation and hypercorrection" (1966, 11).

Related to the physical theory of sound change, but usually rejected out of hand by linguists, are theories that attempt to relate language change to non-linguistic elements such as material culture, heredity, or climate. One scholar, for instance, did not hesitate to claim: "The influence of climate may be seen in the frequency with which (a) is rounded in the direction of (o) in the northern languages of Europe . . . as compared with the southern languages, in which it is generally preserved; this rounding of (a) is doubtless the result of unwillingness to open the mouth widely in the chilly and foggy air of the North" (Sweet 1900, 34).[50] No one has ever been able to show the slightest connection in any meaningful way between such external factors, however, and sound change and therefore they may be dismissed from further consideration.

Another factor that has been invoked to explain sound change is the "Principle of Least Effort." In its simplest and crudest form, this principle states that sound changes tend to proceed in the direction of articulations that require less effort on the part of speakers. It can even be asserted that all human activity tends toward a reduction of effort. Stated in this fashion, of course, it is easy to find many counterexamples, i.e., sound changes that do not involve any simplification or reduction of effort, and even examples of sound changes that seem to require increased effort. Therefore, it is necessary to qualify the principle, since obviously the activity that requires the least effort of all is to cease speaking altogether. A somewhat more adequate formulation might be to claim that speakers tend to reduce the amount of effort involved in speaking in *allegro* styles, provided that they can communicate as well as they can with more effort. In other words, when a certain amount of denotative information is being conveyed by any utterance, and a speaker aims primarily at getting his message across, he may tend to eliminate redundant features. If one can communicate one piece of information with one word as well as with two words, the normal human tendency might be to use just one word, if the communication of this information is the only thing that is important. It would, however, be erroneous to think that this is an established fact—long-windedness and wordiness are common human characteristics. The communication of discrete denotative information is only one function of speech (although probably the most important). Another function is to bolster ego by dominating conversation. Increased effort and wordiness can certainly serve the latter purpose better than can reduced effort.

Even when stated in this limited fashion, the principle must have many further qualifications simply because of the vagueness of the terms used. For example, how do we measure effort? Is it possible to distinguish be-

---

[50] See Lord 1966, 82–87, for a discussion of such notions. Odd ideas of this sort still crop up from time to time: Schmidt claims that the open vowel [a] is a sound of "enormous masses of land of an endless hinterland" while "island languages . . . let the open [o] sound exist . . ." (1956, 167). Brosnahan (1961) is exceptional in that he attempts to link genetic factors to language in a serious and scientific fashion.

tween sounds that require different amounts of effort? Is only articulatory, muscular effort to be considered, or does psychological effort also enter into play? How can information be measured? Is it possible to show that the same amount of information is being communicated by two utterances involving different amounts of effort, however it may be defined?

It can be seen, then, that no precise definition can be given to the term "least effort." Nevertheless, there is undoubtedly a core of truth involved in the claim that speakers seek some kind of balance between what they wish to communicate and the effort they will exert in doing so. Although it may not be possible to elaborate any very precise formula for determining when information and effort are unbalanced, it is nonetheless true that a word that appears very often in the chain of speech will often be subject to considerable abbreviation and simplification of form, undoubtedly because the more frequent a word, the less distinctive it is and the less essential the information it conveys. For example, the modern American greeting "Hi!" is a reduced form of the phrase, "How are you?" When the speaker wishes to ask about the state of health of another person, he will use the phrase in its full form, even though he may actually be quite indifferent to how the other person feels. The reduced form resulted when speakers no longer expected a reply and used the phrase simply as a greeting, first in the form "Hiya?" and then "Hi!" The only information being conveyed was, "Greetings!" and for that purpose one word is much more economical than three, especially if it is used many times a day. Commonly used grammatical particles, for instance, are often reduced to a single syllable for the same reason (see Mańczak 1969).

In contrast, those words or combinations of sounds that appear less frequently will be more distinctive simply because they contain more unpredictable information. Speakers may therefore not be as tempted to reduce them. Dealing with individual phonemes, however, is not the same as dealing with words, and it is not easy to tell which ones are more complex and involve greater effort. Even so, statistical studies have shown that there tends to be a sort of balance in the frequency of usage of different consonants. If a consonant were used more and more often, for example, it would become less distinctive and more predictable, and the same tendency to avoid excessive effort in its articulation would take effect. Perhaps a better term than "principle of least effort" is the one preferred by André Martinet, the "principle of economy" or "technical efficiency" (Coseriu 1973, 204). As we have seen, there are many difficulties involved in making precise calculations of complexity or of effort, but it is undoubtedly a conditioning factor in a number of sound changes, especially those involving a simplification of sound groups.[51] In fact, it is

---

[51] The fundamental work on the principle of least effort is by Zipf (1965; original edition 1935, especially chap. 3, "The Form and Behavior of Phonemes"). The introduction to the 1965 edition by George A. Miller claims that the relations that Zipf found between frequency and shortness of words is strictly the result of the laws of probability because if "word-

possible to consider language as being in a continual state of unstable balance. As Martinet puts it: "Il y a conflit permanent entre la tendance de l'individu à restraindre sa dépense d'énergie et les besoins de la communauté qui réclament la maintien de distinctions jugées nécessaires par l'ensemble des usagers de la langue. C'est ce conflit, que résume la théorie du moindre effort qu'on désigne également comme le principe d'économie" (1965, 86). In summary, it does not seem that "least effort" should be considered a very important factor in linguistic innovation, but rather a sort of moderating influence that affects certain developments (Labov 1973, 245-46).

We have already considered the role that social factors play in sound change. There can be no doubt that the spread of sound change through a linguistic community is intimately related to the evolution of society. No further explanation is needed here to prove that the adoption of a particular pronunciation and its generalization in a language depend on the values and needs of social groups.

Structural Causes of Sound Change

The factors that can account for the spread of a sound change do not, in and of themselves, explain why shifts take place in one direction rather than another. For example, there is nothing in the social matrix of a language that can tell us why the intervocalic /t/ of western Latin simply voiced to /d/ rather than being changed into another consonant altogether, say to /b/. As far as social change is concerned, the spread of /t/ > /b/ is no less likely than /t/ > /d/. In order to understand the direction that sound changes take, linguistic causes of sound change must be discovered.

One basic principle underlying the direction of sound shifts is that phonemes do not exist as isolated entities in a language, but as elements of a total phonetic and phonological system.[52] Thus, Lat. /t/ is not simply an arbitrary symbol like a letter, but must be defined through its relations with other consonants. When it is analyzed in terms of its distinctive features we can more easily see what these relations are. The consonant /t/ can be defined as consisting of three elements: [+stop, +dental, −voice].[53] When

---

boundary markers (spaces) are scattered randomly through a text, then there will necessarily be more occurrences of short than long words" (vii). The same result would appear if a monkey kept hitting the keys on a typewriter. Nevertheless, when one considers the evolution of words and sounds rather than statistical frequency, it seems evident that there is some relation between simplification and frequency. See Mańczak 1965 and 1969. Martinet devotes a number of pages to a consideration of how Zipf's studies may explain certain types of sound change (1955, 130–52).

[52] The following section is based largely on Martinet 1955, 47–62. Good summaries are found also in Anderson 1973 and Bhat 1972.

[53] The "universal set of phonetic features" proposed by Chomsky and Halle (1968, chap. 7) would describe the Latin voiceless dental occlusive in terms of other features which are supposedly more useful because they can be applied to all languages. In terms of these

these features are compared to those of other Latin occlusives, we can see
that all are shared by two or more of them. Thus, /d/ is also a dental stop,
but is voiced, while /p/ and /k/ are also voiceless stops, but are articulated at different points. Therefore, /t/ fits into a matrix of distinctive
features. In terms of the Prague school terminology,[54] /t/ is one unit in a
correlation of six members consisting of three *orders* of location: labial,
dental, and velar, and two series: one voiced and the other voiceless,
voicing being considered the *mark* of the correlation:

$$/p/ \quad /t/ \quad /k/$$
$$/b/ \quad /d/ \quad /g/$$

Because each of these phonemes shares features with others, each can be
said to be integrated in the correlation, and a change in the realization of a
distinctive feature will affect all phonemes sharing it. Therefore, the voicing of /t/ will not occur without also affecting the other voiceless stops.
Likewise, a change in the manner of articulation of any consonant will
affect the manner of articulation of all others sharing that particular feature. In short, the structure of the phonological system will determine the
direction in which sound changes can operate. Not only does the combination of features that make up any particular phoneme have an effect on the
way that it will develop, but also the diacritic function of phonemic oppositions will serve to determine the direction and type of development. The
opposition between /t/ and /d/, for example, served to distinguish
among a variety of words and morphemes, e.g., DĪTŌ 'I enrich' vs. DĪDŌ 'I
distribute'; LŪTU 'plant for making yellow color' vs. LŪDUS 'game'; NŪTUS
'nod (of command)' vs. NŪDU 'naked'; IT 'he goes' vs. ID 'it', etc. Speakers
would find it useful to maintain the distinction between /t/ and /d/ in
order to prevent the confusion of a number of different words. It can be
supposed that if there were any movement that might imperil this distinc-

---

features /t/ could be described as [+obstruent, +coronal, +anterior, -distributed, -voice]
and possibly some others. There is as yet no general agreement on all these features or the
proper labels for them, so for our purposes we can continue to rely on traditional phonetic
terms. They can always be translated into more fashionable terms, in case of need. A dispas-
sionate presentation of the validity of these features is found in Sommerstein 1977, chap. 5.
With regard to vowels it is important to note that the use of discreet distinctive feature
notation may serve to obscure the nature of vowel shift. Weinreich, Labov, and Herzog
remark: "[T]he mechanism of change is not a sudden substitution or addition of higher-level
rules, but rather the application of a continuous function to phonological space at a level
where continuous values are possible. . . . Thus if the historian of language should accept the
distinctive-feature matrix, he loses the possibility of describing in a coherent way a series of
shifts moving around the periphery of the vowel trapezoid" (1968, 149). Another scholar
declares: "The system of distinctive features used in transformational phonology, based on
acoustic analysis, cannot handle satisfactorily historical change in which shifts occur in whole
series of elements" (Foley 1970, 87). Bhat is equally skeptical: "[T]heir [i.e., generativists']
current distinctive feature system would be highly inadequate in taking care of the extreme
complexity that underlies sound changes" (1976, 347).
    [54] See Martinet 1955, 69–73. An earlier article presents the same ideas (Martinet 1952,
especially 13–17).

tion, speakers would react in some way to prevent a merger of two phonemes. The simplest would be to maintain the distinction without change. If, however, there were some other factor at work that made conservation of the original state of affairs impossible, another means would be sought to preserve it.

Every phoneme may be said to have a certain "field of dispersion" in its phonetic realizations that allows it to vary slightly in pronunciation without coming into conflict with other phonemes. This field of dispersion provides a margin of safety against potential confusion of sounds. Let us illustrate this by means of a sketch. If there are three phonemes A, B, and C, each having a phonetic realization bordering on another of the group in its articulatory space (and possibly overlapping at times), each will remain distinct from its neighbors as long as they are balanced:

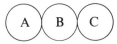

If, however, A should begin to be realized with any degree of consistency within the field of dispersion of B, the distinction between them would be imperiled and speakers would therefore either react against this shift by reestablishing the original pronunciation, or by changing the articulation of B away from A. If this happens, B then begins to impinge on C and C will, in turn, be forced to move also:

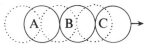

This chain reaction may be labelled a "push chain" because the movement of A served to set the other phonemes in motion. Alternatively one could consider that C might be the first phoneme to move. By shifting out of its normal field of dispersion it would leave a greater margin of safety between it and B, and thus B could be realized in the space formerly occupied by C without endangering the distinction. In this way too it increases the margin of safety with respect to A and thus A too can move. This latter type of shift can be called a "drag chain" or "pull chain":

An example of just this type of chain reaction is the development of the back vowels in the Portuguese dialect of São Miguel in the Azores. In this dialect the vowels have moved up, with each vowel entering the space of its neighbor: /a/ —> /ɔ/ —> /o/ —> /u/. Since /u/ is the highest vowel, it would seem to have nowhere to go to avoid a merger with /o/, but by moving forward as a front round vowel, /ü/, it continues to be distinct from /o/.[55] There are many other examples of sound changes

---

[55] Martinet 1955, 52. A striking parallel is found in the development of the Old French vowels. See Haudricourt and Juilland 1970, chap. 10.

occurring in groups in this fashion so that there can be no doubt that this sort of change must be accounted for. The theory that there is a tendency for speakers to preserve useful distinctions is, to some extent at least, a plausible one. Is it possible, however, to determine whether there is truly a push or a pull involved in this type of change? Most historical cases of chain shifts, and those in progress now, seem to be pull chains, but there are also some examples of push chains too (Labov 1982, 73).[56] One may wonder too why it is that chain shifts do not occur consistently. After all, phonemic mergers do take place from time to time, and languages continue to function. One conclusion might be that since mergers are not always avoided, the idea that useful distinctions tend to be maintained is invalid.[57] And yet it is clear that wholesale mergers of phonemes do not occur either. Why are some mergers prevented and others not?

Martinet suggests that the solution to the problem is "toutes choses égales d'ailleurs, une opposition phonologique utile à la compréhension mutuelle se maintient mieux qu'une autre moins utile" (1955, 42). When attempting to apply this principle to concrete cases, however, one is immediately faced with the difficulty of determining which oppositions are in fact more useful. Martinet concluded that those oppositions that had a greater "functional yield," i.e. served to distinguish greater numbers of morphemes, would tend to be maintained more often than those with a lesser yield. The notion of functional yield is a statistical concept, and therefore should be calculable, although a basic problem is just what should be counted: different morphemes and lexical items or their actual occurrence in spoken discourse? Various attempts have been made to give a precise numerical value to the functional yield of various phonemic oppositions, and in one case to apply it to the explanation of sound changes.[58] So far there is little evidence to support the idea that differences of functional yield have any real relation with mergers or their avoidance by speakers.

One objection that has been raised to the supposed influence of functional yield is that it seems to assume a kind of "phonological consciousness" on the part of speakers: that is, speakers consciously perceive that a

---

[56] King (1969a) concludes that drag chains can be considered a kind of simplification of rules. His article would be more convincing if he were not dogmatically committed to the notion that sound change can never be gradual (however one defines graduality), that it can only be viewed as a change in the "rules" of the "underlying" grammar, and that the phoneme (variously labelled "autonomous" or "taxonomic") does not exist. Anttila observes that: "[R]ule change is not a primary change mechanism, but an effect (on a notation of the 'right' kind) resulting from sound change, analogy, and so on" (1972, 131). Chen (1976) observes that King's belief results from the use of generative notation and its requirement of strict linear ordering.

[57] This is how King reasons. Like so many others, he assumes that no principle can have any validity unless it consistently produces the same results everywhere.

[58] The mathematical problems involved have been studied by Hockett (1967) and Palau Marti (1969). An elaborate study of the whole problem is by Meyerstein (1970). The relation between functional yield and sound change is treated by King (1967) and Mańczak (1970).

useful distinction is menaced and then deliberately set out to change their pronunciation in order to prevent it.[59] There is no proof that a speaker does indeed behave this way. Objections to teleology may be partially based on the assumption that "purpose" must necessarily involve some conscious intent, but one can very well speak of a "teleology of function"[60] without implying such intent. The function of the distinction between /t/ and /d/, for example, is to keep morphemes distinct, but this does not mean that speakers are necessarily consciously aware of it.

Another problem with phonological consciousness is that it is not clear why some oppositions with a very low functional yield are preserved and others with a higher yield are eliminated. One possible view might be that phonological consciousness is a purely negative force, avoiding mergers by exploiting possible alternative realizations of phonemes, but not always succeeding in preventing all of them.[61] One way of avoiding the assumption of some kind of conscious deliberation by speakers would be to assume that mergers will be avoided when some phonetic possibility for doing so already exists in the language. In other words, if phoneme A is close to another phoneme B, but for some reason takes on a phonetic realization [A'] which is non-distinctive, a change of the realization of B into the space formerly occupied by A will not produce a merger because the realization [A'] will now become distinctive, thus maintaining the opposition. For example, the Romance dialect of Castile altered the pronunciation of Late Latin /ļ/ (< l + j, k'l) to /ž/ and the geminate /l:/ became

---

[59] Il faut reconnaître que la prétendue conscience linguistique veille assez mal à la conservation des précieuses oppositions phonologiques. À mon avis, elle n'y veille pas du tout. Il y a des collisions que la conscience linguistique n'accept pas: celles des mots et celles des formes, celles qui compromettent la distinction entre les éléments du contenu, bref la pathologie verbale dont parle Gilliéron. Mais les collisions phonologiques qui n'ont pas de répercussions dans le contenu ne sauraient gêner dans la moindre mesure la conscience linguistique. Les changements phonologiques se réalisent donc aveuglément, d'après les lois phonétiques. . . . Bref, il n'y a pas de conscience phonologique (Togeby 1959–60, 404).

[60] "[T]here is good traditional precedent for thinking of teleology in terms of what nowadays are called 'goal-directed activities,' in which there is persistence towards a terminal state in spite of deviations and set-backs, but not necessarily conscious envisagement of an objective" (Emmet 1958, 51). Andersen states: "The notion of teleology has traditionally been erroneously identified with purpose in the sense of '(conscious) intent': and most students of linguistic change have been wary, and rightly so, of either ascribing (conscious) intent to willful distortions of inherited patterns. However, there is no reason to think of purpose narrowly as 'intent'. It is perfectly proper to speak of some constituent element of a structured system as serving a certain purpose in the sense of 'function' " (1973, 789). An early paper of Roman Jakobson (published in 1928) was the first to speak of teleology in terms only of the pressure of the phonological system on sound shifts; he did not use teleology in the sense of 'intent' (Jakobson 1962).

[61] Weinrich reasons in this manner: when a phonemic opposition is obviously endangered, a sort of "antitoxin" develops, exploiting varieties of pronunciation that will avoid mergers: "Aber das Gegengift ist auch ein Gift," he observes (1959, 53), and in trying to avoid one merger, speakers often end by merging some other oppositions. It is not too exaggerated a conclusion to say that in his view, speakers seem to be people who walk around backward in order to avoid head-on collisions and end up by bumping into things with their backs. Perhaps this is how people act.

palatalized to /l̦/. If /l:/ had palatalized and the previously existing /l̦/ had not changed, a merger would have taken place. Since merger did not occur, it is reasonable to assume that the shift of the earlier /l̦/ to /ž/ was related to the degemination of /l:/. If we suppose that the pronunciation [ž] had already existed in the language, much as modern Spanish /y/ has become [ž] in the region of Buenos Aires, then we could conclude that the palatalization of /l:/ did not provoke a merger simply because speakers could exploit a previously existing pronunciation and thus avoid it ("secondary split")(Lehmann 1973, 161).

It may be too that a concentration on the functional yield of isolated oppositions conceals more than it reveals. As noted previously, every phoneme is a combination of distinctive features that are shared among other phonemes. Therefore, the degree of integration of a phoneme in a phonological correlation would be a powerful factor in maintaining it. In English, for example, the distinction between /θ/ and /ð/ has a very low functional yield, e.g., *thy - thigh*; *mouth* (verb) - *mouth (noun); either - ether*, and a few others. Nevertheless there is little danger of any merger because the feature of voice that separates them is found in many other oppositions with a very high functional yield: /t-d, p-b, k-g, f-v, š-ž, č-ǰ/. Any change that affected this feature could affect the entire correlation. Possibly the chain shifts that occur so often are better interpreted as a result of a change of a distinctive feature as a whole which then exerts pressure on other related features. If one considers the distinctive feature as the relevant item in paradigmatic sound changes, perhaps it might be better to claim not that useful oppositions, but rather distinctive features tend to be preserved. Changes in distinctive features could be described as changes in "rules," provided that one is not thereby committed to the position that such changes are sudden shifts from one rule to another. Although such sudden shifts may occur, there is no plausible reason for assuming that all changes are of this type. Some changes, and especially vowel shifts, may result from what Weinreich, Labov, and Herzog call "the application of a continuous function to phonological space" (1968, 149), and they would therefore be gradual.

In conclusion, the existence of chain shifts of pronunciation seems to prove that the phonological system has a definite effect on sound changes, although it is not clear just how the system does this. In particular, there does not appear to be any necessity for believing that all changes result from the pressure of the system. Assimilation and other syntagmatic sound changes, for instance, do not have anything to do with the avoidance of mergers, even when they result in a systematic restructuring, as in the creation of a new phoneme or series of phonemes. They are usually the result of a relaxation of articulation. The role of the phonological system in these cases seems to be that of channelling the results of a purely phonetic change.[62]

---

[62] See Burger 1955 and Vachek 1965.

Sound Changes Caused by Language Contact ("Substratum" Theories)

One of the most fertile and widely discussed theories of the cause of sound changes is that of the "substratum." In its most basic form this theory attempts to account for linguistic changes through the supposition that one language is able to exert an influence on the development of another and thus be the cause of certain changes. The term *substratum* is usually used to refer to a language that has been replaced by another but has had an influence on the replacing language. Because not all cases of language contact involve this particular type of replacement, other terms have been invented, such as *superstratum*, referring to the language that is brought by an invader and has had an influence on the language of the original speakers, and *adstratum* or *parastratum*, indicating that the influencing language is neither above nor beneath the language influenced.

In reality, the proliferation of terms serves no useful purpose because the linguistic phenomenon is the same in all cases.[63] In fact, it can be fairly claimed that:

> Hablar de 'sustratos', 'superstratos' y 'adstratos' (o 'parastratos') parece invitar a concebir las situaciones de contacto o comercio entre hablantes más-que- monolingües (más bien que bilingües) a modo de sedimentaciones geológicas en las que a cada lengua corresponde una capa. Mucho menos engañoso parece tratar de concebir estos fenómenos de 'aculturación' en términos de interrelaciones entre hablantes de lenguas distintas, uno de los cuales se ve en el trance de tener que echar mano de una lengua ajena que no ha interiorizado a la perfección (Otero 1971, 180).

In such cases the relative social position of the speakers is only a secondary matter, and may be important only as one of the factors that determine the fate of a language. Therefore, the term "substratum" will be avoided whenever possible here; the real topic of discussion is all types of inter-language influence.

The theory of the substratum originated in the nineteenth century as a way of explaining the causes of certain phonetic developments in Romance that purely descriptive historical grammars could not.[64] The basic idea, however, can be traced much earlier. The earliest clear formulation of the theory so far found is that of Lorenzo Hervás y Panduro in his *Catálogo de*

---

[63] The term *substratum* is discussed perspicaciously by Izzo (1972a). Substratum is used to mean both any language that is replaced by another and a language that leaves some trace on the replacing language. The confusion that results from using 'substratum' to refer to lexical borrowing is clearly shown in this article. Many of the ambiguities discovered by Izzo result from his use of the term to refer to borrowed words.

[64] An excellent summary of the development of substratum theory is found in Craddock 1969, 18–47, especially 18–31. An ample bibliography is found in the notes. A first-rate study of a particular problem of substratum, including a lengthy consideration of the whole theory is Izzo 1972.

las lenguas de las naciones conocidas (Madrid, 1800-1804; originally published in Italian in 1784), 6 vols. In the introduction to this work, Hervás outlines the idea of how substratum influence can be conceived:

> Una nación llega a abandonar el idioma propio, cuando de otra ha recibido no solamente las palabras, mas también el artificio y orden gramatical; pero en tal caso conservará siempre muchísimos idiotismos de su lengua antigua, por los que se podrá conocer que no pertenece a la nación que le ha dado el idioma que habla. El francés, que antiguamente hablaba el céltico, y el español, que antiguamente hablaba el cántabro o vascongado, actualmente hablan lenguas que son dialectos de la latina; mas quien atentamente las analice y coteje con la céltica y con la cántabra, fácilmente observará que el francés en su dialecto usa no pocos idiotismos célticos, y que del mismo modo el español en su dialecto latino usa muchos idiotismos cántabros: que tanto el francés como el español conservan muchas palabras de sus antiguos y respectivos lenguajes; y que según el genio gramatical de éstos, han dado terminaciones a muchas palabras latinas. Si todas estas cosas no nos constaran por la historia o tradición, podríamos inferirlas de la observación y cotejo de los dialectos latinos que al presente hablan los franceses y españoles, con el céltico y cántabro, que aun se hablan entre ellos, con el latín antiguo, y con los dialectos puros de éste, que en Italia hablan los descendientes de los romanos. Esta observación y cotejo nos harían advertir y descubrir en la lengua francesa muchas cosas de la céltica, y en la española muchas de la cántabra. Si por ventura ésta y la lengua céltica hubieran perecido, y consiguientemente no pudiéramos hacer entonces cotejo con ellas y los lenguajes que en la actualidad hablan los franceses y los españoles, no obstante, por razón de la diferencia de los idiotismos y de otras cosas en dichos lenguajes, conjeturaríamos que antiguamente los franceses y los españoles hablaban diversos idiomas (cited in Craddock 1969, 21).

It might be possible to find earlier formulations of this idea,[65] for in all probability the basic notion results from a common observation from all times and places: that those who learn a foreign language imperfectly frequently insert in it elements from their first language.

The borrowing of words and even affixes from another language has never been seriously disputed (see Tesch 1978 for details), although the actual number of words or morphemes that can be safely assumed to have come from pre-Romance languages into Latin, for example, is not agreed on by all. Influence on the lexicon, however, is of relatively little theoretical significance since the borrowing of words goes on all the time without affecting the basic structure of a language. In fact, to use the term "sub-

---

[65] The Spanish version is quoted because, as Rodríguez de la Mora (1971) points out, the original Italian version was not just translated into Spanish but also revised. Coseriu suspects that Ascoli, often considered the "father" of modern substratum theories had read Hervás in his youth (1978, 530).

stratum" to refer to the taking of words from one speech community into another confuses matters because extensive bilingualism is not essential for it to occur. As for syntax, relatively little has been done to establish whether such influence is likely, although it seems that there are cases of syntactic patterns being borrowed by one language from another, especially where there are many imperfect bilingual speakers.[66]

It is in the area of phonic interference that the majority of disputes about substratum influence arise, disputes that at times seem to be as acrimonious as those dealing with linguistic theory. As with the matter of the regularity of sound change, some linguists have tended to adopt dogmatic positions. One is that substratum influences are almost invariably denied, for a variety of reasons. A basic assumption of many structural linguists who attempt to explain sound change through the influence of the phonological structure of a language seems to be that it is sufficient to seek internal causes of sound changes.[67] Others have apparently concluded that in most cases no unequivocal proof of interlanguage influence has been yet presented.[68] A pervasive belief in many quarters that linguistic changes can have one and only one cause has likewise blinded many scholars to the true complexity of historical developments (Malkiel 1967). The failure of many substratum researchers to explain adequately just how they conceive of the mechanism of interlanguage influence has probably also led to a certain skepticism about the entire topic.

It is impossible to make any blanket rule about the possibility of one language having had any effect on the phonetic development of another. As with any other historical question, the facts of each case must be examined carefully to determine whether there is any reason to assume such influence: "[E]ach instance of alleged substratum influence must be examined and correlated with the available linguistic and historical data, on its own merits; and conclusions must be reached independently of other instances" (Hall 1949, 155-56). At the same time, certain general minimal conditions under which interlanguage influence is possible can, nevertheless, be given. Fundamental to the concept of this sort of influence is the realization that languages may affect each other not through any kind of vague, mystical union but concretely through the use of two or more languages by the same speakers, that is, through bilingualism or multilingualism. Unless the different languages are kept rigidly apart in a speaker's mind, it seems inevitable that eventually he will use a feature or features from one language when speaking the other. In those cases where one language is the first or dominant one and the other is learned later in life and less thoroughly than the first, the likelihood is that the first language

---

[66] Silvestri (1978) examines in great detail the development of substratum theory since Ascoli. An example of how syntactic influence might be studied is found in Galmés de Fuentes 1956, although, of course, Galmés was studying written texts.

[67] For example, Malmberg has adopted this assumption in his discussion of Spanish phonetic development (Malmberg 1961, and especially 1963). For a summary of the structuralist argument see Lloyd 1971.

[68] For example, Rohlfs 1955.

will be the one that imposes its mark on the second, although there will always be influences in both directions.

The question of whether such influence will become permanent, however, is quite another one:

> Obviously it is a matter of socio-cultural conditions whether the speakers of the "losing" language learn the new language so well as to leave no trace on it, or whether they learn it in an imperfect manner, bequeathing the phonetic and grammatical peculiarities of their speech to future generations in the form of a substratum. Hence, in a language shift, the scholar must look not only for the pressures that determine the choice of language but also for those which decide the thoroughness with which the new language is learned and the flow of leveling, equalizing forces from the unilingual bulk which tend to eliminate traces of the old languages (Weinreich 1953, 109).

Ordinarily, especially in modern societies, the influence of short-lived bilingualism will be ephemeral. If the descendants of bilinguals abandon the language of their parents and grandparents and adopt a new language, they will speak the new language like natives, since the prestige model for them will be those who speak the language well, not those who speak it imperfectly. In the United States, for example, the children of the millions of immigrants from non-English speaking countries learned to speak English like natives, and the pronunciation of most varieties of American English has not been affected in the slightest. Although some might consider that this example proves that the influence of bilingualism can never be permanent, it is more likely that the social situation in the United States was and is fundamentally different from that of Europe one thousand to two thousand years ago. The American system of free, tax-supported public education had as one of its chief tasks the "Americanization" of the foreign-born, and the dominance of the English language has always been one of the primary tools of Americanization, in spite of the fact that the United States has no legally recognized official language.

In the movements of various peoples of Europe in ancient and medieval times, nothing remotely resembling this system existed, and it is fairly certain that the social pressures toward national unity that exist today were also absent in ancient times. The lack of nationalism of the modern type and public education would not, of course, make it any more likely that the effects of bilingualism would have a permanent effect on the pronunciation of the language that finally triumphed. If, however, bilingualism was not just a passing feature of one or two generations but rather became a stable phenomenon during centuries of historical development in which both the older and the new speech lived side by side in active competition, some influence would have had a much greater chance of making itself felt. If the older language only gradually ceded before the pressure of the newer, more socially acceptable language, some sectors of society might have become accustomed to using certain features of pronunciation stimulated by the dying language, and these features could persist even after the period of bilingualism had ended.[69] It may not even be necessary for bilingualism to have endured for a long time, provided that the conditions of life were such that the models for future generations were speakers with some features that had originated in the bilingual situation: "Contrary to what is often said, substratum . . . is most likely to occur not where native speakers of the (future) core-stratum and substratum language are in contact over a long period of time, but rather where native models cease to be present after only a part of the substratum population has learned the new language, and hence the only available 'teachers' are non-native speakers of that language" (Izzo 1972, 193).[70] In all probability each case will be in some way different from all others.

Since bilingualism (or multi-lingualism) is the essential condition for any possible phonic change caused by language contact, the basic requirement for a supposed contact influence is that the sound or sound shift must be found in the influencing language.[71] In the case of languages that are not known today, but which were known to have existed in the past, this criterion may be one of the most difficult to satisfy. Even if there is inscriptional evidence of the lost language, it may be difficult or impossible to be certain of how to interpret it. In that case, any supposed influence on the replacing language will be conjectural at best, and definite proof may never turn up.

The second requirement is that there should be some geographical correspondence between the two languages. This requirement is necessary because a language spoken in one area could hardly have influenced a language spoken elsewhere in the absence of regular communication between the two areas. In other words, bilingualism will probably require some sort of geographical overlap of the two languages. On the other hand, if a change occurs other than in the area of geographical overlap, one cannot thereby assume that no contact influence was possible. This point must be emphasized, because one of the most frequently raised objections to these explanations is that the change in question can be found in a place in which no contact influence was possible: "Many discussions of substratum theory are based on the assumption . . . that the influence of a presumed substratum language must have been present in all regions where the development in question is found, or else not at all. This assumption is not logically consistent. . . . Parallel linguistic develop-

---

[69] An especially interesting essay on the replacement of one language by another is by Terracini 1957.

[70] It is interesting to note that one scholar suggests that certain common changes in the structure of Arabic may well be due to common situations of bilingualism in areas where Arabic spread but was spoken originally only by a few native speakers and many non-native speakers (Versteegh 1982).

[71] This requirement might seem obvious, but on occasion it has been forgotten. Malmberg (1964) claims that the pronunciation of the final /-r/ in Mexican Spanish must be due to the influence of the Nahuatl substratum. The major difficulty with the notion is that there is and was no alveolar trill [r] in Nahuatl, the closest sound being a lateral [l].

ments can perfectly well take place independently of each other both in space and time" (Hall 1949, 150).

One example of this sort of occurrence is the change of Latin /f/ > Castilian /h-/ > MSp. /∅/, which has often been attributed to the influence of Basque, which lacked any consonant like the Latin labial fricative (see chap. 4). This particular change is not limited to this area in Romania, however. In certain sections of Sardinia and Calabria and sporadically in northern Italy and in Rumania as well, the same change has occurred.[72] Some scholars have concluded that this fact completely invalidates any supposed Basque influence because there can be no question of any such substratum in Sardinia, Italy, or Rumania.[73] Therefore some other cause must be sought, probably in the phonological structure of Latin. If one reasons in this way, it would be necessary to look beyond the confines of the Romance family to see if this same type of change has occurred elsewhere in the world. As a matter of fact, it has. In the Malayo-Polynesian languages, for example, the correspondence between Maori and Hawaiian /h/, Fijian /v/, and Samoan /f/ leads to the reconstruction of */f/ in the Proto-Malayo-Polynesian, showing that the identical change has occurred in this family (Arlotto 1972, 96). In Kanarese, a Dravidian language of India, the initial /p-/ changed to /h/ and later to zero from the tenth to the fourteenth centuries (Narasimhia 1941, 1-5). Mongolian, a subgroup of the Altaic language family, also developed an [h] from the bilabial [φ] of Common Mongolian, although in most Mongolian languages this aspirate has disappeared (Poppe 1955, 96). There can be little question of any common substratum or genetic factors in Romance, Malayo-Polynesian, Dravidian, or Altaic, and yet a very similar phonetic change has taken place in all of them. Therefore, to the objection that change must be unique in order for there to have been any contact influence, a simple answer can be made: "The number of phonemes being limited, recurrence of phonemes and phoneme sequences . . . and even recurrence of typical phonological changes, is to be expected" (Pulgram 1949, 243). Therefore, it is sufficient to remark that substratum influence can never be the *sole* cause of a phonetic change. It will be simply one of the factors influencing a change. Similar changes occurring elsewhere may or may not be relevant, depending on the particular circumstances.[74]

Thus, it is not necessary to imagine a complete geographical correspondence between the area occupied by the substratum language and the area in which the change in question is found. The origin of the shift must be

---

[72] Wagner 1941, 90–91, and Rohlfs 1966, 206.

[73] One can, of course, draw just the opposite conclusion and reason that there must have been a common pre-Romance substratum in all of these areas. See, for example, Schuchardt 1866–68, 3: 39.

[74] A very apt remark is the following: "Uno de los aspectos más curiosos de la confusión aludida es el de realizar la búsqueda con el supuesto de que el cambio lingüístico debería tener *una sola causa* genérica. Se piensa que, siendo único el «efecto» (el cambio), también debería de ser única la «causa», y hasta se pretende fundar esta creencia en el principio de que 'las mismas causas producen los mismos efectos.' Pero, en rigor, este principio no es reversible, pues el mismo efecto puede ser producido por causas diversas" (Coseriu 1973, 183).

located in the historical boundaries of the substratum language, to be sure, but once begun the change may be carried far outside its original area. Once a change has taken root in a language, its origins no longer necessarily affect its subsequent spread.

The third requirement for a supposed contact influence is a chronological one. The change which is being explained must date from the period when bilingualism was active. In the past it was sometimes suggested that a change stemming from a substratum language may have appeared centuries after the language itself had disappeared. The only way to explain such a change then would be through some kind of physical inheritance of acquired habits or atavism, a theory that has no scientific standing today (Francescato 1970, 13). Therefore, if a sound change appears after the substratum language has disappeared, there can be no possible influence of the substratum. It is not sufficient, however, to claim that the absence of any documentary evidence of the vanished language proves that it was no longer spoken.[75] A language, or style of language, may persist for hundreds of years, relegated to obscure regions and to unnoticed and insignificant social classes, and the changes provoked by it may likewise remain limited to colloquial, regional usage for a long time before ever coming to the notice of scholars or other socially esteemed persons. After remaining in a "latent state" (Menéndez Pidal 1963) for many years, later social changes may then bring the formerly unnoticed feature to prominence. It can be no objection to possible contact influence that linguistic prestige could not possibly have been attached to the dying language. "Prestige" is not a simple concept; it may apply not only to those in a position of social superiority but also to those admired for some other qualities, not necessarily qualities that speakers will admit they admire. Prestige norms may also change: "It is notable that subculture solidarity may reverse the social evaluation of a change from stigmatized to prestigious, with consequent effects on its progress in the group in question" (Bailey 1975; also Trudgill 1972). It may seem that the change has occurred suddenly, long after the period of bilingualism has ended. Such sudden changes, however, are often only apparent, as was pointed out previously. A better knowledge of the past may often show that it is simply our ignorance that makes it seem that there is a chronological gap between the disappearance of a substratum language and the changes provoked by it in the replacing language.

In summary, these three requirements are only the minimal ones for a substratum language to have made itself felt in the development of another.[76] No further general rules can be formulated, and each individual case must be examined on its own merits. It is likely that language contact, even between dialects of the same language, in so far as they can be considered truly distinct, may have been responsible for many historical

---

[75] Menéndez Pidal (1950a) shows how a feature of language may exist unnoticed for centuries simply because of lack of apparent evidence.

[76] These requirements are similar to those presented by Posti 1965.

changes. In the words of one scholar: "Bilingualism is a universal phenomenon, since no languages we know have been spoken over long periods of
time in complete isolation. It is even possible that bilingualism is one of the
major factors in linguistic changes—a point of view which could be defended by good arguments" (Vogt 1954, 368). Nevertheless, in many instances it is possible that we shall never have sufficient data to allow us to
come to firm historical conclusions, and we will have to be content with
likely conjectures. In any case, such conjectures cannot be simply thrown
out in an off-hand fashion, but must be based on as full a collection of
primary data as can be obtained. It is essential that the investigator make
every attempt to determine just what were the social conditions that might
have permitted the effect of bilingualism to have persisted long enough to
have given rise to an established variable.

Other Causes of Sound Change

The Stress Accent

It is sometimes thought that a strongly accented syllable may absorb
enough articulatory energy from a word to be able to cause speakers to
neglect the unstressed syllables, and finally to drop them altogether and
thus reduce the number of syllables in a word. Syncope and apocope could
thus be attributed to an increasing amount of articulatory stress or muscular effort. The loss of syllables could then be classified as an effect of the
principle of least effort. As the speakers increase the amount of stress on
one part of a word, they reduce it on another and thus economize their
effort. Or, taking another tack, one could conceive of the loss of redundant
syllables as the motive for increasing the amount of stress on the accented
syllable. In Martinet's words: "On pourrait même en arriver à concevoir
que ce n'est pas l'accent dynamique qui estompe le timbre des voyelles et
supprime les syllabes, mais que ce sont les distinctions de timbre inutiles
qui, s'estompant, perdent une partie de leur énergie qui se reporte sur les
zones proprement lexicales du mot qu'elles renforcent" (1955, 169-70).

What is most dubious about such conjectures is that there is no historical
proof (in Romance, at least) that stress on accented syllables has in fact
increased. Such an increase is often assumed because of syncope, but the
only evidence for it is syncope itself. Possibly there is some sort of balance
between stress and the number and quantity of syllables,[77] but syncope

---

[77] A skeptical view is the following:

Acaso para algunas personas el término 'compensación' recuerda el conocido axioma de la
física, según el cual a toda acción se opone una reacción igual y contraria; pero debe tenerse
presente que la reacción y la acción son simultáneas, y que al salir la corriente de aire para
producir un fonema, la reacción tiene lugar simultáneamente en el diafragma, pulmones,
etc. del hablante, como el retroceso al disparar un arma. Quizá se supone, por otro lado,
que los hablantes de una lengua determinada tienen el sentimiento o la impresión de que
las palabras de una categoría particular o las de frases frecuentemente repetidas han de
tener cierta masa o magnitud. En este caso, si hubiera aumentado la intensidad . . . las

alone cannot prove that the stress accent has increased. If unstressed syllables become excessively redundant so that their loss may have no effect on communication, speakers may be tempted to elide or drop them in allegro styles and thus point the way to their complete elimination. Also there may be a close relation between the evolution of accentuation and the general tempo and rhythm of a language (Bailey 1975, 54), but an examination of the prosodic features of speech and their relation to sound change would expand this brief introduction far beyond its necessary limits.

The Influence of Syllable Structure

Another factor that may account for certain changes is the typical or statistically dominant kind of syllable that characterizes a language or family of languages. Romance for instance, has preferred open syllables to closed ones since the time of ancient Latin. The natural way for any Romance speaker to divide words into syllables is to make each syllable end in a vowel whenever possible. Thus, any consonant that necessarily comes at the end of a syllable because it cannot form a unified group or cluster with the following consonant will be subject to some kind of weakening, even if limited to a slight assimilatory change. As will be seen in the section on Latin phonology, the weakness of the syllable-final position resulted in a neutralization of various phonemic oppositions, and in many cases produced the loss of final consonants. Even languages which have more phonemic oppositions in this position than Romance and which have many more closed syllables are more likely to show more weakening of consonants finally than initially.

Force of Articulation

It may be thought that all such reductions of articulatory energy in the final position are simply the result of a lessening of physical energy as a speaker reaches the end of a phonic group (including a single syllable as well as a complete utterance). The next question that one must ask is why it should be true that the end of a group should inevitably require less effort on the speaker's part than the beginning. In part, at least, this phenomenon can be illuminated by a consideration of information theory.

Before one begins to speak, the possibilities that exist for a hearer are almost unlimited. He may expect to hear almost anything. Once the speaker begins, however, the successive parts of an utterance are increas-

---

demás vocales—podría argumentarse—tendrían que reducirse para que las palabras o las frases no tuvieran una masa mayor de la habitual; por tanto, se favorecerían las realizaciones debilitadas de las vocales átonas. Pero no se aplicaría esto también a la pronunciación de los fonemas? (Jungemann 1955, 310–14).

In the Slavic languages, there is evidence of some kind of compensation with regard to differences in syllabic prominence and length tending toward a balance of the syllables of a word. See Avanesov 1949 (information supplied by Henning Andersen, private communication).

ingly limited by what has preceded. In the choice of vocabulary, for example, once the definite article has been pronounced, the speaker must follow it by a noun phrase of some sort, rather than a verb. Once the predicate has been uttered, there are even more limitations. Similarly, in phonology one may expect to hear any combination of phonemes that the language allows, but once a syllable has been pronounced, both the number and types of syllables that can follow are restricted by the phonological structure of the language and its average word length. Within the syllable itself, once the onset has been pronounced, the possibilities for what may follow in the nucleus are sharply limited, and the coda is even more restricted. Thus, as one proceeds, there is a decreasing amount of new information that is being conveyed. In Spanish, for instance, any consonant or no consonant may appear at the onset of a syllable. After a single consonant, on the other hand, only a liquid may appear in the onset, if the consonant is a stop or /f/. In the nucleus only a vowel or a combination of vowels may appear, and in the coda only a limited number of consonants.

Thus once an utterance or part of an utterance has begun, the hearer can predict, to a certain extent, what will come next. In other words, there is an increasing amount of redundancy, and the hearer can miss or disregard what he hears without losing any essential information. The speaker likewise can be more careless in pronouncing toward the end of a syllable or a word with the assurance that the content of what he is saying will still be communicated. There is no absolutely consistent reduction in informativeness from beginning to end of an utterance, however. A psychological experiment conducted a few years ago revealed that the distortion of the beginning of a word caused far more errors in interpretation than distortion of other parts of a word. Also the distortion of the end of a word caused more errors of interpretation than a distortion of the middle (Bruner and O'Dowd 1958).[78]

One may conclude that the initial segments of words and syllables are much more resistant to change than medial and final segments. Historically these theoretical points are borne out by the frequency with which words are shortened through syncope of medial syllables, in contrast with the much more frequent preservation of initial segments. The position that sounds occupy in words and syllables therefore must be a factor favoring change or resisting it.[79]

The Influence of Morphological Patterns on Sound Change

In general, it seems that phonetic change proceeds without regard for the effect it may have on other aspects of language. The Latin case system, for example, should have been severely disturbed by the change in the

---

[78] Probably there is some relation between these findings and the fact that many languages rely on suffixes to convey grammatical information.

[79] Some studies by Bertil Malmberg analyze in greater detail the points covered in this section: Malmberg 1962, 1963.

vowel system of Late Latin and the loss of final /-m/. There is, however, only slight evidence that speakers of Latin reacted against this change in order to preserve the accusative case. The case system collapsed and sound change continued unchecked. Of course, it is probable that the case system would have disappeared anyway without the assistance of phonetic change since the use of other devices (prepositions, word order) increasingly replaced the case endings as indicators of syntactic function. Occasionally though, it appears that phonetic change has been arrested or deflected in a certain direction by some well established morphological patterns. For example, in one area in central France unstressed /a/ becomes /o/. Just to the north of this area, the final /-s/ which had served as a marker of the plural has disappeared, but in this same region the change of /a/ to /o/ has occurred only in the singular of nouns, thus preserving the distinction between singular and plural (i.e., sing. -o, pl. -a). It may appear that one factor in the limitation of this change to the singular was the need to preserve a clear distinction between the singular and the plural (Labov 1972, 109). Malkiel (1968, 1970, 1976; among others) has shown that it is at least possible that certain sound changes were deflected or possibly strengthened in one direction by well-defined morphological developments. In general, however, it seems clear that such influence is extremely limited, and grammars have practically no effect on sound change (Campbell 1974, 89).

Favored Pronunciations?

Many years ago Edward Sapir suggested that some languages may have a drive or "drift" toward certain types of pronunciation, or possibly, away from other types, as in a trend toward the monophthongization of all diphthongs: "It is curious to observe how often languages have striven to drive originally distinct sounds into certain favorite positions, regardless of resulting confusions" (Sapir 1921, 181). In many cases, it is probable that such drift is simply the result of structural readjustments, as related phonemes press against their neighbors. Possibly there are certain distinctive features that are underexploited in the phonological system and that by being utilized more fully are an aid in the over-all economy of the system. At present the concept of favored pronunciations can best be considered simply a covering term for what later research may reveal to be a variety of different things.[80]

The Origin of Sound Changes

In the preceding sections we have examined some of the factors that influence sound change and its direction, and the social factors that may affect its spread. It remains to be seen whether it is possible to determine why and how a sound change gets a start (the "actuation problem" in

---

[80] See Malkiel 1981 for a close examination of the various meanings that Sapir attributed to "drift."

Labov's terminology, 1982, 81). A child who begins learning his first language is naturally exposed to the heterogeneous forms of that language and their social significance, and his contribution to sound change will be a function of his socialization. He will continue to adapt to the usages of his community, whether the changes in progress are internally motivated or result from bilingualism.

No one, however, has yet explained how a sound change begins in the speech of an individual who is not imitating anyone else. As we saw previously, the notion that language change begins with imperfect learning on the part of children has a certain superficial attractiveness, since childhood is the time when a person is still actively acquiring the system of the language of his community. Nevertheless, there is no evidence of regular change between generations, because generations are characteristic of the family but not of the community, which has persons of all ages in it (Labov 1972, 102).

If an innovation of any sort must be some kind of deviation from a norm, it is necessary to explain why such deviations are not corrected, either by the learner himself or by his models. First, a distinction must be made between the surface structure—in the case of phonology, the articulatory and acoustic realizations—and its "underlying representation": that is, the units of a phonological system may not correspond exactly to what a speaker actually pronounces. This is very clear in the case of a phoneme with two or more clearly distinct allophones, as for example, the Spanish /b/ whose realizations are either a voiced bilabial stop or a fricative, depending largely on the phonetic circumstances. The learner hears both allophones, and, in trying to imitate what he hears, eventually classifies both into a single unit, the phoneme /b/. This phoneme, however, is neither a stop nor a fricative but an abstraction whose distinctive features are [+voice, +bilabial, +obstruent]. Although some theoreticians prefer to assume a greater degree of abstractness in phonology than others, all linguists agree on some distinction between surface structure and what may be called the "underlying structure."

In learning the underlying structure, a child must base himself on the behavior that he observes around him. He does not learn the abstract system directly from others. To use a metaphor popular with some linguists today, the child is said to "construct a grammar" which he "internalizes."[81] The following diagram illustrates this process:[82]

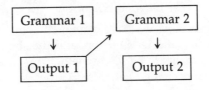

---

[81] An appropriate remark is that: "There is reason to believe that the act of perception is not a purely passive one. It is an act of construction rather than reception" (Rivers 1971, 125).
[82] This diagram is taken from Andersen 1973, fig. 1, on 767. This section is based largely on Andersen's article.

If the learner discovers how to imitate exactly what he hears, then to all intents and purposes, as far as other speakers are concerned, he has learned the same abstract system that they possess. There are, however, in any system certain areas of ambiguity which a learner may interpret in a fashion that differs from that of his models. If the learner speaks according to his own interpretation of the output of his models, but the result does not correspond to their output, he will probably be corrected by others, or notice the difference himself and try to correct his own performance.

In revising his pronunciation he can proceed in two ways: either to alter his "underlying system" so that his output will conform to that of others, or to keep the same system and change his rules for output on an ad hoc basis so that the output will be the same as that of his models. In the latter case, as far as the learner is able to tell, he is now in conformity with the pronunciation of other speakers, and he may not suspect that his abstract system is any different from theirs. Neither the learner nor his models would be aware that their systems are different in some way. The ad hoc rules, which may be termed "adaptive rules" (to use Andersen's term), serve to conceal the differences.

There can be no doubt of the reality of some adaptive rules in language, although they would differ from ordinary phonemic representation rules or morphophonemic rules in that they are limited to certain words or to the output of certain morphophonemic rules. For example, in the English of lower middle-class speakers of New York City, the linguist may assume that the underlying forms of the words *beard, bared,* and *bad* are homonyms whose nucleus is a high ingliding vowel /bihd/. In the spontaneous speech of these speakers these words are all pronounced as homophones [bihd]. In the prestige form of American English these words are not homonyms but are all different: /biːrd/, /beːrd/, and /bæd/. Speakers with underlying homonymic forms are aware that their pronunciation does not conform to the prestige model and, if they wish to adapt their own pronunciation to this model, they can do so, and produce forms that are not homophones: [bihd], [behd], and [bæhd]. These forms are, however, "produced in a most irregular and unreliable manner" (Weinreich, Labov, and Herzog 1968, 134–35). In the phonemic structure of these speakers it might appear that there has been a structural innovation which can be concealed by adaptive rules limited to certain words and not motivated by the structure itself. Because these rules are limited only to specific lexemes, they are not productive. In other instances, an adaptive rule may be employed by speakers in order to produce an "accent" characteristic of some prestige dialect. In such cases a rule is applied to certain classes of sounds rather than to specific words, and is limited by the social circumstances in which a speaker finds himself.

According to this view, the results of a structural innovation may thus be concealed by a system of adaptive rules. As far as the language learners themselves are concerned, they have succeeded in reproducing the same sounds as their models. Since, however, the adaptive rules of this sort are unproductive and unmotivated by the phonological structure, they are likely to become more restricted with the passage of time so that the number of words to which they apply becomes reduced, or the circumstances in which they must be used become less frequent. If, for example, a rule is associated with some social grouping like age, as the members of that group decline in importance, the rule will also become less frequently applied. Since there are many different kinds of groups in any society, the domains of adaptive rules may overlap in a very complex fashion.

If adaptive rules are a valid assumption, structural innovations would appear only gradually in usage and speakers could adjust themselves to new norms. It would not do, however, to think that "adaptive rules" are necessarily the only way that changes can spread gradually through a language for they seem to assume a rather static view of language; that is, they are based on the notion that each speaker has only a single "underlying" form for every word in his lexicon. What proof do we have that speakers who pronounce *bad*, *bared*, and *beard* as homophones in their most informal style necessarily have a single homonymous underlying form for all three words in all of the styles at their command? Why could it not be that they have separate forms for their formal style and homonymous forms for their informal styles, and that they sometimes confuse them in actual practice because their formal style is less controlled than their informal styles? It may be that Bailey is correct in his more psychologically realistic claim that "linguistic competence is polylectal" (1975, 27), i.e. that speakers have command of a variety of systems that they associate with the different social uses to which language is put.

At any rate, it cannot be claimed that ambiguity of surface structure is the starting point of all phonetic changes. In many cases, if not most, we can never be sure what motivates a single individual to make a particular change. And, in the last analysis, it may not even be very important. The distinction is often made between the "origin" and the "propagation" of a phonetic change, and, often enough, it is a most necessary distinction. The origin of a particular change or variant form may be quite unrelated to its further progress in a language. It is possible that one of the important factors in the change of the Latin labial /f/ to an aspirate /h/ was the early bilingual Castilian community in which many speakers of Basque were learning to speak the Romance vernacular (see chap. 4). Lacking the /f/ in their mother tongue, they might well have tended to use a weak labial fricative or even an aspirate as the equivalent of the Latin-Romance /f/. At any rate, once the Romance of Castile was established as a dominant dialect in the Iberian peninsula, the aspirate pronunciation of /f/ was well established as a variant pronunciation of the phoneme, and was carried to new regions along with Castilian. It reached many areas where no bilingualism of Basque and Romance had ever existed; thus in this case the propagation of the change is quite independent of the circumstances of its origin. In other instances, it may not be so easy to distinguish between the circumstances of the origin of a change and its further propagation. Since language is an instrument of communication of a community, then "idiosyncratic habits are not part of language so conceived, and idiosyncratic changes no more so. Therefore we can say that the language has changed when a *group* of speakers use a different pattern to communicate with each other. . . . [T]he origin of a change *is* its propagation or acceptance by others" (Labov 1973, 209).[83] Finally, we may have to content ourselves with the thought that "linguistic reality is too complex to allow for an exhaustive listing of all the causes of all phonological changes" (Martinet 1951, 76).

MORPHOLOGICAL CHANGE: ANALOGY

The preceding section dealt with phonetic change and the problems of general language evolution most closely related to it. Since this book is concerned with both the phonetic and morphological evolution of Spanish, it is fitting to discuss some of the general aspects of morphological evolution also.

First, a few words on what is meant by morphology are appropriate. In its original meaning, the word referred to the study of forms in the biological sciences (Matthews 1974, 2), but in the study of language it soon came to be used to refer to the forms of language above the phonemic and phonetic level. A morpheme is usually defined very generally as "the single minimal or primitive unit of grammar" (Matthews 1974, 78). In many instances, it is fairly simple to determine what these units are. If we take, for example, the single word *libros* 'books', we can separate at least two basic elements: *libro* 'book' and *-s* 'plural'. We can take another derived word, *librero* 'book seller', and similarly separate at least two morphemes: *libr-* 'book' and *-ero* 'agent; one associated in some way with the base word'. Some linguists would prefer to distinguish another morpheme, *-o* 'masculine', since the *-o* of *libro* does not appear in the derived word *librero* immediately after the base. In Latin we might take as an example AMĀMUS 'we love', and separate three morphemes: the root AM- 'love', a suffix -MUS 'first person plural', and a thematic vowel -Ā- that has no special meaning except possibly 'present tense indicative, first conjugation'. Problems of appropriate morphological analysis sometimes become very complex and cannot be dealt with in detail at this point.

It is usual in traditional linguistic studies to distinguish between "lexical" and "inflectional" morphology.[84] Lexical morphology is the study of inde-

---

[83] Labov's point of view echoes Menéndez Pidal:

Sin duda: el individuo por sí solo es impotente para alterar el curso de las modificaciones que el lenguaje tienda sufrir; pero también es evidente que los cambios que se produzcan en el lenguaje, siendo éste un hecho humano, serán siempre debidos a la iniciativa de un hombre, de un individuo que al desviarse de lo habitual, logra la adhesión o imitación de otros, y éstos logran las de otros: en suma, el proceso por el que se propaga cualquier opinión o cualquier costumbre en un grupo humano, hasta hacerse propia de la mayoría (1944a, 17–18).

[84] See Matthews 1974, chap. 3, for a clear exposition of some problems associated with this classification.

pendent lexemes,[85] such as we saw above in the derivation of *librero* from *libro*. Although the relation between these two words may seem somewhat similar to the relation between *libro* and *libros,* i.e., a suffix is added to a base, for the most part the relation is quite different. The formation of *librero* served to create a new lexeme that is in some sense independent of its base. Many other words have been formed in a similar way, e.g., *mesero, cartero, alfombrero, maletero, cuchillero, papelero, lechero, cantinero,* etc., and yet not all substantives can automatically produce a derived form in *-ero*. From *pared* 'wall' one should be able to form **paredero*, and yet it does not seem to exist as a part of the general Spanish lexicon. The same thing is true of **maquinero* as a derivative of *máquina* 'machine' or **presero* from *presa* 'dam', **reactorero* from *reactor,* or many more. In short, formations in *-ero* are greatly limited, in spite of the large number that actually do exist, and the facility with which new ones can be formed. Also, once a word in *-ero* is created, it may eventually lose much of its connection with its base. *Caballero,* for example is now far removed from much association with *caballo* 'horse'. Historical circumstances have given *caballero* a number of meanings that could not be predicted from the base word, 'knight; gentleman'. On the other hand, there is no limit to the formation of plurals from singular substantives, in spite of the fact that a few words may appear only in the plural, e.g., *tijeras* 'scissors', while other words may be quite rare in the plural, e.g., *aguas* 'waters', *harinas* 'flours', etc.

The essentially unlimited morphology such as is found in the formation of plurals, then, and the concordance of adjectives, along with the various tenses and moods of verbs, and the case endings of nouns, are put into the category of inflectional morphology, and are studied in this volume. The problem of lexical morphology (word formation), since it is of a different nature for the most part, will be studied in a second volume.

Morphemes are usually realized by means of phonemes or phoneme sequences,[86] and therefore, if there were no interfering factors, would have no evolution apart from the evolution of the individual sounds or groups of sounds identified with each morpheme. In many cases, in fact, this is just what happens. A word like Lat. CASĀS 'huts' becomes modern Spanish *casas* 'houses', with all of the expected sound changes. Similarly, Lat. **FĀBULŌ* (C.L. FĀBULOR, a deponent verb) evolves into modern *hablo* 'I speak'. The same sort of change affects many other morphemes.

Of course, we must point out that to analyze linguistic evolution solely

---

[85] The distinction between *word* and *lexeme* is found in Matthews 1974, chap. 2. Essentially any linguistic form that can be uttered by itself can be considered a word, while lexeme includes all the various variant forms that may appear in paradigms, e.g. the lexeme *hablar* 'to speak' would be intended to include all of the forms of the verb that may be used by speakers, *hablo, hablábamos, hablé,* etc.

[86] We cannot really say that a morpheme is "composed of" phonemes since in many cases the various elements that go to make up the functional forms of a single lexeme (as in cases of suppletion) have no phonetic connection with each other, e.g. Eng. *goes* (present tense) vs. *went* (past tense). Also certain functions may be conveyed by nothing at all, e.g. Eng. *sheep* (singular) vs. *sheep* (plural).

in this fashion is to omit as much as we include. CASĀS is not exactly equivalent to *casas* because the morpheme -ĀS in Latin was not simply a sign of plurality as it is today, but also included the notion of the case of the substantive: in this instance it was accusative. In other words, the study of morphemes must inevitably include a study of the function and meaning of morphemes and not simply their phonetic form. These functions may change over time, as in the case of CASĀS, or as when the Latin perfect passive AMĀTUS EST came to be reinterpreted as a present passive, e.g., Sp. *es amado* 'he is loved' vs. the Latin meaning 'he *was* loved'. This shift in turn coincided with the disappearance of the paradigmatic pattern earlier employed as a present passive. Once this type of change has been described, our major task is to show the correspondences between the remaining modern and medieval forms and their historical prototypes. In many instances, this involves simply an application of straight phonological rules. In order to divide our material conveniently, however, the study of morphology in this volume will concentrate primarily on form, in so far as it can be divided from function, and the study of morphological functions will be included in a second volume.

Even if we were to attempt to study simply the external form of various morphemes, we should soon find that ordinary phonetic development cannot possibly account for all the changes that we observe. In tightly knit paradigms such as are found in verbal systems, some forms are modelled on others rather than following a straight phonetic development. Even when regular phonetic development could have produced a regular paradigm in a later development, some forms seem to have an expansive force in the linguistic consciousness of speakers and can eliminate phonologically regular changes. For example, we find in Latin that the perfect of the verb TENĒRE 'to hold' was a regular type of formation involving the ending -Uī, i.e., TENUī 'I held, have held'. The form equivalent to this one in modern Spanish is *tuve* 'I had, received', although once again we see that it is not exactly equivalent in function because Latin had no tense like the modern *he tenido* 'I have had'. The Latin perfect included concepts that in Romance became separated with the creation of the compound perfects. It is most unlikely that anyone would be inclined to try to find a phonetic explanation for the Spanish form,[87] and therefore we must look for some other source than simple sound change. In this particular case, it seems clear that speakers abandoned the form TENUī altogether and remade the perfect on the model of another word, Lat. HABUī 'I had, have had', which developed phonetically into Old Spanish *ove* > MSp. *hube*.[88] The close relationship of the meanings of the two verbs (*tener* eventually replaced

---

[87] Possibly some ingenious student might attempt to claim that this case reflects an "*n*-deleting rule," followed by a "rule of consonantization of *u*," etc., but such contortions are rarely worth the effort since they apply for the most part to a few exceptional words rather than to whole series of words.

[88] The modern spelling reflects only a later attempt to make the Spanish written form resemble more closely its Latin etymon rather than any change in the pronunciation of the medial consonant or the initial segment.

haber with the meaning of 'to possess') seems to have served to induce speakers to alter the perfect of *tener* to make it more closely resemble that of *haber,* although other factors may also have been present.

This sort of modelling of one morpheme on another is called *analogy,* which can be defined as a relation of similarity (Anttila 1972, 88). Human beings tend to have a natural facility for perceiving similarities between objects of different kinds even when they base their perception on relatively few features.[89] It is not surprising then that speakers should associate the form of words that are perceived as related in some other way. Speakers generally associate sameness of meaning with sameness of form (or similarity of form) and vice versa. Thus, they expect that there should be a biunique relationship between a phonetic form and its meanings and/or functions. If there is no great similarity of form between one word and another associated with it, it is a very common occurrence for speakers to alter the form of one of the words in order to make their similarity more evident, as in the example above.

Analogical changes are often presented in the form of a proportion (Latin PROPORTIŌ = Gr. ἀναλογία) such as the following:

$$\frac{aver}{ove} : \frac{tener}{X}$$

As in a mathematical proportion one must solve for the unknown X and in this instance X = *tove* (MSp. *tuve*). Of course the fact that one can present the process in this fashion does not make it in any way a genuine mathematical operation. It is rather a simple diagram for illustrating how speakers *may* proceed in the creation of a new form. In some cases, a speaker may actually be conscious of the model he is following. A Danish child is reported to have formed the past tense form *nak* 'he nodded' from the verb *nikke* 'to nod' instead of the correct form *nikkede.* On being corrected, he justified the form by saying, "*Stikker:stak* ('stick:stuck'), *nikker:nak*" (Jespersen 1922, 131).[90]

All sorts of formations of this type can be described by means of proportional models like the one given above, e.g.,

$$\text{Eng.} \frac{drive}{drove} : \frac{dive}{X}$$

---

[89] See Anttila 1977, 45–58, for an extended discussion of this tendency as a feature of human psychology. Esper (1973) shows the strong connection between general psychological principles of analogy and language.

[90] All sorts of "incorrect" verb forms are created in this way. Children who have not learned the standard form of words are especially likely to create analogical forms, e.g. *goed* for *went.* In my neighborhood, for instance, the common use of *got* (from the compound verb *has got*) as a verb meaning 'to have' has induced many children to regularize it and say, "He gots."

which produces the form *dove,* a past tense which exists along with the regular past tense *dived.*

In this particular example we can see several aspects of the problem of analogy. First, although the preceding proportion is undoubtedly a possible model of the actual process that created the form *dove,* we cannot be sure that speakers were necessarily following the pattern of the verb *drive.* There are a number of other verbs having the diphthong /ay/ in the present stem and /ow/ in the past that might have been the model:

$$\frac{\text{thrive}}{\text{throve}} \quad : \quad \frac{\text{strive}}{\text{strove}} \quad : \quad \frac{\text{ride}}{\text{rode}} \quad : \quad \frac{\text{write}}{\text{wrote}}$$

In fact, all these verbs together may have served as models for *dive* and therefore it might be more accurate to put all items meeting the same conditions on the left-hand side of the proportion. The particular conditions may be a similar or identical phoneme or sequence of phonemes in a morpheme or in part of a morpheme, or a similarity or identity of function or meaning, e.g., past vs. non-past in the examples given above. This identity or similarity which serves as the model of an analogy can be called the "focus" of the analogy (Leed 1970, 6).

Second, we have to keep in mind that besides the list of verbs containing /ay/ in the present and /ow/ in the past, there are other verbs having an /ay/ in the present stem that could also be put into a proportion:

$$\frac{\text{fly}}{\text{flew}} \quad : \quad \frac{\text{arrive}}{\text{arrived}}$$

In other words, there are often several patterns that may serve as a model for the formation of any particular word, and we cannot be certain which pattern is likely to exert the strongest influence on any one speaker or group of speakers, any more than we can tell which of several possible analogical results will finally win out and become the accepted one. Indeed, as we see in the case of *dived* versus *dove,* two different results may continue to exist side by side. In many instances, a large number of examples of words which follow a specific pattern may suffice to induce speakers to add more words to the group. In the history of English, for example, the number of verbs containing the suffix -*ed* in the past tense has steadily increased, while the number of "strong" verbs (i.e., those that indicate the past by means of a change of the stem vowel) has decreased. The increasing number of verbs of this type may be a factor in the creation of even more "weak" verb forms. On the other hand, the creation of the strong past *dove* went against the expected tendency. Therefore, it is important to emphasize that simply because one can formulate a particular proportion there is no guarantee that an analogical formation will necessarily result. Undoubtedly many analogical changes are made by speakers all the time but are not picked up by other speakers and thus go unnoticed.

It has been pointed out that, for example, the existence of a proportion such as:

$$\frac{\text{ear}}{\text{hear}} : \frac{\text{eye}}{\text{X}}$$

cannot make it likely that a new verb like *heye* will be formed (Kiparsky 1974, 259).[91] In other words, there must be a regular functional relationship between the elements of a proportion, as in the case of **dive:dove**, i.e., non-past:past, which does not exist in the case of the relationship between **ear** and **hear**. In the case of **dive**, for example, the creation of **dove** may not be due to the large number of verbs meeting the structural requirements of the proportion but to the frequency of usage of the verbs showing the /ay/:/ow/ relation. Thus frequency of occurrence of one pattern may serve to offset to some extent the larger number of items in another pattern. We must conclude that there are usually competing analogical pressures at work on any one lexeme, and that there is always a large degree of indeterminacy in analogical formations, both in the models likely to be followed by speakers, and in the strength of any particular model and in the final results of the various analogical formation. This fact accounts for the great complexity that is found in different types of analogical changes.

A minimal set of the characteristics that allow us to formulate the potential for an analogical formation would then be (following Leed 1970, 6–7):

1) a formal operation or operations (i.e., regular derivation of some sort);
2) identity of focus (i.e., the elements of the proportion must be partially identical);
3) lexical lists which may be open-ended (i.e., indefinitely large);
4) indeterminacy (i.e., unpredictability).

Of course, we cannot always be sure what will strike speakers as similar. Resemblances between different things may not always be perceived by all speakers, and therefore there is no way to formalize similarities (Anttila 1974, 10). This fact alone adds to the indeterminacy of analogy.

One of the most common effects of analogy in morphological systems is the leveling of paradigms so that they gain in uniformity of form. Sound change, for example, can be considered to be a type of analogy (Vennemann 1978), and when one particular sound or group of sounds begins to

---

[91] The fact that we do not find a word like *heye* may be due to chance and may not be an absolute impossibility, as Kiparsky seems to think. In morphological systems and in word formation such isolated creations are rarely found, and yet it is not impossible that in the case of individual pairs of words just such a result might be found.

evolve in a certain direction, all examples of these sounds will tend to follow the same evolution. Thus, the group of a consonant plus a high or mid front vowel and another vowel began to be realized in ordinary conversational Latin in a single syllable rather than in two syllables as in earlier Latin or in careful speech. The result was the formation of a front glide in place of the full front vowel, e.g., VĪNEA 'vineyard' [bi:-ne-a] > [bi:-nja] (Sp. *viña*). All combinations of this type developed a palatal glide or yod in Late Latin. The group /tj/ began to develop a sibilant quality as the dental stop assimilated to the glide and thus eventually produced an assibilated affricate /tˢ/. This should have affected all examples of /tj/, including verb forms such as SENTIŌ 'I feel, perceive', which, had phonetic analogy been consistent, would have produced Old Spanish *sienço*, but we find only *siento*, in which the yod has been eliminated. It seems evident that the lack of a yod in most other forms of the present indicative and in the other tenses induced speakers to restructure the first person singular on the model of the other persons: SENTIS, SENTIT, SENTĪMUS, etc. Analogy here had a conservative effect which undid the effects of sound change, or at any rate, never allowed it to take effect in the first place.

Thus, we can see that ordinary sound change can produce "irregular" forms in a paradigm, i.e., forms whose phonetic shape differs in some way from other members of the paradigm. As long as sound change is unchecked, the result is the creation of allomorphs. Often enough, such varying phonetic shapes can establish themselves as a fixed part of the language. Thus, we find that the process of diphthongization of the mid open vowels of Late Latin produced a whole series of verbs in which a diphthong alternated with a simple vowel, the so-called "radical-changing" verbs of Castilian. We have *siento, sientes, siente, sienten*, contrasting with *sentir, sentimos, sentides*, and *duermo, duermes, duerme, duermen* contrasting with *dormir, dormimos, dormides*. In some languages, this sort of occurrence can produce widespread morphophonemic variation which seems to be quite stable, e.g., Rumanian. Opposed to these verbs with varying vowels in the stem are a large number of verbs with a mid vowel in the stem that did not derive from Latin open mid vowels and thus never diphthongized, e.g., *deber* 'to owe; ought' < DĒBĒRE, *beber* 'to drink' < BIBERE, *correr* 'to run' < CURRERE, *poner* 'to put' < PŌNERE, etc. As a result, speakers had available two models of verbs with mid vowels in the stem: those that diphthongized under stress and those that did not. In a number of instances, the model of the verbs with unvarying stems was followed by speakers and verbs which in the Middle Ages had belonged to the class of radical-changing verbs abandoned the alternation in later Spanish. Thus, OSp. *prestar* 'to lend', *entregar* 'to deliver, hand over', *pretender* 'to attempt' and various others (Menéndez Pidal 1941, 290) had present tenses with diphthongs: *priesto, priestas*, etc., *entriego, pretiendo*, and similarly, while in modern Spanish the corresponding forms are *presto, entrego*, and *pretendo*. If this process had been carried to completion, all radical-changing verbs would have been eliminated.

As pointed out above, however, the process of analogy is indeterminate. As there are multiple pressures at work on any one particular form, not all speakers may follow the same model. The number of radical-changing verbs was large enough and contained enough verbs of common usage to serve as a counter-model to the regular verbs. Not surprisingly, some verbs which formerly did not belong to the class have joined it. In Old Spanish *sembrar* 'to sow' < Lat. SĒMINĀRE, *pensar* 'to think' < PĒNSĀRE (cf. the popular verb *pesar* 'to weigh' which contrasts with semilearned *pensar*) had present tense forms such as *sembran* and *pensan*. Along with these regular forms there arose diphthongized forms such as *siembran* and *piensan* which today have become the norm.

The paradigmatic leveling which we saw in the case of SENTIŌ tends to be conservative in morphological systems and to undo the effects of unrestricted sound change, as we saw in the preceding examples. The same type of leveling can also work in the opposite direction and lead to the creation of new forms unjustified by any phonetic development. Thus, in the case of the radical-changing verbs speakers may be tempted to make the diphthongized stem the unique form and to create new forms within the paradigm containing the diphthong, e.g., *piérdamos* or *piérdanos* 'we lose' (pres. subj.) or *vuelamos* 'we fly', *vuelar* 'to fly', forms found in some dialects of colloquial Spanish in place of the standard forms *perdamos*, *volamos*, and *volar*. The model for the diphthongized forms was obviously the singular form and the third person plural, in all of which the stress fell on the stem. In the history of Spanish, analogical creation is responsible for the perfects in *-ove* mentioned previously, and totally new forms utilizing stems found in a paradigm. For example, Lat. ESSE 'to be', in the present stem, had two different roots: ES- used in forms 2, 3, and 5 of the present indicative, ES, EST, ESTIS vs. the stem SU- found in the remaining forms: SUM, SUMUS, and SUNT. Speakers of Ibero-Romance, following the model of the plurals in SU-, created a new form *SUTIS which later became the OSp. *sodes* (cf. a similar creation in Rumanian *sînteți* 'you [pl.] are').

In some cases, we may not be able to set up a proportion of the type shown above, especially when we have to do with the extension of a morph to words that formerly did not employ it. The extension to new words may not eliminate completely older forms. In English, for example, the increasing use of *-s* as the indicator of plurality in the class of nouns did not necessarily involve a proportion of the following type:

$$\frac{\text{book}}{\text{books}} : \frac{\text{foot}}{\text{X}}$$

One might expect that X would turn out to be **foots,* but it is not unusual to find *feets* (and similar plurals such as *mices* from *mouse*) where the older plural form is retained but the plural morpheme *-s* is added to it. It seems that in such cases the morpheme *-s* exists as an independent form in the speakers' consciousness and can be applied to the old plural form without being a part of a proportion.

Analogy affects all areas of language and not only morphological systems, even though it is in closely knit paradigms where we may see most clearly its effects. Purely chance resemblance of words may provoke reanalysis. Thus, the Old Spanish words *ascuchar* 'to listen' < Lat. AU- SCULTĀRE and *asconder* 'to hide' < ABSCONDERE resembled each other solely in having the same initial syllable, *as-* followed by the occlusive /k/. One rule of Spanish phonology which applied to all words was, and still is, that the consonant group of /s/ plus another consonant develops an epenthetic vowel /e-/ before it, thus producing forms like *escuela* 'school' < Lat. SC(H)OLA, *escala* 'ladder' < SCĀLA, *escaño* 'bench' < SCAMNU, *escoba* 'broom' < SCŌPA (usually SCOPAE, 'twigs; broom'), *escribir* 'to write' < SCRĪBERE, and many more. The great number of words beginning with *es-*, as opposed to these two beginning with *as-*, seems to have stimulated speakers to bring them into the majority group, thus producing the modern forms *escuchar* and *esconder*.

It may be useful now to make a classification of different sorts of analogies in language even when the only examples we have are of individual words or groups of words rather than elements in a morphological paradigm.

1. A word having a similar meaning to another word or one that belongs to the same category as another word may adopt specific phonetic features of the other word. Thus, words which belong to a certain series of the same type may all end up with certain phonetic features in common. The days of the week in Latin, for example, were named after the pagan gods and thus the names of the gods appeared in the genitive case: DIĒS LŪNAE 'the day of the moon, i.e., Monday', DIĒS MARTIS 'Tuesday, the day of Mars', DIĒS MERCŪRIĪ 'Wednesday, the day of Mercury', DIĒS JOVIS 'Thursday, the day of Jupiter', DIĒS VENERIS 'Friday, the day of Venus'. The names for Tuesday, Thursday, and Friday belonged to the third declension and therefore had the genitive singular ending -IS, while Monday and Wednesday belong to other declensions and thus had different genitive endings. Strict phonetic development would therefore have given Sp. **lune* and **mercure.* The actual forms, *lunes* and *miércoles,* show that the -*s* of the other names was borrowed by these words, and, in the case of *miércoles,* the stress on the second syllable was changed to a stress on the first syllable to match all the other names. Similarly, the words for 'mother-in-law' and 'daughter-in-law' in Latin were commonly associated: SOCRUS and NURUS (both in the fourth declension). The /o/ of the stem of SOCRUS was borrowed by NURUS, thus producing the Spanish form *nuera,* instead of **nora.* (Both words were shifted to the first declension when the ending -US became associated exclusively with masculine nouns.) The cases of paradigmatic leveling of verbs all belong to this class too, since the root meaning of the paradigm is the same for all the different forms.

2. A word having the opposite meaning to another word can also adopt some phonetic feature of the other word, especially if both already have

some partial likeness of form. For example, Lat. DEXTER 'right' developed regularly into Sp. *diestro* 'skillful'. Its counterpart, SINISTER 'left' should have resulted in **senestro,* but instead we find OSp. *siniestro* 'sinister, unfortunate, unlucky'. Obviously the diphthong was borrowed from *diestro,* thus making both words more alike in form. Likewise SŪRSUM 'upward' was opposed to DEORSUM 'downward'. This semantic relationship induced speakers to adopt the /u:/ of the first word into the second one, thus once again producing forms of greater similarity: It. *su–giù,* OSp. *suso–yuso.* Such cases of mutual influence can be called "lexical polarization" (Malkiel 1951).

3. Words having a specific function may serve as a model for others having the same function but a different phonetic form. We saw earlier the proportion that allowed speakers to create a new preterite for *tener,* OSp. *tove,* based on the model of *ove.* The existence of these two preterites allowed speakers to associate the segment *-ov-* with the notion of the preterite, since it appeared that what had occurred was the preservation of the initial consonant from the root of *tener* plus the addition of what appeared to be a suffix, *-ove.* Thus a new proportion could be set up:

$$\frac{\text{tener}}{\text{tove}} : \frac{\text{seer}}{\text{X}}$$

in which X = *sove* (Lat. SĒDĪ). From this proportion new analogical formations could be created, applying especially to verbs containing a single syllable in the stem and a root often ending in a vowel. The result was several new preterites like *crove* 'I believed', *andove* 'I moved', *estove* 'I was' (< *estar*).

Thus, from a single proportion speakers extracted what became a relatively independent suffix. Such a reanalysis of forms is not uncommon in language history. The Latin second and third conjugations in -ĒRE, and -ERE, for instance, had no specific passive participial ending. A few verbs having a perfect in -UĪ had a participle in -ŪTUS, e.g., TRIBUERE 'to allot, assign, attribute', passive particple TRIBŪTUS > OSp. *atrevudo* 'dared; daring'. A proportional analogy extended this ending to many verbs in Romance; for HABĒRE 'to have' we find It. *avuto,* Rom. *avut,* Fr. *eu,* and for verbs descended from Late Lat. **VOLERE* 'to wish, want'(C.L. VELLE), It. *voluto,* Fr. *voulu;* and Old Spanish *-er* verbs also often had participles in *-udo* (see Ch. 4), e.g., *temudo* (<*temer* 'to fear' < Lat. TIMĒRE). In modern Spanish, another proportion associating the *-er* conjugation verbs with those of the *-ir* conjugation has extended the participial ending *-ido* to all second conjugation verbs:

$$\frac{\text{viene}}{\text{venido}} : \frac{\text{tiene}}{\text{X}}$$

giving modern *tenido.* This sort of progressive extension of a morpheme to a new set of circumstances is sometimes called "relative analogy" (Wheeler 1887, 31).

Similarly word elements that were not originally morphemes may become separated from their original word and extended to new formations:

$$\frac{\text{alcohol}}{\text{alcoholic}} : \frac{\text{work}}{X = \text{workaholic}}$$

$$\frac{\text{ham}}{\text{hamburger}} : \frac{\text{steak}}{X = \text{steakburger}}$$

$$\frac{\text{water}}{\text{Watergate}} : \frac{\text{Korea}}{X = \text{Koreagate}}$$

These examples show that new affixes may be created by a simple proportional analogy and then become independent morphemes, even when in the original model they had no special meaning; after all, *-holic* contains the suffix *-ic*, but *-hol-* had no meaning by itself. Likewise, *hamburger* was originally a derivative based on the name of the city of Hamburg, and had nothing to do with the meat, *ham*, and yet the fact that *ham* existed as an independent word was sufficient to allow speakers to set up a proportion.

4. Morphemes having sameness or similarity of form but different functions or meanings may lose one function in order to become more alike in meaning. In Latin, for example, the suffix -A had two functions: 1) feminine singular, nominative (first declension), e.g., RŌSA 'rose', FĒMINA 'woman'; 2) neuter plural, nominative-accusative (second, third, and fourth declensions), e.g., ARMA 'arms', FOLIA 'leaves'. In Late Latin the feminine function became predominant, producing a proportion like the following:

$$\frac{\text{MĒNSA}}{\text{MĒNSĀS}} : \frac{\text{FOLIA}}{X = \text{FOLIAS}}$$

with the neuter plurals being identified as feminine singulars, Sp. *hoja, hojas*; Fr. *feuille, feuilles*; It. *foglia, foglie.* Similarly the ending -US had three functions in Latin: 1) masculine singular, nominative (second declension), e.g., BONUS 'good'; 2) neuter singular, nominative-accusative (third declension), e.g., TEMPUS 'time'; 3) feminine singular, nominative (fourth declension), e.g., SOCRUS 'mother-in-law'. The first function became the only one in Late Latin so that neuter nouns of the third declension became identified with masculine nouns of the second. Regular phonetic development of TEMPUS produced OSp. *tiempos*, OFr. *tens.* In Spanish, the identification of the suffix *-s* with the notion of plurality induced speakers to consider *tiempos* to be a plural noun, and thus a new singular was created, *tiempo*, in a process known as *back formation* or the creation of what appears to be the base word from which an apparent derivative was formed. In reality, the supposed derivative is the true base and the new word is based on the derived word. Back formation is simply another form of analogy. The feminine nouns of the fourth declension which referred to females could hardly become masculine nouns, so the *-a* suffix was adopted to replace the former -us, thus giving Sp. *suegra,* It. *suocera.*

Sometimes chance resemblances of form suffice to set up a proportion that results in an altered form. Old French *saucisse* 'sausage' was borrowed into English; if it had retained its original ending it would have become **sausish.* The ending, however, most closely resembled the suffix *-age* found in many words and as a result we now have *sausage.*

One class of analogies is known as *popular* or *folk etymology* in which a meaningless part of a word is identified with another word or morpheme, often bearing a chance resemblance with it. Thus, a word like *vagabundo* 'vagabond' becomes in colloquial Spanish *vagamundo,* through association with *mundo* 'world', possibly aided by the related notion that a vagabond is one who wanders (*vagar*) around the world. Popular etymologies (which might better be termed "reinterpretations" [Anttila 1974, 92]) do not have to make as much sense as the preceding example might indicate. Thus, a word like *asparagus* can be reinterpreted into *sparrow grass* simply because of a vague resemblance to the words *sparrow* and *grass,* even though asparagus is not really a grass and has nothing to do with sparrows. What is most important is that a previously unanalyzable word has been reanalyzed so as to become a compound made up of known elements. Thus, the result seems to make more sense than did the original form.

The force of analogy is pervasive in language development. The association of form and meaning/function is fundamental to language and thus we can expect that speakers will constantly be making changes in the forms of words to make these relations clearer. At the same time, many, if not most, of the analogical creations of speakers are likely to be nonceformations that are not imitated by other speakers. As in the case of sound change, it is not the individual idiosyncrasy that counts but rather the particular change that a community adopts that constitutes true linguistic change. The factors that tend to favor the spread of any analogical creation are probably the same as those that favor the spread of any other linguistic innovation.

Universals of Linguistic Change?

Although the particular mechanisms that affect any area of language are individual, and concerned most directly with the special nature of the elements that are being changed, i.e. phonetic properties in sound change, meaning and function in morphological and syntactic change, it may be possible to perceive some general features that seem to characterize all kinds of language change. We can see that in phonetic and phonological change, internal changes (i.e. those not resulting from language contact) often appear to be the result of the spread of relaxed or rapidly articulated variants of sounds or sound groups to become a new norm, with subsequent elimination of the older more highly distinctive forms. In sound change we may detect:

1) wider application of preexistent features to new circumstances;
2) the elimination of redundancy;
3) the adoption of a less highly marked phonological system as against the conservation of a more highly marked one (Corbett 1970–71, 277)

In analogical change, it may be possible too to classify leveling of paradigms and the extension of one specialized form to all members of the class as a similar sort of widened application of a feature from a limited circumstance to more and more areas of language. We might be tempted to call all of these features a kind of *simplification*, as speakers seek to achieve a closer connection between form and meaning: "Put at its simplest, speakers will, in general, prefer—unconsciously, of course—to organize the material which comprises their language in a maximally regular and economic fashion, a preference which manifests itself in the changes captured by diachronic linguists of various persuasions for many decades, from 'structural pressure' through 'rule simplification' to 'typological consistency' " (Harris 1982, 4).

Of course, it will not do to think that we can define simplicity as a sort of numerical reduction of features. Likewise, as in the case of the theory of "least effort," it can hardly be claimed that all changes necessarily will always produce simpler forms of language. As we shall see in the case of certain phonetic changes, a change which eliminates certain redundant elements, e.g., the syncope of unstressed posttonic vowels, had the effect of producing a number of consonant groups in early Ibero-Romance that were more complex than any that had existed before, and thus a simplification in one subsystem of language may well produce complexity elsewhere. As has often been observed, the progress of regular sound change frequently produces irregularities in paradigms which may then be eliminated by analogical extension of one form and subsequent leveling. Nevertheless, a certain striving toward more general and less highly distinctive forms can be considered a general tendency in language, provided we are aware that language is made up of a complex variety of small subsystems which may work together or may work at cross purposes to each other, thus producing the mixture of simplicity and complexity that we so often see.

Summary of Causes

Before ending our general discussion of causation of phonetic and morphological change, we must take account of the fact that language is not an object in any physical sense, but rather an activity that is expressed by physical means (i.e., the sounds of language). Each speaker in essence creates language each time he or she speaks: "La lengua cambia justamente porque *no está hecha* sino que *se hace* continuamente por la actividad lingüística. . . . [E]l hablar es actividad creadora, libre y finalista, y es siempre nuevo, en cuanto se determina por una finalidad expresiva individual, actual e inédita" (Coseriu 1973, 69). Thus in studying the causes of change, one may legitimately look forward rather than back, and ask what purpose a change will serve in communication in all its aspects: "Los hechos lingüísticos existen porque los hablantes los crean *para algo*, y no son ni productos de una necesidad física, exterior a los hablantes mismos, ni consecuencias necesarias e ineludibles de un estado de lengua anterior. La única explicación propiamente 'causal' de un hecho lingüístico nuevo es que la libertad lo ha creado con una finalidad" (Coseriu 1973, 202).

If one accepts this point of view, the discussion of the causes of sound change and other types of language change should be looked at somewhat differently than the causes of other types of change: "[E]l problema que debe plantearse en cada caso particular no es: ¿por qué (por cuáles circunstancias empíricamente objetivas) ocurrió tal cambio?, sino «para qué (con qué finalidad) yo, disponiendo de tal sistema determinado y hallándome en tales y cuales circunstancias históricas, cambiaría A en B, abandonaría el elemento C o crearía el elemento D?»" (Coseriu 1973, 206).

Coseriu's ideas were anticipated over a hundred years ago: "There is always one element in linguistic change which refuses scientific treatment: namely, the action of the human will. The work is all done by human beings, adapting means to ends, . . . The real effective reason of a given phonetic change is that a community, which might have chosen otherwise, willed it to be thus . . ." (Whitney 1875/1979, 73). Explanations of linguistic change, viewed in this fashion, will be like other historical explanations of changes in human institutions and will often entail a certain circularity. That we cannot predict the course of changes in the future is simply the result of human freedom, the fact that, to some extent at least, people can choose the direction in which they and their society and its institutions will go. The study of the causes of changes must therefore, in as far as possible, be supported by as much evidence as the investigator can obtain, especially extralinguistic evidence.

Summary

The preceding brief survey of sound change and analogy is only a short introduction to a few of the manifold problems associated with some parts of this particular aspect of language change. Although much has been written about both subjects, there is as yet no general agreement among all linguists on all facets of them. It is highly unlikely that any all-encompassing theory of linguistic change will ever be devised, any more than any general theory of human history can be elaborated that will satisfy all scholars. Much will inevitably depend on the investigator's viewpoint, his goals, and the level on which he chooses to work. Some will prefer to deal with the most general and regular types of change, leaving the unusual and limited kinds in a sort of limbo. For others, it will be the exceptional character of the development of some few words that will be most attractive. There should, however, be no true conceptual conflict between scholars who work in these essentially different areas.

What is most dangerous to the progress of knowledge in this area is a desire for simplistic solutions to problems. No progress will be possible for those who impatiently discard all that has been discovered in the past and naively think that some new theory will "explain" everything. The same is true for those who refuse to consider new approaches because they seem unfamiliar and depart from the hallowed paths of established doctrine. The progress of knowledge inevitably involves building upon past accomplishments as well as on new insights into the nature of language and its development. We can expect that in the future the contribution of structuralism, and, more recently, the revealing investigation of the relationship between language change and social attitudes and social change, will become part of the general linguistic knowledge of all students. We may also expect that there may be more attention paid to the matter of the hierarchization of the multiple causes of change, a topic already explored tentatively by Malkiel (1977).[92] Further advances of knowledge will undoubtedly be made, and if linguists of all schools can keep an open mind and a receptive attitude toward new insights, needless quarrels can be avoided and further light can be shed on the nature of language and its processes of evolution.[93]

---

[92] The problem of the ranking of the causes of historical changes in order of importance is one that not many historians have yet tackled successfully. See Berkhofer 1969, 295ff.

[93] Bailey observes aptly: "All these old-fashioned methods still remain valid and should not be forgotten in a misguided zeal to take advantage of newer approaches. The proper thing to do is to use both old and new where they are justified, and neither when not justified" (1975, 55).

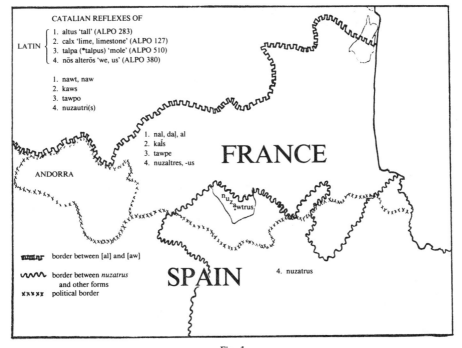

CATALIAN REFLEXES OF

LATIN
1. altus 'tall' (ALPO 283)
2. calx 'lime, limestone' (ALPO 127)
3. talpa (*talpus) 'mole' (ALPO 510)
4. nōs alterōs 'we, us' (ALPO 380)

1. nawt, naw
2. kaws
3. tawpo
4. nuzautri(s)

1. nal, daḷ, al
2. kaĺs
3. tawpe
4. nuzaltres, -us

FRANCE

ANDORRA

nuzₐwtrus

border between [al] and [aw]

border between *nuzatrus* and other forms

political border

SPAIN

4. nuzatrus

Fig. 1

CHAPTER 2

THE LATIN LANGUAGE

THE PHONOLOGICAL SYSTEM OF LATIN

The Vowel System

Phonology

The vowel system of early Latin, as reflected in the variety of language chosen for literary expression (i.e., Classical Latin), consisted of five qualitatively different vowel positions: one low central, two front and two back, both of the latter with distinctions of tongue height, mid and high. For each position, it has been traditional to regard length as phonemic (or prosodemic).[1] Thus, the older Latin vowel system could be represented as a triangular one:

	FRONT		**CENTRAL**		**BACK**
HIGH	/i: i/				/u: u/
MID		/e: e/		/o: o/	
LOW			/a: a/		

---

[1] The question of whether one should speak of ten separate vowel phonemes or five phonemes plus a prosodeme of length cannot be gone into here. The former is the customary answer but it may have no more to recommend it than would a claim that Spanish has ten separate vowels, with one stressed and one unstressed in each position, simply because stress has phonological status in Spanish, e.g., *ánimo* vs. *animo* vs. *animó*. See Pulgram 1975, 66–72, 151–54, for a good discussion of the matter. Another way of looking at the length distinctions is found in Zirin 1970, 79, and Herslund 1974, both of whom claim that long vowels are really a short vowel followed by a semivowel of the same quality. Length, then, is simply the product of a "rule" that converts the semivowel into greater duration. This way of handling length simplifies somewhat the accentuation rule, but is really more a matter of "phonological bookkeeping" (as Pulgram 1975, 68, 253, puts it) than of phonetic reality. An uncommitted observer might conclude that there is more than a bit of game-playing involved in all of this. Some of the problems involved in the phonemic interpretation of vowel length are discussed in Arnason 1980, 186–203.

Alternatively, one could represent the system in terms of distinctive features which are either present (+) or absent (−), as in the following matrix (Rosoff 1974, 59):[2]

	a	e	i	o	u
high/low	−	−	+	−	+
nonhigh/high	+	+	−	+	−
front/back	−	+	+	−	−
long/short	+/−	+/−	+/−	+/−	+/−

Examples of minimal pairs of words containing the different vowels are the following:

/iː/	FĪDĒS 'you will trust' PĪLUM 'javelin' LĪBER 'free'	/i/	FIDĒS 'faith' PILUM 'hair' (ac.sg.) LIBER 'book'
/eː/	LĒVIS 'smooth' LĒGIT 'he read' (perf.) SĒDĒS 'abode'	/e/	LEVIS 'light' (adj.) LEGIT 'he reads' SEDĒS 'you sit'
/aː/	MĀLUM 'apple' LĀBRUM 'washtub' LĀTUS 'broad, wide'	/a/	MALUM 'evil, bad' (ac.sg.) LABRUM 'lip' LATUS 'side'
/oː/	ŌS 'mouth' PŌPULUS 'poplar' SŌLUM 'alone' (m.ac.sg.)	/o/	OS 'bone' POPULUS 'people' SOLUM 'soil'
/uː/	FŪRIS 'of a thief' (gen.sg.)	/u/	FURIS 'you rage'

Phonetics

It appears that at the very earliest period the phonological difference of length in each position was realized primarily by means of greater or lesser duration. Such a conclusion, at least, is suggested by the evidence of Latinisms in other languages borrowed at an early date. In Basque, for example, the following Latinisms seem to show that the articulatory differences between long and short vowels were sufficiently small that Basque speakers could identify them as the same vowel in each position:

---

[2] For those who prefer to treat phonology in terms of distinctive features, the choice of which features to call "distinctive" seems to be fairly arbitrary; Herslund 1974 adopts "polar," i.e., at the extremes of the vowel triangle, plus "high" and "back" as the only distinctive features. Some very apt comments on this sort of classification are the following: "[T]here really is a systematic quality in language. . . . But this is undoubtedly a far more complicated systemic quality than that which is implied by bundles of DF, squares, cubes, matrices, and similar primitive formalizations; and what is more, this systemic quality seems to be always only a tendency" (Voronkova and Steblin-Kamenskij 1975, 88). It is well too to recall the warning found in Weinreich, Labov, Herzog: "[I]f the historian of language should accept the distinctive feature matrix, he loses the possibility of describing in a coherent way a series of shifts moving around the periphery of the vowel trapezoid" (1968, 140).

LATIN	BASQUE
LĪNU 'linen'[3]	*liñu*
FĪCU 'fig'	*piku*
CIRRU 'lock, curl'	*kirru*
PICE 'pitch'	*pike*
SĒMEN 'seed'	*seme*
SĒNSU 'sense; feeling'	*zensu*
TEMPORA 'times'	*dembora*
MŪRU 'wall'	*muru*
MUCCU 'mucus' (C.L. MUCUS)	*muku*
COHORTE 'cohort'	*korta*
CORPUS 'body'	*gorputz*
POPULU 'people'	*populu*

(Caro Baroja 1945, 40–41)

Likewise, we see that in Sardinian, a very conservative Romance language, the long and short vowels in each position were merged into one single vowel when length distinctions were abandoned, again indicating that qualitatively the vowels in each position were very similar if not completely identical:

LATIN	SARDINIAN
URTĪCA 'nettle'	*urtika, urtiga*
PICE 'pitch'	*pike, pige*
MULIERE 'woman'	*mudzere*
TEMPUS 'time'	*tempus*
DŪRU 'hard'	*duru*
BUCCA 'puffed up cheek'	*bukka* 'mouth'
SŌLE 'sun'	*soli*
BONU 'good'	*bonu*

One of the aspects of the phonetic realization of phonological length is that phonetically what is termed length is rarely, if ever, solely a feature of duration and nothing else. Languages which have been studied in modern times (Durand 1946, Straka 1959) reveal that in phonetic terms length is a composite of several features in addition to duration. Thus with duration are usually found differences of tongue position (quality, timbre) and tension. Indeed it may not even be possible to decide which phonetic feature is truly distinctive in phonological terms: "From a general standpoint, if two phonetic features can be shown to be always co-extensive, there is really no solution as to which is redundant, which is not!" (Klau-

---

[3] When Latin words are given as the etyma of Romance words, the usual practice will be to give them in the accusative singular form of nouns and adjectives, minus the final /-m/. When Latin words are cited as illustrations of Latin phenomena, the nominative singular will usually (but not necessarily always) be used.

senberger 1975, 111).[4] Quite early, the Latin long vowels developed a
secondary feature of greater tongue height and tension, while, conversely,
short vowels became lower and more lax.[5] Although /i:/ was still pronounced as a long, high, front vowel [i:], its short counterpart was pronounced as a somewhat lower high front vowel [ɪ]. Likewise, /u/ was
pronounced as a lower, high, back vowel [ʊ], as opposed to the long, high,
back vowel /u:/ [u:]. With the mid vowels, the long vowels were pronounced somewhat above the mid position [e o]. The short vowels tended
to be pronounced more openly [ɛ ɔ]. The /a:/ and /a/ were probably not
distinguished qualitatively.[6]

The phonetic distribution of Latin vowels may be represented as in the
following figure (based on Pulgram 1975, 250):

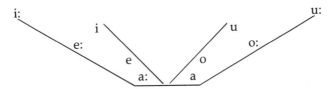

There is evidence that the other languages spoken in Italy which were
related to Latin,[7] Oscan and Umbrian, already had noticeable qualitative
distinctions in their vocalic systems before Latin did (Devoto 1930). As
Latin spread south and north from Rome, engulfing Latium and the neighboring areas where the Italic languages were spoken, it is conceivable that
the Italic speakers who learned to speak Latin continued to use these same
qualitative distinctions when pronouncing Latin and thus helped to reinforce any native tendencies toward an exaggeration of the qualitative distinction between the long and short vowels. It seems most unlikely that
Latin would have failed to develop such distinctions in the absence of
contact with Italic speakers, since, as pointed out above, quantity and
quality usually go hand in hand in those languages which make a phonemic distinction of length in vowels. It is more plausible to think that any
influence of Italic simply contributed to the tendencies already at work in
Latin as part of its long term "drift."[8]

---

[4] Cf. Loicq: "[L]a notion de quantité est une notion essentiellement composite qu'il n'est
pas possible de traduire uniquement en termes de durée physique" (1962, 272).

[5] Terms such as "tenseness" and "laxness" cannot be understood as referring to a single
phonetic feature, any more than can length: ". . . [+tense] vowels appear regularly with
extreme formant position" (Labov, Yeager, Steiner 1972, 41). Tense and lax vowels also
generally seem to follow different paths of development with relation to tongue position,
which cannot be related solely to tongue height, termed "peripherality" in recent research
(Labov, Yeager, Steiner 1972, 42–43).

[6] Lüdtke 1962 believes that there is some evidence for qualitative distinctions between the
low vowels, with /a:/ being realized as a low palatal vowel, and /a/ as a velar vowel. Certain
variant forms of words like JENUA for JĀNUA 'door' and JENUĀRIUS for JĀNUĀRIUS 'January'
(> Sp. *enero*) give some indication of this sort of distinction.

[7] The exact nature of this relationship is not clear. See Beeler 1952.

[8] Coleman offers a further objection to the idea that Oscan and Umbrian substratum

The qualitative distinctions were apparently not the same for the front and the back vowels. The distinctions between /u/ and /o:/ were considerably smaller than those between /i/ and /e:/, since in Rumanian /u:/ and /u/ generally fell together except in a few words (Vidos 1963, 181).[9] In western Romance there are some indications too that /o:/ and /u/ remained qualitatively distinct after /i/ and /e:/ had become identical except for length, especially in those regions more remote from the earlier centers of linguistic innovation, i.e., in Hispania (see further discussion in chap. 4).[10]

The first mention of a difference other than length between /e:/ and /e/ and between /o:/ and /o/ is found in the third century A.D. grammarian Terentian (Keil, VI, 329), and grammarians after him continue to mention these differences.[11] It seems clear, however, that there were noticeable qualitative distinctions between long and short vowels much earlier. Some of the graffiti found at Pompeii (destroyed in A.D. 79) spell words containing /e:/ with the letter I: FILIX, FILICITER, VALIS for FĒLIX, FĒLICITER, VALĒS (Väänänen 1966, 20) In the first century B.C., Cicero remarked on a friend of his who used a rustic pronunciation of /e/ in place of /i/.[12] If Italic influence is considered to be important, one might think that the qualitative distinction between /e:/ and /e/ became general during the first century B.C., since this was the period of the final Romanization of central Italy, and after the Social War (90–88 B.C.), people from Oscan and Umbrian speaking areas came to Rome in large numbers, and

---

influence affected the development of the qualitative distinctions in Latin, namely, that ". . . we should need to assume massive diffusion over the whole Mediterranean extent of Vulgar Latin speech to explain the wide-spread attestation of the phenomena in question" (1971, 182, note 22). This objection cannot stand since it assumes that the conditions in which a phenomenon arises must be the same as the conditions in which it spreads. It is sufficient that a particular linguistic feature should become established as a variable in a language; thereafter it may spread far beyond its area of origin even when the original conditions that led to its establishment have vanished. However, this does not mean that the development of a qualitative distinction between long and short vowels must be due to substratum influence. We can find other languages with phonemic vowel length that have developed qualitative differences between long and short vowels, such as Hungarian (Vidos 1963, 179) and Czech (Pulgram 1975, 70–71).

[9] Latinisms in Albanian also show this same development (Hall 1976, 204, note 11). In Lucania /u:/ and /u/ also fall together, and so do /i:/ and /i/, but since /e:/ and /o:/ also become /i/ and /u/, one may wonder if there is any connection between what happened here and in Balkan Romance (Lausberg 1939, 12–14).

[10] Křepinský (1965) points out that before [n] /o:/ and /u/ give different results in Spain and northern Italy: Lat. GRUNIU > It. grugno 'snout'; Lat. CUNEU, -*A 'wedge' > Sp. cuña, Port. cunha, Cat. cuny, as opposed to Lat. CICŌNIA 'stork' > It. cicogna, Sp. cigüeña, Port. cegonha, Cat. cegonya. Other examples are discussed in the section on vowels in chap. 4.

[11] It is possible that the grammarians who remark on the difference between the articulation of /e:/ and /o:/ and /e/ and /o/, but do not mention any alteration in the pronunciation of /i/ and /u/ were alert to such changes simply because Greek had two different letters for the long and short vowels in the mid position, but only one letter for the high vowels regardless of length (Lambert 1908, 16).

[12] De oratore, III, xii, 46: "Quare Cotta noster cuius tu ille lata, Sulpici, nonnumquam imitaris ut iota litteram tollas et E plenissium dicas, non mihi oratores antiquos sed messores videtur imitari."

Oscan and Umbrian cities began to use Latin as their official language (Devoto 1956).[13] Undoubtedly there were qualitative distinctions of some sort along with length distinctions from earliest times, even before the third century B.C. when the literary standard was being distinguished as a variety of Latin distinct from spoken Latin (Pulgram 1975, 289).[14] Could one conclude, as Pulgram does, that quantitative distinctions were actually secondary for most Latin speakers, excepting, of course, for educated speakers who tried to maintain the most conservative form of the language? No final answers can be given in the absence of anything other than indirect evidence. It might be safest to conclude that although there were certainly qualitative differences of some sort between long and short vowels from the beginning, the differences in tongue height were probably rather slight at first and only gradually became great enough to be obvious to many speakers, as the short counterparts of the long high vowels began to be qualitatively much closer to the long mid vowels than to their original partners. In other words, we are dealing with "the application of a continuous function to phonological space at a level where continuous values are possible" (Weinreich, Labov, and Herzog 1968, 149).

Distribution of Vowels

In certain positions, the distinction between long and short vowels of the same quality was generally neutralized (Kerlouegan 1978). In positions of hiatus, the first vowel had become short in historical times ("vocalis ante vocalem corripitur"), e.g., SUŌ 'I sew' (vs. SŪTOR 'cobbler'), SCIŌ 'I know' (vs. SCĪRE 'to know'), and similarly with all verbs of the fourth conjugation.

In a syllable closed by a consonant only a short vowel appeared unless the second consonant was /s/, e.g., ATTRACTUS 'attracted' (vs. ATTRĀXĪ 'I drew this way, attracted') (exceptions: ĪNFĀNS, ĀCTUS, HŪC, RĒM). Before geminate consonants, the vowel was almost always short, with the geminate /l:/ being the sole exception, and then only in a few words, e.g.,

---

[13] See Devoto 1956 for a study of the spread of Latin in Italy. For an excellent picture of the complicated linguistic situation in Italy when Roman power began to spread, see Homeyer 1957, who points out that bilingualism was common in many parts of Italy until a very late date.

[14] Vidos 1963, 182, claims that /e:/ or /i/ is attested in Plautus, who was an Umbrian. It is well to keep in mind, however, the cautions with regard to the texts of classical authors expressed in Pighi 1951. Speaking of another feature attributed to Plautus, he remarks, "rusus n'est pas «attesté chez Plaute», mais qu'il est «attesté dans les manuscrits de Plaute»: différence que les philologues et les linguistes oublient très souvent" (201). Further on he says, "Nous connaissons la plupart des anciens écrits par le moyen de copies tardives, du IVe-Xe siècle; une petite partie seulement est gardée par des copies du IVe-Ve siècle. . . . On comprend que l'autorité de cette tradition est relative." With reference to a word attributed to Cicero, he says on the same page, "[L]'écriture du palimpseste ne prouve point par elle-même que celle-là fut la graphie du Cicéron, mais elle prouve seulement que dans le V-VIe siècle un éditeur, pour tradition ou conjecture ou préciosité archaisante, employait cette graphie en faisant la copie d'une oeuvre de Cicéron" (205).

STĒLLA 'star', VĪLLA 'villa, farm house', etc. In word-final position, in open syllables only the vowels /a/ and /e/ maintain an opposition between long and short, e.g., ROSA 'rose' (nom.sg.) vs. ROSĀ (abl.sg.), MALĒ 'badly' vs. MALE 'bad' (voc.). In final closed syllables, long vowels only appear before /-s/, e.g., CULTĀS, CULTĪS, CULTŌS, CULTŪS, LEGĀS, LEGĒS, etc. Before all other consonants only a short vowel may appear, e.g., LEGET, AMAT, etc. This restriction especially affects the thematic vowels of verbs in the present indicative, since a long vowel cannot appear before /-t/ or /-nt/, e.g., AMĀS 'you love' vs. AMAT 'he loves' and AMANT 'they love', AUDĪMUS 'we hear' vs. AUDIT 'he hears' and AUDIUNT 'they hear'.

Frequency of Long vs. Short Vowels

Although there were few structural limitations on the appearance of long and short vowels in Latin (as pointed out in the previous section), there were certain preferences that show up in a widely varying discrepancy between the total numbers of long versus short vowels in different positions. A study of the frequency of different types of vowels in various positions of a word reveals that in a frequency count of approximately twenty-five thousand phonemes from a running text, short vowels tend to be much more frequent than long ones. In fact, 70.5 percent of all the vowels in the sample were short (Herman 1968). The following chart shows how the proportion of short to long vowels varies depending on the position of the syllable in the word:

Syllable	Proportion of Short:Long
accented	3 : 2
unaccented, non-final	6 : 1
initial	14 : 1
final	5 : 4

One can conclude from these statistics that distinctions of length were, for the most part, important only in accented syllables and in final syllables (where a number of case distinctions were in fact signalled by the difference). In unaccented syllables (excepting final ones), speakers could easily eliminate all length distinctions with no effect on communicative efficiency. There is evidence that speakers did tend to shorten all long unaccented vowels from a very early period.[15]

---

[15] "[I]l y aurait eu en latin, dans les derniers siècles de la République, mais à des dates légèrement différents ... une double tendance à l'abrègement des voyelles longues: sauf influences analogiques, les antépénultièmes longues des proparoxytons et les voyelles longues inaccentuées seraient devenues brèves, celles-ci dans tous les cas, celles-là dans certaines conditions seulement" (Fouché 1949, 28). See also Safariewicz 1965.

Diphthongs

Classical Latin had only three relatively common diphthongs: /oi/, /ai/, and /au/, written OE, AE, and AU.[16] Earlier states of Latin had had more diphthongs, but most had been monophthongized, or were in the process of monophthongization, at the time when the literary standard was being established.[17] The diphthongs written OE and AE were later spellings of diphthongs that at an early period had been written OI and AI. The change in spelling may show that the semivocalic element had changed and pointed the way to further modifications (Porzio Gernia 1978, 53).[18]

The Consonant System

Phonology

The system of consonants was a fairly simple one. There were two series of occlusives, one voiced and one voiceless, two nasals, two liquids, a labial fricative, and a voiceless spirant. There were no palatal or affricate consonants, and voice was not a distinctive feature of any consonants but the occlusives. The following chart shows the system in a schematic form:[19]

		labial	dental		velar
occlusives	voiceless	/p/	/t/		/k/
	voiced	/b/	/d/		/g/
fricatives		/f/		/s/	
liquids			/r/	/l/	
nasals		/m/	/n/		

The problem of the proper phonemic classification of [kʷ] and [gʷ] has been the subject of much discussion. In some cases [kʷ] behaves like a single consonant which would favor interpreting it as a unit phoneme. The subsequent development of these groups in Romance tends to favor their interpretation as /k/ and /g/ plus a semiconsonant. [gʷ] is found only after a nasal so that it can be considered to be simply an allophone of /w/

---

[16] The combination /eu/ also occurred in words like SEU 'or', NEU 'and not', and HEU 'alas!' but was otherwise uncommon. See Sturtevant 1940, 133.

[17] For example, DEICŌ > DĪCŌ 'I say', JOUXMENTA > JUMENTUM 'beast of burden; horse, mule', MOIROS > MŪRUS 'wall' (Maniet 1975, 70–74).

[18] Such a conclusion is not absolutely certain, since Greeks continued to transcribe AE as AI. See Sturtevant 1940, 129; Kent 1945, 48; Antkowski 1956, 22. Franceschi believes that AE was a spelling for [e:] from the start (1976, 260), which seems unlikely given the findings of Gernia Porzio (1978). See chap. 3 for the discussion of monophthongization of Latin diphthongs.

[19] Although a back aspirate, represented by the letter H, appears in Classical Latin, it was evidently a very weak and unstable consonant which by late Republican times had disappeared from ordinary speech, even though retained in writing. As Sturtevant remarks, ". . . the pronunciation and writing of h was a recognized mark of social prestige . . ." (1940, 156).

(if indeed /w/ is a phoneme). Symmetry, however, would indicate that both sounds be interpreted similarly (Fischer 1979, 307).[20]

The status of the semiconsonants [j] and [w] is also unclear, and it is likely that they were originally asyllabic variants of the vowels /i/ and /u/.[21] There is some evidence that [w] could be considered to be in opposition to [u] in a number of examples:

SERUĪ 'I have tied' [serui:]   SERVĪ 'of a slave' (gen.)[serwi:]
VOLUĪ 'I have wanted' [wolui:]   VOLVĪ 'I have rolled' [wolwi:]
ALUĪ 'I have fed' [alui:]   ALVĪ 'of the belly' (gen.)[alwi:]
SALUĪ 'I have jumped' [salui:]   SALVĪ 'well, safe' (nom.pl.)[salwi:]

The difference between these pairs of words may, however, simply be a matter of syllable division (Touratier 1971). At any rate, the Romans consistently wrote both the semiconsonants and the vowels with the same letters: I and U.[22] Their uncertain status probably reflects an imperfect integration into the consonantal system and a sign that they were in the process of becoming independent consonants.[23]

As with the vowels, consonants also distinguished length, although only between vowels within a word. The long consonants were written with two letters which has given rise to the term "geminates" or "double consonants." They may, if one finds it convenient, be classified as sequences of the same consonant, with one ending one syllable and the other beginning the next one. Although we cannot be absolutely certain of just how they were pronounced, it is quite unlikely that they were really two separate articulations of a simple consonant. Probably they were pronounced as in modern Italian: that is, with greater duration of contact of the articulators.[24] Consonantal length also involved greater tension and muscular

---

[20] For a summary of the arguments see Janssen 1956 and especially the extensive discussion of Devine and Stephens 1977, 12–104: "The Latin Labiovelars." Zirin (1970) interprets QU as /ku/, while Touratier 1971 believes that QU must be considered a unit phoneme. GU, on the other hand, he thinks is simply a post-nasal realization of /w/. The recent study by Marotta 1982 contrasts a Prague-school type of analysis with a generative analysis, and especially tries to show their numerous similarities, but the problem of whether /kʷ/ is an independent phoneme or not cannot be decided definitely by either method of analysis.

[21] Godel 1953 finds the evidence ambiguous. Mariner remarks that "nada se opone, en realidad, a considerar I,V semiconsonánticos como las variantes combinatorias asilábicas de I,V vocales" (1958, 230). Muljačić (1965) believes that minimal pairs of the type given must prove that the semivowels are independent phonemes, and Touratier similarly believes that although [w] and [u] are in complementary distribution, the fact that they can appear in contact shows that they must be different phonemes (1971, 234). Zirin believes that phonemic independence must be related to the loss of phonemic vowel quantity (1970, 81–87).

[22] A lengthened form of the letter I, used to represent /i:/, was sometimes used also to denote the semiconsonant, but this was not a regular practice (Väänänen 1966, 35).

[23] See Hill 1954, 439–47, especially 443, and Hill 1958, 443, Stati 1964, and Zirin 1970, 81–87, and Fischer (1979) who believes that parallelism with [w] and subsequent phonetic development tend to support their interpretation as phonemes.

[24] "Quantity distinctions exist also among consonants. The continuants among them behave like vowels also phonetically in that they can be lengthened or shortened in duration. . . . In the signaling of /tt/ the articulation is usually briefly arrested at the point of implosion of [t] and the explosion is slightly delayed; but no double articulation of [t] takes place. This

force in pronunciation so that these consonants may be described as "fortis" as opposed to the "lenis" or short consonants. With the occlusives, the voiced series rarely occurred as geminates. The following examples illustrate the differences of consonantal length:

SHORT	LONG
RĪPA 'shore, bank'	LIPPUS 'blear-eyed'
ADITUS 'access'	ADDITUS 'added'
VĪTA 'life'	VITTA 'ribbon, headband'
CATUS 'sharp; shrill'	CATTUS 'cat' (Late Lat.)
VACĀ 'empty!' (imperative)	VACCA 'cow'
AGER 'territory; field'	AGGER 'rampart'
CASA 'hut'	CASSA 'empty' (fem.nom.sg.)
PALAM 'openly'	PALLAM 'dress, mantle' (ac.sg.)
CALEŌ 'I am warm'	CALLEŌ 'I am experienced'
CŪRŌ 'I care for'	CURRŌ 'I run'
FERUM 'wild' (ac.sg.)	FERRUM 'iron'
FLĀMEN 'blast; priest'	FLAMMA 'flame'
ANUS 'old woman'	ANNUS 'year'

If we wish to represent the consonant system in terms of various distinctive features, the chart (fig. 2) shows one possible classification.

Figure 2.

Distinctive Features of Latin Consonants

	/p	b	m	f	t	d	n	s	k	g	kw	r	l	h/
sonant	−	−	−	−	−	−	+	−	−	−	−	+	+	+
vocalic	−	−	−	−	−	−	−	−	−	−	−	−	−	−
consonantal	+	+	+	+	+	+	+	+	+	+	+	+	+	−
coronal	−	−	−	−	+	+	+	+	−	−	−	+	+	−
anterior	+	+	+	+	+	+	+	+	−	−	−	+	+	−
high	−	−	−	−	−	−	−	−	+	+	+	−	−	−
low	−	−	−	−	−	−	−	−	−	−	−	−	−	+
back	−	−	−	−	−	−	−	−	+	+	+	−	−	−
rounded	−	−	−	−	−	−	−	−	−	−	+	−	−	−
nasal	−	−	+	−	−	−	+	−	−	−	−	−	−	−
lateral	−	−	−	−	−	−	−	−	−	−	−	−	+	−
continuous	−	−	−	+	−	−	+	+	−	−	−	+	−	+
delayed release	−	−	−	+	−	−	−	−	−	−	+	+	+	+
tense	+	−	−	−	+	−	−	+	+	−	+	+	−	+
heightened subglottal pressure	−	−	−	−	−	−	−	−	−	−	−	+	−	+
voiced	−	+	+	−	−	+	+	−	−	+	−	+	+	−
strident	−	−	−	+	−	−	−	+	−	−	−	−	−	−
long	−	−	−	−	−	−	−	−	−	−	−	−	−	−

(Adapted from Mignot 1975, 214)

---

also creates an audible syllable boundary 'within' the long consonant, that is between implosion and explosion" (Pulgram 1975, 71). Pulgram's statement is probably generally valid, but there is some evidence for rearticulation of geminates (Lehiste 1973).

Phonetics

The voiceless occlusives were probably unaspirated [p t k], judging by their reflexes in the Romance languages. Their counterparts were voiced, and there is some evidence of a prehistoric weakening of their articulation.[25] Latin grammarians describe them as being stops, but in some positions conceivably there were still remains of an earlier fricative pronunciation.

The consonant represented by the letter F is usually considered to have been a labiodental voiceless fricative, as it is today in the majority of the Romance dialects, although it may well have represented in different areas and different times a bilabial fricative [φ]. Sturtevant believes this to have been its articulation in early Latin (1940, 162–63). Since Latin did not inherit any [f] from earlier Indo-European, this consonant must therefore be due to a secondary development. The variant spellings for what was later represented by the letter F might reflect the articulation of a bilabial fricative. A Praenestine inscription that represents the Greek name *Hercules* as *Fercules* would confirm this idea (Pulgram 1979, 698).[26] It is very probable therefore that the pronunciation to be associated with the letter F was often [φ], possibly in free variation with [f], or with geographical variations.

The exact phonetic realization of /s/ is not known for certain either. Most of the Romance languages today have what is often described as a dental sibilant, and on this basis most scholars have assumed that the Latin pronunciation was the same. It is equally likely, however, that the sound of the sibilant in Latin was more that of an apico-alveolar sibilant much like that of modern Castilian [ś], a sound found also in other conservative sections of Romania, and very probably inherited from Indo-European (Martinet 1955, 235–47). An apico-alveolar articulation also would make clearer just how the rhotacism of ancient Latin occurred, when the intervocalic /s/ became the later /r/, an alveolar flap. Also evidence from Arabic transcriptions of Hispano-Romance words containing /s/ frequently used the Arabic letter *šin* which represents a palatal hushing consonant [š] and thus may be an attempt to imitate the somewhat palatal quality of the [ś]. However, there were also other transcriptions, less numerous to be sure, with the letter *sin* (Torreblanca 1981–82). We must also take into account the evidence of Basque which had and still has two different sibilants, an apico-alveolar [ś] written with the letter S, and a predorsal one written with z. The Latin words taken into Basque do not favor the idea that the Latin /s/ was apico-alveolar (Michelena 1968).

---

[25] Martinet (1950) believes that Latin is like the Italic languages in this respect.

[26] The representation of /f/ in Latin orthography suffered certain fluctuations before the digamma was finally chosen (Pulgram 1979). Of course, any of the evidence that Pulgram takes from the fake "Praenestine Fibula" must be discarded (Guarducci 1980).

Although Adams (1975) shows that alveolar or retracted sibilants were much commoner in Europe in the Middle Ages than in modern times, we still have no way of being certain whether the phonetic realization of Latin /s/ was uniform in all parts of the empire. Being the only sibilant, it could have varied considerably from one region to another and over time without there being any difference in its phonemic status or in writing.[27]

The nasals /m/ and /n/ were bilabial and alveolar respectively in syllable-initial position. The velar nasal [ŋ] occurred before nasal consonants, e.g., SANGUIS [saŋgwis] 'blood', HANC [aŋk] 'this' (fem.ac.sg.), and before /n/, where it was written with the letter G, e.g., PUGNA [puŋna] 'fight' (the so-called 'agma').[28] Since in this location it may be considered to be in opposition to a geminate /n:/, some scholars claim that it was an independent phoneme, but such an interpretation depends on analyzing the geminates as sequences of identical consonants rather than as long consonants (Hill 1958, 441). In final position /m/ was pronounced very weakly (except in monosyllables), and, judging by inscriptional evidence, it may have disappeared as a full consonant at a very early period, although it was probably realized as a slight nasalization of the preceding vowel.[29]

The /r/ was doubtlessly an alveolar flap. The liquid /l/ varied noticeably in pronunciation depending on its position in the syllable and perhaps on the preceding vowel also. Latin grammarians distinguished diverse kinds of L's but their terminology for describing these differences is not easy to interpret. We may conclude, at any rate, that the pronunciation was subject to considerable variation, although since the consonant was relatively isolated in the consonantal system, these fluctuations could have no effect on any neighboring consonants until the pronunciation had changed a great deal (Sletsjøe 1959, Nandriş 1965). The semiconsonant [w] seems to have been originally a labiovelar fricative as is indicated by the existence of pairs of related words such as FAUTOR-FAVEŌ, LAUTUS-LAVŌ, NAU-FRAGIS-NAVIS, etc., and Germanic borrowings of Latin words that still have this pronunciation, e.g., Eng. *wine* < VĪNUM, *wall* < VALLU (Sturtevant 1940, 140–43).

---

[27] See also Michel 1953. The dental [s] could be the result of the confusion of /s/ with the reflexes of other consonants (Galmés 1962, 117–26). Torreblanca (1980–81) concludes that the apico-alveolar pronunciation was not inherited from Latin but represents rather an internal development in Hispano-Romance, resulting from the palatalization of /s/ before front vowels. Although this notion is a possibility, the evidence that the apico-alveolar pronunciation was ancient in Latin and inherited from Indo-European is quite strong.

[28] Ward (1944) concludes that there may have been a large number of speakers who pronounced the combination as [gn] rather than [ŋn]. Allen (1965, 24) concludes that it may have been a spelling pronunciation. Zirin claims it is merely the allophone of /g/ before /n/ (1970, 26).

[29] "Il n'y a pas de phénomène 'vulgaire' qui soit plus répandu dans les inscriptions latines que la chute de *m* final. Elle se constate dès l'époque archaïque dans les *tituli* de caractère officiel même, comme les épitaphes des Scipions, du IIIᵉ siècle av. J.-C." (Väänänen 1966, 71). See also Jucquois 1970.

Consonants and Consonant Clusters

In word-initial position all consonants occurred. Indeed, /f/ is rarely found in any other position.[30] Consonants could also cluster, although they were then subject to certain restrictions. No more than three consonants could occur in an initial cluster, and they had to be placed in a specific order: 1) fricatives, 2) occlusives, 3) liquids and nasals (and if [w] is considered a consonant it could occur after /k/, /g/, and /s/). Not all possible combinations were found, and those that did occur were not used with equal frequency, nor were they distributed equally with relation to the following vowel (Benveniste 1939). The clusters actually found were distributed according to the following schema (based on Pulgram 1975, 137):

$$
s + \left\{\begin{array}{c} \left.\begin{array}{c} d \\ t \end{array}\right\} \quad + r \\ \left.\begin{array}{c} p \\ k \\ g \end{array}\right\} \quad \pm w \end{array}\right\} \quad + r/l
$$

$$
\begin{array}{c} b \\ f \\ s \pm \quad w \\ (g + \quad n) \end{array}
$$

Examples of clusters having /r/ or /l/ as the second element are the following:

/pr-/	PRĀTUM 'meadow'	/pl-/	PLACĒRE 'to please'
	PRETIŌSUS 'valuable'		PLĒNUS 'full'
	PRĪMUS 'first'		PLŌRĀRE 'to wail, lament'
	PRŌMITTERE 'to set forth'		PLUMBUM 'lead' (noun)
/br-/	BRACCHIUM 'arm'	/bl-/	BLANDUS 'smooth'
	BREVIS 'brief'		BLATERĀRE 'to chatter'
	BRŪTUS 'heavy, dull, stupid'		BLITUM 'tasteless herb'
/tr-/	TRĒS 'three'	/dr-/	DRACŌ 'dragon'
	TRĀNS 'across, beyond'		
	TRAHERE 'to draw, drag'		
/kr-/	CRĒDERE 'to believe'	/kl-/	CLĀRUS 'bright, shining'
	CRŪDĒLIS 'cruel'		CLĀMĀRE 'to cry out'
	CRUX 'cross'		CLĪVUS 'slope, rise'
/gr-/	GRANDIS 'large, great'	/gl-/	GLADIUS 'sword'

---

[30] Kent (1945, 111–12) points out that medially /f/ is only found after a prefix or in dialectal borrowings, e.g., DĒFERŌ, RUFUS.

	GRĀTIA 'favor, grace'		**GLĀNS** 'acorn'
	GREX 'herd, flock'		**GLŌRIA** 'glory'
/fr-/	**FRĀTER** 'brother'	/fl-/	**FLŌS** 'flower'
	FRIGIDUS 'cold'		**FLUERE** 'to flow'
	FRŌNS 'forehead'		**FLĒTUS** 'weeping'

Examples of /s/ plus a voiceless occlusive are the following:

/sp-/	**SPĪNA** 'thorn'	/st-/	**STĀRE** 'to stand'
	SPECULUM 'mirror'		**STĒLLA** 'star'
	SPATIUM 'space, distance'		**STOREA** 'rush mat'
/sk-/	**SCĀLA** 'ladder'	/skw-/	**SQUĀLOR** 'roughness, filth'
	SCŌPA 'branches, twigs'		
	SCĪRE 'to know'		

The initial cluster written **GN-** was an archaism preserved only in literary usage (Zirin 1970,26), and in all likelihood was simply a spelling for /n-/ or /nn-/, e.g., **GNARUS** 'knowing, acquainted with, expert' (Stephens 1978).

Only four three-consonant clusters occurred, if we exclude /skw-/:

/spr-/ **SPRĒTOR** 'he who scorns; disdainful'
/str-/ **STRINGERE** 'to tighten'
/skr-/ **SCRĪBERE** 'to write'

/spl-/ was found only in **SPLENDERE** 'to shine' and its derivatives. The combination /stl-/ was archaic and found only in **STLOPPUS** 'slap'.

Of the two-consonant clusters /br-/, and /bl-/, and /dr-/ were found mainly in foreign borrowings, except for **BLANDUS**. /gli-/ and /gle-/ were also rare. /skw-/ appeared only before the vowel /a/.

In syllable-final and especially word-final position, restrictions on sequences of consonants were considerably greater. Instead of the thirteen simple consonants possible in initial position, only the stops (excluding /g/, nasals, liquids and /s/ appeared: /p, b, t, d, k, m, n, r, l, s/. /-n/ appeared only in words ending in the suffix -**MEN**, or in Greek loan words. The commonest consonant in word-final position was /s/, followed by /m, t, r, l, d/. (/-d/ was rare except in monosyllables.) Final clusters could occur, but only in the reverse order of initial ones: nasals or liquids, occlusives and /s/. The two-consonant clusters that were found were /-nt, -ns, -ks, -ps (also written -**BS**), -rs/, and in certain verb forms /-rt/ (i.e., **FERT** 'he carries, brings' and its derivatives), /-lt/ (e.g., **VULT** 'he wishes') and /-st/ (in **EST** 'he is' or 'he eats'). Examples of these final groups are the following:

/-nt/	**AMANT** 'they love'	/-ns/	**TRĀNS** 'across, beyond'
/-ks/	**NOX** 'night' (nom.sg.)	/-ps/	**INOPS** 'weak, helpless'
/-rs/	**ARS** 'art' (nom.sg.)		

Some three-consonant clusters also occur, but are even rarer than the two-consonant ones (and usually in the nominative singular form of nouns):

/-rps/ STIRPS 'stalk, stem'   /-rks/ ARX 'stronghold, castle'
/-lks/ FALX 'sickle, reaping hook'   /-nks/ DEUNX 'eleven twelfths'

Medially there were more sequences found since they could be divided between neighboring syllables. There were, however, certain limitations on such sequences: no two stops, one voiceless and one voiced could occur together. The opposition between nasals was neutralized in syllable-final position, with the realization of the nasality being assimilated to the point of articulation of the following consonant, e.g., [m] is found only before labials, [n] only before dentals or alveolars, and [ŋ] only before velars and /n/.

From the restrictions on the occurrence of consonants in syllable- and word-final position, it appears that the syllable-final position was a much weaker one than the initial position, and there tended to be neutralization of consonantal oppositions in this position, as we saw above in the case of nasals. Although /-t/ and /-d/ and /-p/ and /-b/ could be found in opposition in Classical Latin, e.g., AB 'from ', ID 'this, it', IT 'he goes', etc., this opposition was rarely utilized and seems to have been just a transitory feature of the language, since it was not found in ancient Latin. By the middle of the first century, inscriptional evidence reveals that /-t/ and /-d/ were being pronounced alike, as were /-p/ and /-b/ (Safariewicz 1964, Anderson 1964).

Frequencies of Consonants and Consonant Clusters

A study of the frequency with which different consonant phonemes appear in samples totalling 49,488 words of continuous Latin prose (from Cicero and Sallust) reveals the following absolute frequencies:

Phoneme	Percentage of all Consonants	Percentage of all Phonemes
/p/	5.22	2.87
/b/	2.79	1.53
/t/	15.06	8.29
/d/	5.23	2.88
/k/	7.60	4.18
/g/	2.06	1.14
/kw/	3.63	2.00
/gw/	.02	.01
/f/	1.71	0.94
/s/	14.50	7.98
/m/	10.93	6.07
/n/	10.89	5.99
/r/	11.38	6.26

Phoneme	Percentage of all Consonants	Percentage of all Phonemes
/l/	5.69	3.13
/v/	2.27	1.25
/h/	0.99	0.55

(adapted from Devine and Stephens 1977, 175, Table II)

In the biphonemic word-initial clusters, the following frequencies are found:

Cluster	Percentage of all Word-Initial Clusters	Percentage of all Biphonemic Clusters
/pr-/	43.20	5.03
/pl-/	9.40	1.09
/br-/	1.16	0.13
/bl-/	.31	0.03
/tr-/	5.79	0.34
/kr-/	4.15	0.24
/kl-/	2.89	0.33
/gn-/	0.44	0.05
/gr-/	5.41	0.63
/gl-/	2.76	0.32
/fr-/	4.63	0.54
/fl-/	2.31	0.27
/sp-/	4.66	0.54
/st-/	6.33	0.74
/sk-/	6.30	0.73

(Devine and Stephens 1977, 180, Table XII)

The percentages of word-final clusters are the following:

Cluster	Percentage of all Word-Final Clusters	Percentage of all Biphonemic Clusters
/-ps/	0.61	0.06
/-bs/	0.15	0.01
/-ks/	15.97	1.64
/-st/	24.93	2.56
/-nt/	45.67	4.70
/-ns/	7.46	0.77
/-rt/	0.50	0.05
/-rs/	2.04	0.21
/-lt/	0.35	0.03

Medial biphonemic clusters and sequences reveal the following percentages of frequency, if we include geminates as clusters (only those representing more than .2 percent of all clusters are included):

Sequence	Percentage of all Biphonemic Clusters & Sequences	Sequence	Percentage of all Biphonemic Clusters & Sequences
/-nt-/	8.64	/-tr-/	0.91
/-s:-/	5.41	/-m:-/	0.90
/-l:-/	4.71	/-rb-/	0.88
/-rt-/	4.37	/-bv-/	0.82
/-nd-/	3.76	/-r:-/	0.73
/-kt-/	3.59	/-k:-/	0.68
/-st-/	3.29	/-p:-/	0.67
/-ns-/	2.34	/-ng-/	0.66
/-ks-/	2.24	/-bl-/	0.61
/-gn-/	2.24	/-np-/	0.52
/-mn-/	2.11	/-rn-/	0.48
/-lt-/	1.95	/-gr-/	0.47
/-tkw-/	1.61	/-n:-/	0.47
/-mp-/	1.50	/-rv-/	0.42
/-rs-/	1.38	/-f:-/	0.41
/-pt-/	1.38	/-nf-/	0.41
/-skw-/	1.30	/-dv-/	0.36
/-ps-/	1.05	/-br-/	0.27
/-rk-/	1.05	/-rf-/	0.23
/-nv-/	0.98	/-dk-/	0.22
/-mv-/	0.95	/-ds-/	0.21
/-rm-/	0.91	/-rkw-/	0.20

(adapted from Devine and Stephens 1977,
181–82, 184, Tables XIV and XVII)[31]

Further figures on the frequencies of different sequences of consonants in all positions are found in the elaborate study of Devine and Stephens 1977. The figures reveal that biphonemic clusters were much commoner than triphonemic ones, of which only /-str-/ is at all common, followed at some distance by /-nkt-/ and /-ntr-/ (187).

---

[31] The distinction between -NP- and -MP- is undoubtedly purely orthographic. Devine and Stephens do not distinguish between sequences and clusters, but it seems to be a useful distinction, even though in medial position it may not always be easy to determine the syllable border. See Pulgram 1970. I have also assumed that in the column labelled "percentage of all clusters" they mean all biphonemic clusters. They also distinguish between sequences found in non-compounded words and compounds. I have ignored this distinction and have added together the percentages of frequency. Devine and Stephens 1977, Table XIV has the sequence -CS- listed twice: on p. 181 with a total of 244, and on p. 182 with 565. I do not know which one is correct or whether they should be perhaps added together.

Syllabic Structure and Frequency

Syllable structure, which is probably of greater importance than the frequency of occurrence of individual phonemes, has been much less studied. Given the rules governing the combination of consonants, sixteen different types of syllables were possible (C = any consonant, V = any vowel or diphthong):

	CV	CCV	CCCV
V	VC	VCC	VCCC
CVC	CCVC	CVCC	CCCVC
CCVCC	CVCCC	CCCVCC	CCCVCC
		CCVCCC	

In fact, however, syllables with three consonants were rare and the combination of CCCVCCC did not occur at all. A study of the frequency of the different types of syllables reveals the following percentages of each type in a sample of 3000 running syllables from prose texts (Lloyd 1970):

CV	C	CCV	CVC	CCVC	VC	VCC	CVCC	CCCVC
44.9	8.3	3.6	27.2	1.1	11.6	0.9	2.1	(less than 0.1)

Open syllables predominate, making up 56.9 percent of the total and if we include as open syllables word-final syllables ending in /-m/, the total rises to 62.7 percent. This figure confirms the conclusions of the preceding section that the syllable-final position was an especially weak one. The typical syllable in Latin was an open one, and all consonants following the syllable nucleus were especially exposed to erosion.

As far as the general length of Latin words goes, another study (Richman 1967) shows that in a set of 100 common words taken from the standard Romance languages, the Latin etyma averaged 2.8 syllables per word. In units of discourse longer than the word, however, it may well be that Latin had no more syllables than the Romance languages because inflectional endings have been replaced by prepositions in many instances.

Accentuation

The position of the accented syllable in early Latin was determined solely by the phonemic shape of the last two syllables of the word. The general rule was that the accent always fell on the penultimate syllable of all two-syllable words and of those of more than two syllables unless this syllable was light (i.e., ended in a short vowel), in which case the accented syllable was the second from the end (the antepenult). All syllables that were not light were heavy, i.e., contained a long vowel or a diphthong or ended in a consonant, including a geminate consonant.[32] The following examples have the accented syllable marked by an acute accent mark:

---

[32] I follow here the definition of Pulgram 1975, 145: "[A] short-vowel syllable that is open, is light; all other syllables (long-vowel ones that are open or closed, and short-vowel ones that are closed) are heavy."

TWO SYLLABLE WORDS

VĪNUM 'wine'   SÍTIS 'thirst'
CḖRA 'wax'   BÉNE 'well'
PRĀTUM 'meadow'   MÁNUS 'hand'
TŌTUS 'all'   BÓNUS 'good'
MŪTUS 'mute'   LÚPUS 'wolf'

LONGER WORDS WITH HEAVY PENULT

FORMĪCA 'ant'   BALLÍSTA 'catapult'
MONḖTA 'mint, money'   INFÉRNUS 'nether world'
VENĀTUS 'chase, hunting'   CABÁLLUS 'pack horse, nag'
PRAECŌNEM 'public crier' (ac.sg.)
SĒCŪRUS 'safe, secure'   PALÚMBA 'wood pigeon'
BALLAÉNA 'whale'

LONGER WORDS WITH LIGHT PENULT

LÍMPIDUS 'clear, transparent'   CORNÍCULA 'crow'
HÉDERA 'ivy'   GÉNERUM 'son-in-law' (ac.sg.)
PUTÉOLUS 'well, cistern'   MULÍEREM 'woman' (ac.sg.)
TALÉOLA 'shoot, slip'   PARÍETEM 'wall' (ac.sg.)
ÁNIMA 'soul'   ÓRPHANUS 'orphan'
VÚLTUREM 'vulture' (ac.sg.)   PÁUPEREM 'poor' (ac.sg.)

The nature of the Latin accent has been a subject of much dispute. Latin grammarians spoke of the accent in terms that indicate that it was, like the accent in ancient Greek, one of pitch, i.e., the prominence of the accented syllable consisted in its being pronounced on a higher tone than unaccented syllables. Since, however, the terminology of the Latin grammarians is simply translated from Greek and they seem to have taken over wholesale the Greek system of describing accentuation, regardless of whether it could be applied to Latin, we can use their testimony only with a great deal of caution.[33] The best evidence is that the Latin accent was from the beginning one of stress rather than solely pitch (Pulgram 1975, 113–35), although it is not unlikely that speakers of Classical Latin may have, on formal occasions, tried to imitate the pitch accent of Greek (Pulgram 1975, 116).[34]

---

[33] "It is inconceivable that Latin should have developed a system of melodic accentuation that agreed in such minor detail with Greek, and we can only assume that the grammarians have slavishly misapplied the Greek system to the description of Latin" (Allen 1973, 151).

[34] Stress is often thought of as being the same thing as intensity, but such is not necessarily the case. Modern experiments (Bolinger 1958) indicate that a change of pitch level is by far the most important factor in the acoustic perception of stress. Possibly our terminology is too vague. As Allen points out: "[W]e may . . . assume as a working hypothesis that, whereas in the case of pitch the relationship between audition and interpretation, however complex, is relatively direct, stress is primarily interpreted in indirect, 'kinaesthetic' terms, i.e., in terms of the movements the hearer himself would make in order to produce the perceived effect. Much of the confusion regarding the nature of stress probably arises from the fact that it is used to denote 'both an aspect of the articulatory or motor side of speech and also a feature of the sounds perceived by the hearer' " (Allen 1973, quoting in part another scholar, 76–77).

Words containing a consonant cluster of a stop plus an /r/ at the beginning of the last syllable seem to have fluctuated considerably in the position of the accented syllable. In literary usage the rule was supposed to be that the cluster functioned like a single consonant so that if the penult was light the accent would fall on the antepenult, as in the following examples:

ÁLACREM 'lively' (ac.sg.)   CÓLUBRA 'snake'
CÁTHEDRA 'chair' (<Greek)   ÍNTEGRUM 'whole' (ac.sg.)
TÉNEBRĀS 'darkness' (ac.pl.)   TÓNITRUS 'thunder'

There is evidence that in popular usage, the stress fell on the penult, with the proparoxytonic accent being limited to formal literary style (Niedermann 1953, 16–17; Perini 1974; Pulgram 1975, 156–72).[35]

THE MORPHOLOGICAL SYSTEM OF LATIN

The Nominal System

Substantives

In older Latin, the nominal system distinguished three grammatical genders: masculine, feminine, and neuter. Gender, in spite of the traditional names for the three categories, was not related to sex except in the case of animate beings, in which case natural gender predominated over grammatical form. Thus, although most nouns ending in /-a/ (the first declension) were feminine, such nouns as referred to male beings were masculine, e.g., NAUTA 'sailor', AGRICOLA 'farmer', etc. There were also two numbers, singular and plural. Gender was usually expressed by means of concord with the adjective (Mignot 1978).

The function of substantives (and adjectives) in the sentence was indicated to a large degree by the use of case endings. Five different cases were distinguished in literary Latin:

1) the nominative or the case of the subject;
2) the genitive or the case of possession (plus other kinds of relations between nouns);
3) the dative or the case of the indirect object;
4) the accusative, or the case of the direct object;
5) the ablative, which had no one specific function but rather a variety of different uses, most frequently as the object of some very common prepositions.

The general tendency of the Indo-European languages has been to reduce the number of cases, and Latin was no exception to this general drift

---

[35] The complex problem of the muta cum liquida is examined exhaustively by Perini (1974). He concludes that the group of a stop plus a liquid was from ancient times a consonant cluster, but that the accentuation on the preceding syllable was due to the phonetic nature of the /r/ which tended to prolong the articulation of the stop.

(Maurer 1959, 85). The lack of a unified function for the ablative case, for example, reflected the fact that it was the result of a combination of three earlier Indo-European cases: the instrumental, the locative, and the ablative (or "case of separation") (Leumann 1977, 405). Unlike other cases, it rarely appeared alone but was usually governed by a preposition. In the plural, a further collapsing of cases had occurred in Italic (including Latin) so that the dative and the ablative were always identical in form.

Five separate formal classes of substantives were distinguished: the five declensions of Classical Latin. Membership in the classes was determined by the form of the substantive or adjective:

Declension	Number	Nominative	Accusative	Genitive	Dative	Ablative
1 (fem.)	sg.	-A	-A-M	-AE	-AE	-A
	pl.	-AE	-Ā-S	-Ā-RUM	-ĪS	-ĪS
2 (masc.)	sg.	-US	-U-M	-Ī		-Ō
(neuter)			-UM			
(masc.) (neuter)	pl.	-Ī	-Ō-S	-Ō-RUM		-ĪS
			-A			
3 consonant stems	sg.	-S	-E-M	-IS	-Ī	-E
-I stems		-IS				-Ī
(neuter)		-E				
	pl.	-Ē-S		-UM		-IBUS
(neuter)		-A				
-I stems		-IA				
4	sg.	-US	-U-M	-ŪS	-UĪ	-Ū
(neuter)		-U (-Ū)				
	pl.	-ŪS		-UUM		-IBUS
(neuter)		-UA				
5	sg.	-ĒS	-E-M	-(I)ĒĪ	-(I)ĒĪ	-Ē
	pl.	-ĒS	-ĒS	-Ē-RUM		-ĒBUS

The preceding chart cannot include all of the forms of substantives that were found in Classical Latin. The third declension in particular contained a number of words whose nominative did not fit the pattern. Thus there were some substantives lacking one syllable in the nominative singular in comparison with the other singular case forms ("imparisyllabic nouns"). For example, some had nominatives in /o:/, e.g., HOMŌ 'man' vs. gen. HOMINIS, LEGIŌ 'legion' vs. gen. LEGIŌNIS, etc., some had an /-n/, e.g., FLĀMEN 'priest' vs. gen. FLĀMINIS, some had the regular /-s/ ending but had lost the vowel, e.g., PAX 'peace' vs. gen. PĀCIS, NOX 'night' vs. gen. NOCTIS, etc., while others ended in other consonants, e.g., CAPUT 'head' vs. gen. CAPITIS, ANIMAL vs. gen. ANIMĀLIS, etc. Some nouns were not imparisyllabic but ended in consonants other than /-s/ in the nominative, e.g., PATER 'father' vs. gen. PATRIS, MĀTER 'mother' vs. gen. MĀTRIS, etc. The vast majority of all substantives belonged to the first three declensions.

The chart also reveals that there was considerable syncretism of cases. The nominative and accusative were identical for all neuter nouns, as were the plural of all words in the third, fourth, and fifth declensions. The genitive and dative were identical in the singular of the first declension, as were the dative and ablative singular of the second. The weak articulation of the final /-m/, characteristic of the singular accusative of most nouns, meant that the nominative and accusative of the first declension were probably identical in speech at the latest by the first century B.C., and possibly much earlier, as were the ablative and the accusative of the third declension. Thus, even in the very conservative variety of Latin it seems clear that the case system was well on its way to a drastic reduction.

Adjectives

Adjectives were limited in form either to the first and second declensions, or to the third declension. That is, any given adjective would belong either to the class that had the endings /-a/, /-us/ or /-um/ and thus reflect the gender of the noun it modified, or, if it was part of the third declension, did not distinguish between masculine and feminine in form, although the neuter was distinguished from the other genders in the nominative and accusative, e.g., /-e/ for the neuter singular and /-a/ for the neuter plural, versus /-is/ and /-em/ for masculine and feminine singular, and /-e:s/ for the plural.

The formation of the comparative and superlative of adjectives was generally by means of suffixes. The comparative endings were /-ior/ (masc.-fem.) and /-ius/ (neuter), and were declined like third declension adjectives, e.g., FORTIOR and FORTIUS 'stronger', from FORTIS 'strong'. The superlative suffix was /-is:imus/, declined like first-second declension adjectives, e.g., FORTISSIMUS, -A, -UM 'strongest'. There were a number of irregular comparatives and superlatives, e.g., MELIOR 'better' from BONUS 'good', MAJOR 'greater', from MAGNUS 'great', etc. In the case of adjectives whose stem ended in a vowel, however, the comparative and superlative were not formed in the usual fashion, but rather analytically, by use of the adverbs MAGIS 'more' and MAXIMĒ 'most', e.g., MAGIS IDONEUS 'more suitable', MAXIMĒ IDONEUS 'most suitable'. This particular construction pointed the way to future developments.

Personal Pronouns

The personal pronouns of Latin distinguished only four separate cases:

PERSON	CASE	SINGULAR	PLURAL
	nom.	EGO	NŌS
	gen.	MEĪ	NOSTRUM, NOSTRI
1	dat.	MIHI (MĪ)	NŌBĪS
	ac.		NŌS
		MĒ	
	abl.		
	nom.	TŪ	VŌS
	gen.	TUI	VESTRUM, VESTRĪ
2	dat.	TIBI	VŌBĪS
	ac.		VŌS
		TĒ	
	abl.		VŌBIS

In the plural it could be said that only three cases were distinguished. The genitive form was used mostly for the genitive of the whole, e.g., PARS MEĪ 'a part of me' or as the objective genitive, e.g., TIMOR NOSTRĪ 'fear of us'. For possession the possessive adjectives were used.

There was no special pronoun of the third person so that any demonstrative pronoun might be employed to refer to someone other than the speaker and hearer. Commonly the weak demonstratives IS, EA, ID were used in this function.

Demonstratives, Interrogatives, and Relatives

Latin traditionally distinguished three degrees of distance in demonstrative adjectives and pronouns, corresponding more or less to the three persons of verbs (the full declension is omitted):

LOCATION	MASCULINE	FEMININE	NEUTER
1: near speaker	HIC	HAEC	HOC
2: near person addressed	ISTE	ISTA	ISTUD
3: apart from speaker and hearer	ILLE	ILLA	ILLUD

Another third person demonstrative was IS, EA, ID which was evidently weaker in deictic force than ILLE. The intensive pronoun and adjective was IPSE, IPSA, IPSUM.

The interrogatives were QUIS (mas.-fem.) and QUID. Identical except in the nominative case were the relative pronouns: QUĪ, QUAE, QUOD. The interrogative pronouns could also be used as indefinite pronouns while the relative could serve as an indefinite adjective. Certain other forms also served as indefinites, but only the one formed with ALI- plus the other indefinites persisted in Romance, e.g., **ALIQUIS** 'someone', **ALIQUOD** 'something', etc.

The Verbal System

The Latin verbal system was even more complex in its morphological structure than the nominal system. A variety of affixes and modifications of the stem served to distinguish a number of different verbal concepts and functions. Being linked in a tightly-knit set of paradigms, the verbs undoubtedly suggested to Latin-Romance speakers that the core of the form conveyed the abstract notion of the verbal action or state and that the various accretions to that core expressed person, number, tense, mood, aspect, etc. A Latin verb form may be analyzable into quite a number of constituents. A form such as **REFUNDUNTUR** 'they are poured back' consists of several more or less easily identifiable elements which recur with approximately the same meanings in other verbs. The prefix **RE-** figures in such forms as **RE-VENIT** 'he comes back' or **RE-VOCANT** 'they call back'; the root **-FUD-** (discontinuous in **REFUNDUNTUR** which contains the infix **-N-**) appears in **RE-FUD-IT** 'he poured back'; the present infix also appears in **TANGIT** 'he touches' as opposed to **TĀCTUS** 'touched' (the perfect passive participle). The /-u-/ might be considered a tense/mood/conjugational-class marker, as in **CAP-I-U-NT** 'they seize'; /-n-/ is a plural sign, as in **AM-A-N-T** 'they love'; /-t-/ indicates the third person as in **AM-A-T** 'he loves'; the **-UR** marks the passive, as in **AM-Ā-T-UR** 'he is loved'.

Of course, it is most unlikely that any Latin speaker performed such a detailed analysis of individual forms. However, apparently even naive speakers could recognize a division of morpheme chains into stems (**RE-FU[N]D-**) and desinences (**-U-N-T-UR**), since to some extent the chains on either side of the boundary evolved independently of one another. Even a trained linguist at times hesitates to assign a very precise semantic or functional content to a particular segment because not all inflectional categories are consistently marked in the suffix chains that make up the endings. In **REFUNDITUR** 'it is poured back', for instance, no segment can be unequivocally labelled a number-marker signifying 'singular', somehow parallel to the pluralizing /-n-/ of **REFUNDUNTUR**. The result was a tendency to perceive the entire desinence as reflecting a complex of semantic parameters not always easily separable from one another. The presence of /-o:/ and the absence of any other morphs in the ending of **AMŌ** 'I love' can be taken to mean that /-o:/ means 'first person/singular/ present/in-dicative/active'. In this instance, person, number, tense, mood, and voice all find expression in a single morpheme, while in **REFUNDUNTUR** the burden is divided among four different ones.

The description of the Latin verb is usually couched in an "item-and-process" formulation (Hockett 1954), so that the shape of multi-morphemic stems has traditionally been described in terms of the process of derivation, and the makeup and distribution of the endings have ordinarily been treated as inflection. The process image requires a hierarchization of forms which may distort some of the factual details of historical evolution, but it has the virtue of emphasizing the dynamic nature of language.[36]

No account of Latin verb inflection can focus exclusively on the endings, for the conjugation of Latin verbs consisted of two distinct and partially independent subsystems. The first is the set of forms built on the present stem (traditionally known as the INFECTUM); the present tenses, the imperfect tenses, and the future. The second system is the set of perfective forms based on the stem known as the PERFECTUM: the simple perfect, the pluperfect, and the future perfect. The two systems were independent of each other only to a certain extent, but in a number of verbs the relationship between the infectum and the perfectum was quite arbitrary. For example, the verb FERŌ 'I bear, carry' used the stem FER- as the infectum (e.g., FERT 'he carries', FERĒBAM 'I used to carry', etc.), and the stem TUL- as the perfectum (<TOLLERE 'to take away') (e.g., TULĪ 'I bore', TULERIT 'he will have carried'). Few verbs were as irregular in this respect as this one, but nevertheless the particular modification of the verb that might be found in the perfectum had no necessary relationship to the infectum, as will be seen in the section on the perfect.

In spite of the general independence of the perfect system from the present system, analogical pressure often tended to bring the two systems closer together, thus making for a single unified verbal system. From earliest times, some sort of primacy has been attached to the present system, and the perfect stems have frequently been remodeled to match the present. The traditional classification of the verb has been based largely on the present system (Leumann 1977, 605).

Formal Distinctions in the Verb System

A transitive Latin verb had, for the active voice, six indicative tenses, their traditional labels being: present, imperfect, future, perfect, pluperfect, and future perfect. There were also four subjunctive tenses: the present, imperfect, perfect, and pluperfect, as well as a present and future imperative. For each of these active forms there were passive counterparts, formed by means of special endings in the present system and by a special syntactic construction in the perfect system.

The Conjugational Classes

Varro, who was probably the first to write a formal treatment of the Latin conjugation shortly after the middle of the first century B.C., divided

---

[36] The problem of the best possible analysis of the complexities of Latin verb morphology is taken up in exhaustive detail by Matthews. He remarks: "It may be . . . that the most rudimentary segmentation into 'stem' and 'ending' . . . would yield a better hypothesis than the finer segmentation which we have taken for granted " (1972, 121).

the verbs into three classes, using as his criterion the second personal singular present indicative endings (-ĀS, -ĒS, -ĬS). We find the same division in the works of Marius Claudius Sacerdos (early third century) and Probus Grammaticus (third/fourth centuries), though the former mentions that some grammarians preferred to separate the -ĪS verbs from the -ĬS group and call them a fourth conjugation. In the sixth century Priscian adopted this quadripartite classification and effectively established the tradition which has endured until the present. Despite the popularity of this taxonomic scheme, it is deficient in several respects. It somewhat arbitrarily takes the present system as the point of departure, even given that this system was largely dominant. Even so, it collapses into one type verbs of two quite different classes, for the third conjugation contains two distinct subclasses of verbs: those ending in /-o:/ in the first person singular of the present indicative and /-a-/ in the present subjunctive and /-e:-/ in the future, and those with /-io:, -ia-, -ie-/ in these forms. The verbs in this second class behave much more like verbs of the fourth conjugation, e.g., CAPIŌ 'I take', CAPIAM 'I shall take', etc. parallel AUDIŌ 'I hear', AUDIAM 'I shall hear' of the fourth conjugation. The infinitives, however, fit quite neatly into the pattern.

The Infinitive

The verbal noun which came to be used as an infinitive form was formed in ancient Latin by adding *-SE to a stem consisting usually of the verbal root plus a vocalic element, the thematic vowel, which, for the most part seems to be strictly a sign of membership in a particular conjugational class. In a few instances the ending joined the root directly, e.g., ESSE, VELLE, FERRE, POSSE, but these verbs formed such a small subclass that they have generally been regarded as some sort of irregular residue. Since the archaic Latin intervocalic /-s-/ normally became /-r-/ in Latin, the infinitive endings with their characteristic vowels are -ĀRE, -ĒRE, -ERE, -ĪRE. There was also a perfect infinitive based on the perfect stem, ending in -SSE.

For the sake of convenience we can follow the convention of calling the -ĀRE class Conjugation I, and the -ĒRE class, Conjugation II. For clarity we shall label the -ERE verbs of the type LEGŌ 'I read', III-A, and those of the type CAPIŌ, III-B. Finally, we can call the -ĪRE conjugation Conjugation IV.[37]

It is a complicated matter to measure the relative vitality of the various conjugational classes. A tally of each class as represented in the total lexicon yields a set of figures from which one would scarcely be able to predict their fate in later Romance. Conjugation III contained the largest

---

[37] The convention is by no means universal. Meyer-Lübke (1895) labels the -ĪRE class as class II.

number of primary simple verbs, but if one includes the derived verbs, conjugation I far outnumbered it (1800 vs. 570).[38] Both conjugations had a little more than 1800 compound verbs. In contrast, Conjugation II contained but 180 simple verbs and 390 compounds. Nor was Conjugation IV much better represented. It counted some 200 simple verbs, of which a score were deponents, and approximately 335 compounds, including a little over forty deponents.

Although it is not possible to attach any rigid semantic or syntactic significance to the different conjugations, there is at least some evidence that the formal distinction between classes of verbs bore some relation to the function of the verbs in that class. Denominative verbs might appear in any class, although they tended to be more common in Conjugation I (Buck 1928, 267). Conjugation I also tended to have factive verbs. The verbs of Conjugation II, however, tended to be more often iterative and causative verbs (Sommer 1977, 542). There is also some indication that in Ibero-Romance, stative verbs tended to be associated with this particular conjugation, a problem which will be examined later (Montgomery 1978).

Likewise, there may have grown up some linguistic consciousness of a relation between the shape of the root and the conjugational class, but this sort of association was only weakly present for most speakers and never became fixed in any form of Romance, with the exception of the association between the vowel of the root and the conjugational class which later developed in Spanish. Otherwise it appears that only Conjugation I was a truly productive one. The verbs in other conjugations tended to shrink in number over time (with certain exceptions) and to shift from one class to another under varying analogical pressures.

The Present Tenses

The person/number suffixes in the present active voice are identical for all four conjugations. (For the sake of brevity we shall label the singular forms with the numbers 1–3, and the plurals 4–6.)

1. -Ō (ind.), -M (subj.)	4. -MUS
2. -S	5. -TIS
3. -T	6. -NT

However, since the vocalic conjugation class marker we observed in the infinitive occurs in most present tense forms, the result is a characteristic set of endings for each conjugation class, though with considerable overlap (indicated below by braces) between conjugations III and IV. The present indicative endings were as follows:

	1	2	3	4	5	6
I	-Ō	-ĀS	-AT	-ĀMUS	-ĀTIS	-ANT
II	-EŌ	-ĒS	-ET	-ĒMUS	-ĒTIS	-ENT

---

[38] Numerical estimates in this chapter are based on a count of the verbs in Gradenwitz 1904.

	1	2	3	4	5	6
III-A	-Ō	}-IS	}-IT	}-IMUS	}-ITIS	-UNT
III-B	}-IŌ					}-IUNT
IV		-ĪS		-ĪMUS	-ĪTIS	

In the present subjunctive, the thematic vowels were reversed; Conjugation I used /-e:-/ and the other conjugations /-a:-/ as their vowels. In the present subjunctive too the overlap between III-B and IV was complete:

I	-EM	-ĒS	-ET	-ĒMUS	-ĒTIS	-ENT
II	-EAM	-EĀS	-EAT	-EĀMUS	-EĀTIS	-EANT
III-A	-AM	-ĀS	-AT	-ĀMUS	-ĀTIS	-ANT
III-B	-IAM	-IĀS	-IAT	-IĀMUS	-IĀTIS	-IANT
IV						

Even after vowel quantity ceased to be distinctive in Latin, some implications of quantitative contrasts continued to distinguish the Latin conjugations from one another. Word stress, which had been a redundant feature of the oldest Latin phonological structure, acquired contrastive value when oppositions based on vowel quantity were lost. Accentual patterns for conjugations I, II, and IV were identical, but Conjugation III stood apart with a short vowel in a few endings, while the conjugations with long vowels uniformly bore the stress on the endings:

	Infinitive	4	5
I	AMÁRE	AMÁMUS	AMÁTIS
II	DĒBÉRE	DĒBÉMUS	DĒBÉTIS
IV	AUDÍRE	AUDÍMUS	AUDÍTIS
III	PÉRDERE	PÉRDIMUS	PÉRDITIS

The Imperfect Indicative

The imperfect in Latin was characterized by a well defined suffix /-ba-/, which followed the thematic vowel of the conjugational class of the verb (Baldi 1976). Conjugations III and IV have, in Classical Latin, the same /e:/ as Conjugation II:

I	II	III-A	III-B	IV
AMĀBAM	DĒBĒBAM	REGĒBAM	CAPIĒBAM	AUDIĒBAM

There is evidence that Conjugation IV had also an imperfect ending -ĪBA- which reflected more accurately the thematic vowel of the conjugation (Sommer 1977, 522; Leumann 1977, 578).

The Future Indicative

The future, unlike the other tenses of the present system, lacked a single morpheme to indicate it. Conjugations I and II used /-bi-/ or /-bu-/:

	1	2	3	4	5	6
AMĀ-						
DOCĒ-	-BŌ	-BIS	-BIT	-BIMUS	-BITIS	-BUNT

In conjugations III and IV, on the other hand, the future morpheme was a long vowel /-e:-/ (except in form 1 which was identical with the present subjunctive). In this tense, as in the present subjunctive and the imperfect, the overlap of III-B and IV was complete:

		1	2	3	4	5	6
PŌN-							
CAP-	-I-	-AM	ĒS	-ET	-ĒMUS	-ĒTIS	-ENT
SENT-							

The Passive Voice

In the present system, the passive voice was distinguished from the active by a special set of personal endings, most of which contained as chief characteristic a final /-r/:

1. -R	4. -MUR
2. -RIS	5. -MINĪ
3. -TUR	6. -NTUR

The endings were added after the thematic vowel of the conjugation or the tense morpheme, except that in the present tense the /-o-/ of the active ending of form 1 was retained: AMOR 'I am loved', DOCEOR 'I am taught', PŌNOR 'I am placed', CAPIOR 'I am taken', MŪNIOR 'I am guarded'. In form 2 of the future of conjugations I and II, the vowel preceding the ending was /-e-/ rather than /-i-/ as in the active voice, e.g., AMĀBERIS 'you will be loved'.

The Subjunctives

The present subjunctive has been mentioned above. The imperfect subjunctive was formed with the morpheme /-re-/ plus the personal endings:

		1	2	3	4	5	6
AM-	-Ā-						
DOC-							
PŌN-	-Ē-	-RE-M	-RĒ-S	-RE-T	-RĒ-MUS	-RĒ-TIS	-RE-NT
CAP-							
SENT-	-Ī-						

The future had no special subjunctive form; the present subjunctive or some periphrastic construction could substitute for it.

The Perfect

The Latin perfect represented a merger of the earlier aorist and the perfect. A great many verbs had a perfect containing the suffix -v- followed by a specific set of personal endings, not identical in all persons with those of the present system. The extension of the -v- perfect resulted in its becoming the regular form for the vast majority of all first and fourth conjugation verbs, following the characteristic theme vowel:

I, IV

1.   -Ī
2.   -I-STĪ
      AMĀ-V-
3.   -I-T
4.   -I-MUS
      AUDĪ-V-
5.   -I-STIS
6.   -ĒRUNT, (-ERUNT, -ĒRE)

Although these were the forms most commonly used in Classical Latin, in the very earliest literary sources and later, there appear certain forms of the perfect of these conjugations without the characteristic -v- morpheme:

2.	5.	6.
-ĀSTĪ	-ASTIS	-ĀRUNT

Less common but still attested are:

	1	2	3	4	5	6
I	-AI		-ĀUT			
			-ĀIT			
			-ĀT			
IV	-IĪ	-ISTĪ	-IIT	-IIMUS	-ISTIS	-IĒRUNT
	-Ī		-ĪT			-IERUNT
			-ĪUT			

(Leumann 1977, 599–600)

The usual explanation for these reduced forms is that they began in Conjugation IV as a result of the regular phonetic loss of the bilabial fricative /-b-/ between two identical vowels (Leumann 1977, 601).[39] The

---

[39] St. John (1976) suggests that /-u-/ was originally simply a semiconsonant serving as a hiatus breaker that became associated specifically with the perfect, and then spread through the system. Others think it may be an extension of the /u/ of verb roots such as MŌVI, FŪVIT etc. (Leumann 1977, 596).

first conjugation forms would then be due to analogical imitation of Conjugation IV. However, it is equally possible that they are the result of an analogical extension of the thematic vowel /-a:/ which is characteristic of Conjugation I in all the other tenses. These shorter forms were apparently as common in speech as the longer ones, if we may judge by Varro's remark that "amasti dicimus libentius quam amavisti" (cited in Maurer 1959, 148, n. 412), and the evidence of graffiti such as PEDICAUD, DONAUT, PUGNAUT, etc. (Leumann 1977, 599). It is possible too that the long forms characteristic of written texts were not the original ones at all, but were formed analogically on the basis of the U perfects (Bonfante 1941). The presence of the /u/ in form 3, however, shows that these perfect forms were not exclusively literary. The retention of V in the form of a semivowel in this form (-AUT, -IUT) is a regular characteristic of Latin phonology when it appears in an asyllabic position, e.g., AUCELLA 'little bird', the diminutive of AVIS 'bird' (Leumann 1977, 143), so that -AUT, at least, is simply a normal syncopated form. The form -IUT is rarely attested in writing. The ending -AIT appears to be analogical with form 1, while the variant -AT is modelled on forms 2, 4, 5, and 6.

It is in the perfect of conjugations II and III that we see most clearly the independence of the present and the perfect systems, since the verbs in these conjugations did not have a single specific perfect formation associated with each class. In these classes all of the four basic types of formation were found.

The rarest type of perfect was characterized by vowel gradation, i.e., some sort of alteration of the stem-vowel of the present stem. This alteration could be simply a lengthening of the short vowel of the present, as in the following verbs:

PRESENT		PERFECT
LEGŌ	'read'	LĒGĪ
EMŌ	'buy'	ĒMĪ
EDŌ	'eat'	ĒDĪ
MOVEŌ	'move'	MŌVĪ
VOVEŌ	'vow'	VŌVĪ
JUVŌ	'help'	JŪVĪ (-ĀRE)
RUMPŌ	'break'	RŪPĪ
VIDEŌ	'see'	VĪDĪ
VINCŌ	'conquer'	VĪCĪ
LAVŌ	'wash'	LĀVĪ (-ĀRE)
CAVEŌ	'beware'	CĀVĪ

If the vowel of the stem was /a/, there was often a shift to another vowel as well as lengthening, e.g.,

AGŌ	'act; drive'	ĒGĪ
CAPIŌ	'take, seize'	CĒPĪ
FACIŌ	'do, make'	FĒCĪ
FRANGŌ	'break'	FRĒGĪ

A second type of perfect formation was, as was vowel gradation, a relic of processes that had been more actively used in earlier Indo-European: reduplication or repetition of the initial syllable of the verb stem. Usually the first consonant of the stem was utilized as the initial consonant plus the vowel /e/, e.g.,

CANŌ	'sing'	CECINĪ
TANGŌ	'touch'	TETIGĪ
PARIŌ	'bear, give birth'	PEPERĪ
CADŌ	'fall'	CECIDĪ
PUNGŌ	'prick'	PUPUGĪ
DŌ	'give'	DEDĪ (-ĀRE)
STŌ	'stand'	STETĪ (-ĀRE)

If the vowel of the stem was a back vowel, it was usually used in the reduplicative syllable:

CURRŌ	'run'	CUCURRĪ
MORDEŌ	'bite'	MOMORDĪ

The third type of perfect formation was sigmatic suffixation, i.e., the addition of /-s-/ to the verb stem. The majority of sigmatic perfects were found after stems ending in occlusive consonants, especially velars:

PINGŌ	'paint'	PINXĪ
NINGUIT	'it snows'	NINXIT
JUNGŌ	'yoke, join'	JUNXĪ
CINGŌ	'bind, gird'	CINXĪ
DICŌ	'say, tell'	DĪXĪ
DŪCŌ	'lead'	DŪXĪ
FĪGŌ	'fix, fasten'	FĪXĪ
TRAHŌ	'pull, drag'	TRAXĪ
VĪVŌ	'live'	VĪXĪ
RĪDEŌ	'laugh'	RĪSĪ
ĀRDEŌ	'burn'	ĀRSĪ
MANEŌ	'remain'	MĀNSĪ
SENTIŌ	'perceive'	SĒNSĪ (-ĪRE)

The last type of perfect was the most common one: the -v- suffixation, which as we saw above, had become the regular perfect of conjugations I and IV. Because the sound denoted by the letter v (which later merged with the intervocalic /-b-/), was essentially a semiconsonant, it appeared in a different form depending on the shape of the base to which it was attached. After a vowel, it was a bilabial fricative [w] > [ƀ]. A number of verbs in the second conjugation added the v after the thematic vowel, e.g.,

PLEŌ	'fill'	PLĒVĪ
DELEŌ	'destroy'	DELĒVĪ
FLEŌ	'weep'	FLĒVĪ

(In the preceding examples, the stem ended in a vowel so that perhaps it is not precisely correct to speak of the /-e:-/ as a true thematic vowel.)

Some verbs in Conjugation III also had perfects like the preceding ones:

| QUIĒSCŌ | 'rest, be still' | QUIĒVĪ |
| SERŌ | 'sow' | SĒVĪ |

Thus wherever the -v- suffix appeared between vowels, the result was the preservation of the full consonant. Since in conjugations I and IV the -v- always came after the thematic vowels /a:/ and /i:/, the stress also falls consistently on the ending, producing what is often called the "weak" perfect. However, when the suffix was added directly to a stem ending in a consonant, it remained a labiovelar semiconsonant [w]. The accent in this case fell on the stem, rather than on the ending, producing the so-called "strong" perfect:[40]

HABEŌ	'have'	HABUĪ
DĒBEŌ	'owe; ought'	DĒBUĪ
TENEŌ	'hold'	TENUĪ
		(Old Latin TETINĪ)
TIMEŌ	'fear'	TIMUĪ

In the second conjugation this form became the most common type of perfect, and it is often claimed that it is the "regular" second perfect. However, it is by no means limited to this conjugation, e.g.,

DOMŌ	'tame'	DOMUĪ	(-ĀRE)
SONŌ	'sound'	SONUĪ	(-ĀRE)
VETŌ	'forbid'	VETUĪ	(-ĀRE)
MOLŌ	'grind'	MOLUĪ	(-ERE)
GIGNŌ	'beget'	GENUĪ	(-ERE)
PŌNŌ	'put'	PŌSUĪ	(-ERE)

In perfects of this type the semiconsonant lost its connection with the intervocalic /-ƀ-/ (< /-b-/, -v-), and tended to disappear. This phonetic development further accentuated the difference between the rhizotonic and arrhizotonic perfects.

Other Perfect Tenses

Two other tenses formed part of the perfect system: the pluperfect and the future perfect. They were both formed on the same stem as the perfect. The pluperfect was characterized by the morpheme /-era-/ added to the perfect stem and followed by the present personal endings, e.g., PORT-Ā-

[40] "Cette terminologie singulière a été forgée dans le premier quart du XIXᵉ siècle par des germanistes allemands, imbus de l'idée que les irrégularités dénotent plus de vigueur chez un peuple qu'une morphologie normalisée" (Gougenheim 1960, 123). In this text, "weak" forms, stressed on the ending, will be called arrhizotonic, while "strong" forms, stressed on the stem, will be designated rhizotonic.

V-ERA-M 'I had carried', DOC-U-ERĀ-MUS 'we had taught', HAB-U-ERA-T 'he had had', AUD-Ī-V-ERA-NT 'they had heard', etc.

The future perfect morpheme was /-eri-/, e.g., AM-Ā-V-ERI-NT 'they will have loved', etc. In form 1, the /-o:/ of the present indicative appeared, e.g., POS-U-ER-Ō 'I shall have placed'.

The Perfect Subjunctives

There were two perfects in the subjunctive system: the perfect and the pluperfect. The perfect subjunctive was identical with the future indicative in that it used the morpheme /-eri-/, e.g., AUD-Ī-V-ERI-T 'he heard, has heard; he will have heard'. Form 1 differed from that of the future perfect in that it took the personal ending /-m/, e.g., AUD-Ī-V-ERI-M 'I heard, have heard'.

The morpheme of the pluperfect subjunctive was /-is:e-/, followed by the personal endings, e.g., AM-Ā-V-ISSE-M 'I had loved', HAB-U-ISSE-S 'you had had', VĪX-ISSE-T 'he had lived', AUD-Ī-V-ISSĒ-MUS 'we had heard'.

The Perfect Passive

There was no special morpheme for the passives of the perfect tenses, unlike the present. Instead, a periphrastic construction was used: the perfect passive participle and forms of the verb ESSE. The present of ESSE was used to indicate the simple perfect, e.g., AMĀTUS SUM 'I have been loved', AMĀTAE SUNT 'they (fem.) have been loved', etc. The imperfect formed the pluperfect passive, and the future the future perfect passive, e.g., PORTĀTĪ ERANT 'they had been carried', MŪNĪTUS ERIT 'it will have been armed'.

Other Verb Forms: The Imperative

The present imperative was usually formed with the verb stem plus the thematic vowel: I. -Ā II. -Ē III. -E IV. -Ī. The plural imperative added the affix /-te/ to the singular form, e.g., AMĀTE, AUDĪTE, etc. There was also a future imperative, used much less than the other.

Some verbs formed the present singular imperative with the bare verb root and no vowel: DŪCERE 'to lead' - DŪC, DĪCERE 'to say' - DĪC, FACERE 'to do, make' - FAC.

Participles: The Perfect Passive

This participle had begun as a verbal adjective in *-TO which was independent of the infectum and perfectum. It was added to the weak grade of the verbal root, and a few traces of this ancient pattern can still be seen in Classical Latin: LINŌ 'I smear, daub'-LITUS, REOR 'I reckon, think' - RATUS, SERŌ 'I sow' - SATUS, ŪRŌ 'I burn' - USTUS.

The verbal adjective came to be used with the forms of ESSE to form the passive of the perfect system and as a consequence became more and more closely integrated with the other verb forms, especially with the perfect stem. The suffix was joined to a base which could consist of a root or a root plus a vowel. Verbs with perfects in -ĀVĪ, -ĒVĪ, -ĪVĪ, as well as the third conjugation verbs in -UŌ formed a participle with a long vowel before the ending: AMĀTUS, PLĒTUS, AUDĪTUS, INDŪTUS. All other verbs formed their participles in -́ITUS or -́TUS; when the latter followed a dental, normal phonological development produced -SUS, e.g., SESSUS 'seated' ← SEDĒRE, VĪSUS 'seen' ← VIDĒRE, etc.[41]

Participles thus fell into two large groups, arrhizotonic and rhizotonic. Since the only productive conjugations (I and IV) usually had arrhizotonic participles, there existed already in Republican Latin favorable conditions for the analogical spread of this pattern. The -ĀTUS ending was clearly associated with the -ĀRE verbs, and -ĪTUS with the -ĪRE pattern. Of the other weak endings, -ĒTUS characterized only a small number of verbs in the most sparsely represented conjugational class, while -ŪTUS, though perhaps not much more frequent, was linked with the perfects in -UĪ.

The Future Participle

Independent of the regular future formation was a future participle based on the form of the perfect passive participle, with the suffix -ŪRUS, e.g., AMĀTŪRUS 'going to love', MORITŪRUS 'about to die', etc.[42] This participle could be used with the verb ESSE to form a periphrastic future (Leumann 1977, 618).

The Active Participle

There was also a present participle formed with the suffix /-nt-/ which functioned as an imparisyllabic adjective of the third declension: AMĀNS, AMANTIS, AMANTĪ, etc. 'loving'.

The Gerundive

The form known as the gerundive was characterized by the suffix /-nd-/. It was an adjective of the first and second declensions, and functioned as a future passive, AMANDUS 'to be loved', AGENDA (n.pl.) 'things to be done', etc.

---

[41] The -SUS ending was sometimes analogically extended to verbs with roots ending in consonants other than dentals, e.g., LĀPSUS ← LĀBOR 'glide, slide', FĪXUS ← FĪGŌ 'fix, fasten', MULSUS ← MULCEŌ 'stroke', PULSUS ← PELLŌ 'strike, knock'.

[42] Maurer believes that the future participle was never a part of spoken Latin, and that the present participle also disappeared from speech, as we see in Spanish and Portuguese. Its presence in modern French and Italian would then be the result of learned influence (1959, 130).

CHAPTER 3

FROM EARLIER TO LATER LATIN

THE PHONOLOGICAL SYSTEM

Vowels

The Monophthongization of the Diphthongs

The diphthongs found in Latin by the first century B.C. were only the remnants of a previously richer system of off-gliding diphthongs which had steadily yielded to a monophthongizing tendency. The remaining ones eventually monophthongized also, although at widely differing dates. The earliest appears to have been AE /ai/ which, by the first century A.D. at the latest, was being monophthongized as a mid vowel, probably a long open front mid vowel [ẹ:]. The graffiti at Pompeii show this sort of development, e.g., QUERITE for QUAERITE (Väänänen 1966, 23), and reverse spellings like ADVAENTU for ADVENTU, VĪCĪNAE for VĪCĪNE (Väänänen 1966, 18). This change had occurred much earlier in other areas. Umbrian, for example, shows /e:/ for /ai/ by 200 B.C., and in other regions outside of Rome there is evidence for monophthongization about the same time (Leumann 1977, 67–68). Latin inscriptions in northern areas show monophthongs: CEDITO for CAEDITO (Spoletium), PRETOR for PRAETOR in Faliscan areas, etc. (Coleman 1971, 183). Most words originally having /ai/ thereafter developed in the same way as those containing the short front mid vowel /e/:

CAECU 'blind' > [kẹ́ku] (> Sp. *ciego*)
CAELU 'heaven, sky' > [kẹ́lu] (> Sp. *cielo*)
QUAERO 'I seek' > [kwẹ́ro] (> Sp. *quiero*), etc.

A number of words originally containing /ai̯/ apparently, however, monophthongized to /e:/, and thereafter developed as did those containing an original /e:/:

105

CAESPITE 'turf, grass' > [ke:spite] (> Sp. *césped*)
FAECE 'sediment, dreg' > [fe:ke] (> Sp. *hez*)
FAENU 'hay' > [fe:nu] (> Sp. *heno*)
PRAEDA 'booty, prey' > (> Sp. *prea*)
SAEPE 'fence, stockade' > (> Sp. *sebe*)
SAEPTU 'hedge, fence' [se:ptu] (> Sp. *seto*)
SAETA 'silk' [se:ta] (> Sp. *seda*)
TAEDA 'pitchpine torch' > [te:da] (> Sp. *tea*)

In some cases the diphthongal and monophthongal forms competed in writing from a very early date, e.g., FAENUM-FĒNUM, SAETA-SĒTA, TAEDA-TĒDA, SAEPTUM-SĒPTUM, FAEX-FĒX, etc. These early monophthongal forms were rural borrowings from Faliscan (which may best be considered simply a dialect of Latin), Umbrian, and other Italic languages which monophthongized /ae/ before the Latin of Rome did. Evidently they were taken into Latin at a time before there was any very noticeable qualitative difference between /e:/ and /e/. Although probably they were pronounced with an open quality [ẹ:], their greater length would have been sufficient for Latin speakers to identify them with their own /e:/ (Belardi 1979, 32). It is also possible that there was some dialectal difference in the results of the monophthongization of /ai/ with Faliscan and Umbrian having [ẹ:], while Oscan preferred [e] (Porzio Gernia 1978, 59). Later when the monophthongization of /ai/ was generalized in Latin, the quantitative system had been lost or was in the process of disappearing so that the open quality of the monophthong, being the primary distinctive feature of the simple vowels, caused it to merge with the /ẹ/ < /e/. It is possible too that the monophthongization of /ai/ to /ẹ/ took place before the quantitative system was completely gone, but after the qualitative differences between /e:/ and /e/ had developed sufficiently for speakers to identify the result of /ai/ with /e/ rather than with /e:/ (Blaylock 1964–65). The date of the beginnings of monophthongization have been set as early as the third century B.C. (Franceschi 1976, 260), but in Latin-speaking areas dominated by urban standards, there are no examples in writing before the first century A.D., at Pompeii (Porzio Gernia 1978, 59).

The diphthong OE /oi̯/, which was considerably rarer than /ai̯/ also monophthongized to /e:/: e.g., PHEBUS for PHOEBUS (Väänänen 1966, 25), COENA 'supper' > CĒNA, POENA 'punishment' > [pe:na] (> Sp. *cena, pena*).

The diphthong /au̯/ appears as /o:/ at a very early date in a number of words borrowed from Oscan and Umbrian where monophthongization of this diphthong had occurred partially, particularly in rural areas (Ernout 1909, 51–54). Likewise a number of names of persons from the Faliscan territory, and from the Volsci as well as the Umbrians reveal this change, e.g., OLIAMUS, PLOTIDIUS, and POLA, corresponding to the Roman names AULIANUS, PLAUTIDIUS, PAULA, etc. (Bertoldi 1939, 15; Franceschi 1976, 269).

Since the monophthongization had occurred very early in Italic, these words were considered old (as indeed they were) and also rustic, since they came from rural areas outside of Rome. The monophthongized forms, being in harmony with the general Latin tendency to eliminate the diphthongs, were probably accepted with relatively little resistance, especially among the less cultivated speakers. Being mostly rural words, it is not surprising that most of them denote rustic objects or products: ŌLLA 'stewpot' for AULA, CŌLIS 'cabbage' for CAULIS,[1] PLOSTRA 'cart' for PLAUSTRA, and CŌDEX 'tree trunk' for CAUDEX.

A monophthongization of /au̯/ to /a/ is regularly found everywhere before a velar consonant followed by /u/:

AGUSTO < AUGUSTO (> Sp. *agosto*) (Richter 1934, 59)
ASCULTĀRE 'to listen attentively' < AUSCULTĀRE (> OSp. *ascuchar*)
AGURIUM < AUGURIUM 'augury, prophecy' (> Sp. *agüero*)

There are also numerous inscriptional spellings of /au/ as A even when the diphthong does not appear in the same phonetic conditions as the preceding words, e.g., CLADIUS (Numidia) (CIL 8,5948), FASTI (for FAUSTI) (Seville CIL 2, Supp., 6257), PAPERTAT (for PAUPERTĀTE 'poverty' CIL 6, 25741), etc. There are too many of such spellings to make it seem likely that they were only simple spelling errors, especially in view of the fact that monophthongization of the diphthong was to eventually reach so many Romance dialects. Possibly the spelling with A was meant to represent a very open back vowel [ɔ:] from a sporadic monophthongization of /au̯/, paralleling the open front vowel [ɛ] that resulted from the /ai̯/. The spelling could indicate that the openness of the monophthong was what most struck those who spelled in this way, rather than the back quality (Fischer 1968). In general, however, the diphthong AU continued to exist until a later period[2] and in some of the Romance languages persists to this day (Provençal, Rumanian) (Vidos 1963, 184–87).

The Collapse of the Quantitative System

As we saw in chapter 2, in the earliest form of Latin vowel quantity was a distinctive phonological feature, so that potentially a long or short vowel could appear in any syllable of any word and serve to distinguish mean-

---

[1] Although CŌLIS and CŌLICULUS were used by several Latin writers, the evidence in Romance is that CAULIS continued to be used widely (Vidos 1963, 186).

[2] See Bertoldi 1939 for an extensive study of these early monophthongal forms. Malkiel considers the problem of the "slant" of Romance toward monophthongization of /au̯/ (1981, 553–55) and particularly the problem of whether there is any connection between these forms and the later monophthongization which characterizes many of the Romance languages. Can one can really state confidently that /au̯/ and /o:/ belonged to two separate dialects of Latin? There is nothing implausible about the notion that in Italic and rural dialects of Latin, monophthongization of /au̯/ had begun early and affected a number of lexical items, and that many of these words then entered Roman Latin as individual words. Malkiel's argument that the preservation of /au̯/ in rural Romance areas such as Sardinia and Rumania shows that /au̯/ > /o/ was not a rural change is not persuasive. We are actually dealing with two different rural societies: the early Italian one, before standard Latin (presumably the Latin preserving for the most part words with /au̯/) had become the general language of the western Empire, and later rural developments, or, as in this case, lack of development.

ings. There were, as we have seen, certain distributional restrictions, but these did not affect the phonemic distinctiveness of long and short vowels as a system. A characteristic drift of the Indo-European languages in general is the tendency to eliminate phonological quantity as a feature of the vowel system. This tendency reached Latin some time before the breakup of the Roman Empire, producing a vowel system that distinguished only qualitative differences among vowels. Length then ceased to be an independent distinctive feature, and became a non-distinctive phonetic feature that depended on the position of the accent in the word, and on other factors, as will be seen.

First, speaking in general linguistic terms, it appears that duration has been a very unstable contrast in many languages of the world, and has often been lost (Chen and Wang 1975, 271–75). For one thing, although phonetic duration is one of the main phonetic features that distinguishes phonologically long from phonologically short vowels, it is also affected by other phonetic features. For example, the position of a syllable in a word may influence the length of the vowel nucleus. Factors of tempo and emphasis likewise can affect duration. Even more important is stress: the accented syllable in a word is usually longer than the unaccented syllables (Janson 1979, 34). This particular effect of the accent seems to have had the result of making most unstressed vowels short by the second century B.C.[3] As a result of this tendency, it is likely that the distinction of phonological vowel length was largely restricted to stressed syllables alone, with most unstressed vowels being automatically short (Straka 1959, 290ff.).

Another factor that must be taken into account is that of communicative efficiency. Distinctions of length in language are generally limited to two degrees only: long versus short (or better, longer versus shorter since length distinctions are necessarily relative). On the other hand, qualitative distinctions based on tongue height, tenseness and laxness, are not so limited but, in fact, "are more easily articulated and perceived" (Pulgram 1975, 260). This being so, when distinctions of quantity and quality go together, speakers may not be very certain of which trait is primary and which is secondary. One feature is therefore redundant and if one is to be given up, it is more likely that it will be the least efficient one, namely length. The history of the Indo-European languages in general would confirm that length is less important as a feature of vocalic systems than other features and the one that can most easily be abandoned when conditions favor it.

With regard to the particular conditions of Latin, the continuous exaggeration of the opening of the short vowels, and possibly the concomitant raising of the long vowels, eventually resulted in the short /i/ and /u/ becoming qualitatively identical with the long mid vowels /e:/ and /o:/ in many areas of Romania (central and northern Italy, Gaul, Spain and prob-

---

[3] Sturtevant (1940, 180) points out that Plautus and Terence show a shortening of the long unstressed vowels of two syllable words like MIHĪ beside MIHI, MODŌ along with MODO.

ably north Africa). We must emphasize that the following schema applies only to the most advanced form of the vowel system and that retention of a more conservative pronunciation of the vowels in many areas is by no means to be excluded. In particular, it is quite likely that those areas of western Romance more remote from the centers of innovation (i.e., originally Rome and later Lugdunum) may well have retained a higher pronunciation of the short high vowels, especially in the back series (v. Ch. 4). The resulting phonetic system can be diagrammed as follows:

	FRONT	**CENTRAL**	**BACK**
HIGH	[iː]		[uː]
close	[ẹ̆] [eː]	[ọ:] [ọ̆]	
MID			
open	[ẹ] [ọ]		
LOW	[a] [aː]		

Thus, there were still ten vowel phonemes, and although qualitatively /i/ and /e:/ and /u/ and /o:/, were pronounced quite differently, speakers may well have compensated for these qualitative distinctions and still associated the short mid close vowels with the long high vowels as speakers of modern Czech do (Janson 1982, 121). Still, the qualitative identity of the /e:/ and /o:/ and the short close mid vowels meant that the way was open for this perceptual compensation to be lost so that younger and/or less traditionally oriented speakers might begin to associate these sounds as counterparts. As a result, in the consciousness of many speakers length would have been distinctive only for certain vowels, namely the close mid vowels /ẹ/-/ẹ:/, and /ọ/-/ọ:/ and the low vowels /a/-/a:/. The other vowels were distinguished solely by their quality. Therefore, we could diagram the phonemic system as follows:

	FRONT	**CENTRAL**	**BACK**
HIGH	/iː/		/uː/
close	/ẹ/ /ẹ:/	/ọ:/ /ọ/	
MID			
open	/ẹ/ /ọ/		
LOW	/a/ /a:/		

Finally, there may be one other structural feature that can have had some effect on the quantitative system. For many years there had existed a tendency to eliminate long vowels before geminates and consonant clusters. Since length was characteristic of both vowels and consonants, four combinations within words were possible:

1) short vowel + short consonant: ROTA 'wheel'
                                     PILUS 'hair'
                                     LUPUS 'wolf'

2) short vowel + long consonant: GUTTA 'drop'
                                     SICCUS 'dry'
                                     VALLIS 'valley'

3) long vowel + short consonant: TĒLA 'web'
                                     VĪTA 'life'
                                     LACTŪCA 'lettuce'
4) long vowel + long consonant: VĪLLA 'estate, country house'
                                     STĒLLA 'star'

The last combination was considerably rarer than the first three and examples with liquids, nasals and fricatives were the commonest. In ancient Latin all examples of a long vowel or diphthong plus a long stop consonant had been eliminated, usually by shortening the consonant, e.g., *SĒDPARŌ > *SĒPPARŌ > C.L. SĒPARŌ 'I separate', *PRAID(I)CŌ > *PRAECCŌ > C.L. PRAECŌ 'public crier'. Another way of eliminating this combination was to shorten the vowel. The verb MITTERE 'to send, release', for example, had forms illustrating both developments. The stem originally had the vowel /i:/ < /ei/. The infectum then shortened the vowel before /t:/, while the perfectum retained the vowel and shortened the consonant: *MĪSSĪ > MĪSĪ. Even the combination of a long vowel before a long nasal or liquid, which persisted until quite late, tended to show shortening of either the vowel or consonant in imperial times.

The development of STĒLLA 'star' in the Romance languages illustrates this tendency. Sp. *estrella*, Port. *estrela*, Rom. *stea*, and It. *stella* all derive from the form with /l:/. Fr. *étoile* and North It. *steila*, however, must have developed from a variant form, *STĒLA, in which the undesired combination of a long vowel and a long consonant was eliminated by shortening the consonant. The final result of this tendency would have been to eliminate altogether the combination and to make the length of the vowel in many cases dependent on the nature of the following consonant. Although in combination 1) the length of the vowel and the length of the consonant were independent of each other, in the other two combinations they seemed to be interdependent, with the long vowel appearing only before a short consonant and the short vowel only before a long consonant. Thus, in these particular combinations speakers might have been doubtful about whether the significant element was the length of the vowel or of the consonant. Probably consonant length was felt to be distinctive, if we may judge by the large number of words having long consonants resulting from expressive gemination, e.g., LIPPUS 'blear-eyed', FLACCUS 'flabby', CRASSUS 'dense, fat', and many more. The creation of words like these seems to indicate that for Latin speakers consonant length was the most important element. Therefore, in these words the length of the vowel depended on the following consonant, and, being automatically determined, could no longer be phonologically pertinent (Weinrich 1958, 12–42).

All of these factors then affected the vocalic system of Latin: 1) the relative inefficiency of length distinctions as opposed to qualitative distinctions; 2) the limitation of the difference between long and short vowels to three vowel positions only; 3) the effect of the accent, which made length partially dependent on the position of the accent, and thus further limited length distinctions to stressed syllables alone; 4) the tendency to eliminate the combination of long vowel and long consonant so that quantity was to some extent dependent on the following consonant and hence non-phonemic. The concurrence of all these factors resulted in the complete abandonment of quantity as an independent phonological feature of the vowel system. When this happened phonetic length of vowels became a secondary, non-distinctive feature of vowels as it is today in modern Spanish. Another result was that those vowels which had hitherto been distinguished only by length could no longer be kept separate. In the Latin spoken in Hispania, Gaul, and northern Italy, this meant that /e/-/e:/, /o/- /o:/, and /a/-/a:/ merged into a single vowel phoneme for each position.[4] The resulting system was one of seven vowel positions:

	FRONT	CENTRAL	BACK
HIGH	/i/		/u/
MID CLOSE	/ẹ/		/ọ/
MID OPEN	/ę/	/ǫ/	
LOW		/a/	

It is this system that underlies most further developments in the Romance of these areas.

The date of the loss of the quantitative system cannot be determined in any very precise way. One scholar even thinks that length was not a part of the spoken Latin system from the third century B.C. onward (Pulgram 1975).[5] A very early date for the abandonment of phonemic quantity would certainly account for the fact that it was not retained in any form of Romance, no matter how conservative in other areas. Actually, it may well have been the case that for many speakers it was impossible to tell whether they were conscious of length as the distinctive feature rather than quality

---

[4] Haudricourt and Juilland (1949, 23–24) put great emphasis on the monophthongization of /ai̯/ as the stimulus for the loss of the quantitative system. As they conceive it, AE, upon being monophthongized, must have become a long open mid front vowel [ę:], which was different from the short /e/ by being long and also different from the long /e:/ by being open. Since it did not fit into the system, it tended to disrupt it by creating qualitative differences where none had existed before. These assumptions are ingenious but cannot stand up to critical examination. First, the monophthongization of AE as an open /ę/ depended on the previous development of a qualitative distinction between /e/ and /e:/. It cannot be the cause of the qualitative distinction, since as Blaylock (1964–65, 21) shows, early monophthongizations of AE were adopted as /e:/ and not /e/. Secondly, the assumption that a monophthong must always be long because it derives from a diphthong, which is inherently long, is not necessarily true. Michelena (1964, 58) shows that Latin borrowings in Celtic, which treats long and short vowels differently, adopted words with /ai̯/ as though they were a short /e/, which would indicate that the monophthongization resulted in a short vowel. Coleman (1974) likewise believes that there is no causal connection between monophthongization of /ai̯/ and the loss of the quantitative system, arguing against Spence (1974) that vowel quality began to be introduced as a concomitant of length before the monophthongization of /ai̯/ occurred.

[5] See Dressler 1973 for pertinent remarks on stylistic differences within Latin and the coexistence of advanced features in careless and low class speech and conservative features in more formal styles.

(Haudricourt and Juilland 1952). We must assume that the qualitative distinctions must have become noticeable before quantity became dependent on other factors.

It should be noted that the Latin words adopted by the Celts in Britain (i.e., after 54 A.D.), still preserved in modern Welsh, show a clear distinction between long and short vowels, although once again we cannot be certain that what was perceived by Celtic speakers was length rather than quality (Michelena 1964). Once the loss of phonological length started, it spread everywhere, although the actual process may have been "gradual and perhaps for a long time incomplete abandonment . . ." (Janson 1979, 44).[6] Indeed, if Pulgram is correct, the Latin that was taken to all parts of the empire beyond Latium had already lost quantity. In those areas in which the qualitative distinction between long and short vowels had not been adopted, or at least had not been exaggerated, e.g., Sardinia, the result was a merger of the original long and short vowels into a five-vowel system. In Dacia, where the qualitative distinction affected the front vowels but not the back, the back vowels merged long and short /u/ and /u:/ into /u/ and /o/ and /o:/ into /o/. At any rate, in the fifth century St. Augustine remarked that in Africa people could not distinguish between long and short vowels. We may assume that he was referring to literary Latin since most of our evidence would indicate that spoken Latin had discarded quantity as a phonological feature long before then.

Atonic Vowels

Vowels found in syllables not bearing the main stress were more weakly stressed than those in the tonic syllable, but the amount of stress varied depending on the position of the syllable with respect to the main stress and possibly with respect to the position of the syllable in the word.[7] Initial syllables immediately preceding the main stress, and syllables (whether initial or not) two syllables before the main stress, and final syllables, all

---

[6] Janson, in a lengthy discussion of the problems of chronology, shows how difficult it is to be certain of when the phenomenon occurred (1979, 16–27).

[7] It may be argued that the choice of a single system of classification of vowels with reference only to the position of the main stress presents a better picture of their development than one that takes into consideration their position in the word as well. Such a scheme has the advantage of simplicity, but since Latin words had on the average less than three syllables it has a limited value. Also historical development shows that the initial and final positions are stronger, regardless of the position of the main stress. Nevertheless, the close relationship between word structure and stress must be kept in mind at all times (Malkiel 1962–63). A somewhat similar system of classification is Lausberg's (1965, 116, 121, 252). Lausberg divides atonic vowels into deuterotonic (corresponding to Malkiel's countertonic), posttonic and intertonic (corresponding to Malkiel's weakest vowels). Lausberg ties his system directly to the position of the syllable in the word while Malkiel endeavors to keep the position of the main stress as the determining factor. In practice there is little difference between the two systems since Malkiel's moderately weak vowels are those found initially and finally when the main stress comes immediately after the initial syllable and/or immediately before the final syllable. Thus, his system is really lexico-syllabic in spite of his attempt to keep it purely accentual.

had a secondary stress. The changes of pronunciation that were occurring in the tonic vowels also affected the atonic vowels so that the short high vowels became [e] and [o]. The reduced stress, however, made the preservation of distinctions of quality in the mid vowels a very uncertain thing. The result was the coalescence of these vowels into two phonemes only: /i, e:, e/ > /e/, and /u, o:, o/ > /o/. Thus for vowels in these syllables a five vowel system was established:

	FRONT	CENTRAL	BACK
HIGH	/i/		/u/
MID		/e/ /o/	
LOW		/a/	

Some examples are the following:

HĪBERNU 'pertaining to winter' > [ibérnu] (> Sp. *ivierno*)
CIRCĀRE 'to surround' > [kercáre] (> Sp. *cercar*)
VĒNĀTU 'chase, hunting' > [venátu] (> Sp. *venado* 'stag')
SEPTIMĀNA 'related to the seventh' > [set:emána] (> OSp. *sedmana* 'week')
CABALLU 'nag' > [kabal:u] (> OSp. *cavallo*)
FORMĪCA 'ant' [formíka] (> Sp. *hormiga*)
FŌRMĀCEU > [format'u] (> Sp. *hormazo* 'earthen wall')
NUMERĀRE > [nomeráre] (> Sp. *nombrar* 'to name')
SŪDĀRE 'to sweat' > [sudáre] (> Sp. *sudar*)

Syncope

There was extensive syncope of atonic vowels in words having four or more syllables in prehistoric Latin, and this process continued throughout the historical period (Faria 1955,163; Live 1959, 57; Rix 1965). Oscan and Umbrian show more extensive syncope than Latin so it is conceivable that another influence of these languages on Latin may have been to accentuate the tendency to eliminate unstressed vowels. A number of words found in early writers and in inscriptions compared with the usual form in later literature illustrate the process:

BALINEAE 'baths' > BALNEAE
OPIFICĪNA 'workshop' > OFFICINA
COLUMEN 'top, summit' > CULMEN
TEGUMEN, -IMEN 'covering' > TEGMEN

Syncope continued to affect words during imperial times, especially when an atonic vowel was in contact with a liquid or nasal consonant. There was no absolute regularity of syncope at that time since the analogical influence of related words may have tended to maintain the unsyncopated forms.

There are also cases of anaptyxis in which words having the same shape as syncopated forms have added a vowel, e.g., *AGRS > AGER, AGRIS 'field', *FAKLITAS > FACULTAS 'capacity'. The alternations that existed then in written Latin looked exactly like cases of syncope regardless of their origin (Reighard 1974, 255). In earlier periods syncope was variable and affected words in an apparently random fashion. We are informed that the Emperor Augustus, for example, considered CALIDUS 'hot' to be a pedantic pronunciation, and he himself preferred the syncopated form CALDUS. The factor that seems to have had the greatest importance was whether the consonants which came into contact after syncope formed normally occurring groups in Latin. Since these offered no difficulties in pronunciation the loss of a vowel could have only the effect of making a word slightly shorter. Some examples of syncopated words attested in writing during imperial times are the following:

1) posttonic, following a liquid or /s/:
   VIRDIS 'green' < VIRIDIS (> Sp. *verde*)
   POSTUS 'placed' < POSITUS (> Sp. *puesto*)
2) posttonic, preceding a liquid:
   SUSPENDRE 'to suspend' < SUSPENDERE (Väänänen 1966, 90)
   SPECLUM 'mirror' < SPECULUM (App.Pr.) (> Sp. *espejo*)
   OCLUS 'eye' < OCULUS (App.Pr.) (> Sp. *ojo*)
   TABLA 'plank' < TABULA (App.Pr.) (> Sp. *tabla*)
3) pretonic:
   MALDIXI 'I cursed' < MALEDĪXĪ (Väänänen 1966, 89)

Syncope in contact with a nasal occurred only in the word DOMNUS 'lord, master' < DOMINUS (Väänänen 1966, 43), probably because of its very frequent use as a title. Syncope with other consonants also occurred but was much less frequent. FRĪDAM 'cold' < FRĪGIDAM (Väänänen 1966, 44), for example, is evidently a form influenced by CALDUS, rather than a result of ordinary syncope. It was only at a much later period that syncope became a categorical rule affecting all vowels, regardless of the surrounding consonants.

Final Vowels

Final vowels generally received more stress than intertonic ones, possibly in part because case endings were often distinguished by the vowels alone. As case distinctions became less important and the tonic vowels changed, final vowels were also reduced in number, eventually even more than vowels in other positions. At first they, like countertonic ones, were reduced to five vowels.

The vowels in the final syllable in masculine and neuter nouns of the second declension deserve separate consideration. There is some evidence that there was a qualitative difference between the vowels of these endings which persisted for several centuries, as we shall see in the next chapter. However, the influence of the plural in -ōs and the change of tonic /u/ to /o/ was sufficient to eventually produce -o in the singular, although at a fairly late date.

The final /i:/ of the first person singular of the perfect tenses and of the demonstratives persisted for centuries and had a pronounced effect on the tonic vowel in verbs which will be discussed in the sections on morphology in the next chapter.

Accentuation

Since, as we saw in chapter 2, in earlier Latin the position of the accent was dependent on the phonological distinction between long and short vowels, as soon as this distinction ceased to be phonemic, the accent immediately became potentially phonemic, as it is today in Spanish. For example, in earlier Latin the perfect of the verb CADERE 'to fall', CECIDI, was distinguished from the perfect of CAEDERE 'to cut down', CECĪDĪ, by the difference in the length of the vowel in the second syllable. The words were also accented on different syllables, with the stress falling on the first syllable in CECIDI and on the second in CECĪDĪ. When the length of vowels became phonetic rather than phonemic, the position of the accent could no longer be predicted automatically and thus had the potential to distinguish words which otherwise would be identical (Lüdtke 1956, 122ff.).

Those words containing a cluster of a stop and /r/ between the penultimate and the last syllable, which in Classical Latin were supposed to be treated as though the group were a single consonant, did not maintain the proparoxytonic pronunciation, if, indeed, it had ever been common in popular usage. Although there is evidence that there was a proparoxytonic accentuation in some words,[8] the general tendency was to treat these groups like all other groups and to stress the penultimate syllable. The results in Spanish confirm this position of the accent:

> ALÁCRE for ÁLACRE 'lively, animated' (> Sp. *alegre* 'merry')
> CATHÉDRA for CÁTHEDRA 'chair' (> Sp. *cadera* 'hip')
> INTÉGRU for ÍNTEGRU 'whole' (> Sp. *entero*)
> TENÉBRAS for TÉNEBRAS 'darkness' (> Sp. *tinieblas*)
> *COLÓBRA for C.L. CÓLUBRA 'snake' (> OSp. *culuebra*)
> TONÍTRU for TÓNITRU 'thunder' (> Sp. *tronido*)

Is it possible that this preference for the paroxytone was favored by the general structure of these words? If the accent had been on the antepenult, syncope would have produced consonant groups which were not acceptable or were extremely rare in Latin. Thus speakers may have unconsciously avoided a pronunciation which could have led to phonetic difficulties.[9]

In a number of derived words the position of the accent required by the earlier rules was changed by morphological analogy with the base word. Thus RECIPIT 'he takes back, retains', according to the earlier pattern,

---

[8] For example, PULLITRU > Sp. *potro* 'colt', Fr. *poutre*, Port. *poldro*; INTEGRU > OFr. *entre*.

[9] See Spence 1963. In the case of CATHEDRA, it is likely that the stress on the penult reflects the Greek accentuation (Richter 1934, 46).

would have the stress on the first syllable, but the influence of CÁPIT 'he takes' was sufficient to cause speakers to pronounce it RECÍPIT (> Sp. *recibe*). Other examples of this sort of analogical shift, occasionally with recomposition, are: CÓNTINET 'it contains' > [konténet] (> Sp. *contiene*), RÉTINET 'he retains' > [reténet] (> Sp. *retiene*), etc. (showing the influence of the base word TENĒRE 'to hold'), RÉNEGŌ 'I denounce, refuse' > [renégo] (> Sp. *reniego*) (showing the influence of NÉGŌ 'I deny'), etc.

In those words in which the derivation was no longer obvious, there was no change of accent, e.g., CÓLLOCAT 'he places, arranges' (> Sp. *cuelga*), based on LOCĀRE 'to place', CÓMPUTAT 'he calculates, computes' (> Sp. *cuenta*), based on PUTĀRE 'to estimate, reckon', etc.

As for the nature of the accent, it undoubtedly remained what it had earlier been in popular usage, a stress accent (see chap. 2). Those who are convinced, on the basis of Latin grammarians' comments that the Latin accent had been a pitch accent, naturally have to account for the fact that no such accent is found in modern Romance. One popular theory is that the increasing number of Germanic speakers somehow passed their type of accent to Latin-Romance speakers. If, however, the Latin accent had always been a stress accent, no such theory is needed.[10]

The Beginnings of Diphthongization

A wide-spread phenomenon of Romance is the development of diphthongs from what had been simple vowels in earlier Latin. Although any vowel may become a diphthong in the right conditions and in the right place, the most nearly universal form of diphthongization in Romance is that affecting the Late Latin mid open vowels /ẹ/ and /ọ/. It may be claimed, of course, that the conditions under which diphthongs appear vary so much from region to region that they cannot be linked to any single origin[11] and must therefore be studied as unrelated phenomena, sharing only a certain similarity of result. Certainly some forms of diphthongization seem to be unrelated to the most wide-spread type and some diphthongizations originate too late to be connected to any changes in Late Latin, but the diphthongization of Late Latin tonic /ẹ/ and /ọ/ is found so early and in so many widely separated languages that it is legitimate to seek its origins in Late Latin itself (Straka 1953, 247ff.). However, since the problem of Romance diphthongization is far too complicated to be taken up in any great detail here, we must therefore limit ourselves to some general considerations.

---

[10] Weinrich remarks ironically, speaking of this supposed strong stress accent introduced by the Germanic invaders: "Der Intensitätsakzent ist das Phlogiston der romanischen Sprachwissenschaft" (1958, 179).

[11] Cf. Delbouille: "le phénomène se présente, selon les régions, dans des conditions phonétiques différentes et résulte donc des processus indépendants" (1966, 24).

The Process of Diphthongization

Before we look at the possible causes for the diphthongization of /ę/ and /ǫ/, we must define just what a diphthong is. A recent definition of a "segmental diphthong" is: "a single segment whose central phase is acoustically heterogeneous in its temporal development, rather than presenting a steady state" (Andersen 1972, 18). In other words, a diphthong is a single syllable nucleus in which there is some qualitative difference between the beginning or onset of the vowel and its center, or between the center and the end, or coda. This sort of diphthong is defined as a segmental diphthong because it results historically from what was originally a single vowel, as opposed to a "sequential diphthong" which results from the combination in one syllable of two vowels that were originally separated in two different syllables (Andersen 1972, 18).

If the diphthong has a somewhat weaker or non-syllabic element at the beginning the diphthong can be defined as an on-gliding diphthong, while if the center of the vowel is followed by a weaker element, the diphthong is an off-gliding one.[12] The diphthongs resulting from /ę/ and /ǫ/ are almost invariably on-gliding ones: [je, ja, jə, wo, wa] etc. This seems to be one of the more common types of diphthongization, in which "the initial portion of a segment is modified with respect to a feature whose marked value defines that segment" (Andersen 1972, 24).[13]

It might be supposed too that it would be necessary that a diphthongized vowel had become somewhat longer and thus could suffer some alteration in its articulation. Length, of course, is a relative matter, so that it would be sufficient that the vowel be tonic. As noted previously, the former phonological distinction of length had given way to a phonetic distinction, dependent on the position of the accent in a word. All tonic vowels were thus longer than the atonic ones, and we note that, with rare exceptions, it is only tonic vowels that ever diphthongize.

Thus, at the beginning of the process, the onset of the vowel may have

---

[12] For purposes of clarity, I have adopted the terms proposed by Corbett 1970–71, 279: on-gliding diphthongs for those beginning with a close articulation, and off-gliding diphthongs for those ending with a close articulation. Other terms often used are ascending or rising for on-gliding diphthongs, and descending or falling diphthongs for off-gliding ones (Purczinsky 1969–70, 497; Lipski 1974, 415). Romeo 1968, however, uses rising and falling in a different sense (44, n.27). Corbett's terminology seems much simpler and more descriptive, provided it is understood that at the beginning of the process of diphthongization one cannot definitely speak of non-syllabic glides as being present.

[13] I have made relatively little use of Andersen 1972 in view of his reliance on the early form of distinctive feature theory as proposed by Jakobson, especially since "there is little common consensus on the distinctive features to be employed in describing human languages; in particular, no set of features has been shown to triumph over all others on psychological grounds. . . . [T]hus in order for Andersen's claims to have any substance, one must isolate the set of distinctive features operative in any given language, a task which remains unaccomplished" (Lipski 1974, 428). Also Andersen's belief that "markedness" is involved in diphthongization cannot be accepted until it is proved what features are "marked." His conclusions then, "must be regarded as completely hypothetical, although not necessarily invalid" (Lipski 1974, 429).

been somewhat higher than the nucleus. We may symbolize this as follows: [o̞o, e̞e]. Alternatively we may imagine that what occurred was not so
much the raising of the initial portion of the vowel as an exaggeration of
the opening of the central portion, a process which we could symbolize as
[oo̞, ee̞] (Straka 1959, 295; Spore 1972, 299). Further exaggeration of either
the onset or the nucleus or both would have served to separate even
farther the different parts of the vowel so that the onset eventually closed
sufficiently to become a semiconsonant [w, j], while the nucleus of the
vowel could open enough so as to become identical with the preexisting
low central vowel /a/: [wa, ja].

Another conception of the beginnings of the process of diphthongization is that the process was rather one that involved all of the vowels,
which were lengthened under stress, and that what happened originally
was the transformation of the quality of length (which was non-phonemic
in Late Latin) to a semivowel following the vowel nucleus. According to
this view, all stressed vowels could be symbolized in the following scheme:

i̯i	u̯u
e̯i	o̯u
e̯i	o̯u
a̯i (AE)	a̯u (< AU)

a:

(Adapted from Purczinsky 1969, 497)

The long low vowel is thus isolated in this system and therefore speakers
might seek to make it adopt the same pattern as the other vowels and take
a central semivowel following the nucleus, become [aa̯].[14] Therefore
diphthongization must involve a modification of the end of the vocalic
nucleus, not the beginning. "No matter what the final result may be,
diphthongization has at its very roots, in the initial stage, a modification of
the final vowel segment in terms of tension" (Romeo 1968, 41).

The next step would have been the adoption of the mid central semivowel in place of the high semivowel by [e̞i̯] and [o̞u̯] so that they might be
more clearly distinguished from the higher mid vowels [ei̯] and [ou̯]. The
result would have been [e̞a̯, o̞a̯] (Purczinsky 1969, 498).

In support of the idea that diphthongization originally affected only the
first part of the vowel and that the only vowels affected at the beginning of
the process were the Late Latin low mid vowels /ę/ and /ǫ/ is the evidence from the majority of the Romance languages; when diphthongization is found (it is missing in Portuguese, excluding some modern dialects,
Sardinian, and southern Gallo-Romance and Catalan),[15] it is usually just

---

[14] One wonders why Purczinsky includes [ai̯] in his schema when Lat. AE had undoubtedly
monophthongized to /ę/ long before diphthongization began. Also I am not certain what the
real phonetic difference between [a] and [a̯] is supposed to be, unless the latter symbol
represents simply a very short low central vowel or perhaps a somewhat higher central
vowel.

[15] This statement is over-simplified since Provençal and Catalan had diphthongization
preceding a palatal in the Middle Ages, e.g., Old Prov. *lieit* < Lat. LECTU 'bed', *ueit* < OCTO
'eight' (Spore 1972, 160).

these vowels that are affected and the results are always on-gliding diphthongs. We find also that the form of the diphthong resulting from /ǫ/ and /ẹ/ in certain northern modern Portuguese dialects is that of an on-gliding diphthong, e.g., *piera* for *pera* 'pear', *tiempo* for *tempo* 'time, weather', *fuorti* for *forte* 'strong', *fuogo* for *fogo* 'fire', etc. (Spore 1972, 185–86).[16] The same thing is true in the dialect of Quérigut (Ariège) in France; when [ẹ] and [ǫ] diphthongize, they take the form [iẹ] and [uǫ] (Seguy 1954). Of course, these diphthongs are modern and evidently unconnected with the early Romance diphthongization, but they serve to prove that spontaneous diphthongization can take the form of on-gliding diphthongs.

On the other hand, Old French and Old Dalmatian had off-gliding diphthongs, e.g., OFr. *peire* < PIRA 'pear', OFr. *houre* < HŌRA 'hour', etc., Dal. *kajna* < CĒNA 'dinner', *fajn* < FĪNE 'end', *saul* < SŌLE 'sun', etc. Also we notice that the diphthongs that result from the Late Latin /ǫ/ often vary in the articulation of the nucleus of the diphthong, rather than in the onset. Thus the nucleus may become a low vowel [wa] or a front vowel [we] or even a mid rounded front vowel [wö]. It might be concluded that this sort of change implies that originally the nucleus of the vowel was the first portion and that it was the coda that ceased to be articulated in the same manner as the original.[17]

Although there seems to be somewhat more evidence favoring the assumption that the original form of the diphthong was that of an on-gliding diphthong, there are enough indications that possibly the last part of the vowel was the element altered first to make our conclusions uncertain. It should be noted too that the off-gliding diphthongs in Old French involved vowels other than the ones deriving from Late Latin /ẹ/ and /ǫ/. One may ask then whether there is any other reason for assuming that if one type of diphthong is found in one or more areas, it must necessarily follow that all diphthongs must have been of this type. Why could it not be that some kinds of vowels produce certain types of diphthongs and others produce other types? Experimental research in articulatory phonetics reveals that when high vowels, which would include the highest vowels [i u] and the mid high vowels [ẹ ǫ] are lengthened, they tend to close, while the more open vowels [ẹ] and [ǫ] become even more open (Straka 1959, 296).[18] This research has been conducted in modern times, using French speakers as subjects, and thus conceivably is unrelated to the process that took place many centuries ago, but nevertheless it appears to offer a substantial em-

---

[16] In all justice it must noted that some dialects on the Leonese border diphthongize in the opposite direction, with central off-glides following the vocalic nucleus (Fagan 1979).

[17] Purczinsky believes that not only French but also the evidence of conditioned diphthongization supports his theory that originally all vowels that diphthongized were "falling" diphthongs (1969–70, 500–01), with the semivowel added after the nucleus. Strangely enough, in view of the thoroughness with which Purczinsky has surveyed previous theories of diphthongization, he seems to be completely unaware of Straka's work.

[18] Straka's experimental evidence confirms an early hypothesis of Antoine Meillet (cited in Rauch 1967, 92).

pirical basis for the process of diphthongization. The notion that because some diphthongs are of one type, therefore all diphthongs must also be of that same type, or that because some vowels diphthongize, all must therefore have diphthongized, may be the result of a desire to have a simple explanation regardless of any other considerations.[19] It is important too to remind ourselves that our discussion of diphthongization must not be influenced by the necessities of phonetic symbolism which constrain us to represent different portions of a continuum of articulation by means of separate symbols which then may give the impression that we are dealing with truly individual and separate elements.

The preceding remarks are especially necessary in view of a frequent problem that is often dealt with in studies of diphthongization, namely, that of where the accent falls in the original diphthongs. The assumption made by Purczinsky 1969–70 is that since the origins of diphthongization are found in the alteration of the coda of the vowels, all diphthongs are off-gliding ones, with the onset and nucleus having the quality of the original simple vowel with the accent on them while the following semi-vowel is unstressed. Those who favor the idea that all diphthongs are originally on-gliding ones think that the final part of the diphthong has the stress. There are occasional clues that some diphthongs derived from /ẹ/ and /ọ/ are indeed off-gliding and have the principal stress on the initial element. In the Leonese dialect of Sanabria the diphthong from the back vowel is so stressed [ú ə]. Also the development of the Old Spanish possessive adjectives into the forms *mie, tue, sue* < MEA, TUA, SUA might suggest that the Late Latin pronunciation of the nucleus of the syllable was more like [íə] and [úə] and that the pronunciation as [wé] and [jé] represents a later development (Purczinsky 1969–70, 509).[20] The development of the proper name DIDACUS into Sp. *Diego* may also be an indication that the pronunciation in Late Latin was [díego] and this diphthong later went the same way as all others derived from low mid vowels. In the Oxford Psalter, stresses are marked in diphthongs for the convenience of the singers and [ue] is usually marked [úe] (Purczinsky 1969–70, 505).[21]

---

[19] Although the problem of explanations in history is dealt with in more detail in chapter 1, it may be well to recall here the words of Hosper: "A true explanation is often very complicated, and many alleged explanations turn out to be gross oversimplifications which overlook the actual complexity of events" (1946, 346). Thus, Purczinsky offers in support of his idea that all Late Latin vowels must have been off-gliding diphthongs, examples from English, which hardly seems relevant to Romance (497). One might equally cite as relevant the diphthongization of Old High German /ẹ:/ and /ọ:/ into /ie/ and /uo/, a process which parallels exactly the development in Romance (Rauch 1967).

[20] The Old Spanish forms are discussed in chapter 4. We may note here, however, that the modern forms *mi, tu, su*, must be derived from forms stressed on the high vowel.

[21] Purczinsky quotes L. Havet's demonstration that in the oldest French texts, the /ie/ < /ẹ/ or postpalatal /e/ does not assonate with OFr. /ẹ/ (Lat. /e:/), or the /e/ from late /ẹ/ or /e/ from Lat. /a/ in stressed free syllables that do not follow a palatal, nor does it assonate with the apparent diphthong in words like *marier* < Lat. MARITĀRE 'to marry'. Finally he notes that the last syllable in *marié* was long kept separate from the final syllable in *moitié* (505). He believes that this proves that the diphthong must have been a falling one with a

Yet if diphthongs develop from what were originally simple vowels, why should it be assumed that it was necessary at the very beginning that there be a definite split of the vowel into two distinct parts? If an incipient diphthongization is just a variation in the realization of one part of the lengthened vowel, it would appear to the speaker and to the hearer that it was just a single vowel and thus would have the accent on the whole vowel, and not on one part or another. Once again it is essential that we remember that our phonetic symbols may be separate but that they do not necessarily mean that the vowels in question had separated into two distinct parts. A more fertile conception is that of Spore 1972. In his view, since the alteration of /ẹ/ and /ọ/ is only slight at first, the resulting phonetic form may be termed a "semidiphthong" (295). At this stage there are as many monophthongs as diphthongs. In other words, the alteration in the articulation of the vowels may or may not occur, depending on the force of articulation. Being a very slight alteration at first, the speaker will not be conscious that he is articulating anything other than a simple vowel. With the passage of time, the exaggeration of the initial part of the vowel produced a greater closure that eventually turned into a palatal or labio-velar semiconsonant [j w]. However, this would not mean that the higher portions of the vowel were identified with any other element in the phonological system, such as the palatal consonant /j/ or the vowels /i/ or /u/ until a much later period. These semidiphthongs and the resulting diphthongs continued to function as separate phonemes rather than as combinations of phonemes until quite late. Thus as far as speakers of early Romance were concerned, there was likely to be no awareness of any particular difference between the semidiphthong and a simple vowel that maintained the same degree of opening throughout its articulation. The accent fell on the diphthong as a whole, although it probably tended to shift somewhat from one element to another in the realization of the diphthong and thus could develop in some places into an off-gliding diphthong and in others into an on-gliding one, with a further exaggeration of the diphthongal nature of the phoneme. To use Andersen's terminology, what we are dealing with in the beginnings of the process is "phonetic diphthongization" or "a phonetic innovation by which a segment comes to be realized as a segmental diphthong." Only later comes what can be called "phonemic diphthongization," which is "the re-inter-

---

central semivowel. One may wonder whether it actually proves anything other than that the diphthong derived from the Late Latin /ẹ/ was a separate phonological unit in the linguistic consciousness of Romance speakers. As for *marier, marié*, it is quite likely that the units written with the letters I and E were disyllabic at the earliest period and thus could not be considered diphthongs at that time. Even after merging in a single syllable, the result would have been a sequential diphthong and not a segmental one, and thus may still have sounded different to speakers of Old French. The only positive evidence for P's thesis is that words like *crestiien* 'Christian' < CHRISTIĀNU and *moillier* 'woman' < MULIERE do assonate with words like *ciel* 'heaven' < Lat. CAELU, and that triphthongs like /iei/ and /iee/ reduce to /i/. Even here, however, a more conservative conclusion might be that the accent did not fall on any one part of the diphthong but rather on the whole unit.

pretation of a single segment as a sequence of segments" (Andersen 1972, 18).

Most of the evidence presented by Purczinsky to prove that originally all diphthongs must have been off-gliding ones can, in fact, equally well be interpreted to mean that the entire phonemic unit (realized phonetically as a semidiphthong and later as a full diphthong) received the syllabic stress (1969–70, 500–511). Thus it is a reasonable conclusion that at the start of the process, the diphthong was neither on-gliding nor off-gliding but rather a unified semidiphthong that could fluctuate in either direction. Finally, it should be noted that there is no need to assume that diphthongization provides any proof that a new "accent of intensity," essentially different from the accent in earlier Latin, had come to characterize Late Latin.[22]

The Conditions of Diphthongization

We have already discussed to some extent the conditions under which vowels diphthongize: with rare exceptions[23] diphthongs appear only in stressed syllables. In addition, in some of the Romance languages there are further conditions that determine diphthongization. In French and Italian, for example, diphthongization only occurred in free (i.e., ending in a vowel) stressed syllables:

LATIN	FRENCH	ITALIAN
CAELUM 'heaven'	*ciel*	*cielo*
PETRA 'stone'	*pierre*	*pietra*
OVUM 'egg'	*uef* (OFr.)	*uovo*
MOLA 'mill-stone'	*meule*	*muola*

In checked syllables, on the other hand, only a simple vowel appears:

SEPTEM 'seven'	*sept*	*sette*
TERRA 'earth'	*terre*	*terra*
MORTE 'death'	*mort*	*morte*
OSSU 'bone'	*os*	*osso*

In Spanish and Rumanian, however, all low mid stressed vowels diphthongize, regardless of the type of syllable they appear in (certain Spanish exceptions will be discussed in chap. 4):

LATIN	SPANISH	RUMANIAN
PETRA	*piedra*	*piatră*
FERA 'wild beast'	*fiera*	*fieră*

---

[22] For example, Schürr speaks of "la résurrection de l'accent d'intensité dans le latin parlé vers la fin de l'époque impériale" (1970, 7). Spore 1972 likewise believes in an "accent musical cédant la place à l'accent dynamique" (296). Like so many other scholars in Romance they confuse the literary dialect with the Latin language as a whole.

[23] The twelfth century diphthongization in Walloon in which both atonic and tonic vowels diphthongize is a notable example (Delbouille 1966, 25, note 8).

LATIN	SPANISH	RUMANIAN
MOLA	*muela*	*moară*
SEPTEM	*siete*	*şapte*
TERRA	*tierra*	*ţară*
MORTE	*muerte*	*moarte*
C(H)ORDA 'string'	*cuerda*	*coardă*

Some other Romance dialects have the same type of diphthong pattern as Spanish and Rumanian. For example, Friulian has forms like *t'era* < TERRA, *m^{u}art* < MORTE (Schürr 1970, 62).

In some areas, diphthongs only appear before palatals. Thus, in Old Provençal we find *glieiza* < ECLESIA 'church', *pieitz* < PECTUS 'chest', *plueia* < PLUVIA 'rain', *nuoit* < NOCTE 'night', etc. (Schürr 1970, 75). In some dialects in central and southern Italy, there is diphthongization of /ẹ/ and /ọ/ before a final high vowel, producing a system of internal inflexion for forms of the same lexemes, e.g., *cuntientu, cuntienti* 'content' versus *cuntenta, cuntente*, and *gruossu, gruossi* 'fat' versus *grọssa, grọsse* (Schürr 1970, 23). In other dialects there are further conditions on the appearance of diphthongs whose discussion here would involve an extension of this section far beyond the limits of this book. These few examples of the differing conditions under which diphthongization is found in Romance should suffice, however, to show that these conditions vary considerably from place to place. A natural question would be whether any of the conditions reflect the original ones found at the very beginning of diphthongization in Romance or whether they are later developments from conditions which perhaps no longer prevail anywhere in Romania. The usual approach to the problem has been to assume that one set of conditions must reflect the original ones and that those dialects showing any deviation from the "norm" must be later developments. Thus, some have assumed that diphthongization originally appears only in stressed free syllables as in French or Italian and that in order to account for the appearance of diphthongs in checked syllables in other Romance languages, one must assume that in those languages the syllable was structured differently so that consonant sequences of all types began syllables. It is supposed that in early Spanish words like Lat. SEPTEM or MORTE were syllabized [se-pte] and [mo-rte] (Corbett 1970, 287). Considering the general pattern of syllable structure in all the Romance languages, however, such a conclusion seems unjustified and needed only to support a hypothesis of the priority of Gallo-Romance or Italo-Romance in the process of diphthongization.

Another theory is that originally all diphthongs were conditioned by final high vowels and result from an anticipation of the following high vowel through addition of a higher element to the onset of the stressed vowel (Schürr 1975, 298). The spread of diphthongs to all tonic syllables could then be considered a generalization resulting from the loss of the conditioning factors. For example, in the dialect of Rome, the diphthongs /ie/ and /ue/ originally resulted from the metaphonic influence of final /-i/ and /-u/, but from the sixteenth century onwards they appear in all

tonic syllables. Their generalization can be attributed to the replacement of
the final /-u/ by a final /-o/ under Tuscan influence. With the consequent
loss of the conditioning factor and insecurity on the part of speakers about
where diphthongs should appear, they could spread to syllables that had
not had them previously (Schürr 1964, 148). Possibly in very early times
something similar happened in all areas where diphthongs later appeared
in syllables not followed by high vowels.[24] Others, however, reject the
notion that diphthongs like [je] and [we, wo] could be the direct result of
metaphonic influence. Purczinsky for example, asks:

> Can the influence of a following articulatory position leap over the
> stressed vowel to produce a high semivowel before it? Certainly not. The
> assimilation of a stressed vowel to a following tongue-position is, in
> physiological terms, ANTICIPATION. The speaker, unconsciously,
> shifts the position of the tongue too soon. . . . Since the speaker is
> unaware of the muscular shift involved in anticipation, it is inconceiv-
> able that he first lifts the tongue to adjust it to the sound which is to
> follow the stressed vowel, then lowers it again to the correct position.
> No, if he raises the tongue, unconsciously, either only the part of the
> vowel nearest the following will be affected or the whole vowel . . .
> (1969–70, 501).

Purczinsky, of course, in this quotation is advocating his theory that all
diphthongs were originally off-gliding ones. His reasoning appears plausible, but one may wonder if it is based more on speculation about how
phonetic developments ought to occur rather than on more solid evidence.[25] Even given, however, that one may reasonably accept on-gliding
diphthongs as the result of metaphonic influence, there is too little proof
that such conditioned diphthongs were the original ones throughout Romania and that all diphthongs must result from a generalization by analogy to all stressed syllables. Nor does this theory explain why some dialects generalized only to free syllables and others made no such restriction.
It seems odd that analogy should act this way (Purczinsky 1969–70, 518).

The Causes of Diphthongization

Just why diphthongization of /ẹ/ and /ọ/ should have occurred at all is
a difficult question to answer. A great many scholars seem to believe that
the fundamental cause of diphthongization is lengthening of the vowel

---

[24] Ferguson (1976, chap. 7) supports Schürr but claims to have formulated his theory
independently and solely on the basis of comparison (126, note).

[25] See chap. 1, note 20, for a good example of how speculation about phonetic change can
seriously mislead a scholar. As Andersen remarks, with regard to one linguist's rejection of a
certain phonetic change on the basis that he cannot imagine its taking place: "He does not
show why a general linguist should trust his own imagination rather than consulting the
pertinent scholarly literature for such matters of fact" (1972, 14, n. 3).

under stress (Purczinsky 1969–70, 519–20). They assume that once /e/ and /o/ in tonic syllables became long as did all other stressed vowels, they then began to become "acoustically heterogeneous" solely because of their greater length.

Another theory is the one advocated by Wartburg 1950. According to him, the Germanic-speaking invaders who established themselves in various parts of western Europe, i.e., the Franks in northern Gaul, the Burgundians in the south, the Langobards in northern Italy, and the Visigoths in Hispania, all imposed a linguistic superstratum that affected the Romance of the areas in which they were most numerous. In Wartburg's view, one of the chief features of this superstratum was a strong accent of intensity that served to give greater emphasis to accented vowels and thus induced them to split into diphthongs.

Another, somewhat similar theory, is that of Alarcos Llorach 1958, who believes that diphthongization arose in Hispania because Latin was adopted by speakers of a language (or languages) like Basque which had only two mid vowels. When trying to pronounce the /ẹ/ and /ọ/ which did not exist in their native tongue, they would have tended to exaggerate them by adopting the mid position of their own mid vowels and then opening further the end of the vowels, thus producing the diphthongs.

Other theories of the causes of diphthongization put primary emphasis on the vowel system as a whole. Thus, Romeo believes that: "A basic weakness of the Vulgar Latin system is that the front and higher e/o is a little too close to the lower mid e/o in terms of linguistic comfort. In other words, the margin of tolerance between /e/ and /ẹ/ and /o/ and /ọ/ is not enough for phonemic security"(1968, 63).

Because of the reduced margin of tolerance between the mid vowels as compared with the earlier Latin system, there is a tendency for speakers to increase the difference between the open and close mid vowels by diphthongizing the lower mid ones. The direct cause of this movement is said to be the existence of the last remaining diphthong of the earlier Latin system: /aų/. The monophthongizing movement that had eliminated all other Latin diphthongs undoubtedly exerted pressure on /aų/ to simplify also, as it finally did in many Romance languages.

We saw that in the case of /aị/ the resulting monophthong merged with the results of the former short mid vowel /ẹ/. Very likely the monophthongization had been to a very open front vowel [aẹ] which was too close to the /ẹ/ to be kept apart from it. If /au/ was also tending to monophthongize as a very open back vowel, it would have exerted extra pressure on the /o/ which could, as in the case of the front vowels, simply produce a merger (as it did eventually in Castilian and a number of other Romance languages) or alternatively speakers might have been tempted to alter the pronunciation of /ọ/ in some way. Thus, they could have resisted the final monophthongization of /aų/ for a long time, long enough so that diphthongization had gone to completion before final monophthongization took place.

In this view, diphthongization must have begun with the /ǫ/. As for why the initial segment invariably becomes a semiconsonant, Romeo simply states that it is one way of exaggerating the difference of openness between the mid vowels: "Since the distinctive feature (quality), differentiating the close /o/ from the open /ǫ/ could best be heightened by increased opening, the u-glide, taken from the highest level of the back series, was utilized as an initial element to accentuate the open nature of the low-mid by contrast, resulting in the diphthong /uǫ/" (1968, 71). Although the pressure of the tendency to monophthongize the /au̯/ might then account for the beginnings of diphthongization in the back vowels, it does not explain why the front mid vowel should have diphthongized also. The /ai̯/ diphthong had already merged with /ę/ in the same direction. Possibly then the only reason could be the pressure of parallelism between vowels in the front and back series: "As a correlative partner of the former /ǫ/, the front mid-open vowel phoneme /ę/ is now subjected to the pressure of equipollence, and by a similar process utilizes the highest vowel in the front series, i.e., /i/ as an initial glide, resulting in /ie/" (Romeo 1968, 71).[26]

The theory that holds that originally all stressed vowels diphthongized also seeks to find an explanation for this in the patterning of the vowel system of Late Latin. Thus, Purczinsky explains the system presented earlier, in which all vowels end in a semivowel,[27] as the result of a process of simplification. Assuming, as he does, that there were two diphthongs already existing in the system, the change of all vowels into diphthongs would result in "THE APPROXIMATION OF ALL STRESSED SYLLABLES TO A SINGLE TYPE" (497) (capitals in the original). Thus, the cause of the change can be considered the unconscious desire to simplify the structure of the vowel system.

The theory that attributes the original formation of diphthongs to those syllables preceding final high vowels sees the cause of these diphthongs as simply a physiological adaptation of a vowel through anticipation of the following vowel. The spread of the diphthongs to syllables lacking the conditioning factor would then be seen as simply analogical extension of the diphthongs to all stressed syllables once speakers no longer had a sure guide as to the form of the vowel they should use.

Finally, there is a somewhat simpler structural theory that sees in the two open mid vowels a condition that may have favored further development. The necessity of keeping /ę/ and /ǫ/ distinct from /e/ and /o/ encouraged speakers to exaggerate the openness of the open vowels. Thus,

---

[26] Support for the principle of equipollence or parallelism between front and back vowels is given in Weinreich, Labov and Herzog: "[W]e recognize front-back symmetry as one of the near-universal conditions of linguistic change" (1968, 175).

[27] As Purczinsky expresses it: "[S]yllables which once ended in non-phonemic length came to end in a semivowel" (1969–70, 497) (repeated in the next sentence). It may strike some as odd to speak of a syllable as "ending" in length, but his meaning is clear.

as a speaker began to pronounce [ẹ], he opened even farther the nucleus of the vowel, thus producing something like /ẹae/ which was, at the beginning, only slightly diphthongized, i.e., a semidiphthong (Spore 1972, 299). Similarly, in an effort to exaggerate the /ǫ/, the speaker opens even more the nucleus and produces [ǫə]. If one wonders why it should be just the lower mid vowels that are exaggerated rather than the close mid vowels, one explanation could be sought in the notion that /ẹ/ and /ǫ/ were in a sense "intruders" in the previous three-level system (Weerenbeck 1930). Deriving as they do from what were originally phonologically short vowels, upon being lengthened under stress they would have gained the tension that was associated with long vowels (whether previously long phonologically or not). Tense vowels tend to be higher than lax vowels,[28] or, alternatively, high vowels tend to be tenser than low vowels. If speakers translated this greater tension into greater tongue height, they would have risked a merger with the close mid vowels. Therefore they would have been tempted to raise the initial portion of the vowel and, possibly, to exaggerate the nucleus, as stated previously.

The evaluation of the various theories of causation is difficult. The notion that lengthening alone is a sufficient condition for diphthongization does not explain why it is just the open mid vowels that are the ones that most often diphthongize in Romance. Of course, if Purczinsky's theory that all vowels do in fact diphthongize is accepted, this objection vanishes. It is notable, however, that Purczinsky does not attribute diphthongization to this cause but rather to the supposed effort to make all stressed syllables similar. While it may be true that there is a general tendency in all languages for syllables to form certain basic patterns, it cannot be proved that all syllables must necessarily form a single pattern without any variation possible. The fact that some vowels developed into diphthongs cannot be taken as proof that all vowels must have so developed, any more than we can assume that because some diphthongs are on-gliding or off-gliding therefore all diphthongs must be of the same type.

As for Wartburg's theory of the influence of Germanic-Romance bilingualism, we would need to have proof that the accent in Germanic was any stronger or more intense than that of Romance. Also this theory does not explain why it is the mid open vowels that are affected; stress would affect all vowels equally. Finally, the theory would not account for the existence of diphthongization in those regions not affected by Germanic influence (Dacia, Dalmatia, and southern Italy). Similarly, the theory that it is pre-Romance bilingualism in Hispania that causes diphthongization has little to recommend it in view of the fact that diphthongization appears

---

[28] Tenseness and laxness are phonetic terms related in a general way to relative muscular tenseness or lack thereof, in the articulation of a sound. As Corbett puts it: "Les voyelles [e, o, a] et le **chva** [ə] sont relativement rapprochés à la position de repos des organes de l'articulation, tandis que la prononciation des voyelles [i, u, e, o] exige un effort de déplacement plus marqué" (1976, 124–25).

in many parts of Romania where this sort of bilingualism is not found. Nevertheless, it may well be that the Germanic invaders and the pre-Romance speakers in Hispania had a more indirect influence in the areas where they were preponderant in that they could have served as a sort of barrier against the conservative tendency to reject the diphthongizing fashion altogether, or to limit the new diphthongs to certain narrowly circumscribed phonetic conditions. By weakening the older Latin tradition, such groups of people would have provided the conditions that favored the spread and acceptance of new modes of pronunciation, which, of course, included the new diphthongs (Purczinsky 1969–70, 513–14).

As for the theory that seeks to account for diphthongization in the narrow margin of security between the two mid vowels in front and back, it alone cannot explain why diphthongization should have affected only the open mid vowels (if we leave out of account French and Dalmatian). Four-level systems are not inherently unstable and can endure unchanged for centuries; Italian and Portuguese still have such systems. In addition, Italian did diphthongize /ę/ and /ǫ/ in open syllables and still maintains a distinction between the open and close mid vowels in many words (Corbett 1970–71, 282).

As for the influence of the monophthongization of /au̯/ on the open mid back vowel, with its consequent dragging of the front open mid vowel, one wonders why this particular diphthong should have been powerful enough to have such a far-reaching effect. There is no evidence that it was frequent enough to have had this effect. If the monophthongizing tendency was that powerful, one could ask why it would not have simply merged with /ǫ/ as /ai̯/ merged with /ę/.

The theory championed by Schürr (conditioned diphthongization with subsequent generalization of diphthongs to all syllables as the basic source of all diphthongs) seems to overgeneralize the factors that do indeed condition the appearance of diphthongs in some dialects (Castellani 1965; 1970). It would seem more fruitful to look for the basic cause of diphthongization in those more modest theories that concentrate on the factors that were more likely to affect just the mid open vowels. The increasing length and tension that affected these vowels when they were stressed could be sufficient to account for the beginnings of diphthongization, especially if we adopt Spore's idea that at the very beginning the phonetic realization of these vowels was a semidiphthong. At this stage, we would have to do with a vocalic phoneme that was realized with a slight differentiation between the beginning and the end, not really a full diphthong of a glide accompanying a full vocalic nucleus. As a facultative variant of a non-diphthongized /ę/ and /ǫ/, it could appear whenever some greater emphasis was put on the vowel.[29] Under less stress, only the simple

---

[29] Menéndez Pidal, in *Orígenes* §22.1, lays great stress on the notion that diphthongization is not the result of a relaxation of pronunciation but rather of an exaggeration. Purczinsky (1969–70, 509) questions this idea and thinks it is more likely that stressed forms are conservative.

lengthened vowel without differentiation would be heard. It could therefore appear in any type of syllable. At this point, further exaggeration of
the vowel could take place tending toward a full diphthong, or, alternatively a conservative resistance to the new pronunciation could make itself
felt and cause the vowel to be monophthongized once more. As further
exaggeration of the differentiation gradually made the semidiphthong
evolve toward a full diphthong, certain conditions that would favor or
inhibit this exaggeration could come into play. The most conservative
dialects (excluding those that never adopted any kind of diphthongization,
like Portuguese) might accept diphthongization only before a palatal articulation (as in Provençal) or before a high final vowel (as in southern Italian
dialects). Less conservative dialects would accept diphthongs in syllables
having the greatest length in the articulation of the nucleus, i.e., in open
syllables, while monophthongizing the semidiphthongs in closed syllables.
As for the matter of stress, it would become a problem only after the
semidiphthong approached the status of a full diphthong and then could
clearly fall more toward the beginning in some areas or more toward the
end in others, thus producing off-gliding diphthongs in the first case and
on-gliding ones in the second. The conditions that governed the appearance of diphthongs and the form that they actually took pertain rather to
the individual histories of each Romance dialect and are far too complicated to be discussed here.[30] Their development in Castilian is taken up in
the next chapter.

The Date of Diphthongization

If we accept the idea that diphthongization began in the form of a
semidiphthong, it would be impossible to say exactly when it occurred,
especially if speakers were at first not conscious of the semidiphthong as
something different from the simple vowel. Only after the semidiphthong
had been further exaggerated so that the glide and the vocalic nucleus had
definitely become a diphthong would speakers have been likely to be
sufficiently aware that they were dealing with something other than a
simple vowel. Even so, being a feature of popular speech, we would not
expect that it would appear in writing very often, given the tendency of
writers to follow the conservative spelling norm, even after popular pronunciation had gone completely over to the diphthong.

A number of examples of what appear to be diphthongs have been cited,
but the only ones whose readings can be reasonably accepted are an
inscription dated about A.D. 120 from Rome: NIEPOS CN. COMITI TROPHIMI,
with NIEPOS for NEPOS, and one from Moesia dated A.D. 157 with the word

---

[30] Fuller discussion of various theories on diphthongization are found in Purczinsky, and
Spore 1972, as well as in the excellent articles by Corbett. Schürr (1970) gives a good
summary of his own ideas on diphthongization. Discussion of Spore (1972) by a number of
scholars is found in *Revue Romane* 1974.

PUOSUIT for POSUIT (Tovar 1976, 244–45).[31] In view of the paucity of trustworthy examples from this early period, it might be well to be cautious about accepting these as proof that diphthongization existed at this period (as Schürr 1970 does). They might be simple cutters' mistakes.

Valuable evidence of diphthongization of tonic /ẹ/ and /ọ/ is found in three fifth-century commentators on the grammarian Donatus: Pompeius, Servius and Sergius, all from North Africa. Sergius says, with regard to the pronunciation of the short /e/: "quando e correptum est, sic sonat, quasi diphthongus," and Servius states similarly that "e quando producitur, vicinum est ad sonum i litterae, ut meta; quando autem correptum, vicinum est ad sonum diphthongi, ut equus" (Wright 1982, 58–59).[32] In view of the result of the latter word in Castilian, *yegua* 'mare' < EQUA, it is evident that Servius was referring to something like [jekwo]. Pompeius actually gives a diphthongized spelling in order to illustrate how to avoid the mistake of confusing long and short vowels. As an example, he chooses the name RŌMA which, as it contains a long vowel, would not diphthongize. One who mixes up long and short vowels would be likely to pronounce the O as though it were short: "facimus vitium, ut brevis syllaba longo tractu sonet aut iterum longa breviore sono; siqui velit dicere Ruoma" (Wright 1982, 59). Apparently he considered the correct pronunciation of the short /o/ to be [uo].

From a later period, under the Visigothic kingdom in Hispania, several examples of what look to be diphthongs are attested: UALIENTEM for VALENTEM (before the seventh century), CURRIENTE for CURRENTE (682 A.D.), PARIENTIBUS for PARENTIBUS (end of sixth or beginning of seventh centuries). Although these may indeed be examples of diphthongization, there is also a possibility that the first two reflect some confusion of -I- stems with non-I stems in the third and fourth conjugations. In the case of the last example, there may be seen the influence of PARIENTIA 'obedience' which may reflect analogical influence of words like CONSCIENTIA, OBOEDIENTIA, PATIENTIA, etc. (Gil 1970, 53). Nevertheless, the fact that the later results in Castilian of these words is *valiente*, *corriente*, and *pariente*, and that we find in Mozarabic evidence of the spread of diphthongization before the eighth century, means we need not be too skeptical in accepting them as genuine examples of diphthongs.

At any rate, we cannot give any clear *terminus a quo*, and must be satisfied with a reasonable guess that the stage of semidiphthongization may have begun in the third or fourth centuries and was then subject to further evolution according to the special conditions of each Romance-speaking region (Spore 1972, 321).

---

[31] Tovar also lists several forms from inscriptions that he believes show diphthongization at an early period, but Herman (1971, 203) shows that all but the two cited in the text are false readings. Tovar also erroneously cites the last word in the form POUSUIT.

[32] Allen 1978, 49, believes that the reference to a "diphthong" must refer to the digraph AE. However, since AE had ceased to represent a diphthong centuries before, this conjecture is most unlikely (Wright 1982, 59).

Vowel Harmony in Latin?

One of the most wide-spread features of the Romance languages is the existence of vowel harmony, also called umlaut or metaphony (Leonard 1978). The form that this metaphony takes in most Romance languages is that of some alteration of a vowel in a syllable preceding a final high vowel /i:/ /u/. In standard Castilian and French, the only traces of metaphony are found where a final /i:/ appears in the verb system in the perfects of certain verbs: Lat. FĒCĪ > OSp. *fiz(e)*, Fr. *fis* (Lausberg 1965, 249).

In many Italian dialects, the effects of the final high vowels are far more extensive. We saw above that one of the theories seeking to explain diphthongization was based on the occurrence of diphthongization in Italian dialects. There are other types of changes as well, often involving a raising of the preceding vowel, with all sorts of complex results stemming from a limitation in some dialects to only the front high vowel, and subsequent analogical reformation of the results, especially when speakers exploited the originally phonetic phenomenon for morphological purposes (Lloyd 1977). The details of development are far too complicated to be gone into here, but can be found in Leonard 1978.

Since this sort of vowel harmony is so limited in the most well known literary Romance languages, it has often been considered a limited and unimportant phenomenon by many scholars. Nevertheless, it is found in so many regions of Romania, including very archaic ones, that we may be justified in thinking that it must have begun at a very early period (Lausberg 1965, 248). Leonard 1978 is convinced that metaphony must date from the very earliest period and claims that various later regional developments must have been found as early as the fourth century B.C., i.e., at the time that Latin was the language of a very limited area in central Italy (198). While it is certainly not impossible that phonetic vowel harmony existed in incipient form in very early spoken Latin, as with diphthongization, it is hardly necessary to see it as fully developed in a modern form at such an early date. It is sufficient to think of it as a slight phonetic feature that in differing circumstances could develop farther or be limited to a few words.

Consonants

The Phonemicization of the Semiconsonants

As was mentioned earlier, the semiconsonants [j] and [w] were probably originally only asyllabic allophones of the high vowels /i/ and /u/. The [w] appeared automatically whenever /u/ preceded a vowel in the same syllable. When, however, the older form HOIC became HUIC [(h)úik] 'to this' (dat. sg.) and CUI and CUIUS 'to whom', 'of whom' (dat. and gen.) were pronounced [kúj, kújjus], the appearance of [w] as a realization of /u/ before another vowel was no longer predictable and thus /w/ was an independent phoneme (Hill 1958, 443).

The Latin consonant system had previously lacked any voiced fricatives, and therefore /w/ as an independent phoneme was a kind of intruder in the system. Its articulation was then strengthened so that it was pronounced as a bilabial fricative [b̄]. As such it became the voiced counterpart to /f/, which, as noted previously, was probably a voiceless bilabial in many places. When this shift occurred, it then collided with the intervocalic realization of /b/ which may already have become a voiced bilabial fricative. Thus, from the first century A.D. onward, we find confusion of the letters v and B in many written documents, e.g., IUVENTE for IUBENTE (first century), IUBENTUTIS for IUVENTUTIS (155 A.D.), LIVERTUS for LIBERTUS (207 A.D.), etc. (Richter 1934, 60). The evidence of later developments in Romance indicates that the merger of /b/ and /v/ was limited to the intervocalic position, with a distinction remaining in initial position. Inscriptional evidence, however, does not seem to reveal any distinction in any position, since incorrect use of the letters B and v(u) is found initially also (Herman 1971, 209), e.g., BALIAT for VALEAT, BACCULEIEUS for VACCULEIEUS (Väänänen 1966, 51). Possibly there would have been a complete merger in all positions throughout Romania if the later voicing of the intervocalic /-p-/ had not reintroduced a medial voiced stop. After /r/ and partially after /l/, /v/ may have become an occlusive, thus being identical with /b/ in this position as well (Barberino 1978). (The fate of /w/ after a consonant is taken up in the section on the palatalization of /k/ before front vowels.)

The palatal semiconsonant [j] likewise strengthened its articulation about the same time so that it too became clearly consonantal and developed a strongly fricative pronunciation in word- and syllable-initial position, e.g., ZANUARIO for IANUARIO, in which the letter z may represent something like a palatal fricative [ž] or an affricate [dž].

The Reduction of Hiatus and the Formation of the "Yod"

The consonantization of [j] and its pronunciation as a fricative must be related to a whole series of changes in the pronunciation of Latin that produced a new series of palatal, fricative, and affricate consonants that had not existed previously. The elimination of the combination consonant-semiconsonant-vowel was an ancient tendency in Latin, e.g., archaic Latin DUENOS > BONUS 'good', DUIS > BIS 'again'. Possibly then the elimination of hiatus was part of the tendency which in turn may be part of the drive toward the CV type of syllable (Kiss 1972, 96–97). Vowels which had been in contact but had maintained their individual character by being pronounced in separate syllables began to be fused into a single syllable with the following vowel. The first result of this fusion was simply the pronunciation of /i/ in hiatus as a palatal semiconsonant [j] (a "yod"). The next step was the change of /e/ in hiatus to a yod. This change may have occurred fairly early. An inscription dated 125 B.C. has PARIAT for PAREAT (CIL 2, 592/10). Inscriptions from Pompeii also illustrate this same change: VALIA for VALEAT, ABIAT for HABEAT (Väänänen 1966, 51, 37).

The loss of hiatus after /t/ produced another change, an assibilation, as the tongue passed from a dental occlusion to the yod [t^{sj}]. In the second century A.D. inscriptions begin to reveal this pronunciation: CRESCENT-SIANUS for CRESCENTIĀNUS (A.D. 140), VINCENTZA for VINCENTIA, LAU-RENTZIO for LAURENTIO, MARSALIS for MARTIALIS (4th cent.) (Richter 1934, 81).

The group formed by /k/ plus a yod likewise began to develop an assibilated pronunciation. The passage of the tongue from the velar con-tact to the palate had the effect of advancing this contact farther forward in the mouth exactly as the yod after the /t/ tended to retract the stop from a dental position to an alveolar or prepalatal one. Thus, these two combina-tions began to approach each other in their realizations, although without becoming identical. Probably [t^j] became a completely alveolar affricate [t^s] while [k^j] was still a prepalatal affricate [t^j]. Evidence of their similarity is found in inscriptions where they are sometimes confused: MUNDICIEI for MUNDITIEI (A.D. 136), TERCIAE for TERTIAE (A.D. 179), FATIO for FACIO, NUNCIARE for NUNTIARE, DEFINICIO for DEFINITIO (A.D. 222–35) (Richter 1934, 88, 83, 88). Although in many areas, including Hispania, these two groups eventually fell together into the same phoneme, at the beginning they remained distinct and in some Romance languages have remained so to this day (Posner 1979, 47).

Parallel developments were occurring with the voiced stops /d/ and /g/. As indicated earlier, with reference to the pronunciation of /b/, it is possible that these consonants were articulated laxly. Thus, when the yod began assimilating the /t/ and /k/, the /d/ and /g/ became completely assimilated to the yod since the occlusion was not strong enough to pro-duce an assibilation or affrication as in the case of the voiceless consonants. The combination of [dj] and gj] then became identical with intervocalic [-j-] and suffered all the changes that affected this consonant. Intervocalically they were pronounced as geminates [j:] as intervocalic /i/ had always been. Their realization could be either fricative [j:] or affricate [d:^{j}], de-pending both on the position of the sound in the spoken chain and on the general force of articulation. Inscriptional evidence for the merger is found from the first century onward: AIUTOR for ADIUTOR, AIUTORIS for ADIU-TRIX (Väänänen 1966, 63), IOSIMUS for ZOSIMUS (< Gr. Ζώσιμος) (Väänänen 1966, 49),[33] ZIOMEDIS for DIOMEDIS, ZEBUS for DIEBUS, ZONI-SIUS for DIONISIUS (beginning of third century), MADIAS for MAIAS (A.D. 364) (Richter 1934, 85, 87), ZABULUS for DIABOLUS (Gil 1970, 76).[34]

---

[33] Kent (1945, 41) points out that inscriptions often have a double letter for the intervocalic -I-, e.g., EIIUS for EIUS.

[34] Väänänen 1966, 49, says that the spelling with Z does not necessarily mean that initial [j] was pronounced as a [z] or [dz], but only that this was the closest sound to the Greek consonant. Fischer (1980) suggests that this example may be just a spelling error, especially if someone unfamiliar with the Greek alphabet was trying to write the letter z. At any rate, it seems most likely that the assibilated pronunciation of the medial yod did not originate until later. Gavel (1953) believes that the evidence of Gregorian chant, which was constituted in the fourth and fifth centuries, suffices to demonstrate that hiatus had completely disappeared by that time.

cted by the yod were /l/ and /n/,
letely and thus becoming palatalized

eyard' > [biɲa]
ider' > [araɲa]
es' > [foḷa]
w' > [paḷa]

easily palatalized tended to lose the
t vowels, e.g., **PARETE** 'wall' < **PARIE-**
ubj.) < **QUIESCANT** (Richter 1934, 49).
a consequence an apparent shift of
llowing vowel in many words, such as
the ones cited above or in cases like **MULIEREM** 'woman' which originally
had four syllables, [mu-lí-e-rem], and thus later had three following the
palatalization of the consonant [mu-ḷé-re]. Actually, if one considers that
the accent in a word falls on a whole syllable rather than on the vowel
alone, this shift is more apparent than real. The only essential change was
the fusion of two syllables into one, with the accent remaining on the new
syllable (Skårup 1966). This new pronunciation was probably general in
Latin by the fourth century A.D., if not much earlier (Gavel 1953).

In many cases the yod persisted quite late without fusing with the
preceding consonant, and in some words it remains until today in Spanish:

RUBEU 'red, reddish' > [rubjo] (> Sp. *rubio* 'blond')
CEREU 'waxen' > [kerjo] (> Sp. *cirio* 'candle')
*****NERVIU** 'sinew' (C.L. **NERVUM**) > [nerbjo] (> Sp. *nervio*)

The Development of Postconsonantal [w] and [kʷ] and [gʷ]

The alteration in the pronunciation of word- and syllable-initial [w] to
/ɓ/ left the postconsonantal [w] isolated, since it did not change in the
same way. Along with this structural isolation went the general tendency
to eliminate hiatus, which, as we have just seen, led to the creation of a yod
in the case of front vowels in hiatus with a following vowel. As the
labiovelar semiconsonant did not lend itself to the same sort of absorption
into the preceding consonant that the yod did, the simplest way of remov-
ing all trace of hiatus was to drop the semiconsonant altogether:

BATTUŌ 'I strike' > [bat:o:] (> It. *batto*, Sp. *bato*)
MORTUU 'dead' > [mortu] (> Fr. *mort*, It. *muorto*, Sp. *muerto*)
QUATTUOR 'four' > [kwat:or, -ro] (> Fr. *quatre*, It. *quattro*, Sp.-Port.
cuatro, Rum. *patru*)
FEBRUĀRIU 'February' > [febrariu] (> Fr. *février*, It. *febbraio*, Sp.
febrero)
CONSUERE 'to sew' > [kosere] (> It. *cucire*, Sp. *coser*)

The combinations of /kʷ/ and /gʷ/, as we saw in the previous chapter,
were possibly at an early period phonemically distinct from the simple

velars /k/ and /g/, but in Late Latin both had become identified as a velar plus the vowel /u/. In line with the general development of postconsonantal [w], the tendency with these groups was also toward the elimination of the semiconsonant:

QUŌMODŌ 'how' > [komo] (> It. *come*, Sp. *como*)   (see p. 231 also)
  ANTĪQUU 'old' > [antiku] (> It. *antico*, OSp. *antigo*)

Only in the case of the combination of /kʷ/ and the vowel /a/ did the semiconsonant tend to remain in some Romance languages, especially when the /a/ is accented:

QUANDŌ 'when' > It. *quando*, Sp. *cuando*
QUANTU 'how much' > It. Port. *quanto*, Sp. *cuanto*
QUĀLE 'which' > It. *quale*, Sp. *cual*
AQUA 'water' > It. *acqua*, Sp. *agua*
AEQUĀLE 'equal' > It. *uguale*, Sp. *igual*

The combination /gw/ did not appear in word-initial position in any Latin words, but was introduced in a number of words borrowed from Germanic in which the initial consonant was a labiovelar [w-]. Since the earlier /w/ had shifted to /ƀ/, the sound was unfamiliar to speakers of Late Latin who substituted /gu-/ for it:

WERRA 'war' > /guer:a/ > Sp. It. *guerra*
*WARDON 'to guard, protest' > /guardare/ > It. *guardare*, Fr. *garder*,
  Sp. *guardar*
*WARNJAN 'to provide, equip with' > /guarnire/ > It. *guarnire*, Fr.
  garnir

The combination in these words and others like them then developed as it did medially in Latin words.

The Palatalization of Velars Before Front Vowels

A somewhat later change related to the palatalizations before yod was the tendency to palatalize /k/ and /g/ before the front vowels /e, i/ without subsequent loss of the vowel. Apparently, at first there was just a slight fronting of the velar contact which was clearly distinct from the similar fronting with assibilation which occurred when /k/ was followed by a yod. Like the palatalization with the yod, it was originally only a phonetic change which had no effect on the phonological system. As time went on, the fronting became more pronounced, although this in itself might have produced no systematic change as long as the palatal realization of /k/ and /g/ was identified with the non-palatalized allophones. The phonetic movement at work which we discussed in the preceding section directly affected, however, the phonemic status of the velars before /e/ and /i/. The weakening and loss of the labiovelar semiconsonant in the group /kʷ/ left only the velar /k/ before a following front vowel:

$$[k^w] > [k] / +front[k] > [k^j] / +front$$

As can be seen, with the loss of the [w], the fronted variant of /k/ would then have been perceptibly different from the [k] which resulted from the former /kʷ/. In short, before a front vowel two different velar articulations could appear: [k] versus [kʲ]. When this happened the palatalized velar could then no longer be considered just an allophone of the phoneme /k/, and thus it must have been an independent phoneme.

Some have sought to explain the palatalization of the /k/ before front vowels as the result of the pressure of the shift of /kʷ/ to /k/ (Alarcos 1968, 228). Others have looked to another development as the triggering force: the reduction of hiatus of /k/ plus /u/ plus a front vowel, e.g., *ECCU HĪC ([ek:u-i:k] > [ek:wi:k]), *ECCU ILLE ([ek:u-il:e] > [ek:wil:e]) (> Sp. *aquí, aquel*). The change of /kui/ to [kʷi] could be considered to have exerted pressure on the previously existing /kʷ/, thus obliging the /k/ before front vowels to shift forward in its realization. In view of the fact that the results of earlier /ku-V/ and /kʷ-V/ both merged in Ibero-Romance, it seems hardly likely that there was any very strong movement among most speakers to keep them apart. On the other hand, the evidence of Italian indicates that an effort to preserve a distinction between them was indeed active at one time, e.g., *ECCU HĪC > It. *qui* [kwi], versus QUĪ > It. *chi* [ki]. The palatalization of velars before front vowels has often occurred, and some have argued therefore that a similar development in Romance did not need to depend on the development of /k/ before a back vowel; in other words there was no need for any sort of a push from /kʷ/ to serve as the motive force in the whole process. At the same time, as one scholar argues: "It cannot be argued that a push shift is to be discounted here on the ground that there are so many cases of palatalization of dorsals which certainly do not result from a pressure upon /ki/ exerted by /kwi/ and /kui/. There is no valid reason for assuming that the ultimate cause of such a palatalization is necessarily the same in all cases" (Martinet 1952, 12).

Undoubtedly we have to do in this case with several different factors operating together to produce the same effect (González Ollé 1972, 314). The disappearance of the postconsonantal [w] was a general movement in Latin-Romance which did not go to completion in all areas and in all phonetic circumstances. At the same time the fronting of velars before front vowels was a dominant movement in most areas of Romania (Sardinia and, in part, Dalmatia, alone escaped it). Therefore, the pressure of the need to maintain a distinction between the results of /ku-i/ and /kʷ-i/ would have been a concomitant factor working in the same direction, although it was less strong, as is shown by the fact that in western Romance both groups fell together. In Rumanian both /ku-i/ and /kʷ-i/ coalesced with the original /ki/, e.g., *cine* 'who' /čine/ < Lat. QUEM, *aci* 'here' /ačí/ < *ACCU HĪC. Possibly in Rumanian we may be seeing simply the result of a slower working of the palatalizing movement which did not become clearly palatal until after both /kui/ and /kʷi/ had become /ki/ and thus could share the same fate as the original /ki/. In the other parts of Romania, in contrast, when the /w/ was lost, the palatalized velar was phonetically too different from the /k/ < /kʷ/ for them to be identified.

The /g/ before front vowels also began to evolve in a similar fashion, i.e., by fronting. When, however, the point of articulation had reached the palatal area the occlusion weakened, or perhaps because it sounded so similar to the /g/ plus yod, it became identified with it and from then on shared its fate.

The palatalization of /k/ and /g/ before the front vowels is a later phenomenon than the palatalization before yod and it may indeed have been provoked by the latter. There is no inscriptional evidence of it until the fifth century, although it may have begun long before, and it continued to be an active process after the Visigoths reached Hispania, since Gothic names containing velar stops sometimes undergo palatalization as do native Latin words, e.g., Port. *Cintães, Sintião* < KHINTILA (Lapesa 1980, 126).[35] Alarcos (1968, 235–36) and Gamillscheg (1968) contend that borrowings in Basque and Germanic in which the velars are preserved as stops, e.g., *Kaiser* 'emperor' < Lat. CAESAR, *Keller* 'cellar' < Lat. CELLARIUM, show that as late as the fifth century the velars had not become palatalized. It is not necessary to assume that no palatalization had occurred until then, however. It could have been just that the palatal realization of /k/ was still not phonemic and thus the [kʲ] was still identified with the phoneme /k/, realized as [k] before other vowels. Undoubtedly the phonemic status of [kʲ] was not settled until about the fifth century, or even later.

Summary

The result of these palatalizations was the creation of a series of palatal and affricate consonants in Late Latin-early Romance. The results of /t/ and /k/ plus yod, although originally only phonetic accommodations of the stop to the yod, eventually became single consonants as their assibilation became more pronounced and absorbed the original palatal.[36] Al-

---

[35] Some names of Gothic provenience do not palatalize /k/, but this may be due to the fact that Germanic voiceless stops are generally more aspirated than Romance stops and thus would have sounded noticeably different from the unaspirated Latin-Romance voiceless occlusives. Gamillscheg (1935, 52) believes that the difference in treatment is due to the names' being preserved in both a Latinized form and in the Gothic form until the end of the Visigothic kingdom. Then at a later period the Gothic names were again romanized, this time after the result of /k/ before front vowels had become an independent consonant phoneme.

[36] It would, however, be erroneous to assume that Latin developed a correlation of palatalization for all consonants as does Petrovici 1958, as not all consonants were in fact palatalized. The general Romance developments may be sketched as follows:

Earliest phase:		/tj/	/kj/	/k/ + front V
Second phase:				
	(central)	[ts]	[tj]	/kj/
		[ts]	[t:j]	[tj]
	(marginal)	[ts]	[t:j]	[tš]
	(Rumanian)	[ts]		[tš]
Third phase:				
	(Italian)	[ts]	[t:s]	[ts]
Fourth phase:	(Ibero-Romance)			
	initially	[ts-]		
	voicing bet. vowels	[-dz-]		

(Adapted from Alarcos Llorach 1968, 239)

though [kʲ] and [tʲ] were originally articulated distinctly, the margin of security between them was small, and the palatalization of /k/ + front vowel must have added even more pressure to create a single articulation for both. Italian, of all the Romance languages, managed to keep them apart, e.g., Lat. PLATEA 'open space; square' > It. *piazza* [-t:ˢ-] vs. Lat. LAQUEU 'halter, snare' > It. *laccio* [-č:-]. In the other Romance languages, at least two of the results of /tʲ/, /kʲ/, and /k/ + front vowel merged into a single consonant, although the effort to maintain a distinction may account for the puzzling results in Castilian (see chap. 5), where eventually all three merged into a single consonant, if we disregard for the moment the later voicing of the intervocalic single voiceless consonants.

The voiced counterparts of the preceding consonants, [gʲ] and [dʲ], merged with /-j:-/, realized variously as [j:] or possibly [d:j] or [dᶻʲ] in strong positions (word initially or postconsonantally). For the Latin of the Iberian peninsula the result was then the addition of four new consonant phonemes to the system: tˢ/, /j/, /ņ/, and /ļ/. This was not the only effect of the yod, as is seen in the next chapter in the section on the development of the vowels in Old Spanish.

The Simplification of the Syllable: Reduction of Consonant Groups

As mentioned in chapter 2, the open syllable predominated in Latin. The history of Latin-Romance indicates that there was a general movement in the language as a whole toward this type of syllable from the very earliest times. It might almost be said that speakers of Latin had in their minds a model syllable, which was open, to which all the syllables of the language had to conform. Syllables not fitting the model were therefore subject to various alterations tending to adjust their structure to the model. There is evidence from languages of unrelated families that those tongues in which open syllables predominate also share a tendency toward certain general phonetic developments, such as the monophthongization of diphthongs (such as we have already seen in Late Latin) as speakers sought to eliminate the semivocalic element following the vowel nucleus and thus reduce, as far as possible, all syllables to the CV type (Porzio Gernia 1976). Some consonant changes may also result from the same tendency to make all syllables open: the palatalization of consonants, affrication of palatalized dental stops, the elimination of gemination, and the simplification of consonant groups (Shevelov and Chew 1969).

In prehistoric Latin a large number of consonant groups were reduced to one or two consonants with the assimilation of one or more of the consonants to one of the others (Live 1959, 42; Maniet 1975, 56, 188; Porzio Gernia 1976). The forms of a number of words in Latin reveal this simplification of consonant groups. For example, the prefix EX- appears in the form Ē- before roots beginning with a voiced consonant, e.g., ĒMERGERE 'to bring forth'. In others a medial consonant has been absorbed by surrounding consonants, e.g., TORQUEŌ 'I twist', perfect TORSĪ, perf. passive part. TORTUS (Kent 1945, 126). Thus, the indications are that the development of consonant sequences in Late Latin are nothing new, but on the contrary were part of a characteristic "drift" of the language throughout its history.

Groups Containing a Fricative

One of the earliest groups to be simplified in historical times was /-ns-/, which as early as the third century B.C. appears in inscriptions written with a single S: COSOL, CESOR for CONSUL, CENSOR (CIL I, 31). Later inscriptions reveal the same thing: PRESUS for PREHENSUS 'seized, grasped' (pass. part. of PREHENDERE) (Väänänen 1966, 68). Even the most elegant users of Classical Latin probably never pronounced the /n/ represented in spelling; Velius Longus tells us that Cicero "libenter dicebat foresia, megalesia, hortesia . . ." (Lindsay 1894, 69).

There are occasional indications that the groups /-nf-/ may have assimilated the nasal to the /f/, e.g., inscriptional evidence of forms like COFĒCĪ, IFERŌS for CONFĒCĪ 'I made, prepared', INFERŌS 'lower regions, Hell'. It may be, however, that we have to do here with an incipient tendency that never became established as a general change. The Romance languages, at any rate, appear to have kept the group for the most part, possibly through analogical restructuring on the basis of the common prefixes IN-, CON- (Maurer 1959, 61).

Another early change was the reduction of /-rs-/ to /s:/. Manuscripts of Plautus, for example, show RUSSUM for RURSUM 'backwards', SUSUS for SURSUS 'upwards' (Richter 1934, 41). The group /-ps-/ also became /s:/: e.g., ISSE for IPSE 'himself' (Väänänen 1966, 65).

Groups Containing an Occlusive as First Member

These groups also tend to be simplified, although there are regional variations in the form of the simplification. The sequence /-pt-/ becomes /t:/ everywhere, e.g., SCRĪTUS for SCRĪPTUS 'written' (A.D. 19), SETEMBRE for SEPTEMBRE (A.D. 219), SETIMIO for SEPTIMIO, OTIMO for OPTIMO 'best', CATTUS for CAPTUS 'seized, caught' (pass. part. of CAPERE) (Richter 1934, 88).

Groups with /k/ as the first member, e.g., /-ks-/ as in TAXUS 'yew', MAXILLA 'jaw', /-kt-/ as in FACTUM 'done', LECTUS 'bed', LACTEM 'milk', /-kl-/ as in SPECLUM 'mirror' (< SPECULUM), OCLUS 'eye' (< OCULUS), and including the group /-tl-/, which, being unknown in Latin except in a few foreign borrowings, uniformly was replaced by /-kl-/, e.g., VECLUS 'old' (< VETULUS, dim. of VETUS), all develop differently. The weakening of the velar stop produced, instead of an assimilation of the /k/ to the following consonant, a fricative that soon became a palatal semivowel in western Romance [i̯] which later affected the consonant in some dialects (see chap. 4 for examples).

If /g/ appeared as the first member of a group, it was treated usually like the voiceless velar stop before /l/. In the group spelled GN, which we recall represented a velar nasal followed by the alveolar nasal [ŋn], the first nasal assimilated to the second, the cluster resulting in a geminate /n:/.

Other Consonant Groups

Medial consonant groups that contain other consonants as the first member, namely those with a liquid or nasal, remained stable until a later period when those with the liquid /l/ tended to vocalize and those with stops following a nasal tended to be reduced in parts of the Ibero-Romance territory. A sequence of a sibilant plus another consonant tended to be stable, e.g., POSTUS 'placed' (< POSITUS, pass. part. of PŌNERE) (> Sp. *puesto*). The group of a bilabial nasal /m/ followed by another nasal likewise assimilated to the second nasal producing a geminate /n:/, e.g., DOMNUS 'lord, master' (< DOMINUS) (> Sp. *dueño*).

The Development of Intervocalic Consonants

Under this general heading is included a large number of closely related phonetic and phonemic changes that distinguish the Romance of the western Empire.[37] In chap. 2 some examples of the opposition between long (geminate) and short consonants were given. The system of consonants in medial position was as follows (omitting voiced geminate stops which were, in any case, very rare):

OCCLUSIVES

	Labials	Dentals	Velars
Geminates	/-p:-	-t:-	-k:-/
Voiceless	/-p-	-t-	-k-/
Voiced	/-b-	-d-	-g-/

OTHERS

Laterals	Alveolars	Nasals Bilabial	Alveolar	Sibilants
/-l-	-r-	-m-	-n-	-s-/
/-l:-	-r:-	-m:-	-n:-	-s:/

The new palatal consonants of Late Latin also fitted into this system:

Affricates	Palatal Fricatives
/-č-	-j-/
/-č:-	-j:-/

---

[37] The division of Romania into "East" versus "West" is traditional (Wartburg 1967, 55–57), but the customary criteria for this division, i.e., the voicing of intervocalic stops in the west and the loss of final /-s/ in the east, present many complications. See Vidos 1963, 287–89, and Weinrich 1958, 46.

(The phonetic realizations of the palatals, of course, may well have varied from one area to another.)

Although the structure of the system itself remained unaltered, a series of changes in the phonetic realizations of the occlusive consonants ended by affecting the whole system. First, as we saw above, the intervocalic /-b-/ came to be pronounced as a fricative rather than a stop. This pronunciation produced a merger of /-b-/ with the bilabial pronunciation of the older [-w-] > /-ƀ-/. From this confusion of two phonemes we are led to wonder whether or not the other voiced occlusives were not similarly weakened in pronunciation. There being no other phonemes with which they might have been confused (except for /j/ in some positions) there would be no trace of this change in writing, because for Latin speakers a fricative pronunciation of /-d-/ or /-g-/ would alter nothing in the phonological system as did the weakening of /-b-/. Therefore they would not have been especially conscious of any change and would not have been tempted to make any changes in spelling.

Second, the voiceless stops were assimilated to their vocalic surroundings and pronounced with voicing. Last, the geminates came to be pronounced with reduced tension so they became short voiceless stops. (The liquids and nasals developed somewhat differently.) There is no doubt that all these changes are related and in some way interdependent so that a schematic representation of the process shows a kind of chain reaction. If, for example, we take the labial consonants /-p:-, -p-, -b-/, as representative, the following stages can be observed:

		Initial	Intervocalic
Stage 1 (earlier Latin):			
	/p:/		1. [-p:-]
	/p/	1. [p-]	2. [-p-]
	/b/	2. [b-]	3. [-b-]
	/v/	3. [ƀ-]	4. [-ƀ-]
Stage 2:	/p:/		1. [-p:-]
	/p/	1. [p-]	2. [-b-]
	/b/	2. [b-]	3. [-ƀ-]
	/v/	3. [ƀ-]	4. [-ƀ-]
Stage 3:	/p/	1. [p-]	1. [-p-] (< p:)
(Phonemicization)			
	/b/	1. [b-]	2. [-b-] (< -p-)
	/ƀ/	2. [b-]	3. [-ƀ-] (< -b-, -ƀ-)

(based on Alarcos 1968, 237)

The second part of the schema can be labelled "variation" (to adopt the term used by Weinrich 1958, 49), i.e., the development of a "weak" or lax variant as opposed to a "strong" or tense variant for each consonant phoneme among the occlusives. The final step was the phonemicization of the shift: i.e., the identification of the new [-b-] (</-p-/) with the word initial /b-/ instead of with its former counterpart /p-/, and the identifi-

cation of the new [-p-] (</-p:-/) with the word initial /p-/, e.g., Sp. *escoba* 'broom' < Lat. SCŌPA, Sp. *copa* 'goblet, wineglass' < Lat. CUPPA.

One effect of the development of variation was to produce varying phonetic realizations of simple consonants in word-initial position. Since the strong variant appears after consonants, as well as after pauses, while the weak variant would appear after a vowel, the particular allophone that would appear at the beginning of a word would be dependent on the preceding word. That is, we assume that any single word would undoubtedly not be separated in the chain of speech from other words but would form rather a single phonic group. Thus, if a single consonant appears at the beginning of a word following a word ending in a vowel, it would have been realized by the same variant that is found between vowels in the middle of a word. On the other hand, if the preceding word ended in a consonant, we must presume that the strong variant would then have been used. If we represent this in a schematic fashion, using the /t/ phoneme to illustrate, we would find the following variants in word initial position (-s can represent any word-final consonant):

Initial		Medial	
/-a ta-/	/-as ta-/	/-ata-/	/-asta-/
[-a da-]	[-as ta-]	[-ada-]	[-asta-]

This particular development had a pronounced effect on the development of initial consonants and will be discussed at greater length in the next chapter.

The cause or causes of the variation are closely related to the conditions in which the weak and strong variants of the simple consonants occur. The weak variant appears most in those positions in which it stands in opposition to a long consonant. Undoubtedly the need to preserve a clear distinction between long and short consonants is involved. Now the development of a voiced allophone of /-p-/ is not the only way that the opposition between geminates and simple consonants may be maintained. One way would be simple conservatism: the maintainance of a difference of length and tension between the two phonemes, i.e., no change at all. The contact of the articulators in the realization of /-p:-/, for example, would be held sufficiently long so that it would not be confused with /-p-/.

Another way would be the one found in part of Tuscany, the so-called "gorgia toscana." Here voiceless stops have become either aspirates or fricative. Thus, in the dialect of Iano in northern Tuscany, /p/ and /t/ are realized intervocalically with a strong aspiration: standard Italian *nipoti* 'grandchildren' is pronounced [nipʰótʰi]. Intervocalic /k/ becomes completely fricative: It. *giuoco* 'game; joke' is [jóho]. Other possible realizations of the weak variants could be: voiceless fricatives [φ, θ, h], voiced fricatives [ƀ, đ, ǥ], half-voiced stops [p, ţ, ķ], fully voiced short stops [b, d, g], or voiced long stops [b:, d:, g:]. All of the preceding realizations are attested in modern Italian dialects without phonemicization of the variation.[38] Al-

---

[38] See Weinrich 1958, 50–60, for examples of variation in different Italian dialects.

though there are different phonetic outcomes, the underlying phonological process seems to be the same for all. The strong similarity between these modern dialectal phenomena and the ancient voicing of the intervocalic stops might suggest that there is some connection between them. In other words, modern variation in Italy could be a reflection of a similar process in the west.

There is, however, no evidence that the *gorgia toscana* (and, we presume, related phenomena in other dialects) originated before the sixteenth century, and if we assume that voicing is connected in some way with it and similar processes in other dialects, it would have had to have originated much earlier, perhaps as much as a thousand years before (Izzo 1972). While this may not be impossible, there is no evidence for it. As far as we can tell, therefore, variation developed in western Romania independently of later developments in Italy (excluding northern Italy).

As for the date of the beginnings of variation, we find that there is no trace of it in Dalmatian or Rumanian (Hadlich 1965, Nandriş 1963, 108, 124, 151) although there is some indication of it in some Sardinian dialects which are otherwise quite archaic (Lausberg 1965, 350–52). Since Dacia was officially abandoned by the Romans in A.D. 270 it may be presumed that the appearance of variation postdates this time (Wartburg 1950, 34–36).[39] The third stage seems not to have been attained everywhere until several centuries later.

The causes of variation and voicing have been a subject of dispute for many years, and several hypotheses to account for them have been conceived. According to one, a primary cause of the development would be the tendency to reduce the amount of effort required to pronounce the long consonants. In this view, as more and more geminates appear in a language, the amount of information they convey becomes correspondingly reduced so that speakers may be tempted to expend less energy in their articulation and thus achieve greater economy of expression. This pressure from the geminates threatens confusion with the simple consonants. The latter therefore develop a different articulation in those positions where long and short consonants are in opposition, as discussed previously. If the voiced stops were already pronounced intervocalically with weak contact or fricatively, it would have been even easier for the voiceless stops to move into this vacant slot by becoming voiced (Martinet 1952, 198–99).

According to another view, we should start from the features that distinguished the consonant phonemes in the Latin phonological system at

---

[39] Lozovan 1954 points out that although official links with Italy were broken in A.D. 270 there were undoubtedly continued communications, on a reduced scale perhaps, after that date with the rest of the empire, and imperial authority was reestablished at intervals until the Slavic invasions of the sixth century finally broke all links with the West. One may wonder whether these continued communications were of a nature and intensity sufficient to bring linguistic innovations (assuming that variation originated at this early date). Lozovan recognizes that Rumanian is characterized by its conservatism. It may be in fact a direct result of its early separation from the rest of the empire.

various articulatory points. There are three principal ones: length, voicing, and continuity. With regard to the last feature, in earlier Latin continuity distinguished only the voiceless fricative consonants /f/ and /s/. Thus, the voiced stops could adopt the feature of continuity and become fricatives without causing any confusion in the system. They would simply have been moving into a phonetic and phonological space that was unoccupied. Then as [b̵ d̵ g̵] become the normal intervocalic allophones from the earlier voiced occlusives, it would have been superfluous to signal the distinction between /b d g/ and /p t k/ by means of the feature of voice. Thus, the voiceless stops could simply assimilate to the surrounding vowels and adopt voicing. The distinction between these two orders of phonemes would then be conveyed by means of the remaining feature: continuity. At this stage, as voice became the normal feature of the former medial voiceless stops, length no longer served any purpose. The presence or absence of voicing would then suffice to distinguish the long consonants from the short ones. Length being now redundant, it could be abandoned with no loss in communicative efficiency (Corbett 1970–71, 276).

We are faced then with the question of whether it is possible to tell at which end of the chain reaction the whole process began. There can be no question that the simplification of geminates was an active factor outside of Italy,[40] since all the Romance languages with the exception of the most conservative ones, i.e., Sardinian and Italian, have abandoned consonantal length as a distinctive feature, even where the result has been a merger of the simple and the geminate consonants as in Rumanian (Nandriş 1962, 108, 117, 120, 123, 130, 139, 143, 151). It might be argued that in view of what happened in Rumanian and because documentary evidence elsewhere reveals that the simplification of geminates was a fairly late phenomenon (Politzer 1966), that it is essentially unrelated to the problem of variation and voicing. A counter-argument would be that the simplification of the geminates is indeed a motivating force, a force so powerful that it overcame the tendency to preserve useful distinctions in those areas where ancient variation did not develop. The fact that the geminates appear to have simplified only after the voicing of the simple stops can be considered precisely a result of the need to preserve useful distinctions. In other words, the geminates would have exerted pressure on the simple consonants, but would not lose their length until it was possible for them to do so without danger of confusion, that is, after the simple stops had become voiced (Martinet 1965, 101). One not committed to either theory may wonder why it is not possible that both factors operated in tandem: the pressure of the geminates on the simple consonants at one end, and the extension of preexisting distinctive features of consonants at the other.

It is also possible that this tendency to reduce the geminates is related to the assimilations and reductions of consonant groups discussed earlier:

---

[40] Corbett (1970–71, 276) says that Martinet has postulated the simplification of geminates *ex nihilo* as the cause of the process. This is hardly the case, as can be seen in an examination of Martinet 1952.

that is, it could result from the same tendency to make all syllables open ones by eliminating the postvocalic element (Malmberg 1959, 196). It would then be characteristic of those regions where Latin was imposed on speakers of different languages who would tend to favor a more primitive syllable structure, i.e., one with open syllables. It may be debatable whether this fact alone would explain why such speakers would prefer open syllables, but there is no question that they most probably learned Latin first from soldiers and traders speaking a variety of Latin character- ized by popular traits, one of which would undoubtedly have been the tendency to favor open syllables. It is undeniable too that those languages in which Latin was native or learned by speakers of closely related lan- guages (Italy) have preserved the geminates intact to this day and have even increased their number (Grandgent 1927, 82–85).

Although the tendency toward economy of effort and the drive toward the open syllable can be considered powerful factors in the origin of an- cient variation, several problems still remain. Why did variation not de- velop everywhere? Why did it take the form of voicing in western Roma- nia? The answer to the first question may be simply a chronological one. If variation developed after Dacia and Dalmatia had been effectively cut off from linguistic innovations from the west, these areas would never have picked it up. The answers to the other questions may be found in the hypothesis of the influence of another linguistic system.

The Celtic Substratum

The Celtic languages known to us today have all undergone a phonetic change known as "lenition" which was essentially a weakening of the simple consonants between vowels. It is a development remarkably similar in structure to "variation," except that in Celtic it must have affected all consonants, and not just the stops. It is not surprising therefore that some scholars have attempted to associate the two phenomena and have sup- posed that the origin of variation must be a result of the influence of Celtic speakers who learned Latin but maintained some of the pronunciation habits of their former languages (Jungemann 1955, chap. 6).

In order for us to accept the idea of Celtic influence, some assumptions must be made. The Celtic spoken in Gaul, Spain and elsewhere on the European continent before it was displaced by Latin ("continental" Celtic), has disappeared and the only Celtic languages remaining today are repre- sentatives of "insular" Celtic: Irish, Welsh, Breton, etc. Therefore, it is necessary to hold that the process of lenition evidenced in the latter tongues must also have affected the continental languages before Latin arrived or possibly at the same time that Latin was being introduced.[41]

---

[41] This assumption is, by itself, sufficient to condemn the whole hypothesis for Malmberg (1959, 305). He remarks: "En réalité, le système celtique primitif—qui aurait été adopté aussi par les populations romanisées—est une reconstruction faite pour expliquer l'état de choses actuel. Sous ces conditions, l'idée d'un rapport intime entre les deux phénomènes (lénition celtique et affaiblissement) me semble, si non absurde, quelque peu risquée."

Second, we assume that there existed a sufficiently long period of bilingualism for speakers of Celtic to have been able to transfer to their spoken Latin the same features of weakening of the intervocalic consonants that they had in their original speech. We know that Gaulish continued to be spoken in Gaul as late as the fifth century A.D., so we may suppose that the Celt-Iberians, whose center of heaviest settlement was in northwestern Hispania, might also have maintained their language that late.[42]

As for evidence that continental Celtic underwent lenition, there are a number of Celtic inscriptions that have spellings that appear to indicate that there was a voicing of intervocalic voiceless stops and a weakening of the voiced ones. For example, in an inscription dated A.D. 152 the tribal name AVOLGIGORUM is found. This name appears to contain the suffix -ICUS (Tovar 1948, 270). There are a number of other Celtic inscriptions which give evidence of the writing of G for C which likewise may be interpreted as evidence of voicing. Other examples are ethnic names based on place names ending in the Celtic root -BRIGA or -BRIGO (cf. Port. *Coimbra* < CONIMBRIGA), in which the intervocalic /-g-/ is written with the letter C, e.g., CAELOBRICOI, derived from CAELIOBRIGA (Tovar 1948, 273). These spellings may be interpreted as examples of hypercorrection.

Although there are numerous examples of an apparent voicing in Celtic inscriptions, there are no certain cases of voicing in Latin inscriptions in imperial times.[43] It may be argued that there is no relationship between the Celtic phenomena and voicing in western Romance since the only examples we have of the Romance change postdate the extinction of Celtic. It may also be held that these spellings in Celtic only tell us that Celtic speakers did not distinguish phonemically between voiced and voiceless consonants,[44] and therefore that they could hardly have favored voicing. Another argument against the Celtic hypothesis is that there are areas in which voicing appears but where the Celts never settled, such as Venetia.

None of these arguments is, however, conclusive. The lack of inscriptional evidence in Latin for voicing at an early date cannot be considered proof that there was no voicing in speech, merely that it was not recorded. The claim that the prestige of the Latin tradition was sufficiently strong to prevent any written evidence of voicing (Tovar 1952, 11) can hardly be accepted in view of the large number of errors evidenced in inscriptions, in spite of the tradition of "good" Latin. A more cogent view would be that as long as voicing existed at the stage of variation, i.e., as a phonetic phenomenon with no effect on the phonological system, speakers would have been

---

[42] A description and analysis of the gradual extinction of Celtic is found in Terracini 1957, 15–48.

[43] See Weinrich 1960 for a detailed examination of examples of supposed voicing in Latin inscriptions.

[44] This seems to be Lapesa's argument (1980, 44–45). Apparently he is unwilling to accept the Celtic hypothesis since he remarks that these spelling variations represent vacillations, and "hubieron de constituir base favorable para la sonorización de las oclusivas sordas intervocálicas." This "base favorable" could hardly have been an active factor.

largely unaware of it and thus would have felt no temptation to write the voiceless stops with anything but the traditional letters, P, T, C. One may compare this state with a similar phenomenon in some varieties of modern English. In many dialects of American English, the intervocalic /-t-/ is pronounced as a voiced flap, identical with the realization of its voiced counterpart, /-d-/. Although this pronunciation is widely found, most speakers are probably unaware of it and would never write this /-t-/ with the letter D (Malécot and Lloyd 1968). It would be only when the variation became phonemicized that speakers would have become aware of the difference between their own speech and the older Latin spelling tradition, and this stage may well have been reached long after the period of extensive Latin-Celtic bilingualism had passed. If voicing had been phonemicized in Celtic before it was in Latin, this fact would account for the appearance of examples of voicing in the spelling of Celtic names which lacked a strong orthographic tradition. The arguments that the known fluctuations in spelling indicate that Celtic speakers did not distinguish between voiced and voiceless stops is contradicted by the evidence of the Celtic languages. Finally the argument that the area of Romance voicing is greater than the area of Celtic settlement can be valid only if we assume that voicing could not have spread beyond the region in which it originated.

It is worth noting too that voicing did not take hold everywhere in Iberia. In upper Aragon, for example, in the area closest to the Pyrenees, the voiceless stops were consistently preserved in all native words (Zamora 1967, 227–30; Politzer 1954). Being an isolated region where no Celts settled, it seems to have escaped the innovation, whether it came from the western, Celtic area or elsewhere, and thus in all probability it simply preserved the older pronunciation, as did other isolated areas like Sardinia and Rumania. In southern Hispania as well, there were some regions where voicing appears not to have been accepted. Although there were some Celtic settlements in what was later to be called Al-Andalus, they were more scattered, and with the Islamic invasion this section of the peninsula was isolated from the north and thus may have preserved the older pronunciation in part (see chap. 4 for more details).

Voicing: Conclusions

There is no essential conflict between explanations concentrating on the internal structural factors leading to variation and voicing and those which claim some relation between Celtic lenition and western Romance voicing. Neither explanation excludes the other, and they may, in fact, be complementary. The structural pressures favoring the development of variation (pressure of the geminates, or alternatively, the fricatization of the voiced stops through extension of the existing feature of continuity to voiced consonants, the tendency to eliminate or modify closed syllables) undoubtedly exerted an influence. On the other hand, the Celtic influence can hardly explain the existence of variation in central Italy and Corsica in modern times. Celtic influence would lie behind the adoption of voicing as the phonetic realization of variation in the west and its subsequent phonemicization, while in Italy simple conservatism would explain why the geminates were preserved. The Celtic substratum would have been a concomitant factor in the change, one which could have helped to determine the direction that it took in western Romance.[45]

Vocalic Epenthesis Before /s/ Plus Consonant

During the second century A.D. there began to appear in writing sporadic examples of a vowel, probably /i/,[46] before the so-called "impure" /s/, i.e., /s/ followed by a consonant at the beginning of a word. In earlier Latin the only word initial combinations of /s-/ plus a consonant were those in which the second consonant was voiceless occlusive: /s + p, t, k, kʷ/. In Latin poetry this particular group was treated as somehow not a cluster like others since poets appear to have been doubtful about whether a word-final short vowel preceding such a group was the nucleus of a light or a heavy syllable (Collinge 1970, 192). Probably the poets' hesitation in such matters is due to the fact that in word-internal position, /s/ did not form a cluster with the following consonant but was counted as part of the preceding syllable, e.g., AS-TŪ-TI-A'skill, cunning', DE-TES-TOR 'I curse, execrate', etc., thus making that syllable a heavy one (Anderson 1972, 34). The very earliest example of a prothetic vowel is found in words not native to Latin which contained an /s-/ before a consonant which was not an occlusive: ISMURNA for SMYRNA, found at Pompeii (Löfstedt 1961, 108) (unless it was a matter of Hellenistic Greek meter not being applicable without violating the older Latin tradition). The next earliest example is another borrowed word beginning with the same group: ISMARA(G)DUS 'emerald' found at Rome, A.D. 105 (Löfstedt 1961, 108). In these two cases the addition of the vowel was undoubtedly a native Latin response to an unfamiliar sequence of consonants. By adding a vowel, the /s/ became part of a separate syllable as in native Latin words, such as we saw above.

The generalization of the word-internal rule that separated the /s/ from a following consonant so as to include the initial /s/ plus consonant groups was probably aided by the phonetic character of [s] as compared

---

[45] Vendryes (1925, 262–73) suggested that the influence of Celtic was in the nature of a guide to pre-existing tendencies: "L'action du substrat sur la prononciation des intervocaliques aurait donc consisté à favoriser les tendances naturelles de la langue et à en précipiter" (273).

[46] The western Romance languages have /e-/, but in Italian and Sardinian the vowel is [i]. It should be noted too that vocalic epenthesis before /s-/ and a consonant is not confined to Romance but is found in a number of languages around the world (Omeltchenko 1971, 506), such as Greek, Armenian, Persian, Magyar, Turkish (Löfstedt 1961, 108), and Alabaman, a Muskogean language (Andersen 1972, 35, n. 19).

with the stops [p t k] (Politzer 1959). Phonetically speaking [s] has greater acoustic power than the stops. Since in general there is a tendency to begin syllables at a point of minimum acoustic power and then to reach maximum power in the nucleus, the transition from [s] to the following consonant could give the impression of a transition from one syllable to another. If the [s] were pronounced with greater emphasis, there would be a greater effort on the part of the speaker to make it a separate syllable with a vowel preceding it, since in Latin (as in Romance) a syllable must contain a vowel. The following sketch may give an idea of how the custom of putting a supporting vowel before the [s] could have arisen: [s-sC] > [is-sC] > [is-C] (Şiadbei 1958).

Obviously the use of a supporting or prothetic vowel would not be necessary in those cases in which the word preceding the one beginning with an impure /s/ already ended in a vowel and thus provided a vowel to which the /s/ could attach itself. Thus, at first the appearance of the prothetic vowel was undoubtedly conditioned in just this way: [V sC-], but [-C isC-]. Modern Italian preserved this system to some extent, e.g., *la Svizzera* 'Switzerland' but *in Isvizzera* 'in Switzerland',

The evidence from inscriptions and Low Latin texts, however, does not reveal the sort of phonetic conditioning that we postulate must have determined the original appearance of the prothetic vowel (Prinz 1937, 109), and the initial I- or E- can appear equally well after a word ending in a vowel as after one ending in a consonant. One reason why this irregular distribution of the prothetic vowel is found may be that those words that in Latin began with the prefixes EX- or INS- would have been pronounced in Late Latin as [es-] and thus would have appeared to speakers to be simply examples of phonetic vowel prothesis, not conditioned by the preceding word. In some early Low Latin manuscripts, there is obvious confusion of the two prefixes, e.g., INSTRUCTUS 'provided, equipped' and EXTRUCTUS 'piled up' are confused in the Benedictine Rule (Löfstedt 1961, 112, n. 2) and in other texts similar words often appear without the prefix, e.g., STRUCTUS, STRUMENTUM (113). This process is reflected in the form that a number of Latin words take in Italian. Some words beginning in Latin with (H)IS- or similar prefixes drop everything but the /s/ in Italian: HISTORIA 'story, history' > *storia*, HISPANIA > *Spagna*, INSTRUMENTUM 'instrument' > *strumento*, etc.

Inscriptional evidence indicates that the phenomenon originated in Rome (Omeltchenko 1971, 506). In those regions where many final consonants fell at an early period (Italy and Rumania), the prothetic vowel never established itself strongly, so that today Rumanian has no trace of it at all, and Italian has it in a few cases as a part of syntactic phonetics. In western Romania, however, where final consonants (the /-s/ of the plural of nouns and adjectives and the consonant endings of verb forms) were retained, the appearance of the vowel was much more common. Therefore in these areas it came to be regarded as an inherent part of the word rather than a feature of syntactic phonetics.[47] The final result was that the prothetic /e-/ was generalized in western Romance[48] so that it appeared invariably before impure /s-/ regardless of the ending of the preceding word, e.g.,

SCHOLA 'school' > [iskola] (> Sp. *escuela*, Fr. *école*)
SPERĀRE 'to hope' > [isperare] (> Sp. *esperar*, Fr. *espérer*)
STARE 'to stand' > [istare] (> Sp. *estar* 'to be')

THE MORPHOLOGICAL SYSTEM

The Nominal System

As pointed out in the previous chapter, the general drift of many of the Indo-European languages has been toward a reduction in the number of case distinctions. Latin had already fewer cases than many other I.E. languages, and during the course of its development, it continued this same drift toward a reduction in the number of cases. In Romance the final step was taken and all case forms were eventually eliminated except in Rumanian.[49]

The chief causes of this drift were two: phonetic development and the increasing use of word order and prepositions to indicate syntactic relationships. One of the most ancient sound changes in Latin was that of the weakening of final /-m/. In archaic Latin it had apparently become a very weak sound, being omitted in some ancient inscriptions as well as in later imperial inscriptions. Although it continued to be written in Classical Latin, Quintilian noted that it was scarcely pronounced (Leumann 1977, 224–25). We may imagine that he was referring to the very "best" type of speech and that in the speech of most speakers of Latin it had disappeared completely. The result was the merger of the singular nominative and the accusative of the first declension in the single ending /-a/. In the third declension the ablative and the accusative of most nouns would likewise have merged in the single ending /-e/.

---

[47] Politzer 1959 suggests that the increasingly strong stress accent (which, as we have noted before, is popular with many scholars) would serve to mark word boundaries more clearly and thus make the prothetic vowel seem part of the word rather than the sentence or word group. Even if one doubts that the stress accent was becoming stronger all over western Romania, there can be no doubt that word boundaries were more clearly marked by the identification of the initial consonant with the strong variant of medial consonants. See chapter 4, in the section on degemination.

[48] Prinz concluded that the prothetic vowel was more frequently found in North Africa and in Rome than in other areas, and that Semitic influence might be responsible for its introduction into Latin (1937, 97ff). Löfstedt believes that absolute numbers cannot be used as a guide because Prinz had not calculated the percentage of occurrences with reference to the total number of cases where prothesis might occur (1961, 107). He, as well as Dressler (1965), is skeptical of any foreign influence since prothesis is found all over the empire.

[49] Old French and Old Provençal retained both a nominative and an oblique case. The case system of Rumanian includes a nominative-accusative and a combined genitive-dative. Formally, it is based principally on the article rather than on the noun or adjective stem.

The development of the vowel system would also have had an impact on the different forms of certain cases, leading to further syncretism. Thus, in the first declension again, the only distinction between the nominative and the ablative singular was length: ROSA (nom.) vs. ROSĀ (abl.). With the abandonment of phonological length, all unaccented vowels became short and thus the nominative, accusative and ablative would have been identical:

First Declension	Third Declension

The merger of the short /u/, when it had opened to [ǫ] in Later Latin, with the long /oː/, also [ǫː], must have affected the second declension. The neuter nominative and accusative and the masculine accusative, with the loss of final /-m/, would have tended to become identical, with the ablative and dative singular in /-o/:

If the final vowel in the masculine nominative singular in /-us/ had followed the regular vocalic development, it too would have become identical with the accusative plural ending in /-oːs/.[50] There is some evidence, however, that the vowel in the ending -US remained distinct from that in the ending -UM and the vowel in the accusative plural ending -OS for some centuries. In Gothic, loanwords fom Latin masculine nouns, for example, retained the -US ending, e.g., Goth. *asilus* < ASINUS 'ass', *aggilus* < ANGELUS 'angel', *diabaúlus* < DIABOLUS 'devil', etc., while the neuter nouns in -UM were apocopated, e.g., Goth. *wein* < VĪNUM 'wine', *akeit* < ACĒTUM 'vinegar', *balsan* < BALSAMUM 'balsam', On the basis of these examples, it may be reasoned that there was a difference in the quality of the vowels at the time that these words were borrowed (Blaylock 1964–65, 267). The maintenance of this distinction, however, seems to have been limited both in time and space so that most Romance languages of the west have merged the vowels of both endings into /o/.[51]

The singular of the nominative and the accusative in the third declension may have remained distinct in the same fashion, i.e., through preser-

---

[50] In Old French these forms did become identical: MURUS and MUROS > *murs*.

[51] Some central Italian and Asturian dialects still preserve a distinction between the final vowel from Lat. /-um/ /-us/ endings and the vowel /oː/, as in the ablative singular, accusative plural, e.g., Cabranés *ibiernu* 'winter' < (H)ĪBERNU, vs. *como* 'how' < QUŌ MODŌ (Maurer 1959, 16).

vation of a distinction between the -IS and the -E(M) endings. Once again, however, the opening of the atonic short /i/ would have threatened a merger when the /-s/ became identified as the mark of plurality.

Even more important than the changes in the pronunciation that could lead to increased syncretism of previously different cases was an increased tendency to make use of word position and prepositions to make clear the function of words in syntagmas.[52] If the distinction between different case forms had been an element of the core of the language, the confusion of case endings threatened by phonetic change would undoubtedly have been repaired by extensive analogical reconstruction of the endangered endings. It is evident, however, that speakers did not feel that case distinctions were as important as, for example, the person, number, and tense distinctions of the verbal system. The function of cases being taken over by other means, the remaining forms could be eliminated without any loss of communicative efficiency. Thus, the subject of a sentence could easily be distinguished from the object by its position. The concept of the genitive could be conveyed equally well by the use of a preposition such as EX 'from' or DĒ 'from, out of, of'. In fact, from early times we find examples of the use of the dative instead of the genitive, showing that the distinction between these two cases was not necessarily clearcut (Maurer 1959, 91). The dative, in its function as the indirect object case, could be realized as well by the use of the preposition AD 'to', and the ablative, having few clear functions, could simply be abandoned, with the accusative taking its place after various prepositions. There is evidence from early times that the accusative had already replaced the ablative after prepositions that classical usage required with the ablative, e.g., CON TIRONES 'with the recruits', CON MĀTREM MEAM 'with my mother' instead of the correct forms CUM TIRŌNIBUS and CUM MĀTRE MEĀ (from a letter dated at the beginning of the second century A.D.) (Díaz y Díaz 1962, 21, line 94).

It is likely then that even during the period in which the great classics of Latin literature were being written in the conservative Classical Latin dialect, i.e., the first century B.C., in popular speech the number of cases had already been somewhat reduced, perhaps to a maximum of three: a nominative, a combined genitive-dative case, and an accusative. As indicated above, not all declensions would have retained even this many case distinctions. The use of the forms of the dative and the genitive to indicate the function of possession is attested in inscriptions and in Low Latin texts,

---

[52] Suetonius records, in his sketch of the life of Augustus, that the emperor preferred to use prepositions in some cases where their omission might make his meaning obscure, in spite of the artistic grace such omission might add: "quod quo facilius efficeret aut necubi lectores vel auditores obturbaret ac moraretur, neque praepositiones urbibus addere neque conjunctiones saepius iterare dubitavit que detractae afferunt aliquid obscuritatis etsi gratiam augent" (Liber II, 86; Rolfe 1913, 252). Maurer (1959, 85) quotes this passage differently with VERBIS instead of URBIBUS, which changes the meaning somewhat since URBIBUS would seem to refer to the use of a preposition with the name of a city to convey the same notion as the accusative of motion, rather than, as Maurer would have it, the use of prepositions with all words.

e.g., **MAGISTER CONVIVIO** 'master of the banquet' (Apuleius), and **FILIUM DUCI** 'the son of the leader', etc. (Dardel 1964, 14–15). This usage in writing may be a reflection of a merger of these two cases in Late Latin.[53]

As we have seen before, the distinction between the nominative and accusative singular of many nouns was already extinct. In the plural, we noted that in the neuter gender the nominative and the accusative were always identical (as well as in the singular), and in the third declension the two cases were also identical. In the first declension, although Classical Latin had the nominative plural in -AE, from an early period there are examples of the use of -AS as a nominative ending also, e.g., from Pompeii, **BENE QUIESCANT RELIQUIAS** 'let the relics (remains) rest well' (Väänänen 1966, 83ff). The spread of this ending may have been stimulated by a similar nominative plural in -S found in Oscan and Umbrian whose speakers, on learning Latin, would likely have tended to favor the form most like one in their first language (Gerola 1950, 334). All the evidence is that this form of the nominative plural spread over the entire Romance world, and thus was probably favored in spoken Latin from an early period (Aebischer 1971). The system of cases then in Late Latin may well have been more or less as follows (using **TERRA** 'earth', **LUPUS** 'wolf' and **REX** 'king' as examples:)

s	nom.	/tẹr:a/	/lọpus/	/rẹks/
i	gen.-dat.	/tẹr:e/	/lọpo/	/rẹje(s)/
n	acc.	/tẹr:a/	/lọpo/	/rẹje/
g.				
p	nom.	/tẹr:as-ter:e/	/lọpi-lopos/	/rẹjẹs/
l	gen.-dat.	/tẹr:-is, -aro/	/lọp-i, -oro/	/rẹj-ẹbọs, -ọ/
u	acc.	/tẹr:as/	/lọpọs/	/rẹjẹs/
r.				

(Based on Maurer 1959, 92–93)

Given the identity between the nominative and the accusative for most nouns it is even more likely that this system was, in effect, to a large extent simply a two-case system in many parts of the Empire: a nominative vs. accusative system, which was the ancestor of the Old French and Old Provençal system, and in other areas simply a nominative-accusative vs. genitive-dative system (possibly retained in the Daco-Romance area and reflected in modern Rumanian) (Hall 1980).

The identity of the nominative and accusative forms in all declensions except the second in the plural would have been a powerful incentive to speakers to reform the nominative plural in /-i/ to make it conform to the

---

[53] The persistence of certain fixed expressions indicating possession without any preposition in Old French, Old Provençal, and Old Italian is evidence of this combined case, e.g., OFr. *le tens ancienor* 'the time of the old ones', *la geste Francor* 'the deed(s) of the Franks', both show the Lat. genitive plural ending -ŌRUM, otherwise found in the genitive-dative pronoun Fr. *leur*, It. *loro*, Rum. *lor* < ILLŌRUM (Dardel 1964).

pattern of all other nouns and thus produce a nominative plural in /-os/ (Menéndez Pidal 1941, 208). Even the reduced two-case system would probably have been preserved only in very conservative areas. In Hispania, at any rate, there is no trace of any functional case system for nouns and adjectives from the very earliest written sources. The result of the elimination of the case system in most of Ibero-Romance meant that the ending /-s/ came to be associated exclusively with the concept of plurality, as it is today.

The Elimination of the Neuter Gender

One effect of the reduction of cases and the unification of all nouns and adjectives into one class, distinguished only by the type of final vowel, was that there was no longer any formal distinction between neuter and masculine nouns in the singular. The fact that even in early Latin many of the masculine and neuter forms had been identical is attested by confusions of forms in those cases where they should have been distinguished. In place of C.L. BALNEUM 'bath', CAELUM 'sky, heaven', LIGNUM 'wood', TEMPLUM 'temple', etc. we occasionally find BALNEUS, CAELUS, LIGNUS, TEMPLUS in the second declension, and accusatives like LACTEM 'milk', PECTOREM 'chest', etc., in place of the expected LAC and PECTUS in the third declension. The uncertainty about the formal distinction between masculine and neuter nouns is further revealed in certain hypercorrections of nominatives such as GLADIUM 'sword', PUTEUM 'well', etc. in place of GLADIUS and PUTEUS (Maurer 1959, 78). Thus,the neuter nouns that remain in Romance usually became masculine, e.g., Sp. *baño, cielo, leño, templo, pecho(s)*.

In the plural, all neuters ended in /-a/ in the nominative-accusative.[54] With the identification of the final /-s/ as the only ending for the plural in western Romance, such forms came to represent an anomaly. They seemed to be identical with the feminine nouns of the first declension. Therefore, in many instances speakers took them to be feminine singular nouns, thus producing the Romance forms: FOLIA ← FOLIUM 'leaf', PIGNORA ← PIGNUS 'pledge, pawn', CILIA ← CILIUM 'eyelid', VOTA ← VOTUM 'vow', etc. > Old Castilian *foja, péñora-pendra, ceja, boda*. Even in written Latin of early times, a few originally plural nouns had been treated as feminine singulars: ARMA, CASTRA ← ARMUM 'arm, weapon', CASTRUM 'camp'. Some forms kept some plural function and then adopted a new plural in *-s*: OSp. *gestas* 'heroic deeds', *bodas* 'wedding' (Alvar-Pottier 1983, 53–55).

Thus, with loss of any clear formal distinction between neuter nouns and those of the other two genders, the neuter gender simply ceased to exist as an active part of the grammatical system.[55] It may be too that the

---

[54] This ending had apparently originated in a feminine collective singular (Leumann 1977, 452).

[55] Some formal remains are found in the Italian plurals for formerly neuter nouns: *braccia* 'arms', *ciglia* 'eyebrows', *ginocchia* 'knees', *labbra* 'lips', etc., which are syntactically plurals, but are morphologically feminines from masculine singular nouns: *braccio, ciglio, ginocchio, labbro*.

function that originally was associated with the neuter, namely that of 'inanimate' (i.e., lacking an inherent power) was a factor in the loss of this gender. Thus, the results in Romance might as well be considered not simply the result of a phonetic merger of certain forms but rather the result of a gradual breakdown of an earlier system in which gender was more closely related to function. As gender became more of a purely formal distinction, the neuter had less reason to be distinguished from the masculine and feminine (Chevalier 1975, 186).

There is what may be a curious trace of the neuter in a formal distinction still preserved in the Asturian dialect. Adjectives,when modifying indefinite amounts of something or a noun designating a material in general take the ending /-u/, regardless of the normal gender of the noun. Thus, one can say, "la cebolla blancu" 'the white onion' when referring to onions in general, as opposed to a specific onion, where the adjective takes a regular feminine ending, "la cebolla blanca." Many of the substantives which govern this kind of distinction were neuter in Latin, e.g., VINUM, OLEUM, LIGNUM. Therefore, some have thought to see in it a fossilized trace of the ancient neuter gender (Alonso 1962, 125–34), although others are skeptical, since, as one scholar puts it, "we detect nothing in Latin or in the Italic dialects that foreshadows the crystallization of either metaphony or the collective neuter"(Blaylock 1964–65a, 270).

Neuter substantives of the third declension, having no ending that could be clearly seen to be masculine or feminine could therefore adopt either gender. The various Romance languages do not all agree on the gender chosen for every formerly neuter noun, which would indicate that they were not uniformly classified in Late Latin. SAL 'salt' and LAC, LACTIS 'milk', for example, have become feminine in Spanish and masculine in French: Sp. *la sal, la leche*, Fr. *le sel, le lait*.

Changes in Declension

The five formal classes of nouns in Latin were reduced in time to three. The fourth and fifth declensions were already relatively unimportant in view of the small number of nouns in each class. The fourth declension had some forms in common with masculine nouns of the second declension:

		Second	Fourth
sing.	nom.	LUPUS	FRŪCTUS 'fruit'
	acc.	LUPUM	FRŪCTUM

This formal similarity of some forms of the nouns of the fourth declension with those of the second, and their small number, plus the lack of any adjectives in this class, led the majority of fourth declension substantives to be associated with the masculine nouns of the second declension. There are very early traces of a shift from the fourth to the second, e.g., SENĀTĪ (gen.) 'senate' instead of SENĀTŪS (Leumann 1977, 441). The dative-ablative plural ending was already identical with the same case ending of the third declension, although an analogical form, -UBUS, is also attested. (It may be simply orthographical, cf. OPTUMUS for OPTIMUS.)

The fifth declension was even more sparsely represented, although it did contain a few frequently used nouns: DIĒS 'day', FACIĒS 'face; surface', RABIĒS 'anger', etc., plus a number of derived nouns containing the suffix -ITIĒS. For the most part, these words became identified with the nouns of the first declension and adopted a final -A in place of earlier -E(S). Thus, the form *DIA must have existed along with the earlier form, and in spite of its ending, it has kept the masculine gender up to the present in Sp. *día*. The suffix -ITIĒS became identified with the first declension suffix -ITIA.[56]

The reduction of the number of case distinctions made the classification of words into declensional patterns in Ibero-Romance essentially meaningless, since with the final elimination of all case endings, the only remaining inflection was that of the plural. Because the vast majority of nouns then were derived from the first three declensions, the only meaningful distinction was between those that formally distinguished their gender by means of the endings /-o, -a/, and those that did not, i.e., nouns derived from the third declension which ended in /-e/ and might be of either gender. There then occurred a certain restructuring of genders because of this formal identification of /-o/ with the masculine gender, and of /-a/ with the feminine gender, as will be seen in the following section.

Hypercharacterization of Gender

The existence of different declensions in earlier Latin had made the identification of a particular phonetic shape of words with a specific gender a less than critical matter. Thus, in the fourth declension, a number of words were feminine, although the majority of words in this class were masculine. There was no formal distinction, however, between words of either gender. With the elimination of the neuter as a separate gender, the ending /-a/ became more closely associated with the feminine gender. As pointed out above, some of the feminine nouns of the fifth declension adopted the suffix /-a/ in place of the original /-e/, thus marking their gender more clearly, e.g., *RABIA, *GLACIA, SANIA (> Sp. *saña*), MATĒRIA for RABIĒS, GLACIĒS, SANIĒS, MATERIĒS.

When the nouns of the fourth declension that resembled masculines referred to females, speakers simply put them into the first declension. Thus, SOCRUS 'mother-in-law' and NURUS 'daughter-in-law' were shifted to SOCRA and NURA (also NORA) (> Sp. *suegra, nuera*); both are condemned in the *Appendix Probi*. A few other of the nouns of the third

---

[56] The suffix itself did not disappear (phonetically, at least) and is seen in the Sp.-Port. ending -ez, e.g., *acidez* 'acidity' as opposed to the suffix -eza, found in other deadjectival formations such as *pobreza* 'poverty'.

declension also showed a tendency to adopt /-a/, e.g., *PUPPA < PUPPIS 'doll', *NEPTA 'granddaughter' < NEPTIS (> Sp. *nieta*), probably for the same reason that the fourth declension nouns were made more obviously feminine. Occasionally masculine nouns of the third declension were given the /-o/ ending, e.g., PASSER 'sparrow; bird' > *PASS-ERO, -ARO 'bird', PALUMBES 'dove' > PALUMBUS (*Ap.Prob.* 99) (> Sp. *pájaro, palomo*). Some third declension nouns in -x adopted the /-a/ ending, e.g., TENAX (> Sp. *tenazas* 'pincers' plus some dialectal forms) (Alvar-Pottier 1983, 73).

A few adjectives of the third declension were shifted among some speakers to the first and second declensions, e.g., PAUPER 'poor' > PAU-PERA, TRISTIS 'sad' > TRISTUS, ACER 'bitter' > ACRUS, and a few others, but not all of these new forms became established everywhere so that some Romance languages continued the older Latin forms: Sp. *pobre, triste*, but OSp. *agro*.

The other nouns of the fourth declension that did not refer to animate objects all became masculines ending in /-o/, e.g., FRAXINUS 'ash tree' > Sp. *fresno*, ULMUS 'elm' > Sp. *olmo*, PĪNUS 'pine' > Sp. *pino*, etc. In a few rare examples, the feminine gender is retained along with a change of the ending to /-a/, e.g., ALATERNUS 'evergreen buckthorn' > OSp. *aladierna*, which existed along with a form which had changed gender, *ladierno* (Menéndez Pidal 1941, 213). In one example only did the ending remain as /-o/ while at the same time the original feminine gender was retained, MANUS 'hand' > *la mano*.

The Personal Pronouns

Although the specific usage of personal pronouns, like the creation of a definite article, belongs more properly in the area of syntax, the forms of the pronouns should be mentioned here. The first and second person pronouns have remained much as they were in Latin, although affected by whatever sound changes occurred. The first person pronoun EGO seems to have developed very early a reduced form *EO which is the base for Sp. *yo*, OFr. *jo*, It. *io*, Rum. Port. *eu*. Otherwise the only notable change of the other pronouns is the loss of any case distinctions beyond the nominative, dative and accusative.

The dative singular forms, MĪ < MIHI, and *ti* < TIBI,[57] and the accusative forms *me* and *te* probably retained a case meaning for a while, but later lost even this distinction and became specialized as conjunctive and disjunctive pronouns. In the plural the case distinctions were lost completely and NŌS and VŌS became the sole forms.[58]

Early Latin had had no specific pronoun for the third person and speakers relied on various demonstratives when specific reference was

---

[57] Although it is evidently an analogical formation based on *mi*, the analogy evidently worked in the reverse direction as well, e.g., Mozarabic *mib*, paralleling *tib* < TIBI (Gifford and Hodcroft 1966, 109, l. 4).

[58] NŌBĪS and VŌBĪS persisted in some areas, e.g., OIt. *bobe* (Maurer 1959, 106).

necessary. In Late Latin, the demonstratives ILLE and ILLA became special-ized as third person pronouns and lost their original force as demonstra-tives, possibly as part of the specialization of the same pronoun as a definite article. The objective case uses of ILLE, being atonic and used with greater frequency than the subject forms, apparently developed reduced forms: *ILU, *ILA, *ILU < ILLUM, ILLAM, ILLUD.

Demonstratives

The earlier Latin system of three-person demonstrative adjectives was continued in some areas and abandoned in favor of a two-person ("here" vs. "there") system. In Ibero-Romance the three person system continued to be used, with one change common to all Romance: the replacement of the first person demonstratives, HIC, HAEC, HOC, by the second person demonstratives, ISTE, ISTA, ISTUD . Undoubtedly this change was the earli-est to occur since it is found everywhere. The shift of ISTE had the natural effect of leaving the second person slot open, and in a number of areas it was occupied by the former intensifier IPSE. The third person demonstra-tive ILLE remained, but with the additional uses of the third person pro-noun, and, in a reduced form in most of Romania, as the definite article.

There was in Late Latin a strong tendency to supplement the demon-stratives with a deictic particle such as ECCE 'lo, behold'. The use of ECCE obviously underlies the demonstratives of Italy and Gaul. In other areas, such as Dacia and Hispania, ECCE was changed to something like *ACCU. The source of the final /-u/ may be HUNC 'this' or HOC 'this' (masculine and neuter singulars respectively), while the /a-/ can be seen to derive from the conjunction ATQUE or AC 'and on the other hand' (Malkiel 1982b, 255–56). It is even possible that ATQUE alone would have produced the same result (González Ollé 1977). The resulting combined forms in Ibero-Romance were probably something like:

1	2	3
/akːu-iste/	/akːu-isːe/	/akːu-ilːe/

It is only in the third person that the deictic particle became firmly welded to the demonstrative; in the other forms, the demonstratives without it continued to be used, along with the amplified ones (Maurer 1959, 108–12).

The Definite Article

Latin originally had no articles, but in Late Latin several demonstratives began to be used more and more with the function of definite articles. In most of Romania the demonstrative which became the article was ILLE, although for a long time it was in competition in many areas with IPSE (Aebischer 1948; Lapesa 1961). The increasing frequency of usage led to a reduction in the form so that /ile, ila, ilud/ must have existed along with the original forms.

Relative and Interrogative Pronouns

In Late Latin the distinction between the masculine and feminine relatives was suppressed with the masculine QUĪ taking over for both genders. The neuter QUOD was largely replaced by its interrogative equivalent QUID. The three case system was probably retained in the relatives in the form:

nom. QUĪ

dat. CUI

acc. QUEM

The interrogative QUIS seems to have been replaced by QUĪ, in a general merger of these two categories. The genitive CUIUS had long been taken to be an adjective, appearing as such even in the works of stylists like Cicero, Vergil, and Pliny, although some considered such usage to be rustic (Maurer 1959, 113–15).

The Verbal System

The verb system of Latin-Romance remained much better preserved than did the case system of nouns and adjectives. The tenses and personal and mood forms remained more or less intact, although some forms were heavily influenced by a certain amount of analogical restructuring. In some instances, a complete category has been lost in its ancient form and replaced by a new form with the same function as the former one.

Loss of the Synthetic Passive

As pointed out in the previous chapter, the present system formed the passive voice by means of endings. The perfect system, however, was distinguished by the lack of any endings for the passive and the use of a periphrastic construction to correspond to the present system: that is, to form the passive voice of any perfect tense Latin used the perfect passive participle ending in -TUS, with forms of the present system of ESSE 'to be'. Thus, corresponding to AMOR 'I am loved' was AMĀTUS SUM 'I was, have been loved', etc. In Late Latin this periphrastic construction was expanded to fill the entire passive system simply by the reinterpretation of AMĀTUS SUM as a present tense, meaning 'I am loved'. The perfect forms of the passive were then expressed through the use of the perfect forms of ESSE: PORTĀTUS FUIT 'he was carried', etc. The endings of the present system, having no further function, disappeared.

Elimination of Deponent Verbs

Classical Latin possessed nearly a thousand verbs which, while active in meaning, were conjugated only in the passive, the deponent verbs.[59] Their

---

[59] In this chapter, as in chapter 2, the source is Gradenwitz 1904.

distribution among the conjugational classes rather closely paralleled that of the non-deponent verbs. Well over half (647) belonged to the first conjugation, while the second most numerous group (184) belonged to the third. The fourth conjugation and the second accounted for but a fraction (63 and 33, respectively). The anomalous nature of these verbs led to the formation of active forms based on the verb stem, some of which appear in the earliest Latin literary works. Thus, for HORTOR 'I call', LUCTOR 'I wrestle, struggle', SORTIOR 'I cast lots; allot' we find in Plautus HORTŌ, LUCTŌ, SORTIŌ. In Cato we find NASCŌ 'I am born' for C.L. NASCOR, and similar formations appear in other authors. The replacement of the present passive system by the periphrastic construction was the *coup de grâce* for these verbs, many of which were simply replaced by the active formations of the type that we have just seen, while others disappeared. In syntax, however, the deponents may have had some effect on the formation of the new compound perfect tense.

Other Losses

The synthetic future also gave way to various circumlocutions, and forms like PORTĀBIT 'he will carry', AUDIAM 'I shall hear', and others were replaced by constructions such as those based on the wide-spread construction PORTĀRE HABEŌ 'he is to, must, carry'. The future perfect indicative and the perfect subjunctive disappeared with their original function, being replaced in the system by the newly created compound tenses formed with HABĒRE. The present imperative also extended its field to include that originally covered by the future imperative which disappeared. Finally, among the impersonal verb forms, the perfect infinitive (e.g., PORTĀSSE), the future participle (e.g., PORTĀTŪRUS), the supine (e.g., PORTĀTŪ, PORTĀTUM), and possibly the present participle (e.g., PORTĀNS, -ANTIS), also were lost.

Changes of Conjugational Classes

As we saw in the previous chapter, Conjugation III was distinguished from all the others in certain forms by having a stress on the stem: in the infinitive, forms 4 and 5 of the present indicative. Daco-Rumanian has maintained stem-stress in all three forms, and Italian, Sardinian, Rhaeto-Romance (Engadine, Sursilvan), French, Provençal, and Catalan have all preserved a rhizotonic infinitive. Spanish and Portuguese, alone among all the Romance languages, completely eliminated the third conjugation stress pattern, adapting all verbs from this conjugation now to the vocalic pattern of the second, now to the fourth.

In many cases, the second conjugation attracted a number of verbs from the third because of the identical quality of the thematic vowel when unaccented. The loss of quantitative distinctions of vowels and the merger of unstressed mid front vowels produced a merger of the third conjugation

endings with forms 2, 3, 4, and 5 of the second conjugation: -ES, -ET,
-ĒMUS, -ĒTIS, thus taking these conjugations one step nearer a complete
merger. In Late Latin some verbs of III-A had evidently already entered
Conjugation II. The evidence of the Romance languages guarantees the
existence of *CADĒRE for earlier CADERE 'to fall' (> Sp. *caer*), *SAPĒRE for
SAPERE 'to taste; know' (> Sp. *saber*), plus the formation in this conjugation of new infinitives to replace the irregular infinitives mentioned earlier:
*VOLĒRE for VELLE 'to want' (replaced by QUAERERE 'to seek' in Spanish
and Portuguese), *POTĒRE for POSSE 'to be able' (> Sp. *poder*). The fact that
the stress on forms 4 and 5 was different in the two conjugations was
apparently insufficient to keep the two conjugations apart, given that only
forms 1 and 6 differed in their theme vowels. For the most part, verbs of
the second conjugation dropped the /-e-/ for form 1 so that, for example,
DĒBEŌ 'I ought, should; owe' was replaced by *DĒBŌ (> OSp. *devo*). Form
6 then adopted the second conjugation ending -ENT, as opposed to the
generalization of -UNT in the other Romance languages, e.g., It. *devono* vs.
Sp. *deben*.

Some verbs in III-B, because of their resemblance to verbs in IV had
already in earlier Latin developed infinitives in this conjugation: PARERE
'to give birth' also has the infinitive PARĪRE(> Sp. *parir*), MORĪ 'to die' is
also found as MORĪRĪ (> Sp. *morir*), CUPERE 'to desire' has also CUPĪRE in
competition with it (Leumann 1977, 545). In general, however, the direction in which verbs of the third conjugation develop in Castilian is determined by factors other than the resemblance of some forms to forms of
either the second or fourth conjugations.

The -ESCERE/-ĪRE Pattern

An innovation in the conjugation of verbs in Conjugation IV reached
most areas of Romania. In Latin a number of verbs existed which contained the inchoative suffix -SCERE. Usually these verbs were derived from
simple verbs and served to indicate the beginning of the action or state
conveyed by the simple verb, e.g., TREMĒSCERE 'to begin to tremble',
derived from TREMERE 'to tremble', OBDORMĪSCERE 'to fall asleep', from
DORMĪRE 'to sleep', etc. A number of these verbs were derived from verbs
of Conjugation II: CALĒSCERE 'to become hot', from CALĒRE 'to be hot',
CŌNSENĒSCERE 'to grow old', from SENĒRE 'to be old', FLŌRĒSCERE 'to
begin to flower' from FLŌRĒRE 'to bloom, flourish', HORRĒSCERE 'to grow
rough' from HORRĒRE 'to dread, shrink from; to be rough', etc. Given the
meaning of many of these verbs, i.e., 'to become (adjective)', a number of
other verbs based directly on adjectives were created; MĀTŪRĒSCERE 'to
grow ripe' from MĀTŪRUS 'ripe', OBMŪTĒSCERE 'to grow mute' from
MŪTUS, GRANDĒSCERE 'to become large' from GRANDIS 'large',
MOLLĒSCERE 'to become soft' from MOLLIS 'soft', etc.

At the same time, there were a number of other verbs in -ĪRE, based on adjectives, which were transitive, e.g., GRANDĪRE 'to make large', MOLLĪRE 'to make soft', etc. The -ĒSCERE forms existed only in the present paradigm; the perfect was shared with that of the -ĒRE verbs, e.g., FLŌRUIT 'it began to bloom' or 'it bloomed', CALUIT 'it grew warm' or 'it was warm'. The closeness of meaning of the verbs in -ĪRE and -ĒSCERE evidently led to their being fused into a single pattern. As MOLLĪTUS EST 'it became soft', 'it was made soft' was associated with MOLLĒSCERE as well as with MOLLĪRE, a conjugational pattern was gradually created for verbs in Conjugation IV whereby the infinitive -ĪRE was associated with -ESC- as an interfix in forms 1–3 and 6 of the present tense. The reason for the limitation to these particular forms in the earliest development of the pattern was apparently that with the loss of semantic distinctiveness of the ending, speakers could adapt the pattern to a new function. That function seems to have been the establishment of a consistent accentual pattern in the present tense. The traditional present tense pattern in Latin had stem stress in forms 1–3 and 6 but stress on the thematic vowel in forms 4 and 5 (except for Conjugation III). The use of the -SC- interfix in the former rhizotonic forms allowed stress to fall consistently after the stem. Since forms 4 and 5 were already so stressed, they did not need the new interfix (Allen 1977–78, 209).

A number of -ĪRE verbs with no semantic connection with the original inchoative meaning began to join the pattern so that, for example, FĪNĪRE 'to end' must have developed a by-form, *FĪNISCERE 'to come to an end', and PERĪRE 'to perish' and ADDORMĪRE 'to begin to go to sleep' likewise developed froms like *PERESCERE and *ADDORMESCERE. This particular innovation must have begun to flourish in Late Latin at a time when some of the Romance dialects had been sufficiently cut off from the newer modes of speaking so that they never adopted it, e.g., Sardinian and Southern Italian. In Ibero-Romance, the new pattern began to make some headway, but, except for Catalan, was eventually ousted by further developments (Wilkinson 1967, 26–28; Maurer 1959, 133–35).

Special Developments of Form 1

Many of the verbs with form 1 in -ĪŌ behaved like those of the second conjugation and abandoned the yod, aligning the first person stem with that of the other persons. Thus, *SENTŌ 'I feel, perceive' must have replaced earlier SENTIŌ, and *MENTŌ 'I lie' replaced MENTIOR, eventually resulting in Castilian *siento* and *miento*. Some traces of the yod remain in a few verbs in which the stem consonant fused with the yod:

AUDIŌ 'I hear' > /oj:o/ (> OSp. *oyo*)
FUGIŌ 'I flee' > /fuj:o/ (> OSp. *fuyo*)

Apparently the tendency was to preserve the yod when it followed one of the consonants that normally palatalized:

TENEŌ 'I hold' > /teno/
VENIŌ 'I come' > /beno/
VIDEŌ 'I see' > /bej:o/
FACIŌ 'I do, make' > /fatˢo/

Portuguese tended to preserve the yod longer than Castilian; we find Old Port. *senço* and *menço*, later replaced by *sinto* and *minto*, as well as the forms that remain until today: *tenho, venho, faço, vejo*. The persistence of yod in Late Latin is revealed by the metathesis of the yod which affected some verbs:

CAPIO 'I take, seize' > /kaipo/ (> Sp. *quepo* 'I fit')
SAPIAM 'I know' (subj.) > /saipa/ (> Sp. *sepa*)

It may be that a dual development occurred with competing forms existing for a while. Thus, /*fako/ may have existed along with /fatˢo/, its final /-k/ supported by verbs whose stems already ended in /-k/ such as DĪCŌ 'I say' and DŪCŌ 'I lead' (Wilkinson 1980, 41).[60]

One class of verbs was distinguished from others by the presence of a consonant sequence /-ng-/ at the end of the verb stem, as in the following examples:

CINGERE 'to surround, encircle'
EXTINGUERE 'to extinguish'
FRANGERE 'to break'
IMPINGERE 'to pin to, thrust, dash'
JUNGERE 'to join'
PLANGERE 'to bewail'
PUNGERE 'to prick, puncture'
STRINGERE 'to draw tight; prune; graze lightly'
TANGERE 'to touch'
TINGERE 'to dye, color'
UNG(U)ERE 'to annoint'

These verbs were no different from any other in earlier Latin. As soon as the /g/ preceding a front vowel began to change into a palatal [j], however, the stem would have developed two allomorphs, depending on whether the ending following it contained a front vowel or not. For example, the present indicative of FRANGERE would have had the following forms:

1. /frango/ (< FRANGŌ)
2. /franjes/ (< FRANGIS)
3. /franjet/ (< FRANGIT) or /franjent/
4. /franjemos/ (< FRANGIMUS)
5. /franjetes/ (< FRANGITIS)
6. /frangont/ (< FRANGUNT)

---

[60] Wilkinson bases himself on the pattern found in Rumanian: *fac* 'I do', 'they do' < FAC(I)Ō, FAC(I)UNT. Malkiel (1973–74) does not take Rumanian into account in his study of the velar insert.

In the present subjunctive form there would have been no change since the thematic vowel was /a/, e.g., FRANGAM, FRANGAS, etc. This contrast between the stem forms /franj-/ and /frang-/ might have been maintained, but, as so often happens in the history of the development of verbs, the tendency of speakers to unify the forms of verbs according to a standard model often led to an analogical extension of one form of the stem to all positions.

In the case of the verbs with stems ending in /-ng/, the most common form would have been the one with the yod in the present indicative, and this could have been generalized to all forms of the verbs.[61] At the same time there were other verbs in which the stem was followed by a yod. As mentioned previously, they generally were those in which the consonant was one that normally palatalized when followed by a yod, such as /n/. Thus, VENĪRE 'to come' and TENĒRE 'to hold' had forms 1 with a palatalized /ɲ/: /beɲo/ and /teɲo/, contrasting with other forms with a stem ending in a simple /n/: /ben-es/, /ten-es/, etc. (VENIS, TENES). That the forms 1 postulated above actually existed is proved by Port. *venho, tenho*, and similar forms in other languages, e.g., Old It. *vegno, tegno* (Wilkinson 1978, 25). Along with these common verbs, others almost as common undoubtedly developed in the same way: Lat. RE-MANEŌ 'I remain' must have produced /remaɲo/ (> Old It. *rimagno*). The common verb PŌNERE 'to place, put' was the only surviving verb of Conjugation III whose stem was a single syllable ending in a single /n/, and it was therefore drawn to other verbs with a similar structure, producing a form /poɲo/[62] > Port. *ponho*.

The result of the establishment of a number of verbs with form 1 ending in /ɲ/ and the establishment of a series of verbs of the /-ng/ type with all forms of the present indicative having the stem in /-nj/ except for form 1, was that the scene was set for some mutual analogical influence of one type on the other. The individual verbs of the /ng/ class were not used with any special frequency, but the existence of a large number of verbs all sharing the same phonetic features was undoubtedly sufficient to make these features distinctive in the economy of the verbal system. The mutual influence we posit for both kinds of verbs would be most likely to occur when speakers began to analogically extend the stem ending in /-nj/, or its more advanced form /ɲ/, to form 1 of verbs such as FRANGERE or TANGERE. Thus, when they began saying /franj-o/ or /fraɲ-o/ or /taɲ-o/ instead of /frango, tango/, it is not surprising that they would then be

---

[61] The problem of the specific phonetic development of the yod after a consonant is a separate problem and will have to be taken up in the next chapter since it varies from one region to another and thus must not be a single, general Romance development.

[62] The form PONIAMUS is found in a Spanish document written in 844, evidently a representation of [poɲamos] (Gifford and Hodcroft 1966, 23, l. 11).

inclined to feel that they could alternate /-ngo/ and /-ņo/ as more or less equivalent forms. Therefore those verbs which already had form 1 in /-ņo/ could easily develop forms ending in /-ngo/, e.g., /tengo/ beside /teņo/ and /ɓengo/ along with /ɓeņo/ (Wilkinson 1978, 28–29). It may be that this identification of verb stems in /ņ/ and those in /ng/ occurred in a broad area in central Romania before there had been any sharp division of dialects since several languages have these forms: Sp. *tengo, vengo, pongo*, Provençal and Gascon *tenc, venc, remanc, ponga*, Catalan *tinc, tinga, vinc, vinga*, Italian *tengo, vengo, rimango, pongo* (and, of course, all present subjunctive forms).[63] The absence of any forms in writing in Castilian (which at this time did not exist as such, but only as one of a variety of more or less differentiated dialects and dialect groups) in /-ņ/ might lead us to suspect that the loss of the yod in north central Hispania occurred earlier than in other areas (Lenfest 1978, 901). It is possible too that the final palatalization of the stem final /n/ did not occur at the same time in all areas and that the morphological equivalence of /-ng/ and /-ņ/ did not occur either. What seems most likely is that there was no uniformity but rather a number of fluctuating norms that coexisted for a time before a specific variable or tendency gained predominance, and, in some areas, drove out all others. It seems likely too that the yod persisted after the /n/ long enough to raise the preceding vowel and thus prevent diphthongization of the /ę/ in Castilian (Lenfest 1978, 900).[64] The subsequent development of these verb forms is discussed in the next chapter.

Some Other Common Verbs

Several frequently used verbs such as ESSE 'to be', DĀRE 'to give', STĀRE 'to stand', etc. were also reshaped by analogy in Late Latin, but since many of the problems associated with them are more closely related to early medieval Romance, they are dealt with in the next chapter.

---

[63] Wilkinson believes that since the results of the phonetic development of the -NGERE verbs are not all found in contiguous areas therefore "this is not a case of a local variety expanding outward from one centre; what we have to do with is a common tendency, based on parallel developments in each language, and expressing itself to a greater or lesser extent in one area or another" (1978, 26). Lenfest observes, however, "The languages in which the velar infix appears stretch in an unbroken chain from Spain to Italy, and the ones in which it does not appear are found on the fringes of this area" (1978, 903). Lenfest, of course, is speaking of the standard languages and not dialects. The question of just how contiguous these areas are deserves some study. Wilkinson believes that the absence of the /-ng-/ in northern Italy serves to set off central Italian from the remaining areas.

[64] Lenfest believes that the forms /*teņo/ and /*beņo/ must have existed in early Castilian and not /teņo/ and /beņo/. I wonder if we can be so certain that the forms with the /ņ/ did not exist in this area. They may have existed in competition with /tengo/ and /bengo/ but have been driven out at a very early period by the /-g/ forms, especially after voicing had added to the number of verb stems ending in /-g/ (see next chapter for fuller discussion).

The Imperfect

The reflexes of the Latin imperfect endings in many of the Romance languages indicate that the intervocalic /-b-/ of the suffix must have disappeared quite early from the endings of all conjugations except the first, e.g., OFr. *-eie*, Rum. *-ea*, Sp.-Port. *-ía*, etc. These results could have come from forms in Late Latin like /-ea/ or /-ia/. The fact that in Sardinian, the most archaic of the Romance languages, the imperfect endings also lack the medial /-b-/ shows that the loss of the consonant was a fairly early change, although the preservation of the medial labial was not unusual either (Alvar-Pottier 1983, 240–41).

Why this /-b-/ should have disappeared has not yet been explained satisfactorily. The loss of the consonant is found in some words, e.g.,

> GINGĪVA 'gum' > OSp. *enzía*
> PRIVĀTU 'private' > OSp. *priado*
> PAVŌRE 'fear' > Fr. *peur*
> VĪVENDA 'victuals' > Fr. *viande* 'meat, food'

One might conclude that this loss is regular between vowels, except when the same vowel appears before and after the /b/, e.g., FABA 'bean' > OSp. *faba*, Fr. *fève*, etc. Or possibly one could think that this was a regular phonetic change that was stopped before reaching completion (Posner 1961). We know that the imperfect in Conjugation IV was often -ĪBA-, instead of C.L. -IĒBA- (Alvar-Pottier 1983, 239; Maurer 1959, 140–41), and if this ending was extended analogically to Conjugations II and III, it would account for the forms found in Spanish and Portuguese.

Another suggestion has been that possibly the verbs having a /b/ in their stem underwent a dissimilatory loss of the same consonant in the imperfect endings. Thus, verbs like HABĒRE 'to have' and DĒBĒRE 'to owe, ought' might have developed imperfect forms like /aβéa/ and /deβéa/. Being frequently used verbs, they could have influenced other verbs of Conjugations II-IV to adopt the shortened endings (Maurer 1959, 140).

The change of the endings of these conjugations probably must be related to their general tendency to be grouped together in opposition to Conjugation I, where the ending has retained the /-b-/, e.g., OFr. *-eve*, OSp.-Port. *-ava*, etc. Thus, the change would have helped to set these conjugations off more clearly. Another possibility is that there was some relation between these new reduced endings and the creation of the new tense, the future of the past or conditional, which arose once the new Romance future composed of the infinitive and the verb HABĒRE became established. The use of the imperfect of HABĒRE-HABĒBAM, HABĒBAS, with the infinitive would have tended to reduce the forms of HABĒRE since there is a strong tendency for very frequently used forms to be reduced in bulk (Mańczak 1969). Given the close relationship between the forms of the conditional and the imperfect in most Romance languages, the adoption of a shortened form in the conditional could have influenced the imperfect.

Another factor that may have affected this particular development was the growth in Late Latin of a number of new perfect verb forms in Conjugations II, III, and IV, containing /-u-/, as in the perfect of HABĒRE. The forms of the verb that were used for this tense were reduced to the minimum necessary to still remain distinctive:

1. /aio/		4. /emos/
2. /as/		5. /etes/
3. /at/		6. /ant/

(cf. Alvar-Pottier 1983, 234)

The problem of why the older future was replaced is essentially one of syntax that must be discussed elsewere.

The Perfect

In chapter 2 we saw that certain forms of Conjugations I and IV did not commonly contain the element /-ui-/ - /-ue-/ in spoken Latin. The extension of the same pattern to form 4 would be a natural analogical development, thus producing a pattern of the perfect in which all endings consisted of a single syllable following the thematic vowel (Craddock 1983, fn. 44):

Forms:	1	2	3	4	5	6
I:	-AI	-ASTI	-ÁUT	-ĀMUS	-ASTIS	-ĀRUNT
IV:	-II	-ISTI	-ÍUT	-ĪMUS	-ISTIS	-IĒRUNT (-ĪRUNT)

The endings for form 3 seem to be later forms, developed originally from the /-vi-/ perfect endings, while the other forms are likely to have been original. We can see that form 3 offered speakers a clear model of the verb root plus a stressed theme vowel, plus the ending /-ut/ which could then be imitated by other verbs, as will be seen in the next chapter (Craddock 1983, 6). Some examples of the Late Latin perfect forms are found in the graffiti at Pompeii: COMMODASTI, IURASTI, PROBASTI, CURARUNT, LOCARUNT, etc. (Väänänen 1966, 40). The new pattern inspired the elimination of some of the perfects that in earlier Latin had not followed the majority of the verbs in Conjugations I and IV:

	Older Perfect	Late Perfect
CREPĀRE 'to creak, rattle'	CREPUĪ	*CREPAI
CUBĀRE 'to lie down, recline'	CUBUĪ	*CUBAI
LAVĀRE 'to wash'	LAVĪ	*LAVAI
FRICĀRE 'to rub'	FRICUĪ	*FRICAI
SECĀRE 'to cut'	SECUĪ	*SECAI
SONĀRE 'to sound, resound'	SONUĪ	*SONAI

(Maurer 1959, 144)

The ending /-ui/, which became the typical perfect ending of Conjugation II verbs, was extended to those verbs which had not had this form of the perfect:

	Older Perfect	Late Perfect
CADERE 'to fall'	CECIDĪ	*CADUI
CAPERE 'to seize, take'	CĒPĪ	*CAPUI
SAPERE 'to taste; know'	SAPĪVĪ	*SAPUI
SEDĒRE 'to be seated'	SĒDĪ	*SEDUI

Even in Classical Latin we can see reflections of a tendency to remake older and less frequent perfects according to more active models. Thus, the relic forms showing reduplications, for example, often were replaced by sigmatic perfects:

PANGERE 'to fasten, fix'	PEPIGĪ	PANXĪ
PARCERE 'to spare, economize'	PEPERCĪ	PARSĪ
MORDĒRE 'to bite'	MOMORDĪ	MORSĪ

The old Latin TETINĪ, the perfect of TENERE 'to hold', had already been replaced in Classical Latin by TENUĪ, and in compounds of CANERE 'to sing', the perfect CINUĪ replaced CECINĪ (Leumann 1977, 587). Thus, not only did we find PARSĪ but also PARCUĪ (Leumann 1977, 605).

Large numbers of verbs with reduplicating perfects or perfects showing vowel gradation simply disappeared from the language altogether, replaced by other verbs. Thus, CANERE was replaced by an iterative derivative, CANTĀRE. Some of the very commonest verbs, however, remained: VĪDĪ, 'I saw', VĒNĪ 'I came', FĒCĪ 'I did', DEDĪ 'I gave'.

Sigmatic perfects were more resistant and often survived through the Middle Ages, as is seen in the next chapter. Although reduplication as a system of forming the perfect vanished completely, one of the verbs with a reduplicating perfect had far-reaching effects on the formation of many perfects in Late Latin and early Romance: DEDĪ, perfect of DĀRE. The frequency of use of this verb may have been sufficient to induce speakers to use it as a model for other verbs. Those verbs which had an irregular perfect similar to DEDĪ, in many Romance dialects shifted in form to resemble it more closely by adopting -DEDĪ as the ending with stress on the ending rather than on the stem as previously. Thus, the following verbs were reshaped:

CRĒDERE 'to believe'	CRĒDIDĪ > *CREDÉDI
PERDERE 'to lose'	PERDIDĪ > *PERDÉDI
REDDERE 'to give back'	REDIDĪ > *REDEDI
VENDERE 'to sell'	VENDIDĪ > *VENDEDI

The existence of a core of verbs with this type of formation was sufficient to attract other verbs whose perfects had not had a form similar to DEDĪ, but whose stems ended in /d/ as did the verbs of the original group. So DĒSCENDERE 'to descend' and RESPONDĒRE 'to answer' also joined the group with new perfect forms, *DESCENDÉDI, *RESPONDÉDI. This new perfect was destined to produce further changes in the Romance languages at a later stage of development (Maurer 1959, 146; Lausberg 1966, 2:345ff).

Other Perfect Tenses

As we saw in the previous chapter, the future perfect and the perfect subjunctive were distinguished only in form 1: AMĀVERŌ 'I shall have loved' vs. AMĀVERIM 'I (may) have loved'. At the same time, the adoption of reduced forms of the endings in the perfect indicative induced speakers to reduce in a similar fashion the other perfect tenses. Thus, for example, AMĀVERAM 'I had loved' gave way to AMĀRAM, and the pluperfect subjunctive AMĀVISSEM was replaced by AMĀSSEM, etc. The same process then reduced the future perfect to AMĀRO, AMĀRIS, AMĀRIT, etc. and the perfect subjunctive to AMĀREM, AMĀRIS, AMĀRIT. With the merger of /i/ and /e/ in unstressed syllables these reduced forms must have become identical with the imperfect subjunctive: AMĀREM, AMĀRĒS, AMĀRET, and thus all three tenses would have become identical in form with the exception of form 1, where AMĀRO and AMĀRE must have coexisted. The result of this coalescence of tenses was the loss of these forms in their original function. In Ibero-Romance, the forms of the verbs then adopted new meanings, which in Castilian was to become a new tense, the future subjunctive, which had not previously existed in Latin.

The loss of the perfect and imperfect tenses of the subjunctive left the pluperfect subjunctive isolated, and, as the only remaining past subjunctive, it lost its specific tense meaning and took the place of the two lost tenses and remained as the only past subjunctive.

The Compound Perfect

In Late Latin a new construction made up of the forms of HABĒRE 'to have' and the perfect passive participle began to gain ground with the function of a perfect as distinct from the aorist or simple past. The forms of HABĒRE were, as in the new future tense, reduced in form with forms 1–3 and 6 consisting of single syllable. In forms 4 and 5, the root /ab-/ was sometimes retained so that both longer and shorter forms coexisted: /aḃemos/ vs. /emos/ and /aḃetes/ vs. /etes/.

The creation of this new tense allowed speakers eventually to extend its range to cover the pluperfect and the future perfect as well as the various subjunctive tenses, thus replacing the former synthetic tenses. It appears, however, that the creation of these new compound tenses was a slow process that required many centuries. The synthetic pluperfect, for example, was used with its original meaning in Castilian and Portuguese throughout the Middle Ages, and only gradually began to take on a different meaning.

The Past Participle

The regular past participles of Conjugations I and IV need no special treatment since they evolved normally. In the second and third conjugations, however, a new pattern became established in Late Latin. Earlier Latin had had no one pattern for the verbs of these conjugations, so that both weak participles in -ĒTUS and -ŪTUS and strong participles, -ĪTUS, -TUS were found. The relationship between the perfect in -UI and the participles in -ŪTUS, as in TRIBUERE 'to allot, assign' - TRIBŪTUS, STATUERE 'to place, set up' - STATŪTUS, BATTUERE 'to strike' - BATTŪTUS, evidently induced speakers to extend this suffix to other verbs and to eliminate many arrhizotonic participles. Many new -ŪTUS participles must have been created in early imperial times. Latin cognomina like CREDŪTA, SALŪTUS, VENŪTUS, and gentilicial or tribal names like ALBŪTIUS, CANNŪTIUS, CREMŪTIUS, DOLŪTIUS, TOLŪTIUS, VOLŪTIUS surely derive from unattested participles in -ŪTUS (Zimmerman 1904).

CHAPTER 4

FROM LATE LATIN TO OLD SPANISH

INTRODUCTION: IBERO-ROMANCE WITHIN THE WESTERN ROMANCE COMPLEX

The various changes in Late Latin discussed in the previous chapter were, for the most part, general to all the various Late Latin-Early Romance dialects. Undoubtedly the language of the late western Empire was characterized by the regional and social differentiation which is only to be expected in any far-flung language. Students of the period are, however, faced with an extreme lack of data when attempting to find out just what features may have been typical of different regions. The system of written Latin continued to be that of much earlier times, namely "Classical Latin." The morphological changes in the spoken language which had led to a great reduction in the number and function of the various cases in the nominal system were, for the most part, unreflected in most written texts which strove, wherever possible, to retain all the distinctions that had been found in earlier Latin. The system of orthography was not adjusted to reflect any of the sound changes that had been occurring, since it offered the average literate native speaker of Latin-Romance no particular difficulty in reading or in writing. For example, one could easily learn that the direct object of verbs must be written with a "silent" -M, for most nouns. Even vocabulary that had vanished long before from conversational Latin could be learned as a part of a special lexicon needed only when one set pen to paper. Thus, when reading most texts from late imperial days and early medieval times, we find only brief and tantalizing hints about what actual speech may have been like. In general, we are limited to what we can reconstruct from the comparison of medieval written Romance and occasional "mistakes" in texts by writers less skilled in reproducing correct Classical Latin, plus some unpretentious non-literary works, or lists of glosses explaining unfamiliar vocabulary that may contain more features of spoken Romance than the average official text.

171

Two phonetic changes in particular have often been singled out as marking the most important differences between the Latin-Romance found in "Western" as opposed to "Eastern" Romance (i.e., the dialects to the north and west of the "Spezia-Rimini" line vs. those to the south and east of it, with appropriate adjustments for Sardinia and Africa). The retention of the final /-s/ and the voicing of the intervocalic voiceless consonants as against the loss of /-s/ and the retention of the voiceless consonants, following the inspiration of Walther von Wartburg, is often held to be basic in making this great overall division of the Romance languages. There are many reasons for questioning whether two phonetic features such as these should be sufficient to distinguish such a fundamental division, but a full discussion of the problems involved cannot be taken up here.[1]

Suffice it to say that there are valid reasons for perceiving within the general context of "Western" Romance, some phonetic features that may have characterized Ibero-Romance during late imperial times and the early Middle Ages as opposed to other regional varieties. These features may well have been the retention of a more conservative vowel system, in which the high short vowels had not opened as far as in more advanced dialects, the possible shift of initial consonant groups with the liquid /l/, i.e., /pl-, kl-, fl-/ to the affricate /č/, the maintenance of a voiceless articulation of intervocalic consonants, and a generally slow adoption of syncope. All of these conservative phonetic features may then have been overlaid by innovations like the basic seven vowel phonemic system of Western Romance and, possibly, the tendency toward the reduction of unstressed vowels to a mid central vowel or schwa [ə], from more tone-setting dialects centered probably around Lugdunum (modern Lyon) and the area of the Narbonensis, as Rome lost its position as the cultural center of the western Empire after the third century. The important study of Malkiel (1983) examines in detail many of these phenomena which are discussed in somewhat more detail in the appropriate section of this chapter.

The Constitution of the Castilian Dialect

Although this text is primarily an "internal" history of the development of the Spanish language, it is impossible to deal with language development purely and simply in terms of language structures themselves with no consideration for the social context in which language exists. The evolution of language does indeed respond to various internal structural pressures, but, as was pointed out in the discussion of the nature of language change in chapter 1, the choice of the features to be emphasized and those to be left to wither is often determined by factors that are to some extent

---

[1] For a thorough discussion of Walther von Wartburg's *Die Ausgliederung der romanischen Sprachräume*, see Malkiel 1972, 863–68.

independent of language. This is especially true when certain changes are determined by contact with speakers of other languages. Therefore, in the following pages some consideration must be given to the external factors that contributed to the evolution of the Romance dialect of Castile, the dialect that eventually became identified as the Spanish language.

The distinguishing feature of medieval Spain was the Moslem invasion and occupation of much of the peninsula that split ancient Hispania into two sections and made it a frontier area as compared with the rest of western Europe. The late Visigothic kingdom had been increasingly weakened politically in the seventh century. During the latter half of that century especially, the ruling class of the nobility was principally concerned with the pursuit of personal and factional goals rather than with national ones (García Moreno 1975, 211). As the different factions of the nobility sought to control the monarchy or to weaken it if they could not control it, these divisions became more and more sharply accentuated, leading to frequent revolts. Along with the political dissension that did so much to break up the precarious unity of the kingdom, a variety of natural disasters contributed to social discontent: poor harvests, famines, and numerous outbreaks of the plague. As if natural calamities were not enough, the hand of the royal tax collector had come to weigh so heavily on the masses of the poor that a notable increase in rural banditry occurred the in second half of the seventh century. Harsher laws punishing escaped slaves and those who aided them, evidence of greater numbers of suicides, and of poor free men selling themselves into slavery all indicate that popular disaffection was on the rise, and, in some cases, was reaching the point of despair (García Moreno 1975, 47–82). The invasion by Moslem forces from Africa in response to a call for help by one faction of the nobility in an internal conflict in A.D. 711 led to the sudden and precipitous collapse of the Visigothic kingdom.

The first reaction of the majority of the inhabitants of the peninsula to the Moslem invasion was, for the most part, apparently fairly mild, especially in the southern regions. Some of the Gothic nobility managed to make a deal with the new rulers and thus kept their lands and their position in the country. The conquerors were, in general, liberal in their treatment of the Hispano-Roman and Gothic peoples. No conversions to Islam were forced on Christians, and, for the great mass of the poor who had suffered under the monarchy and the quarrelling Gothic-Roman nobility the change from one overlord to another could hardly have been a cause for much regret. Their life went on under the emir (later caliph) much the same as it had under the Christian kings.

In the north, on the other hand, the situation was rather different. The most northerly areas had not been a highly civilized region under imperial and Visigothic rule. Roman culture had reached there, but it was undoubtedly somewhat attenuated by the lateness of its penetration and by the lack, in most areas, of the extensive urbanization of the south and the eastern coastal areas. The north was, in general terms, marginal with respect to Roman culture and can be considered to have been only half-Romanized in contrast with other parts of the peninsula (Sánchez Albornoz 1956, 74).

The period in which the native languages of the north (and others as well) were finally replaced by Latin is one still wrapped in a mystery.[2] Romanization, which included the adoption of Latin as the general language of all persons, had been rapid in the urbanized south and in the Levant, but we have no certain knowledge of when the rural areas also adopted Latin. The persistence of Basque in the Pyrenees and in adjacent territories is clear evidence that Latin did not become dominant everywhere. It is quite likely that in other northern areas the indigenous languages remained in use until the beginning of the Middle Ages (whenever that may be). In other words, there may well have been many speakers of pre-Romance tongues at the time of the Moslem invasion. As pointed out by García y Bellido (1967), the decisive blow against the native languages was probably the conversion of their speakers to Christianity, since the new religion in the west brought with it Latin as the language of the church and intellectual life. Written Latin, as the official language of the western church, favored the use of the Romance vernacular, since for native speakers of Romance, there was probably no general consciousness of Romance as a language distinct from the way it was written. People spoke in one way and wrote in another way, one that looked more archaic, but as far as they were concerned it was all one language. In the places where Basque continued to be spoken, however, the native tradition evidently was strong enough to persist even after the Basques had become Christians.

The area which was eventually to become Casti(e)lla had not had any special importance during imperial times or under the Visigothic kingdom. It had not even constituted a unified area, but had been part of one of the various provinces of the peninsula, divided differently at different times (Lapesa 1980, 184). The native tribes that inhabited the region were not unified either: the Cantabri, the Autrigoni, the Caristi, the Barduli, the Berones, the Turmogi, etc. are today little more than names handed down by history. Their culture and their languages are the subject of much speculation and few hard facts (Caro Baroja 1943, 39–41).[3]

At the time of the initial Moslem invasion, the north-central and northwestern areas were not immediately subjected to the domination of the new rulers as the south was. Being generally mountainous, especially in

---

[2] "Las lenguas indígenas de la Península debieron de pervivir en ciertos vicos y aldeas rurales hasta muy entrada la Edad Media" (García y Bellido 1967, 28). Hard facts on just where and how long the native tongues endured are not available.

[3] The Berones, Autrigones, and Turmogi were probably Celtic-speaking tribes (Sánchez-Albornoz 1974, 210). Sánchez-Albornoz speaks of them as belonging to the Celtic "race," whatever that may be. It is a well established principle of modern anthropology that physical race and language are entirely different things and should not be confused.

the lands closest to the coast, and lacking the urbanization of the south, the north did not attract any permanent Moslem settlement.[4] The conquerors seem to have regarded it primarily as a collection of places available for raiding. Raids tended to be frequent and often enough included not only pillaging but also a general massacre of the population (Sánchez Albornoz 1966, 257–59). The inhabitants of these areas were therefore concerned for a number of years simply with protecting themselves, and they consequently took refuge in the mountains. By the middle of the eighth century an independent monarchy had been established in Oviedo, and the king, Alfonso I, undertook a policy of concentrating as much of the population as possible in the mountains, creating thereby an uninhabited zone in the valley of the Duero River to serve as a sort of no-man's-land between his territories and the south.

Alfonso's policy was a necessary one at the time in view of the primitive kingdom's limited population and resources, especially in comparison with those regions under Islamic control, but it was not to be permanent. The political disunion that frequently troubled the Emirate and Caliphate of Córdoba discouraged the Moslem states from mounting a long-term, concerted campaign to reduce the north to permanent submission. Attacks became less frequent toward the end of the eighth century. The population of the kingdom of Oviedo, later called Asturias, began to increase, and it became possible for Christian monarchs to think of extending their borders to the south. The "Reconquest" could begin.

The area that became Castile was originally a small region just south of the Cantabrian chain, west of the valleys of Mena, Losa and Valdegovia. Southern raiders could move up the valley of the Ebro River fairly easily until reaching this place (Sánchez Albornoz 1966, 292–93). Since it lay outside of the natural defenses of the mountains, those who began to settle there found it essential to construct fortifications to protect the new settlements. Some of these, indeed, had begun to appear as early as the reign of Alfonso I. The number of fortresses eventually became sufficiently large to be perceived as a distinctive characteristic of the area, so that toward the beginning of the ninth century the popular description of it was "the place of castles" < Lat. CASTELLA (provided that we do not have a mental image of a castle as necessarily something like the huge stone keep of the late Middle Ages or of modern popular fiction). The name was at first simply a descriptive term, but by the middle of the ninth century it had become a proper name and began to be applied to a more extensive territory as the process of settlement continued (Sánchez Albornoz 1951), although the older name of Bardulia was still remembered ("Bardulies quae nunc appellatur Castella" [Pérez de Urbel 1969, 87, note 16]).

---

[4] In speaking of the "north," it is necessary to exclude much of the northeast where there are cities such as Zaragoza. Zaragoza (< CAESARAUGUSTA) did indeed become a Moslem city for a long time. I refer mainly to the Cantabrian chain that runs parallel to the northern coast of the peninsula.

We cannot give here a history of the origins and development of Castile aside from the brief sketch provided above. At first simply one part of the kingdom of Asturias, it gradually became a "county," i.e., a district under the command of a count appointed by the Asturian, and later the Leonese, king, and eventually an independent kingdom.[5] For our purposes, what is most important to note is how the gradual formation of the new community affected the Romance dialect(s) of the region. The precarious conditions of life for many years meant that for centuries Castile, as it spread to the south, remained a frontier area. Although no universal rule can be made regarding the conditions that are found on all frontiers throughout history,[6] in this particular case, the previous depopulation of the valley of the Duero and other northern regions meant that there was a serious shortage of people to undertake the repopulation of these empty lands. Kings and other lords, and monastic establishments, who wished to attract settlers, had to make the conditions of settlement favorable to them.

Toward the west, in León proper, which considered itself the successor to the primitive Asturian monarchy, settlement was by and large under the control of the king, the great lords, and various ecclesiastical and monastic establishments. In Castile, on the other hand, the occupation tended to be of a much more popular character. Rather distant from the capital, Castile developed a sentiment of detachment from the center of the kingdom, accentuated by the different conditions of life. In many cases, the shortage of population was such that it was not sufficient for settlers to be offered new land; in addition, other benefits and advantages had to be given: the reduction of taxes and feudal obligations and of other limits on personal freedom.

Los medios ordinarios de atracción se cifraban en una mejoría de condición social de los entonces vecinos o primeros pobladores que llamara a otros nuevos. En las colonizaciones difíciles, se llegaba a prometer la extinción de las obligaciones contraídas en el pasado por los nuevos pobladores, tanto si eran originadas en el contrato como en el delito. Estas repoblaciones enfranquecidas engendraron una floración de comunidades vecinales, mitad guerreras, mitad agrarias, con una base social igualitaria y una autonomía política muy acentuada, extendidas principalmente por los sectores fronterizos del alto Duero y alto Ebro, es decir el núcleo originario del reino de Castilla (Font Rius 1957, 268–69).[7]

---

[5] Pérez de Urbel 1969, Font Rius 1957, and, of course, the *Orígenes* are the most useful sources, along with some of the articles cited.

[6] An interesting comparison of different types of moving frontiers is found in Mikesell 1968.

[7] "El carácter popular de la repoblación castellana—que provenía de la ascendencia norteña de sus pobladores: cántabros, vascos— contrastó bien pronto con el tinte más aristocrático y monacal de la gallega y leonesa, por la profusión de abades y señores que, con sus monjes, colonos y gasalianes, emprendieron la explotación de granjas y villas, levantadas, a veces, tomando como centro una fundación monástica" (Font Rius 1957, 268).

A natural result of these policies was the establishment of a community of a generally more open social character, lacking the rigidly stratified classes of earlier and later times: "The warlike frontier of early medieval Spain was a miniature 'wild west', attractive to adventurous, combative men who were willing to live dangerously and uncomfortably rather than submit to established hierarchies" (Jackson 1972, 36–37). Thus, opportunities abounded for a man of low birth, but ambitious and talented, to become free and relatively independent, and possibly, if he could gain some spoils from military attacks upon the south, to enter the ranks of the lower nobility and bring up his children as **fijos dalgo**. Inhabitants of this territory could gradually come to feel themselves to be a people apart. Group solidarity would then be expressed in certain features of their dialect that came to be thought of as distinctively Castilian, serving to identify Castilians as a group with a certain **ethos**, a certain way of looking at the world.

One of the effects of the social mobility that characterized early Castilian society would have been a greater unity of language as people from different areas mixed together in the newly populated regions (Lantolf 1974, 264), and abandoned isolated dialectal features. A large degree of homogeneity was, in fact, an early feature of the emerging Castilian dialect (*Orígenes* §94).

One other element in primitive Castilian society must also be considered: the presence of another language among many of the settlers of the newly occupied areas, namely, Basque. The Basque-speaking regions of Spain today are limited to the areas closest to the western end of the Pyrenees, on both sides of the mountain chain. The frontier between Basque and Romance has been steadily moving toward the north for many centuries as the number of Basque speakers has shrunk (see the map in *Orígenes* §96), but during the first few centuries after the Moslem invasion, Basques were found in a much larger area and may even have occupied lands close to the city of Burgos (founded in A.D. 882). The evidence of place names and family names indicates that in the advance of the Christian peoples toward the south, Basques played a prominent role. The following quotation can serve to illustrate this point:

> Muchos [i.e., toponyms] conservan recuerdo de grupos de colonizadores. Abundan los que atestiguan las presencia de emigrantes vascos. Recibieron el nombre de Bascones lugares de Castella Vetula, Lantarón, Lerma, Osma, Palenzuela, Saldaña (de Ojeda), Valdivia, Valdivielso y de tierras de Palencia. Existían varias Villa de Bascones: Villa Bascones de Sotoscuevas, Villa Bascones de Bezana, Villa Vascones en Cardeña; algunos Basconcillos: de Toso en Villadiego, de Muñó cerca de Burgos y otros en Cardeña y en Levilla; un Bascoñuelos en Vallarcayo, un Bascuñana en Belorado y un Vizaínos en tierras de Lara y Salas.
>
> Otros por su estirpa éuscara acreditan, también, migraciones colonizadoras vascas. Aparecen especialmente en Oca y Briviesca: Amunartia, Arcaya, Ayabarre, Cihuri, Esquerra, Galarde, Galbarros, Herramel, He-

terrena, Larrahederra, Urrez, Urquiza, Zaballa, Zabarrula, Zalduendo, Zorraquín, Zuneda y un Xafarruri (Sánchez Albornoz 1966, 314).

In fact, settlers with Basque names form the largest single identifiable group beside that of persons with Roman and Gothic names. Towns and villages such as those mentioned above and others like *Váscones, Basconcillos, Bascuñuelos (-las), Villabáscones* (*Orígenes* §98.1; Menéndez Pidal 1960, xlv-slvi) continued to be founded in the eleventh and twelfth centuries, and also appear in areas far outside of the early limits of Castile (Lantolf 1974, 324).[8]

One might ask whether this deliberate identification of groups of settlers as Basques necessarily means that all these persons were speakers of Basque, or whether they could simply have been persons with Basque names who spoke Romance. No positive answer can be given, but the existence of Basque speakers is guaranteed in La Rioja (on the border between Castile and Navarre) in the *Glosas emilianenses* in the tenth century. Two of the glosses are written in Basque along with the remaining Romance-Latin glosses (*Orígenes* §97.2). As late as the thirteenth century, the inhabitants of Ojacastro in La Rioja had the right to testify in court in the Basque language (*Orígenes* §41.6). These few data allow us to conclude that during a fairly long period, Basque and Romance were both used and that there were undoubtedly numbers of bilinguals. One additional fact deserves to be stressed: during the earliest years of the constitution of the county and kingdom of Castile, when the inhabitants were gradually coming to identify themselves as Castilians and to think of themselves as a people separate from their neighbors, neither Basque nor Romance were considered as anything other than household tongues, useful for ordinary conversation alone. There was for a long time no special Romance literary form of the language distinct from standard written Latin. Of equal importance was the fact that for many centuries the principal element that served to unite and distinguish all settlers was not ethnic or linguistic origin, but religion.[9]

---

[8] "Estos grupos originarios de Occidente tuvieron escasa importancia en el poblamiento del país castellano en comparación con el aluvión humano procedente de Vasconia y, sobre todo, de Cantabria, que suministró el mayor contingente de repobladores hasta la línea del Duero. Fueron éstos, principalmente, los que imprimieron su espíritu y marcaron de modo indeleble la futura existencia del reino castellano. También de procedencia vascona fueron la mayoría de habitantes que pasaron a establecerse en las comarcas de la Rioja y alto Ebro" (Font Rius 1957, 286). ". . . [E]n estos primeros documento de la repoblación castellana [i.e. in the ninth century], y que conviene comentar, es la presencia casi exclusiva de nombres latinos o ibéricos. En Mena, en Losa, Brañosera y en Valdegovia, los repobladores son cántabros, astures o vascones; cántabros sobre todo. Los cinco primeros habitantes de Brañosera se llamaban Félix Valero, Zono, Cristuébalo y Cervello; los primeros compañeros de Vítulo en Mena: Ervigio, Armentario, Iñigo, Eugenio, Belastar, Gersio, Nona, y así en todas partes" (Pérez de Urbel 1969, 148).

[9] Failure to consult original sources, which demonstrate conclusively the massive participation of Basques and Cantabrians in the early repopulation of Castile, accounts for claims such as Castro's: "El no haberse romanizado lingüísticamente descubre, sin más, su escasa participación en la vida del resto de la Península" (Castro 1966, 151), on which Izzo (1977) bases his claim that it is most unlikely that there can be any Basque influence in the well-

Eventually the speakers of Basque who participated in the Reconquest gave up their original language, and as they came to feel themselves to be Castilians, adopted the Romance dialect. However, the long period of bilingualism can well be imagined to have had an effect on certain features of the evolving Romance of Castile. That is, during the period in which the Basques were ceasing to think of themselves as Basques, and were taking Romance as their language, there were undoubtedly many who still kept some feature of Basque in their pronunciation of the evolving Castilian dialect. These are discussed at greater length in this chapter. Suffice it to say at this point that one was possibly the favoring of a particular articulation of Latin /f-/ and the other the merger of the voiced and voiceless sibilants. It is hardly necessary to conceive of these phenomena as having been general among all Romance speakers in early Castile. Such forms of pronunciation merely had to become established as viable alternate forms of speaking (variables) among certain groups of speakers. Once established, they would then be learned by younger speakers who knew nothing of Basque. They could then spread to those regions where no Basques need ever have gone, carried by settlers from the primitive Castile. It is possible too that these variables were looked down on as vulgar pronunciations and were avoided by the better class of speakers.

We should note too that once Castile had become an independent kingdom and the dominant power in northern Spain and had moved south of Burgos, especially after the conquest of Toledo in 1085, it lost much of its early egalitarian character. The area to the south of the Guadarrama mountains even took a new name, "New Castile," which differed noticeably from "Old Castile." The repopulation of this area was not by popular settlement (**presura**) as in earlier centuries but was formally and effectively directed by the crown and council. The military orders, created to protect the land from the Almohads, also took charge of repopulation, with a strong influence of manorial and latifundist type of settlement (Font Rius 1957, 270–73).

The social fluidity that had characterized early Castilian society gradually gave way to a fairly rigid social structure (Lantolf 1974, 266). The conquest of Toledo and especially the establishment of the dialect of Toledo as the prestige model for the emerging literary language also may have served to keep some features of pronunciation in a position of social inferiority for some time. The spread of elements of lower class speech may have been aided, however, not only by the continuous movement southward of people from the north, but also by another factor, namely, covert prestige. In literary usage and in the estimation of the members of the upper classes, who became increasingly separated from the lower classes

known shift of Lat. /f/ > /h/. It is obvious that there were two groups of Basques: the ones who stayed home and kept aloof from the affairs of the rest of the peninsula, as, for example, in Navarre where Lat. /f/ was maintained, and those who became immigrants and participated fully in the organization of the evolving territory of Castile.

as the Middle Ages wore on, the use of [h] for /f/ and the abandonment of voiced sibilants may have been considered somewhat vulgar. It is entirely likely that among many speakers there existed at the same time a hidden, but no less real, admiration for these aspects of Castilian as somehow characteristic of a tough, aggressive attitude toward life. Such covert prestige is often a powerful factor in the maintenance of socially disapproved aspects of life.[10] It is also possible that the great population shifts of the sixteenth century which led to the migration of large numbers of people from northern Castile to the south with the breakdown of the internal economy may have reinforced the shift to phonetic features characteristic of the north, in other words, those influenced by Basque-Romance bilingualism (Sturcken 1969, 304).

In short, as Castile developed into a distinctive entity in the life of early medieval Spain, consciously asserting its personality as somehow different from that of the other Christian kingdoms of the north, its language likewise came to be distinctive. As a twelfth-century writer expressed it: "Castellae vires per saecula fuere rebelles" (*Orígenes* §99.4c). Its language was also rebellious to some of the norms of early Ibero-Romance, as will be seen.

THE PHONOLOGICAL SYSTEM

Vowels

The vowel system of Ibero-Romance was the one that had resulted from the changes that had affected all vowels in Late-Latin: namely, the loss of the quantitative system and those changes that occurred in western Romance: the merger of /i e:/ > /ẹ/, /u o:/ > /ọ/, and /a a:/ > /a/. As pointed out briefly in chapter 2, there is a sufficiently large number of words in Spanish which retain /u/ as the medieval and modern reflex of the Latin short /u/ as to lead us to believe that the merger of /u/ and /u:/ occurred after the merger of their front counterparts (see the next section). The vowel system that was eventually established (as opposed to the outcome of any one word or group of words) was the seven vowel system that we saw in the preceding chapter:

	FRONT	CENTRAL	BACK
HIGH	/i/		/u/
MID CLOSE	/ẹ/		/ọ/
MID OPEN	/ɛ/		/ɔ/
LOW		/a/	

Some examples of the results of the Late Latin tonic vowels in Castilian are given below, with the exception of the mid open vowels /ɛ/ and /ɔ/.

---

[10] See the section on sound change in chapter 1 for some remarks on covert prestige. One who assumes that there is only one type of prestige can hardly ever account for the persistence of condemned features of speech in the face of overt disapproval.

From this point on, Latin etyma will be given in the form of the accusative singular, minus the final /-m/:

/iː/ > /i/
FĪCU > *figo* 'fig'
FĪLIA > *fija* 'daughter'
GINGĪVA > *enzía* 'gum'
PĪNU > *pino* 'pine tree; fir'
SCRĪPTU > *escrito* 'written'
VĪTA > *vida* 'life'

/i/ /eː/ > /ẹ/
AURICULA > *oreja* 'ear'
CAPILLU > *cabello* 'hair'
CIPPU > *cepo* 'stake; branch'
VIRIDE > *verde* 'green'
PARIĒTE > *pared* 'wall'
PLĒNU > *lleno* 'full'
RĒGE > *rey* 'king'
SĒMITA > *senda* 'path'

/uː/ > /u/
ACŪTU > *agudo* 'sharp'
DŪRU > *duro* 'hard'
FŪMU > *humo* 'smoke'
LACTŪCA > *lechuga* 'lettuce'
NŪDU > *nudo* 'knot'
SĒCŪRU > *seguro* 'secure'

/u/ /oː/ > /ọ/
BUCCA 'puffed cheek' > *boca* 'mouth'
CUBITU > *cobdo* 'elbow'
ROTUNDU > *redondo* 'round'

(H)UMERU > *hombro* 'shoulder'
FORMŌSU > *hermoso* 'beautiful'
*NŌMINE > *nombre* 'name'
PRAECŌNE > *pregón* 'crier'
SŌLE > *sol* 'sun'

/aː/ /a/ > /a/
ARĀNEA > *araña* 'spider'
MĀTRE > *madre* 'mother'
PĀNE > *pan* 'bread'
PRĀTU > *prado* 'meadow'
ANNU > *año* 'year'
PATRE > *padre* 'father'
STABULU > *establo* 'stable'

The Final Results of /u/ vs. /uː/

If we take the preceding outline of the seven-vowel system as the norm for all of western Romance, it would be essential to consider any words whose phonetic outcome does not reflect this norm to be in some way aberrant. As we saw briefly in our discussion of the problem in chapter 1, when such exceptions to a particular "sound law" are few and easily accounted for, they usually merit little discussion in a text that seeks to deal with the average, or normal development. As their number increases, however, we may find ourselves in somewhat of a dilemma. How many examples do we need to establish a general law, and, conversely, how many exceptions to a putative law are required to invalidate such a law?

We would expect that the vast majority of examples of words in Latin with the short high back vowel /ŭ/ in tonic syllables would show the outcome we have just seen in the preceding section, and indeed, we can find many examples of a regular development to /o/ in addition to the few examples given there. It would not do, however, to leave out of consideration at this point the fairly large number of words that show the change /ŭ/ > /u/:

CRUCE 'cross' > Sp. *cruz*
SUMMA 'sum; gist, main point' > Sp. *suma*
JUGU 'yoke' > Sp. *yugo*
DUBITA 'doubt' > OSp. *dubda*, Port. *dúvida*
MUNDU 'world' > Sp. *mundo*
NUMQUAM 'never' > Sp. *nunca*
JUNCU 'reed' > Sp. *junco*
PUNCTU 'point, small hole' > Sp. *punto*
FURTU 'robbery, theft' > Sp. *hurto*
SULCUS 'furrow, trench' > Sp. *surco*, Port. *sulco*
PUGNU 'fist' > Sp. *puño*
*CUNEA (C.L. CUNEUS) > Sp. *cuña* 'wedge'
RUBEU 'reddish' > Sp. *rubio* 'blond', Port. *ruivo*
PLUVIA 'rain' > Sp. *lluvia*, Port. *chuva*
FUGIŌ 'I flee' > Sp. *huyo*
LUCTA 'struggle' > Sp. *lucha*
TRUCTA 'trout' > Sp. *trucha*
CONDUCTU > Sp. *conducho* 'a dish eaten with bread'
A(U)SCULTŌ 'I listen' > OSp. *ascucho*
MULTU 'much' > Sp. *mucho*
VULTURE 'vulture' > Sp. *buitre*
DULCE 'sweet' > OSp. *duz/duce* (MSp. *dulce*)
*CULMINE 'top, summit, ridge' (C.L. CULMEN, neuter) > Sp. **la cumbre**
PULPA 'meat, flesh' > Sp. *pulpa*
VULTU 'face' > Sp. *bulto* 'form, shape; bulk'
IMPULSU 'push' > Sp. *empujo*
SULPHURE 'sulphur' > Sp. *azufre*

Some Portuguese words contrast conspicuously with their Castilian cognates that show the normal western change to /ǫ/:

CURTU 'shortened' > Port. *curto* 'short' (Sp. *corto*)
CURVU 'crooked' > Port. *curvo* 'curved, arched' (Sp. *corvo*)
FUNDU 'deep' > Port. *fundo* (Sp. *hondo*)
URSU 'bear' > OPort. *usso*, Mod. Port. *urso* (Sp. *oso*)
SURDU 'deaf' > Port. *surdo* (Sp. *sordo*)
PLUMBU 'lead' > Port. *chumbo* (Sp. *plomo*)

As we remarked in chapter 1, it would be possible to settle matters simply by deciding that all words showing the change of /ŭ/ > /u/ must have been "learned," i.e., borrowed from the innovative pronunciation of medieval Latin, rather than being ordinary popular words. Such a solution is certainly not impossible in a number of cases in which the word may have appeared frequently in religious contexts such as *cruz*, *mundo*, and *suma*. In a number of cases, too, it might well be that special phonetic conditions favored the retention of the older [u], e.g., when /u/ was followed by an implosive nasal, which, as we see in other words, sometimes does have the tendency to close slightly the preceding vowel, e.g., COMITE > *conde*, OSp. *cuemde* 'count', HOMINE > Sp. *hombre* (found along with OSp. *huembre*). And, as we shall see later, the presence of a following yod can account for /u/ rather than /o/ in words containing the group /kt/, or the combination /-ult-/ (see the section on the various yods). When we have to do with other words containing an implosive liquid /-l/ the outcomes seem to be most irregular. In the case of *cumbre*, *empujo*, and *azufre*, the liquid has simply disappeared altogether. How then do we explain *dulce*? In medieval Castilian, in addition to the forms cited above we also find *doz* and *doce*, paralleling Port. *doce*. Evidently speakers created a number of by-forms which competed with each other until the modern form *dulce* came to dominate. And lastly we note those words containing another liquid, a syllable-final /-r/, such as *hurto*, and Port. *surdo*, *curto*, *curvo*.

In the end too, we are still left with a few ordinary rural agricultural terms like *yugo* and *surco* that cannot be easily explained through any special phonetic conditions or as the result of learned transmission. A full analysis of the special circumstances surrounding each word would take up more space than is available here, but the little we have presented should suffice to show that there are enough cases of the preservation of /u/ as /u/ rather than /o/ to need careful attention rather than a wholesale dismissal of all such examples as unimportant aberrant developments. A number of cases could be accounted for through a sort of zig-zag movement, i.e., the assumption that in Late Latin the short /u/ consistently merged with /o:/ and then was pulled back up to /u/ again by special phonetic conditions, such as the yod. An attractive alternate explanation is that of Malkiel 1983. In his view, Ibero-Romance had originally had a very conservative vowel system that much more closely approximated that of early Latin, such as that found in archaic areas like Sardinia. It was then overlaid by a dynamic innovating vowel system, the one usually attributed to "Western Romance," illustrated in the preceding section. The scene in Hispania as he views it, is that of a very conservative form of Latin-Romance, which from the third to the sixth centuries A.D., was swept by a newer fashion in pronunciation that identified not only the Latin short high front vowel and the mid long front vowel, but also their back counterparts. As the new fashion of pronunciation reached the peninsula, its effect was the creation of a number of articulatory doublets of existing words. In most cases the more advanced forms with the vowel /o/ eventually managed to make themselves the common norm. During the period of competition of the older and the newer standards, however, special phonetic conditions could tend to favor the older forms, while the area most distant from the center of innovation (i.e., Galicia and subsequently Lusitania) might retain even older forms simply through general conservatism. Isolated rural areas too, might have tended to be somewhat more resistant to the newer fashions.[11]

The Diphthongization of /e/ and /o/

As was pointed out in the previous chapter, it is likely that the mid open vowels had been subjected to some kind of differentiation in their realization, resulting in an incipient diphthong with a tendency to exaggerate the difference in the articulation of the beginning and the end. Even when the articulation of these vowels had become more clearly diphthongal, they probably continued to function phonologically as single phonemes. It seems likely too that the phonetic realization of the diphthong could vary considerably, even in the pronunciation of a single speaker. In some isolated modern Leonese dialects (and formerly in Aragonese), for example, there is no clear-cut phonetic norm for the realization of the diphthong. In these Leonese dialects, the reflexes of /o/ and /e/ may be [wo], [wö], [wa], [úə], and [ja], [je] (Zamora Vicente 1967, 91–92; Catalán 1956–57, 79–85).[12] The accent can fall more perceptibly on the initial portion of the diphthong, although it is more likely to fall on the middle. There are certain regular phonetic developments that indicate that the early Castilian diphthongs must have been like these.

A good example is the development of the group -ORIU as in Lat. CO-RIUM 'leather'. The anticipation of the yod following the /r/ must have produced a combination of vowels like [oi] which was identified by speakers as the same diphthong as the one resulting from the breaking of /o/. thus in modern Spanish the form that CORIUM took is *cuero*. If the /o/ had gone immediately to [we], it would not have sounded similar to [oi̯] and CORIUM might have remained as *coiro*, as indeed it does in Portuguese *coiro*. The Latin AUGURIUM developed in the same way into Sp. *agüero*. Likewise the development of Lat. QUŌ MODŌ 'how' > OSp. *cuemo* shows that the segment [uo] must have been interpreted by speakers as a realization of the diphthong from /o/. It therefore shared the same fate as all diphthongs from /o/.[13] Both of these cases indicate that

---

[11] A full consideration of all aspects of this topic would require far more space that can be given here, and would inevitably involve consideration of the shift of /ĭ/ > /i/.

[12] Catalán and Galmés 1954 point out that speakers are frequently unaware of phonetic diphthongs in their own speech: "los diptongos en su época originaria pueden pasar inadvertidos al propio hablante para quien no son sino variantes especialmente expresivas de la vocal larga. Esta inconsciencia la encontramos hoy en algunas regiones en que la diptongación es, hasta cierto punto, incipiente: así por ejemplo en Ancora (Miño portugués) un individuo que decía *puorto, puoco*, creía pronunciar solamente «*o muito fechado*»"(96).

[13] It is sometimes thought that the development of /e/ before /ļ/ < /l:/, which regularly becomes /i/ in Castilian, can be considered a further example of fluctuating accent on the diphthong, e.g CASTELLU 'castle' > *castiello* > MSp. *castillo*. It is assumed that if the diphthong had originally been pronounced as an on-gliding one, with stress clearly on the /e/, i.e. [jé], it would hardly have monophthongized to /i/. With the accent not clearly on

the very earliest Castilian diphthongs had fluctuating realizations. Ibero-Romance diphthongization (excluding the westernmost areas where it did not occur and Catalan which only has diphthongization of the Provençal type) is characterized by its appearance in all stressed syllables, which may be an archaic feature, if we suppose that at the beginning of the process, when the realization of the vowel was as a semidiphthong, the semidiphthong could appear in all syllables (Spore 1972, 176). Castilian thus resembles the other Ibero-Romance dialects which diphthongize in this respect. Two special features, however, distinguish it from the surrounding dialects:

1) The absence of diphthongs before a yod, including those verb forms that contained a yod in Late Latin:

NOCTE > *noche* 'night' (Leon. *nueche*)
HODIĒ > *hoy* 'today' (Leon. *vué, ué*; Aragonese *güey*)
OCULU > *ojo* 'eye' (Leon. *ueyo*; Aragonese *güello*) (Mozarabic *ualyo*
   [*Orígenes* §25.3)
TENEŌ > *tengo* 'I have' (Leon.-Arag. *tiengo*)

(examples from Zamora Vicente 1967, 93, 93, 218,
93, 218, 98, 218)

This particular feature of Castilian makes it doubtful that diphthongization was controlled in any fashion by the presence of palatals, as it was in Provençal and Catalan.

It is, of course, entirely possible that Castilian originally diphthongized before a yod as its neighboring dialects did, but then monophthongized the diphthongs to /e/ and /o/ which thereafter remained unaltered. But then we cannot account for the diphthongization in all other syllables, unless it is supposed that Castilian adopted the diphthongs from other dialects with which it came into contact as it spread beyond its original confines. This is possible, but so far no explanation has been offered as to why Castilian, once it had begun its march to the south, should in this case have borrowed a linguistic feature from other dialects.[14] What most probably happened in Castilian was that the /ę/ and /ǫ/ followed by the yod were raised by anticipation of the following high element. As we will see later this kind of anticipation was a very common occurrence. In all other tonic syllables not so affected, the process of diphthongization could go to completion.

2) The early establishment of a single realization of the diphthong from /ǫ/ was as /ue/. The perpheral areas of Castile may have continued to maintain the older, fluctuating realizations, or preferred a more archaic

---

the last portion, or even on the initial portion, the change to /i/ is more comprehensible, but this example may not be a good one in view of the possibility of analogical influence. The ending -*illo*, after all, is a diminutive suffix. It is more likely that this particular change may owe more to the influence of the other diminutive suffixes, -*ito*, -*ico*, -*ín* than to phonetic change (Malkiel 1968, 55–63; RPh 23, 188, note).

[14] See especially Alonso 1962, 37–45.

diphthong [wo]. In the most northern part of primitive Castile (Valpuesta, Santander) and in the south, as late as the twelfth century, this form of the diphthong may have been found, although undoubtedly other realizations may also have existed at the same time.[15] Around Burgos, however, from the tenth century onward, the modern /ue/ became fixed as the dominant result, expelling all other variants.

The reason why this particular form of the diphthong was chosen may be simply analogy with the other diphthong /ie/. In some contexts, a word containing the /ie/ diphthong would have alternated frequently with another word with the diphthong from /o/: *bien* 'well' < BENE — *buono*, *bueno* 'good' < BONU (Corbett 1970–71, 289). Another factor that may have influenced the choice of /ue/ was the acoustic quality of the vowel [e]. [e] of all the vowels combines the greatest amount of perceptibility with the greatest degree of sharpness. If, for example, the vowels are ranked by perceptibility, they go in the following order from grave to sharp: [u o a e i]. If placed on a two dimensional graph the following results are seen:

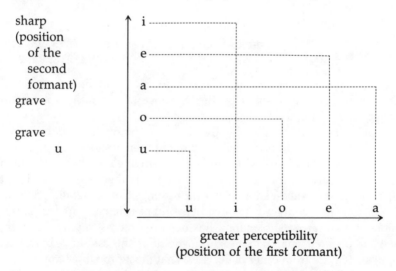

greater perceptibility
(position of the first formant)

It can be seen that [e] represents a mid-way point between the maximum sharpness of [i] and the maximum perceptibility of [a]. Since one of the characteristics of Castilian from its earliest days has been the clarity and precision of its vowels, /ue/ was therefore the best choice for the result of diphthongization in this dialect (Badía Margarit 1962).

Once the elements of the diphthongs had ceased to be felt by speakers to be single phonemic units and the glides were identified with the asyllabic allophones of the high vowels /i/ and /u/, the vowel system of Castilian

---

[15] Some of the rimes in the text of the *Cantar de mio Cid* seem to reflect the [wo] diphthong. Menéndez Pidal therefore assumes that the original form of the text had a fairly archaic linguistic aspect, but his view has been sharply contested in recent years (Smith 1972, xlv).

had only five vowels, as it does today: /i e a o u/. Some examples of the
diphthongs resulting from the Late Latin /ę/ and /ǫ/, are the following:

/ai̯, ę/ > /ie/

CASTELLU > *castiello* 'castle'
FERRU > *fierro* 'iron'
PETRA > *piedra* 'stone'
VENIT > *viene* 'he comes'
CAECU > *ciego* 'blind'
GRAECU > *griego* 'Greek'
QUAERŌ > *quiero* 'I want'

/ǫ/ > /ue/

BONU > *bueno* 'good'
COLLOCŌ > *cuelgo* 'I hang up'
FORTE > *fuerte* 'strong'
LONGE > *lueñe* 'far, distant'
SOLU > *suelo* 'soil, earth'

Atonic Vowels

Since the diphthongization of the lower mid vowels only occurred in
accented syllables, in atonic syllables the distinction between the two kinds
of mid vowels was not exaggerated, and only two mid vowels remained:
/e/ and /o/ < /ę ę/ and /ǫ ǫ/. Thus, the result is a five vowel system:
/i e a o u/. Some examples in word-initial syllables are the following:

/iː/ > /i/

CĪVITĀTE > *cibdad*
HĪBERNU > *ivierno* 'winter'
TĪTIŌNE > *tizón* 'firebrand'

/i eː e ai̯/ > /e/

LIGŌNE > *legón* 'type of hoe'
VINDICĀRE > *vengar* 'to avenge'
SĒCŪRU > *seguro* 'secure'
MENSURA > *mesura* 'measure'
SENIŌRE > *señor* 'lord'
LEGUMINE > *legumbre* 'vegetable'
PRAECŌNE > *pregón* 'crier'

/aː a/ > /a/

ABSCONDERE > *asconder*
ALIĒNU > *ajeno* 'alien'
PĀNĀRIA > *panera* 'breadbasket'

/uː/ > /u/

DŪRITIA > *dureza* 'hardness'
SCŪTELLA > *escudiella* 'bowl'

/u oː o au̯/ > /o/

SUSPECTA > *sospecha* 'suspicion'
RUGĪTU > *roído* 'noise'
FORMĀCEU > *formazo* 'earthen wall'
NŌMINĀRE > *nombrar* 'to name'
AUTUMNU > *otoño* 'autumn'
AURICULA > *oreja* 'ear'

Non-initial and non-final pretonic and posttonic vowels were generally
lost, since they were the most weakly accented of all (chap. 3, note 7). They
are discussed in the section on syncope. Vowels in word-final position
continued to be five in number for many centuries, although there was a
strong tendency to merge the high and mid vowels which eventually
triumphed. During the earliest centuries, however, say up to the eleventh
century, the five vowel system remained for the most part intact. Some
words in later literary Castilian such as *otri* 'another' < ALTERĪ 'others',
and *nadi*, which is more likely to have been influenced by *otri* than to be a

direct descendant of NĀTĪ 'born' (Malkiel 1945), persist with a final /-i/, but it is likely that these forms were maintained because of their association with *qui* 'who' < QUĪ. From documentary evidence it appears that final /-i/ was tending to be merged with /-e/ from a fairly early period, especially in Castile. As we shall see later, it may be that the loss of final /-e/ began with the loss of /-i/ first.[16]

The preservation of the distinction between /-u/ and /-o/, derived from the Late Latin case endings /-us, -um/ versus /-os, -o/, lasted longer. Early documents such as the glosses of San Millán and Santo Domingo de Silos show many examples of a clear distinction between these vowels (provided that we can be certain that the spelling reflects the phonetics): *nafregatu* 'shipwrecked', *cadutu* 'fallen', *kematu* 'burned', *illu* 'that, the' (*Orígenes* §35). One possibility is that the final -U represented a sort of high mid labialized vowel that later became identified with either /-o/ or /-u/ depending on the dialect (López García 1977–78). The form derived from the accusative singular -UM was strongly influenced by the plural -OS, so that frequently the singular appears in the glosses with a final -O, as in later Castilian, e.g., *terzero* 'third', *nuestro dueno* 'our lord', *elo* 'the', etc. This analogical influence was probably the principal factor in the final merger of /-o/ and /-u/ into the medieval and modern /-o/. Other Hispanic dialects continue to show traces of the Latin /-u/ in the singular versus /-os/ in the plural (Blaylock 1964–65a, 268–69).

Monophthongization of Off-Gliding Diphthongs: /ai/ > /ei/ > /e/

In Late Latin a number of words and some affixes developed a new off-gliding diphthong (a sequential diphthong) /ai̯/, distinct from the older Latin AE which had monophthongized to /ę/ long before. Some of the words in which it appeared were from non-Latin sources, while in other cases the palatal off-glide developed from the voiced velar /g/ before a front vowel. Since it was evidently more weakly articulated than the palatal resulting from /d/ and /g/ plus a yod, it was absorbed by the front vowel, and if the preceding vowel had been /a/, the result was /ai̯/, unless, of course, the /i/ was stressed/. Finally, the first person singular of the perfect of Conjugation I verbs had become /-ai/ following the loss of intervocalic -V-:

VAIKA (Pre-Roman) 'plain' (> *vega*)
LAICU 'lay; non-clerical' (> *lego*)
MAGICU 'magical' > [mai̯go] (> OSp. *mego* 'affable')
PLANTAGINE 'broom plant' > [plantai̯ne] (> *llantén*)
SARTAGINE 'frying pan' > [sartai̯ne] (> *sartén*)

---

[16] The final /-i/ vs. /-e/ in Castilian is difficult to study because of the problem of apocope, which probably started with the /-i/. Likewise with /-u/ vs. /-o/ there is undoubtedly much analogical influence of the plural morpheme -*os* on the singular form.

FARRAGINE 'fodder' > [far:aịne] (> *herrén*)
*AMAI 'I loved' (> *amé*)

Another source of this new diphthong was the yod produced when a non-palatalizing consonant was followed by a yod which was later anticipated and metathesized into the preceding syllable:

-ĀRIU (agential suffix) > -*airo* (> -*ero*)
ĀREA 'threshing floor' > [aịra] (> *era*)
GLĀREA 'gravel' > [glaịra] (> *glera*)
CAPIAT (← CAPERE 'to take', seize') > [kaịpat] (> *quepa*)
SAPIAT 'he may know' (← SAPERE) > [saịpat] (> *sepa*)
CASEU 'cheese' > [kaịsu] (> *queso*)

A final source of /aị/ was the yod produced by the syllable-final /-k/ preceding a consonant:

LACTE 'milk' > [laịte] (> *leche*)
FACTU 'done; deed' > [faịtu] (> *fecho*)
TAXU 'yew tree' > [taịsʲu] (> *texo*)
AXE 'axis' > [aịsʲe] (> *exe*)
FRAXINU 'poplar' > [fraịsnu] (> *fresno*)

In the most archaic regions, e.g., in the south after the Moslem conquest, /ai/ seems to have been widely preserved (*Orígenes* §18.2), but in the north an assimilation of the nucleus of the diphthong produced the diphthong /eị/ in most areas, e.g., Port. *carreira, leite, amei*, etc. Castile distinguished itself by monophthongizing the /eị/ to /e/, although once more the most northerly regions preserved the /eị/ longer than the area around Burgos. Those words containing the /aị/ from a late contraction of the /a/ and /i/ in separate syllables (e.g., -[aịn] < -AGINE) preserve a diphthongal form as late as the thirteenth century.

$$/au/ > /ou/ > /o/$$

A similar evolution affected the back diphthong /aụ/, producing the assimilated diphthong [oụ], which apparently was fairly unstable in comparison with [eị] (*Orígenes* §§19–21). Castile and Aragon eliminated the diphthong by the eleventh century at the latest, monophthongizing it to the modern /o/:

CAUSA 'cause; motive; thing' > *cosa* 'thing'
AUTUMNU 'autumn' > *otoño*
TAURU 'bull' > *toro*
MAURU 'from Mauretania' > *moro* 'Moor; Moslem'

As pointed out in the preceding chapter, when /aụ/ preceded a velar consonant followed by /u/, it was simplified to /a/ in Late Latin:

AUGUSTU 'August' > *agosto*
AUGURIU 'omen' > *agüero*

A secondary /au̯/ also appeared as a result of the evolution of form 3 of the Latin perfect of Conjugation 1: -ĀVIT > -AUT. In Castile this ending quickly became -ó (-ót, -ód), e.g., AMĀVIT 'he loved' > amó.

As we saw in the section on the outcomes of words containing the Latin /u/, the development of the implosive /-l/ was subject to all sorts of special outcomes. The commonest tendency seems to have been to convert the /-l/ to a vocalic articulation. Thus, another secondary /au/ developed from a vocalization of the implosive /-l/ after /a/ and preceding a consonant. The lateness of this development meant that it appeared at the time that the original /au/ had become /o/, or was almost completed in Castile, and thus the new diphthong tended to remain rather isolated. In the tenth and eleventh centuries a variety of forms are attested:

ALTĀRIU > Leon. *autario, autairo, octejro, otero* 'hill'
SALTU > Port. *sauto, souto*; Leon. *sauto, soto* 'small woods'
ALTU 'high' > Cast. (Villa) *auta, Villota, Oto, Otura* (place names)
ALBU 'white' > (Penna) *Alba, Auba, Ova*; (torre) *Torroba, Torralba* (place names)
CALVU 'bald' > *Cobos* (near Burgos, formerly *Calbos*), *Coviella* (Asturias); *Calvela* (Galicia)

The result in Castilian vocabulary has been to have some forms accepted that reflect a popular change of the late /au̯/ to /o/:

ALTERU > *otro* 'other'
ALTĀRIU > *otero* 'hillock, knoll'
CALCE > *coz* 'kick'

However, in the twelfth century a preference for the more conservative forms expelled all intermediate forms (spelled variously OU, OK, OB) so that a number of other words have come down without any change of the original group:

ALTU > *alto* 'tall'
SALTU > *salto* 'jump'
ALBU > OSp. *albo* 'white'
CALVU > *calvo* 'bald'
CALCEA > *calça* 'trousers'

Only in the case of two words, Lat. SALICE 'willow' and CALICE 'chalice', which developed the diphthong /au/ fairly late, was the intermediate form able to survive: *sauce* and *cauce* 'river bed'. Because of the reaction against the change, this particular development never became general; in other words, it was "terminated" before it was "completed" (Hsieh 1972).

Vowels in Hiatus

Vowels that appeared in hiatus were by and large eliminated in Late Latin so that relatively few persisted in Romance. Ordinarily either one vowel was simply dropped, e.g., BATTUERE > *batir* 'to strike', COQUERE >

cocer 'to cook', or, if one of the vowels was a front vowel, it became a palatal semiconsonant, i.e., the various yods examined in the previous chapter.

If, however, one of the vowels in hiatus was a high vowel and was ·accented, it could not develop into a yod as in other syllables, especially if the high vowel appeared in the penultimate syllable. Thus, in a limited number of words, the high vowel remained stressed and in hiatus in Romance. Examples of such words are the following:

VIA 'road'	TUA 'your' (fem. of the
*DIA (C.L. DIĒS)	possessive adjective)
FUI, FUIT 'I was; he was'	SUA 'his, her' (fem.)
(perfect of ESSE)	GRUE 'crane'

The results in Spanish, *vía*, *día*, *fui*, *fue*, OSp. *túe*, *súe*, and *grúa* (with hypercharacterization of gender through the addition of the feminine ending -*a*, Mod. Sp. *grulla*), would seem to indicate that the hiatus produced a dissimilation of the accented vowel (Lüdtke 1956, 143–44). This dissimilation acted against the normal development of the short high vowels that otherwise would have become /e/ and /o/. Possibly we can imagine that this dissimilation was caused by the effect of the development of a glide between the accented vowel and the following vowel (Meadows 1948). After a front vowel a palatal glide would have developed and after a back vowel, a labiovelar glide. These glides could have served to keep the high vowels intact so that they did not follow the normal development of tonic vowels.

The Combination /eu/

When the accented vowel in hiatus was /e/, its development is somewhat more obscure. The diphthong /eu/ appeared but rarely in older Latin, being found only in five words of native origin: NEU 'and/or not', SEU 'or if', CEU 'like, as', HEU 'alas!', NEUTER 'neither'. It also appeared in a few Greek borrowings like EUROPA, but the native Latin words containing the diphthong all disappeared from popular speech and the Greek words were part of the learned vocabulary and did not form part of the popular lexicon.

In Late Latin-early Romance, a number of words are found in which the combination of the vowels /ẹ/ and /u/ appears. In earlier Latin these vowels had been in hiatus, but it is likely that at this period they were pronounced as a diphthong (a sequential diphthong, unlike the segmental diphthongs resulting from /ę/ and /ǫ/) (Malkiel 1975–76). The words in which this combination appears are:

MEU 'my' (masc.)
DEUS 'god'
JŪDAEU 'Jewish'
*RŌMAEU 'pilgrim headed for Rome'
*EO (< EGO) 'I'

The modern reflexes of MEU and JŪDAEU are *mío* and *judío*; DEUS has produced *dios* [djos], *EO has become *yo*, and *RŌMAEU is now *romero*, obviously an analogical form using the agential suffix *-ero*. Given the varying results and the small number of words involved, one may wonder whether it is possible to know whether this particular combination was a diphthong at an early period rather than two vowels in hiatus. One indication in favor of the diphthongal solution is Portuguese which consistently shows the diphthong [ęu] in its reflexes of these words: *meu, deus, judeu, eu,* and OPort. *romeu*.

If this evidence from another branch of Ibero-Romance is accepted, then it may be legitimate to see this late and rare diphthong in the context of the other off-gliding diphthongs just studied above. Since Castilian was in the process of monophthongizing /ai̯/ and /au̯/, it seems likely that if [ęu] had existed at this time, it would have been swept along by this same structural current. In that case, the modern results with [jo] should be compared with the medieval reflexes of MEU and JŪDAEU which, in fact, turn out to have been *mió* and *judió*. A reasonable conclusion might be that the off-gliding diphthong /ęu̯/ was replaced by an on-gliding one, /jo/.

In the case of /ai̯/ and /au̯/, however, we see an assimilation of the nucleus to the glide with the raising of the nucleus to a mid position and a subsequent absorption of the glide. The development of /eu/ seems fundamentally different from them.

First, the regular development of /é/ was to /je/. There is no reason for supposing that the vowel would not diphthongize in this combination to [jęu̯] (Wilkinson 1977, 22). An examination of modern Western Asturian dialects reveals forms like the preceding plus further developments:

EGO 'I'	/jeu/		/jou/
MEU(M) 'my'	/mjeu/	/mjeu/	/mjou/
DEUS 'god'	/djeus/	/djeus/	/djous/
DEDIT 'he gave'	/djeu/	/djeu/	/djou/

Since it is not at all unusual for a dialect or dialect group to preserve the stages of phonetic development through which another, closely related, dialect has passed, we may safely conclude that these developments plausibly represent those in early Castilian (Craddock 1983, 2).

The shift of a front vowel [e] to a back vowel [o], however, may not be a purely phonetic change. The pronoun /jeu/ < E(G)O undoubtedly appeared frequently in syntagmas such as /jeu vou/ < EGO VĀDŌ 'I go' and /sou jeu/ < SU(M) EGO 'it is I', and similar ones in which the monosyllabic verbs derived from VĀDŌ, DŌ, SU(M), and STŌ all develop in parallel fashion. These syntactic combinations could well have induced speakers to rime the pronoun with the verbs and thus produce /jou̯ vou̯/, /sou̯ jou̯/, etc. The shift of /jeu̯/ to /jou̯/ very likely had further analogical influence on the corresponding first person possessive adjective /mjeu/ which would thus have become /mjou/. Form 3 of the verb *dar*, /djeu/, would

Environment 2 and 3, in which the yod is preserved, shows the same kind of raising:

SUPERBIA 'pride' > Sp. *soberbia*
*NERVIU 'sinew' > Sp. *nervio*
PRAEMIU 'prize' > Sp. *premio*
GREGE 'flock, herd' > Sp. *grey*
SEDEAT (subj. of SEDĒRE) > Sp. *sea*

Before the group /kl/, we are faced with a scarcity of data. The only words that can be used as examples are Sp. *viejo* 'old' < Late Lat. VECLU < Lat. VETULUS, a diminutive of VETUS, -ERIS, and *espejo* 'mirror' < SPE-CULU.[20] Judging by the evidence of /o/, which is raised to /o/ by the yod, one might be inclined to think that *espejo* represents the normal development and that some particular explanation must be sought to account for the diphthong in *viejo*. Thus, Menéndez Pidal 1941, 57, believed that there must have been some influence of Leonese on the word. Another possibility is that the diphthong might have been borrowed from OSp. *viedro* < VETERE (Schuchardt, Romania 13, 286, n. 4). Corominas (DCELC IV 727a) argues that it is hardly likely that a rare word like *viedro* or a dialectal form would have influenced a word as common as *viejo*, which must always have formed part of the basic vocabulary of the language.

If *viejo* then is to be considered the regular development, some explanation would then have to be sought for the lack of a diphthong in *espejo*. The reflexes of the word in other languages, e.g., Basque *ispilu* and Catalan *espill*, can be taken to show that the etymon must have been SPICU-LUM, rather than SPECULUM. There may have been also a form in Latin like SPĒCULUM or SPICULUM (García de Diego 1951, 59). We would then be left with only one word having the /e/ before /l/ and would have to conclude that for some reason /e/ was not raised by this yod. Some doubts remain, however. The lack of parallelism with the inflection of /o/ by the /ļ/ causes some surprise. Corominas' argument that /ę/ diphthongized before /ǫ/ is not convincing when we see that there is no diphthongization in verb forms like *tengo* and *vengo* < TENEŌ and VENIŌ.[21] The fact that a word is very common is no argument that it cannot have been influenced by similar forms from dialects in contact with Castilian. Finally one may feel somewhat uneasy at having to construct a sound law on the basis of a single example. It might be best to refrain from making a final decision until there is more conclusive evidence.[22]

---

[20] *Reja* is given by Menéndez Pidal 1941, 49, as an example of /ę/ raised by /ļ/. However, the C.L. form is RĒGULA 'rule, pattern'.

[21] As for /ę/ before /ņ/, Alarcos Llorach discounts the evidence of *engeño* < INGENIU 'nature; invention' because he believes it to be a late word which may be semilearned (1965, 946).

[22] It should be pointed out too that an undiphthongized form, *beia, ueia* appears in the thirteenth century in the *Fuero de Madrid* (Madrid, 1963). Lapesa, in his linguistic study of this *fuero*, remarks that the standard form *viejo* is "contrario a la evolución normal del vocalismo

The Results of /ǫ/

The vowel is raised in all three environments and fails to diphthongize:

OCTO 'eight' > Sp. *ocho* (Port. *oito*)
NOCTE 'night' > Sp. *noche* (Port. *noite*)
OSTREA 'oyster' > OSp. *ostria*
NOVIUS 'somewhat new' > Sp. *novio* 'bridegroom'
HODIĒ 'today' > Sp. *hoy*
MODIU 'corn measure' > Sp. *moyo* 'wine measure'
PODIU 'balcony' > Sp. *poyo* 'stone bench'
FOLIA 'leaves' > Sp. *hoja* 'leaf' (Port. *folha*)
CORDOLIU 'heartache' > Sp. *cordojo*
OCULU 'eye' > Sp. *ojo* (Port. *olho*)

We must pay special attention at this point to the result of words ending -ORIU in Latin. As mentioned previously in the section on diphthongization, we cannot treat a word like CORIUM 'leather' like other examples of /ǫ/ before a yod. We would expect that the yod would raise the vowel and thus prevent diphthongization, but the result in Castilian *cuero*, has what appears to be an ordinary diphthong. As we saw before, the Portuguese *coiro* reveals what must have happened: the metathesis of the yod produced a group that sounded like a diphthong and thus was so treated.

Before /ɲ/ *sueño* 'sleep, dream' and *lueñe* 'far' show a surprising lack of inflection. In the case of *sueño*, it is entirely possible that there never was a yod if the etymon was SOMNUS since this would have developed regularly to *sueño*. Evidently there was a confusion of the two words in Latin, SOMNIUM 'dream' and SOMNUS 'sleep', as in Castilian the same word has both meanings (cf. also Port. *sono*; It. *sogno, sonno*). The evidence of *lueñe* may also be doubtful, in view of the results of Latin /-nge-/ in other words, e.g., *RINGELLA > *renziella* 'quarrel'.[23]

The Results of /ę/

In environments 1 and 3, where the yod disappeared, the mid close front vowel is not raised any further and remains unchanged:

CERV- -ISIA, -ĒSIA 'beer' > OSp. *cervesa* (Port. *cerveja*)
STRICTU 'close, tight' > Sp. *estrecho* 'narrow' (Port. *estreito*)
CORRIGIA 'string, strap' > Sp. *correa*
DESIDIU 'erotic desire' (Late Lat.; C.L. DESIDIA 'idleness') > Sp. *deseo* 'desire'

---

castellano" (157). It is difficult to judge whether to accept this form as a typical Castilian one since one of the chief characteristics of the language of the *fuero* is the relative scarcity of diphthongs. Lapesa believes that this feature may prove only that the diphthongs in this area were still just expressive variants of /e/ and /o/.

[23] The development of yod after /n r l/ has implications beyond those of simple phonetic change, and is discussed more fully in the section on morphological development.

VIDEAT 'he may see' (subj.) > Sp. *vea*
CILIA 'eyelids' > Sp. *ceja* 'eyebrow' (Port. *celha*)
APICULA 'bee' > Sp. *abeja*
SIGNA 'signs' > Sp. *seña* 'flag, sign'
LIGNA 'firewood' > Sp. *leña*

In environment 2, in which the yod remains, the vowel is regularly raised to a high vowel:

VINDĒMIA 'harvest' > Sp. *vendimia*
SEPIA 'cuttlefish' > OSp. *xibia*
VITREU 'made of glass' > Sp. *vidrio* 'glass'
LIMPIDU 'clear' > Sp. *limpio* 'clean' plus many other words in -IDUS[24]

The Results of Lat. /u/ /o:/

We saw previously in the section of the development of the Latin short high vowel that there are many examples which seem to show that it remained as such in Ibero-Romance. Many of these words are those preceding a yod. One can, to be sure, assume that what occurred was a sort of "zig-zag" movement, to use Malkiel's term (1983, 212) from a general merger of /u/ and /o:/ to /o̜/ in Late Latin in the western Empire to a subsequent raising again to /u/ by the yod (Craddock 1980, 65–66). Such a shift is not impossible, but one may wonder if it is really necessary to make this assumption. Could we not as easily conceive of the yod as having preserved the high quality of the original /u/ when the new wave of merger reached Ibero-Romance? Whatever the truth of the matter, the results in Castilian are clear: /u/ remains in all environments in almost all examples.

LUCTA 'struggle' > Sp. *lucha* (OPort. *luita*)
TRUCTA 'trout' > Sp. *trucha*
CONDUCTU (pass. part. of CONDŪCERE 'to bring together') > Sp.
  conducho 'a dish eaten with bread'
A(U)SCULTŌ 'I listen' > OSp. *ascucho*
MULTU 'much' > Sp. *mucho* (Port. *muito*)
VULTURE 'vulture' > Sp. *buitre*
RUBEU 'reddish' > Sp. *rubio* 'blond'
PLUVIA 'rain' > Sp. *lluvia*
PUGNU 'fist' > Sp. *puño*
*CUNEA (C.L. CUNEUS) > Sp. *cuña* 'wedge'
CUNEU > Sp. *cuño* 'die for stamping coins'
FUGIŌ 'I flee' > Sp. *huyo* (Port. *fujo*)

---

[24] TEPIDU > *tibio* 'warm, tepid' must be explained as a result of a diphthongization of /e̜/ to [tiebio] with later loss of the more open element between two high vowels, as in DEUS > [dieos] > *díos* (Malkiel 1952).

We find, however, that the /ḷ/ < /-kl-/ does not preserve the /u/ (or, alternatively, raise the /ǫ/):

GENU- -*CULU 'knee' > OSp. *e-, i-nojo* (OPort. *geolho*)
CUSCULIU 'kermes oak' > Sp. *coscojo*

Several words containing the endings -UMNIA, -ŌNIA, or -ŌNEU show varying outcomes:

CALUMNIA 'trick; false accusation' > *caloña*
SYMPHONIA 'concert' > *zampoña* 'rustic flute'
CICŌNIA 'stork' > *cigüeña*
RISŌNEU > *risueño* 'smiling, laughing'
TERRŌNEU > *terruño* 'native soil'

The forms with a diphthong before the /ṇ/ seem to resemble the results of CORIU, A(U)GURIU, etc. in which an anticipatory metathesis of the yod produced a vowel combination that resembled the ordinary diphthong /ue/ and was absorbed into it. We cannot then account for the result *-uño*, if we take into consideration only phonetic circumstances. If, however, we consider these endings as separate suffixes, they may be seen to be two variant developments of the same Latin suffix which became established as independent suffixes in Castilian. Thus, what appear to be two groups of words may in reality be only two separate morphemes. Thus, words like *risueño, halagüeño, pedigüeño*, etc. may be creations of medieval Castilian with the suffix *-ueño*, rather than Latin formations that developed as whole words. *Caloña* and *zampoña* would require separate explanations. *Zampoña* is a late borrowing, first attested in A.D. 1335 according to the BDELC, and thus may not represent a popular development.

The Yod Before Certain Consonant Groups

In some cases where a yod is formed, the syncope of a posttonic vowel produced a consonantal group that prevented any further change of the preceding consonant. In these cases, the yod was preserved as a semivowel:

PECTINE 'comb' > *peine*[25]
SEX 'six' (before words beginning with consonants) > *seis*
MULTU 'much' > *muit* (before words beginning with consonants) > *muy*
VULTURE 'vulture' > *buitre*

In other cases the yod was absorbed by a preceding /i/ before any change of the consonant occurred:

---

[25] See Malkiel 1953. The preservation of the diphthong /ei/ is unusual because most words in which it was formed later monophthongized to /e/, e.g., PIGNORA 'pawns, pledges' > OSp. *peindra, prenda*, PECTORALE 'chest covering' > OSp. *petral* 'strap put in front of a horse's chest', FRAXINUS 'ash tree' > *fresno*. Malkiel believes that the /ei/ was held back here by the existence of other words having the root *peñ-*: the descendants of two Latin words, PIGNUS 'pawn' > OSp. *peños*, and PINNA 'battlement' > *peña* 'stone, rock' (77).

FĪCTU (C.L. FĪXUS, pass. part. of FĪGERE 'to fix, fasten') > *hito* 'fixed; milestone'

FRĪCTU 'fried' > *frito*

The Yod and the Pretonic Vowels

A yod invariably raises pretonic vowels, even when it subsequently disappeared or if it resulted from the diphthongization of /ẹ/:

COGNATU 'related' > *cuñado* 'brother-in-law'
COCLEARE 'spoon' > OSp. *cuchar*
AUSCULTĀRE 'to listen' > OSp. *ascuchar*
MULIERE 'woman' > OSp. *mugier*
TONSIŌNE 'fleece; > OSp. *tusón*
CAEMENTU 'cement' > *cimiento*
FENESTRA 'window' > *finiestra*
FERVENTE 'boiling' > *firviente*
GENESTA 'broom plant' > *hiniesta*
TENEBRĀS 'darkness' > *tinieblas*

Many of the yods found in the *-ir* conjugation have the effect of raising the pretonic vowel, even when the yod subsequently disappeared:

DORMIĀMUS 'we may sleep' (pres. subj.) > *durmamos*
SENTIĀMUS 'we may feel' (pres. subj.) > *sintamos*

The other forms with pretonic raising are 3 and 6 and the present participle in all of whose endings a yod appears: *durmió-durmieron, murió-murieron, pidió-pidieron, sintió-sintieron, durmiendo, sintiendo,* etc. The medieval perfects and imperfects in *-ié-* also exhibit pretonic vowel raising: *durmié, durmiedes, sintié, sintiemos, sintiedes.*[26]

Syncope and Its Effects

The loss of the vowels in posttonic syllables in contact with liquids and some sibilants has been discussed in chapter 3 as a common phenomenon of Latin from a very early period. It was at first a sporadic phenomenon, limited in practice to certain syllables and certain words. Syncope can, however, be conceived of as a variable rule of Latin which gradually expanded to more and more words and to more and more phonological conditions until finally it became a categorical rule of the language (Reighard 1974). With the increasing separation of the various parts of the Empire, resistance to syncope seems to have weakened in western Romance, most notably in Gallo-Romance. In most of Ibero-Romance the result was the elimination of all pre- and posttonic vowels which were neither initial nor final, with the exception of /a/:

---

[26] The reason for the restriction of the influence of yod to verbs of the *-ir* conjugation is discussed later in this chapter.

ORPHANU 'orphan' > *huérfano*
ORGANU 'organ' > *huérgano* (Leonese)
RAPHANU 'radish' > *rábano*
ANATE 'duck' > *ánade*
PASSAR (C.L. PASSER) 'sparrow' > OSp. *pássaro, páxaro* 'bird'

The force of syncope was weaker the farther west one goes, so that the results in Galician-Portuguese differ notably from those in central and eastern Ibero-Romance.[27] The chief structural effect of this reduction in the number of syllables in some words was to produce some closed syllables which had not existed before.

Consonant plus Liquid

As remarked before, syncope in contact with liquids had occurred quite early (first century B.C.) so that when this tendency was carried to its ultimate conclusion the result was the formation of some new groups. If the loss of a vowel produced a sequence[28] of an occlusive plus a liquid, the new sequence matched previously existing syllable-initial clusters:

FĀBUL- -*ĀRE (C.L. -ĀRĪ) > *fablar* 'to speak'[29]
*MO-BILE (C.L. MŌ-) 'movable' > *mueble* 'piece of furniture'
NEBULA 'cloud' > *niebla*
NUBILU 'cloudy' > *nublo*
STABULU 'stable' > *establo*
RŌBORE 'oak' > *robre* (MSp. *roble*)
LABŌRĀRE 'to work, toil' > *labrar* 'to farm, work the earth'
HEDERA 'ivy' > *yedra*

The pronunication of /b/ was as a fricative [b̄] which might account for its assimilation to the /l/ in a few words, producing a geminate that later palatalized:

INSŪBULU 'cloth beam, warp rod' > *enxullo*
TRIBULU 'threshing sledge' > *trillo* 'spike-toothed harrow'

Voiceless stops became voiced and produced clusters similar to those already produced by syncope alone, although probably they differed in being realized as occlusives [b] [d] rather than as fricatives, thus matching

---

[27] This conclusion seems reasonable as in northern Gallo-Romance all posttonic vowels are lost or reduced to [a], while Galician-Portuguese, the most western Romance variety, retains many posttonic vowels, e.g., CUBITU 'elbow' > *cóvedo*, DEBITA 'debt' > *dívida*, MACULA 'stain' > *mágua*, etc. (Williams 1962, 53).

[28] In this section, as previously, I follow the usage of Pulgram 1970 and use the term *cluster* to refer to groups of consonants that occur within a single syllable, and *sequence* to refer to consonant groups whose members belong to different syllables.

[29] Although the infinitive has the syncope preceding the accent, the most used of the finite forms have the stress preceding, e.g., *hablas, habla, hablan*, etc.

preexisting clusters /-pl-/, /-pr-/, and /-tr-/ which had voiced intervocalically:

DUPLICARE 'to bend double' > *doblegar* 'to fold'
POPULU 'people' > *pueblo*
CAPRA 'goat' > *cabra*
APERĪRE 'to open' > *abrir*
COOPERĪRE 'to cover' > *cobrir*
LEPORE 'hare' > *liebre*
LĀTRĀRE 'to bark' > *ladrar*
PETRA 'stone' > *piedra*
ITERĀRE 'to plow a second time' > *edrar*
VETER-E 'old' > *viedro*

If the syllable preceding the new group ended in a liquid, a nasal or /s/, the resulting sequence was stable:

*COMPERĀRE 'to buy' (C.L. COMPARĀRE) > *comprar*
TEMPORĀNU 'early' > *temprano*

The extensive assimilation of syllable-final consonants to the following consonant in Late Latin had left the language with only liquids, nasals, and /s/ as possible syllable-final consonants. Syncope left some of these consonants that had formerly been intervocalic in a syllable-final position. Since they matched previously existing sequences, they were stable. Voicing of intervocalic occlusives had occurred in most cases before syncope, although in a few examples syncope occurred before voicing. In the case of /s/, syncope evidently occurred consistently before voicing, while with occlusives, voicing occurred before syncope:

*CONSUĒTŪMINE 'custom' > *costumbre*
CONSUTŪRA 'seam; sewing' > *costura*
VĒRITĀTE 'truth' > *verdad*
VERĒCUNDIA 'shame' > *vergüe-ña, -nça*
EREMU 'barren; desert' > *yermo*
CORŌNĀTU 'crowned' > *cornado* 'copper coin'
ALIQUOD 'something' > *algo*
DELICĀTU 'delicate; > *delgado* 'thin'
FAMĒLICU 'famished' (← FAMĒS 'hunger') > *jamelgo* 'nag, jade'
PULIC-A (C.L. PULEX, -ICIS) 'flea' > *pulga*

Nasals plus Consonants

When syncope resulted in bringing an /n/ into contact with an occlusive, the sequence was similar enough to preexisting sequences so as to be accepted with only slight adjustment. That is, the alveolar [n] that came into contact with a dental assimilated to the dental articulation, and the [n] that came into contact with a velar likewise automatically became a velar nasal:

BONITĀTE 'goodness' > *bondad*
REPAENITERE 'to repent' > OSp. *rependir*
VĪCĪNITĀTE 'neighborhood' > *vezindad*
DOMINICU(S) (DIĒS) > *domingo* 'Sunday'
MANICA 'sleeve' > *manga*
TUNICA 'tunic' > *tonga*

New Consonant Sequences

Syncope also brought into contact consonants that had never before formed sequences in Latin-Romance. Such sequences are treated differently from those which fitted smoothly into the existing patterns. Apparently the separation between the new syllable-final consonants and the following consonants was maintained for a considerable period of time so that these consonants did not really form sequences of the same type as the others. It might be, as Menéndez Pidal says, that the speakers had a "living memory" of the lost vowel (*Orígenes* 58.6b), and expressed it by making these syllables more distinct from the following one than were those with the accepted syllable-final consonants. Phonetically, it is likely that these new final consonants were pronounced slightly longer than the others. In writing these syllables scribes occasionally put a vowel after the consonant, although not necessarily the original vowel.[30]

The structural result was that there was now a new kind of syllable in the language, one that was not as smoothly linked to succeeding syllables as were the vast majority of others. Given the aberrant nature of these syllables, they were inherently unstable since they formed only a small class, and did not fit into the structure of the typical syllable. Thus, although they persisted in the language for several centuries at least, speakers began making adjustments to them from the beginning, until finally they eliminated them altogether.[31]

---

[30] For example, *cuempetet* < COMPUTAT 'he calculates, counts' (*Orígenes* §32.5). The conflict of older and newer norms led to cases of anaptyxis when scribes thought that certain consonant sequences must have been due to syncope and tried to restore (incorrectly) the vowel they assumed had been lost, e.g., *gelemo, ellemo* for the correct form *yelmo* 'helmet' < Gmc. HELM (*Orígenes* §40.2).

[31] Catalán claims that syncope produced a new syllable structure in Old Spanish in which open syllables were not preferred: "Me parece claro que el español antiguo . . . no estaba estructuralmente inclinado a dar preferencia al paradigma silábica /c_1v/, y que la tendencia del español del español moderno, no puede considerarse como una característica estructural que presida ininterrumpidamente la evolución diacrónica del español desde la época latina hasta nuestros días" (1971, 81). In support of his conclusion, however, Catalán simply lists a number of words containing the new consonant sequences taken from documents from a variety of different places and widely differing dates covering several centuries of development without any consideration of their total number nor of their frequency of appearance. Only if such sequences had become statistically important would we be justified in speaking

In a few cases new sequences were established, but only when the syllable-final consonant was one that had previously appeared in this position. Thus, where /r/, /n/, or /s/ became final, even when the following consonant was one that had not existed in this combination before, the basic structure of the syllable was in no way different from that of preexisting syllables:

ASINU 'ass' > *asno*
RESECĀRE 'to cut off, cut back' > *resgar, rasgar* 'to tear, rip'
SŌRICE 'shrew mouse' > *sorze*
UNDECIM 'eleven' > *onze*
QUĪNDECIM 'fifteen' > *quinze*
QUATTUORDECIM 'fourteen' > *catorze*

Syllable-Final Nasals

When the bilabial appeared in a syllable-final position, it remained bilabial for some time, although before a dental consonant assimilation began quite early:

COMITE 'companion' > *comde/cuemde* 'count' (> ModSp. *conde*)
LĪMITE 'boundary line' > *limde* 'border' (> ModSp. *linde*)
SĒMITA 'path' > *semd*a (> ModSp. *senda*)
SANCTĪ EMETERĪ > *Sandemder* (> ModSp. *Santander*)

This sequence was sometimes made clearer by the development of an epenthetic consonant which may be simply a reflection of the open of the lips in the transition from the bilabial to the dental: *limbde*. When a bilabial nasal came into contact with a liquid, a regular epenthesis of /b/ occurred, probably because the opening of the lips in this position is more noticeable:

CAMERA 'chamber, room' > *canbra*[32]
CUCUMERE 'cucumber' > *cogonbr-o*
MEMORĀRE 'to remember' > *membrar*
TREMULĀRE 'to tremble, shake' > *temblar*
(H)UMERU 'shoulder' > *onbro*

When /m/ came into contact with /n/, the two nasals were apparently clearly separate so that there was no assimilation of the /m/ as in the

---

as Catalán does. For example, on the basis of words in modern Spanish such as *vals*, *angstrom*, *transparencia*, *constitución*, etc., would we be able to claim that the modern Spanish syllable prefers to end with two or more consonants?

[32] The nasal before a bilabial was often spelled with the letter N (or the tilde over the preceding vowel), but this does not mean that we must interpret it as an alveolar. Juan de Valdés in the early sixteenth century in the *Diálogo de la lengua*, however, says of this spelling: "Bien sé que el latín quiere la m, y que a la verdad parece que stá bien, pero, como no pronuncio sino n, huelgo ser descuidado en esto, y assí, por cumplir con la una parte y con la otra, unas vezes escrivo con m y otras n" (80, l. 9).

original Latin group /mn/ which had produced a geminate /n:/. The resulting sequence was maintained in many Ibero-Romance dialects. In Castile a dissimilation of the /n/ to /r/ took place, with subsequent epenthesis of a bilabial /b/ between the nasal and the new liquid:

AERĀMINE > *aramne* 'wire' > Cast. *alambre*
HOMINE 'man' > *omne/uemne* > Cast. *(h)ombre*
*NŌMINE 'name' > *nomne* > Cast. *nombre*
FĒMINA 'woman' > *femna* > Cast. *fembra*
FAM- *INE (C.L. FAMĒS) 'hunger' > *famne* > Cast. *fambre*

The clear separation between the two nasals before the dissimilation of /n/ became popular is illustrated in certain spellings with the letter P between them:

costumpne, sempnadura (Cast. *costumbre* 'custom', *sembradura* sowing') (*Orígenes* §58.1, note 2)

Final /n/

The /n/ in syllable-final position before a dental or a velar consonant has already been mentioned. Before other consonants the /n/ was much less stable. When immediately followed by /r/, for example, the difficulty of producing a trill after the alveolar contact gave rise either to a prolongation of the [r] or a metathesis:

CINERE 'cinder, ash' > [tˢerne] → *cernada* 'cinder, leach ashes'
GENERU 'son-in-law' > *yerno*
TENERU 'tender' > *tierno*
VENERIS (DIĒS) > 'Friday' > *viernes*
HONŌRĀRE 'to honor' > *honrar* [onr:ár]

Another solution to the problem of the transition from /n/ to /r/ was the epenthesis of a /d/ between them:

CINERE 'ash' > *cendra*
INGENERĀRE 'to engender, generate' > *engendrar*
HONŌRĀRE > *ondrar*

If /n/ preceded another nasal, the eventual result was a dissimilation of the /n/ to a liquid:

ANIMA 'soul' > *alma*
MINIM-*-ĀRE > *mermar* 'to shrink, decrease'

If /n/ preceded two consonants of which the last was also /n/, a dissimilation occurred:
*GLANDINE (C.L. GLANS, GLANDIS 'acorn') > *landre* 'tumor'
*LENDINE (C.L. LENS, LENDIS 'louse egg') > *liendre* 'nit'
INGUINE 'groin' > *ingle*
SANGUINE 'blood' > *sangne* > *sangre*

Other Consonants

The coming into contact of /p/ or /ƀ/ plus a /t/ produced the group /ƀd/:

CAPITĀLE > *cabdal* 'abundance, wealth; principal, foremost'
CAPITELLU (dim. of CAPUT 'head') > *cabdiello* 'chief, leader'
*RE-CAPITĀRE > *recabdar* 'to gather, collect'
BIBITU 'drunk' > *bebdo*
CUBITU 'elbow' > *cobdo*
DĒBITA 'debt' > *debda*
DUBITĀRE 'to doubt, hesitate' > *dubdar*
CĪVITĀTE 'body of citizens' > *cibdad* 'city'

The bilabials before other consonants were rare and considerably less stable than before dentals:

FABRICA 'forge' > [fraƀga] *frauga* > *fragua*
-IFICĀRE > [-ibgar] *-iguar*, e.g., *apaziguar* 'to pacify', etc.

By and large, syllable final dentals were rather unstable and subject to a variety of changes, the most common being metathesis:

CATĒNĀTU 'chained' > *cadnado* 'lock' > *cañado/candado*
LEGITIMU 'legitimate' > [lidmo] > *lindo* (OSp. *mugier linda*
    'legitimate wife') 'fair; pretty'
*RETINA (← RETINĒRE 'to hold back') > *rienda* 'rein'
SEROTINU 'late' > *serondo/seroño* 'late, as referring to fruits'

The combination /dg/ produced a fricative [đ] which has remained until today, although the spelling has changed:

JŪDICĀRE 'to judge' > *judgar* (MSp. *juzgar*)
-ĀTICU > *-adgo*, e.g., *portadgo* 'road toll', *mayoradgo* 'primogeniture;
    inheritance' (MSp. *-azgo*)
NATICA (C.L. NATĒS) 'buttocks' > *nadga* (MSp. *nalga* < Leonese)

If a dental appeared before an affricate, it was absorbed into the occlusive element of the affricate:

D(U)ODECIM 'twelve' > *doze*
TRĒDECIM 'thirteen' > *treze*

Although the new sibilant affricates could appear in syllable-final position, they became stable only in word-final position. If an affricate appeared before a dental, it remained for a while and later absorbed the dental:

PLACITU 'pleasing, agreeable' > *plazdo* 'term extension of time' > *plazo*
RECITĀRE 'to recite, read aloud' [r:e^{z}dar] > *rezar*
AMĪC- *ITĀTE (← AMĪCUS 'friend') > *amizdad, amizad* (*amiçtad* >
    MSp. *amistad*, may be semilearned)

Reduction of Consonant Sequences

In a few cases the syncope resulted in a sequence of three consonants. If the last two consonants did not form a syllable-initial cluster, the middle consonant was dropped, producing a more normal two consonant sequence with the intervocalic voiceless stop having voiced normally:

PENDICĀRE > *pingar* 'to hang, drip'
VINDICĀRE 'to lay claim, avenge' > *vengar*
*RENDITARE > *arrendar* 'to tie a horse by the reins'

If we consider the Latin geminate /l:/ to be two consonants, then the development of COLLOCĀRE 'to place' would fit into this group as well, > Sp. *colgar* 'to hang up'. In the case of the affricates /t^s/ < /k/ plus a front vowel, a similar development is found, although one may also assume that when the middle consonant was a /d/ it was simply absorbed in the new prepalatal affricate:

UNDECIM 'eleven' > *onze*
QUATTUORDECIM 'fourteen' > *quatorze*
*DOMNICILLA > *donzella* 'maiden'

A number of words which would be expected to fit into the preceding group with normal development, show an apparent lack of voicing of an originally intervocalic voiceless stop:

*ANTEPARARE > *amparar* 'to support, help'
EPISCOPU 'bishop' > *obispo*
COMPUTĀRE 'to reckon, calculate' > *contar*
HOSPITĀLE 'pertaining to a guest, or host' > *hostal*
MASTICĀRE 'to chew' > *mascar*
PANTICE 'bowels, belly' > *pança*

Words like *preste* 'priest' < PRESBYTER, *renta* 'income' < *RENDITA, and *venta* 'sale' < VENDITA which show no diphthongization, are probably Gallicisms, since in northern Gallo-Romance syncope often preceded voicing (Penny 1983, 138). The case of *costumbre* 'custom' < *CO(N)SUĒTŪDINE probably should be excluded from this group since syncope between /s/ and /t/ occurred very early (see p. 000). *Costura* 'seam, stitching' < *CONSŪTŪRA, should probably be classed with *costumbre*, although it is not impossible that a form like *cordura* < /cosdura/ may have been the original one (it is found in Asturias [Penny 1983, 139]).

In the case of the group of native words which do not show voicing, it may be that voicing of the intervocalic voiceless occlusives did occur normally, but that when syncope occurred, forming a three-consonant sequence, if the medial consonant was voiceless, the following consonant assimilated partially to it by unvoicing. The medial consonant would then have disappeared as in all other examples.[33] (A very full discussion of syncope and its results is found in Pensado Ruiz 1984, 225–457.)

The Development of the Apocope of Final /-e/ in Old Castilian

A feature of medieval Castilian that came to characterize much of the literature written in the twelfth and thirteenth centuries was the widespread loss of word-final /-e/. In modern Spanish the results of this apocope are limited to words in which the /-e/ follows a single apical consonant: dental, liquid, sibilant, or nasal, i.e., /d, l, r, s, θ, n/, as in the following examples:

VĪTE 'vine' > [bide] > *vid*
AMĀTE 'love!' (imp. pl.) > [amade] > *amad*
SŌLE 'sun' > [sole] > *sol*
MARE 'sea' > [mare] > *mar*
PĀCE 'peace' > [pad^ze] > *paz*
TRĀNSVERSE (C.L. -A) 'crossways, obliquely' > [trabese] > *através*
MĒNSE 'month' > [meze] > *mes*
PĀNE 'bread' > [pane] > *pan*

If more than one consonant precedes the /-e/, it remains:

PONTE 'bridge' > *puente*
FORTE 'strong' > *fuerte*

If the final /-e/ is a morpheme, as in numerous verb forms, it does not drop even when preceded by an apical consonant:[34]

VĒNĪ 'I came' > *vine*
FĒCĪ 'I made, did' > *hice*
TENET '(he) holds' > *tiene* 'he has'
PETIT '(he) seeks, requests' > *pide*

As was pointed out in chapter 3, the change from the quantitative to the qualitative system had affected atonic vowels differently from those in tonic syllables. The atonic vowel system had been reduced to five vowels, and, by the time that Castilian had become a literary language, the word-final vowels had been further reduced to three by merger of all front vowels to /e/ and all back vowels to /o/.

The question of when the further reduction of the five vowel system in

---

[33] The only apparent exception to the preceding rule is the case of *revolcar* 'to roll over, roll around' < REVOLVICĀRE (Penny 1983, 140).

[34] In words which had a consonant group before -e until quite late, the -e remains: *siete* 'seven' < SEPTEM, *doze* 'twelve' < DUODECIM, *treze* 'thirteen' < TREDECIM, *peine* 'comb' < PECTINE, *sauce* 'willow' < SALICE, etc. The rule also applies to popular words only. Learned and semilearned words, and some borrowed words, may or may not retain final -e, *ápice*, *enlace*, *envase*, *fase*, *sacerdote*, *confite*, etc.

final syllables occurred is not easy to determine. Several modern Asturian dialects still preserve the final /-i/ derived directly from Latin /i:/. Forms such as *elli, eli, li* < Late Latin /el:i/, *lis* < ILLĪS, are found along with form 2 of the preterite ending in /-sti/ < -STI.[35] In the manuscripts of the works of Gonzalo de Berceo from the first half of the thirteenth century are found forms like *aquesti, esti* < *ACCU-ISTĪ, *li* < ILLĪ, *lis* < ILLĪS, etc. (Montgomery 1975, 359; Lüdtke 1970, 52). It is likely that a similar situation prevailed in Castile in the pre-literary period and that the final vowel that tended to drop in relaxed pronunciation was the same reflex of the Late Latin /-i/. Thus it is conceivable that it had first become a rather open high front vowel [-i], somewhat like that found in modern conservative dialects in Asturias (Montgomery 1975, 360). It may also have been rather laxly articulated and thus especially exposed to influences tending toward apocope. The evidence of texts like the *Fazienda de Ultramar* and the translation of the Bible is that apocope occurs with greatest frequency in just those words that had this final vowel rather than the one derived from /-e/, which would justify our presuming that apocope began first with the high vowel and later spread to /-e/ as speakers merged both vowels. These purely phonetic conditions, however, were not the only factors that must have influenced the rise of apocope in Old Castilian (Montgomery 1975, 351).

As far as can be determined from the surviving documents, the Romance of northern Spain, with the exception of Ribagorza and Catalonia, up the middle of the eleventh century generally maintained the final /-e/, although there was an incipient tendency to drop it after the consonants which eventually became final. Apocopated forms like *carral, segur, pergaminar, sal*, are attested along with conservative forms: *messe, pane*. A sign of the persistence of the final /-e/ can be observed in hypercorrect forms like : *matode* for *matod* 'he killed' (< -AUT < -ĀVIT), *kede* 'what, which' for *ked* < QUID (Lapesa 1951, 188).[36]

The progress of the apocope of /-e/ seems to have gone hand in hand with the triumph of the syncope of atonic vowels. The reduction and transformation of medial consonant sequences in Late Latin-early Romance had resulted in a limitation of syllable-final consonants to /r, l, s, m, n/, or, in other words, to most of those consonants after which final /-e/ was beginning to drop. In the tenth and eleventh centuries syncope finally eliminated all posttonic vowels except /a/, and thus created a number of

---

[35] According to Granda Gutiérrez: "[N]os encontramos ante zonas de conservación de un estado fonético proto-romance en que aún no se había realizado la neutralización de las oposiciones *-u-o, -i-e* enposición final" (1960, 133).

[36] Preservation of final *-e* and hypercorrect forms (the "paragogic" e) were used by epic poets and later appeared in medieval ballads as a poetic device for gaining additional rimes or to add an archaic flavor to this kind of poetry, e.g., "Burgeses e burgesas por las finiestras sone/ plorando de los ojos, tanto avien el dolore" (*Cid*, 17–18), or in the *Romance del Marqués de Mantua*: "Al cabo de una gran pieça/ que ambos cansados estane/ el marqués al ermitaño/ comiença de preguntare" (Menéndez Pidal 1944a, 3.1181).

new syllable types in which consonants not previously found in a postnuclear position could now be syllable-final, as we saw in the preceding section. With the existence of words like *cobdo, riepto, judgar, plazdo, comde, setmana, sangne*, etc. the way was clear for the final /-e/ to drop after these consonants as well.[37] In the middle of the eleventh century forms like *adelant* are attested sporadically in Old Castile (Lapesa 1951, 193). Along with the loss of /-e/ in single words went the linking of the enclitic atonic pronouns *se, le, me, te*, to a preceding word that ended in a vowel, with subsequent dropping of the /-e/: *lexol* 'I leave to him/her' for *lexo le, levós* 'he took himself away' for *levó se, quem quadra* 'which suits me' for *que me quadra*, etc.

Thus, by the end of the eleventh century not only had the spontaneous tendency to drop final /-e/ after apical consonants become strong, but the tendency to "extreme apocope," i.e., the dropping of /-e/ after any consonant regardless of its point of articulation, and even after consonant groups like /-nt/, /-rt/, /-lt/, was beginning to make itself felt. The language was ripe for a continued change in the same direction.

A push toward the confirmation of the extreme apocope of /-e/ and occasionally of /-o/ was given by the increasing introduction into the peninsula at just this time of a large number of prestigious persons from France, and possibly also from Catalonia. Sancho el Mayor, king of Navarre (A.D. 1000–1035), later heir to the county of Castile, and finally of much of Leon, changed the pilgrim road to Santiago de Compostela in Galicia from its previous route through the hilly coastal country of Alava and Asturias to an easier route through the plains further inland, through Logroño, Nájera to Briviesca, Amaya and Carrión. Before long this new road became an important and active medium of communication between France and the Iberian peninsula (*Orígenes* §96.4). Colonies of "Franks" were established along it in a number of towns during the eleventh century. Sancho also established the Cluniac rule in the monasteries of Navarre and Castile, thus opening another way for Gallic influence to make itself felt. With the reign of Alfonso VI (1072–1109), Gallic influence reached its height. Alfonso established a connection with Cluny in an effort to win its support against the pope, Gregory VII, who was claiming to be the temporal overlord of Leon and Castile, as he already was of Aragon. Finally, through the intercession of Abbot Hugh of Cluny, the pope did not press his political claim, but did demand that the kingdom accept the common western or "Roman" liturgy in the church (it had already been adopted in Aragon in 1074). The Council of Burgos of 1086

---

[37] Exact parallelism between syllable-final medial consonants and word-final consonants cannot be found. Certain consonants were almost never found medially but appeared in word-final position and vice versa, e.g., *-f*, < *-ve* is found in a number of words *nief, nuef* for *nieve* 'snow', *nueve* 'nine', and final groups like *-at, -nt*, and *-rt* never appear syllable-finally in medial position (Lapesa 1975, 17). Also the chronology of the disappearance of medial syllable-final consonants and word-final consonants differs considerably.

officially established the new liturgy and relegated the older Hispanic or "Visigothic" liturgy to a limited number of places (Wright 1982, 209–212). With the introduction into Spain of the Roman liturgy came the new pronunciation of written Latin which had been established centuries before in northern France and had gradually become the norm in France. The new liturgy and the new spoken standard required the presence of numerous non-Hispanic clerics trained in the new system. A number of French monks came to Spanish monasteries, and the chief ones were reformed as branches of Cluny. The French abbot of the monastery of Sahagún, Bernard de Sédirac, became archbishop of Toledo in 1086, shortly after its fall to Castilian troops. In 1097 Bernard brought other Cluniac monks to be bishops of Osma, Sigüenza, Segovia, Palencia, Zamora, Braga, and Santiago. During the twelfth century bishops of Gallic origin are found in different sees in Castile, Leon, Toledo, or Galicia. In the "fuero" of Oreja, granted by Alfonso VII, six of the seven bishops confirming it have French or Occitanian names. These bishops undoubtedly had numbers of their countrymen as their assistants. Finally, the older Gothic handwriting was replaced by the modern Carolingian script, thus marking another break with the past. King Alfonso himself married several foreign women, two of them known to be of French origin, one from Aquitaine and the other from Burgundy.

The linguistic influence of persons from Gallo-Romance speaking areas must have been considerable because, in addition to imposing the letter-by-letter pronunciation of written Latin, they must have had much to do also with the authorship of religious literature in the new literary representation of the vernacular, and also have been involved in preaching. In fact, it seems that the regions in which the greatest amount of apocope of /-e/ is found are precisely those in which are found dioceses ruled for a long time by French bishops. One of the notable characterics of French and Catalan is the consistent loss of all final vowels, except /-a/ > /-ə/, even when there is also a final /-s/:

Latin		French	Catalan
PONTE 'bridge'	>	*pont*	*pon(t)*
VALLE 'valley'	>	*val*	*vall*
HERĪ 'yesterday'	>	*hier*	*ahir*
VĪNU 'wine'	>	*vin*	*vi*
AMĪCU 'friend'	>	*ami*	*amic*
MŪRŌS 'walls'	>	*murs*	*murs*
PĀNĒS 'breads'	>	*pains*	*pans*
FLŌRĒS 'flowers'	>	*fleurs*	*flo(r)s*
CURRIT 'he runs'	>	*court*	*cor*

Thus, the natural tendency of speakers of Gallic or Catalan origin would have been to follow the practice of their own Romance vernacular and to exaggerate the apocope of /-e/ when speaking Castilian. Being men of considerable prestige, favored by the kings and in positions of eminence and authority, their type of language would have represented a prestige norm for others to imitate. The non-ecclesiastics would still have had a different type of prestige, that associated with a refined courtly life typified by the regional courts of southern France. Poets and singers of lyric poetry or thrilling epics also would have provided different linguistic models for native Castilians.

Since the various Romance dialects of western Europe were at this time much more similar in general appearance than they were in later centuries, there would have been no particular reason to differentiate sharply between Castilian and Gallo-Romance or eastern Ibero-Romance. The habit of ending words with practically any consonant and certain groups of consonants would have carried over into speaking Castilian. All Romance dialects were undoubtedly considered by some to be varieties of the same basic system, as indeed they were in a very real sense. It would be easy in these circumstances to insert Gallicisms into Castilian texts without the feeling that one was thereby altering its essential nature. The use of Gallicisms and Catalanisms would simply have added to the atmosphere that favored extreme apocope of /-e/. One must also take into consideration the possibility that many documents written during this period were authored by Gallic scribes whose knowledge of Castilian was fairly superficial. This possibility would explain why certain documents are written in what appears to be a mixture of dialects. One striking example is the "fuero" granted to the town of Valfermoso de las Monjas by the convent that had been founded there. The abbess was Nóbila de Périgord and her chaplain, Ebrardus, wrote the "fuero" in a strange mixture of Provençal, Latin, Castilian and Mozarabic with all sorts of apocopes that go far beyond anything tolerated by monolingual Castilians (Lapesa 1975, 20). The *Fuero de Avilés* likewise mixes Castilian, Provençal, and barely adapted Latinisms.

Examples of extreme apocope between 1179 and 1212 are: *regnant, suert, est dono, a tot el convent, present, part, puent, semient, ond*, etc. along with various Gallo-Romance words not found in Castilian: *argent, domen* (< Prov. *domenh*), *pleit, arciprest, ardiment, duc, estrument, tost, consentiment, franc, gambax*, and many more. Such borrowings undoubtedly helped to reinforce the tendency to drop all final /-e/'s (Lapesa 1951, 200). It should be noted, however, that in no case did apocope go as far as it had in French, which allowed morphemes like /-s/ and /-t/ to appear after a root ending in a consonant.

The influence of these prestigious French- and Provençal-speaking persons was not the only stimulus for the fashion of apocopation. With the progress of the reconquest into the southern areas of New Castile, colonists from the north were needed to organize the new towns that were being founded. In this way Navarrese and Aragonese settlers, whose dialects, like Catalan and Gallo-Romance, dropped final /-e/ and occasionally other vowels as well, mixed with Castilian settlers and helped to reinforce the preexisting tendencies. Then with the conquest of Toledo and areas further south, there were brought into Castile many speakers of Arabic, which had had a profound influence on the Romance of the south during the centuries of Moslem domination, stimulating the loss of many final vowels, e.g., *sinab* < SINAPI 'mustard', *lait* < LACTE 'milk', *dols* < DULCE 'sweet', *komt, kond* 'count' < COMITE (Lapesa 1951, 189).

From the facts presented above it might seem that the drive toward the complete elimination of all final /-e/'s must have been so powerful that it would eventually triumph in all forms of Castilian. As with other phonetic changes, however, we have here two competing norms, one limiting apocope to the postapical position and the other extending it to all consonants. The struggle between these norms was by no means one-sided. Along with examples of extreme apocope, one is as likely to find conservation of final /-e/ even in words that are completely popular Castilian; in the *Fuero de Valfermoso*, for example, we find *lidiare, sennale, pane, pastore, pare* along with *coger, par, pastor, amistat*, and *deuant* (Lapesa 1951, 205). Similar examples of extreme apocope and conservation of /-e/ are found in many documents, but in literary works, especially in epic poetry and ecclesiastical works the apocopating custom predominated and seemed destined to triumph as the wave of the future. In the early thirteenth century in all Castile, forms with loss of /-e/ far outweigh those preserving it, by three to one in a study of sixty-six notarial documents (Lapesa 1951, 208). The occurrence of apocope may have been related to the position of a word in a breath group; possibly it was more likely at the end of a sentence where the last word would be at the end of an intonational curve. There are some indications that this may be the case since apocope was especially common in the imperative singular form of verbs: *recib, sub, sab, escriv, met, bat*, etc. for *recibe, sube, sabe, escrive, mete, bate* (Lapesa 1975, 17).

CONSONANTS

The Beginnings of the Change /f-/ > /h-/

One of the most characteristic features of the Castilian dialect was the shift of Latin initial /f-/ to an aspirate /h-/ under certain specific phonetic conditions. This /h-/ later disappeared in northern Spain and in standard Spanish, although it is widely preserved in the popular Spanish of southern Spain and in Spanish America. At this point we will examine the conditions and possible causes of this particular change.

The Position of /f-/ in Latin: Phonology and Phonetics

/f-/ in Latin was found solely in initial position in authentic Latin words, as we saw in Ch. 2. The limitation of /f-/ to this position is so strict a rule of the native Latin lexicon that its presence in medial position is a sure sign that the word is a borrowing from another language, e.g., RŪFUS 'red, reddish' (Ernout 1909, 75). Of course, there were a number of derived words based on simple words beginning with /f-/: DĒFENDERE 'to defend, ward off', DĒFERRE 'to carry away', CONFUNDERE 'to mingle, mix up', OFFOCĀRE 'to strangle, choke', etc., but the /f/ was clearly initial from a morphological point of view, with few exceptions. In addition to the distributional restrictions on /f/, the consonant was weakly integrated into the consonantal system. It was the only labial fricative and had no other fricative counterpart except /s/. It was, in other words, relatively unprotected by the structure of the system itself and was therefore particularly exposed to possible phonetic change; any change in its realization would have had no effect on any other consonants.

As mentioned in chapter 2, the articulation of the consonant represented by the letter F may not have been that of a labiodental fricative [f] but rather that of a bilabial fricative [φ]. With the evidence available to us today, we cannot be at all certain of which was the commonest pronunciation in older Latin, or even if there were some regional differences during imperial times. Because of the isolation of /f/ in the phonological system, it could have been pronounced either way or have changed from one type of articulation to the other without leaving the slightest trace in writing or even attracting anyone's attention. Some scholars are convinced that the bilabial articulation was a specific development in Castile and other northern areas (Steiger 1932, 219–21, 223), possibly through the influence of Indo-European dialects having the [φ] (Torreblanca 1983–84, 280), and not a general pronunciation in all of Hispania. Although this is a possible hypothesis, there is no way that it can be confirmed. At any rate, it is extremely probable that the bilabial articulation was widespread in the Middle Ages, whether because this was the pronunciation of most of Ibero-Romance, or because it was brought by the Castilians to the areas they conquered. The existence of [φ] in many areas of the modern Spanish-speaking world could then be seen not as an innovation but rather the preservation of an ancient tradition. The existence of the labiodental pronunciation in much of western Romance (Portuguese, Catalan, French, Italian) and in Rumanian, can be accounted for then as a generalization of the [f] realization, which could well have been widespread in Latin. It is likely that the [f] pronunciation was strengthened by the parallel development of medial [b̄], the Late Latin reflex of the merger of earlier intervocalic /b/ and /v/. The bilabial voiced fricative could either remain as such, as it had done in much of northern Spain and other areas (see the subsequent sections on the development of medial /b d g/), or could develop into a labiodental [v]. This latter change occurred in Gaul, Italy, parts of the Iberian peninsula and Rhaetia (Lausberg 1965, I.356). The development of the labiodental articulation would have strengthened the labiodental pronunciation of /f/ since now both sounds would be counterparts in the correlation of voicing. Castilian did not adopt the new [v] articulation and thus /f/ continued to remain isolated in the consonantal system.

The Development of [φ] in Castilian

The bilabial voiceless fricative pronunciation of /f/ tends to be inherently unstable and subject to phonetic modification by neighboring sounds. If we were to describe the sound in terms of its articulatory features, we could put it as follows:[38]

+ consonantal
+ labial
+ fricative
− tense
− voice

The combination of bilabiality with laxness means that the slightest relaxation of the lip position will in effect almost eliminate the lips as articulators, something which is especially likely to happen as the lips are not rigid. Thus, [φ] before a vowel, pronounced with slightly more laxness, will result in a voiceless air stream followed by the vibration of the vocal cords required by rthe following vowel. The effect of this lax articulation would tend therefore to that of a glottal fricative (Steiger 1932, 221; Penny 1972a, 466–67). This type of development is more likely to occur with back vowels since the lip-rounding required in pronouncing them conflicts to some extent with the lip-spreading needed in articulating [φ]. Before the semiconsonant [w] (usually in the combination [we] < Late Latin /ǫ/), there would probably have been less of a relaxation of the labial articulation because the labiovelar [w] would have worked against it, but partial relaxation could have produced a partial glottal fricative followed by the original bilabial voiceless fricative, i.e., [hφ]. To put this once again in terms of phonetic features, we can describe the resulting allophones of /f/ as follows:

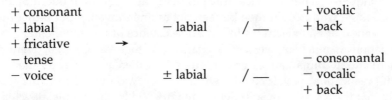

Before front vowels and the palatal semiconsonant and other consonantal articulations, the original bilabial fricative pronunciation would not have been drawn away from its original shape. Thus there would have existed three allophones of /f/ at the earliest period:

---

[38] Although in this particular case the use of the distinctive feature notation with + and − values is useful, it is not universally valid because this type of notation requires that we label a feature as being either present or absent. In many cases, the difference between various articulations is not a simple presence or absence, however, but of more and/or less of one type of articulation. See chapter 2, note 2, for some comments on how distinctive feature notation distorts our understanding of the evolution of vowels. The same thing is true in the development of certain consonants as well.

[h] before /o u/

[hφ] before [w][39]

[φ] elsewhere, i.e., before /i e a j r l/

In addition to these allophones of /f/, the presence of a nasal immediately preceding the [φ] could have served to strengthen the labial quality of the sound by pushing it toward an occlusive articulation, [p] or even [b].[40]

When allophonic variation of this sort exists, there is always a potential for change in the distribution of the allophones. That is, one of the realizations can become felt by speakers to be a "normal" pronunciation, at least for certain purposes. They may then extend it to positions that it formerly did not occupy. Thus,we see that in Gascony, on the other side of the Pyrenees, the [h] allophone was generalized to all positions:

FRATRE 'brother' > *hray*

FRUCTU 'fruit'> *heruto*

FESTA 'feast, holiday' > *hesto*

FĪLU 'string' > *híu*

FATU 'fate'> *hado*

CŌNFĪNE 'having common borders > *couhí*

PROFUNDU 'deep' > *prouhoun*

(Rohlfs 1970, 145–49)

It is worth noting too that there are other areas of Romania in which this same change has taken place. In Italy, for example, [h] is found for Latin /f/ in Calabria, in the provinces of Catanzaro, Cosenza, and Reggio, e.g., FABA 'broad bean' > *hava*, FĒMINA 'woman' > *hímmina*, FERRU 'iron' > *hierru*, FĪCU 'fig' > *hicu*, etc. Also in northern Italy in the province of Brescia we find similar examples, e.g., FAMEN 'hunger' > *ham*, FARĪNA 'flour' > *harina*, FEBRUĀRIU 'February' > *hebrer*, FOLIA 'leaves' > *hoja*, etc. (Rohlfs 1966, 206). In rural dialects of Rumanian in Moldavia and in Macedo-Rumanian are found examples like: FĪLIU 'son' > *hiu*, FERRU 'iron' > *hier*, FĪLU > *h'ir*, etc. (Lakovary 1955, 311). In some areas of Sardinia, the reflexes of Latin /f/ have disappeared altogether. In Barbagia and Baronía are found FOCU 'fire, hearth' > *oku*, FUMU 'smoke' > *úmmu*, FAECE 'dregs' > *eke*, etc. (Wagner 1941, 94). As was noted in chapter 1, the change of /f/ to /h/ is one of the commonest changes in all kinds of languages around the world, and is not limited to Romance.

In northern Castile and eastern Leon, the evidence is that a similar

---

[39] It does not matter too much how we represent this articulation. Doman (1969) prefers the symbols in reversed order [φh]. The important thing is that the shift to a purely aspirate articulation was countered by the labial quality of [w].

[40] Menéndez Pidal (*Orígenes* §41.6b) believes that this sort of development can account for the ancient toponyms *Porma*, *Borma*, *Puerma*, if the etymon of this name is Lat. FŌRMA 'form; river bed, aqueduct', but this etymology may not be certain. Torreblanca 1983–84 associates it rather with the Indo-European root *POR- *PER- 'to pass, cross, transport' plus the suffix *-MA.

leveling of allophones took place, with [h] being substituted for [φ] or [f] before all vowels, and not just back ones. The use of the letter H in early documents or the absence of any letter at all in words derived from Latin words beginning with /f/ may be considered proof of this shift. The earliest documentary examples of a change in the realization of /f/ are seen in Castile (including La Rioja), in the ninth century. In one document dated A.D. 863 the Latin name FORTĪCIUS appears in the form *Ortiço*. Later the same name appears in the form *Hortiço* (A.D. 927). Hypercorrections also appear, as, for example, in the name *Albari Ferrameliz* (A.D. 923), where F is written instead of the correct form with H, *Herramelliz*.

In the eleventh century increasing numbers of examples are found, not only in Castile but in other areas. On the border between Castile and Pamplona in A.D. 1016 the toponym *Garrafe* is written *Garrahe*. The Oja river, which gives its name to the region of La Rioja, may be derived from Lat. FOLIA, but never appears with the initial F. In Aragon the personal name FORTIS appears in 1099 as *Hortiz*, and in 1100 as *Ortíz*. There are many other examples,[41] but the ones given here show that from the earliest written sources the spelling with the letter H existed alongside the older spelling with F, from which we may conclude that in speech the change of /f/ > /h/ existed even earlier. Of course, we have no way of knowing whether this variant pronunciation was general throughout Castile or was confined to certain social classes, possibly on the lower end of the social scale. It is possible that more conservative speakers preserved the labio-dental [f] or the bilabial [φ] in all positions, or kept [h] only before back vowels. Such notions are, however, merely speculations since spelling can never be a certain guide to pronunciation except when a new spelling appears. Those who spelled words with the letter F could well have pronounced [h]. At any rate, all of these very early examples are grouped in the extreme north between the river Porma in the east of Leon and in the Cinca in Aragon, being especially typical of the northern part of Castile and La Rioja (*Orígenes* §41).[42]

There is also a precious bit of direct phonetic evidence that cannot be dismissed as any sort of spelling confusion. An Arabic history referring to the descendants of Sancho el Mayor of Navarre, makes particular reference to one of the brothers of Sancho Garcés de Nájera, stating that he went to the land of the Moors and burned the mosque at Elvira and died

---

[41] Numerous examples are given in *Orígenes* §41, and in a slightly more condensed fashion in Catalán 1967–68, 414–18.

[42] Menéndez Pidal (*Orígenes* §41.6b) makes much of the appearance in a document in Leon of the year 905, of the place name *Fonte Fascasia* in place of the true name *Pascasia* (today *Fontasquesa*). He believes it to be a case of a hypercorrection by someone who believed that the initial [p] must have been an error for *f*. He relates this item to the modern Basque tendency to use a labial occlusive in place of [f], e.g., *pago* < FAGU 'beech tree', *besta* < FESTA 'feast', etc. He may be right, but it might be better not to put too much weight on a single, isolated example like this one, especially when it may equally well be that the writer made a mistake in writing, influenced by the F of *Fonte*.

violently in 1083. The history states that he was given the name "ilhante," "changing the f to h in speaking, and its meaning among them is 'son of a king' " (Catalán 1967–68, 412–13). It is clear from what is said about this person that those who called him *ilhante* were from La Rioja. It is also a fact that the author of the quotation used the Arabic letter **hā'** ه   to indicate the pronunciation and was aware that it corresponded to something that he identified with the Arabic **fā'** ف .[43]

Further proof that the letter **F** was associated with the pronunciation [h] is seen in foreign borrowings. When the Old French words containing an initial aspirate such as *hardi* 'bold, daring', *honte* 'shame' and *heraut* 'herald' were taken into Castilian, they were often written with **F**: *fardido, fonta,* and *faraute,* although they also appear written with H: *hardido, honta, haraute.* A word derived from Frankish *FALDA* appears in Old Spanish with a suffix as *haldeta* 'shirt-tail' (Penny 1972a, 475). Some words taken from Arabic which contained [f], also appear in Old Spanish with **H**:

FUNDUQ > *alhóndiga* 'corn market'
SAFUNĀRIYA > *çanahoria* 'carrot'
FANIQA > *hanega* 'dry measure'

(Penny 1972a, 475)

It is always possible, of course, that this particular development occurred after these words were borrowed into Old Spanish.

Even more common are examples of Arabic words that in their original form contained various back fricatives: the pharyngeal fricative [ḥ] ح , the glottal fricative [h] ه , and the dorsovelar fricative [x] خ . Many of these words came into Old Spanish spelled with **F**:

HADIYA > *alfadía* 'bribe'
HURI (Hisp.-Ar.) > *alfolí* 'granary; salt bin'
HAKIM> *alfaquín* 'Moslem physician'
ḤAUZ > *alfoz* 'district under the control of a city or a castle'
ḤATTA> *fa(s)ta* 'until'
XAJAR> *alfarje* 'lower millstone of oil press'
XAJJAM > *alfajeme* 'barber surgeon'
XURJ > *alforja* 'saddle bag'
XUMRA> *alfombra* 'carpet'

(DCELC I, 109–18)

There are many more examples, but these are sufficient to show that an aspirate could be considered the equivalent of a labial fricative in certain circumstances. As one scholar puts it: "[E]n el sentimiento del hablante la

---

[43] The spelling with the letter ل *lām* before the **F** probably does not reflect the Romance pronunciation but rather serves to show that the following consonant was strengthened since in Arabic the /l/ of the prefixed definite article *al-* assimilates to certain following consonants, resulting in a geminate. Thus, the title *al-raḥman* 'the merciful one' (one of the names of God) is pronounced [ar:aḥma:n], but the spelling of the definite article remains unchanged.

sustitución de *h* por *f* no comportaba ningún cambio de significación; fonológicamente, eran variantes de un solo fonema. Para los cultos, entre estas dos variantes había cierta relación valorativa: la *f* era más culta, ha *h* más rústica; ambos sonidos eran, pues, variantes estilísticas de un solo fonema'' (Alarcos Llorach 1951, 39).

The medial geminate resulting from the assimilation of /n/ to /f/ in the original group /-nf-/ was treated like an initial /f-/, since, as we shall see, the results of the geminates were identified with word-initial simple consonants. Thus Latin INFANTE 'child' usually appears written as *ifant* or *iffante*, but the Arabic testimony mentioned above shows that it could also be pronounced with [h]. Based on CONFECTUS (pass. part. of CONFICERE 'to manufacture, prepare') is the verb *cohechar* 'to bribe a public official; to prepare the land for sowing', and the nouns *cohecho, cohecha*. From *CONFORTIU derive *cohuerço* and *cofuerço* 'funeral banquet', from CONFORTĀRE 'to comfort' came *cohortar*, along with the learned *confortar*.[44] From CONFUNDERE derive *cohonder* and *cofonder*'to confound'. There are other examples as well, but these should suffice to show that /-nf-/ developed like a geminate /f:/, as it did in cases like OFFOCĀRE 'to strangle, choke' > *ahogar* 'to drown' (Catalán 1967–68, 420–33). Other words containing a prefix before a base word beginning with /f-/ developed similarly: SUBFŪMĀRE > *sahumar* 'to smoke meat', CANNAFERULA > *cañaherla* 'giant fennel' (Menéndez Pidal 1941, 132).

On the other hand, if the /f/ was intervocalic and speakers lost any sense of its being part of a derived word, it developed as did other voiceless consonants, voicing to a bilabial fricative, e.g., PROFECTU > *provecho* 'benefit, advantage'.

Although the shift of [φ] to [h] occurred only before vocalic articulations, the frequency of occurrence of this sound apparently led to its being extended to some preconsonantal positions as well. Thus the initial group /fl-/ may have occasionally been realized [hl-], since in a few words, especially in some toponyms, the result was a simple /l/: FLACCIDU 'flabby, weak' > *lacio* 'faded, withered; lank', FLAGINU > *Laíno*, FLAMMULA > *Lambla, Lambra*, FLAVIANA > *Laviana*, FLACCIANA > *Laciana* (Menéndez Pidal 1941, 126). In general, however, the [φ] remained as such before all consonantal articulations, and [hφ] was kept before [w].

/f-/ > /h-/ and Basque-Romance Bilingualism

The explanation which has most commonly been given for the start of the shift of /f-/ > /h-/ is the one particularly associated with Menéndez Pidal: that of a ''Basque-Cantabrian-Iberian'' substratum.[45] In its simplest

---

[44] Some words which appear to be based on this etymon are more likely to be learned words based on COHORTĀRĪ 'to encourage, cheer up' (Catalán 1967–68, 427).

[45] Actually the theory of a Basque-Cantabrian substratum influence on the shift goes back much farther than Menéndez Pidal. Lorenzo Hervás, in his *Catalogo delle lingue*, published in 1784, remarks: ''Vedesi, che lo Spagnuolo costantement rifiuta la lettera *f* delle parole

and crudest form, this explanation holds that the shift of the articulation of /f/ occurred when speakers of Basque and Cantabrian (and possibly Iberian), who lacked any [f] in their own language, attempted to learn the Latin-Romance [f]. Having no sound similar to it in their first language, they substituted for it a simple aspiration [h], thus imitating the fricative quality and ignoring the labiodental articulation with which they were unfamiliar. As this pronunciation became established in Castilian and other dialects influenced by it, it was spread south along with the expansion of Castile. It did not immediately replace /f/ but existed in competition with it as a popular variable that only later managed to become accepted as the norm in the standard literary dialect in the sixteenth century. Proof of the influence of Basque (and any other pre-Romance language sharing its lack of /f/), is seen in the fact that, as pointed out above, the earliest written evidence of the use of the letter H, or nothing, in words in which F would be expected appears in the northern parts of Castile and in La Rioja (see p. 177). The Arabic history mentioned above likewise confirms that the pronunciation of [h] for /f/ was established in La Rioja in the eleventh century at the latest. Since these areas are the ones closest to that of the Basques, and since Gascony, on the other side of the Pyrenees, is also a region inhabited by Basque speakers, and likewise shifts /f/ to /h/, it seems to be a reasonable hypothesis at first glance.

Certain objections have been raised to some points of this theory. First of all, we cannot be certain that [h] existed in medieval Basque, although it is not impossible (Martinet 1955, 371–88). In view of this uncertainty, is it reasonable to believe that those lacking /f/ in their own language would have substituted [h] for [f]? Also, Menéndez Pidal assumes that the Latin-Romance consonant was definitely a labiodental [f] rather than [φ]. We might ask too whether it would really have been impossible for Basque speakers to imitate the Latin-Romance [f], especially in view of the fact that some Basque dialects developed an intervocalic [f] from an earlier voiced bilabial fricative [ƀ] (Torreblanca 1983–84). As one eminent scholar of Basque puts it: "[l]os vascos no parecen haber encontrado demasiadas dificultades para pronunciarlo a partir de fecha bastante antigua" (Michelena 1957, 126).

Another argument against the Basque "substratum" is that in Navarre, where many Basque speakers lived, the initial /f/ was preserved in the Romance dialect (Alvar 1952). If the presence of Basque speakers was so important, it can be argued that they should have had an effect on Navarrese (Izzo 1977). Others have objected to the theory on more general

---

Latine, e vi sostituisce l'*h*, la quale non si pronunzia se non in alcuni paesi delle Andaluzie, ove le si dà un'aspirazione assai forte, che si accosta al *jota* Spagnuolo, prova, che esso anticamente parlò una lingua, ove forse mancava la *f*; ed appunto nella lingua Cantabra, che era l'antica Spagnuola, pochissime voci incominciano colla *f*." In several other places he says more or less the same thing, e.g., "Il rifiuto, che della lettera *f* hanno fatto gli Spagnuoli in moltissme parole Latine, prova parimente la loro tenacità per conservare l'antica pronunzia Cantabra" (Coseriu 1978, 529).

grounds. Since the change /f/ > /h/ is found elsewhere in Romance-speaking areas, why is it necessary to posit any special influence of Basque? Some scholars believe that if one can find an internal structural reason for the change, no other causal factor need be sought. Thus, if we conceive of the change as simply the loss of a redundant phonetic feature, namely, labiality, in an area rather isolated from many of the phonetic developments found in other western Romance areas, no other cause is needed (Malmberg 1958; 1961, 75).

One more internal explanation is that of Naro (1972) who sees the development of /f/ as part of a supposed "initial palatalization" of all consonants in Romance. There is no evidence of any such change, however. The change of initial /l-/ to /l̯-/, which he cites as evidence, is an essential part of the identification of medial geminate consonants with their corresponding word-initial consonants and has nothing to do with any general palatalization.

One isolated view of the cause for the innovation was that of Orr (1936), who cited examples of place names far from the Basque region which seem to show the existence of the change, e.g., *Hinges* (Pas-de-Calais) < fīnibus, *Honvault, Honvaux* < fundu, etc. According to Orr, the substitution of [h] for [f] was found elsewhere in Romania and so could not be due to Basque influence. It is certainly true that the change is found in other regions, as we noted above, but the place names cited by Orr cannot be safely derived from Latin etyma that he claims for them and therefore ought not be cited as evidence (Rohlfs 1938).

Tentative Conclusions

Many of the studies of the problem of /f/ > /h/ have been characterized by gross oversimplification, and ignorance or disregard of the existing scholarship. Both supporters of a "substratum" explanation and its opponents have been all too ready to look for a single cause of the phenomenon and have arbitrarily rejected the possibility that it was not due to any one single factor but rather to a variety of different circumstances which, acting in concert, could have set the innovation in motion.

The use of the term "substratum," for instance, is most unfortunate because it gives the impression (whether intended or not) that the change must go back to the very first centuries in which Latin was being introduced into the Iberian Peninsula. Izzo (1977) argues against this idea very cogently, and is then led to reject any possibility of bilingual influence. As was pointed out at the beginning of this chapter, the sources of the characteristic sound changes of the Castilian dialect must, in most cases, be sought in the period in which Castilian was taking shape as an independent dialect and not before. If Basque-Romance bilingualism had any effect on the development of the developing Castilian it would have been during the eighth to the tenth centuries when large numbers of Basque speakers were participating in the expansion of the new county. Thus, the influence would have been that of an adstratum (if indeed we need such terms). Nor have the proponents of a Basque influence ever attempted to determine just how the influence of the Basque speakers could have made itself felt in the early Castilian speech community. It should be pointed out clearly too that not all advocates of bilingual influence have thought that it could be the sole cause of the change. Menéndez Pidal, for example, was well aware that there were other causes, which he did not examine in detail (*Orígenes* §41.6c).

Those seeking an internal cause have more often tended to reject even the possibility of any Basque influence. Thus, Malmberg claims that only "positive modifications" can be attributed to linguistic interference: "Pour qu'il soit entièrement légitime de parler d'interférences, la modification doit se produire dans un sens positif. Je veux dire par là que la simple perte d'une catégorie—d'une opposition phonématique, d'une catégorie grammaticale ou d'une distinction sémantique—ne suffit pas en elle-meme pour prouver une action modifiante d'une langue sur une autre" (1973, 42). This limitation, however, is a purely arbitrary one and appears to be a dogma announced *ex cathedra*, to be accepted on faith alone. The same is true of the claim that the existence of the change of /f/ > /h/ in other areas of Romania makes it impossible for Basque-Romance bilingualism to have had anything to do with it in Ibero-Romance. Only a belief in the theory of "single causes" of linguistic changes could justify this claim. Those who have argued that the innovation started too late to have resulted from Basque influence have either been ignorant of the early examples discovered or have arbitrarily disregarded them as "insufficient" (Malmberg 1963).[46] Even those who have tried to examine seriously all previous scholarship have not considered the evidence found by Catalán (1967–68) (e.g., Izzo 1977). The general view of all those who reject the possibility of Basque influence seems to be that the early appearance of the innovation in the areas closest to the Basque territory is due simply to chance (Gavel 1936) or isolation from other Romance areas.

Is it possible, however, to disregard the points made by Menéndez Pidal (*Orígenes* §41.6b)? They are: 1) the change, although not unique in Romance, nor even in a variety of other languages, is unique in its density and geographical extension in two languages, otherwise rather different from each other: Spanish and Gascon; 2) these two languages are geographically contiguous; 3) both Gascon and Spanish (i.e., early Castilian) are found on a common historical and ethnic base: the Hispano-Iberian and Aquitanian-Iberian; 4) these two languages are still linked geographically by a pre-Romance tongue that formerly lacked [f]; 5) in early Castilian there was some vacilation between the letters /f/ and /p/ and between /f/ and

---

[46] He remarks in reference to this change: "Si je préfère exclure du débat sur le passage *f* > *h* en Castillan le facteur substrat, c'est parce que notre documentation ne me semble pas assez riche pour justifier une supposition de ce genre" (44). The deciding factor seems to be personal preference rather than anything else.

/h/, as was seen in Basque, which serves to demonstrate that the change was one of "acoustic equivalence" rather than an evolutive process.

While it cannot be claimed that Basque is the same as Iberian (Lapesa 1980, 28), nevertheless it is true that Basque historically appears to have lacked [f] in its earliest stages. At the same time, it cannot be ignored that the phonological status of /f-/ in Latin-Romance was that of an isolated consonant, unsupported by any counterpart having most of its distinctive features (until many dialects adopted the labiodental pronunciation for Late Latin /ƀ/). Also, if the assumption of Penny (1972a), and others, is correct, the pronunciation of /f-/ as a bilabial fricative [φ] was one of the most widespread articulations in Ibero-Romance, or at least in the Romance of north-central Hispania. It may be asked then whether this articulation alone would not be sufficient to account for the shift to [h] before syllabic vowels. Even if the change were largely an internal one, we would still have to account for the fact that both early Castilian and Gascon were the Romance dialects in this area that adopted the innovation first and generalized it. We could claim that it was simply a coincidence, but after all, there is no reason to assume that internal, structural developments cannot work in tandem with inter-language influences (Weinrich 1958, 104).

Given that large numbers of Basque speakers participated in the organization of the emerging county of Castile in its earliest days and that they did influence the development of the voiced sibilants, as we shall see later, it is entirely plausible that they also helped to favor the innovation of /f/ > /h/. Although it is difficult to reconstruct the phonetic history of Basque, it is likely that in addition to lacking any [f] in the earliest form of their language, the Basques during the Middle Ages had a bilabial aspirated stop [pʰ] (Martinet 1955, 371–88; Lafon 1960). Those Basque speakers who came to form part of the primitive Castilian community would have been more likely to favor the articulation [φ] of their Romance-speaking compatriots since it more closely resembled their own [pʰ]. Strongly supported by the large number of bilingual speakers, the change of [φ] > [h] would have easily have taken root as a variant pronunciation of /f-/. Other regions farther removed from the Basque-speaking area would not have been pushed in the same direction and could rather follow the general western Romance drift toward the labiodental articulation of both [b] and [φ]. In Navarre, by way of contrast, where the Basques remained at home and did not mingle actively with Romance speakers to form a new linguistic community as in Castile, the Romance dialect was not impelled to adopt the innovation.

Naturally much depends on whether [φ] was actually the pronunciation of /f-/ in Ibero-Romance, or at least in the Romance area that was to become Castile. The evidence favoring it seems reasonably strong, and if this was indeed the typical pronunciation, the subsequent phonetic developments and the phonological restructuring of /f-/ are most easily comprehensible. If, however, the pronunciation of the phoneme /f-/ was as a labiodental [f], then the role of Basque-Romance bilingualism would have been even stronger since it would have involved more of an active substitution of [pʰ] or [φ], as stressed in Menéndez Pidal's point 5, and not just the reinforcement of a previously existing [φ]. No absolutely certain conclusions are possible at present, and may never be, in view of the lack of sure data on early pronunciation, but such uncertainty is often found in history. At present, it seems most probable that [φ] truly was the general articulation of /f/ in Castile.

Once established as a variable, [h] existed along with [φ] and possibly also [f] during the rest of the period of the reconquest, carried south by many of the **pobladores**, although some cultivated speakers may have preferred the labiodental [f] as the more traditional or refined pronunciation. In the next chapter we will examine just how the [h] developed further, and also how the modern standard pronunciation [f] came to be identified with the letter F in the educated norm.[47]

Initial Consonant Groups

The initial consonant groups in Latin were limited to combinations of a stop or /f/ plus a liquid (with */tl/ and */dl/ lacking), if we disregard for the moment groups of /s/ plus a consonant, which were eliminated by the epenthesis of initial /e-/ in late western Romance. Those clusters containing a consonant plus /r/ have remained stable to the present:

BRĀCCHIU 'arm' > *braço*
DRACŌNE 'dragon' > *dragón*
GRANDE 'large' > *grande*
PRAECŌNE 'crier' > *pregón*
TRAHERE 'to drag, draw' > *traer*
CRESCERE 'to grow, increase' > *crescer*
FRONTE 'forehead' > *fruente* (> MSp. *frente*)

Clusters containing the lateral /l/ have undergone a variety of developments, and, taken in their entirety, present an extraordinarily complicated picture.

/bl-/, /gl-/ > /l-/

The simplest evolution is seen in groups containing a voiced stop. There

---

[47] The history of the scholarship of this problem is too complicated to be examined in detail here. The older treatments are discussed in *Orígenes* §41.1, and Jungemann 1955, with a briefer study by Alarcos Llorach 1968. None of the foregoing mention Lázaro Carreter 1949 or Nielsen 1952. Baldinger 1972, 22–27, 397–401, and Izzo 1977 also examine many previous studies, but Izzo makes no mention of Catalán 1967–68, and does not refer to primary sources for the study of the origins of Castile. It is interesting to note that Espinosa 1927, in his review of the first edition of the *Orígenes*, was not happy with the notion of an immediate substitution of [h-] for [f-]. He believed, as does Penny 1972, that the original pronunciation of F- was probably as a voiceless bilabial fricative [φ].

were in Latin relatively few words beginning with /bl-/[48] and most of them have disappeared so that there is little evidence on which to base a reconstruction of their development. Of those that survive in modern Spanish, some seem to show preservation of the cluster:

BLANDU 'smooth, soft' > *blando*
BLITU 'tasteless vegetable used in salads' > *bledo*

Others have lost the /b/:

BLATTA 'insect which shuns the light' > *lad-illa* 'crab louse'[49]
BLASPHĒMĀRE 'to revile, slander' > [*blastimare] > *lastimar* 'to damage' (Malkiel 1976–77)

Evidently statistics alone cannot suffice to tell us which developments should be considered typical. If we assume that *blando* is a learned word, we are left only with *bledo* to account for. Actually this word is rather rare and is today limited to the expression *no se me da un bledo* 'I don't give a hoot', so that possibly it did not suffer normal popular development (Bonfante 1935).

Words containing /gl-/ are also rather rare in Latin,[50] but their development offers fewer problems since most popular words that have remained in the language have lost the /g/:

GLATTĪRE 'to give short, sharp barks (dogs)' > *latir* 'to beat'
GLĪRE 'dormouse' > OSp. *lir* (MSp. *lirón*)
GLANDINE (C.L. GLANS, GLANDIS) 'acorn' > *landre* 'tumor'
GLOBELLU 'small globe' > OSp. *loviello* (MSp. *ovillo* 'ball [of yarn])'

Other Spanish words with initial /gl-/ are evidently learned words: *gloria*, *globo*, *glotón*, etc. We may conclude therefore that in the normal popular development of both these clusters the initial consonant was lost.

/kl-/, /pl-/, /fl-/ > /l̯/

The development of these clusters presents a far more complex picture than that encountered with the voiced consonants plus /l/. First of all, there are many more words beginning with these clusters and the variety of results shows that a number of different linguistic forces have been at work affecting their development, so that one cannot set up a simple straight line of change from Latin to Spanish.

The evidence of Italian and Rumanian indicates that the first change that occurred was a palatalization of the /l/ after /k/. This change can be conceived of as beginning as an assimilation of the dorsovelar articulation of /k/ to the succeeding lateral. The raising of the back of the tongue

---

[48] *Harper's Latin Dictionary* contains only nine.
[49] If BLATTA is the source of *ladilla* we must suppose that an alternate form was the real root word: *BLATA*.
[50] *Harper's Latin Dictionary* has eighteen (not counting proper names or their derivatives).

caused the tip to be retracted toward the palatal area. The allophonic
distribution of initial clusters with /l/ would originally have been as follows: [pl], [fl], [kl̦]. The spread of the palatal [l̦] to the other clusters cannot
be understood then as a similar phonetic development but rather as the
allophonic unification of all clusters, with the palatal /l̦/ of the last group
being adopted by speakers as the articulation for all clusters (Tuttle 1975,
407–08). This pronunciation, in fact, is still found in a very conservative
area of Hispania, upper Aragon, known for its preservation of other archaic phonetic features (Viudas Camarasa 1979).

These new clusters, however, are somewhat "heavy" in articulatory
terms, and those areas of Romania that adopted this shift (Rumanian,
Italo-Romance, central and western Ibero-Romance) soon made further
changes in the direction of a simpler pronunciation. Thus, in a movement
similar to that affecting /gl-/ and /bl-/, the initial consonant was
dropped, leaving the palatal /l̦/ as initial consonant:

PLANCTU 'beating of the breast, lamentation > *llanto* 'weeping'
PLŌRĀRE 'to cry aloud, wail' > *llorar* 'to weep'
PLAGA 'bleeding wound' > *llaga*
PLICĀRE (back formation of APPLICĀRE 'to board, approach') > *llegar*
  'to arrive'
PLENU 'full' > *lleno*
PLUVIA 'rain' > *lluvia*
CLAMĀRE 'to call' > *llamar*
CLĀVE 'key' > *llave*
FLAMMA 'flame' > *llama*

Some have associated this initial consonant loss with pre-Romance languages, since Latinisms containing initial clusters in Basque drop the first
consonant (Lapesa 1980, 43). Similar developments are found in southern
Italian dialects, however, which leads us to suspect that this may be primarily a Romance development (Tuttle 1975, 427; Schürr 1959), although
undoubtedly Basque-Romance bilinguals would have favored it.

Dialect Borrowings?

As Castilian was carried south with the reconquest, this change, along
with others, was brought into regions which had either preserved the Latin
clusters intact, as in Catalan and Mozarabic, or areas such as the northeast
and its dependents, where the typical development of these clusters is to [č]
(later [š]), e.g., Port. *chave, chuva, chegar, chamar* etc. < CLĀVE, PLUVIA,
PLICĀRE, CLAMĀRE. Certain words now part of the Spanish lexicon, which
show a different result of the Latin clusters, may have been adopted in
these parts, e.g., *chopo* 'black poplar' < Late Lat. *PLOPPU (C.L. PŌPULUS),
choza 'hut' < PLUTEU 'framework of boards with which soldiers protected
themselves', *chub-asco -azo* 'shower' (apparently based on Gal.-Port.
chuva 'rain').

It has been suggested that instead of being dialect borrowings into Castilian, such words may rather be the relics of an original early Ibero-Romance development of the Latin clusters which were later overlaid by the palatalizing innovation from central Romania (Malkiel 1983, 229–230). In view of the very small number of such cases in the Castilian lexicon, and especially the difficulty of accounting for the development of the clusters directly to [č] without passing through a previous stage of palatalization of /l/,[51] an alternative explanation may be more likely. As is seen later in this chapter, the normal development of a palatal in medial position after a consonant is to an affricate. Indeed, such is the normal development of clusters plus /l/ in Castilian when in this position, e.g., AMPLU 'ample, wide' > *ancho*. It is easy to conceive that this development was then generalized to all positions in Galician-Portuguese, while Castilian continued to preserve the palatal /l̯/ in word-initial position. In view of the preservation of the very first stage of the palatalized pronunciation /pl̯-, kl̯-, f l̯-/ in the conservative Upper Aragonese dialect, this line of development seems quite plausible.

Learned Influence and Resolution of Possible
Homonymic Clash

In other cases it seems that possible lexical conflicts were settled by the adoption of doublets, with one word showing the typical popular development, and the other some other solution, usually a retention of the Latin group:

CLĀVU 'nail' > *clavo* (contrasting with *llave* < CLĀVE)
PLAGA 'stretch, space, zone' > *playa* 'beach' (contrasting with *llaga* 'wound')
PLICĀRE 'to bend, fold' > *plegar* (contrasting with *llegar* < (AP)PLICĀRE)

Determining which is the truly "popular" development of the cluster /f l-/ is no easy task, and indeed may be impossible. There were apparently only six words in Latin beginning with this cluster that were preserved in Castilian:

FLACCU 'flabby' > *flaco*
FLOCCU 'lock of hair, down' > OSp. *flueco* (MSp. *fleco*)
FLUXU 'flowing, loose; careless' > *floxo*
FLŌRE 'flower' > *flor*
FLAMMA 'flame' > *llama*
FLACCIDU 'flabby' > *lacio* 'languid, withered; straight, lank'

---

[51] Malkiel states: "The relation of /č/ to /λ/, though seemingly easy to describe in geographic terms, fails to lend itself to any smooth interpretation on other levels of analysis" (1983, 229). But is not a phonetic development such as I suggest much simpler and more likely than a direct change of /kl-/, /pl-/, and /f l-/ > /č/?

Were there no other clusters to be taken into account, it would be easy to decide on the basis of numbers alone that the preservation of the cluster represented the "normal" development and that some special explanation was required for *lacio* and *llama*. The fact that the normal development for /pl-/ and /kl-/ seems to be to /ḷ-/ has led many to the conclusion that such should be considered the "regular" change for /fl-/ also and thus only *llama* needs no explanation. Once /f l-/ > /ḷ-/ is established as a "sound law," all sorts of explanations, tortured or otherwise, needed to be devised to explain why *flor*, *fleco*, *flojo*, and *flaco* are "irregular." The ordinary solution has been to declare them to be "learned" words and thus not subject to popular phonetic development. This conclusion then made it necessary to think of some reason why such common words should have been taken directly from the Latin vocabulary. It is certainly possible to do so in case of need (Wright 1982, 10–12). Thus, Malkiel (1963) declared that generic words are frequently learned (29–31), although he gave no reason for thinking so. *Flor* would necessarily be learned[52] (disregarding for the moment the fact that Italians seemed to have no difficulty in using a popular form of the word, *fiore*). He likewise thought that it was possible that speakers needed to delineate the word more sharply from those derived from PLŌRĀRE > *llorar*.

In a number of examples, the retention of the original group may have a different explanation, based on the phonetic conditions of the word. As we saw above, the single initial /f-/ had developed a variant pronunciation as [h] which would not normally in Romance form any kind of cluster with any other consonant. Speakers who began to pronounce the /f-/ as [h] would have simply omitted the [h] altogether and thus ended with *lacio* as we saw above. We find similar developments of toponyms like *Laíno* and *Lambra*.

Likewise the existence of a palatal farther on in the word might have provoked a dissimilatory action on the incipient palatalization of the /l/. This sort of dissimilation may well account for other cases of preservation of the initial group since during the period in which both older and newer variants of the words coexisted, speakers could easily have preferred the older form which avoided two palatal articulations in succession (cf. Wright 1976). Thus, in the following examples speakers may also have retained the initial cluster for the same reason:

playa 'beach', contrasted with *llaga* 'wound'
PLANGERE 'to strike one's breast or head in token of grief' > *plañir* 'to lament, grieve, bewail', contrasted with *llanto* 'weeping'.
CLAVICULA, dim. of CLĀVE 'key' > *clavija* 'peg, pin', contrasted with *llave*
PLATEA 'street' > *plaça* 'public square'

---

[52] Some toponyms the development *llor-* is found, e.g., *Lloredo* < FLŌRĒTUS 'flowery', etc.

PLACITU > *plaz(d)o* 'term'
FLUXU 'flowing, loose, slack, limp' > *floxo* 'lax, lazy'

Consonant Clusters in Medial Position

When the consonant clusters containing an /l/ appeared in a medial position, immediately after a consonant, they normally result in an affricate /č/:

AMPLU 'ample, wide' > *ancho*
IMPLĒRE 'to fill' > *fenchir*
INFLĀRE 'to inflate' > *finchar*[53]
CONCLĀVĀRĪ 'to settle in a room' > *conchavar* 'to unite; hire the services of someone'

The Development of /b d g/ and the Spread of Voicing

The process of voicing seems to have been in full swing when the Moslem invasion of the early eighth century effectively cut off the Romance of the southern areas of the peninsula from the northern dialects, but it evidently had not reached the point of completion. Manuscripts of the ninth and tenth centuries (and occasionally earlier) show that voicing existed as a variant pronunciation of intervocalic voiceless stops in many areas. It is likely that in popular speech it had become the norm in the north, but the older norm of voicelessness may still have been actively competing with it to some extent. The earliest written examples are from the seventh century, before the Moslem invasion: PONTIVACATUS for PONTIFICATUS 'office of the pontiff' (A.D. 652), LEBRA (7th century) for LEPRA 'leprosy', IUBENTUDIS (seventh century) for IUVENTUTIS 'youth' (gen. sing.), EGLESIE (A.D. 691) for ECLESIAE 'of, to the church' (gen., dat. sing.). All of these examples are from the southern part of the peninsula (*Orígenes* §46.6b). In the eighth century other examples are found: FELGARIAS (A.D. 775, Asturias) for FILICARIA, and SEBARATUS (*Orígenes* §45.1). Further documents from Leon in the ninth century testify to the voiced pronunciation, and in the tenth and eleventh centuries more and more examples appear in writing. It is especially worthy of note that in the northwest, i.e., the western part of the kingdom of Leon and in Galicia, voicing seems to be most firmly rooted. The strength of the new norm is revealed particularly in words that were now purely literary, probably having disappeared from popular usage: *perpedua, abut,cíngidur, áliga, digunt*, etc. for earlier PERPETUA 'continuous', APUD 'at, nearby', CINGITUR 'it is bound', ALIQUA 'some(one)' (fem.), DĪCUNT 'they say'. Such spellings show clearly that earlier voiceless stops were read as voiced stops and that

---

[53] The origin of the initial F- is a separate problem. See Malkiel 1954, Meier 1970–71. Malkiel suggests that there may be some relation between medial /-č-/ and the non-organic /f/, since it is only in Castilian that the phenomenon is found (1963, 168).

some scribes were so uncertain of proper spelling that they probably did not realize their errors in writing. Hypercorrect forms in which Latin voiced consonants are spelled with P, T, K reveal this same sort of ignorance of proper spelling norms: *intecra, pupliga, iuco* for correct INTEGRA 'whole, upright', PUBLICA 'public', IUGUM 'yoke', and many others (*Orígenes* §45).

It is possible that voicing was most popular in the northwest because it was in this area in which the heaviest settlement of Celtic-speaking peoples had occurred. Such, at least, is the conclusion of Menéndez Pidal (*Orígenes* §46.5). Later research in notarial documents has confirmed that the spread of voicing is from west to east (Politzer 1954), but the question still remains open as to whether this movement can be specifically related to a Celtic language substratum in the Iberian peninsula. The greatest difficulty lies in determining when variation involving voicing took root and whether the Celtic languages lasted long enough in Iberia to have had this sort of effect on Romance. There may be no definitive answer simply because the evidence at our disposal, for all its value, is not a record of living speech but a stylized variety of a literary dialect.

The strongest resistance to voicing, or, to phrase it differently, the greatest conservatism, is visible in the areas near the Pyrenees. The preservation of voiceless stops was characteristic of the oldest strata of Upper Aragonese dialects, as can be seen in the comparison of Aragonese words with Castilian ones (regardless of whether the etyma are all Latin):

Aragonese		Castilian
krapa	'goat'	*cabra*
cocote	'back of the neck'	*cogote*
pocilca	'pig sty'	*pocilga*
marito	'husband'	*marido*
taleca	'bag, sack'	*talega*
		(*Orígenes* §46.3)

This particular feature has been attributed to some kind of non-Romance influence, specifically Iberian. It is not really necessary in this particular case to posit the influence of language contact to account for simple conservation in an area remote from the centers of linguistic innovation,[54] although the presence of non-Romance speakers may have been a concomitant factor.

Voicing may still have been in competition with the preservation of voiceless stops in the early eighth century as may be seen in the strongly conservative area in southern Iberia, cut off, as we remarked earlier, from the northern Ibero-Romance dialects. As we have already seen, there are examples of voicing from this area before the eighth century. However, there is some indication of the preservation of the voiceless consonants.

---

[54] See Zamora 1967, 227–30, for bibliography and discussion. Posner 1966 refers to this preservation as a pseudo-problem (329).

Menéndez Pidal attributes the phenomenon to an Arabic literary taste for conservative standards rather than to a true popular preference for the older forms and is convinced that voicing was the norm in popular speech as it was in the north (*Orígenes* §46).

In support of his opinion is the fact that the transcription of Romance words in Arabic script in the *Vocabulista in Arabico* of the thirteenth century, in the harjas (over a range of several centuries), and in the *Botánico anónimo* (eleventh and twelfth centuries), the medial /-t-/ and /-k-/ are consistently spelled with t ط (a velarized alveolar stop) and q ق (a uvular stop).[55] In all other positions the consonants having their source in Latin /t/ and /k/ are represented by t ت and k ك as are the consonants derived from Latin medial geminated /t:/ and /k:/ (Hilty 1979, 152). Galmés (1977, 280; 1983, 9–100,175–79, 201–02, 236–39) points out that the original pronunciation of the "emphatic" (i.e., velarized) consonants in Arabic was that of voiced stops.[56] There is even evidence of some fricative articulation as well so that it seems safe to conclude that voicing of medial stops was widespread in Mozarabic (Corrientes 1978, 217).

On the other hand, one bit of evidence that would support the conclusion that voicing had not become the norm everywhere is the existence of a large number of Mozarabic words in the modern Castilian vocabulary such as *alcaparra, almatriche, alpatana, anapelo, canuto, capacho, caroca, cernícalo, cópano, cornato, horchata, marchito,* etc., not to mention an abundance of placenames such as *Belchite, (Puerto) Lápiche, Estepa, Játiva, Júcar,* etc. (Griffin 1958, 60–61). If these words are indeed of Latin-Romance origin, one might conclude that some words in Mozarabic still retained the older voiceless pronunciation and it would be reasonable to conclude that voicing, although strongly established in most dialects, was not completely dominant everywhere in southern Hispano-Romance by the eighth century.[57] The subsequent disappearance of the southern dialects, or rather, their absorption by northern Castilian during the reconquest, makes it impossible to be absolutely sure that the newer norm had triumphed in all areas. In the north, by way of contrast, the innovation of voicing eliminated almost all traces of the former pronunciation. Some typical examples of the results in Castilian are the following:

/-p-/ > /-b-/

APICULA 'bee' (dim.) > *abeja*
CAPILLU 'hair' > *cabello*
LUPU 'wolf' > *lobo*
APRĪLE 'April' > *abril*

---

[55] Since Arabic has only one bilabial consonant /b/, we cannot be certain what sound is represented by the letter ب *bā'*.

[56] Torreblanca (forthcoming) claims that ق ٩ was used not to indicate voice but rather a lack of aspiration (16). According to him, Hispano-Latin voiceless stops were aspirated. He does not say how he knows this.

[57] Hilty (1979) ignores these words in his criticism of Griffin 1958 (148).

CAPRA 'goat' > *cabra*
DUPLARE (Late Lat.) 'to double' > *doblar*
POPULU 'people' > *pueblo*

/-t-/ > /-d-/

ACŪTU 'sharp' > *agudo*
DELICĀTU 'dainty, nice' > *delgado* 'thin'
PRĀTU 'meadow' > *prado*
VĪTA 'life' > *vida*
PATRE 'father' > *padre*
PETRA > *piedra*

/-k-/ > /-g-/

FĪCU 'fig' > *figo*
LACTŪCA 'lettuce' > *lechuga*
SĒCŪRU 'secure, safe' > *seguro*
SŪCU 'juice' > OSp. *xugo*
ACR- *-U 'sharp' > OSp. *agro*
LUCRU 'gain, profit' > *logro*
MACRU 'thin, poor' > *magro*
ECLĒSIA 'church' > *iglesia*

The Development of /kʷ/ in Castilian

As was pointed out in the previous chapter (pp. 134–35), /kʷ/ and /gʷ/ usually lost the semiconsonant in Late Latin. If the /k/ then appeared between vowels, it became voiced as did other examples of voiceless consonants:

ALIQUOD 'something' > *algo*
ALIQUEM 'someone' > *alguién* (Malkiel 1948)
ANTIQUU 'old' > OSp. *antigo*
SEQU- *ĪRE (C.L. SEQUOR, SEQUĪ) > *seguir*
VACUU 'empty' > *vago*

If the resulting /k/ appeared word-initially or after a consonant, it remained without further change:

*QUALANIA (← QUĀLIS) > OSp. *calaña* 'model, pattern'
QUATTUORDECIM 'fourteen' > *catorze*[58]
NUMQUAM 'never' > *nunca*[59]

---

[58] We must presume that the preservation of kʷa/ in *cuarenta* < QUADRAGINTA 'forty' was influenced analogically by *cuatro* 'four' < QUATTUOR (Menéndez Pidal 1941, 187). *Cuatro* did not have a similar influence on *catorze* 'fourteen', probably because of the stronger influence of *quince* < QUĪNDECIM.

[59] There is some evidence that NUMQUAM was still pronounced /nunkwa/ in Old Spanish, probably along with the pronunciation /nunka/ (González Ollé 1972, 298).

SQUALIDU 'rough, dirty' > OSp. *escalio*
SQUALIDARE 'to make dirty' > OSp. *escaliar, escalidar*
SQUĀMA 'scale' > *escama*
TORQUĀTU 'wearing a twisted collar or necklace' > *torcado*
QUEM 'whom' (acc.) > *quien*

If the combination of /k/ plus the vowel /u/ before another vowel produced the phonetic result [kʷ], the semiconsonant was lost exactly as it was in the original QU:

*ACCU HAC > *acá* 'here'
*ACCU HĪC > *aquí* 'here'
*ACCU ILLE > *aquel* 'that' (plus the other demonstratives)

Only when /kʷ/ appeared before a tonic /a/ did the semiconsonant remain. Between vowels, the /k/ voiced regularly:

AEQUĀLE 'equal' > *igual*
AEQUĀRE 'to equalize' > OSp. *iguar*
ALIQUANDŌ 'sometime' > OSp. *alguandre*
ANTĪQUA 'old' (fem.) > *antigua*
AQUA 'water' > *agua*
EQUA 'mare' > *yegua*
*EXAQUĀRE > OSp. *enxaguar*

In initial position, of course, the /k/ remained unchanged:

QUĀLE 'which' > *cual*
QUANDŌ 'when' > *cuando*
QUANTU 'how much' > *cuanto*
QUATTUOR 'four' > *cuatro*

(The results of /gʷ/ are discussed in the section on /g/.)

Intervocalic /-đ-/

As we recall from the discussion in chapter 3, the voicing of the intervocalic voiceless occlusives entailed the fricatization of the voiced occlusives. This process produced a set of voiced fricatives, limited in distribution to the interior of words (excepting for the moment the /ƀ/). The former voiceless stops, having become voiced, would now be associated with the initial voiced stops. For example, the /t/ of Lat. VĪTA had been the intervocalic counterpart of the word initial /t-/ of words like TERRA, but after having become voiced to /d/, would have been identified as the same consonant found at the beginning of words like *dar* 'to give' < DĀRE. The medial /d/ would have become a fricative /-đ-/.

Evidently the fricative was very weakly articulated since in western Ibero-Romance it disappeared in almost all words. Probably it ceased to be pronounced first between identical vowels:

COMEDERE 'to eat' (C.L. EDERE) > *comer*
DISCĒDERE 'to separate; depart' > OSp. *deçir* 'to descend'
*SEDENTĀRE 'to seat' > *sentar*
SEDĒRE 'to be seated' > OSp. *seer* 'to be'

Next, the presence of any one front vowel became sufficient to stimulate the loss of /-đ-/:

CRŪDĒLE 'cruel' > *cruel*
FIDE 'faith' > *fe*
JŪDICE 'judge' > OSp. *júez*
LAMPRĒDA 'eel' > *lamprea*
CADERE 'to fall' > *caer*
RŌDERE 'to gnaw' > *roer*

The shift of /-đ-/ was not completed entirely in the preliterary period, nor was it universal in Ibero-Romance. It seems to have been most consistently adopted in the westernmost areas, with less application the farther east one goes. The manuscripts of Berceo, for example, who was from La Rioja, show many examples of /d/ alternating with zero. In Castilian a number of exceptions to the loss are found. An examination of the phonetic environment of words which still contain medial /đ/ < /d/ reveals that if it was flanked by two back vowels or by /a/ and a back vowel, it is retained (Dworkin 1974, 172):

ALAUDA 'lark' > OSp. *aloda* (> MSp. *alondra*)
CAUDA 'tail' > OSp. *coda* (> MSp. *cola*)
CRŪDU 'crude, raw' > *crudo*
NŪDU 'naked' > *(d)es-nudo*
NŌDU 'knot' > *nudo*
SŪDĀRE 'to sweat' > *sudar*
SŪDŌRE 'sweat' > *sudor*
VADU 'ford' > *vado*

There are some examples of words with similar phonetic shapes in which the /-đ-/ has disappeared, but apparently this occurred only when the /-đ-/ was on a morpheme border:

ADHŪC 'thus far' > OSp. *ahú/aún* 'still, yet'
*ADOCULARE > *aojar* 'to bewitch'
ADORĀRE 'to adore, worship' > OSp. *aorar* (MSp. *adorar*)
ADŪNĀRE 'to join, unite' > *aunar*
MEA DOMINA 'my mistress, lady' > OLeon. *miona* 'noble lady'

The preservation of /-đ-/ was not, however, automatic in these phonetic circumstances. The pressure to eliminate it in so many places led speakers to create forms without the /-d-/, and numerous Old Spanish sources show that it was frequently lost in forms in which it is now

standard: *aloa, coa, crúo, desnúo, suar, suor*. It would not be unreasonable
to reconstruct also **grao, *núo*, and **vao* as having existed also, perhaps as
ephemeral variants along with the forms retaining the /-đ-/.

The spread of the loss of medial /-đ-/, as can be seen in the forms cited
above, was evidently a process that lasted over several centuries since,
although many words had lost all trace of the consonant in preliterary
times, there are numerous texts that reveal its continuing presence along
with the more evolved forms. Many verb forms continued to retain the
/-đ-/, at least in some texts, and we see forms like *odió, odieron, cadió,
credió, sedió*, etc. for *oyó, oyeron, cayó, creyó, seyó* (Dworkin 1974, 52).
Occasionally the /-đ-/ appears also in the medieval imperfect in /-ié/:
cadié, credié, etc. (Dworkin 1974, 73).[60] The appearance or loss of /-đ-/
then was conditioned by a complex concatenation of factors: geographical
distribution of the loss, greater or lesser archaism of the text, and, by
implication, the personal preferences of different authors.

The conditions that favored the preservation of /-đ-/ seem, however, to
have been primarily phonetic, namely the presence of a low vowel /a/
and a back vowel /o, u/. The reasons for this particular exception to the
general rule can be found in the effect that loss of medial consonants had
on the structure of the syllable and the word. Speaking in general terms,
the preferred form of the syllable in Spanish, as it was in Late Latin, was
the CV type, statistically dominant as we saw in chapter 2. The type CCV
was a secondary type, providing the two consonants formed a cluster. As
we saw earlier, many of the developments of the syllabic structure of Late
Latin seem to result from a drive to eliminate the final consonant of closed
syllables, leading to the creation of open syllables.

The elimination of /-đ-/ would, however, result in a number of vowels
coming into contact. As we observed previously, vowels in hiatus were
also generally antithetic to the linguistic feeling of Latin-Romance
speakers. Thus, two different phonetic movements, the elimination of a
weakly articulated medial consonant and the avoidance of hiatus, worked
against each other. In a language like French, the drive to eliminate many
medial consonants, including /-đ-/, was evidently so strong that speakers
became used to vowels in hiatus for a fairly long time before they finally
disposed of many of them.[61] Portuguese likewise lost medial /-l-/ and
/-n-/ and was therefore somewhat in the same position. In Castilian,
however, speakers who were faced with the necessity of adopting either a
more advanced form with hiatus or a conservative form without it could
choose the older form when the vowels surrounding the /-đ-/ seemed to
be more "hiatic" than others, i.e., were low or back.

Another way of avoiding the undesired hiatus was to choose some sort

---

[60] The case of *vide* and *vido* is at least as much a problem of morphology as of phonetic
development (Malkiel 1960).

[61] In the thirteenth century, according to Pope 1934, 108–11.

of consonant that would serve as well as the preservation of the /-đ-/ to keep the vowels apart. Thus, a number of verb forms that would have had /a/ in hiatus with a back vowel in form 1 of the present indicative developed a preference for [-j-] as the appropriate antihiatic consonant

CADŌ 'I fall' > *cayo*
TRAHŌ 'I draw, drag' > *trayo*

It is possible that the choice of [-j-] as the antihiatic consonant was influenced by a number of verbs that had developed this consonant naturally, when a /đ/ was followed by a yod:

AUDIŌ 'I hear' > *oyo*
SEDEŌ 'I am seated' > *seyo*
VIDEŌ 'I see' > *veyo*

In fact, the loss of /-đ-/ may have been aided by the structure of such verbs in which the evolution of /d/ plus a yod had eliminated the /d/ in form 1, thus producing a contrast between this form and the other verb forms that had no yod to absorb the /đ/ (Dworkin 1974, 46).

This particular antihiatic consonant spread to other verb forms, such as the variant forms of the infinitives: *cayer, creyer, oyir, rayer, reyir, seyer, veyer* for *caer, creer, oir, raer, seer, veer*. Such forms continue to be found in modern Leonese and Aragonese (Dworkin 1974, 177). The [j] spread to other word classes too as a convenient hiatus breaker, regardless of the nature of the vowels potentially in contact, e.g., *aloya, desnuyo*, and *peyón* for *aloda, desnudo, peón*, and modern Asturian *feyo* 'ugly' vs. Cast. *feo*, *nuyo* vs. Cast. *nudo*.[62]

Other consonants were used on occasion with the same function, such as /-ƀ-/ and /-ɡ-/, e.g., *juvezes* for *juezes* (*Fuero Juzgo*), *juvizio* for *juizio* (*Cid* 3226, 3239, 3259), *oviestes* for *oístes* (*Cid* 2314, Yúçef A, 67d), *feguza* 'confidence' vs. Cast. *fe-, fi-uza*. A few modern dialectal forms such as *pegulio* 'louse' (Cabraniego) for Cast. *piojo*, Ast. *fego* for Cast. *feo*, Santander *peganio* 'of lower rank' (applied to judges) for *pedáneo* (Dworkin 1974, 178).

An alternate method of eliminating hiatus was to merge the vowels in contact into a single syllable, something that eventually happened to many words whenever one of the vowels was a high vowel: *crüel* > *cruel* [krwel], *fiel* > *fiel* [fjel]. This particular solution was favored when the /-đ-/ appeared between two atonic syllables as we can see in the numerous examples of the adjectival suffix -IDUS:

FLACCIDU > *lacio*
LŪCIDU 'shining, bright' > *luzio*

---

[62] There is a question of whether the modern dialectal forms go back to an earlier period or are modern formations (Levy 1973).

NĪTIDU 'shining; slippery' > *nidio*
RANCIDU 'rank, stinking' > *rancio* 'old, ancient; stale'

(Dworkin 1974, 94)

Intervocalic /-g-/

The development of medial /-g-/ is very similar to that of /-đ-/. It will be recalled that /-g-/ was subject to phonetic change in Late Latin when it preceded a front vowel and was reduced to a palatal fricative. We must therefore eliminate from consideration all examples in which this change has occurred. This process left only a relatively small number of words with the intervocalic /-g-/ as compared with /-đ-/ and /-b-/. One might conclude, on the basis of a number of examples, that the general tendency was the same as with /-đ-/, i.e., elimination, especially when /-g-/ was preceded by a front vowel:

INTEGRU 'whole, entire' > *entero*[63]
LĒGĀLE 'legal' > *leal* 'loyal'
LĪTIGĀRE 'to quarrel, dispute, brawl' > *lidiar* 'to fight'
PIGRITIA 'indolence, sluggishness' > *pereza*
RĒGĀLE 'royal' > *real*
FŪMIGĀRE 'to fumigate, smoke' > *humear*
RŪMIGĀRE 'to ruminate' > *rumiar*

One may question whether the three verbs given should count as three separate examples since in all of them the same suffix appears: -IGĀRE, which could therefore count as a single example. Also *leal* and *real* are closely associated with base words that had contained a /-g-/ before a front vowel and therefore had developed a palatal consonant: *ley* 'law' < LĒGE and *rey* 'king' < RĒGE.

It is necessary too to take into account a number of words containing /-g-/ which had preserved the consonant:

A(U)GUSTU 'August' > *agosto*
A(U)GURIU 'omen' > *agüero*
ASPARAGU 'asparagus' > *espárrago*
JUGU 'yoke' > *yugo*
PLAGA 'wound' > *llaga*

In the examples just given, we have a non-front vowel before the /-g-/ so that perhaps we could assume that the consonant is preserved only in this particular circumstance (cf. however, the common form *iuvo* instead of *yugo* [*Fuero de Usagre*, p. 290]). There are, on the other hand, several words having a front vowel before the /-g-/ which still preserve the consonant:

---

[63] As we saw in the examples of intervocalic voicing, the liquids following a consonant act as though they were vowels.

LEGŪMINE 'vegetable' > *legumbre*
LIGŌNE 'hoe, mattock' > *legón*
NIGRU 'black' > *negro*
NEGĀRE 'to deny' > *negar*
FUSTIGARE 'to lash, whip; harass' > *hostigar*
LIGĀRE 'to bind' > *ligar*[64]
NAVIGĀRE 'to sail, navigate' > *navegar*
CASTIGĀRE 'to reprove, chasten; punish' > OSp. *castigar* 'to advise'

Comparing the two sets of examples with /-g-/ after a front vowel, we might be tempted to conclude that when the consonant disappears it is the result of an association of the word with another word in which the /g/ had become palatalized (e.g., *leal*, *real*), that the result of the group /gr/ is best explained by a syllable division between the two consonants producing a yod that was subsequently absorbed by the preceding vowel (*entero*, *pereza*), and that the verbs containing the suffix -ĪGĀRE show a special development > -*ear*, -*iar* perhaps through association with -*ear* < -IDIĀRE, as opposed to the development of -ĪGĀRE. Another possible explanation for the preservation of the /-g-/ in verbs could be that the consonant is kept when the accent falls on the immediately preceding syllable in most forms of the present tense (*hostigar*, *negar*), while it falls when in these forms the accent falls on a preceding syllable (*humear*, *lidiar*, *rumiar*) (DCELC III 90a). We would then have to classify *ligar* and *castigar* as learned forms in view of the preservation of the short /i/ as /i/. An older form of *navegar* is *navear*, which would have to be balanced against the base word *navío* < NĀVIGIU 'ship'. We would be left finally with *legumbre*, *legón*, and *negro* for which we can find no good explanation if we assume that all medial /-g-/'s should disappear.

Faced with arguments of apparently equal weight in favor of both hypotheses (i.e., 1. that all medial /g/'s disappear after a front vowel; 2. all medial /g/'s remain, with special associations accounting for occasional disappearances), the investigator can with safety only conclude that the evidence is not really sufficient to allow us to decide which should be the "regular" outcome. Considering early Romance /-g-/ as part of the system of voiced fricatives which includes /b̵/ and /d̵/, we may observe that it seems to be halfway between them: /-d̵-/ disappears with few exceptions while /-b̵-/ is preserved with rare exceptions.

Initial and Intervocalic /b̵/

As we saw earlier, in intervocalic position Latin /-b-/ and /-b̵-/ (< [w]) merged everywhere in Romania at a fairly early date, although in initial position they remained phonemically distinct. In many areas the original bilabial pronunciation changed to a labiodental articulation, probably as a

---

[64] *Liar* is a borrowing from Fr. *lier* (BDELC 353a).

result of its association with the voiceless fricative /f/, especially where, as in northern Gallo-Romance, the other voiced fricatives disappeared early (Galmés 1961, 27). We might conclude that since /f/ was found almost exclusively in word-initial position it was in this position that the labio-dental pronunciation first became established, spreading next to the medial position. The position after a liquid consonant is likewise usually treated as though it were word-initial.[65]

In the Iberian peninsula the labiodental pronunciation is found today in Portuguese, in certain Catalan-speaking areas, and in a few southern dialects of Castilian.[66] It cannot be proved that the labiodental ever existed in northern Ibero-Romance. Alarcos Llorach (1968, 258) suggests that the lack of [f] and the presence of [ƀ] in the Cantabrian area prevented the more modern pronunciation from ever developing.[67]

Because of the phonemic merger in intervocalic position, medieval scribes (like some modern ones) had at their disposal two letters to represent the same sound. It is not too surprising then to find that they often used them indifferently in writing the same words: *bebetura*, *ueuetura*, *debisa*, *deuisa*, *habet*, *hauet* (*Orígenes* §10.2). Eventually the orthographic system of Old Spanish became relatively fixed and the letter u (v) was used to represent the bilabial fricative:

CABALLU 'nag' > *cavallo* 'horse'
FABA 'broad bean' > *fava*
LEVARE 'to raise' > *levar* (MSp. *llevar*)
NOVEM 'nine' > *nueve*
BARBA 'beard' > *barva*
SERVU 'slave, servant' > *siervo*

The voiced occlusive resulting from the Latin medial /-p-/ was usually written with the letter B: SAPERE 'to taste; know' > *saber*, etc. (see p. 230) (Alonso 1962, 169).

Initial /b-/ and /ƀ-/

The phonemicization of the former phonetic "variation" (see chapter 3) produced the restitution of the stable initial word boundary which we see in the identification of Lat. /p-, t-, k-/ with the results of the former medial geminates /-p:-, -t:-, -k:-/ (Weinrich 1956, chaps. 3, 4) which we will discuss shortly. If this same phonemicization acted in the same way with regard to the voiced stops of Latin, the result would have the identification

---

[65] Rumanian, for example, merges /b/ and /v/ after a liquid, but not initially.
[66] See Jungemann 1955, 337–41, for a description of the areas where [v] and [b] are found.
[67] Söll 1964, 93, agrees with this idea, but misinterprets him to have said that [v] had once existed but then shifted back to [b]. However, Alarcos simply says: "Es muy posible que, desde el principio, la zona donde nació el castellano ignorase la articulación labiodental y mantuviese para /v/ . . . la pronunciación bilabial" (258).

of the Late Latin initial /ƀ-/ and the medial /-ƀ-/. This was indeed the result in the other Romance languages:

Initial /b-/ vs. /ƀ-/

	French	Italian	Portuguese
BENE 'well'	*bien*	*bene*	*bem*
BUCCA 'puffed up cheek' > 'mouth'	*bouche*	*bocca*	*boca*
VACCA 'cow'	*vache*	*vacca*	*vaca*
VINU 'wine'	*vin*	*vino*	*vinho*

Medial /-ƀ-/

CABALLU	*cheval*	*cavallo*	*cavalo*
FABA	*fève*	*fava*	*fava*
NOVA 'new' (fem.sg.)	*neuve*	*nuova*	*nova*

In contrast with the results in these languages, the earliest evidence we possess from northern Ibero-Romance areas reveals frequent use of the letter B where we would expect to find V (U). Thus, in the *Glosas emilianenses* of the tenth century we find *bertiziones, beces, bergu[n]dian* instead of *vertiziones, veces, vergundian* (*Orígenes*, pp. 3, 6), and in the *Glosas silenses* many more: *basallos, bientos, betatu, bicinos, betait*, all of which could be expected to appear with initial U (*Orígenes*, pp. 20, 21, 22). Reverse spellings also are found: *ueuetura* (p. 14) shortly after *bebetura*.[68] Other early documents present a similar picture: *binea* for *vinea* (several times), *bolumtate* for *voluntate* (both dated 1062 A.D., *Orígenes*, p. 40).[69] The greatest number of examples of confusion seem to come from the northernmost areas. It is interesting to note that the Gascon dialect has merged initial /b-/ and /ƀ-/, e.g., VETULU 'old' > *bielh*, VACCA > *baca*, etc. (Baldinger 1958, 246).

A plausible conclusion might be then that in word-initial position the two consonants merged at an early period (Alonso 1962, 167). Another possible conclusion might be that such confusions as are in early documents are simply sporadic spelling errors, since the majority of words are spelled in accordance with their Latin etymology. If this is true, the complete merger of /b/ and /ƀ/ would have to be a later development.

If we turn back to the situation in Late Latin when variation was still a living process, we can see that the initial /b-/ would have had two realizations: [b-] after pause or consonants, and [ƀ] after words ending in a vowel, while /ƀ-/ would have had one invariable articulation as a bilabial fricative. In other words, the realizations of /b-/ would have been just what they are in modern Spanish. This same phenomenon of a dual realization

---

[68] Perhaps this example should be left out of consideration since the presence of two B's might have produced some mutual influence.

[69] Other examples are given by Alonso 1962, 162–65.

for the phoneme /b-/ and the bilabial fricative articulation is not restricted to Castilian alone, but is also found in Galicia and in northern Portugal, Leon, and Extremadura (except in the areas of Cáceres that have labio-dental [v]), Aragon, Catalonia and Valencia (except for western Valencia which also has [v]), Gascony, Languedoc, Guienne, and Sardinia (Penny 1976, 154–55). The distribution of the phenomenon suggests that this is not a relatively modern change that has been spread by the influence of Castilian but rather a very old, conservative feature, namely the preserva-tion of ancient variation of /b/, and probably also /d, g/ (Söll 1964, 89). The double realization of /b-/ would also account for the numerous spelling errors in early documents that we have noted. Since /b-/ after vowels would have had the same articulation as /ƀ-/, scribes would have occasionally confused them in writing. The total confusion of the two consonants in word-initial position would have resulted from a further development of the articulation of /b-/. A bilabial fricative could very easily become a stop consonant after nasal consonants, and, in fact, it is difficult to articulate a bilabial fricative in this position. Also the easiest articulation after a pause would be a stop. In other words, with the further development of these occlusive pronunciations of /ƀ-/, the only remain-ing positions in which /b-/ and /ƀ-/ would have remained distinct would have been after words ending in non-nasal consonants. As there are only a few of these, the inevitable result would have been that speakers lost all consciousness of the two consonants as distinct phonemes; in short, they merged them.

When this merger occurred in initial position is difficult to determine. Alonso believes that they had merged completely from the very earliest times in northern Spain (1962, 231–33). Penny believes that if they had completely merged there would have been much more confusion in writ-ing them than we actually find, and that etymological consistency cannot explain the regularity in writing that we do actually find (1976, 156). These contrasting views are by no means mutually exclusive. It is evident that merger did in fact occur, but there is no reason to think that it must have occurred at exactly the same time in all parts of northern Spain. Given the conditions that favored merger, it is not difficult to imagine that it occurred first in the areas least affected by the Latin tradition (or possibly in several different areas), i.e., those same regions that were the cradle of the original Castilian dialect, and then spread to other lands. Alonso finds that in documents from Castile the greatest number of examples of confusion of both phonemes appear in the earliest and most northerly ones (1962, 163).[70] This fact would confirm our hypothesis.

The distinction between medial /-b-/ and /-ƀ-/ in word-medial posi-tion would not have been immediately affected by merger in word-initial

---

[70] It would not, however, be necessary to assume that Castilian influenced all the dialects that merged /b-/ and /v-/, since "similar circumstances everywhere produced similar re-sults" (Penny 1976, 157).

position. Intervocalically /b/ would still have been an occlusive and /ƀ/ a fricative. Nevertheless, the initial merger could be a source of danger to the continued distinction in the middle of words, since speakers might be tempted to follow the same rules for articulation in both positions. Also there may have been a structural factor that would have influenced further development, namely the "increasing disfavor shown by Castilian toward oppositions which function only internally and are neutralized in initial position" (Penny 1976, 157).[71] Probably the /ƀ/ following nasal consonants had already developed an occlusive articulation as it had initially. If speakers then began to imitate the fricative pronunciation of /b-/ after vowels, they would have taken a great step toward complete merger. Again, as with the initial /b-/ and /ƀ-/, the distinction would finally have been limited to postconsonantal position (excluding nasals).[72] And, once more, the force of tradition would not have been sufficient in itself to preserve the phonemic distinction in the face of such extensive neutralization.

A number of scholars have concluded that the absence of a labiodental [v] in Basque is causally related to this eventual merger of all cases of /b/ and /ƀ/ in Castilian. In view of the fact that the bilabial pronunciation of the results of Latin v seems to be a Romance archaism rather than an innovation, we may wonder whether this is so. It seems more likely that in this case the role of Basque-Romance bilingualism was limited to favoring the retention of a conservative pronunciation (Jungemann, chap. 15), especially since it would have been aided by the voiceless counterpart [φ].

Summary

The final development of /đ/ and /g̶/ was probably very similar to that of /ƀ/, except that since there was no special letter to represent the fricative articulation, we can only study the alternation of /d/ and /g/ with zero. We can assume that northern dialects preserved the variation of Late Latin, and that in medial position the /-d-/ and /-g-/ < Lat. /-t-/ and /-k-/ represented an occlusive articulation during the early part of the Middle Ages. The conditions under which the fricative allophones appeared in word-initial position would then have influenced the pronunciation of the medial stops as well. Since most examples of medial /-ƀ-/ and /-g̶-/ < Lat. /-d-/ and /-g-/ had disappeared, it would have meant that by and large the number of occurrences of voiced stops far outweighed that of voiced fricatives. As with the merger of /b/ and /ƀ/, it is conceivable that the adoption of a medial fricative pronunciation was based at first on an imitation of the rules for alternation of fricative and stop in word-ini-

---

[71] The unvoicing of medial sibilants would be another example of this factor.

[72] In some regions of America (Nicaragua, El Salvador, Costa Rica, Colombia), postconsonantal /b d g/ are still realized as occlusives (Canfield 1962, 77–78). This feature may be a conservative one, dating back to medieval usage. It should be noted that the phonemic distinction is not preserved and that the results of Lat. /b/ and /v/ are treated alike.

tial position. (A far more elaborate and detailed discussion of the whole subject of the intervocalic voiced stops is found in Pensado Ruiz 1984, 21–175.)

Degemination and the Strengthening of Word-Initial Consonants

The simplification of the Latin geminate consonants is intimately related to the voicing of simple intervocalic stops as we saw in chapter 3. Whether or not the pressure to simplify geminates can be considered as an important factor in the voicing of the stops, there can be no doubt that once these stops were voiced there no longer remained any structural reason for maintaining them. The voicing left a hole in the pattern that could easily be filled by reducing the amount of effort required to produce the geminates, thus changing them into voiceless stops. The phonological system itself was not changed since the same number of phonemes was found, but greater economy of articulation was achieved.

Some typical examples are the following:

$/p{:}/ > /p/$

CAPPA (Late Latin) > *capa* 'cape'
CIPPU 'boundary marker; column; stick' > *cepo* 'foot of tree trunk; stake'
CUPPA (Late Latin) > *copa* 'cup'
STUPPA 'tow, oakum' > *estopa*

$/t{:}/ > /t/$

CATTU (Late Latin) 'cat' > *gato*
GUTTA 'drop' > *gota*
MITTERE 'to send' > *meter* 'to put into'
SAGITTA 'arrow' > *saeta*

$/k{:}/ > /k/$

BUCCA 'puffed out cheek' > 'mouth' > *boca*
PECCĀTU 'sin' > *pecado*
SICCU 'dry' > *seco*
VACCA 'cow' > *vaca*

The simplification of the voiceless geminate occlusives, however, could not occur without affecting all geminates, regardless of their type. This means that there would also be strong structural pressure on the liquids $/l{:}/$, $/r{:}/$, the nasals $/m{:}/$, $/n{:}/$, and the sibilant $/s{:}/$, and of course, on the few examples of voiced geminate stops $/d{:}/$ and $/g{:}/$. In the case of the simple sibilant $/\acute{s}/$, being a voiceless consonant, it could adopt the same feature as the voiceless stops, namely voicing, and thus become [ź]. The geminate $/\acute{s}{:}/$ could then simplify to $/\acute{s}/$:

CASA 'hut' > *casa* [ź] 'house'
FORMŌSU 'beautiful, handsome' > *hermoso* [ź]
ŪSU 'usage' > *uso* [ź]

MENSA > *mesa* [ź]
SĒNSU 'sense, intelligence' > *seso* [ź]
OSSU 'bone' (C.L. OS, OSSIS) > *huesso* [ś]
PRESSA > *priessa* 'haste' [ś] (MSp. *prisa*)
GROSSU 'fat' > *gruesso* [ś]
FOSSA 'ditch' > *fuessa* [ś]

The standardized Alfonsine orthography maintained the Latin spelling for the phonemes: -s- /ź/ and -ss- /ś/.

For voiced geminates the voicing solution was obviously impossible. One possible change was simplification and merger with the simple consonant. This particular change did in fact occur with the voiced stops which were, in any case, very rare, e.g., Late Lat. *INADDERE 'to add' (C.L. ADDERE) > OSp. *eñadir, anadir* (MSp. *añadir*). The geminate bilabial nasal /m:/ also simplified, e.g., FLAMMA 'flame' > *llama*. This geminate also was very rare, and in addition labial articulations tend to be inherently weaker than apical ones and thus provide less resistance to the pressure toward reduction of effort. As for /r:/, no change at all occurred and thus the geminate has been preserved until today, although there is some evidence that it is now changing in pronunciation in some Hispanic dialects[73] as it did several centuries ago in French and has done in some dialects of Portuguese.

The lateral /l:/ and the nasal /n:/ could have followed either of the preceding courses, but other factors intervened. First, they were phonetically strong or fortis in articulation, and were found in many more words than the /m:/, /d:/, or /g:/. Thus, any merger with the simple consonants would have produced more confusions of words than with the other consonants. This fact alone would not have sufficed to preserve the distinction between the simple and geminate consonants, but it helped to incline speakers to seek some other solution. In terms of articulation, there was a simple solution which would preserve the distinction: a change to some other type of articulation. Since geminates are articulated with greater force than the simple consonants, this greater force could be realized in some other way than simply by prolonging the contact of the articulators. The tongue, for example, could spread out in its contact with the alveolar-palatal area. Instead of greater duration, the realization would then have a palatal quality which would be sufficient to distinguish the geminate from its simple counterpart. In much of the Iberian peninsula this is just what occurred: the /l:/ became /ļ/ and the /n:/ became /ņ/:

CABALLU > *cavallo* [ļ]
CAPILLU 'hair' > *cabello*
CULTELLU 'knife' > *cuchiello*
MEDULLA 'marrow' > *meollo*

---

[73] See, for example, Granda Gutiérrez 1966.

VALLE 'valley' > *valle*
ANNU 'year' > *anno* [ņ]
CANNA 'read' > *canna*
GRUNNĪRE 'to grunt' > *grunnir*
PANNU 'piece of cloth' > *panno*

The geminate /n:/ resulting from the assimilation of [ŋ] and [m] to a following /n/ developed in the same way:[74]

LIGNA 'firewood' > *lenna*
PUGNU 'fist' > *punno*
SIGNA 'signs' > *senna* 'sign; flag'
AUTUMNU 'autumn' > *otonno*
DAMNU 'loss, harm' > *danno*
SCAMNU 'bench' > *escanno*

The standard orthography followed the Latin system with /l/ represented by LL and /n/ by NN. An alternate to NN in medieval spelling was as Ñ and this symbol came to be used exclusively in modern Spanish: *año, caña, gruñir, paño, leña, puño*, etc.

The palatalization of /l:/ had one further consequence. The yod following /l/ in Late Latin had produced a palatal /ļ/. If this consonant had continued to be pronounced as a palatal it would have merged with the new /ļ/ < /l:/, as did the /n/ plus yod with the /ņ/ < /n:/. The original /ļ/ had, however, developed a more fricative pronunciation which at first was probably a non-distinctive feature. Once the new /ļ/ was established, this fricative element was now distinctive and thus became the voiced palatal sibilant /ž/ which was a particular feature of Castilian in contrast with the other Ibero-Romance dialects (see the next section on palatals).

The Strengthening of the Initial Consonant

One change characteristic of the whole Iberian peninsula is the change of the initial vibrant from a simple to a geminate pronunciation /r-/ > /r:-/:

RATIŌNE 'reason' > *razón* [r:-]
RĒGE 'king' > *rey* [r:-]

If we may judge by Italian, in which initial /r-/ is a single trill, more like the medial /-r-/ than /-r:-/, it is likely that in Latin the word-initial vibrant was also a simple trill. In considering why this change should have

---

[74] For a detailed study of the results of /-l:-/ and /-n:-/ in Hispanic dialects, see Catalán 1954. A summary is found in *ELH* 1, cxxxi-iv, by Menéndez Pidal. It should be noted that in Portuguese medial /n/ and /l/ vanished altogether, thus leaving room for /n:/ and /l:/ to simplify to /n/ and /l/.

occurred, we must keep in mind the changes that affected other initial consonants and their relation to the geminate and simple medial consonants.

When the intervocalic stops began to develop a weak variant between vowels, it can be assumed that words beginning with a simple stop also suffered the same change when following a word ending in a vowel. Thus, when PRĀTUM 'meadow' began to be pronounced [pratu] or [pradu], the initial /t-/ of TERRA was probably also pronounced with voicing when it appeared in a breath group after a word ending in a vowel, e.g., ILLA TERRA 'that land' [il:a der:a]. After words ending in a consonant the voice-less pronunciation would have been maintained, e.g., ILLAS TERRAS [il:as ter:as]. As long as variation was a phonetic process, the weak (partially or fully voiced) variant of the initial consonant would have been identified with the medial weak variant of the voiceless stop. Speakers probably would have been unconscious of the difference in the pronunciation of initial consonants since it made no difference in meaning.

When, however, the medial consonant became fully voiced and varia-tion was phonemicized, it would not be possible any longer to maintain a variation in initial position since it would have meant that the same word would have two different phonemes at the beginning, a voiced stop /d/ after a vowel and a voiceless stop /t/ after a pause or another consonant. Alternations of phonemes would have produced a confusion of all initial stop consonants and, for example, words which had always had an initial /d-/ like DĀRE 'to give' would have developed forms beginning with /t-/. The way to avoid such confusion was to maintain a stable, consistently realized voiceless stop at the beginning of words, thus preventing the identification of medial /-d-/ < /-t-/ with initial /d-/ < /d-/. Thus, variation of the initial consonant ceased and the strong variant was con-sistently used. The pronunciation of geminate consonants required greater articulatory effort so that they were in effect "strong" consonants, as opposed to the intervocalic simple consonants. When the initial stop was consistently pronounced as a voiceless consonant, it was undoubtedly identified with the medial geminate, especially since the simple medial stop was no longer voiceless, e.g., the initial /t-/ of TERRA was identified with the /-t:-/ of GUTTA 'drop', etc.[75]

The variation of the stop consonants in initial position must also have affected other inital consonants, that is, there would have developed a strong and weak variant of all consonants depending on the ending of the

---

[75] It is entirely possible too that the word-initial position was considered a "strong" one not only because of the existence of final /-s/ in plural noun phrases, but also because a number of prepositions and the conjunctions ET and AUT ended in consonants, and thus would have been followed by strong variants of consonants. For example, in some Italian dialects a geminated or reinforced consonant is found initially after such words that in Latin had ended in consonants, although they have subsequently disappeared, e.g., *e tterra*, *au tterra* < ET TERRA, AUT TERRA, etc. (Hall 1964, Di Pietro 1966).

preceding word. If we represent the strong variant of /r-/ by [R] and the weak variant by [r], the distribution would have been as follows: (-A represents any vowel) [-a ro-] but [-as -Ro-], e.g., ILLA ROTA 'that wheel' [il:a roda] vs. ILLAS ROTAS [il:as Rodas]. Similarly one would expect to find strong and weak variants of initial /n-/ and /l-/. Then when the geminates simplified and either merged with the simple consonants or changed their pronunciation, the initial consonants would have changed in exactly the same way.

Thus, the initial /r-/ was associated exclusively with the medial /-r:-/ which was still phonetically a geminate but phonemically was isolated in the consonantal system because of the disappearance of the correlation of length as a distinctive feature. Initially all words beginning with /r-/ would be phonetically strong and the result was as we see it today, with the pronunciation of all initial /r-/'s as [r:-].[76]

It should be noted that the strengthening of initial /r-/ is not limited to the Iberian peninsula alone, but is found in much of southern Italy, in Apulia, Calabria, Sicily and southern Corsica. Although it is possible that there is no connection between these areas and Spain, some believe that this particular pronunciation was brought to Hispania by colonists from these areas of Italy. In other words, the initial /r-/ in Hispanic Latin was a multiple trill from the beginning.[77] If this is true, there is no need to seek a specifically internal structural explanation, but there is no inherent conflict between the two explanations and they may be complementary: that is, the habit of pronouncing the initial /r-/ strongly would have been reinforced by the structural developments of Late Latin-early Romance.

In the case of initial /r-/, Castilian goes along with the general developments of Ibero-Romance. If it had been completely consistent, however, it would also have adopted the palatals /ʎ/ and /ɲ/ in word-initial position also. Catalan, for example, regularly has /ʎ/ < /l-/, e.g., *lluna* < LUNA, *llet* < LACTE 'milk', etc. Castilian has not followed this path and the weak consonants /l-/ and /n-/ have remained. In the case of /l-/, it is possible to see here the influence of the initial /ʎ-/ derived from the initial clusters /pl-/, /kl-/ (and occasionally /fl-/) as the determining factor. Since these groups were developing into /ʎ-/, the adoption of /ʎ-/ as the reflex of Latin /l-/ would have resulted in a further merger. In reaction against this threatened merger the weak consonant /l-/ was chosen in all word-initial positions. Catalan and some other Ibero-Romance dialects chose the strong consonant, either because the Latin consonant clusters with /l/ remained intact or had changed to some other phoneme that did not offer the

---

[76] See Weinrich 1958, 64–78, for an explanation of the reestablishment of a stable word-initial consonant.

[77] Menéndez Pidal 1954 seeks to relate Asturian [tˢ] < Lat. /-l:-/ and /l-/ with the south Italian [-d:-] < Lat. /-l:-/. His theories are opposed by Rohlfs 1955a, and Alonso 1962, 138–39, points out that the places in Sicily in which this pronunciation is found are colonies established by settlers from northern Italy during the Middle Ages.

possibility of a merger. There remains only one problem. Why does Castilian keep /n-/ in initial position rather than changing it to /ɲ-/? There is no apparent explanation, except the possibility that Basque influence may have been decisive here.[78] Initial palatal /ɲ-/ is not unknown in Spain, but is typical of rustic speech in much of Leon, e.g., *ño, ñascer, ñuestro*, etc. It has been consistently rejected in the standard language.

Palatal Consonants

As pointed out in chapter 3, the reduction of vowels in hiatus in Late Latin had resulted in the creation of a number of new palatal consonants when the first vowel was a front one. All single consonants that could easily absorb the yod fused with it to form these new consonants. Thus, /n/ and /l/ plus a yod had become /ɲ/ and /ʎ/, the /ɲ/ later merging with the results of the degimination of /n:/:

VINEA 'vineyard' > *viña*
SENIORE 'elder' > *señor* 'lord, sir'
FOLIA 'leaves' > /foʎa/ > Cast. *foja*
MELIORE 'better' > /meʎore/ > Cast. *mejor*
MULIERE 'woman' > /muʎere/ > Cast. *mugier*

The further development of /ʎ/ will be discussed below.

Medial /-j:-/ < Lat. /-j:-/, /g, d/ plus Yod

The long medial palatal /-j:-/ was affected by the degemination of all the long consonants, and thus became a simple consonant /-j-/:

EXAGIUM (Late Latin) 'act of weighing' > *ensayo* 'attempt'
FĀGEA 'beech tree' > *faya*
FUGIŌ 'I flee' > *fuyo*
MAJŌRE 'greater' > *mayor*
MĀJU 'May' > *mayo*
PODIU 'stone bench' > *poyo*
RADIĀRE 'to radiate, emit rays' > *rayar* 'to line, mark'

Where the preceding vowel was a front vowel, the geminate had already been partially absorbed, producing a single palatal (at least in Castile) which was later treated exactly like all single medial palatals (< /g/ plus /e, i/), i.e., it disappeared (Alarcos Llorach 1954, 337):

CORRIGIA 'leather strap, thong' > *correa*

---

[78] Martinet 1955, 285, note 59, suggests this explanation without going into detail. Catalán 1954, 44, also comments on the lack of explanation for the development of initial /n-/, but offers no theory of his own. The problem of Leonese remains apart since /l-/ and /pl-, fl-, kl-/ all become [ʎ] or [tˢ]. See Catalán 1967. As Alarcos Llorach says, resistance to merger cannot be rejected in all cases simply because merger does occur in some areas. Evidently other factors were more powerful here (1968, 251).

FASTIDIU 'loathing, disgust' > *fastío*
PEJORE 'worse' > *peor*
PRAESIDIA 'defenses; protection' > *presea* 'furniture, house adornment'
*PULĒGIU (C.L. PŪLĒGIUM) 'pennyroyal' > *poleo*

Medial [-j-]

As we saw previously, the development of Lat. /g/ plus a front vowel was similar to that of the /g/ plus a yod in that there was an assimilation of the velar to the vowel resulting in a palatal [j]. This palatal was then absorbed by the vowel and disappeared completely, e.g., DIGITU > [dejedo] > [deedo] > *dedo*:

DIGITU 'finger, toe' > *dedo*
MAGISTRU 'master, teacher' > *maestro*
RĒGĪNA 'queen' > *reína*
SEXAGINTA 'sixty' > OSp. *sessaenta*
SIGILLU 'small figure' > OSp. *seello* 'seal'
VĀGĪNA 'sheath' > *vaína* 'pod'

Initial [j-] Before Front Vowels

In initial position the /g/ before a front vowel produced the same palatal as medially. In the earliest period Castile preserved this consonant:

GERMĀNU 'having the same parents' > *iermano* 'brother'

This development parallels that of other Ibero-Romance dialects:

Leonese *jermanos, iermanos, giermanis*, etc.
Mozarabic *yenesta* 'broom plant' < GENESTA
yenair 'January' < JENUĀRIU (C.L. JANUĀRIUS)

(*Orígenes* §42.1)

Castilian, however, soon distinguished itself by dropping the initial [j-], in contrast to other dialects that not only preserved it but even strengthened it to a palatal hushing fricative [ž] or an affricate [ǰ]:

	Portuguese [ž]	Catalan [ǰ]
GENESTA 'broom plant'	*giesta*	*ginesta*
GINGĪVA 'gum'	*gengiva*	*geniva*
JA- JENUĀRIU 'January'	*janeiro*	*gener*

Possibly this particular change in Castilian can be linked with the early establishment of the realization of the diphthong resulting from tonic /ę/ as [je] in Castile. Diphthongization was at this time closely linked with stress, there being no segmental diphthongs in any unstressed syllable. Castilian speakers may have felt that [je] belonged only in tonic syllables and that the unstressed [je], even though it came from another source, was somehow out of place. Since the atonic equivalent of [je] was [e], they simply dropped the initial palatal element:[79]

GENESTA > *hiniesta*
GEN- *UCULU 'knee' > *hinojo*
GINGĪVA > *enzía*
JENIPERU (C.L. JUNIPERUS 'juniper tree') > *enebro*
JACTĀRE 'to throw' > *echar*
GELVĪRA (Germanic proper name) > *Elvira*

When the initial [j-] is found in a stressed syllable, the diphthong [je] would have absorbed the palatal so that it cannot be determined whether or not it had disappeared as in the preceding examples:[80]

GENERU 'son-in-law' > *yerno*
GEMMA 'bud; gem' > *yema*
GELU 'ice' > *hielo*
GENTE 'nation, people' > *yente*

Initial [j-] Before Other Vowels

Our view of the development of [j-] before non-front vowels, i.e., /a o u/ will inevitably be colored by the lexical items selected to illustrate it. If we take the following words as examples, the result is obvious:

JUNCTA 'joined, connected' > *yunta* 'yoke of oxen'
JŪRĀRE 'to swear' > *yurar*

---

[79] This is the explanation given by Malkiel 1973, 232, apparently following Meyer-Lübke 1936, 29. A somewhat similar opinion is found in García de Diego 1951, 67, who associates the change with the regular alternation of /e/ and /ie/ in the conjugation of the radical-changing verbs and the contrast between derived words such as *terruño* and its base *tierra*. Alarcos Llorach 1954, 337, objects that there are words which have lost the [j-] which have no association with any derived word, but he does not take into account the possibility suggested by Malkiel who offers as further proof of his contention the fact the MS O of the *Poema de Alexandre* has *azer* for *yazer* 'to be lying, stretched out' < JACĒRE (1973, 234). In Aragonese a common realization of the diphthong from /ę/ was [ja], so that the scribe of MS O apparently made a similar sort of association between stress and diphthongization, thinking that the [ja-] of *yazer* must have come from /ę/. Alarcos Llorach (1954) believes that the initial yod must have disappeared in all words, whether accented on the first syllable or not, offering as proof the lack of diphthongization in the present tense forms of *echar* < JACTĀRE 'to throw' which he supposes would necessarily have been *yecho, *yechas, etc., if the yod had been preserved. Verb forms, however, are poor examples on which to base sound changes, and it should be noted that the E of *echar* may well be the result of the monophthongization of the [-ai̯-] from the development of /-akt-/ and thus would not have been associated with /e/.

[80] The problem of *yeso* 'plaster' < GYPSUM, then, remains to counter the idea that all examples of initial [je-] necessarily derived from the diphthongization of /e/. Alarcos believes that it is a late word that may have entered Castilian from some dialectal source.

JUGU 'yoke' > *yugo*
JAM 'already' > *ya*
JACET 'he lies' > *yaze*
JACOBE 'James' (vocative) > *Yagüe*

If, on the other hand, we take numerous other examples from the medieval lexicon, we would have to come to a different conclusion, since the result is initial [ĭ] or [ž] (spelled J):

JOCU 'joke, jest' > *juego* 'joke; game'
(DIES) JOVIS 'Thursday' > *jueves*
JŪDAEU 'Jewish' > *judió, judío*
JŪDICE 'judge' > *júez*
JŪDĪCIU 'judgment' > *juicio*
JŪDICĀRE 'to judge' > OSp. *judgar*
JŪNIU 'June' > *junio*
JUNCTU 'joined' > *junto* 'together'
JUNCTA > *junta* 'assembly'
JŪLIU 'July' > *julio*
JUVENE 'young' > *joven*
JUSTU 'just' > *justo*
JAM MAGIS > *jamás* 'never'

On the basis of the preceding examples and proper names such as *Jacob*, *Joan*, *Juan*, *Judas*, *Judea*, etc. we would have to conclude that the regular development of [j-] before a back vowel was /ĭ/ or /ž/. On closer examination, however, these words take on a rather different aspect. The words from the area of administration and justice (*júez*, *juicio*, *judgar*, *justo*) may well be learned words, taken directly from written Latin with some adjustment to popular phonetics. *Justicia* 'justice' is clearly a learned word too in view of the form of its suffix, which contrasts sharply with the popular form of the same suffix, -*eza*. *Juego* and *jugar* 'to play' may be words borrowed from Gallo-Romance, to be classed with *juglar* 'minstrel'. *Judío* may likewise be considered of Biblical provenience, properly classed with the names given above, i.e., learned words. *Junio* and *julio* may also be attributed to a Latin written source in view of the lack of popular development of the rest of their phonetic shape (popular development would have produced **juño* and **jujo*). *Joven* in the meaning of 'young man' was never a popular word in the Middle Ages, the concept being conveyed rather by *moço* and *mancebo*, and it therefore may also be a learned word.

The existence of doublets like *yunta-junta*, *yurar-jurar*, *ya-ja(más)* may then be a clue to a possible solution to the problem of the appropriate "sound law" to be constructed in this case. We may assume that the most ancient stratum of the Castilian vocabulary preserved intact the Late Latin [j-]. Then, when a number of words containing /ž/ were borrowed from other Romance languages and were taken directly from written Latin with

/ž/ as the reflex of Latin J-, they so overwhelmed the few original words
that the normal outcome appeared to be /ž-/ rather than /j-/ (Malkiel
1976a).

Therefore, all the previously cited words must be classified with the
numerous words beginning with /ž-/ before a front vowel, whether in
initial position or not:

1) (from pagan antiquity): *gigante* 'giant'
2) (from Biblical tradition and the church): *Jeremías, Jerusalén, ángel,
    ymagen* 'statue; idol'
3) (abstract words): *general, gesto* 'bearing, appearance'
4) (from Gallo-Romance): *gemir* 'to sigh, moan', *gentil* 'noble, ele-
    gant', *girgonça* 'hyacincth', *viage* 'journey' (and all other words
    containing the suffix *-age* < Lat. -ATICU), *ligero* 'light, fast', *ver-
    gel* 'flower garden'
5) (from Arabic): *alfaja* 'clothes, adornment, jewels', *alfajeme* 'sur-
    geon, barber', *gengibrante* 'ginger', etc.

(Malkiel 1976a, 30–31)

If Malkiel's assumption is correct, the very earliest Castilian community,
or its immediate predecessors before Castile came into existence, must
have been extremely conservative in their treatment of palatal consonants
and avoided the new strengthened palatal [ž]. When, however, the new
pronunciation of Late Latin /ļ/ as /ž/ became standard in Castile, this
new sound, which had not been found elsewhere in popular Castilian
Romance, constituted a revolutionary change in the phonetic appearance
of many words. The early "aversion" (to use Malkiel's term) to [ž] was lost
and with the borrowing of large numbers of foreign words containing the
sound and the adoption of many Latinisms, Castilian came to resemble its
neighbors more closely in this respect.

If we take into account place names like *Junquera, Junco, Juncosa, Jun-
car, Junta, Las Juntas*, etc. which are found all over the peninsula, and
must in medieval Spanish have been pronounced with [ž], we might see in
them further indication that initial [ž-] was a later innovation. There are in
the center and south of the peninsula some remains of forms with [j-]:
Yuncos in Toledo, *Yunco* in Almería, *Yunquera* in Guadalajara, Albacete
and Málaga, and *La Yunta* in Guadalajara, which may be evidence of the
earliest pronunciation, later overlaid by the innovating Castilian
(Menéndez Pidal 1941, 125, note).[81]

Another explanation is that given by Alarcos Llorach 1954, 340–41,
which sees the development in connected discourse of variant pronunciations of the same word. A word beginning with [j-] in Late Latin could,
after a word ending in a consonant, have become pronounced with initial

---

[81] Alarcos Llorach (1954, 340–41) suggests that /ž-/ was typical of the north, but that as
Castilian was carried south with the reconquest it adopted some words from conservative
southern dialects having [j-].

[ž-] (cf. below the development of [j] medially after consonants), while when pronounced after a word ending in a vowel the original [j-] would have been maintained, e.g., *elo júez* [elo júetˢ] vs. *elos juezes* [elos žuedᶻes]. Then when one variant was chosen as the only form of the word, sometimes [j] was selected and sometimes [ž], with the quality of the following vowel being the determining factor in most cases.

Possibly there is some relationship between the loss of word-initial [j-] before /e/ and the disappearance of [j-] before other vowels as in the following examples:

JĀJŪNU (C.L. JĒJŪNUS 'hunger, fasting') > *ayuno* 'fast'
JUNGERE 'to yoke, join' > *uñir, uncir*

With these two words may be included the toponyms *Unquera* in Oviedo and Santander and *Valluquera* in Burgos, Segovia and Guadalajara. Possibly this loss was aided by the presence of a following palatal which may have stimulated a dissimilation.

It may be too that the dropping of the initial semiconsonant is related to a somewhat similar change in the treatment of words of germanic origin beginning with [w-]. We recall that when such words were borrowed into Late Latin, the labiovelar semiconsonant which was foreign to Latin-Romance speakers was identified with the native /gu-/, e.g., WERRA > [gwer:a] (> Sp. *guerra*) 'war', WARDON > [gwardare] (> Sp. *guardar*) 'to guard', etc. In some words beginning with an unstressed [w-], there is an early tendency to eliminate the semiconsonant after /g/:

*WITHRALAUN > *gualardón* > *galardón* 'prize, reward'
WRANJONS 'stud jackass' > *guaranyón* (Aragonese) > *garañón*

There was a period of free variation when either /gwa-/ or /ga-/ could be used, e.g., *galardón* is found in the *Cantar de Mio Cid* while other medieval works use *gualardón*. The later addition of many words from the New World beginning with /gwa-/ appears to have prevented the development of a regular loss of the semiconsonant.[82]

/k/ and /g/ in Syllable-Final Position

In chapter 3 we discussed the development of consonants in syllable-final position. In general, the assimilation of the consonant to the following consonant produced a geminate which was then treated like all other geminates. When the final consonant was a velar stop, the occlusion weakened, resulting in a fricative [x] which might vary in the place of articula-

---

[82] This is the explanation given in Wright 1976b. The preservation of /kwa-/ in *cuaderno* 'notebook' < QUATERNU, *cuaresma* 'Lent' < QUADRAGESIMA, etc., makes it appear that the development of pretonic /gwa-/ is somehow anomalous. As he puts it, [wa] remains before /d/ and /r/, but loses the [w] before /s/ or /z/. This sort of distribution does not seem to be related to any special phonetic environment, so perhaps we are dealing with a tendency that never managed to develop into a full-fledged change. See also Malkiel 1973, 226–28.

tion depending on the preceding vowel.[83] This particular development, which fits in perfectly with the weakening of all consonants in syllable-final position in Late Latin, is sometimes attributed to the effect of a Celtic substratum on the group /kt/.[84] Such an influence is not impossible, but would have been simply a minor concommitant of a general movement in Late Latin. The development of other sequences containing a syllable-final /-k/ shows that this change occurred before all consonants and not just before /t/. Having become a fricative and then a palatal semivowel, the resulting combination was treated differently both according to the geographical region and according to the nature of the following consonant:

/-kt-/ > /-it-/

FACTU 'done' > [faito]
LACTE 'milk' > [laite]
LECTU 'bed' > [leito]
OCTO 'eight' > [oito]

/-g, -k/ plus /l/ > [i̯l] > [ḷ] (> ž)

LENTICULA 'lentil' > [lenteḷa] (*lenteja*)
OCULU 'eye' > [oḷo] (*ojo*)
SPECULU 'mirror' > [espeḷo] (*espejo*)
VERMICULU 'little worm' > [bermeḷo] 'red' (*bermejo*)
COAGULU 'curds' > [koaḷo] (*coajo*)
REGULA 'metal bar' > [r:eḷa] 'plowshare' (*reja*)
TEGULA 'roof tile' > [teḷa] (*teja*)

/-ks-/ > [-i̯s-] > [š]

DIXI 'I said' > [diše] *dixe*
MAXELLA (C.L. MAXILLA) 'jaw' > *mexiella* 'cheek'
MATAXA 'skein' > *madexa*
TAXU 'yew tree' > *texo*

The /l/ and /s/ absorbed the semivowel early enough to produce a palatal consonant in most areas of the peninsula, while the group [-i̯t-] persisted without further change in most areas, unless the semivowel was absorbed by the preceding vowel, e.g., Arag., Port. *feito*, Cat. *fet* (cf. Fr. *fait* [fe]). Castilian then separates from the surrounding dialects by fusing the palatal into the occlusive and producing an affricate /č/:

[faito] > *fecho*
[laite] > *leche*
[leito] > *lecho*
[oito] > *ocho*

---

[83] Lausberg 1965, 380, gives [*noxte, *textu] from NOCTE, TECTU.
[84] See Jungemann 1955, chap. 9, for a thorough consideration of the problem.

If, however, the vowel preceding the [-i-] is /i/, it absorbs the semivowel and the /t/ remains unchanged:

FĪCTU 'fixed, nailed' (C.L. FĪXUS) > *fito* 'boundary marker'
FRĪCTU 'fried' > *frito*
VĪCTU 'conquered' > *vito*

$$/\text{-ult-}/ > /\text{-u}\underset{.}{i}\text{t-}/$$

Another group that generates a palatal semivowel is /-ult-/,whose final result is exactly like that of /-kt-/:

A(U)SCULTĀRE 'to listen' > *ascuchar*
CULTELLU 'knife' > *cuchiello*
MULTU 'much' > *mucho*

If the group of [-i̯-] plus a consonant occurs before another consonant, the development to a palatalized consonant is blocked and the [-i̯-] either remains or is absorbed by the preceding vowel:

PECTINĀRE 'to comb' > *peinar*
PECTORĀLE > *peitral* 'breast strap of a harness'
VULTURE 'vulture' > *buitre*
FRAXINU 'ash tree' > *fresno*

In syntactic phonetics similar results are seen. The following words often appear directly before words beginning with a consonant (the final /-o/ of [muito] drops with syncope):

SEX 'six' > *seis*
MULTU (used as intensifier) > [muit] > *muy* 'very'

$$/\underset{.}{l}/ > /\check{z}/$$

Another development peculiar to Castilian was the shift of the /ļ/ to a palatal sibilant /ž/. Apparently this change was stimulated by the palatalization of /l:/ to /ļ/ (discussed in the section on degemination):

[lenteḷa] > *lenteja*
[oḷo] > *ojo*
[foḷa] > *foja*
[meḷore] > *mejor*

As we can see, the orthographic representation in Medieval Castilian was usually by means of the letter J, although before /e/ and /i/, the letter G (GI) was also used: *ojo*, *mugier*. The voiceless counterpart was represented by the letter X: *dixe*, *texo*.

Postconsonantal Palatals

When a palatal consonant is preceded by a syllable-final consonant, it usually assimilates to the preceding consonant by developing an occlusive element. The general solution seems to have been a voiceless affricate, identified with either CH /č/ or ç /tˢ/. Thus, postconsonantal /l/ derived from [-il-] < /-g'l-/ gives /č/, as does the /ļ/ < /-pl-, -f l-/, as we saw previously:

CONCHULA 'small sea-shell' > *concha* 'sea-shell'
TRUNCULU 'small tree trunk' > *troncho* 'stalk'
MACULA 'stain' > [mankula] > *mancha*
HINNIT- *ULĀRE > *reninchar* 'to whinny' (> MSp. *relinchar*)
MASCULU 'male' > *macho*
CICERCULA 'blue vetch' > *cizercha*
SARCULĀRE 'to weed' > *sachar*

The geminate palatal from /dj/ also produced an affricate ç [tˢ]:

(FARRA) GRANDIA 'thick flour' > *granças* 'chaff, dross'
HORDEOLU > *orçuelo* 'sty; snare, trap'
VIR(I)DIA 'greens; herbs' > *verça* 'cabbage'
VERĒCUNDIA 'shame' > *vergüe-nça, -ña*
SĒMENTIA 'seed' > *simiença*

Along with the preceding group of words, we should probably also include some Old Portuguese forms that show similar developments, even though Old Castilian did not parallel the western forms:

ARDEŌ 'I burn' > OPort. *arço* (Sp. *ardo*)
*PERDIŌ 'I lose' (C.L. PERDŌ > Sp. *pierdo*) > OPort. *perço*
            (possibly influenced by contrast with INVENIŌ 'I find'
                              [Malkiel 1984b, 10, note 7])

What is most striking about the preceding words is that although the Latin etyma all contain a liquid followed by a /d/ plus a yod, the results in Old Spanish and Portuguese all have a voiceless affricate /tˢ/ ç instead of what might be reasonably expected, namely its voiced counterpart /dᶻ/. Inevitably we must look for some explanation of why the result of a voiced consonant should be voiceless in these circumstances. One possible reason might be that in the period when these sequences were coalescing into a new and relatively unusual sequence, the sequence of /n/ or /r/ followed by a dental plus a yod, /t/ or /d/ + /j/, by far the larger number of examples were of /tʲ/, e.g., MARTIU 'March', TERTIU 'third', FORTIA 'strength', and many more. Possibly speakers preferred to save themselves the trouble of forming two new consonant sequences by condensing both into the one they were more familiar with, namely, /tʲ/ (Malkiel 1984b, 13).

Since /n/ is especially susceptible to palatalization, we find that in a few cases the palatal has simply been absorbed by the /n/, producing /ņ/:

CINGULU 'girdle, sword belt' > *ceño* 'iron ring, band'
SINGULĀRIU 'alone, single' > *señero*

UNGULA 'fingernail' > *uña*
SCANDULA (for SCANDALA) 'spelt' > *escaña*[85]

A later development of the postconsonantal palatal derived from /g$^{e, i}$/ is found, although with some important deviations from the results that we might expect if we consider the pattern presented above. A number of words show a palatalization of /n/ when followed by this palatal:

CINGERE 'to gird on' > *ceñir*
FINGERE 'to feign, pretend' > *feñir*
FRANGERE 'to break' > *frañ-ir, -er* (Aragonese)
JUNGERE 'to yoke, connect' > *uñir*
TANGERE 'to touch, play [an instrument]' > *tañir*
RINGI, -*ERE 'to show the teeth, snarl' > *reñir* 'to scold, quarrel'
TINGERE 'to dye' > *teñir*
LONGE 'distant, far' > OSp. *lueñe*

In these examples, the palatal derived from /g$^{e, i}$/ has been treated as a Late Latin yod: that is, it palatalized the /n/ in the same way as did the yod in *señor* < SENIŌRE. However, there are some other examples which show a development right in line with that of other postconsonantal palatals, namely the articulation of an affricate: /d^z/ z:

SING- *-ELLU (C.L. SINGULUS) 'single, separate' > *senziello* 'simple'
GINGĪVA 'gum' > *enzía*
JUNGERE 'to yoke, connect' > *unzir*

Especially interesting are the doublets *frañir/franzir, uñir/unzir* and the postverbal derivatives of *reñir, reñilla/renziella* 'dispute, quarrel'.

If the preceding consonant is /r/, the result is invariably z:

ARGILLA 'white clay, potter's clay' > *arzilla*
BURGĒNSE 'burger, townsman' > *burzés*
ĒRIGERE 'to raise up' > OSp. *erzer* (MSp. *erguir*)
EXTERGERE 'to clean up' > *estarzir* 'to stencil'
SPARGERE 'to scatter, strew' > *esparzir*
TERGERE 'to wipe, scour' > *terzer*

The contrasting development of the palatal from /g$^{e, i}$/ after /n/ and /r/ deserves a closer examination. The lack of uniformity of results may be related to the nature of the words in which they appear. The first list of words, in which the /n/ was palatalized to /ɲ/, are, with one exception, verbs, and the difference in the treatment of the postconsonantal palatal may be the result of the conflict between the morpheme boundary between the root of the verb and its endings, and the natural syllable boundary.

---

[85] This particular development seems to have been limited mostly to /-g'l-/. Another development is a strengthening of the palatal, producing a /d/, e.g., SINGULOS > *sendos* 'one each', AXUNGIA > *enxundia* 'animal fat', or the variant form of *escaña, escand(i)a*.

The natural syllable division in Romance is between consonants that do not form a cluster. In other words, if the postconsonantal palatal from /g^{e, i}/ is considered to be just another consonant, the natural division of FRANGERE and TINGERE, for example, would be [fran-je-re, ten-je-re]. When dealing with verbs, however, speakers are usually conscious of a morpheme division between the stem of the verb and its endings. Thus, the morphemic separation of the preceding verbs is as follows: [franj-ere], tenj-ere]. In words in which this sort of morphemic division is not found (or is much less obvious than it is with verbs), the normal syllable division results and the development is the same as with other postconsonantal, syllable-initial palatals, i.e., into an affricate. When the morpheme boundary and the syllable boundary do not coincide, however, speakers might feel some conflict. They could ignore either one or the other. In this instance, the phonetic nature of the consonant preceding may have been decisive in most words. In Romance /r/ does not normally palatalize so that there would be no temptation for speakers to merge the palatal with the consonant. Thus, the result would be what we find: RZ. With /n/, on the other hand, palatalization of the consonant before a yod is the normal outcome. Therefore, it may be that when speakers treated the palatal from /g^{e, i}/ as a normal yod, since the morpheme boundary came after it rather than before, the result was /ṇ/. The few doublets may have been produced by different speakers who did not follow the general pattern in resolving the potential conflict. This conflict was by no means limited to Ibero-Romance since some doublets are found in other Romance languages, e.g., JUNGERE > OProv. *ionher/ionger* [joṇer/jonĵer], PUNGERE 'to prick' > It. *pungere/pugnere* [púnĵere/púṇere] (Craddock 1970).

The difference between word-initial palatals that do not become affricates and postconsonantal palatals that do, is evidently a problem of differing phonetic developments in different phonetic conditions, as we have seen above in the development of /-j:-/ < /-dj-/ and /l/ which become affricates in postconsonantal position (Fontanella de Weinberg 1971, 323–24).

Two questions still remain. One is why the affricate should have been /d^z/ rather than /ĵ/. In this case, we may seek some evidence in the early Castilian avoidance of [ž] which was discussed earlier. Speakers who preferred not to use [ž] or [ĵ] in word-initial position might have been equally disinclined to adopt a similar sound postconsonantally, and would therefore have preferred to use the affricate /d^z/ which already existed. Thus, the development could be seen to be a part of early Castilian's general economy of expression (Malkiel 1982).

The other question is why the palatal from /g^{e, i}/ should have become a voiced affricate in postconsonantal position rather than a voiceless one as do all the other palatals in this position. One possibility is that there has been some influence from a regular morphological alternation in a number of verb forms. Very commonly used verbs like *fazer* 'to make, do' < FACERE, and *dezir* 'to say' < DĪCERE show a regular alternation between a form 1 with the root ending in /g/, while all other forms have /dᶻ/, e.g., *fago, fazes, faze*, etc., *digo, dizes, dize*, etc. Therefore it may be that these verbs had some influence on the verbs mentioned previously which developed a stem ending in -NZ- < -NGᵉⁱ. Could it be that speakers accustomed to pronouncing /dᶻ/ in *fazer* and *dezir* then extended this same voicing to those verbs with a postconsonantal palatal following /r/ and /n/, and thus set the pattern even for non-verbal developments?[86] It seems likely that once again we are dealing with a variety of different factors whose coalescence effectuates a particular change.

Other Affricated Palatals

The affricate which developed from /kᵉ˒ ⁱ/ appears to have been originally of the hushing palatal type [č], if we may judge by the articulation of this consonant in linguistically conservative varieties of Romance (i.e., Italian, Rumanian, Rhaeto-Romance, Norman, Picard, Mozarabic [Lausberg 1965, 316]). This consonant did not retain the same articulation in most areas of western Romance, but advanced to a more forward pronunciation, perhaps through merger with the affricates resulting from the /t/ and /k/ plus yod (Alarcos Llorach 1968, 238). The exact articulation of the more evolved western Romance affricate is not absolutely certain, but all the evidence indicates that it was pronounced principally with the predorsal area of the tongue making contact with the front part of the hard palate (Galmés 1962, 72–74). The tip of the tongue was not involved in the articulation except in a negative sense, i.e., that it would be placed against the lower teeth, or might touch the edges of both upper and lower incisors without affecting the fundamental pronunciation of the affricate. We shall represent it as /tˢ/ (spelled ç or simply c before the letters E and I).

In word-initial position it was kept as a voiceless consonant:

CAEPULLA 'onion' > *çebolla*
CĒNA 'supper' > *çena*
CENTU 'hundred' > *çiento*
*CINQUE (C.L. QUINQUE) 'five' > *çinco*

After a medial consonant also a voiceless affricate resulted:

CALCE 'kick' > *coçe*
MANCIP(I)U 'slave' > *mançebo* 'boy, youth'
TORQUĒRE 'to twist' > *torçer*

---

[86] Menéndez Pidal (1941, 138) remarks that the infinitive *franzer* soon disappeared in the Middle Ages. Corominas DCELC (under *fracción*) cites only an Aragonese *franzido*. A detailed discussion of the issues involved is found in Craddock 1970. Malkiel 1968 and 1969 thinks that the production of an affricate is due to the analogy with verbs like *fazer* and *dezir*, which seems unlikely in view of the more plausible phonetic explanation, especially since he failed to consider all postconsonantal palatals. There may have been some influence in the matter of voicing, as pointed out in the text. Malkiel 1982 considerably modifies his earlier views and discusses in great detail all matters related to the /gᵉ˒ ⁱ/ group in Old Spanish.

Intervocalically the consonant voiced to /dᶻ/ z, as did all other simple voiceless stops:

ADDŪCERE 'to lead' > *aduzir*
DECEMBRE 'December' > *diziembre*
LŪCE 'light' > *luze*[87]

/tʲ and /kʲ/

As we saw in chapter 3, the assimilation of the yod to /t/ is a fairly early change found everywhere in Romance; it resulted in an assibilated affricate [tˢ]. The similar evolution of /k/ plus yod occurred somewhat later (Lausberg 1965, 452). The prepalatal pronunciation of /tʲ/ and the fronting of the stop in /kʲ/ caused these two consonants to tend toward a similar palatal articulation. Nevertheless, there seems to have been some difference in their pronunciation for a long time. Italian (Tuscan) continues to maintain a distinction in their modern reflexes until today, with /tʲ/ having resulted in /t:ˢ/ (written -ZZ-), e.g., PUTEU 'well' > *pozzo*, while /kʲ/ became /č:/ (written -CC-), e.g., FACIE 'face' > *faccia* (Lausberg 1965, 398, 394).[88]

In Ibero-Romance both combinations merged into a single sound. Following a consonant, the results of /tʲ/ and /kʲ/ were a voiceless prepalatal affricate /tˢ/, identical with the results of /kᵉ, ⁱ/:

MARTIU 'March' > *março*
TERTIĀRIU (C.L. TERTIUS) > *terçero*
LENTEU (C.L. LINTEUM) 'linen cloth' > *lienço*
LANCEA 'lance' > *lança*
URCEU 'pitcher, water pot' > *orça*
CALCEU 'shoe, half boot' > *calça*
ASCIOLA (dim. of ASCIA 'adze') > *açuela*
ASCIATA > *açada*
FASCIA 'bandage, strip of cloth' > *faça*

The change found in the last three examples of the group /skʲ/ to /tˢ/ distinguished Castilian from the other Ibero-Romance dialects which, in

---

[87] With the loss of final -E, which became increasingly common from the eleventh century onward, a number of words in which z had been intervocalic came to end in this consonant. It is not certain whether it continued to be voiced. In view of the unvoicing evident in other consonants that had become final, e.g., *nueve* 'nine' *grande* 'large', which were written *nuef*, *grant*, it is most likely that /dᶻ/ also became /tˢ/. It continued to be spelled z, however, and to alternate consistently with the voiced medial z, e.g., *luz-luzes* 'light(s)', *paz* 'peace' - *(a)paziguar* 'pacify' and many more. See especially Malkiel 1971, 14.

[88] See chapter 3, note 36, for an outline sketch of the development of these sounds. One should not assume, however, that the development of /tʲ/ and /kʲ/ is simple everywhere except in Castilian. It suffices to look at words in Old Italian such as *palagio* vs. Mod. It. *palazzo* 'palace' < PALĀTIU, to realize that there are many complications elsewhere. See Tekavčić 1972, 347–54.

contrast, palatalized the /š/, e.g., Leonese, Aragonese *a[š]ada*, Port. *faixa*, *faxa*.

The development of intervocalic /tʲ/ and /kʲ/ is one of the most complicated and difficult to unravel in all of the sound changes of Castilian. The reflex of /kʲ/ seems to have remained usually unvoiced in western Romance, if we may judge by the results of a number of words in some other languages:

Latin	Old French	Provençal	Portuguese
FACIĒ 'face'	*face*	*fassa*	*face*
ACIĀRIU 'steel'	*acier*		*aceiro*
ĒRICIU 'hedgehog'	*hérisson*		*ouriço*
SAETACEU 'seive'	*sas*		*cedaço*
PELLICEA 'fur coat'	*pelisse*	*pelissa*	*peliça*

In short, the results of /kʲ/ are identical to those of words in which we can find evidence in Latin of a geminate /k:/ followed by a yod:

BRACC(H)IU 'arm'	*bras*	*brats*	*braço*
BRACC(H)IA 'fathom'	*brasse*	*brassa*	*braça*
COCC- EU, -EA 'pod, hull'	*cos*	*cos*	
PITACCIU 'piece'		*pedas*	*pedaço*
(C.L. PITTACIUM < Gr.)			

The results of these last examples in Old Castilian is right in line with those of other western Romance languages: *braço, braça, pescueço, pedaço*.

Would we then be justified in assuming that in Late Latin all examples of /kʲ/ became geminated, even where we have no written evidence for such a change? It is possible to conceive that the yod following the stop was interpreted by speakers as the initial element of the following syllable before the yod had become so fused with the stop that it was no longer perceived as a separate element. The preceding stop would then have been syllable-final and treated like a geminate which always closed one syllable and opened the next. In central and southern Italy and in Sardinia, for example, gemination of the consonant before a yod became the rule (Lausberg 1965, 386–87),[89] e.g., It. *bestemmia, vendemmia, sappia, abbia,* etc. < BLASPHEMIA, VINDĒMIA, SAPIAM, HABEAM (Tekavčić 1972, 360–62).

The development of /tʲ/ is somewhat more complicated since some words show voicing and others do not:

Latin	Old French	Provençal	Portuguese
RATIONE 'reason'	*raison*	*razó*	*razão*
SATIONE 'sowing, planting' > 'season'	*saison*	*sazó*	*sazão*

---

[89] Evidence in support of the syllable division proposed here may be seen in the result of /nʲ/ in Sardinian, where it becomes [ndᶻ], e.g., VĪNEA > *bindza* (Lausberg 1965, 392). The affricate pronunciation must be the result of a syllable break after the /n/, [vin-ja]. Gavel (1952) expounds the idea of regular gemination before yod, although he has relatively few data.

Latin	Old French	Provençal	Portuguese
POTIONE 'draught, esp. of poison'	*poison*	*pozó*	
PLATEA 'street; open square'	*place*	*plassa*	*praça*
PUTEU 'well'	*puis*		*poço*

The difficulty for Old Castilian, and to some extent Portuguese, lies in the fact that the results of medial /tʲ/ and /kʲ/ are so unpredictable that it is impossible to set up any kind of set of regular sound correspondences. The intervocalic reflexes of these consonants are as likely to be voiced as voiceless:

/-tʲ-/ > /-dᶻ-/

*ACŪTIARE 'to sharpen' > *aguzar*[90]
PUTEU 'well' > *pozo*
PIGRITIA 'laziness' > *pereza*
RATIŌNE 'reason' > *razón*
SATIŌNE 'season' > *sazón*
TĪTIŌNE 'firebrand' > *tizón*
VITIU 'fault, blemish' > *vezo* 'habit'

/-tʲ-/ > /-tˢ-/

CAPITIA (pl.) 'heads' > *cabeça*
*MATEA 'club' > *maça*
PLATEA > *plaça* 'square'
PLUTEA (pl.) 'hut(s)' > *choça* (< Western Ibero-Romance?)
PET-, PEC-IOLU > *peçón* (with change of suffix) 'nipple, stem'
PŌTIŌNE 'draught' > *poçón, poçoña* 'poison'[91]

/-kʲ-/ > /-dᶻ-/

ACIĀRIU 'steel' > *azero*[92]
CORTICEA 'bark, rind' > *corteza*
LAQ(U)EU 'noose, snare' > *lazo*
LĪCIU 'warp, leash' > *lizo*
MINACIA 'threat' > *amenaza*

/-kʲ-/ > /-tˢ-/

CORĀCEA 'cuirass' > *coraça*
PELLĪCEA 'fur coat' > *pe(l)liça*

In view of the preceding results, one could certainly make the blanket assumption that wherever we have ç in Old Castilian, the origin must be

---

[90] Perhaps this word should be excluded as a derived word containing the suffix -*zar* (Malkiel 1971, 33).

[91] This word also may have been subject to special pressure. See Malkiel 1959.

[92] Malkiel (1971, 11) believes that this word should be excluded from consideration here because it probably was associated with *az* < ACIE 'edge'.

sought in a geminate /k:/ or /t:/ before a yod in Late Latin.[93] Western Ibero-Romance would seem, on the basis of a number of words in Portuguese, to have suffered from a similar irregular development, although in a different direction from Castilian. We find such contrasts as *priguiça*, *pegriça/pereza, cortiça/corteza, -aço/ -azo, -iço/-izo*.[94] There does not appear to be any principled basis on phonetic grounds alone for accounting for this lack of regularity.

One particular feature of this tangled problem stands out very clearly: the remarkable paucity of primitive, non-derived words containing intervocalic /-t^j-/ and /-k^j-/. The vast majority of words with reflexes of these consonants are derived words in which the z or ç appears in a suffix of some kind: the verbal suffixes *-zar, -izar*, the adjectival or substantival suffixes *-azo, -izo*, the deverbal *-azón*, the substantival suffixes *-ez, -eza, -ece, -ice, -icia, -icie*. Such being the case, it is possible that what appears to be a genuine phonetic anomaly is in reality a problem most closely connected with morphology, specifically with word formation (Malkiel 1971). In other words, in the absence of more than a few non-derived words from Latin with these consonants, it is impossible to set up any kind of "sound law" or "rule" as the truly regular one since analogical developments and the mixture of suffixes (e.g., -ACEUS and -ACIS) may have overwhelmed the few cases that might serve as examples of a regular development.

Malkiel (1971) points to the fact that the vast majority of derivational suffixes in Castilian contained either resonants (i.e., liquids or nasals) which were naturally voiced, or voiced obstruents, e.g., *-al, -il*, etc. *-ar, -ero*, etc., *-ano, -ino, -iño, -ido, -ajo*. He concludes that the existence of voice in most of these suffixes (omitting the diminutives in *-ito, -ico*, which have a special semantic range) may have been the model for suffixes that originally did not contain a voiced consonant. Thus, the original /-t^s-/ could have been replaced by /-d^z-/ in suffixes in order to conform with the general pattern of derivational suffixes.

Given the complications that can be barely sketched in this book, it is clear that a truly adequate study of the problem cannot be limited to Castilian or even to Ibero-Romance but must be pan-Romance in scope. It would also require extensive analysis of numerous individual word histories in order to trace the influence of learned words and many analogical formations. The extraordinary complexity of the problem of the medial /-t^j-/ and /-k^j-/ has been realized by few scholars. Most studies have

---

[93] This is the reasoning followed consistently by Wilkinson 1976.

[94] Discrepancies of this sort between what one might expect on the basis of evidence from Gallo-Romance are undoubtedly what caused Williams to remark, "Latin T plus yod preceded by a vowel did not develop regularly in most cases" (1962, 80). Such a conclusion is justified only if one assumes that the results in French must be the norm for all western Romance. Later studies, on the basis of what can be described as "majority rule" conclude that the voiceless affricate is the normal result in Portuguese (Carvalho 1956, Lüdtke 1957). Wilkinson (1976) assumes that both ç and z are normal in Portuguese but that ç derives from forms that geminated the /t/ before a yod. (He is not acquainted with the two earlier studies.)

contented themselves with examining relatively few examples and constructing theories on them alone. As Menéndez Pidal remarked about the totally opposite conclusions of previous scholars, "El haberse podido apoyar en series de etimologías estas dos opiniones opuestas, indica lo embrollado de la derivación" (1941, 151). Lausberg attempts to explain the odd behavior of these consonants in Old Castilian by presuming that gemination of /k/ before yod was general throughout the Romance-speaking world, so that when degemination occurred the result was a voiceless consonant everywhere. As opposed to this, Lausberg sees no such gemination of /t/ before yod so that voicing should have occurred everywhere that other intervocalic voiceless consonants voiced. The results in Old Castilian, however, can be fitted into this scheme only by excluding large numbers of words that do not develop in this fashion (1965, 387, 394). As he remarks, "Es peculiar la posición del español" (396). Malkiel's 1971 study is fundamental for any serious approach to the problem because he subjects the entire range of vocabulary in Old Spanish containing the voiced and voiceless affricates to a minute analysis. Wilkinson (1976) attempts to relate Ibero-Romance to the results in all western Romance including North Italian.

One complicating factor that has not been emphasized is the matter of the adequacy of medieval spelling of these affricates. Menéndez Pidal remarks in *Orígenes* (§9.2): "[L]a escritura francesa empezó usando ç también para el sonido sonoro, lo mismo que la escritura visigoda; esas voces se escriben con z en la ortografía nebrixense; el empleo de çz o ç exclusivamente para el sonido sordo, a diferencia de z sonora, se manifiesta con claridad sólo desde los primeros años del siglo XIII, y no se afianza y generaliza sino desde hacia 1240." Thus, it may be that in the earliest period we simply do not have the written evidence most necessary for a resolution of our difficulties. If in early documents the same symbols are used indifferently for the voiced and voiceless affricates, it may be forever impossible to know what the true pronunciation was.

In spite of the difficulties involved in attempting to determine just how Late Latin /t^j/ /k^j/ developed, it is still clear that there was a phonemic distinction between the voiced and voiceless affricates in medial position that was observed by the speakers of medieval Romance. The correlation of voicing was valid for a variety of phonemes and the affricates were no exception. Nevertheless, as we shall see, these affricates were also sibilants and thus subject to the special development of the sibilants that spread through Castilian during the Middle Ages.

Other Consonants Plus Yod

A yod could appear after other consonants in Late Latin, but since they were not consonants that could palatalize easily, the results tended to be different from the preceding ones. The labials /b/ and /m/ simply preserve the original yod:

PLUVIA 'rain' > *lluvia*
RUBEU 'reddish' > *rubio* 'blond'
*RABIA (C.L. RABIĒS) 'rage' > *rabia*
VINDĒMIA 'harvest' > *vendimia*
PRAEMIU 'prize' > *premio*

After /p/ and /r/, the yod is sometimes preserved as in the preceding examples:

SĒPIA 'cuttlefish' > *xibia*
CĒREU 'wax candle' > *cirio*

The more usual development, however, was an anticipation of the yod, resulting in a metathesis so that it appeared at the end of the preceding syllable:

A(U)GURIU 'omen' > [agoi̯ro] > *agüero*
CORIU 'leather' > [coi̯ro] > *cuero*
-ARIU (agential suffix) > *-airo* > *-eiro* > *-ero*
SAPIAT (SAPERE, 'to taste; know', pres. subj.) > [sai̯pa] > *sepa*
BASIU 'kiss' > [bai̯so] > *beso*

The results of /d/ and /g/ plus yod seem to have provided a model for some words containing other consonants. At any rate, we find that in some examples the labial has been absorbed by the yod:

FOVEA 'small pit, ditch' > *foya*
RUBEU 'reddish' > *royo* (cf. *rubio*)
HABEAM (HABERE 'to have', pres. subj.) > *haya*

The Assimilation of /mb/ to /m/

This particular consonant sequence is found in only a few words, and the assimilation is not limited to Castilian but is found all over northeastern Iberia and in Gascony and much of southwestern France:

CAMBIĀRE (Late Lat. < Celtic) 'to change' > *camiar*
AMBŌS 'both' > *amos*
PLUMBU 'lead' > *plomo*
LUMBU 'loin' > *lomo*

The first two examples were later replaced by the learned forms *cambiar* and *ambos*.

The Sibilants

As we saw in chapter 2, Latin had a single sibilant /s/, whose articulation was very likely to have been that of an apicoalveolar [ś] in many areas, including much, if not most, of Hispania.[95] Like other consonants, it could

---

[95] Thus, there is no real need to speak of an "apicalization" of the Latin /s/ in Castile (as in Otero 1971, 309).

appear long in intervocalic position, and, as we saw above, the processes of degemination and voicing reduced the geminate /s:/ to a simple /s/ and voiced the simple medial /s/ to /z/ (examples on p. 000).

The assibilated affricates /tˢ/ and /dᶻ/ were derived from a variety of sources discussed in the preceding sections. A third pair of sibilants was that composed of the voiced and voiceless palatal hushing fricatives /ž/ and /š/, spelled respectively J or GE, GI for /ž/ and X for /š/. The voiced palatal sibilant derived from the Late Latin /l̦/ and the large number of learned words and foreign borrowings. The voiceless palatal, on the other hand, originally resulted only from the combination /-ks-/, and thus was sparsely represented in the early Castilian lexicon, being especially rare in word-initial position. A number of words which in Latin contained the sibilant /s/ shifted the sibilant to /š/ in early medieval times. Thus, we find medially:

VĒSSĪCA (C.L. VĒSĪCA) 'bladder' > *vexiga*
PASSARU 'sparrow' > *páxaro*

Along with these shifted forms are found others with /s/: *vessiga*, *pássaro*.

A larger number of examples of this shift appear in word-initial position:

SAPŌNE (Late Lat. < Germanic) 'soap' > *xabón*
SĒRICA 'Chinese; pertaining to silk' > *xerga* 'serge, rough cloth'
SIRICU > *sirgo* → *xilguero* 'goldfinch'
SŪCU 'sap' > *xugo* 'juice'
SĒPIA 'cuttlefish' > *xibia*
SYRINGA 'reed' (< Gr.) 'syringe'> *xeringa*[96]

Along with these forms, we find also ones with /s/: *serga, silguero, sugo*.

The substitution of /š/ for /s/ is sporadic and did not constitute a general change. The phonetic conditions under which it occurs are not clear either. In some cases we can detect the effect of a supporting phonetic factor: namely the presence of a high front vowel /i/ following the /s/, as in *vexiga, xilguero,* and *xibia*. The sibilant /s/ was pronounced with the tongue tipped upward toward the alveolar ridge so that the resulting sibilant tended to have a somewhat palatal articulation. Thus, the presence of the vowel with the most palatal qualities could induce a speaker to retract the tongue further and thus articulate a clearly palatal sibilant, but such a factor would explain only a few of the examples found.

Possibly in other examples we may think of the influence of a preceding consonant in derived words based on the words in question. Thus, corre-

---

[96] The examples given in the text reveal that both forms with [s] and [š] existed. The examples are merely those that eventually settled on the form with [š] in standard Spanish. In medieval texts there are many other pairs in which the etymologically correct form happened to win out: *cessar-cexar, xistra-sistra, sarcia-xarcia, sastre-xastre, samugas-xamugas, Suárez-Xuárez* (both forms of this name still exist today), *Messías-Mexías, Quesada-quixada, salma-xalma, sobeo-xubeo, servilla-xervilla,* etc. (Alonso 1947, 2).

sponding to *xabón* is the verb *enxabonar* 'to cover with soap', from *xerga* is *enxergar*, and based on *xugo* is *enxugar* 'to wipe off; dry'. In these examples, we may consider that the alveolar /n/ immediately preceding the sibilant might have induced a retraction of the tongue that shifted the sibilant into the palatal range. The palatal sibilant in the derived word could then have been extended analogically to the base word.

This still leaves some words unaccounted for, so other reasons for the substitution must be sought. Even without any special analogical or phonetic influence, it is still true that the apicoalveolar /ś/ has the acoustic quality that makes it resemble /š/ rather closely so that some substitutions can have occurred simply by chance (Menéndez Pidal 1941, 197). Of course, such acoustic equivalence cannot explain why, when such substitutions did take place, they always occurred in the direction of /s/ > /š/, and not vice versa. Here we may consider as a motivating factor for the direction of the shift the relative scarcity of examples of /š/ at the earliest period. Given this scarcity, the /š/ was undoubtedly the more expressive of the two sibilants and speakers would have been more likely to use it when, for some reason, they wished to give a slightly more expressive tone to a particular word (Michelena 1975; Martínez Álvarez 1976). In medieval Castilian the only words beginning with /š/ that did not result from its substitution for an original /s/ were a few from Arabic:

> *xaque* 'king (in chess)' < ŠAH (DCELC II 1034a)
> *xáquima* 'rope headstall' < ŠAKIMA (DCELC II 1035)
> *xara* 'rockrose' < popular Ar. ŠA'RA 'woods, thicket; bush' (DCELC II 1035b)
> *xarabe* 'syrup' > ŠARAB 'drink; potion; syrup' (DCELC II 1039)
> *xarifo* 'showy, elegant' < ŠARĪF 'noble, illustrious' (DCELC II 1039)
> *xebe* 'rock alum' < ŠABB 'vitriol' (DCELC II 1045a)
> *xábega* 'fishing net' < ŠABAKA (DCELC II 1019b)

Thus, there were originally no words distinguished only by the opposition between initial /ś/ and /š/ so that substitution of /š/ for /ś/ would have had no functional effect.

One of the earliest explanations for the sporadic substitutions we have seen above was the influence of speakers of Arabic in southern spain. In some areas such an influence is not unlikely, as in some place names in southern Spain: *Xátiva* < SAETABI, *Xúcar* < SUCRO, *Xalón* < SALONE, *Xarama* < SARAMBA. Such examples are, however, limited to areas where Arabic persisted for some time and are not found in Old Castile or other northern regions. It is impossible then to account for all examples of the shift by this supposed influence (Alonso 1947, 5).

Last, a structural factor has recently been adduced for the substitution. As we saw above, with the voicing of the intervocalic voiceless consonants, word-initial consonants were usually associated with the former medial geminates, now distinguished in some other fashion than by length from the former simple unvoiced consonants. The sonorants /l:/ and /n:/ both replaced length by palatalization and produced the Castilian /ļ/ and /ņ/. It has been suggested that during the period when variation was still in effect, before the final phonemicization of the medial voicing, when both strong and weak variants of consonants could appear in word-initial position, that the palatal [š-] could have been adopted by some speakers as the strong variant of /ś/ (Martínez Álvarez 1976, 232). Although ingenious, this theory seems rather unlikely especially since Castilian did not generalize the medial palatals /ņ/ and /ļ/ in initial position. Also, if it is thought that bilingual speakers of Basque and Romance might have tended to use [š] because of the influence of Basque, we would have to consider the problem of the lack of any [š] in medieval Basque. It is more likely that the various phonetic, structural and analogical factors mentioned above suffice to explain the substitutions that we do find. Finally, we may take into account a possible general tendency to strengthen explosive consonants in order to distinguish them more clearly from implosive, syllable-final realizations (Granda Gutiérrez 1966, 127).

The Beginning of Unvoicing

The sibilant system that we find for early medieval Castilian is the following:

	apicoalveolar	predorsodental affricate	palatal hushing
voiceless	/ś/	/tˢ/	/š/
voiced	/ź/	/dᶻ/	/ž/

Examples of these sibilants are the following minimal pairs:

/ś/	/ź/
posso 'push'	*poso* 'I stop'
osso 'bear'	*oso* 'I dare'
cosso 'running'	*coso* 'I sew'

/tˢ/	/dᶻ/
façes 'bundle of sticks'	*fazes* 'you do'
foçes 'sickles'	*fozes* 'throat'
deçir 'to part, separate; descend'	*dezir* 'to say'

/š/	/ž/
puxar 'to push'	*pujar* 'to bid up the price'
coxo 'lame'	*cojo* 'I collect'
fixo 'fixed'	*fijo* 'son'

In word-initial position only /š/ and /ž/ were in opposition. The other sibilants neutralized their opposition in both word-initial and word-final position with only the voiceless phoneme appearing here.[97] The examples

---

[97] In final position the affricates were usually spelled with the letter z, but as we saw in note 85, it is likely that the articulation in this position was unvoiced. Occasional spellings of ç instead of z seem to confirm this idea, e.g., *Guterreç* (1197, DLE 153:5, 15) from Villagonzalo Pedernales near Burgos, *Martineç* (same aMS: 6, 7, 9, 17, 18); *Beatriç* (1226, DLC 176:16, 18) from Bugedo de Juarros, southeast of Burgos; *Diaç* (same MS:19); *Roiç* (same MS:19).

given above show that although there were a certain number of minimal
pairs in which one word was distinguished from another only by the
presence or absence of voicing in the sibilant, the words in these pairs do
not belong to the same morphological or semantic categories so that the
elimination of the distinction between them would have had little effect on
communicative efficiency. Both these facts indicate that the distinction
between the voiced and voiceless series was functionally weak.

By the end of the sixteenth century, in most areas where Castilian was
spoken the voiced series had vanished and only the voiceless sibilants
remained, with phonetic realizations evolving differently in different regions. This change is unique in western Romance. The other western
Romance languages have all preserved to this day a distinct voiced and
voiceless series of sibilants (often with some reduction in the number of
sibilants through merger of the original affricates and the simple sibilants).
Some examples from Old French and Portuguese will show this:

Latin	Old French	Portuguese
GROSSU 'fat, thick'	*gros*	*grosso*
URSU 'bear'	*ours*	*usso* (MPort. *urso*)
PLATEA 'street, open space'	*place*	*praça* 'square'
*CAPTIARE 'to hunt'	*chacier*	*caçar*
PULSARE 'to push'	*pousser*	*puxar*
COXU 'lame'		*coxo*
ROSA 'rose'	*rose*	*rosa*
CAUSA 'cause; thing'	*chose*	*coisa*
PLACERE 'to please'	*plaisir*	*prazer*
SATIONE 'sowing'	*saison*	*sazão* 'season'

In view of the preservation of the voiced sibilants in the other western
Romance dialects, the functional weakness of the voiced-voiceless opposition cannot be considered a cause of the merger, although it undoubtedly
facilitated it. Nor can it be attributed to any general unvoicing of the voiced
consonants since voicing remains an important distinctive feature of the
obstruent series. Some other factor must therefore have been at work to
make Castilian go in a direction contrary to that of general western
Romance.

Some time ago it was noticed that the merger of the voiced with the
voiceless sibilants resulted in a system strikingly like that of modern
Basque:

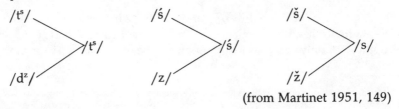

(from Martinet 1951, 149)

Modern Basque has three simple sibilants with three corresponding affricated sibilants:

	predorsal	apicoalveolar	palatal hushing
sibilant	/s/	/ś/	(/š/)
affricate	/ts/	/tś/	/tš/

Some examples are the following:

/s/: *zu* 'you' (pl.)   /ś/: *su* 'fire'
     zuri 'white'   *sagar* 'apple'
     gizon 'man'   *guraso* 'parents'
     ezker 'left'   *esker* 'grace'

/ts/: *atzo* 'yesterday'   /tś/: *atso* 'old' (fem.)
     bizitza 'life'   *aratsalde* 'afternoon'
     (h)otz 'cold'   *(h)ots* 'sound'
     zortzi 'eight'   *zentsu* 'sense'

/tš/: *txori* 'bird'
     etxe 'house'
     itxaso 'sea'

One noticeable feature of the Basque system is the lack of any voiced sibilants. It is possible that medieval Basque did not have a sibilant system exactly like that of the modern dialects. The palatal sibilants, for example, are likely to be a fairly recent phenomenon, resulting from the palatalization of the predorsal and apical sibilants (Michelena 1957, 119).

Still, it is not sufficient to point out this parallelism in order to prove that Basque influence must have been the active agent at work in this particular change. Basque has been in retreat from the spread and prestige of Castilian for many centuries and has been heavily influenced by Castilian since the Middle Ages. In view of the prestige that Castilian has enjoyed for so long, and in view of the lack of such prestige associated with Basque, we cannot conceive of this change as having occurred in the sixteenth century. If the unvoicing of the voiced sibilants was provoked by Basque in some way, it must have had its origin not after Castilian had become the dominant dialect of central Spain, but much earlier, at the time when Castile was developing as an independent area with its own distinctive ethos. As pointed out at the beginning of this chapter, during the very earliest period of the formation of the Castilian dialect Basque and Romance speakers mingled together in the resettlement of the empty lands south of the Cantabrian chain and probably on terms of rough equality. Both Romance and Basque had relatively equal prestige, although, of course, Romance was tending to predominate. During those early years, persons speaking with a slightly different "accent" could easily have been leaders and men of importance in the developing frontier community.

We must now try to imagine how speakers of Basque at this very early period would have pronounced the Romance sibilants that they heard from their neighbors. The system of early Basque probably only had two sibilants, a predorsal /s/ and an apicoalveolar /ś/, plus their affricated counterparts which were probably distinguished from the simple sibilants only intervocalically (Michelena 1957). As far as we can tell, it is reasonable to suppose that the primary distinction between the different series of consonants in the Basque phonological system was between the features tense vs. lax, rather than voiced vs. voiceless. The difference between the sibilant and the affricate would then have been perceived essentially as the difference between a laxly articulated sibilant and a tensely articulated one. Thus, with neutralization of the opposition in word-initial and word-final position, the phonetic system would have been as follows:

Initial		Medial		Final	
+tense	−tense	+tense	−tense	+tense	−tense
	s-	-ts-	-s-	-ts	
	s-	-ts-	-s-	-ts	

(Lantolf 1979, 301)

To the speaker whose primary linguistic system was Basque, voicing would have been an irrelevant feature in the pronunciation of sibilants. On hearing the voiced and voiceless sibilants of the Romance speakers, he would have recognized only those features that were pertinent to his own native system. Accompanying the feature of voice in Romance was a concommitant feature of laxness, while voiceless consonants were generally characterized by being also tense. The Basque speaker would have therefore interpreted this tenseness and laxness as the primary features and in trying to speak Romance, he would most probably produced phonetic realizations like those of Basque. That is, he would identify the voiceless sibilants as his own tense sibilants, and the voiced ones as his own lax sibilants. For example, trying to imitate words like *sole* 'sun' and *cielo* 'heaven', the Basque speaker would have been able to imitate the first accurately since the initial apicoalveolar sibilant corresponded exactly to his own lax sibilant; the second, however, he would have been likely to produce at first as [s]*ielo*, using the predorsal sibilant of his own primary system, since the affricate did not appear initially. In Romance non-affricate dorsal sibilants were not, however, opposed to affricates. (Also, as will be seen in chapter 5, the loss of the occlusive element was to become general in western Romance.) Therefore, such a pronunciation could easily pass unnoticed.

In medial position, however, if the Basque speaker heard the words *posso* [pośo] and *poso* [pożo], he would have been likely to pronounce the first as *po[tˢ]o* and the second as *po[ś]o*. That is, he would have heard the tenseness of the Romance voiceless /ś/ as the equivalent to his own tense affricate /tś/. The laxness of the voiced /ź/ he would probably have heard as his own lax sibilant /s/. Similarly, on hearing the words *dezir* and *deçir*, he would probably have perceived the distinction between /dᶻ/ and /tˢ/ as that between a lax and a tense consonant and would therefore have pronounced them *de[s]ir* and *de[ts]ir*. To the Romance speaker, it would have seemed that the Basque speaker was pronouncing them both almost alike, if we assume that the occlusion was less noticeable than the position of the tongue.

Basque speakers, on being corrected (or on correcting themselves) and attempting to pronounce more accurately the Romance system, would easily have identified the difference between the alveolar and dorsal sibilants, since these distinctions corresponded to a similar distinction in their own system. And they could also have learned to disregard the equivalence of tenseness and affrication and to redistribute the occurrence of affricates and non-affricates, once again because in their own primary system there was a distinction between these two types of articulation. The one thing they would have found most difficult to learn, however, would have been to use voice as a relevant distinctive feature of the sibilants, since this feature was totally foreign to their own system. Those who practiced and made a special effort, could, of course, learn the correct pronunciation. If, on the other hand, there were many persons who did not think (i.e., subconsciously) it worth the extra effort and who were content with a close approximation as long as they could be understood, then it would have been possible for the merger to become established as a viable mode of pronunciation. Once this variable was established as a feature of the Castilian of a sufficient number of persons, and especially once children began to learn to speak in this fashion, it would have been accepted as a norm of pronunciation, at least among certain groups of the population.[98]

One might think that such a pronunciation would have caused some communicative difficulty since there existed, as pointed out above, a number of minimal pairs distinguished only by the difference between the voiced and voiceless sibilants, but the minimal pairs given previously are

---

[98] Allen (1964) points out that from the tenth century onwards manuscripts from various areas of Castile begin to use the graphemes FF-, SS-, and RR- to represent word-initial /f-, s-, r:-/, corresponding to the voiceless medial sibilants and the multiple trill. Such graphemes become commoner throughout the Middle Ages and were used in precisely the positions in which either the voiceless or tense fricatives appeared (medially in opposition to a voiced or weaker consonant). Allen seems to attribute this new spelling to a general "tensing" trend. There is no internal reason for any such tensing to have occurred, and it is quite possible to see in the new spelling simply a generalization of the custom of using SS and RR to represent tense phonemes for those sounds that did not have any special letter to represent them (Lantolf 1974, 212–14). This graphemic system finally broke down when the initial /f-/ was replaced by /h-/ and the sibilants merged. Allen contends that the scribal practices he finds are confirmed by Nebrija's description of Spanish voiceless versus voiced consonants as "apretadas" vs. "floxas" (311–12). Renaissance grammarians, however, were not usually aware of the role of voicing in articulation and thus used other terms to describe these differences (Lantolf 1974, 127). The maintenance in spelling of F in some words and FF in others may indeed be an indication that scribes were trying to make a spelling distinction between [h] and [f], with the double letter standing for the labiodental or bilabial articulation. Blake (forthcoming) finds numerous examples of an attempt to make this kind of distinction, especially in the names of places where it was essential to keep apart the names of places which were identical or almost identical in two or more areas.

the only ones that have been discovered. Most of these words belong to different form classes, and do not appear in the same contexts, e.g., *osso* 'bear' vs. *oso* 'I dare'. Even when both words belong to the same form class, their semantic difference is so great that it is most unlikely that anyone would have misunderstood someone who pronounced both alike, e.g., *foçes* 'sickles' vs. *fozes* 'throat'. In other words, the functional yield of the voiced-voiceless opposition in the sibilant system was not great and its abandonment led to no real confusion in actual discourse (Lantolf 1974, 249–51).

It is worth pointing out too that in at least one pair of sibilant phonemes, the voiceless partner is far more frequent in medial position. When one omits the suffixes *-ez(a)*, *-azo*, *-izo*, *-azón*, etc., it turns out that words with ç outnumber those with z perhaps two to one (Malkiel 1971, 7, n. 2).[99] Thus, it is likely that the occurrence of voiceless sibilants in general outweighed that of their voiced counterparts. Also the fact that the voiced sibilant z so often was associated with derivational suffixes may have induced speakers to associate voicing or its absence with morphological rather than purely phonological circumstances. It seems true too that Castilian speakers tended to disfavor oppositions that functioned only word-internally (Penny 1976, 157).

In short, the influence of Basque-Romance bilingualism could make itself felt in this area because of the lack of any strong factors which favored the maintenance of tradition. The merger of /ź/ and /ś/ and of /tˢ/ and /dᶻ/ had little practical effect on communication. The lack of voiced sibilants made the pronunciation of those who adopted the merger sound distinctive, but not so outlandish as to be unacceptable as a plausible variant form of the pronunciation of Castilian.[100]

The next problem to be considered is why the voiced palatal sibilant /ž/ also became unvoiced. As indicated above, the palatal sibilant /š/ does not seem to have been part of the Basque phonological system in medieval times. The merger of /ž/ and /š/ is, therefore, not directly attributable to Basque speech habits. Nevertheless, such a merger would have fitted in perfectly with the other mergers. Those who lacked voiced sibilants in

---

[99] It is not clear from Malkiel's statement whether his figures refer to medial position alone, or all positions. Lantolf refers to Malkiel but extends what he says to include all sibilants. This is not to deny, of course, that these figures may be correct for *all* sibilants (1974, 248).

[100] For a similar situation today, see Echaide's (1966) discussion of the influence of Basque pronunciation habits on the pronunciation of modern Castilian. It is interesting to note that modern speakers of Basque in Guipúzcoa, when speaking Castilian, substitute a sibilant, either /s/ or /ś/, for the modern interdental fricative /θ/, and interpret initial stops in accordance with the Basque system which has [-tense] in this position. Thus, /k/ and /g/ alternate initially, since to a Basque speaker the distinction is not significant: *gambión* for *camión*, *gorbata* for *corbata*, *goliflor* for *coliflor* (522). Echaide notes that this kind of interference is most noticeable among older speakers, while young people generally speak Castilian correctly. The overwhelming prestige that Castilian has today, coupled with the massive influence of modern methods of communication and the modern educational system, creates a situation far different from that prevailing a thousand years ago.

their primary system would hardly have been likely to learn one that did not exist at all in that system. The new articulation that they did learn would have fitted into the sibilant system, but the feature of voice would have been treated as it was in the other sibilants.[101]

One additional factor that favored the merger is the general linguistic tendency of mergers to spread at the expense of distinctions. Of course, one should not underestimate the power of tradition. Although this particular merger can be conceived of as the result of the creation of a new linguistic norm among a group of speakers heavily influenced by Basque-Romance bilingualism, it was certainly not a general feature of the Castilian dialect. It must be thought of as a feature of a certain class of early Castilian speakers quite possibly lacking any special social prestige in the early Middle Ages. The written evidence that has been discovered so far seems to point to the city of Burgos and nearby areas as the original focus of the merger. The literary standard, however, was based principally on the Castilian dialect of Toledo and thus favored the older Romance standard for the pronunciation of the sibilants, at least as far as spelling is concerned. As García de Diego points out, Castilian even in its earliest years, was a diasystem, including a mixture of dialects and did not present a completely unified, homogeneous dialect structure; it shared characteristics with other dialects and had also certain individual features not found elsewhere: "el castellano, geográficamente unas veces un rincón fonético y otras la mayor parte de la nación" (1950, 108). Thus, the merger of voiced and voiceless sibilants in favor of the voiceless sibilants was a feature of the popular pronunciation of an increasing number of speakers, probably at first of the lowest and least prestigious class, although as we have noted previously, early Castilian society was characterized by a fluidity of social class that was in sharp contrast with its later rigidity. As Castile spread its power and its language to the south, unvoicing was carried along with it.

The Chief Phonetic Characteristics of Castilian

In their coalescence into the group that formed the core of the early Castilian county and later the independent kingdom of Castile, the Castilians selected a range of phonetic developments that, taken together, help to set their speech off in a clearly defined way from their Romance-speaking neighbors. We have discussed these phonetic characteristics in the preceding sections. At this point we shall summarize them briefly. Most were not limited to early Castile alone but were shared in part with the other Ibero-Romance dialects, all of which had features that reflect the

---

[101] Lantolf points out that a similar change is now occurring in the Spanish of the Plate region in Argentina. The merger of /l/ and /y/ into /ž/ has created an unbalanced system with a single voiced sibilant. As there are no other voiced sibilants in the system, this phoneme is isolated and many speakers are abandoning voice altogether, producing a new phoneme /š/ (Lantolf 1974, 254; Guitarte 1955).

common phonetic developments of Late Latin in the Iberian peninsula. The development of the vowel system, the monophthongization of /ai̯/ and the formation of yods were common to all of Romania.

The changes common to all of Ibero-Romance (and in part to all of western Romance) are the following:

1) The formation of the sequential diphthong /ai̯/, which formed a counterpart of the earlier Latin diphthong /au̯/ which had largely remained unchanged;

2) The palatalization of /g/ before front vowels;

3) The voicing of the intervocalic voiceless consonants (if we omit the remnants of the earlier voiceless consonants in upper Aragon and Andalusia).

Other features were found in much of Ibero-Romance but were not accepted everywhere. Thus, diphthongization was not accepted in the western dialects (which became Galician-Portuguese), and the palatalization of the word-initial clusters containing /l/ was not accepted in Catalan.

The following phonetic developments came to characterize Castilian Romance:

1) the early monophthongization of /ai̯/ to /e/, and /au̯/ to /o/;

2) the establishment of the results /ue/ and /ie/ as the only forms of the diphthongs from Late Latin /ę/ and /ǫ/, and the identification of the on-glides as non-syllabic allophones of the vowels /i/ and /u/;

3) the absence of diphthongization before yods (including form 1 of the verbs *tener* and *venir*);

4) the disappearance of /j/ before front vowels, and an early resistance to the voiced palatal fricative /ž/;

5) the loss of the initial consonant of the groups developed from occlusives plus /l/;

6) the change of early /l̦/ to /ž/;

7) the change of /-i̯t-/ to /č/;

8) the change of Late Latin /-skj-/ to /tˢ/ rather than to /š/ as in other dialects;

9) the assimilation of /-mb-/ to /-m-/ (shared with some other eastern dialects);

10) the beginnings of the shift of /f/ to /h/;

11) the beginnings of the merger of the voiced sibilants into the voiceless ones (*Orígenes* §§100–101).

Not all of these phonetic changes began at the same time nor were all completed at the same time, but by the eleventh century they had come to characterize phonetically most of the Castilian dialect, centered originally most probably in the area around the city of Burgos. To the north of Burgos, some of the early phonetic developments of Ibero-Romance were preserved as late as the eleventh and twelfth centuries. Thus, we find the the diphthong /ei̯/ < /ai̯/, earlier forms of the diphthongs from /o/ and /e/, and the preservation of Late Latin final /-u/ distinct from /-o/

(*Orígenes* §99.1). In contrast with its distinctive phonetic pattern, it is likely that in morphology and lexicon Castile was much less distinctive in relation to its Romance neighbors.

THE MORPHOLOGICAL SYSTEM

The Nominal System

As we saw in the previous chapter, the reduction in the number of cases in Latin eventually led to an extreme reduction in most of the Romance languages to a single singular and plural form for most substantives and adjectives, with the /-s/ typical of the accusative plural of most nouns being identified with the general function of plurality in western Romance. The question of which case form must be the one most substantives and adjectives in Romance derive from is not easy to determine (Orbán 1972, Penny 1979–80, Iliescu 1969), since the majority of words had an invariable stem in all cases.

Nevertheless, in a few clear cases, a stem derived from a specific case form other than the nominative-accusative had obviously been preserved. We can determine these words by their peculiar phonetic development. The majority of words retain the vowel characteristic of their ancestral Latin declension: /-a/ from first declension nouns and neuter plurals, /-o/ from second declension and some fourth declension nouns, and /-e/ from the third declension (unless lost after apical consonants). A few of the neuter singulars preserved from the third declension with the ending /-os/ < -US are

PECTUS 'chest' > *pechos*
PIGNUS 'pledge, pawn' > *peños*
OPUS 'work' > *huebos* 'deeds' (also in the expression *uebos me es* <
     OPUS MIHI EST 'it is necessary for me')
TEMPUS 'time' > *tiempos*
VIRTUS 'manliness; bravery; virtue' > *virtos* 'army'

Although these words preserved their form in /-os/ for centuries, they appeared to be masculine plurals and eventually through back formation new singulars were created: *pecho, tiempo, virto* 'force, violence', etc.

A larger number of nouns come from the nominative case. Some are names, usually of persons, and thus more likely to appear as subjects of sentences or as vocatives:

CAROLUS > *Carlos*
DEUS 'god' > *diós*
DOMINICUS > *Domingos*
JESŪS > *Jesús*
MARCUS > *Marcos*
PAULUS > *Pablos*
RUMICIS VALLIS > *Roncesvalles*

Others are names of professions and occupations and thus also more likely to have appeared as subjects of verbs:

COMPANIŌ 'companion' > *compaño* (cf. *compañón* < COMPANIONE)
MAGISTER 'master (of a military order)' > *maestre*

Some others from the nominative case are not native Castilian words but derive from other Romance languages:

CANTOR 'precentor; singer' > OFr. *chantre*
PRESBYTER 'priest' > OFr. *prestre* > OSp. *preste*
SARTOR 'tailor' > Cat. *sastre* (replacing OSp. *alfayate* < Arabic, in the
   later Middle Ages)

In a few other cases we cannot be sure just why the nominative was preserved:

AVIS STRUTHIO 'ostrich' > *avestruz*
PUMEX (C.L. PŪMEX) > *pómez*
TĪTIŌ 'burning brand' > *tizo*
CURCULIŌ 'weevil' > *gorgojo*

One name derived from the vocative is *Santi Yagüe* 'St. James' < SANCTE JACOBE. Similar forms of names have been found such as *Iessu-criste*, and *Sixte*. Possibly the title *maese* 'master' may be considered to reflect an old vocative too (Alvar-Pottier 1983, 68).

The preservation of a distinctive genitive form occurs only in two-word groups in which one word depended on another. Thus, the names of the days of the week were in the genitive because the head noun was under-stood to be DIĒS (Late Lat. DIA):

MARTIS 'day of Mars: Tuesday' > *martes*
JOVIS 'day of Jupiter: Thursday' > *jueves*
VENERIS 'day of Venus: Friday' > *viernes*

The names for 'Monday' and 'Wednesday', being from other declensions, did not have the -IS ending of the third and therefore would have given: **lune* < LŪNAE and **MERCURE* < MERCURIĪ. Through analogy with the others, however, they too came to end in -*es*: *lunes* and *miércoles*.

Many of the other examples of genitive forms are names of places in which the head noun indicates some object or item of terrain or a place:

CASTRUM SIGERICĪ > *Castrojeriz*
CASTRUM PETRĪ > *Castropetre*
VĪLLA GOTTHŌRUM > *Villa Otoro* > *Villatoro* (Burgos)
VILLA VALERIĪ, > *Villavaler*
VILLA ALBONIĪ, > *Villaboñe*
CAMPĪ GOTTHŌRUM > *Campotoro* > *Toro* (Tierra de Campos)
TURRE MAURĪ > *Tormor*

In some toponyms the head noun has disappeared altogether, especially when a church is referred to (ECLĒSIA):

ARMENTARIĪ > *Armental*
ASINIĪ > *Asín*
*CARDELLĪ > *Cardeli*
(COSTA) SAXŌRUM > *Sasor*
*FORMOSELLĪ > *Fermoselle*
GAUDIĪ > *Goge*
GOTHŌRUM > *Toro*
GALLŌRUM > *Gallur*
MAURŌRUM > *Mauror*
RIVĪ ANGULU > *Riaño, Rianjo*
RIVĪ PRESSA > *Represa*
SANCTĪ ANTONINĪ > *Santulín*
SANCTĪ EMETERĪ > *Santemder, Santander*
SANCTĪ FĒLICIS > *Santelices, Sanfelices* > *Safelices* > *Sahelices* > *Saelices*
SANCTĪ JOHANNIS > *Santianes*
SANCTĪ JULIANĪ > *Santillán, Santullán*
SANCTĪ JUSTĪ > *Santiyuste*
SANCTĪ PONCIĪ > *Santiponce*
SANCTĪ QUĪRICĪ > *Sanquirce*
SANCTĪ SATURNINĪ > *Saornil*
SANCTĪ TORQUATĪ > *Santorcaz*
SANCTĪ VICTŌRIS > *Sahechores*

A couple of other terms are titles of persons:

COMITE STABULI 'master of the stable' > *condestable* 'high royal official'
FĪL(IUS) ECLĒSIAE 'son of the church' > *feligrés* 'worshiper, parishioner'

Some family names result from the use of the genitive case of the father's name after the name of the child:

MAURATĪNĪ > *Moratín*
PONTIĪ > *Ponce*
ROMANCĪ > *Romance*

Two others are objects:

AURĪ FRESU > *orfrés, orofrés, orifrés* 'gold braid'
PEDIS UNGULA 'hoof' > *pesuña, pezuña*

Finally a few words were preserved with the form of the ablative because they became adverbs:

HĀC HŌRĀ 'at this hour' > *agora* 'now' > MSp. *ahora*
HŌC ANNŌ 'in this year' > *ogaño*
LOCŌ 'on the spot' > *luego* 'immediately' (MSp. 'later')

(Menéndez Pidal 1941, 207–09;
Alvar-Pottier 1983, 65–71.)

Pronouns: First and Second Persons

The pronominal system of Late Latin developed regularly in Castilian. The reduced form of the first person pronoun /*eo/ < EGO may have diphthongized to [jeo] thus giving the form *yo* (Alvar-Pottier 1983,117–18). TŪ, NŌS, and VŌS remain unchanged in *tú, nos,* and *vos.* The dative singular forms MĪ and TIBI remain as *mí* and *tive,* although the latter form was analogically remodelled on the basis of *mí* to *ti.* In Mozarabic the first person pronoun also appears in the form *mibi,* clearly based on the second person form (Alvar-Pottier 1983, 118). The accusatives MĒ and TĒ likewise remain unchanged, but in Romance the distinction of cases is replaced by a distinction between stressed and unstressed forms, with *me* and *te* being specialized in Castilian as the atonic ones, and *mi* and *ti* as tonic forms. The same development affected the third person reflexive pronouns SĒ SIBI > *se* and *sí.*

One special development must be noted. The preposition CUM 'with' was used enclitically after the first and second person pronouns: MĒCUM, TĒCUM, NOBISCUM, VOBISCUM (NŌSCUM and VŌSCUM in Late Latin with the generalization of the accusative as sole oblique case). With the loss of case distinctions, the regular tonic pronoun was used, giving **migo, *tigo* (OPort. *mego, tego*), and *nosco, vosco* (Leonese, Portuguese). Since regular phonetic development had voiced the intervocalic /-k-/, the final element was no longer recognizable by speakers, who then proceeded to add the preposition *con* once more: *conmigo, contigo, consigo, con nusco,* and *con vusco.* The back high vowel /u/ in the last two forms probably reflects the front high vowel of the singular forms.

Third Person Pronouns

The specialization of ILLE and ILLA as subject pronouns for the third had already occurred in Late Latin. Through regular phonetic development they gave *elle* and *ella.* With the apocope of *elle* the result would have */el/,* but because the palatal lateral /l̦/ cannot appear in word-final position in Castilian, the form *el* became more frequent. The plural forms were the accusatives ILLŌS and ILLĀS which developed regularly to *ellos* and *ellas.* The neuter ILLUD became *ello.*

The object forms are reduced to a single syllable, probably because of their frequency of use (Mańczak 1969) and because they were atonic. The final syllable is the one that remains, undoubtedly because it is the one which clearly indicates the gender of the object: ILLUM > *lo,* ILLAM > *la,* ILLŌS > *los,* and ILLĀS > *las.*Unlike the first and second person pronouns, the third person ones preserved a distinction between the dative and the accusative: ILLĪ > *li* (preserved dialectally) > *le,* ILLĪS > *les.* The combination of*ILI-ILUM, -ILAM very early developed into /l̦elo, -la, -los, -las/ (cf. It. *glielo, gliela*). Regular phonetic development of /l̦/ gave/že-/, written *gelo, gela, gelos, gelas.* Although the original form of these combinations was limited to the dative singular, it was soon extended to the plural as well.

Possessive Adjectives

The first person singular adjectives MEUS and MEA had functioned as first-second declension adjectives in Latin. The regular development of /meo/ with diphthongization of /e/ or, alternatively, the development of the diphthong /eu/ > /ió/ (see p. 000), would give *mió* or *mío* (*mieo* is found in Leonese). The feminine form is similar: *mía*. An even commoner form was *míe* (analogically *mié*). With the apocope of final /e/, the latter form became *mi* and eventually replaced *mío*. It was aided, undoubtedly, by sentence phonetics since *mío* usually appeared before a noun and thus could syncopate the /-o/ as part of an accentual group.

The second person singular adjectives TUUM and TUAM gave *to* and *túa*. The feminine form shows a raising of the first vowel to a high vowel, probably through the influence of a transitional glide between the vowels in hiatus (Meadows 1948). The pronominal use of the second person adjective apparently was influenced analogically by *cuyo* < CUIUS 'of whom' > *tuyo* (and *suyo* as well).

The Latin third person reflexive possessive SUUS was generalized as a common third person possessive whose form developed like those of the second person adjective: *so, sua*.

The first person and second person plural possessives NOSTRUM and VOSTRUM developed regularly: *nuestro, vuestro*.

The feminine forms of all singular adjectives also appeared in a by-form competing with the regular one ending in *-a*: *míe, túe, súe*. The origin of the *-e* ending is obscure. With the apocope of final /-e/ they became *mi*, *tu*, and *su*.

The Definite Article and the Demonstratives

The article developed from the full and reduced forms of ILLE of Late Latin. Both the full and the reduced forms appear from the beginning: *el* would be the normal reflex of *ILE and *ela* < *ILA, and the plural *elos, elas*. It is possible too that *el* derives from an earlier /elo/ < ILLUM, with syncope of /o/ but, is seen below, the nominative origin is more likely. Occasionally there is trace of the full form: *ellos ifantes, ir alla cort* from the *Cid* (Menéndez Pidal 1941, 261). The full form is commonly found also when the article precedes a word beginning with a vowel: *ell estudio, ell espada* (assuming that the -LL- represents /l/).

The question of the case from which the articles and the demonstratives derive has been controversial. With the feminines, of course, the nominative and accusative became identical with the loss of final /-m/. The masculines, however, would have remained distinct in form even without /-m/. In early documents from Leon, Aragon, Navarre and northern Castile, the demonstratives and articles appear in the forms *eli, li, esti*, *aquesti, essi, aquessi*, and *aquelli*. In Upper Rioja these forms remain as late as the fourteenth century. The origin of the final vowel is unclear, although it seems most likely that it reflects a Late Latin analogical extension of the final /-i/ of the interrogative pronoun *qui* 'who' (Gulsoy

1969–70, 183–84). The forms that the demonstratives took in Castilian are often the apocopated ones: *el, est, aquest, es, aques, aquel* (see section on the beginnings of apocope).

The forms ending in *-i, -e*, or nothing, appear to be derived directly from the nominative case in Latin, although some have argued that possibly the letter -E in a number of examples represents the vowel /-o/ from the Late Latin /-u/, in a weakened articulation just before its syncope in syntagmatic combinations (Lapesa 1979, 197). At any rate, early documents written in Low Latin show that most often the article and the demonstratives, when used as subjects of sentences, end in *-e*, e.g., ". . . dedit *ste* episcopus . . ." (A.D. 864), ". . . presot *ille* comite . . ." (c. A.D. 1030), etc. (Lapesa 1979, 201). These uses contrast with the forms that appear as objects of verbs or prepositions which usually ended in -/o/. Very rare were uses of forms in -/o/ as subjects.

The preservation of a distinct nominative case for masculine articles and demonstratives was undoubtedly influenced by the need to maintain a clear distinction between masculines and the neuters ISTUD, IPSUM, ILLUD, all of which produced forms ending in /-o/: *esto, eso, ello, aquello*. Thus in the most primitive form of Castilian, there was probably still a case distinction in masculine articles, with *ele* and *el* as the nominative forms (leaving aside for the moment *ell*), and *elo* and *lo* as the oblique forms. This distinction would account for the fact that all examples of the article *lo* in Castile are found after prepositions. However, the distinction of case could not be maintained, unsupported by a similar distinction of feminine articles or by a case distinction in substantives and adjectives (unlike the situation in Old French). Very soon then mixture of the two forms appear, e.g., "non se cuempetet *elo* uamne in siui" (*Glosas emilianenses*, tenth century). Aiding this movement probably was the apocope of *elo* and *ele*, since in syntactic phonetics the final vowels would have been treated as medial atonic vowels, subject to the same syncope that affected individual words. The resulting form *el* became dominant in Castile at the latest by the middle of the twelfth century (Lapesa 1979, 206–07). An even more reduced form *l*, found after words ending in a vowel, produced the combinations *al* and *del* which have remained up to the present. In medieval Spanish the article could fuse with any preposition ending in a vowel: *fazal alba, contral monte, sol manto* (Menéndez Pidal 1941, 262). The contact of the final /-n/ of *con* and *en* also tended to produce assimilated forms: *conno, -a, enno, -a*,etc., but such assimilated forms became rare in Castile after the thirteenth century. In Leonese and Aragonese they remained much later.

The disappearance of the neuter gender of substantives left the neuter article isolated, although the use of the neuter to indicate an indefinite attribute of the adjective remained and the article could accompany it. Thus *lo bueno* and other pronominal uses, e.g., *lo que, lo de*, could remain with a specific function, i.e., that of referring to things with no gender, such as abstract notions and qualities or unidentified objects (Lapesa 1979, 206).

The Verbal System

The Personal Endings

The personal endings for the present tenses remain as they were in Late Latin, except insofar as they were altered by normal sound change:

1. -o (pres. ind.)   4. -mos
   -ø for other tenses
2. -s   5. -des
3. -t   6. -n

The ending of form 3 remained for a considerable period. Judging by the spelling in a number of early documents, it was undoubtedly pronounced rather weakly since we see it often written -D. In an inscription of 958 are found *despiciad, corriagad* from the eleventh century are *remmansid, dedid*; from the twelfth century, *derelinquid, ueniad, abed*, etc. (*Orígenes* §70.4). In Leon, on the contrary, verbs in form 3 are frequently written without -t. We may conclude that the more conservative norm competed with the loss of the consonant for several centuries. As late as the early thirteenth century, the Fuero de Madrid contains a number of forms with -t along with many without it. The final -t of form 6, on the other hand, evidently had disappeared much earlier as it does not occur except very sporadically, even in documents that contain abundant examples of the singular -t (*Orígenes* §71).

Diphthongized Stem Vowels

The process of diphthongization of Late Latin /e/ and /o/ affected verb forms in which these vowels were stressed, namely forms 1–3 and 6 of the present indicative and subjunctive. Thus, through diphthongization a class of irregular verbs was created in which the stem vowels /e/ and /o/ alternated with /ie/ and /ue/:

Infinitive with /e/	Form 3[102]
FERĪRE 'to strike, hit' > *ferir*	FERIT > *fiere*
LEVĀRE 'to raise' > *levar*	LEVAT > *lieva*
PERDERE 'to lose' > *perder*	PERDIT > *pierde*
SENTĪRE 'to feel' > *sentir*	SENTIT > *siente*
TENĒRE 'to hold' > *tener*	TENET > *tiene*
TENTĀRE 'to test' > *tentar*	TENTAT > *tienta*
TREMULĀRE 'to tremble' > *temblar*	TREMULAT > *tiembla*

With /o/	
COLLOCĀRE 'to place' > *colgar*	COLLOCAT > *cuelga*
COQ(U)ERE 'to cook, bake' > *cocer*	COQ(U)IT > *cuece*

---

[102] To save space, the infinitive is given as a sample of all arrhizotonic verb forms, and form 1 or 3 of the present indicative as representative of all rhizotonic forms (excluding those that adopt the /g/ augment, like *tengo, vengo*, etc.).

With /o/

DORMĪRE 'to sleep' > *dormir*	DORMIT > *duerme*
MORDĒRE 'to bite' > *morder*	MORDET > *muerde*
X ⊣ MORĪ 'to die' > *morir*	*MORIT > *muere*
PROBĀRE 'to test' > *provar*	PROBAT > *prueva*
SOLĒRE 'to be in the habit of ' > *soler*	SOLET > *suele*

Were phonetic considerations alone determinant, every verb that persisted from Late Latin into Castilian with rhizotonic forms containing /-e-/ or /-o-/ would have a diphthong in these forms. And, indeed, in the Middle Ages a number of verbs that in modern Spanish have no diphthong belonged to the radical-changing class, e.g.,

CONFORTAT 'he strengthens, comforts' > *confuerta*
EXPENDIT 'he pays out, spends' > *espiende*
INTEGRŌ 'I make whole, heal' > *entriego* 'I hand over'
NECAT 'he kills' > *aniega* 'he drowns (someone)'
PRAESTŌ 'I perform, fulfill' > *priesto* 'I lend'
PRAETENDIT 'he alleges; pretends' > *pretiende*
TEMPERAT 'he moderates' > *tiempra*
VETAT 'he forbids' > *vieda*

There are other verbs that had diphthongs in earlier times. As we know, verb form, as parts of closely knit paradigms, are often more subject to analogical changes than are more isolated words. Thus, although the rhizotonic forms of the verb are likely to be more frequently used than other forms, the arrhizotonic forms are the majority of the paradigm and so may tempt speakers to regularize all forms by modelling the forms with diphthongs on those without them (see chap. 1). The examples given in the last group, for instance, have all been regularized in modern Spanish so that they do not contain a diphthong in any form.

Another factor that undoubtedly influenced speakers in their choice of the proper form was the existence of many verbs that contained /-e-/ and /-o-/ < Late Lat. /-ẹ-/ and /-ọ-/. The speaker of medieval Romance would have had no way of knowing when the verbs he used with these vowels derived from the close mid vowels rather than the open mid ones, aside, of course, from the alternation between diphthongized and undiphthongized forms. In the arrhizotonic forms, the speaker who said *ofender* 'to offend, insult' and *defender* 'to defend' would have no way of knowing by the form alone that although one must say *ofendo* (probably a Latinism), it was necessary with the other verb to use a diphthong and say *defiendo*. Therefore, from the point of view of the average speaker the choice of whether to use a diphthong was purely arbitrary, determined strictly by tradition rather than any clear-cut phonetic factors. Thus, it is not surprising that some verbs with /e/ and /o/ < /ẹ/ and /ọ/ should have followed the pattern of the diphthongizing verbs, some of which were very common. Along with the phonetically regular *pensa* and *sem-*

bra, some said *piensa* and *siembra* (< PĒNSĀRE 'to weigh mentally, think' (cf. *pesar* 'to weigh', the popular form) and SĒMINĀRE 'to sow'. Other verbs which adopted diphthongal forms in opposition to their etymological origins in verbs without open mid vowels are *feder* 'to stink' < FOETĒRE 'to stink', *comenzar* 'to begin' < *CUM-INITIĀRE, *consolar* 'to console' < CONSŌLĀRĪ, *plegar* 'to bend, fold' < PLICĀRE, *fregar* 'to rub' < FRICĀRE, and a few others (Menéndez Pidal 1941, 291–92).

The Conjugational Pattern

As mentioned in the previous chapter, central and western Ibero-Romance was distinguished by the complete elimination of the Latin conjugation in -ERE with the consequent reduction of the number of conjugations to three, all with arrhizotonic infinitives and forms 4 and 5 in the present tenses. The largest number of verbs was still found in Conjugation I, which has remained until today as the only living conjugation in Spanish.

The endings of the present, through normal sound change, became identical in all verbs of the -*er* and -*ir* conjugations with the exception of forms 4 and 5 in the present indicative which still continued the vowels of Late Latin: the characteristic thematic vowel /-e-/ of form 6 replaced the /u/ of the Latin pattern:

4. *-e-mos*   5. *-e-des*
   -i-mos   *-i-des*

In all other tenses, both conjugations have identical endings. It might seem that they would be destined eventually to fall together into a single conjugation, with analogical merging of the infinitives and of forms 4 and 5. Such has not been the case, however. The two conjugations have continued to remain clearly distinct until modern times.

Other factors must have been at work, maintaining the distinction between the two conjugations. One of the principal ones in determining membership in one conjugation or the other was the quality of the stem vowel. The verbs found in the -*er* conjugation excluded all high vowels, while verbs in -*ir* always include some forms with high vowels. Verbs containing the low vowel /a/ may appear in either conjugation (Montgomery 1975–76). It is this basic phonetic principle that determined whether verbs from the Latin conjugation III went to -*er* or -*ir* in Castilian. Thus, the following verbs with a high stem vowel joined the -*ir* conjugation:

ADDŪCERE 'to lead' > *aduzir*
DĪCERE 'to say' > *dezir*
FRĪGERE 'to fry, roast' > *freír*
RECUTERE 'to strike backwards; rebound' > *recudir*
SCRĪBERE 'to write' > *escrevir, escrivir*
VĪVERE 'to live' > *vivir, bevir*

So strong was the movement of verbs with high vowels into the *-ir* conjugation that verbs from Conjugation II, whose members normally remain in the *-er* conjugation, which had a high stem vowel also joined this conjugation:

LŪCĒRE 'to shine' > *luzir*
RĪDĒRE 'to laugh' > *reír*

The association of verbs with mid vowels in all forms of the stem with the *-er* conjugation meant that most Conjugation III verbs of this type joined this conjugation; among those of greatest frequency were:

ABSCONDERE 'to hide' > *asconder*
BIBERE 'to drink' > *bever*
CERNERE 'to discern, distinguish' > *cerner* 'to sift'
COGNOSCERE 'to be acquainted with' > *conosçer*
COLLIGERE 'to pick up, gather' > *coger*
COMEDERE 'to eat' > *comer*
CONFUNDERE 'to confuse' > *cohonder*
COQ(U)ERE 'to cook' > *cocer*
CRĒDERE 'to believe' > *creer*
CURRERE 'to run' > *correr*
ERIGERE 'to straighten up' > *erzer*
LEGERE 'to read' > *leer*
MOLERE 'to grind' > *moler*
MITTERE 'to send, release' > *meter*
PŌNERE 'to place' > *poner*
REDDERE 'to give back, render' > *render*
RUMPERE 'to break' > *romper*
VENDERE 'to sell' > *vender*
VINCERE 'to conquer' > *vencer*
VOLVERE 'to turn, return' > *volver*

(Montgomery 1975–76, 286; Penny 1972, 346)

It might be more accurate to consider what happened in early Castilian (or possibly late north-central Ibero-Romance) not as the preservation of the Latin conjugations II and IV at the expense of III, but rather "the emergence of two new paradigms, each marked by interdependence of stem and ending" (Montgomery 1975–76, 287). This change was an ongoing process rather than an instantaneous reclassification of all verbs. The basic principles or "rules" that governed the classification were the following:

1) verbs excluding high stem vowels > *-er*;
2) verbs allowing high stem vowels > *-ir*;
3) stems with /-a-/ are neutral (Penny 1972).

These principles apply in a majority of cases. However, there are certain modifying factors that make certain verbs fluctuate in the direction they go. Thus, verbs whose root-final consonant is a palatal (most of whose stems end in /-ng-/) go into the -ir conjugation even though they contain only mid vowels:

>   CINGERE 'to gird on; surround' > ceñir
>   FINGERE 'to disguise, contrive' > feñir
>   IMPLĒRE 'to fill up' > fenchir
>   JUNGERE 'to join, yoke' > unzir, uñir
>   *RINGERE (C.L. RINGĪ) 'to show the teeth, snarl' > reñir
>   STRINGERE 'to strip'; draw tight' > estreñir
>   TINGERE 'to dye' > teñir

Although, as stated above, verbs containing the stem-vowel /a/ are generally neutral as to conjugation, by and large those of Conjugation III tend to enter the -er conjugation:

>   BATT(U)ERE 'to beat' > bater
>   CADERE 'to fall' > caer
>   CAPERE 'to seize, take' > caber 'to fit'
>   FACERE 'to make, do' fazer
>   FRANGERE 'to break' > frañer, franzir
>   INNADDERE 'to add' > eñader (cf. MSp. añadir)
>   *NASCERE (C.L. NASCI) 'to be born' > nascer
>   *PASCERE (C.L. PASCI) 'to graze' > pascer
>   PLANGERE 'to lament, bewail' > llañer (cf. plañir)
>   RADERE 'to scratch, scrape' > raer
>   SAPERE 'to taste, know' > saber
>   TANGERE 'to touch' > tañer 'to play (an instrument)'
>   TRAHERE 'to drag, pull' > traer
>   VERRERE 'to sweep, brush' > barrer

There seems also to be a tendency for verbs with the stem vowel /u/ to enter the -ir conjugation, even if they were in Latin Conjugation II:

>   COMPLĒRE 'to fill up' > cumplir (semilearned)
>   FUGERE 'to flee' > fuir, foir
>   FUNDERE 'to melt, pour out' > fundir
>   PŪTRĒRE 'to rot' > podrir, pudrir
>   RECUTERE 'to strike backwards, rebound' > recudir
>   SUFFERRE 'to suffer' > sofrir, sufrir
>   TUNDERE 'to beat, hammer' > tundir

Some exceptions to this tendency do appear: CURRERE 'to run' > correr, RUMPERE 'to break' > romper, FUT(U)ERE 'to fuck' > joder, etc. In only one example do we see a Conjugation IV verb going to the -er class: TUSSĪRE 'to cough' > toser.

In general, these shifts into a new pattern did not involve a wholesale change of forms. As we have seen, the endings of the non-ar verbs had fallen together for the most part; therefore the only changes that occurred apart from regular phonetic developments were the necessary changes in the infinitive, in forms 4 and 5 of the present indicative, and the plural imperative. Thus, in a way the citation of the infinitive as the example form tends to overstate the degree of change that actually took place.

Vowel Dissimilation

One factor that served to alter the phonetic shape of a number of verbs in the -*ir* conjugation was a general tendency, that increased in extent of application, to dissimilate to a mid vowel /e/ any /i/ that appeared in a verb stem before a stressed ending with /í/: /i/ - /í/ > /e/ - /í/. This change is similar to the development that we see in VĪCĪNU 'neighbor' > *vezino*. Thus, verbs that appear in some of the preceding lists such as DĪCERE, RĪDĒRE, FRĪGERE, SCRĪBERE, VĪVERE, etc. adopted as the most frequently found forms of the infinitive (and also similar forms in forms 4 and 5) *dezir*, *reír*, *freír*, *escrivir*, *bevir*. Although this dissimilatory tendency became increasingly strong during the Middle Ages, it was never an absolute rule. Exceptions appear sporadically in a variety of documents: *firid* 'strike!' (*Cid* 597), *pidimos* (*Cid* 1885), *dizir* (*Pérez de Guzmán*), *dizimos* (*Fernando I of Aragon*, 1412), *dizimelo* (*Roncesvalles* 22), *escribir*, *vivimos* (*Berceo*), etc. (Penny 1972, 347, notes 2, 3).

In the back series of vowels, however, there was a different tendency at work, one that tended to reserve /u/ for the -*ir* verbs, and /o/ for -*er* verbs. In many cases, the /u/ was the etymologically correct vowel, while in the -*er* verbs no verb in Latin had had a /u/ as a stem vowel. Another factor aiding the preference for /u/ is a general preference among speakers for vowel harmony before stressed /í/: /o/ - /í/ > /u/ - /í/. Vowel harmony of this type is not limited to -*ir* verbs, but appears as well in verbs like *sospirar* 'to sigh' > *suspirar*, and adjectives and substantives like *omilde* 'humble', *sotil* 'delicate, subtle' > *sutil*, *roydo* 'noise' > *ruido*, etc. (Penny 1972, 344). In general, this movement toward vowel harmony was a slow one in taking effect, and did not reach completion until the end of the Middle Ages. Also there appears to have existed in early Romance a tendency to regularize those verbs in which a stem vowel /o/ was raised by a yod to /u/, e.g., PŪTREAM > *pudra*, SUBEŌ 'I climb, go up' > *subo*, COOPERIŌ 'I cover' > *cubro*, ABHORREŌ 'I am averse to, shrink from' > *aburro* 'I bore, annoy', etc. All of these tendencies worked together to associate /u/ with the -*ir* class, even more strongly than the association of /i/ with this conjugation. We note that other verbs in which one would expect to find /o/ usually have /u/ if they have entered the -*ir* class: TONDERE > *tundir* 'to trim', SARCĪRE + SURGERE > *surzir* 'to patch, mend', etc.

Operating against the identification of /u/ as the stem vowel of the -*ir* conjugation was the regular phonetic change of Latin /u ō/ to /ǫ/ > Castilian /o/. The vast majority of examples of /ǫ/ remained as Castilian

/o/, and verbs were no exception. Therefore the common forms of verbs with the stem vowel /ǫ/ in Late Latin still have /o/ in medieval documents: *complir, cobrir, foír, sobir, sofrir*, etc.

Some other verbs developed forms in *-ir* which had originally been in the *-er* conjugation: *batir* replaced older *bater, hervir* takes over from *herver, nozer* < NOCĒRE 'to harm' later becomes *nucir, render* gives way to *rendir* and *erzer* is replaced by *erguir, emer* < GEMERE 'to sigh, moan' drops in favor of *gemir*. In some cases the newer forms in *-ir* are semi-learned ones, e.g., *cumplir, aburrir, arrepentir* 'to repent' < PAENITĒRE.

One of the factors that may in some measure account for the sporadic shifts into the *-ir* conjugation of verbs that should have been or actually were earlier of the *-er* class (had the rules of development been followed with absolute regularity), is the geographical position of early Castilian; in other dialects, other factors override such associations. Thus in western Ibero-Romance there is a preference for putting Conjugation III verbs into the *-er* class. As examples we shall give Portuguese verbs contrasted with Castilian:

Portuguese	Castilian
aduzer	*adozir*
dizer	*dezir*
encher	*(f)enchir*
escrever	*escrevir*
morrer	*morir*
sofrer	*sufrir*

Since early Castilian was located in the north central area of the peninsula, it is not surprising that it should have shown some fluctuation in the choice of conjugational class for some verbs, as we saw above. The movement seems to have been always in the direction of *-ir* verbs, when earlier forms belonged to the *-er* class. But it may be that when forms in *-er* appear in documents where the later form is in *-ir*, the source of the *-er* infinitives was a more western area. The result was that early Castilian speakers sometimes had two choices available: *bater, abater* vs. *batir, abatir; combater-combatir; esleer-esleír* < ĒLIGERE 'to choose'; *nozer-nozir; llañer, plañer-plañir; render-rendir, converter-convertir*, etc. (Nelson 1972–73).

Further contrast between eastern and western Ibero-Romance can be seen in the following chart which gives Galician-Portuguese forms and Aragonese-Catalan ones:

Western	Eastern
esconder	*escondir*
atrever	*atrevir/atrivir*
esleer	*esleyr/elegir*
execer	*exercir*
ler	*leyr/llegir*

Western	Eastern
obter	*obtenir*
poseer	*possed(d)ir*
tecer	*tecir / teixir*

(Based on Nelson 1972–73, 281)

Thus, when we compare the preceding chart in which Castilian goes along with the west in its preference for *-er* verbs with the ones before in which Castilian speakers go rather with the east, we can see that Castilian was "a classic example of a language in maximum flux, caught between the W[estern] dialects which favored the *-er* marker and the E[astern] dialects partial to the *-ir* marker" (Nelson 1972–73, 280).

The *-ESCERE* Conjugational Pattern

As indicated in the previous chapter, Late Latin began to develop a new conjugational pattern for *-ir* verbs which added the interfix *-esc-* to the rhizotonic forms of the verb. Modern Spanish and Portuguese have no such interfix in the *-ir* verbs. The verbs that do exist today, derived for the most part from adjectives, as were the original verbs in Latin, seem simply to preserve the older Latin pattern, especially since in Castilian the inchoative meaning is still associated with most derivatives in *-ecer*, e.g., *engrandescer* 'to enlarge' ← *grande* 'large', *embravecer* 'to make fierce' ← *bravo* 'wild, fierce', etc. We might conclude therefore that Castilian and Portuguese never had anything to do with the Late Latin *-esc-* conjugational pattern for *-ir* verbs. In some very early texts, however, there are found sporadically verb forms that show that possibly in the very earliest preliterary period Castilian was also beginning to adopt the new pattern. Thus, in the *Cantar de mio Cid* some verb forms in the infinitive, forms 4 and 5 of the present indicative, the plural imperative and the non-present tenses appear without the *-ec-* of later Spanish. In other words, the lack of *-esc-* is found exactly where it does not appear in the common Romance pattern: e.g., *fallir* 'to expire, decease', *gradimos* 'we are thankful', *cuntió* 'it happened', *gradió* 'he was grateful', *adurmió* 'he lulled to sleep', etc. corresponding to later *fallescer*, *agradescemos*, *acontesció*, *agradesció*, *adormesció* (Wilkinson 1967, 30). The fact that a number of verbs from Germanic in *-ian* were taken into Romance in the *-ir* group, e.g., WARNJAN 'to warn; provide, arm' > *guarir* 'to cure', BASTJAN 'to build' > *bastir* 'to supply, provide; dispose; arrange', SCARNJAN 'to scorn, mock' > *escarnir*, etc. and in Castilian all have the *-escer* suffix, e.g., MSp. *guarnecer*, *abastecer*, *escarnecer* without any inchoative meaning, would be sufficient evidence that the original conjugational pattern of common early Romance was found in very early Castilian. In other words, the modern forms result from a generalization to all of the forms of these verbs of the interfix originally found only in forms 1–3 and 6 of the present indicative. Further proof of the existence of the *-esc-* interfix pattern in very early Castilian is seen in certain Latin verbs that remain in Castilian with the -*escer* suffix, usually without any inchoative meaning:

OFFERRE 'to present, offer' > *ofrescer*
PARERE 'to appear, be at hand' > *parescer*[103]
*PATERE (C.L. PATĪ) 'to suffer' > *padescer*
PERĪRE 'to perish' > *perecer*

In one case both the earlier and the later forms have been preserved as doublets with differing meanings: *aburrir* 'to bore, annoy' and *aborrescer* 'to abhore'.

In this development, as in others, Castilian was a meeting ground of linguistic tendencies from opposite directions: the -*esc*- interfix as part of the -*ir* pattern without any independent meaning, and the conservative western pattern that kept the inchoative significance of the affix and used -*esc*- in all forms of the verb. The struggle between the two tendencies was generally decided in favor of the conservative pattern in the preliterary period, but remnants of the innovative pattern continued to appear for several centuries, aided perhaps by the greater preference for -*ir* verbs in Castilian as compared with the west. Medieval literary works such as the *Cid* and the *Libro de Alexandre* reveal traces of the struggle (Nelson 1972–73, 282–86).

The -er Verbs and Stative Meaning

One other factor must be taken into consideration in the distribution of verbs in the -*er* and -*ir* conjugations in Castilian: namely, the definite tendency for auxiliary verbs and verbs with stative meanings to appear in the -*er* conjugation. Stative verbs are those that instead of referring to actions, as do the majority of all verbs, denote an imperfective, durative meaning. Auxiliaries, of course, are verbs that, for the most part, do not function alone but always as parts of verbal locutions, e.g., *poder* 'can, be able', *soler* 'to be accustomed to (doing something)', *haber* 'to have'. Stative verbs can be seen best in examples, such as *ser* 'to be', *querer* 'to want', *saber* 'to know', *deber* 'to owe; ought', *tener* 'to have', *creer* 'to believe', *conocer* 'to be acquainted with', *parecer* 'to appear, seem', *valer* 'to be worth', *yazer* 'to lie, be stretched out', *caber* 'to fit', *doler* 'to hurt, pain', *entender* 'to perceive, understand', *poseer* 'to possess', *pertenecer* 'to belong to' *plazer* 'to please', *aborrecer* 'to abhore', *merecer* 'to merit, deserve', *pender* 'to hang', etc. Other examples are *estar* 'to stand; be' *bastar* 'to be enough', *amar* 'to love', *osar* 'to dare', *pesar* 'to weigh', *pensar* 'to think', etc. We note that more of the preceding examples are from the -*er* conjugation. Thus, we can perceive a general connection between the imperfective meaning of stative verbs and this particular conjugation. Of

---

[103] The unusual shift of PARERE to the verbs to the -ESCERE class is perhaps assisted by the need to distinguish it from *parir* 'to give birth'.

course, this association is only a general tendency and not a fixed rule. Nevertheless, a statistical study of the number of stative verbs preserved in the -*er* conjugation reveals that such preservation exceeds the general percentage of preserved verbs, and that verbs with dynamic connotations more often tended to be lost when they belonged to Conjugation II in Latin. Thus, of the seventy-five commonest verbs from samples of Classical Latin texts, of twelve stative verbs in Conjugation II, ten remain in Spanish: *deber, haber, yazer, permanecer, merecer, plazer, tener, temer, valer,* and *veer*. The two verbs which disappear are GAUDĒRE 'to rejoice' and LICĒRE 'to be allowed' (Montgomery 1978, 910). In contrast with the association between stative verbs and the -*er* conjugation, one notes the tendency to associate dynamic verbs with the -*ir* conjugation; most verbs of motion, for example, belong to this conjugation, e.g., *ir* 'to go', *venir* 'to come', *fuir* 'to flee, etc. When a larger number of verbs is taken into account, 432 vs. the 75 mentioned above, the connection between stativity and the -*er* conjugation becomes even clearer. The overall retention rate of these verbs in Spanish is 31 percent but with the stative verbs of Conjugation II, the retention rate is 52 percent (Montgomery 1978, 911). By way of contrast, we see that dynamic verbs in Conjugations II and III were most frequently lost; only 20 percent were retained, these being the most frequently used verbs, like *correr, romper, meter, leer, vencer, hacer,* etc.

The general association of -*er* verbs with stativity may indeed explain, at least in part, why some of the verbs that we noted above have shifted from an early association with -*er* into the -*ir* pattern, e.g., *batir* 'to beat', *erguir* 'to raise up' for *erzer*, etc. Thus, we can see from the preceding considerations that not only phonetic factors but also general semantic ones may have worked together to distribute the conjugational patterns of Spanish. Of course, this association is only a general tendency since if the relation between sounds and meaning were constant there would be severe limitations on the creative potential of language. The -*ar* conjugation, for instance, as the largest conjugation in terms of the number of verbs it contains, has many dynamic verbs, as well as a couple of common stative ones, e.g., *quedar* 'to remain', *estar* 'to be' (originally 'to stand'). It is especially interesting to note, however, that the commonest dynamic verbs in the -*ar* class often represent innovations from the point of view of their Latin meanings. Thus, *hablar* 'to speak' has broadened its meaning from Lat. FABULĀRĪ 'to chat, gossip', *llegar* 'to arrive' < (AP)PLICĀRE 'to board (a ship), approach', *mirar* 'to look at' < MIRĀRĪ 'to wonder at', *hallar* 'to find' < AFFLĀRE 'to breathe upon; sniff out', etc. (Montgomery 1978, 913). Thus, -*ar* verbs are often characterized by their neologistic character, as opposed to the far more stable stative verbs of the -*er* type. Of course, one must not exaggerate; since the -*ar* conjugation is the only living conjugation, i.e., the only one to which any newly created verb must be added, it is to be expected that it would contain many neologisms. A reasonable conclusion may be the following: "Harmony or interplay of form and content, essential to artistic use of language, is present in spontaneous expression as well, and begins in the basic elements of linguistic form, the sounds and words" (Montgomery 1979, 237).

/-e-/ > /-i-/: Radical-Changing Verbs in the -ir Conjugation

A small group of verbs in the -ir class are set apart as a special group. If their historical sources are taken into account, they should belong to the larger class of radical-changing verbs which contain a diphthong in the rhizotonic forms of the stem. Thus, PETERE 'to seek, look for' would, if ordinary diphthongization alone had made itself felt, have produced forms like those of *perder* 'to lose'. That is, we would expect to find **piedo, *piedes, *piede*, and **pieden*. In fact, however, we find from the earliest written sources *pido, pides, pide, piden*.[104] Other verbs in this same pattern are the following:

REGERE 'to rule' > *regir*
*SEQUERE (C.L. SEQUĪ) 'to follow' > *seguir*
SERVĪRE 'to serve' > *servir*

A number of other verbs in Old Spanish whose stems in Late Latin had not contained /e/ also belonged to this same pattern with /i/ in the stem in rhizotonic forms alternating with /e/ in other forms:

CINGERE 'to surround, gird on' > *ceñir*
CON-CIPERE 'to conceive' > *con-cebir*, plus all other derivatives of
  -CIPERE: *apercebir* 'to prepare, warn, advise', *recebir* 'to receive', etc.
CONS-TRINGERE 'to bind fast, restrain' > *costreñir* and other deriva-
  tives of STRINGERE: *estreñir* 'to restrain', *restreñir* 'to hold back,
  restrain'
DISCĒDERE 'to part, separate' > *descir* 'to descend'
IMPLĒRE 'to fill' > *(f)enchir*
*METĪRE (C.L. METĪRĪ) 'to measure' > *medir* and a derivative *comedir*
  'to consider, think'
REDIMERE 'to redeem' > *redemir*
TINGERE 'to dye' > *teñir*
VĪVERE 'to live' > *bevir*, plus the other verbs with the stem-vowel in
  /i/ discussed above: *dezir, escrevir, reír*.

We have seen that verbs in the -ir group are those that allow some forms to have high vowels, and undoubtedly this tendency to associate the high stem vowels with the -ir conjugation was an aid in allowing this small class to become established. Nevertheless, this association alone would not have

---

[104] The *Glosas Silenses* have *pitent*. Diphthongized forms do appear, but rarely: *pieden* is found in the *Libro de Alexandre*, O 2183c (Malkiel 1966, 456), and *piede* in the *Fuero Juzgo* (Wilkinson 1971, 9).

sufficed to lead to a rhizotonic /i/ for these verbs from Late Latin /e/, as a number of verbs in -*ir* show the ordinary sort of diphthongal distribution, e.g., *ferir* 'to strike, wound' < FERĪRE, *mentir* 'to lie' < MENTĪRĪ, *sentir* 'to feel' < SENTĪRE, etc.

There are many cases of the raising of a mid vowel to a high vowel in anticipation of a following yod (see p. 198), e.g., SĒPIA 'cuttlefish' > *xibia*, VINDĒMIA 'harvest' > *vendimia*, etc. This same metaphonic effect of a yod applies even more to pretonic vowels, since even the palatal resulting from diphthongization has this effect, e.g., GENESTA 'broom plant' > *hiniesta*. In the verbs of the -*ir* class, a yod appears in the preterite in forms 3 and 6 (and in all forms of the past subjunctive and the pluperfect in -*ra*), and in the present participle. Its effect is the same as in other instances: e.g., *sentir, sint-ió, -ieron, -iendo*, etc., *ferir: fir-ió, -ieron, -iendo*, etc. There are also traces of a metaphonic shift in pretonic vowels of forms 4 and 5 of the present subjunctive. In Latin all verbs of Conjugation IV had had a yod in the present subjunctive, e.g., SENTIAM, SENTIES, SENTIAT, etc., DOR-MIAM, -IAS, -IAT, etc. but there is no evidence of its preservation in Spanish. The rhizotonic forms that remain all show normal diphthongization in the indicative. However, it appears that the Late Latin yod in forms 4 and 5 had the same effect as other yods and the stem vowel is raised, e.g., *sint-amos, -des, durm-amos, -des*. The same effect would be seen in all verbs with mid vowels in their stems, if this is indeed the main cause of the alternation, e.g., VEST-IĀMUS, -IĀTIS > *vistamos, -des*, SERV-IĀMUS, -IĀTIS > *sirvamos, -des*, etc.

Purely phonetic reasons alone cannot explain this particular development. Verbs in -*er* never show any kind of metaphonic alteration of stem vowels; thus *comamos, temamos* are never replaced by **cumamos, *ti-mamos*. The sole exception is the verb *poder* whose present participle is *pudiendo*. Therefore, the phonetic influence of the yod must have gone hand in hand with the growing association of high stem vowels with the -*ir* conjugation. The presence of the high vowels in the stem in pretonic position cannot, however, account for its presence in the rhizotonic forms of verbs with /e/ since only a few verbs, relatively speaking, form this class (Malkiel 1966, 435). In spite of this limitation to a few verbs, however, some have suggested that it is indeed a yod which has raised the stem vowel in some of these verbs. Thus, the yod in **MĒTIŌ* and VESTIŌ has been thought to explain *mido* and *visto* (Menéndez Pidal 1941, 293). A similar explanation could be given for verbs in -*cibo* < -CIPIŌ. In response to such a claim one must then ask why we do not find **sinto* < SENTIŌ, or **minto* < **MENTIŌ* (C.L. MENTIOR), etc.,[105] especially in view of the fact that the yod following /t/ is precisely the yod that does not affect vowels

---

[105] It is interesting to note that *sinto* and *minto* do appear in Old Portuguese but seem to be analogical forms (Williams 1962, 215).

(see p. 193). We must take into account also Port. *meço* and *peço* in which the yod after /t/ has developed normally by forming an affricate.

The formation of the class of /e/ > /i/ radical-changing verbs must be due therefore to some special combination of factors. One thing that is notable is that some of the verbs in the class show dialectal variants with the diphthong /ie/ rather than /i/. We find *sieguen* sporadically east and west of Old Castile, *sierva, sierve, sierven, vieste, viesten, mieden, miedan, riendo* (sources given in Malkiel 1966, 455–56). Thus, it is plausible to reconstruct such regularly diphthongized forms for the very early stages of Castilian as well. At a later period in the development of medieval Castilian there is a tendency to monophthongize diphthongs under certain special circumstances. The monophthongization of /ie/ to /i/ before /l̦/ is an early characteristic of Castilian, although it seems to be less a purely phonetic development than a morphological one. A similar shift of /ie/ to /i/ in the vicinity of /s/, especially when preceding a consonant and when a liquid /r/ or /l/ is also present (see chap. 5 for fuller discussion), e.g., *víspera* 'eve' < OSp. *viéspera* < VESPERA 'evening star', *prisa* 'haste' < *priessa* < PRESSA, etc. Thus, we might expect that an ancient **siervo* could have gone in this same direction and produced *sirvo*.[106] Likewise **viesto*,although lacking the frequently found liquid, could have followed this path. And **siego*, even without the consonant after the /s/, could have been attracted in the same direction. Coupled with the phonetic movement may be the development of the verbs in -INGERE. Although the /i/ of earlier Latin should have given /e/ in Late Latin, the influence of the lengthened vowel /i:/ which appears in the perfect forms, e.g., CINGERE - CĪNXĪ 'I surrounded, girded on', plus the influence of the nasal palatal which sometimes seems to raise a preceding vowel may have been additional factors. And, of course, we must keep in mind the identification of *-ir* verbs with the high vowels. All of these circumstances helped to shift these verbs into this small class.

Last, there is the influence of the pattern established by the frequently used verbs containing an /i/ in the stem which developed regularly from Latin: *dezir, escrevir, reir, bevir*, which were discussed above. These latter verbs may well have fixed the general pattern for the whole class in view of the fact that they regularly dissimilated /i/ to /e/ before stressed /i/, e.g., *digo, dizes* vs. *dezimos, dezides* (Wilkinson 1971, 13).[107] The cause of the shift of *pedir* to the pattern is not clear, but it may, after all, be due to a sporadic metaphony such as we see in Port. *durmo* < DORMIŌ, *sirvo* < SERVIŌ. *Pido* would then be simply an analogically attracted member, because of its phonetic resemblance to *medir*. Thus, a combination of

---

[106] The similar form in Portuguese can hardly be explained in the same way (Williams 1962, 209–12).

[107] Malkiel disregards the possibility of such an influence, although he does say that it lends it "partial support" (1966, 454).

various impulses, phonetic, morphological and morphological, can be seen
to have contributed to the establishment of the pattern, assisted perhaps
by the parallel development of the /o/ - /u/ alternation.

The Velar Insert

   In the previous chapter, we saw that the group /-ng-/ was a widespread
alternative for stem-final /-ɲ/ in form 1 of the present indicative and in
the present subjunctive in those Romance languages in which Late Latin
/ng/ before front vowels and /n/ plus yod had both produced the palatal
nasal /ɲ/ (Wilkinson 1978, 29). Thus, at a very early stage of Castilian, or
perhaps early north-central Ibero-Romance, forms like *cingo* and *ci*[ɲ]*o*,
tango and *ta*[ɲ]*o*, *frango* and *fra*[ɲ]*o*, and all other verbs in the -NGERE
class, were available as alternate forms for form 1 and the entire present
subjunctive. Romance speakers, of course, had no idea which verbs with
the stem-final [-ɲ] had developed this consonant by regular sound change
and which ones had gotten it through analogical extension from other
forms. Thus, the existence of *te*[ɲ]*o* and *ve*[ɲ]*o* < TENEŌ and VENIŌ (and
related subjunctive forms) (cf. Port. *tenho, venho*) would, for most
speakers, have been on a par with the verbs of the -NGERE class. Therefore,
tengo and *vengo* would seem to be appropriate verbs in form 1. It is
possible too that *tengo* was adopted in order to avoid any possible homonymy with the results of TINGERE 'to dye' (Wilkinson 1978, 29).[108]
   Malkiel believes that the use of /ng/ in form 1 is the result of proto-
Castilian speakers' desire to avoid a weak contrast between this form and
the other forms of the present indicative (1973–74, 325). In other words,
the contrast between /n/ and /ɲ/ was somehow felt to be too slight to
give proper emphasis to the difference between form 1 and the other verb
forms. In support of his position, he cites the somewhat parallel examples
of other verbs that would, given regular sound change, have had a contrast
between /tˢ/ and /dᶻ/ in the stem. Thus, from Latin FACIŌ, JACEŌ, and
PLACEŌ we find in Old Portuguese the regularly derived forms (provided
that /kʲ/ can be assumed to produced regularly /tˢ/ *faço, yaço, plaço*). If
these forms had existed in proto-Castilian, they would have provided a
similarly "weak" contrast between form 1 and the other forms of the
present indicative. Thus, he supposes that the forms that we do find, *fago*,
yago, and *plazco* (a form based on the -ESCERE verbs) while in Old Leonese we see *plago* (316), are all analogical, resulting from the same desire to

---

[108] Wilkinson suggests that *pongo* owes its choice to a desire to distinguish *poner* more
clearly from PUNGERE. Malkiel (1973–74, 328, note 45) claims that the influence of PLAN-
GERE, FRANGERE, and other -NGERE verbs in creating an association between /ɲ/ and /ng/
must have been slight because none of these verbs is nearly as frequent in usage as are *tener*
and *venir*. As Wilkinson (1978, 28), however, points out, this association grew up at a very
early period when these verbs were probably more used than later. Besides, although any one
or two verbs of this class is much less frequently used than *tener* or *venir*, there is a large
number of verbs in the whole class of -NGERE verbs and the total number of examples may
well have been equal to that of *tener* and *venir*.

distinguish form 1 clearly from the other forms. the choice of /g/ in these verbs may be safely attributed to the existence of very commonly used verbs that alternate stem-final /g/ and /dᶻ/ through regular phonetic development: *digo* 'I say' and *adugo* 'I lead' < DĪCŌ, ADDŪCŌ vs.*dizes, dize*, and *aduzes, aduze* < DĪCIS, DĪCIT, ADDŪCIS, ADDŪCIT. The absence of any evidence in writing for early Castilian forms like **faço, *yaço*, or **plaço* or **teno* and **veno* merely indicates that these changes all took place at a very early stage, before there was any need to write Castilian.

It may be asked, however, if there is any proof that the contrast between /n/ and /ɲ/ and between /tˢ/ and /dᶻ/ was really felt to be insufficient in verbal paradigms (Lenfest 1978, 869–97). Since *tengo* and *vengo* appear to have existed from the beginning, why is it not sufficient to suppose that the Late-Latin/Early Romance association of /ɲ/ and /ng/ in form 1 of the present indicative and in all forms of the present subjunctive made available competing forms that early Castilian speakers could choose from? One of the characteristics of Castilian, as opposed to other, neighboring dialects, was its relative homogeneity and rapid elimination of competing norms of speech. Therefore, the choice of the /ng/ form may have been made because it was supported by the existence of other very common verbs with a /g/ preceding the /-o/ and /-a/. Lenfest (1978) assumes that the elimination of yod which we see in *fago* and *yago* and in many other verbs was likewise extended to *tener* and *venir* and that the early proto-Castilian forms were **teno* and **veno*, rather than competing *tengo-*teno* and *vengo-*veno*. Thus, he sees the adoption of /g/ after stem-final /-n/ as the result of a desire on the part of speakers to make form 1 conform in phonetic bulk to form 2, 3, and 6. In other words, one can describe the phonemic structure of these latter forms as follows: CVVCV(C) (C = consonant, V = vowel), because the diphthong [je] must be considered a combination of two vowels, i.e., /ie/(Lenfest 1978, 900). Thus the form **veno* had the structure CVCV. The adoption of the /g/ insert allowe speakers to have form 1 with a similar number of phonemes as forms 2 and 3. This explanation seems most unlikely. First, we cannot be sure that the forms posited ever existed. Second, and more important, the assumption that for early Romance speakers the diphthong from Late Latin /ę/ was immediately perceived to be a combination of two separate vowel phonemes, as it is in modern Spanish, is untenable. All the evidence we have shows that for a long time phonetic diphthongs were not perceived as anything other than special forms of simple vowels (see pp. 184–87). Thus, on the phonemic level, forms 2, 3, and 6 had the canonical form CVCV(C) for centuries until early Castilian speakers adopted the fixed realizations of [je] and [we] for both diphthongs and thus could identify the initial glide with the vowels /i/ and /u/. The adoption of the /g/ insert occurred much too early for any such factor as "equal bulk" to have entered into the choice.

One wonders then if it is truly necessary to assume anything more than that the alternation of /ng/ and /ɲ/ and the existence of a stem-final /-g/

in commonly used verbs like *digo*, and *fago* and *adugo* sufficed to produce mental identification of the /g/ as somehow characteristic of form 1 of the indicative and all of the present subjunctive for some verbs. The early adoption of the /g/ in *poner* was undoubted due to the similarity of the structure of this verb with the leader verbs *tener* and *venir*, both of which had a stem consisting of one syllable ending in /n/. Once /-g/ became associated these forms in some very common verbs, the way was open for its occasional extension to other verbs of similar structures, i.e., verbs whose stem contained a single syllable of the CVC pattern. Given the fact that nasals and liquids frequently behave in similar ways, we are not surprised to find that along with the regularized forms of the verbs *valer* 'to be worth' < VALĒRE 'to be healthy, strong', and *salir* 'to go out' < SALĪRE 'to jump up, leap', whose form 1 would have had stem-final /ḷ/ with regular phonetic development, but actually became *valo* and *salo*. The augmented forms *salgo* and *valgo* appear much later than do *vengo* and *tengo*, and only very slowly managed to become the standard forms of modern Spanish. Some dialects even carried the process farther and add the /g/ to other verbs of similar structure: *duelgo* - *duelo* 'I hurt' < DOLEŌ, *suelgo* 'I am accustomed to' - *suelo* < SOLEŌ, and even a form like *tuelga* 'he may take away' < TOLLAT (←TOLLERE). One example of the addition of /g/ to a verb with a stem ending in /r/ is found: *fírgamos* 'let us strike' (*ferir*) (Malkiel 1973–74, 326).[109] In Castilian, only the very commonest verbs adopted the /g/, however, while the majority of verbs followed the road of regularization.

The Anti-hiatic Y

The formation of a palatal from the normal development of /g/ and /d/ plus a yod in Late Latin had the effect of causing certain verbs whose stem had ended in these two consonants to develop some forms, at least, with a stem ending in /y/. Thus, we find the following verb forms:

AUDIŌ 'I hear' > *oyo*
FUGIŌ 'I flee' > *fuyo*
RĪDEŌ 'I laugh' > *riyo*
SEDEŌ 'I am (seated)' > *seyo* 'I am'
VIDEŌ 'I see' > *veyo*

The corresponding present subjunctive forms ended in -*ya* (Malkiel 1973–74, 333). Some other verbs whose stems ended in /-d/ lost the consonant through regular development:

CRĒDŌ 'I believe' > *creo*
RĀDŌ 'I scrape' > **rao*

---

[109] Again we see parallel forms in Italian: *dolgo, salgo, valgo, sciolgo, (s)velgo* (Malkiel 1973–74, 327).

RŌDŌ 'I gnaw' > *roo*

VĀDŌ 'I go' (replacing the present tense of ĪRE) > **vao* > *vo*

(The present subjunctive of *ir*, based on this same stem, was *vaa*.)

Two other verbs entered this class through loss of stem-final /-g/, probably in all forms except form 1 and then analogically in this form too:

LEGŌ 'I read', LEGIS > *leo, lees*

ĒLĪGERE 'to choose' > *esleer*

A verb like Lat. CADERE 'to fall' probably had an alternative conjugation in -er (the infinitive *CADĒRE is guaranteed by the evidence of the other Romance languages) and thus may have had forms like *CADEŌ, *CADEĀS etc. which may explain the old Castilian forms *cayo, caya*.

A verb like *traer* 'to bring' < TRAHERE 'to draw, drag' had no stem-final consonant and thus came to look like a member of the preceding group. Form 1 therefore adopted the /y/ analogically: *trayo*. General phonetic development produced an absorption of the /y/ by a preceding front vowel and thus gradually *riyo, veyo, seyo* gave way to *río, veo, seo*, while after non-front vowel /a o u/ the palatal remained. After a stem ending in /-a/, speakers evidently felt no need to prevent hiatus, and if the following vowel was not /a/, we find *caes, cae, traes, trae*, etc. Occasionally variants like *caye* appear (mostly in Navarro-Aragonese). The ancestral /-d/ is also sporadically preserved in some forms, e.g., *cadio, cadisse* (Gifford and Hodcroft 1966, 31), *kaderat* (132). In the case of the subjunctive of these verbs and VĀDERE, i.e., VĀDA(M), -S, -T, the hiatus of two /a/'s is seen sporadically in *vaas, vaa*, but the general tendency would be for them to merge in a single vowel as is seen in form 4 *vamos* 'let's go' < VĀDĀMUS. The /y/ was then extended to these forms to prevent hiatus: *caya, traya, vaya*. Although it is possible that in Late Latin the expected /abja/ of the verb *haber* 'to have' had already been replaced by /j/ (Menéndez Pidal 1941, 305), an alternative explanation is that it was an analogical extension from verbs like *seya* in early Castilian (Malkiel 1973–74, 336, note 19). In the case of *foir-fuir* and *oír*, the back vowel before the vowel /e/ did appear for a brief while, e.g., *foes, oes* < earlier *odes* < AUDIS, but when stressed also adopted the /y/ to separate the vowels, thus giving *oyes, oye, oyen* and *fuyes, fuye, fuyen*. *Fuir* had great influence on the semilearned verbs ending in -uir, e.g., *destroir* 'to destroy' < DĒSTRUERE, and similarly structured verbs, *arguir, construir, atribuir*, etc. so that they adopted forms with /y/: *destruyo, destruyes, destruye, destruyen*, etc.

Finally, the verb *traer* appeared with two different form, the *trayo, -a* one mentioned above, and *trago, -a* which in all likelihood comes from a Late Latin variant *TRAGO. Thus, in medieval Castilian both forms competed with each other as standard forms.[110]

---

[110] Malkiel suggests that possibly the form without any stem-final consonant may have come from *TRAGO (1973–74, 337).

Other Irregular Verbs

In chapter 3, we mentioned the creation of the new compound perfect in Late Latin with the verb HABĒRE plus the past participle. In this new tense, reduced forms of the verb were employed in forms 1–3 and 6. These forms develop normally, except that the /-o/ of form 1 is eliminated in favor of a single syllable form:

1. HABEŌ > /ayo/ > /ei/ > *e*   4. HABĒMUS > *avemos, emos*
2. HABĒS > /as/ > *as*   5. HABĒTIS > *avedes, edes*
3. HABET > /at/ > *a*   6. HABENT > /ant/ > *an*

The verb SAPIŌ 'I taste, know' in form 1 and in the present subjunctive, developed as most late yods did, i.e., with metathesis of the yod, > /saįpa/ < SAPIA(M). These forms developed normally, with the yod serving here to act as a semiconsonant and thus to prevent voicing as did /aų/: /seįpa/ > *sepa*.[111] CAPIŌ (←CAPERE 'I seize, take' develops in the same way from metathesized /kaįpo/, /kaįpa/ > *quepo, quepa* 'fit'. On the basis of this last verb we could expect /saįpo/ to have produced **sepo*. However, it seems that the influence of *aver* produced a parallel analogical form **/saio/ > sé* (Menéndez Pidal 1941, 305). The remaining verb forms of these verbs develop normally: CAPIS, -IT > *cabes, -e*, SAPIS, -IT > *sabes, -e*, etc.

As mentioned above, forms of the present tense of VĀDERE 'to ford' replaced most of the present tense of ĪRE 'to go' in Late Latin. The loss of stem-final /-d/ resulted in the following paradigm:

1. VĀDŌ > /ɓao/   4. VĀDIMUS > /ɓamos/
2. VĀDIS > /ɓaes/   5. VĀDITIS > /ɓades/
3. VĀDIT > /ɓaet/   6. VĀDUNT > /ɓan/

In forms 4 and 5, the older forms from ĪRE also continued to exist: *imos* < ĪMUS, *ides* < ĪTIS. The regular development of these forms would have given *vo, *vaes* (dialectal *beis* is found as well as Port. *vais*), **vae* (Port. *vai*), *vamos, vades, van*. The plural forms 4 and 5 may well have been reduced to two syllable forms /ɓamos, ɓatis/ before the singular ones were cut to a single syllable through syncope of the posttonic thematic vowel. The limitation of forms 2 and 3 to a single monophthongal syllable *vas* and *va* is probably due to the influence of the plural as well as the parallelism of other single syllable verbs like *dar* and *aver*. Finally, we may think of the effect of the lack of a clearly distinguishable verb stem *va-*, in contrast with verbs like *caer, traer, raer*, etc.

DĀRE 'to give' and STĀRE 'to stand' may also have adopted form 1 forms

---

[111] This diphthong was evidently not formed early enough in the west to prevent voicing. Thus, we find Port. *saiba*. The lack of assimilation of /a/ to /i/ would also indicate that the form must have been metathesized later than the majority of /aį/ diphthongs which normally give /eį/ (Williams 1962, 29).

like that of VĀDERE, */dao/ and */stao/. Regular development then would have produced *do* and *estó* (cf. Port. *dou, estou*), although some feel that such forms are unnecessary for Castilian where the Latin DŌ and STŌ would have given the same results (Alvar-Pottier 1983, 228). The present of ESSE 'to be' remained for the most part, except for some analogical restructuring of forms 2 and 5. Form 5 adopted the root SU- of the other plural forms and thus became *SUTIS > *sodes*. The regular development of form 2, however, would have given *es* (cf. Port. *es*), and with the loss of final /-t/ in form 3, both 2 and 3 would have been identical: *es*. The form that takes the place of second person *es* is *eres* which appears to be the reflex of the Latin future form ERIS 'you will be' (Pariente Herrejón 1969; Alvar-Pottier 1983, 225).[112] The question remains, however, of whether any forms of the Latin future could have persisted in speech long enough for this form to have replaced the older one when the final /-t/ of form 3 disappeared. We recall that this ending continued to be used as late as the eleventh and twelfth centuries in many regular verbs, although possibly in the combination *-st* it might have disappeared much earlier. Surely all traces of the old Latin future would have disappeared, at least as futures. It is not inconceivable, however, that a few isolated forms may have persisted as alternate forms for the present, but naturally with loss of their original meanings. One plausible conclusion might be that perhaps *eres* is an analogical form based on the stem *er-* from the imperfect tense forms, *era, -s*, etc. (Montgomery 1983):

1. SUM > *so*   4. SUMUS > *somos*
2. ERIS (?)> *eres* (C.L. ES)   5. *SUTIS > *sodes*
3. EST > *es*   6. SUNT > *son*

Although one would expect the preservation of a final /-m/ in a monosyllabic word, e.g., CUM > *con*, the limitation in Ibero Romance of final /-n/ in verbs to form 6 would have made this solution impossible, unlike It. *sono* or Rumanian *sînt*. The forms with /ę/ in the stem evidently were generalized in their atonic forms and thus did not diphthongize as they did in the dialectal forms *yes* and *ye*.

The verb SEDĒRE 'to be (seated)' was closely associated with ESSE, particularly in its locative sense. Thus, the infinitive ESSE disappeared and was replaced by *seder, seer*. The present tense of SEDĒRE developed regularly:

1. SEDEŌ > *seyo*   4. SEDĒMUS > *sedemos, se(y)emos*
2. SEDĒS > *siedes, sieyes*   5. SEDĒTIS > *seedes, seyedes*
3. SEDET > *siede, seye*   6. SEDENT > *sieden, seyen, seen*

The increasing mixture of ESSE and SEDERE led to the eventual abandonment of the present tense of *seer*. Only the present subjunctive forms, *sea*

---

[112] Portuguese avoided homonymy by retaining *es* in the second person and dropping the *-st* of form 3, > *é*. Other dialects eliminate the final *-st* also.

< SEDEAM, -S, etc. remained as forms corresponding to the regular indicative from ESSE, replacing the earlier Latin forms, SIM, SIS, SIT, etc.

The Imperfect

Regular phonetic development of the ending -ĀBA in Conjugation I produced the standard ending -*ava* in Old Spanish. The loss of medial /-b-/ discussed in Chapter 3, gave rise to the ending -*ía* for verbs in the -*er* and -*ir* classes. This ending later came to compete with a new imperfect ending -*ié* during the thirteenth and fourteenth centuries (see chapter 5 for a full discussion). The only irregular imperfects were ERAM > *era* (ESSE), and ĪBAM > *iva* from ĪRE. For some reason, the medial /-b̄-/ was retained in *iva* as it was not in any other form (cf. Port. *ia*) (Alvar 1952a). In all imperfects, the accent position was regularized to fall on the first syllable of the ending of form 4 and 5: -*ávamos*, -*ávades* < -ĀBĀMUS, -ĀBĀTIS; *éramos*, *érades* < ERĀMUS, ERĀTIS.

The Preterite (Simple Perfect)

The regular phonetic development of the reduced perfect endings of Late Latin in Conjugation I resulted in the following system in Old Spanish:

1. -AI > /-eị/ > -*é*   4. -ĀMUS > -*amos*
2. -ASTĪ > -*aste*   5. -ĀSTIS > -*astes*
3. -AUT > /-oụt/ > -*ó(t)*   6. -ARUNT > -*aron*

Developing similarly to Conjugation I, Conjugation IV likewise had the shortened forms which then developed regularly:

1. -IĪ > -*í*   4. -ĪMUS > -*imos*
2. -ISTĪ > -*iste*   5. -ISTIS > -*istes*
3. -IUT > (-*ío*)   6. -IĒRUNT > -*ieron*[113]
                             (-ĪRUNT > -*iron* Leonese)

We note that the accentuation in form 3 probably paralleled that of the same form in Conjugation I: -AUT > -*ou* > -*ó*. It should be pointed out too that in Old Spanish the plural endings were often of the form -*iemos*, -*iestes*.

Thus, it appears that the pattern for form 3 was that of a stressed theme vowel, /é/ or /í/, followed by the ending -*ut*, as mentioned in chapter 3. The morphological transparency of the form, coupled with the frequency of use of the verbs in these conjugations, must have made them popular models for analogical reconstruction of other verbs (Craddock 1983, 6). The pattern of stress on the theme vowel still exists in eastern Leonese -*íu* and in Portuguese (Menéndez Pidal 1941, 313).

---

[113] It is entirely possible that Sp. -*ieron* does not derive from Lat. -IĒRUNT, which could have simplified early (Malkiel 1975–76, 470; Wilkinson 1977, 29).

As we saw in chapter 2, there was no completely regular conjugational pattern in the perfect of Conjugations II and III, although the general tendency was to reserve the -UĪ ending for Conjugation II. The Old Castilian paradigm for *-er* verbs, also found in Central Asturian, was as follows (taking *perder* 'to lose' < PERDERE as a model):

1. *perdí*	4. *perdiemos*
2. *perdiste*	5. *perdiestes*
3. *perdió*	6. *perdieron*

The singular forms look to be identical with those of the *-ir* conjugation, but the plural forms contained the diphthongs descended from Late Latin /ę/. It is interesting to compare the preceding paradigm with that of Old Portuguese (taken as representative of the most western Hispano-Romance dialects):

1. *perdí*	4. *perdẹmos*
2. *perdẹste, -iste*	5. *perdẹstes*
3. *perdẹu*	6. *perdẹrom*

(based on Williams 1962, 194)

The question of greatest importance is whether this pattern in Portuguese represents the preservation of the original "Proto-Hispano-Romance" (or Late Hispanic Latin) one, or is rather an innovation limited to the west alone. If the former conjecture is correct, we should have to suppose that "Proto-Castilian" (or "Central Proto-Hispano-Romance") also shared this pattern and then dropped it in favor of an analogical one. In view of the fact that the western dialects tend to be very conservative, this is perhaps the best assumption (Craddock 1983, note 45). Is it possible that the limited Latin perfect in -ĒVIT is involved, e.g., IMPLĒVIT 'he filled' > Port. *encheu*? Although this is the opinion of many scholars (Malkiel 1975–76), the great difficulty with the theory is that the -ĒVIT perfect was quite rare in Latin (Wilkinson 1977, 29–30). It would seem more likely that some other analogical influence was at work.

We recall that a number of verbs had perfects ending in /-didi:/, e.g., VENDIDI, PERDIDI, etc. One early change was a haplological reduction of the second syllable of the ending which exactly parallels the same reduction in the perfect of Conjugations I and IV (Craddock 1983, note 44). We may presume too that form 3 adopted the same ending as in these conjugations, -UT, possibly with loss of the preceding /d/, thus producing the perfect paradigm in the most conservative forms of Ibero-Romance as follows:

Earlier Latin

1. PERDIDĪ	4. PERDI(DI)MUS
2. PERDI(DI)STĪ	5. PERDI(DI)STIS
3. PERDIDIT, -*UT	6. PERDI(DE)RUNT

"Proto-Hispano-Romance"

1. /perdédi/	4. /perdemos/
2. /perdésti/	5. /perdestes/
3. /perdé(d)ut/	6. /perderont/

If we assume that the final /-i/ of form 1 caused metaphony of the stressed /e/, we can see that this conservative pattern accounts perfectly for the Old Portuguese preterite given above.

The Castilian pattern, however, can be better explained through the regular development of an analogical pattern based on the verb DARE, such as that sketched in chapter 3. DĀRE itself had produced the following paradigm in Old Spanish:

1. DEDĪ > *dí*	4. DE(DI)MUS > *diemos*
2. DE(DI)ISTĪ > *diste*	5. DE(DI)STIS > *diestes*
3. *DED-UT > *dio*	6. DE(DE)RUNT > *dieron*

If the forms of the perfect of DĀRE had been substituted for the /-didi:/ endings, the results would have been what we saw above:

1. *PERDÉDĪ	4. *PERDÉ(DI)MUS
2. *PERDÉ(DI)STĪ	5. *PERDÉ(DI)STIS
3. *PERDÉ(D)-UT	6. *PERDÉ(DE)RUNT

In form 1, regular phonetic development, with the loss of /d/ normal before a front vowel would have produced /perdieị/. The simple form *dieỵ*, for instance, is attested dialectally (Menéndez Pidal 1941, 317), although some feel that the final -ī would have prevented normal diphthongization in Castilian (Alvar-Pottier 1983, 257). The usual development of the combination /ieị/ would have given /-í/, thus resulting in a form identical with the same one in the -*ir* conjugation. One would expect that form 2 would have become *perdieste*. The ending with the diphthong is a relative rarity, however, *perdiste* being the usual form, probably through the strong analogical influence of form 1. The plural endings present no unusual changes.

In form 3, the result would have been -*ió* < /-eụ/, as presumed by Malkiel (1975–76), but the development of the same form in the -*ir* conjugation cannot be explained in the same way since the /-dedi/ perfect originally was found only in those verbs descended from Latin conjugations II and III. It is more likely that the -*ió* ending was the result of the analogical association of the -*er* and -*ir* conjugations. We have seen that in the present indicative these two conjugations had the same endings, except in forms 4 and 5, and in the imperfect they shared all endings. Although the two conjugations did not completely coalesce, their endings were so close in form that in the preterite they also eventually became identical. Thus, the plural endings -*iemos*, -*iestes*, and -*ieron* appeared in both the -*er* and the -*ir* conjugations, so it is much more likely that the -*ió* of the -*ir* conjugation was borrowed from the -*er* preterite. One theory espoused by some scholars is that the ending *-ió* results from the general tendency to eliminate hiatus, and so could be simply a development of the original *-ío*, cf. MSp. *periodo* < earlier *período*, paralleling OSp. *reína* > MSp. *reina*, but Castilian has had from early times a large number of words ending in *-ío*, e.g., *río*, *frío*, etc. and none of them have shown the slightest tendency to change to *-ió* (Craddock 1983, 11). It is only those words descended from the Hispano-Romance /-eu/ which finally became *-ió*.[114]

Analogical Influences of One Form on Another

The tendency for speakers to model one form on another within the same paradigm is especially notable in the preterite. Thus, we find that the influence of form 1 on form 2, i.e., the basic forms of any dialog, is very strong. In the *-ar* conjugation, form 2 adopted the tonic /-é/ of form 1 and became *-este*. In medieval texts this form frequently appears in competition with the original *-aste*. In Leonese the same vowel is seen in forms 4 and 5, *-emos*, *-esteis*, and *-emos* is still found in popular Spanish in Castile (Menéndez Pidal 1941, 312). It is likely that the ending *-iste* in the *-er* conjugation is as much a reflection of the vowel of form 1 as a borrowing from the *-ir* conjugation. As noted above, the regular form *-ieste* was fairly rare. There is also a close association between forms 2 and 5, but in general the parallelism of the first and second persons is stronger. Therefore in the plural the first and second persons also usually resemble each other closely.

In Aragonese and Leonese-speaking areas, the *-ió* of form 3 influenced the plural form, resulting in *-ioron*, e.g *touioron* 'they had' (Aguilar de Campó, 1223-*DLE* No. 28, l. 34), *partioron* 'they departed' (l. 117), *quisioron* 'they wanted' (l. 116), etc. The influence of one tense on another is seen in the adoption in some dialects of the personal ending of form 6 from the present, imperfect and future and conditional in a new preterite ending *-ión*, e.g., *perdión* 'they lost' (Malkiel 1975–76, 448).

Rhizotonic ("Strong") Preterites

In spite of the label applied to this class of verb forms, it should be noted that stem stress is not consistent throughout their conjugation in the preterite. Stress falls on the stem only in forms 1 and 3, while the other forms are all stressed on the ending, exactly as in the "weak" conjugation. The personal ending for form 1 is phonetically regular, /-i:/ > /-e/, but the ending for form 3 was analogical, evidently adopted from the Late Latin ending -UT which, as we saw previously, was taken from form 3 of Conjugations I and IV: /-a:-ut/, /-i:ut/.

---

[114] This entire problem is extremely complex, and cannot be examined in detail here. For an analysis of all studies of the weak perfect see Malkiel 1975–76, 445–71, and Wilkinson 1977; of special importance is Craddock 1983.

Although the majority of rhizotonic preterites in Latin were replaced by regular ones, some of the most commonly used verbs retained their ancient pattern. Many of them belonged to Conjugation II in Latin and were patterned like the preterite of HABĒRE 'to have': HABUĪ, HABUISTĪ, HABUIT, etc.: that is, their stems had the pattern: C(C)-/a/-C, e.g., JACĒRE 'to be lying' - JACUĪ, JACUISTĪ, PLACĒRE 'to please' - PLACUI, PLACUISTI. A couple of other verbs that had had different perfects in earlier Latin remade their perfects according to the -UĪ pattern, e.g., SAPERE 'to taste; know' - *SAPUĪ (C.L. SAPĪVĪ), CAPERE 'to take, seize' - *CAPUĪ (C.L. CĒPĪ). An early development was an anticipation of the posttonic [w], much like that seen in some of the yods, e.g., CAPIŌ > /kaịpo/ > *quepo*. Thus, the [w] was metathesized so that it now formed a diphthong with the stem vowel:

HABUĪ > /au̯bi/ > *ove*
JACUI > /jau̯ki/ > *yogue*
PLACUI > /plau̯ki/ > *plogue*
*SAPUI > /sau̯pi/ > *sope*
*CAPUI > /kau̯pi/ > *cope*[115]

The increasing similarity of meaning of *aver* and *tener*, which from its original meaning of 'to hold' became more and more used to indicate possession, led to the analogical creation of the preterite *tove*. This pattern of *-ove*, found in such commonly used verbs was sufficiently striking to cause speakers to generate other rhizotonic preterites ending in *-ove*, especially in verbs having a single syllable stem. Thus, we find:

CRESCERE 'to grow' > *crescer - crove*
CRĒDERE 'to believe' > *creer - crove*
AMBITĀRE 'to go around' (?) > *andar - andove*
SEDĒRE 'to be seated' > *seer - sove*
STĀRE 'to be standing' > *estar - estove*
TRIBUERE 'to assign; allow' > *atrever* 'to dare' - *atrove*

The /-o-/ of the stems of all of these verbs even appears in a widespread form of the preterite of *traer*, *troxe* 'I brought', possibly adopted by speakers not only through analogy with the other verbs of the pattern *-o-C-e*, but also as a way of eliminating a peculiar shift in verb stems which would have resulted from regular phonetic development. The Latin perfect of TRAHERE was TRAXĪ, which, if it had changed regularly, would have become *trexi*. This sort of vowel alternation between present and preterite forms was found nowhere else. Thus, *troxe*, paralleled in Old Portu-

---

[115] The fact that in Portuguese the /au̯/ of the stem does not prevent voicing of the medial labial consonant, e.g., *soube* vs. Cast. *sope*, *coube* vs. *cope* < Late Lat. /saupi/, /kaupi/ < *SAPUĪ, *CAPUĪ leads Williams to suspect that the anticipation of the [u] was relatively late in Portuguese (1962, 88). One may wonder whether this is true since it is only the labial that is affected. Other consonants are voiced in Castilian as well as in Portuguese, e.g., *plogo* < PLACUIT.

guese *trouve* and *trouge*,[116] and dialectal Old Spanish *troge* (Malkiel 1967–68, 491–93), provided speakers with a way out of a possible dilemma in the formation of the preterite of *traer* (Malkiel 1967–68, 495).

Most sigmatic perfects of Latin disappeared in Late Latin also, but some survived to medieval times:

MĪSIT 'he sent' > *miso* 'he placed'
QUAESĪVIT 'he sought' > *quiso* 'he wanted' (with analogical loss of -ĪVĪ ending)
POSUIT 'he placed' > *puso* (with the vowel from Form 1)
(RE)MANSIT 'he remained' > *(re)maso*
RĪSIT 'he laughed' > *riso*
SCRĪPSIT 'he wrote' > *escriso*

Other verbs closely related in form to *querer* also adopted an /-s-/ preterite:

CONQUIRERE 'to collect; search for' > *conquerir* 'to conquer' - *conquiso*
REQUIRERE 'to search for; demand' > *requerir* - *requiso*

Several verbs with different perfects in Latin imitated the preceding ones and developed new perfects in /-s-/:

DISPENDIT 'he spread out, extended' > *despiso*
EXPENDIT 'he expended' > *espiso*
PRENDIT 'he seized, took' > *priso*
*(RE-)PAENITUIT 'he repented' > *repiso* (extremely rare)
RESPONDIT 'he answered' > *respuso*

In the case of these last verbs, it is likely that the preterite was altered by analogy with the past participles of these verbs:

EXPENDERE - EXPENSUS
PRENDERE - PRĒNSUS (← PRAEHENSUS)
RESPONDERE - RESPŌNSUS (Mourin 1976)

Verbs whose stems ended in /-k/ before /s/ developed regularly, i.e., to a palatal hushing sibilant /š/ (written x, see p. 253):

ADDŪXIT 'he led' > *aduxo*
CINXIT 'he girded on' > *cinxo*
COXIT 'he cooked' > *coxo*
DESTRUXIT 'he destroyed' > *destruxo*
DĪXIT 'he said' > *dixo*
EXĪ(V)IT 'he left' > *yxo*
TINXIT 'he dyed' > *tinxo*

---

[116] It is not certain whether *trouge* represents [trouže] or [trouge], given the lack of consistency in spelling in medieval texts (Malkiel 1967–68, 492).

Several other verbs with different perfects in Latin joined this group and formed new preterites in /š/:

FUGIT 'he fled' > *fuxo*
RASIT 'he scratched, shaved' > *raxo*
TETIGIT (TANGERE) 'he touched' > *tanxo* 'he played (an instrument)'

As pointed out in Chapter 2, the pattern of reduplicating perfects in Latin was a small and dying one, and in Romance only two very common verbs of this group remained: DĀRE 'to give' - DEDĪ, and STĀRE 'to stand' -STETĪ. The perfect of *dar* has been mentioned previously with regard to the -DEDĪ perfects. Its development was phonetically regular in the plural: forms 4 and 6, DEDIMUS > *diemos*, DEDERUNT > *dieron*. Form 5 analogically became *diestes*. The singular forms may have developed partially through normal phonetic change, but may equally well have adopted the standard "weak" pattern of -*er* and -*ir* verbs: DEDI > ?[diei] > *di*, DEDISTĪ > *diste*, DEDIT, *-UT > *dio*.

STARE > *estar* develops as expected in the perfect:

1. STETI > **estide*	4. STETIMUS > *estidiemos*
2. STETISTI > *estediste*	5. STETISTIS > *estidiestes*
3. STETIT > *estiedo*	6. STETERUNT > *estidieron*
(Leonese), *estido*	

(Malkiel 1980–81)

Some other verbs were influenced by the preterite of *estar* and developed preterites in /-ide/: *entrar* 'to enter' - *entride*, *andar* 'to go' - *andide*, *demandar* 'to ask, request' - *demandido* (Menéndez Pidal 1944a, l. 283).

One verb showing vowel gradation in the perfect has remained, *ver* 'to see' < VIDĒRE. The commonest pattern of the preterite shows an odd distribution:

1. VĪDĪ > *vide*	4. VĪDIMUS > *vimos, viemos*
2. VĪDISTĪ > *viste*	5. VĪDISTIS > *vistes, viestes, vidiestes*
3. VĪDIT > *vido*	6. VĪDĒRUNT > *vieron, veyeron, vidieron*

The preservation of medial /-đ-/ in this paradigm does not appear to reflect purely phonetic conditions, even given the difficulties in determining the exact fate of medial /đ/ in Castilian (see pp. 232–36). The whole problem of the development of various forms is far too complicated to be discussed in detail here (see especially Malkiel 1960), but the evidence indicates that it was actually form 3 which was preponderant in medieval Castilian. Form 1 would have given originally [ƀiđi] in its most primitive form, and with the increasing loss of final /-i/ and later /-e/, the result would have been *vid*. Given the rarity of final -*d* in verb forms, particularly in form 1, the result *vi* would be then expected. And in fact in medieval usage, *vido* is far more common than *vide*. A reasonable conclusion is that the form *vide* that does appear is probably analogical, based on *vido*, rather than being a direct descendant of VĪDĪ (Malkiel 1960, 331–32). Even so, this does not explain why such form should have persisted so long, only gradually replaced by *vi* and *vio*. Malkiel believes that the pressure of the general pattern of rhizotonic verbs must be considered the decisive factor. Most of these verbs have a pattern of a CVC- stem, followed by the personal endings. At a time when medial /-ð-/ was in the process of disappearing from many words, speakers would have been tempted to prefer the stem *vid-* because it fitted neatly into the general pattern of rhizotonic preterites (Malkiel 1960, 315), while *vi* and *vio* or *vío* represented too great a deviation from the model. The arrhizotonic forms 5 and 6, which contain /-d-/ are limited apparently to Navarro-Aragonese; *vidieron* was the favorite form of Gonzalo de Berceo, from La Rioja. In short, the preservation of *d* was part of a general pattern of conservatism. One other verb was influenced by *vido*: *catar* 'to look at' < Late Lat. CAPTĀRE, originally 'to grasp' ← CAPTUS 'taken seized', pp. of CAPERE, whose preterite *catido* is obviously borrowed from *vido*.

Two other preterites that do not fit into any of the previous patterns are *visque* 'I lived' and *nasque* 'I was born' (*vevir, nascer*). Although these are the only two verbs with this type of preterite formation, certain ephemeral analogical formations appeared in other verbs: *paresco* 'he appeared' from *parescer*, *remasco* 'he remained' from *remaner*, *conquisco* 'he conquered' from *conquerir*, and *amasco* 'it dawned' from *amanescer*. Being fleeting forms, they can be ignored. Slightly more common were *fusco* 'he fled' from *foir* and *trasco* 'he brought' from *traer*. The forms most commonly found are form 3 of the preterite, and less commonly, some other preterite-related tenses. Since no known model or possible sound law can account for these forms, some other source must be sought. Although some have thought of a possible metathesis of a learned pronunciation /ks/, the most likely source is Old Provençal in which one of the commonest patterns for rhizotonic preterites was the one in which /k/ was added to the verb stem, partly through regular phonetic development from a remade perfect, *NASCUIT (C.L. NĀTUS EST) which appears in the Iberian peninsula in the form *nasco* (Alvar-Pottier 1983, 261), and partly from analogy. The extension of the pattern VĪVERE can be seen as the result of the semantic link between 'to be born' and 'to live'. The popularity of the two forms in medieval Castilian, then, can best be understood as part of the strong Gallic influence that began to be felt in the peninsula in the twelfth and thirteenth centuries and that had so much to do with the popularity of the extreme apocope of *-e* (Blaylock 1975).

The forms of the preterite derived from ESSE 'to be' also were distinct from the regular patterns in that they were based on the stem FU-:

1. FUĪ > *fúe, fúi, fui, fu, fi*   4. FUIMUS > *fuemos, fuimos, fimos*
2. FUISTĪ > *fuiste, fueste*   5. FUISTIS > *fuestes, fuistes*
3. FUIT > *fú(e), fo, fué*   6. FUĒRUNT > *fueron*

Regular phonetic development would have produced *fue, fueste, fue*, but the forms that eventually won out were those most similar to the arrhizotonic preterite endings. The forms *fi* and *fimos* seem to be reduced forms of *fui* and *fuimos* (Alvar-Pottier 1983, 265).

There are other forms attested with single vowels in the root:

1. *fo*   4. *fomos, fumos*
2. *fuste, fust, foste, fusti, fuste*   5. *fostes, fustes*
3. *fot, fo, foe, foy, fu*   6. *foron, furon*

These have been reconstructed to possibly similar forms in Late Latin, with a consistently structured root *FU- followed by single syllable endings (Alvar-Pottier 1983, 266).

Metaphony of the Stem-Vowel

One of the commonest features of general Romance is the influence of a final high vowel on a preceding vowel, or metaphony (Leonard 1978). In early Castilian, the evidence for metaphony is found mostly in verb forms as it was in the perfect that the high front vowel appeared in form 1. The effect of /-i/ was to raise the preceding stem vowel in anticipation of the final high vowel. Thus, the two verbs which conserve the last traces of the vowel gradation (aside from *ver*, which we discussed above) are affected by metaphony: *fazer* 'to make, do' < FACERE and *venir* 'to come' < VENĪRE:

1. FĒCĪ > *fize*   4. 5. 6. regular
2. FĒCISTĪ > *feziste*
3. FĒCIT > *fezo*

1. VĒNĪ > *vine*
2. VĒNISTĪ > *veniste*
3. VĒNIT > *veno*

A similar development occurred in verbs with a back vowel in the stem:

FUĪ 'I was' > *fúe*
COGNŌVĪ 'I placed' > *conuve*
POSUĪ 'I placed' > *puse*
POTUĪ 'I was able' > *pude*

The influence of form 1 was sufficient to extend the /u/ and /i/ to other forms so that very early we find *fiziste, fizo, viniste, vino, estidiste, pudiste, pudo, pusiste, puso*. Form 2, however, frequently shows the same sort of vowel dissimilation that we noted before: a mid vowel is preferred before a stressed high vowel. Thus, *feziste, veniste, podiste*, and *posiste* persisted long after form 3 had adopted the high vowel. In the case of verbs like *querer* and *prender*, whose sigmatic perfects were discussed previously, it seems more likely that it is identification of these verbs with those whose stems had inherited the high vowel from Latin, such as *dixo, miso*, etc. (Menéndez Pidal 1941, 320).

In the plural forms, the endings containing a yod /-ie-/ may have changed the stem vowel through the raising effect of a yod on a preceding unstressed vowel (see pp. 000–000), e.g., *feziemos > fiziemos*, etc. as well as by analogy with the singular. Such forms existed in competition with the older perfects, such as *fezimos*, until the end of the Middle Ages.

In the *-ir* conjugation, the yod of endings 3 and 6, /-ió/ and /-ieron/ also raised the stem vowel of those verbs that were radical-changing in the present tense, just as forms 4 and 5 of such verbs in the present subjunctive (see pp. 291–94). Medieval *-iemos* and *-iestes* likewise had the same effect. Thus, taking *dormir* 'to sleep' as a model we find:

1. *dormí*	4. *dormimos, durmiemos*
2. *dormiste*	5. *dormistes, durmiestes*
3. *durmió*	6. *durmieron*

Competing Forms in Old Spanish

In the preceding section the various analogical and regular formations have been treated separately. The effects of analogy, however, were never simple, and in a number of verbs, different preterites were created for the same verb, especially in the case of certain verbs of high frequency of usage. Thus, we find as the preterite of *estar* such varying forms as *estide*, the inherited form, *estove*, analogically based on *ove* and the other *-ove* preterites, and *estude*, based on the regular preterite of *poder, pude*. *Andar*, a verb of disputed etymology, had a similar variety of preterite forms: *andove, andude, andide*. A verb like *traer* revealed a great proliferation of preterites. Regular phonetic development of Lat. TRAXIT produced *trexo*, a form attested but rare. As mentioned above, however, the alternation between a present stem-vowel /a/ and a preterite stem-vowel /e/ was unprecedented, and apparently speakers preferred to try to avoid this unique pattern by analogical formations. Thus, a rare *trasco* appears, based on verbs like *visco, nasco*; alternatively we find *troge* or *trogue* which may possibly derive ultimately from a Late Lat. *TRAGERE, and *tro(u)xe* with the vowel borrowed from the *-o-c-e* verbs, while *trouve* appears in Old Portuguese, obviously based on descendants of HABUĪ. Other forms maintain the present stem-vowel: *traxo*, or shift to the regular conjugational pattern: *trayó*. Thus, we see a lack of stability in the forms of irregular verbs that characterize much of the development of Castilian in the Middle Ages.[117] In part, the great variety of forms reflect the dynamic movements of phonetic shifts over a period of many centuries, with newer forms in constant competition with older ones. The forms of *oír* and *ver*, for example, appear in different places and times with or without the medial /-d-/ as speakers gradually accustomed themselves to the new forms of words without the consonant. Likewise, the effect of the yod on stem-vowels competed with the older form of verbs without raising. Thus, *fezieste* is set against *fizieste*, while the raised vowel of form 1 gives further impetus to the shift. At the same time, the pressure of the inherited *-iste* ending worked against the same tendency to raise the stem-vowel because of the general tendency to dissimilate a mid vowel before stressed /í/, so that *feziste* tended to be strengthened. Some variant forms are limited to certain geographical areas, e.g., *trasco* from *traer* is found mostly in La Rioja and areas close to it in upper Aragon (Malkiel 1967–68, 488), while the variant ending *-ioron*, based on the singular *-ió*, is found in Leon and Aragon, but very rarely in Castile. Similarly, extension of the stressed /ó/ of form 3 to other forms is found in upper Aragon, e.g., 4. *aduxomos* 'we brought', 5. *compróç* 'you bought' (*Orígenes* §75.2). And, working against the preservation of inherited or analogical rhizotonic preterites, was the constant pressure of the majority group of regular verbs. Thus, in the *Cantar de mio Cid* we find *creçió* 'he grew' for *crovo* and *metió* 'he placed' for *miso* (Menéndez Pidal 1944a, l. 277), while in the same text the preterite of the verb *exir* 'to go out' < EXĪRE appears as *yxo* and *exo* as well as *yxió* (l. 279).

If we lump together all the variant forms that we find in texts from a number of different centuries and from different levels of transmission and different dialectal areas, one may easily gain an impression of a chaotic lack of standards (e.g., Lapesa 1980, 212–13). Such an impression may be largely an illusion. It is true that there was less standardization of *literary* norms than there has been since the Renaissance. Also medieval speakers certainly did not feel the pressure to adhere to a single standard in the forms of words to the same extent as do modern speakers, especially literate ones, and thus could more freely use alternate forms as they desired or as the context may have required. But can we be sure that a single speaker would alternately use, say, eight different forms of form 2 of the preterite of *fazer* all at roughly the same time and in the same context? Alternation of two or three forms might well have occurred with more frequency than it does today, but in the usage of single speakers, given the absence of records of the spoken language, we may never be certain of just how much variation actually existed at one time or place, and whether it was really much greater than that existing today. At any rate, as we shall see in the next chapter, the general movement toward greater uniformity eventually led to a great reduction in the number of rhizotonic preterites.

The Other Perfect Tenses

The pluperfect in its reduced form e.g., *amara, -as, -a*, etc., remained with its original meaning, although the existence of the compound tense, *avía amado*, increasingly threatened its integrity throughout the Middle Ages, and eventually led to its specialization as a subjunctive form. The form of the endings of the *-er* and *-ir* verbs reflects the popularity of the *-iemos, -iestes, -ieron* endings of forms 4–6 in the simple preterite, since the diphthong appears regularly in all persons, and in all the other past tenses related to the preterite. The tendency to regular placement of the stress on the same syllable of all forms led to the creation of proparoxytonic forms for forms 4 and 5: *amáramos, amárades* < AMĀ(VE)RÁMUS, AMĀ(VE)RÁTIS.

The pluperfect subjunctive likewise developed normally: *amasse, -es, -e*, etc., with the function of a simple past subjunctive. The other past subjunctives which had merged with the future perfect remained as a future subjunctive. Form 1, through normal phonetic development, became *amaro, podiero, fuero*, etc. up to the end of the fourteenth century (Menéndez Pidal 1944a, l. 277), with the other forms ending regularly in *-res, -re*, etc. The general pattern of the past tenses, however, had identical endings for forms 1 and 3 (excepting, of course, the simple preterite): *-sse, -ra, -ava, -ía*, and this pattern eventually led to the elimination of the *-o* in form 1 and its replacement by *-e*. Form 5 very frequently syncopated the posttonic vowel so that forms like *casardes* from *casar* 'to marry', *ouierdes* from *aver* 'to have', *fallardes* from *fallar* 'to find', etc. appear (Menéndez Pidal 1944a, l. 278).

The Future and Conditional

The Romance pattern of infinitive plus the present indicative of *aver* formed the basis of the future, while the imperfect endings of *aver* were used for the conditional, originally a future of the past. Although there was a considerable degree of fusion of the two elements into one simple verb form, for a long time they continued to exist as relatively independent parts of a syntagma, so that object pronouns could appear between the infinitive and the forms of *aver*, e.g., *amar lo é* 'I shall love him'. The tendency toward fusion, however, was strong and with the formation of a single form, regular phonetic tendencies began to have their effect. A unified future form with stress on the ending left the vowel of the infinitive ending in a pretonic position and thus subject to syncope as in all other words. Since /a/ was not syncopated normally, futures of the *-ar* conjugation were not affected.

In the *-er* and *-ir* conjugations, however, syncope could take effect. When the stem-final consonant and the infinitival *-r* formed an existing consonant cluster, no further change would be likely. Thus, we find the following new future forms:

/-b, -ƀ/ + /r/	/-đ-/ + /r/
bever - bevrá	*arder - ardrá*
aver - avrá	*eñader, -ir - eñadrá*
vivir - vivrán	*entender - entendremos*
mover - movrás	*prender - prendría*
caber - cabrá	*perder - perdrás*
concebir - concibredes	*comedir - comidrás*
recebir - recibrían	

/-t/ + /r/	/-r/ + /r/
consentir - consintrás	*ferir - ferredes*
mentir - mentrién	*conquerir - conquerrá*
partir - partremos	*parir - parrás*
repenter, -ir - repentremos	*querer - querrá*

When the stem-final consonant did not form an existing cluster, e.g., /-n + r/, /-m + r/, /-l + r/, the resulting phonetic difficulty was overcome in several ways. Very common was the epenthesis of another consonant. A nasal plus /r/ often resulted in this sort of solution. Otherwise the /r/ was prolonged to /r:/, occasionally with loss of the nasal. Alternatively there could be a metathesis of the consonants, resulting in a familiar sequence:

Epenthesis

/-m/ + /r/	/-n/ + /r/
comer - combré	*remaner - remandrá*
	poner - pondré
	tener - tendré
/-l/ + /r/	*venir - vendré*
doler - doldrá	
fallir - faldrá	
moler - moldrié	
salir - saldré	
valer - valdré	

/tˢ/ + /r/	/-dᶻ + /r/
fallescer - falleztrá	*bendezir - bendizdré*
conoscer - conoztría	*yazer - yazdrá*

Strengthening of /r/ to /r:/

| *poner - ponrrá* | *salir - salrrá* | *valer - valrrá* |

Elimination of nasal

| *poner - porrá* | *tener - terría* | *venir - verrá* |

The combination of an affricate and /r/ was unusual (see p. 205), but could occur. Thus, a simple sequence of /tˢ/ and /dᶻ/ plus /r/ could be found: *yazer - yazremos, dezir - dizré, luzir - luzrá*. Alternatively there could be epenthesis of an occlusive consonant, as we saw above. Finally the combination could be eliminated simply by dropping the affricate: *aduzir - adurá, dezir - dirá, fazer - fará*.[117] We note that the *-ir* verbs frequently contain a high vowel in the future and conditional forms.

---

[117] The whole story of the preterites of *traer* is far too complex to be discussed in this book. See Malkiel 1967–68, especially 485–501, for a full description of the variants and their sources and attestations.

The Past Participle

The regular past participles of *-ar* and *-ir* verbs need no special comment as they developed regularly to *-ado* and *-ido*. The new -ŪTUS participle of Late Latin, extended to a number of verbs with perfects in -UI, e.g., BATTUERE 'to beat, strike' - BATTŪTUS, so that for the central Romance languages and Rumanian, the -ŪTUS ending became the standard one for verbs derived from Conjugations II and III, e.g., HABĒRE and VENDERE 'to sell', > Fr. *eu, vendu*, It. *avuto, venduto*, Prov. *avut, vendut*, Rom. *avut, vindut*, etc.[118] A number of *-udo* participles appear in Old Spanish and Old Portuguese, but the evidence indicates that in all probability the *-udo* ending never became firmly established in central and western Ibero-Romance.[119]

The *Fuero de Avilés*, long thought to be the oldest preserved Spanish text, has a marked preponderance of *-udo* participles, as one might expect in a text with a generous admixture of Provençal elements (Lapesa 1948). The kindred *Fuero de Oviedo*, however, usually has counterparts in *-ido*: only seldom do we find the reverse situation. Some examples of words from the Fuero de Avilés are the following (the number in parentheses is the the line number): *mouuda* (9), *uenzudo* (14), *cognozudo* (15), *esmoludo* (24), etc. In the *Fuero de Oviedo*, in the same lines, we see: *mouyda, uencido, connoscido, molido*.[120]

The same pattern in found in other texts, with *-ido* endings generally predominating except in those texts strongly influenced by Gallic models. The number of Spanish and Portuguese *-udo* participles in the twelfth century and the early decades of the thirteenth is quite small, even when we take into account the exiguous quantity of preserved texts. The extraordinary vitality they acquire toward the end of the thirteenth century can be due in no small measure to the intensified contact with trans-Pyrenean dialects.[121] Almost immediately after the Gallic cultural links weakened, the *-udo* pattern in Spanish and Portuguese entered into a rapid and irreversible decline.

---

[118] It is possible that the reduced infinitive form found in *fará* may not be the result of a phonetic change in the future form but rather the use of the analogically formed infinitive of Late Latin *fare*. See Malkiel 1977–78.

[119] Lausberg distinguishes an archaic zone from an innovating zone and links the development of an -ŪTUS participle to the rise of a Conjugation IV pattern amplified with an -ESC-suffix (1966, 357–59; 363).

[120] References are to the edition by A. Fernández Guerra y Orbe, *El Fuero de Avilés; Discurso leído en junta pública de la Real Academia Española* (Madrid, 1865).

[121] An illustration of the popularity and decline of the *-udo* participles can be seen in a legal formula. Starting about 1220, the preferred formula for beginning a Castilian legal text was *connoçuda cosa sea*, which replaced the Latin phrase NOTUM SIT OMNIBUS HOMINIBUS. For a time *connuçuda* occasionally alternated with *sabida* (less often *sabuda*) *cosa* . . . , and in the last decades of the thirteenth century we find *connocida cosa*, which shortly afterwards yielded to *sepan quantos* . . . , the formula which has survived to this day.

The various rhizotonic participles of Latin were often preserved, with normal phonetic changes. Thus, of those in which the -TUS ending came immediately after a stem-final consonant (sometimes following syncope), the /t/ did not voice:

APERTU 'opened' > *abierto* (APERĪRE)
COOPERTU 'covered' > *cobierto* (COOPERĪRE)
EXPERGITU 'awakened' > *despierto* (EXPERGERE)
MORT(U)U 'dead' > *muerto* (MORĪ)
POSITU 'placed' > *puesto* (PŌNERE)
RUPTU 'broken' > *roto* (RUMPERE)
SCRĪPTU 'written' > *escrito* (SCRĪBERE)
TORTU 'twisted' > *tuerto* (TORQUERE)

If the stem-consonant was /-k/, normal phonetic development of /kt/ produced /č/:

COCTU 'cooked' > *cocho* (COQUERE)
DUCTU 'led' > *ducho* (DŪCERE)
DICTU 'said' > *dicho*[122] (DICERE)
CORRECTU 'corrected, put straight' > *correcho* (CORRIGERE)
FACTU 'done' > *fecho* (FACERE)
TRACTU 'drawn' > *trecho* (TRAHERE)

If the vowel preceding was high, the yod from /-k/ was absorbed by it: FRĪCTU 'fried' > *frito* (FRĪGERE). In cases where the stem-final sequence was /-nk/, the nasal prevented the formation of the yod:

CĪNCTU 'girded' > *cinto* (CINGERE)
JUNCTU 'joined, yoked' > *junto* (JUNGERE)
TĪNCTU 'dyed' > *tinto* (TINGERE)

A few participles ended in -SUS and some remained in medieval Castilian:

INCĒNSU 'ignited, burned' > *enceso* (INCENDERE)
DĒFĒNSU 'defended' > *defeso* (DĒFENDERE)
EXPĒNSU 'paid out, expended' > *espeso* (EXPENDERE)
PRENSU 'seized' > *preso* (PREHENDERE)

Some others that remain in the lexicon are no longer participles but adjectives: TENSU 'outstretched' > *teso, tieso* (TENDERE), RASU > *raso 'smooth, flat'* (RĀDERE), etc.

The influence of some verbs on others led to the analogical creation of new participles in Later Latin. Thus, C.L. VĪSUS from VIDĒRE 'to see' must

---

[122] Perfectly regular development would have given **decho* (cf. It. *detto*). Since Leonese has this form, we may assume that it existed originally in early Castilian too and that the vowel now found is analogical with the finite forms (Menéndez Pidal 1941, 324).

have been replaced by *VISTUS > *visto*. QUAESITUS from QUAERERE 'to seek' gave way to a rhizotonic form whose reflex in Old Spanish is *quisto* 'desired'. The arrhizotonic participles VOLŪTUS from VOLVERE 'to turn, revolve', and SOLŪTUS from SOLVERE 'to loosen, free', were also replaced by stem stressed ones which give *vuelto* and *suelto*. A new formation for C.L. SUBLĀTUS from TOLLERE 'to take away', based on the stem TOLL- gave *tuelto*. FALSUS from FALLERE 'to deceive', was also replaced by a new form in -ITUS, which became medieval *falto*. Only one new analogical participle in /s/ appears, *repiso* 'repented' from *arrepentir*, along with the regular *arrepentido*.

As with other rhizotonic verb forms, the analogical pressure of the vast majority of arrhizotonic forms led to the replacement of many of the traditional ones by new regular ones. Thus, we find in medieval texts *veído* (*Auto de los Reyes Magos*, Gifford and Hodcroft 1966, 37, l. 3), *rompido*, *querido*, for *visto*, *roto*, and *quisto*. Most of the commonest verb forms, however, managed to maintain themselves.

Other Verbal Participles

The remaining participles of Latin disappeared as active parts of the verbal paradigms with the exception of the gerund in -NDŌ which remained as a present participle: *amando*, *comiendo*, *viviendo*, etc., showing the regular diphthong in the -*er*, -*ir* verbs.

Imperatives

In general, the imperative forms developed as one would expect with regular phonetic change. Thus, the singular forms ending in a simple vowel and the plural in -TE produce the following endings: -A > -*a*, -Ī > -*e*, -E > -*e*, -TE > -*d*. When the apocope of final -*e* became popular, imperative forms went along with the majority:

DESCENDE 'descend!' > *descend*
*FACE (C.L. FAC) > *faz*
FERĪ 'strike!' > *fier*
PETE 'ask, request!' > *pide* > *pit*
PŌNE 'place!' > *pon*
PROMITTE 'promise!' > *promed*
SALĪ > *sal* 'leave!'
VENĪ 'come!' > *ven*

Only the most common verbs remained with apocopated forms. The verb *tener* which should have become **tien* in the imperative, was influenced analogically by *ven* in which the high final vowel had raised the stem-vowel so that it did not diphthongize, thus giving the form *ten*.

CHAPTER 5

FROM MEDIEVAL TO MODERN SPANISH

THE PHONOLOGICAL SYSTEM

Vowels

The vowel system that developed out of the Late Latin system had, by the twelfth or thirteenth century, if not considerably earlier in Old Castile, perhaps by the tenth century at the latest, become what it has remained until today. Once the diphthongs /je/ and /we/ had become identified with combinations of the high vowels and the mid front vowel /e/, the system was a five vowel one:

/i/				/u/
	/e/		/o/	
		/a/		

The diphthongs were still largely associated with the tonic syllable, but the way was clear for them to spread through analogy to atonic positions. Thus, we find words like *mueblería* 'furniture store' derived from *mueble* 'piece of furniture' < Lat. MOBILE, where we would expect, on a purely historical basis, something like **moblería*.

Sporadic Monophthongization of the Diphthongs

Although for the most part the diphthongs were stable once they had become phonemic combinations of vowels, there was a tendency for certain factors to favor a further simplification of the diphthongs, with /ie/ becoming /i/ in a number of words, and /ue/ becoming /e/ in a smaller group.

The first phonetic factor that appears to have induced the monophthongization of /ie/ > /i/ is the presence of a following palatal lateral /l/. The very earliest written evidence of -*ill*- instead of -*iell*- is found in northern Castile and in Burgos in documents dated in the tenth century:

316

Castillo for *Castiello* (A.D. 921), *morcillo* for *morciello* (A.D. 981, *Orígenes* §27.2). In the eleventh and twelfth centuries more and more examples appear, with the greatest number in Burgos in the thirteenth century, followed by La Montaña and Campó and La Rioja. At that time, there was evidently a reaction against the use of -*ill*- in northern Castile and more examples of -*iell*- appear. The literary standard preferred -*iell*- and the written use of -*ill*- did not become common in New Castile until the fourteenth and fifteenth centuries, although undoubtedly in familiar speech it was common much earlier (*Orígenes* §28).

The development has sometimes been seen as the effect of the palatal consonant on a form of the diphthong stressed more on the initial glide than on the /e/. In other words, if we assume that the diphthong originally was not clearly stressed on /e/ and that phonetically the diphthong was [íe] (Alarcos Llorach 1968, 144), then the passage to a monophthong is more comprehensible. It is, however, most doubtful that, regardless of the original stress pattern of semi-diphthongs and diphthongs in early Romance, as late as the tenth century there should have still been any speakers in Castile who pronounced /ie/ as [íe] rather than [jé]. A purely phonetic explanation lacks something. A more plausible account is the one that looks beyond the narrow phonetic circumstances in which the change occurs. The first thing to be noted is that the combination /iel̯/ is found in the diminutive suffix -*iello* < Late Lat. -ELLU. Since the other diminutive suffixes -*ito*, -*ico*, -*ín* existed in competition with -*iello*, it is far more likely that the substitution of /i/ for /ie/ was due to the analogical influence of the other suffixes which are all distinguished by the presence of tonic /í/. The peculiar phonetic circumstances were at most a supplementary factor (Malkiel 1976, 761). The overwhelming majority of the examples of the shift of -*iell*- to -*ill*- are, in fact diminutive formations: *Fermosilla* (A.D. 1082), *portillo* (A.D. 1067) *Cordouilla* (A.D. 1150) and many more (*Orígenes* §27.2). Such was the strength of the innovation that even when the combination did not appear in a diminutive suffix, e.g., *siella* < SELLA 'saddle, seat', *castiello* < CASTELLU 'castle, fortress', *Castiella* 'Castile' < CASTELLA 'castles', the change was adopted just the same.

Aside from this early instance of monophthongization, there are a number of other words containing the diphthong in different phonetic circumstances which at a later period began shifting from /ie/ to /i/:

aprisco 'I gather sheep in the fold'; 'sheep-fold' ← *APPRESSICĀRE, derivative of PRESSUS, passive part. of PREMERE 'to press, squeeze'
avispa 'wasp' < *aviespa* < VESPA
mirl-o, -a 'blackbird' < *mierlo* < MERUL-A, -U
níspero 'medlar-tree', *níspola* 'medlar-fruit' < *niéspera* < MESPIL-U, -A
pingo 'I drip' < *PENDICŌ ← PENDERE 'to hang'
prisa 'haste' < *priessa* < PRESSA
prisco 'kind of clingstone peach' < *priesco* < PERSICU (MALUM) 'lit. Persian apple'

remilgo (refl. verb) ' I am affectedly nice, squeamish'; (noun) 'affected gravity, prudery' < a verb based on *miel* 'honey' < MEL, and the verbal suffix -ICĀRE

ristra 'string, row, file' < *riestra* < RESTE (fem.) 'rope'

sirvo 'I serve' < *siervo* < SERVIŌ

siglo 'world; century' < *sieglo* < SAECULU

víspera(s) 'eve' < *viésperas* < VESPERA (HŌRA)

(Malkiel 1976, 767)[1]

Examination of the phonetic conditions in which the diphthong monophthongizes shows that in almost every case the word contains /e/ (often in sequence with a following consonant) and a liquid /l/ or /r/. Evidently too the presence of a labial consonant also favored the change in some way, although the role played by these consonants is not very clear. It is true that the Castilian apico-alveolar sibilant [ś] tends to have a more palatal quality than the sibilant in standard French or Italian, by itself it cannot be the direct cause of monophthongization. We find other words containing /s/, even in a consonant sequence, in which the diphthong appears to be stable: *fiesta* < FESTA, 'feast; holiday', OSp. *finiestra* < FENESTRA 'window', *siesta* 'noon time; afternoon rest' < SEXTA HŌRA 'sixth hour', etc. The labial and liquid consonants have no special palatal qualities that would tend to make the diphthong unstable. By themselves they certainly do not tend to influence monophthongization, e.g., *pierna* 'leg' < PERNA, *tierno* 'tender, young' < TENERU, etc. It seems to be the combination of all of these consonants that tends to favor monophthongization, if and when it does take place.

Once again, however, it may be that phonetics alone cannot account for this limited sort of change. Another morphological analogy can be taken into account which could plausibly have induced speakers to consider that the shift of /ie/ to /i/ in the presence of /s/ grouped with another consonant was desirable: namely the competition in Old Castilian between the two forms of the preterite. As we saw in chapters 3 and 4, the development of the -DEDĪ perfects in Late Latin produced in the plural, in forms 4, 5, and 6, endings with the diphthong /ie/: -*iemos*, -*iestes*, -*ieron*. Medieval texts show that during the thirteenth and fourteenth centuries, there was a general preference for the -*ie*- plurals, but that after 1400 the fashion rapidly faded and the endings with -*i*- in forms 4 and 5 became dominant. (Other details are discussed in the section on morphology.) The popularity of form 2 in -*iste* may have led speakers to prefer -*istes* over -*iestes* in form 5, and thus to feel that /i/ for /ie/ was part of the same new fashion, even in non-verbal forms. Thus, the morphological preference for -*imos* and -*istes* could have been a sort of clinching factor in inducing some speakers

---

[1] *Prista* fpr *priesta* 'he lends' < PRAESTAT appears only once in writing, in *Elena y María*, and may have been blocked in particular because of the limitation of forms alternating /e/ and /i/ to the -*ir* conjugation (Malkiel 1976, 767).

to prefer the variant *ristra* over the older, and more strongly entrenched *riestra*, plus the few other words whose phonetic structure resembled it in some way. The monophthongization did not become a general movement, however, and was limited to the examples given previously.

A somewhat similar development of the diphthong /ue/ into /e/ occurred later and affected only a very few words:

> *afrenta* 'dishonor' < *afruenta* ← *afrontar* 'to insult', based on the same etymon as that of
> *frente* 'forehead' < *fruente* < FRONTE
> *culebra* 'snake' < *culuebra* < COLOB-RA (C.L. COLUBER)
> *fleco* 'fringe, flounce, raveled edge' < *flueco* < FLOCCU
> *serba* 'serviceberry' < *suerba* < SORBA (pl. of SORBUM)

We may include the following placenames as well:

> *Bureba* < *Burueva* < BOROVIA
> *Noreña* < *Norueña* < NORONIA
> *Ureña* < *Urueña* < ORONIA

In the preceding examples, the presence of a labial consonant grouped with a liquid seems to be the phonetic requirement that triggers the shift, although perhaps the last two place names should be classed with examples of the suffix *-ueño* rather than with the others. In this case too we may see the agency of a morphological rivalry as an assisting factor. In particular there are two separate suffixes that revealed a competition between a form with /ue/ and one with /e/ that may have to be taken into account. The first is the suffix *-ero* < -ĀRIU (through *-airo* < *-eiro*) and the suffix *-(ad)uero* < -(AT)ŌRIU, e.g., *cuchillero* 'knife maker, seller', *asmaduero* 'worthy of esteem', *cobdiciaduero* 'desirable, provoking lust', etc. Around 1300 we see that adjectives in *-duero* began to be merged with their counterparts in *-ero* so that today the only form of the suffix is *-dero*, e.g., *hacedero* 'feasible'. Another pair of adjectival suffixes was *-ueño* < -ONIU, e.g., *risueño* 'smiling' ← *risa* 'laughter', and *-eño* < -INEU, usually used to indicate the place of origin, e.g., *madrileño* 'pertaining to, from Madrid', etc. In this case, *-eño* did not replace *-ueño*, which still exists, although it is no longer actively used in new formations any more. Still, the fact that two such similar suffixes could be seen to be somehow related might have reinforced the stronger stimulus given by the shift of *-duero* to *-dero*.

We may conclude then that possibly these morphological shifts served to push a small number of words with especially complex phonetic structures toward monophthongization. We may also conclude that the much more limited, and considerably later, shift of /ue/ to /e/ (*culebra* and *frente* do not appear in writing until the end of the fifteenth century)[2] may also be in part conditioned by the previous shift of /ie/ to /i/. The two

---

[2] The lateness of the literary appearance of these words is in no way an indication that they did not exist much earlier in speech.

diphthongs frequently move in parallel ways, and, we must remember, after the thirteenth century at the latest, the diphthongs were no longer independent phonemic units but clusters of vowel phonemes and thus structurally different from what they had been originally. Once more we see that several interlocking factors are the likely stimuli for a phonetic change, even one as limited in scope as these were (Malkiel 1976, 775).

The Elimination of Hiatus

The tendency to eliminate the hiatus between vowels in contact in different syllables is a permanent one in Latin-Romance. We have seen that some forms of verbs whose roots end in a vowel tended to eliminate the hiatus by adopting an analogical palatal [j] from other verbs, e.g., *cayo*, *trayo*, etc. where a straight-line phonetic development would have given **cao* and **trao*. Another way of avoiding hiatus was the merger of vowels into a single vowel. Thus, *veer* 'to see' and *seer* 'to be' are eventually replaced by monophthongal *ver* and *ser*, although *ver* retains the older stem *ve-* in the imperfect. *Leer* 'to read' continues to keep the older form although Portuguese *ler* shows the same tendency carried to completion.

In the case of words containing an accented high vowel in hiatus, another solution to the problem was to merge the two syllables into one with a consequent shift of the accent from the high vowel to the lower one so that the vowels form a diphthong. Thus, older *reína* 'queen' < RĒGĪNA, *vaína* 'sheath, pod' < VĀGĪNA, *veínte* 'twenty' < VĪGINTĪ, *treínta* 'thirty' < TRĪGINTA, *béodo* 'drunk' < BEBITU, *víuda* 'widow' < VIDUA, gradually gave way to modern *reina*, *veinte*, *treinta*, *beodo*, *viuda*.[3] The same process is at work in modern times. The words *período* and *océano* and the adjectival ending *-íaco* (e.g., *Austríaco* 'Austrian') which were standard in the nineteenth century are now most frequently pronounced with stress on the lower vowel *periódo*, *oceáno*, *-iáco*. In popular speech the process affects words that in educated Spanish still require a hiatus: *páis* 'country', *bául* 'trunk', and the ending *-áino* instead of the "correct" forms *país*, *baúl*, and *-aíno*.

The Further Development of Final -e and Its Apocope

As we saw in chapter 4, the apocope of /-e/ was due to a native tendency to drop the vowel after an apical consonant, pushed to an extreme of dropping after almost any consonant or consonant sequence by the prestige of Gallo-Romance speakers who occupied high positions in the government and the church during the eleventh to the thirteenth

---

[3] It is usual to include *díos* 'god' < DEUS with this group of words. However, in view of the special development of the diphthong /eu/ in Late Latin, it seems more probable that the monosyllable *diós* was the original one, although an occasional bisyllabic *díos* cannot be ruled out (Craddock 1983, 11).

centuries. It might have seemed as though Castilian would eventually go to the extreme of French and Catalan.

The strong connections between the royal house of Castile and France that had characterized the twelfth and the beginning of the thirteenth centuries began, however, to weaken. Intermarriage between Hispanic and Gallic royalty continued, but by the reign of Alfonso VIII (who married the daughter of Henry II of England and Eleanor of Aquitaine) the number of French officials in the royal court had diminished considerably. As the danger of the attacks of the Almoravids lessened, the aid of French knights came to be less appreciated and native military orders were founded to defend the Christian territory. The failure of the French knights to assist in the crucial battle of Las Navas de Tolosa at the beginning of the thirteenth century was one more sign of waning Gallic influence and of an increasing nationalistic (or, at least, non-French) feeling.

The final union of the crowns of Castile and Leon in 1230 and the conquest of Seville and Córdoba strenghthened the independence of the Christian monarchs of Iberia. At the same time, a movement to eject foreign prelates was a sign of an increased nationalization of the Hispanic church. The declining prestige of French models eventually made itself felt in a decreasing amount of apocope of -e. Although examples of extreme apocope are very common in writing throughout the thirteenth century, toward the middle of the century there is a perceptible decrease in the number of apocopated forms as compared with non-apocopated ones. The well known story of how Alfonso X began correcting the language of the translations of learned works that he sponsored (in the *Libro de la Ochava Esfera*) reveals that the king must have felt that the extreme apocope was to be rejected (". . . cuanto en el lenguaje, endreçólo él por sise"). When one compares the royal prologues, written by the king himself, with the language of the texts, it is noticeable that Alfonso used few apocopated forms other than those that have remained to the present, while the texts themselves frequently have a great abundance of apocopated forms (Lapesa 1951, 218).

In addition to the change in the prestige norm that now showed less favor toward the extreme apocope, we must take into account internal factors as well. As written Romance became more common, writers were growing more accustomed to following indigenous uses and thus were less likely to show an exaggerated respect for foreign models. Also an increasing consciousness of the formal identity of words and a tendency to maintain a single form would have helped to act against extreme apocope. The plurals of nouns and adjectives had always kept the /e/, unlike French, thus providing a model for the singular with a final -e.

From this period on, the extreme apocope began to decline in popularity. In some regions (La Montaña, Alava, Rioja Alta, Murcia) apocopated forms continued to be common in the fourteenth century, and especially in popular speech which, as often happens, continued to respect a linguistic norm that had fallen out of favor with the upper classes. The Archpriest of

Hita, in the first half of the fourteenth century, reveals in the manuscripts of the *Libro de Buen Amor* a number of extreme apocopes: *ribal* 'rascal' for *ribaldo, nief* 'snow' for *nieve, promed* 'promise!' for *promete, yot* for *yo te, pagan* 'pay me!' for *págame*, especially in passages that try to represent rustic speech.

From the last half of the fourteenth century to the present, apocope of *-e* has generally been limited to words having apical consonants before the original *-e*. In the fifteenth century a few words that today are impossible were still found: the enclitic pronouns *le* and *se*, attached to words ending in vowels, lost the *-e*, and the verb form of some very common verbs that ended in *-e* like *diz, fiz, tien, val*, etc.[4] Thus, we can see that the extreme apocope of final *-e* resulted from a combination of different factors: a tendency to drop *-e* after apical consonants, aided by the triumph of syncope which allowed a certain number of consonants to become syllable-final in the middle of words, the arrival of a number of prestigious personages from areas in which extreme apocope was the norm, the borrowing of Gallo-Romance words in apocopated forms and of a number of Arabic and Hebrew words from bilingual speakers from southern Spain. In literature the linguistic norm came to favor extreme apocope for a while until a reaction against it set in. In no case should it be assumed that apocope of final *-e* was imposed on Castilian from without;[5] it was a native tendency, part of the general western Romance movement toward the weakening and loss of final vowels, whose exaggeration, especially in literature, was encouraged by non-Castilian writers and speakers. When the circumstances that had favored this exaggeration changed, it ceased to be acceptable and disappeared, rapidly in writing and more slowly in speech.

Consonants

$/f/ > /h/ > /0/$

In chapter 4 the origins of the shift of /f/ to /h/ were discussed (to use a handy cover label for a complex process). As we saw there, the original substitution of an aspirate [h] for the bilabial or labiodental fricative [φ] or [f] which had developed before back vowels, was generalized to the position before all vowels so that the system of many speakers in northern Old Castile and eastern Leon from the tenth century onward was probably as follows:

[φ] before /r l j/
[h] before syllabic vowels /i e a o u/
[hφ] before [w]

---

[4] Modern *quizá(s)* 'perhaps' < OSp. *qui sab* 'who knows?' is a relic of such forms as is the American Sp. *dizque* 'it is said that' < *diz(e) que*.

[5] This is just what Catalán (1971, 79, n. 4), seems to assume that Lapesa does. Lapesa 1975 answers his objections fully.

The preceding system was undoubtedly the most popular or evolved one, while conservative speech could well have kept [f] or [φ] before all vowels, as a reaction against this popular change. The other northern dialects can then be seen as having similarly leveled the allophones in favor of [f] or [φ] rather than [h]. The last allophone listed in the chart above was a natural development before a semiconsonantal glide that resembled the vowel /u/ but was asyllabic.

This advanced phonetic system spread to the south with the political and linguistic expansion of Castile, and is essentially retained in this form in the twentieth century in the "rural speech of eastern Asturias, western Santander, Extremadura and western Andalusia" (Penny 1972a, 470). The retention of [h] before vowels is found likewise in American Spanish in popular usage, indicating that the [h] was brought by the colonists in the sixteenth century and was reinforced by subsequent immigrants with the same pronunciation.

The pronunciation of [φ] before /r l j/ and in words of learned origin adopted from the standard literary language is overwhelmingly attested in western Andalusia (based on the ALEA, Penny 1972a, 471) and in modern American Spanish (Doman 1969, especially 430–36).[6] Evidence for retention of the sound posited before [w], namely a combination of a labial and velar articulation [hφ] is clear too, although in many dialect studies there is considerable variation in the symbols used to represent the sound. In reality, the use of a digraph, whether the one preferred by Penny or the [φ^h used by Espinosa (cited in Doman 1969, 430), the *ju* used by Flórez (Doman 1969, 433), etc. may suggest that the sound described is a combination of two successive articulations rather than a single one. It is best to keep in mind that the sound is an "aspiración velar emitida con aproximación de los labios" and that "no se trata aquí de una sucesión de dos sonidos, sino de un sonido compuesto, sentido como único por el hablante, por lo cual sería quizá preferible representarlo en lo futuro por un solo signo" (Boyd-Bowman, cited by Doman 1969, 441).

Preservation of [φ] in the rest of the Castilian area and in Castilianized parts of Leon and Aragon is probable but cannot be proved at present because of lack of information. The evidence that the articulation of /f/ in American Spanish is almost always [φ] in the pronunciation of speakers of average culture or below is overwhelming (Doman 1969), with the labio-dental pronunciation being characteristic of educated speech only (on the peninsular model). Even well educated speakers may use the "velarized"

---

[6] Doman (1969) is a valuable survey of American dialectal pronunciation of /f/, but it is marred somewhat by her failure to take into account the information available in the *ALPI* and the *ALEA* which shows clearly that the bilabial voiceless fricative [φ] is widespread in rural Spain today, and also by her belief that the various labio-velar pronunciations of /f/ can have no historical connection with the development of the language of the peninsula. By assuming that the original pronunciation of /f/ was everywhere a labiodental [f], she can see no connection between modern American Spanish pronunciation and the ancient developments.

articulation in spontaneous speech (Doman 1969, 427). And in some areas there has been a mixing of the [hφ] and the [φ] so that they no longer correspond to their original phonetic distribution, just as the [h] allophone, at first probably limited to the position before back vowels, was later generalized so that it could appear before any vowel. Only some similar process of generalization of the [hφ] articulation can account for pronunciations such as are found in Ecuador: *juamilia, enjuermo, juin,* etc. for *familia, enfermo, fin.* This sort of pronunciation is found also in Guatemala, and may well exist elsewhere, unnoticed by dialectologists.

Although the evidence seems clear enough that the sounds represented by the letter F in Old Spanish were commonly [φ], [h], and [hφ], as we have seen, we have no way of knowing that the labiodental pronunciation [f] did not also exist, perhaps among more conservative speakers. In the absence of any direct information on articulation in the Middle Ages, we must remain in the dark. At any rate, it is clear that in modern standard Spanish, the labiodental represents the educated norm for all words written with F. The essential question then is, how did the [f] become functionally distinct from [h] and [hφ]? Probably the cause of this phonemic split is the result of the introduction of large numbers of Latinisms into the Spanish lexicon from the twelfth century onward. The spread of the reform of the liturgy at that same period probably brought with it the reformed pronunciation of written Latin, strongly supported by the large numbers of Gallic clergy brought to Spain to institute the reform. As native clerics were trained in the new pronunciation of Latin, they undoubtedly learned to use exclusively the [f], the pronunciation typical in Gallo-Romance, to represent the letter F. Thus, as Latinisms like *fin, figura, forma, fortuna,* etc. became part of the Castilian vocabulary, the initial consonant would most likely have been pronounced [f] (Wright 1982, 37).

As a result of the reinforcement of the use of [f], there would have been a serious weakening of the phonetic associations among the allophones of /f/. [φ], [hφ], and [h] could appear to be acoustically similar enough to be felt as members of the same phonetic unit, but it is less likely that [f] would continued to be considered just another form of [h] when a great many Latinisms containing [f] entered the language. They could, of course, have remained as *stylistic* variants of the same phoneme for some time, but the potential for a phonemic split began with the possibility of two words with different articulations being given different meanings. Thus, when the word pronounced [fórma] < Lat. FŌRMA took the general meaning 'form, shape', the popularly pronounced [hórma], with the specialized meaning 'shoemaker's last' could then be felt to be a different word, and thus a new phonemic opposition was established. Similarly, when the past participle of the verb *fazer* 'to make, do' < Lat. FACERE was used in the expression *fecha carta* '(this) letter written', the word *fecha,* pronounced [feča] could adopt the meaning 'date', and be phonemically distinct from the popular form of the past participle, *hecho* [(h)ečo]. In a number of examples although doublets were not produced, some forms of words retained the popular [h], e.g., *humo* 'smoke', *a la he!* 'by my faith', other forms were established with the labiodental [f], e.g., *fumar* 'to smoke' < Lat. FUMARE, *fe* 'faith' < FIDE.

The next change that occurred was the gradual loss of [h-], a change which probably began in the region of Burgos, and then spread to both the urban and rural areas of Castile. From then on, the system carried to urban areas in the speech of the educated was one in which [f] could appear initally before either consonants (including semiconsonants) or vowels, or could alternate with zero before vowels. The system in rural Castilian, on the other hand, was more conservative and differed from the earlier one in the loss of [h-] before vowels. This system was carried to all of rural Castile and eastern Andalusia and to Castilianized parts of Leon and Aragon. The loss of [h-] did not spread everywhere, of course, since it was a relatively late innovation. Nebrija, for example, at the end of the fifteenth century, described [h] as a regular part of the phonemic inventory of Spanish. Today [h-] is still found in popular speech in Extremadura, Huelva, Sevilla, Cádiz, Córdoba, Málaga and the western portions of Granada and Almería (Penny 1972a, 470), as well as in many parts of Spanish America. The influence of educated pronunciation on popular pronunciation has been continuous and may have implanted [f] in a number of areas; probably there are stylistic variants of many sorts ranging from the "correct" labio-dental [f] to "vulgar" [φ] with many intermediate sounds between the two extremes.

The allophone [hφ] was not affected by the loss of [h-] and could be retained, as we saw above. Alternatively, before the loss of [h-] had become general it could have given way to the pressure of [h-], e.g., [hwerte] for *fuerte*. This particular solution seems to be rather rare, probably because the use of [h], where retained, is socially condemned as being uncouth (Penny 1972a, 472). A more common solution would be the use of [φ]: [φwerte] which is more likely to be favored because it seems closer to the educated norm.

Another complication in the sixteenth century was the evolution of older /š/ into the velar fricative /x/. Being pronounced in the same area of the mouth, the older [h], in those areas where it had not disappeared, was identified with the new sound (see below for a discussion of the evolution of the sibilants). Thus, today both sounds have merged into one which may be velar [x] or more glottal [h].

The matter of orthography of /f/ in Old Spanish is at times complicated. At the beginning, of course, as long as [φ], [h], and [hφ] were in their original complementary distribution, with solely phonetic factors determining that distribution, the spelling with the letter F would have been considered proper, especially since most of the words with these sounds derived from Latin words spelled with F-. The existence of the aspirate [h-], however, particularly after it had been generalized to the position before all syllabic vowels, would be more noticeable to those from other areas, because of its lack of the labiality that characterized the other allophones.

Castilians may well have been unaware that F represented a labiodental sound in other Romance areas, and even if they noticed the [h] as more different in articulation than [φ] and [hφ], there would have been no need to change the spelling, since the aspirate could easily be considered simply a stylistic variant of [φ] or [f]. Still, as we saw in chapter 4, there were occasional spellings with the letter H-, in the names of places and persons, possibly because the connection with their Latin source was less obvious, and thus the Latin spelling tradition would have exercised less pressure on scribes when writing such words. At the same time, the Latin tradition may, for the most part, have considered the letter H not as a real "letter" (i.e., representing any real sound or phoneme). There is frequent use of the double grapheme FF- in the latter half of the thirteenth century and during the fourteenth century in a number of documents which may be an indication that scribes are trying to use this new grapheme to indicate a conscious differentiation of different sounds (Blake, forthcoming). The relatively sudden use of double FF may well correspond to a desire on the part of scribes to make clear that those words written with it are to be pronounced with the labiodental [f], while the grapheme F can be interpreted as the ordinary aspiration [h], which was now being established as the common prestige norm. Eventually H became the norm in spelling before syllabic vowels in popular words; it has been kept as the spelling norm until today even though it no longer represents any sound in standard educated Spanish. Some words that have become accepted in the standard vocabulary but which came from dialects that preserve the older [h] are now spelled with J, e.g., *jamelgo* 'nag, jade' < FAMĒLICU, *juerga* 'carouse, spree' < OSp. *fuelga* ← *folgar* 'to rest; be idle; to be merry, amuse oneself' < Late Lat. FOLLICĀRE 'to pant' (← FOLLIS 'bellows') (cf. standard *huelga*'strike; leisure') (DCELC II, 930b).

The Merger of /b/ - /ƀ/, /d/ - /đ/, /g/ - /ǥ/

The date of the final merger of /b/ and /ƀ/ cannot be established with certainty. Söll 1964 is convinced that by the eleventh and twelfth centuries the change had already taken place. In order to explain how it was, as pointed out by Alonso, that in medieval documents words containing reflexes of Latin /-p-/ are consistently represented by the letter B and those with the reflexes of Latin /-b-/ and /-v-/ were written with the letter U (1962, 168), Söll supposes that medieval scribes could easily have been drawn to the conclusion that Latin -P- was to be represented by B, just as Lat. -T- and -G- corresponded to Spanish D and G (1964, 93).[7] Can we be sure, however, that scribes would have been so consistent without support from speech? Alonso (1962) studies rimes in the poetry of the fifteenth and sixteenth centuries and concludes that the merger had taken place by the

---

[7] Consistency in writing B where Latin had P would also have depended on a clear recognition of the Latin etyma of Spanish words (Söll 1964, 93).

middle of the fifteenth century, and had its roots in the fourteenth century or possibly even earlier.[8] Once more we would be in error if we concluded that the merger was adopted simultaneously everywhere.[9]

It seems clear too, on the evidence of Portuguese and some modern Spanish dialects, that in the southern half of the peninsula the labiodental articulation of **B** was typical during the Middle Ages (Penny 1976, 158–59). The establishment of the capital of Portugal at Lisbon at an early date meant that its speech became the standard for Portugal, while in Spain the triumph of northern features, which characterizes so much of the phonological history of Spanish, here also ensured the complete merger of the voiced labial consonants. The labiodental [v] was found as late as the sixteenth century in Andalusia and was carried to America (Lapesa 1980, 370) although it soon gave way to the bilabial fricative sound of popular Spanish.

The date of the final merger of /d/ and /đ/ and /g/ and /ɡ/ is no easier to determine than that of the labial merger. Torreblanca (forthcoming/a) points out that until the twelfth century the Arabic letters ﺩ *dāl* and ﺫ *ḏāl* were used to represent Romance /d/ and /đ/ respectively, but from then on both letters were used indiscriminately for either sound. We note too that in the fourteenth century the verbal desinence for form 4, *-des*, began to alternate with forms without the /đ/: *enfiés, entendés*, along with *avedes, olvidedes* (*Libro de la miseria de omne*); *soes, bayaes, yrés, abrés, esteys, darés, tenés* (*Danza de la muerte*) (Lapesa 1959, 177). This sort of change would have been possible only if medial /-d-/ had developed a fricative pronunciation. A reasonable conclusion would be that the merger of all formerly separate occlusive and fricative voiced consonants was complete at about the same time, i.e., the fourteenth century, although the beginnings of the merger may be found much earlier in some areas.

Although the pairs of occlusive and fricative phonemes merged into single phonemes with varying allophones, the distribution of these allophones is not the same everywhere. In some Central American dialects we find the occlusive allophone in some postconsonantal positions that in most other regions utilize the fricative ones (Canfield 1962, 77–88). A reasonable conclusion would be that these articulations are a reflex of an archaic distribution which was still found in the Spanish brought to the New World in the sixteenth century.

---

[8] Alonso (1955) thought that the merger was much later, but later D. Alonso (1962) believes that this opinion was excessively influenced by the Renaissance grammarians on whom he based his studies: "Es muy posible otra interpretación: que no hubiera una gran propagación del fonómeno en esos pocos años del siglo xvi, que lo que se moviera, lo que progresara, fuera el conocimiento de los hechos mismos, sin que éstos sufrieran gran alteración (1962, 160).

[9] The question of whether there really was any further phonemic opposition in the linguistic consciousness of speakers after the fricative pronunciation had been adopted intervocalically is difficult to determine. Alarcos Llorach 1968 thinks that the merger had occurred by the time of Alfonso X in the thirteenth century.

The Further Development of the Sibilants

The system of sibilants in Old Castilian, especially in the standard that was codified in Alfonsine Spanish, was the result of the development of the Latin sibilant (both single and geminate) and the various palatalizations of Latin consonants in Late Latin and early Romance, as described in more detail in chapter 4:

	alveolar	prepalatal affricate	palatal
voiceless	/ś/	/tˢ/	/š/
voiced	/ź/	/dᶻ/	/ž/

The spellings fixed as appropriate for the representation of these sibilants were the following:

voiceless	s-, -ss-	ç	x
voiced	-s-	z	j, g (+ e, i)

The letter ç deserves some comment here since it was a new letter and not one inherited from the Latin tradition. The form of the letter developed over a long period of time, and, in fact, it was not until the twelfth century tha the modern form of the cedilla became generalized. The letter had originated in the Visigothic style of handwriting when the letters c and z were combined with the c being placed over the z: ʒ. Gradually the c moved down into the line of writing and the z was written as a sort of appendage. The specialization of the two letters ç and z to represent the voiceless and the voiced phonemes respectively was also a gradual process: "Los escribas de letra visigoda no intentaron ningún empleo distinto de las dos letras z y ʒ; para ellos eran dos modos de escribir la z, y no se les ocurrió usar una para el *sonido sordo* . . . y otra para el *sonoro*" (*Orígenes* §9). It was not until the thirteenth century that this specialization occurred.

The Spread of the Merger of Voiced and Voiceless Sibilants

The system outlined above was, of course, the more conservative one, and contrasted with a less marked system among substantial portions of the population. The latter system, as we saw in the preceding chapter, was probably produced originally under the impact of Basque-Romance bilingualism, and contained only voiceless sibilants in place of the voiced ones. Undoubtedly for a long time it was a popular norm only, restricted to oral usage and avoided by the more conservative upper class speakers. Thus, it could spread to the south with the continued migration of northern Castilian speakers and yet appear only sporadically in documents, since most writers, regardless of their own usage, preferred to follow the literary norm, at least in spelling (Lantolf 1979, 306).

Nevertheless, there are numerous early examples in writing of a confusion of the representations of the alveolar sibilants /s/ and /z/, with -s-, -ss- alternating in the spelling of the same sound. ç and z also seem to be

frequently confused, although here we may be faced with a lack of orthographic standardization as mentioned above. Even so, it is noticeable that
the spelling "errors" that are found appear earlier and in greater numbers
in documents from Castile.[10] In addition to the misspellings in documents
from Galicia from the thirteenth century onward (Alonso 1962, 93). In
documents from Aragon, the substitution of the letter x for earlier LL /ḷ/ in
the fifteenth century reveals the adoption of a norm lacking voiced sibilants.[11] The same thing is found earlier in Leonese (Alonso 1962, 94–95;
Catalán 1956–57, 75) and even in the *Fuero de Madrid* of the thirteenth
century.[12] All of these phenomena indicate that the unvoicing norm had
spread widely but was still resisted in the usage of the court and of those
influenced by it. There is evidence of unvoicing in the early sixteenth
century in American Spanish (Parodi 1976, 124). With the establishment
of the new capital in Madrid in the middle of the sixteenth century, and
with the vast movements of population from northern rural areas to the

---

[10] Some examples from DLE are the following: *mandasen* (147:20), *pectasen* (24), *presiese*
(33), *diesen* (36), *troçiese* (44), *extidiesent* (34) (in the same MS *exissen* also appears, l. 22),
1100, from Frandovínez, twelve km. east of Burgos; *fiço* (153:4), 1197, from Villagonzalo
Pedernales, near Burgos; *ficiere* (155:12), 1200, Palazuelos de la Sierra, Burgos; *uasalos*
(41:33), 1202, from Oña; *uendiesen* (41:31), *enpenasen* (31), *enagenasen* (41:33), *fiziesen*(34),
perdisen (34), 1202, Oña; *pasare* (158:14), 1207, Burgos; *ficiere* (161:12), 1209, Burgos;
ficiestes (162:7), 1211, Burgos; *iacer* (43:18), 1213, Miranda de Ebro (alternating with *iazer*,
lines 30, 40, 44); *diçen* (167:6), 1220, Burgos; *fiçieron* (28:99), 1223, Campó; *ficiere* (171:23),
1224, Hoernillos (Burgos); *façemos* (171:12), 1224, Burgos; *façemos* (174:7), 1225, Burgos;
deçiembre (174:26), 1225, Burgos; *diçen* (169:6), 1220, Burgos; (172:11), 1224,Burgos; (173:8),
1224, Burgos; (175:7), 1226, Burgos; (177:5), 1227, Burgos (all these documents written by the
same scribe); *defaçer* (176:13), 1226, Bugedo de Juarros, southeast of Burgos; *ueçes* (176:9,
11), 1226, Bugedo de Juarros; *criaçon* (91:42), 1237, San Millán de la Cogolla; *contradicim-
jento* (126:15), 1272, Alfaro in Rioja Baja; *diçie* (64:21), 1278, Frías (Briviesca); *fiçolo* (64:19);
saçon (62:84), 1270, Frías; *vaça* (64:27), 1278, Frías; *deçir* (64:27); *façer* (62:53), 1270, Frías;
fiçiemos (62:77) (64:42); *deçiembre* (106:41), 1282, Haro; *ffaçedores* (141:35), 1288, Vitoria.
These are only the examples gathered so far and do not include any from the fourteenth
century onward. They are not only earlier but more abundant than examples from Galicia
and Aragon. Dámaso Alonso's statement regarding these documents is incomprehensible:
"No veo en Castilla la Vieja, repasando los *Documentos lingüísticos*, publicados por Menéndez
Pidal, nada que ni remotamente se parezca a esos resultados de Aragón y Galicia" (1962, 93).

[11] It should be noted too that the examples that Alonso gives from Aragon, which he thinks
indicate an early unvoicing (1962, 91), are, without exception, of words having a sibilant or
affricate following another consonant, e.g., *Belgit, Belchit, Sanxo*, etc. rather than between
vowels. In postconsonantal position, one of the characteristic developments of Aragonese in
precisely this position is the voicing of the voiceless occlusives after liquids and nasals, e.g.,
Lat. PLANTA > *planda*, BANCU > *bango*, SORTE > *suarde*, etc. Since affricates are partially
occlusive, it is not surprising that there should have been some hesitation on the part of
scribes about whether they should be voiced or voiceless in the same position (Zamora
Vicente 1967, 234–43). Alonso remarks in a note: "Es probable que especialmente tras *n*
hubiera una vacilación articulatoria, por lo que toca al punto de articulación y a la sonoridad o
no sonoridad" (91, note 251). If this point is taken seriously, it would be well to be extremely
cautious about drawing any sweeping conclusions regarding an early unvoicing in Aragon.

[12] The occasional preservation of words in Leonese with a voiced consonant which seems
to derive from the old voiced sibilant, e.g., *bodina* 'vocina, juerga' < *vozina, bederro* 'calf' <
bezerro (Maldonado de Guevara 1958–59, 161) or *fader* 'to make, do' < *fazer*, are likely to be
simply the result of sporadic interchanges of consonants at a very early date rather than any
kind of preservation of the voiced sibilants (Catalán 1956–57, 75–76).

cities, the court language, reflecting in writing by and large northern pronunciation features, finally accepted the merger (Sturcken 1969;
Menéndez Pidal 1962).[13] As late as the last decade of the sixteenth century,
there is evidence of a maintenance of the phonemic distinction between
/ś/ and /ź/ in parts of the south (Kiddle 1975, 97), although it was
undoubtedly archaic then.

On the Articulation of the Sibilants

At this point in our discussion, it might be useful to discuss briefly the
matter of the articulation of sibilants in order that we may comprehend
more clearly the subsequent development of the affricates. First, it is important to keep in mind that in the pronunciation of sibilants the acoustic
effect produced is what gives these sounds their essential character, while
the place of articulation is far less important.[14] According to Heffner
1949:"The acoustic analysis of [s] and [z] sounds shows them to have a
principal characteristic of very high frequency, of the order of 6,000 and
7,800 cycles per second." In speaking of the English /s/, he remarks
further:

---

[13] Alonso (1962) (possibly on the basis of his incorrect reading of early Castilian documents) concludes that there must have been some general substratum influence common to
all of northern Spain. Catalán, however, judges this hypothesis unfounded:
[O]n studying the loss of distinction between /v/:/b/ and the voiceless sibilants of the
northern fringe of the Peninsula (from Galicia to Catalonia), he suggests the effect of a late
substratum common to all, without stopping to think that during Romanization (that is
when there were generations of bilingual speakers) no native language covered a similar
area, and that those which were spoken did not belong to the same language family. In
reality, I am not able to understand how the influence of the substratum languages could
be manifest in the Latin of bilingual speakers so that in Romance times, after the formation
of the several Hispanic languages and dialects, a whole series of voiced sibilant phonemes,
developing late and from different origins in different linguistic domains, would tend to
devoice throughout an entire region. A hypothesis based on diffusion seems more plausible to me (1977, note 819).
[14] Alonso analyzes a great number of grammatical descriptions from the sixteenth and
seventeenth centuries and concludes that "z y ç eran APICODENTALES, lo mismo cuando
eran africadas que cuando se hicieron fricativas" (1955, 374). From the quotations which
follow his conclusion, it appears that he gives primary importance to descriptions of the
position of the tip of the tongue, i.e., touching the edges of the upper and/or lower teeth, e.g.,
"1532 Busto: ç 'los dientes cerrados y la punta de lengua en ellos'; h. 1560, Corro: c, 'poniendo la lengua junto a los dos órdenes de dientes" ' etc. Galmés 1962, 53, argues in favor of
the "carácter predorsal o coronal de las sibilantes españoles antes de llegar a la pronunciación
ciceante interdental." This discrepancy is explained by the fact that although both scholars
utilize the same facts, and Galmés adds some to those collected by Alonso, Alonso seems to
put primary attention on the position of the tip of the tongue and assumes that it is necessarily
involved as the principal articulator. Galmés, on the other hand, takes into account the area of
the tongue in which the current of air is constricted to produce the acoustic effect of the
phoneme. Naturally, in dealing with articulators in which there is no clear separation of one
part and another, as in the frontal areas of the tongue, one cannot claim that an articulation
involving the predorsal area necessarily excludes any constriction of the apex. Neither
scholar, however, nor others who have written on the topic, pay much attention to the
manner of articulation of these sounds, although Alonso 1955 refers to it briefly in his
summary of the problem (406). The articulations described can easily fit the pronunciation of
a flat fricative.

This constriction is produced in the alveolar or gingival region by raising the apex of the tongue and the blade just behind it, so that a very small round opening is left over a ditch or groove along the medial line of the tip of the tongue. The breath stream is forced through this narrow groove with relatively high velocity. . . . [V]ery high-pitched sounds are produced as the breath strikes the air around this opening. . . . *The exact point of articulation, or the precise point at which the jet of air is released may vary over a considerable range* (157; emphasis mine).

He points out further that what makes a sibilant different from other types of anterior fricatives is not the position of the tongue: "They differ from [s] and [z] in that the form of the constriction produced is that of the narrow slit and not that of the groove" (158). Hockett likewise points out that different positions of the tongue tip may still produce identical sounds: "It is also possible to make a lamino-alveolar rill spirant; many speakers of English do this for their *s*, holding the tip of the tongue down behind the lower teeth, and the acoustic effect can be quite indistinguishable from that of an apico-alveolar [s]" (1955, 36). (By apico-alveolar Hockett means, "the front edge of the tongue closes against the upper teeth or the gum on both sides. . . ." In other words he is not referring to a sibilant like the apicoalveolar sibilant of Castilian in which there is less of a rill than in the English /s/.) It seems clear, then, that an excess of emphasis on the position of the tip or blade (predorsum) of the tongue does not really help in determining how a sibilant sounds.

/ś/ and /ź/

The original sibilant /ś/ was pronounced with the tongue curved upward in a concave shape. The acoustic quality of the apical /ś/ was undoubtedly much like that of modern Castilian (Navarro Tomás 1957, 105); that is, because of the nature of the space formed by the tip of the tongue near the alveoles, the sibilant quality of the sound was likely to be somewhat different from that of other kinds of sibilants since the channel through which the stream of air passes is a bit broader than that of a narrow rill [s] in which the friction is produced mainly in the predorsal area. As Joos puts it, the apico-alveolar /ś/ "has a lower resonance and sounds rather 'blunt', somewhat like [š], while [s̩] [Joos's symbol for the dorsal [s] has a higher resonance and sounds relatively 'sharp'" (1952, 232). Such apico-alveolar sibilants were formerly found in a much wider area in Europe than they are now (Galmés 1962, Adams 1975).

ç and z

As we saw in chapter 4, originally the sounds represented by these letters were affricates, /t^s/ and /d^z/. The occlusion was probably formed by the contact of the apex of the tongue and possibly the forward part of the blade against the upper teeth and alveoles. The first change that occurred was the loss of this occlusion, which left a fricative articulation that was probably fairly sibilant in character, i.e., formed with a rill in the center of the tongue, of varying degrees of wideness. As a result of this change, the situation of the former affricates was rather like that found in some very conservative northern Portuguese dialects today, in which the distinction between the two different types of sibilants has been maintained through some exaggeration of the distinct qualities of each type (Galmés 1962, 107–08). Thus, the sibilant from the former affricate was probably much like that found today in modern Andalusian Spanish. That is, it could be either a narrow rill sibilant or could have a flatter quality with the air striking a broader portion of the predorsum, producing an acoustic effect that results from lower acoustic frequencies. In other words, its sibilant quality was less noticeable than was that of the apico-alveolar /ś/.

Very probably the articulation of the ç varied in much the same manner as the modern Andalusian fricative varies. This sound is described by Navarro, Espinosa, and Rodríguez Castellano as follows:

> La corona lingual se estrecha contra la parte más baja de la cara de dichos incisivos [i.e., the upper teeth], elevándose en forma más o menos convexa, de la cual participa también el predorso, y el ápice entretanto forma contacto con los dientes inferiores. Hay escasísima diferencia, como se ve, entre esta clase de ceceo y la articulación de la s predorsal o coronopredorsal. Con la misma disposición de los órganos y sin otra modificación que la de dar a la estrechez linguodental una forma más o menos acanalada o alargada, el sonido pasa casi insensiblemente del timbre seseante al ceceante, o viceversa (1933, 270; see also Alonso 1955, 406).

The acoustic effect of this type of articulation could vary slightly as the speaker gave his tongue a narrower space in the center for the air to pass through or a more slit-like opening. As Alonso remarks: "Lo peregrino del timbre de la ç española tenía que consistir en una mezcla de siseo-ciceo" (1955, 403). Because of the variable nature of the articulation, it could be described as being the result of a variety of tongue positions, as we see in the descriptions of early grammarians. It is interesting to note how an observant foreigner, César Oudin, secretary and interpreter of Henri IV of France, tried to describe the sound of ç in 1619, "le ç . . . se prononce avec la langue grasse que nous disons en grassayant, et non pas si rudement que l's" (Alonso 1955, 208).

This kind of sound is probably a rather unstable one since it is neither a pure sibilant or a pure non-sibilant. As Joos 1952 remarks: "[We] may guess that a phonemic opposition of /s̠/ and /s̩/ [i.e., /ś/] would not very long resist heavy social pressure such as is present in situations of dialect mixture" (223). It is likely that this sort of sound would be unstable even in the absence of dialect mixture simply because of the possibility of confusion with the apico-alveolar sibilant. We may assume that it would then tend to move toward either extreme, and, in cases where the rill variant became more frequent, the danger of merger with /ś/ would increase, as in fact happened in most of western Romance,[15] including the Andalusian dialect of Castilian (*ceceo-seseo*).[16]

The date of the deaffrication of ç and z has been disputed. A number of sixteenth century grammarians speak of these consonants as though they were still affricates (Alonso 1955, 365–72)[17] and various authors compare the sounds with the Italian z and zz. However, there are abundant indications that the occlusive element had been lost much earlier, at least in some regions (probably in the north first) and in the lower social strata. Medieval Jews in Spain preponderantly transcribed ç with the letter *samech* rather than the letter *tsade* from the thirteenth to the fifteenth centuries (Galmés 1962, 65–66). This custom would indicate that in popular speech deaffrication had occurred as early as the thirteenth century. No doubt conservative speech retained the affricate pronunciation longer, which might account for the fact that so many sixteenth century grammarians sought to describe (when they did describe rather than simply copy their predecessors) only the "best" speech.

---

[15] The result in French and Portuguese (as examples of most of western Romance) was the elimination of the apico-alveolar sibilant where it existed, and the generalization of the sibilant resulting from the deaffricated /tˢ/ and /dᶻ/:

Latin	French	Portuguese
*PLATTEA (C.L. PLATEA) 'street, square'	*place*	*praça*
*CINQUE (C.L. QUINQUE) 'five'	*cinq*	*cinco*
PRESSA 'haste'	*presse*	*pressa*
SICCU 'dry'	*sec*	*seco*

The same sibilant is found in all these words today in spite of the different spellings which have been retained from a time when they actually represented phonemic differences.

[16] Joos supposes that Old French passed through a stage like that of Spanish, when the older ç lost its occlusion and became a sibilant. There are indications that Old French had an apicoalveolar [ś], probably inherited from Latin, in French words borrowed into Middle English. Many of those which had s in French were borrowed with a hushing sibilant [š]: *casse* > *cash*, *pousse* > *push*, Anglo-Norman *bousselle* > *bushel*, *coussin* > *cushion*, plus the verbs *polish*, *finish*, etc. English speakers probably heard the slightly hushing quality of the OFr. [ś] and interpreted it as the equivalent of the English hushing palatal sibilant /š/. Words in English derived from Fr. ç on the other hand, invariably have /s/, e.g., *face place*, etc. (1952, 230). See also Galmés 1962, 148.

[17] Alonso was convinced that both phonemes were affricates through most of the sixteenth century (1955, 377), and that the ç became deaffricated first, so that by 1600 it was widely pronounced without occlusion (381–82). It seems most unlikely that any great gap of time separated the deaffrication of both consonants. In postconsonantal position the affricate quality was probably maintained longer since the movement from the occlusion required by a liquid or nasal undoubtedly gave the phonetic effect of an affricate. This is one of the facts that invalidates Alonso's claim that the affricate pronunciation lasted until the sixteenth century. He cites (365) words preserved in Judeo-Spanish with an affricate pronunciation as proof that ç and z were still affricates in 1942. Almost all the examples he cites, however, have /l, n, r/ preceding the sibilant: *katordzi*, *kindzi* < *catorze*, *quinze*, etc. The only exceptions are *dodzi* < *doze* and *tredzi* < *treze*, which are probably influenced by the other numbers. As Galmés points out also, these words all result from the contact of a Latin /d/ and an affricate and thus can be seen as simply very conservative pronunciations (1962, 93).

By the end of the sixteenth century, however, even many conservative speakers had adopted the fricative pronunciation. The establishment of the modern interdental pronunciation was a continuing process that evidently did not become firmly fixed until quite late. As pointed out above, it seems likely that once deaffrication had occurred, the resulting fricative was rather unstable and could tend to evolve in the direction of a flat slit fricative or a pure rill sibilant. The tendency to make the sound an interdental would have resulted from the exaggeration of the purely non-sibilant element and the elimination of all sibilant qualities. There is some indication that at least some speakers had an incipient interdental pronunciation of ç very early in sixteenth century. We find the word *capuz* spelled *capud* in 1495, for example (Frago Gracia 1985, 214). Pedro de Alcalá, writing in 1501, describes the pronunciation of the Arabic letter ث *thā'* as follows: "Mas el son y pronunciación de esta letra *c* es de la manera que pronuncian la *c* los ceceosos, poniendo el pico de la lengua entre los dientes altos y baxos" (Alonso 1955, 104). Alonso disregards this description of an interdental sound, claiming it was a "defecto personal." In 1547 there appear such spellings as *Trinidaz*, and *paternidaz* for *Trinidad* and *paternidad*.In the sixteenth century MS of the *Cancionero* of Pedro del Pozo, written in the Arabic alphabet, the Castilian words *ciento*, *cinco*, and *certificado* have their initial consonants transcribed with the letter ث *thā'* (Frago Gracia 1985, 215), representing the interdental voiceless fricative. A Morisco text of the sixteenth century writes the words *ciudad* and *roz* with the ث *thā'*. We may conclude that the authors of these texts had heard the interdental pronunciation to the exclusion of other articulations, at least a few times (Sánchez Álvarez 1979).

It is evident that Alcalá was not describing a generally recognized articulation, however, since other writers do not speak of it. The mixture of the qualities of a rill and a slit fricative made it difficult to describe precisely. For example, John David Rhys, a Welsh writer who lived in Italy for many years, refers to the Spanish pronunciation in the following terms in 1569: "Pues los españoles, junto con los portugueses, aplicada la punta de la lengua a la fila inferior de los dientes anteriores, expulsan cierto silbo sutil y flatuoso por entre los intersticios de los dientes casi juntos, como en riña canina" (Alonso 1955, 157). Juan López de Velasco, writing in 1578, speaks as follows: "El sonido y voz que la ç con cedilla haze es (como queda dicho) el propio que le da su nombre, que se forma con la estremidad anterior de la lengua casi mordida de los dientes, no apretados sino de manera que pueda salir algún aliento y espíritu, como en lo alto del paladar se forma la *s*, de donde nace la dificultad que los estrangeros sienten en pronunciar la ç cedilla, diziendo siempre *se* por *ce* (Alonso 1955, 289–90). This description seems to refer to a pronunciation much like that typical of many areas of modern Andalusia, not quite an interdental but a slit fricative with the tip of the tongue between the teeth ("casi mordida de los dientes").

Juan de la Cuesta in 1584 describes the ç as an affricate while at the same time condemning the widespread confusion of ç and z (in reality the unvoicing of the voiced sibilants). It is interesting to note that he describes the letter z in the following terms: "La z . . . tiene su sonido más floxo, y se pronuncia abriendo algo los dientes y metiendo la punta de la lengua entre ellos, que salga la lengua un poco fuera" (Alonso 1955, 300). This description very clearly refers to an interdental pronunciation, although probably not as pronounced as today. It is curious to observe that an Englishman, John Minsheu, in his 1599 *Dictionarie in Spanish and English* says that the sound of c is like that of *ths*, thus perhaps stressing the interdental quality of the sound as well as its slightly sibilant quality.[18]

Sebastián de Covarrubias, a native of Toledo, in his *Tesoro* of 1610, describes the ç purely and simply as an interdental: "La c con la lengua entre los dientes" (Alonso 1955, 321).[19] During the seventeenth century, the habit of making a pure slit fricative became more strongly established.[20] Apparently by the beginning of the eighteenth century the interdental slit fricative, which has remained until today, was fixed as the normal realization of the former ç z in all of Spain north of Andalusia. At any rate, it is then that we find the first comparisons of the Spanish z with

---

[18] Alonso gives little credit to Minsheu's spelling, and claims that what Minsheu was doing was to copy the earlier work of Richard Percyvall, *The Spanish Grammar*, published in 1591, in which Percyvall stated that ç was pronounced like the English TS "but not altogether so strong upon the *t* . . ." Alonso 1955, 243). Alonso believes that the spelling THS was simply a way of saying the same thing (249). Since it is clear that Minsheu copied extensively from other authors without giving them any credit, Alonso may be correct. Nevertheless, the pronunciation described can easily be that of a flat fricative, pronounced with the tongue held right behind the point of juncture of the upper and lower teeth. The letter s would then be a way of representing the slightly sibilant quality of the articulation.

[19] Alonso 1955 claims that Covarrubias does not mean what he says since he distinguishes ç and z and because, according to him, "entre los dientes" is an old formula for describing the dental pronunciation (321). Thus, Alexo Vanegas in 1531 describes T as being pronounced "poniendo el pico de la lengua entre los delanteros dientes ansí de arriba como de abaxo" (Alonso 1955, 117, note 20). This is no guarantee, however, that Covarrubias was using this style of description rather than actually describing a true interdental.

[20] Alonso makes much of the silence of English writers of the sixteenth and seventeenth centuries with regard to any comparison of ç and z with the English /θ/ (and, as pointed out above, he disregards Minsheu's description of the pronunciation of ç): "Este silencio de los ingleses y la falta completa de comparación con la theta griega en los helenistas españoles tan amigos de comparaciones fonéticas de idioma a idioma, nos fuerzan a limitar el *ciceo* hasta 1600 a un estado inicial" (1955, 404). If we are thinking of the *ciceo* of modern Castilian Spanish, and of the pronunciation of the upper classes of the sixteenth and seventeenth centuries, he is probably correct. Navarro Tomás describes the modern Spanish interdental as follows: "la punta de la lengua . . . se coloca entre los bordes de los incisivos, apoyándose suavemente contra los superiores. . . . El sonido de la *th* inglesa en palabras como *third*, *truth*, se parece mucho al de la española, si bien ésta resulta de ordinario un poco más enérgica y un poco más interdental que la inglesa" (1952, 93). He also remarks that "el efecto acústico de la articulación de la θ es semejante al de la *f*." The early pronunciation of this phoneme, however, was still less interdental and probably somewhat sibilant in nature and thus not really a pure slit fricative, so that English speakers would not have thought of it as exactly comparable to their own /θ/ until such time as it had been exaggerated so as to lose all sibilant quality.

the English /θ/ (Alonso 1955, 409). Possibly English-speaking authors of grammars had felt themselves constrained, before that time, from accepting as "standard" anything but the descriptions of older grammarians (Lapesa 1980, 374).

Çeçeo-zezeo: The Merger of /ś ź/ and /s z/

As was noted above, the opposition between /ś/ and /ź/ and /s/ /z/ < /tˢ/ /dᶻ/ must have become somewhat unstable after the loss of the occlusive element of the affricates. The acoustic quality of /s/ /z/ was undoubtedly closer to that of /ś/ /ź/ than that of the latter sounds to /š/ /ž/ (although, as pointed out below, even these last sibilants were close enough to /ś/ /ź/ to be occasionally confused). Castile and the areas in which northern speech habits predominated avoided the danger of a merger by exaggerating the fricative quality of ç, thus pushing the sound to the interdental slit fricative found today.

The merger of the two sibilants (or pairs of sibilants), however, was the norm for western Romance, if we disregard for the moment the feature of voice. In fact, the only exceptions to the merger were Castilian and some dialects of northern Italy (Tekavčić 1974, 189). Andalusian and American Spanish, on the other hand, followed the trend of the majority of the other western Romance tongues in collapsing the two sibilants into one. The results of the merger are now called *ceceo* or *seseo*, depending on the phonetic realization of the remaining sibilant. In areas in which *ceceo* is found,[21] the acoustic effect of the sibilant is more or less that of an interdental fricative, although a purely interdental articulation is not necessarily a distinctive feature. The so-called "coronal" sibilant, in which the tongue is held flat or is curved downward, with the stream of air passing over most of the area of the predorsum of the tongue, is the articulation found in most of Andalusia. In the *seseo* areas, on the contrary, the sibilant is realized as a rill sibilant, even when the general shape of the tongue is the same as that used in the *ceceo* areas. The rill produces a sound acoustically distinct from the *ceceo* because of the higher frequencies that result from the air passing through a narrow space in the center of the tongue.

In considering the origin of this merger, it is essential to disregard the definitions of the terms *seseo* and *ceceo* given above since they refer only to the *modern* uses of these terms. The term *seseo*, in fact, does not even appear before the early part of the seventeenth century (Catalán 1956, 308). During the Middle Ages the verb *cecear* and its variants, *çacear*, *çaçavear*, and the adjective *ceceoso* were employed as synonyms of *tartamudear* and *tartamudo*, that is 'to stammer, speak with some kind of speech defect, especially, to be tongue-tied' or 'to have an excessively large tongue', 'stammering'. These meanings are documented in writings from

---

[21] A detailed description is found in Navarro, Espinosa, Rodríguez-Castellano 1933.

the thirteenth century through the seventeenth century (Catalán 1956, 311–12).

Along with these meanings of *cecear*, however, in the fourteenth and fifteenth centuries we find what seems to be a different one. A fairly large number of persons are said to "cecear un poco", which may lead us to suspect that what was intended by such an expression was something other than the sudden mysterious increase in the number of persons with some kind of physical defect in their mouths.[22] Our suspicion that *cecear* in many cases did not refer to the condition of being tongue-tied is confirmed by the fact that a number of those so described are at the same time praised as excellent speakers. Thus, the bishop of Burgos, Alfonso de Santa María, is described by Fernando del Pulgar in these terms: "Fablava muy bien e con buena gracia, çeçeava un poco" (Alonso 1969, 129). Another bishop, Don Francisco, from Coria, was said to be ". . . muy gran predicador y çeçeava un poco . . . su órgano resonava muy claro e tenía singular gracia en sermonear." It seems inconceivable that persons having irradicable speech defects caused by some physical incapacity should be esteemed as great preachers, especially in the terms of praise used by Pulgar.[23] Further indication that the term *cecear* represented a feature of speech that was considered to have a kind of charm and grace is a remark in a poem by Fray Iñigo de Mendoza (fl. second half of the fifteenth century) published in 1511, in which a monk is told that he should avoid various kinds of unseemly behavior, including:

no por gracia el cecear
contrahaziendo el galán (Alonso 1969, 129).

It appears from these lines that the *ceceo* was something that one could imitate, a feature of speech that was characterized in certain persons as a "gracia", rather than an incurable physical defect.

Just what this pronunciation was may be inferred from the remark of Pedro de Alcalá mentioned above. There he describes "ceceosos" who pronounce the c with the tip of the tongue between the upper and lower teeth (Alonso 1969, 132). It is fair to conclude, then that along with the traditional meaning of *cecear* 'to stammer, be tongue-tied', there existed another meaning: 'to substitute ç for s'. That this is the appropriate interpretation of the verb is also confirmed by the fact that it is the *only* term used in the sixteenth century when çeçeo became more widespread. What

---

[22] Such a belief evidently underlies Alonso's comment:"En los siglos XIV y XV, y también en los dos siguientes, los ceceosos o zazos (defecto personal, lengua con frenillo) debieron de ser frecuentes en España, a juzgar por el número de personajes históricos y literarios de que tenemos noticias" (Alonso 1969, 128). Catalán 1956 categorizes this remark as an "ingenuo comentario" (313, note).

[23] Alonso, however, apparently found no inconsistency in these contrary notions since he describes the fact that people found a certain charm in this "defect" as something "de capital importancia" (1969, 129).

struck those speakers who continued to distinguish phonemically between /ś-ź/ and /ç-z/ was that *ceceosos* used the sound associated with their own /ç-z/ in place of the apico-alveolar sibilant, thus confusing what they considered two different phonemes. In 1611 Sebastián de Covarrubias gave just this definition: "*Cecear*. Hablar *ceço*, pronunciando la *c* por *s*, como por *señor* dezir *çeñor*" (Galmés 1962, 80). A few years later in 1614, Bartolomé Ximénez Patón says the same thing: "en Sevilla ordinariamente convierten la **s** en **c** y pienso que de vicio, diciendo *Cevillano, ceñor, ci*" (Alonso 1969, 68).

Although this is undoubtedly what had happened, there were those who spoke of an indiscriminate confusion of ç and s. If it is true that /ç/ had replaced the former apico-alveolar /ś/ completely, it is difficult to understand why anyone should have thought that the reverse process also had occurred, i.e., the use of /ś/ in place of /ç/. There are too many references to this sort of thing, however, to be disregarded. Arias Montano, in 1588, in speaking of how Valencians and Andalusians resemble each other, says: ". . . both change *s* for *zz*, and contrarily the Castilian *zz* or *ç* for *s*" (Alonso 1969, 48).[24] The quote from the preceding paragraph by Covarrubias also appears to make the same claim: "Otras tienen el vicio en contrario, que pronuncian la *s* por *ç*, como *sebolla* por *cebolla*." Such statements seem to contradict the claim that *çeçeo* is the substitution of /ç/ for /s/.

If these statements are to be taken in the sense that s refers only to the apico-alveolar sibilant, one would have to conclude that /ś/ continued to exist in those areas in which the phonemic distinction between the two types of sibilants was lost,[25] but it alternated chaotically with ç. If this is true, however, it is necessary to explain how it came about that practically no trace of /ś/ can be found today in any of the areas that practice *ceceo-seseo*.[26] With few exceptions, the sibilant found in these areas is not apico-alveolar at all, but some variant of a sibilant pronounced with the tongue tip *not* near the alveolar ridge (the actual shape of the tongue can vary [Galmés 1962, 81]).

The apico-alveolar /ś/ formerly existed in Andalusia. Transcriptions of Spanish words in Arabic letters most often represented s with the letter ش *šīn*, which stands for the palatal sibilant [š] (Alonso 1969, 111–16). Arabic has another sibilant, س *sīn* which represents a dental sibilant [s] which

---

[24] "Cum utrisque pro *s*, *zz*; et contra pro *zz*, sive pro Castellanorum *ç*, *s* usurpetur."

[25] This seems to be just what Amado Alonso believed actually happened: "El ceceo, *c* por *s*, y el seseo, *s* por *c*, son dos estratificaciones relativamente modernas de un mismo fenómeno fonemático que duró los siglos XVI y XVII: el trueque anárquico de *s* y *c*" (Alonso 1969, 140–41). If this were true, it would be essential to account for the fact that the term *seseo* appears so late, and that *ceceo* is the first, and for many years, the only term used to describe the process of merger.

[26] In Fuente del Maestro (Badajoz) there is *seseo* with an apicoalveolar /ś/ (Galmés 1962, 81), and in a few places in America there are traces of /ś/: in Antioquia in Colombia and some spots in Puerto Rico (Canfield 1962, 79).

could have been used to represent a Romance sibilant, if it had resembled the Arabic sibilant. The distinctively semipalatal quality of the apico-alveolar /ś/ has already been mentioned, so that it seems evident that Arabic writers, who were trying to represent the Romance sound they heard, paid more attention to the palatal quality, and thus preferred to write سٜ *sīn*. We cannot be certain, however, that the non-alveolar sibilant never appeared, since occasionally s is represented by the letter *sīn* (Torreblanca 1981–82), and thus may have existed as an occasional pronunciation. On the other hand, two early authorities, Pedro de Alcalá and Antonio de Nebrija, both state clearly that in the late fifteenth and early sixteenth centuries the Arabic *sīn* was like the ç of Spanish (Alonso 1969, 117), rather than like s, i.e., [ś].

From these considerations the most likely conclusion is that the modern Andalusian and American Spanish /s/ is the descendant of the former ç. How then can we account for the statements that c and s alternated, if, in fact, the apico-alveolar /ś/ had actually been lost? The most plausible explanation is that the term *çeçeo*, and the more recent term *seseo*, had come to have different meanings. In other words, *cecear* had ceased to mean 'to substitute ç for s' and had adopted its modern, more restricted meaning, 'to articulate with a flat or interdental fricative'. This is especially likely since the period when *ceceo-seseo* became established in Andalusia was the same one in which speakers in Castile were exaggerating the ç to make it more of an interdental fricative, a sound less like the older ç, which continued to be pronounced in Andalusia (Lapesa 1957, 81–86).

As long as *ceceo* was used with its older meaning, it was not possible to speak of substitutions of s for ç rather than vice versa. When, however, people began to pay attention to the acoustic effect of the sibilant rather than to the phonemic merger, they would have associated the rill sibilant with the northern apico-alveolar sibilant, rather than the ç, which was now on its way to losing all of its sibilant qualities. Thus, those who used a rill sibilant for both ç and s would indeed be pronouncing s for c, "el vicio en contrario", as Covarrubias says. It was in order to describe this particular pronunciation that the term *seseo* was coined, with a concomitant limitation of the meaning of *ceceo*.

Therefore, it would have been possible for some time for there to have been an overlapping of the older and newer meanings of *ceceo*. Castilian speakers from north of Andalusia who maintained the old phonemic distinction between ç and s used *ceceo* in the old sense, since what they heard was the use of the sound they associated with the letter ç in place of the sound they associated with the letter s. Andalusians who spoke of an alternation of ç and s, on the other hand, were probably referring to the distinction between a flat fricative (*ciceo*) and a rill sibilant (*seseo*). As the old ç became increasingly less sibilant in the north, northern speakers would also have adopted the new meanings of the term *ceceo* (Lapesa 1957, 91). An additional problem was that of spelling; those who now had only one sibilant in their speech had two letters (or four, after unvoicing) to represent it. They were constantly tempted to misspell words, as will be seen below, and such misspellings give the impression of a chaotic mixing of sibilants (Kiddle 1977).

In modern Andalusia, the *ceceo* is considered to be the most popular and least cultivated form of pronunciation, while *seseo* is acceptable in all kinds of discourse, although Andalusians who move to the north will often adopt the distinction between /θ/ and /s/ which they did not have before. Geographically *seseo* is found in the more northern of those areas of Andalusia that do not maintain the distinction between /s/ and /θ/, and also in the city of Seville (Zamora 1967, 301–03, and map next to 308). We do not know if the geographical and social limitations of *ceceo-seseo* were the same in past centuries, but it is at least likely that *seseo* had from the start a greater social acceptability, possibly because it seemed less unlike the northern speech pattern. In America, *seseo* with a dental or predorsal sibilant is universally found, although *ceceo* is occasionally found in a few areas: el Salvador, Honduras, Nicaragua, parts of Venezuela and Colombia and part of Puerto Rico (Canfield 1962, 79).

The date of the origin of *çeçeo* cannot be established precisely, but the *terminus a quo* must necessarily be the same as for the deaffrication of the /ç z/ (which was not necessarily the same for both consonants). This particular change probably began in the thirteenth century as a variant of /tˢ/ and /dᶻ/, as mentioned above, and then spread both geographically and socially, until its final triumph in the sixteenth century in Andalusia. Once the medieval affricates became sibilants, the danger of merger with /ś ź/ became increasingly likely. As we saw above, the closeness in the points of articulation and the acoustic similarity made it imperative to alter the pronunciation in some way if these pairs of consonants were to be kept distinct. Even in the dialects of relatively isolated and conservative areas of northern Portugal that have kept the distinction, unlike the standard Portuguese of Lisbon which has followed the common western Romance path of *seseo*, there has been an exaggeration of the articulation of both. The /ś/ has become more palatal (closer to [š]), and the ç more sibilant (Galmés 1962, 107–09).

Since it is in the fourteenth and fifteenth centuries that we hear of historical personages noted for being said to "cecear un poco", it is a reasonable conclusion that almost as soon as the deaffricated forms of /ç z/ became possible variants in Castilian, some speakers began to merge them with /ś ź/. This feature was not a consistent one, but was limited to certain words, or, possibly, to certain types of situations, and was considered to be a "gracia," as mentioned previously. At first limited to certain social situations, it was then adopted by the common people of Seville and by the gypsies who arrived there in the early part of the sixteenth century (Catalán 1956, 316), from where it spread to other areas of Andalusia. It seems that by the end of the fifteenth century, *çeçeo*, realized phonetically as a voiceless dorsodental fricative (Catalán 1956, 327), already characterized the speech of the great mass of Sevillians, although undoubtedly the conservative upper classes would have preserved the Toledan norm for a longer period.

At any rate, as early as the formation of the *Cancionero de Baena*, that is, before 1445, the compiler of the collection, Juan Alfonso de Baena, born near Marchena (the southeastern portion of the modern province of Seville), makes certain spelling errors that reveal, if not complete *çeçeo*, at least a beginning: *çatan* for *Satan*, *çedal* for *sedal*, *escaçeza* for *escaseza*, *çenado* for *senado*, *bruçelas* for *Bruselas*. In 1475 in the Gaya of Pedro Guillén de Segovia, we find *çemençera* for *semençera*, *çenzilla*, -o, for *senzilla*, -o, *deçensiones* for *disensiones* (Lapesa 1957, 72–73). Although some of these examples can be considered the result of assimilations or dissimilations within words already containing ç or s, the fact that they can occur so often reveals, if nothing else, a great insecurity about their distribution. In 1487, in a book of accounts of Pedro de Toledo, almoner of Isabel the Catholic, and canon of Seville, we find many examples of misspelling such as *Roblez, inglez, fijoz, Andrez, Blaz*, with z being written in place of s, and others with the opposite phenomenon: *viscayno, sanches, Gomes, durasnos, Beatris*. Although these examples only reveal confusion in syllable-final position, a naturally weak position in which there are some confusions in writing as early as 1324 (Alonso 1969, 79ff), they are an indication of the direction of the evolution of the sibilants. In Granada, in the oldest documents preserved in the Archivo Municipal dated in 1495, we find a number of examples of confusion of sibilants: *disen, faser, plaser, aseyt, servas*, etc. In other documents we find *haser, disen* (1500), *pontesuela* (1501) (Menéndez Pidal 1962, 121).

Given the date of the confusion of the sibilants, there can be no serious doubt that the *seseo* of American Spanish derives from the *çeçeo* of Andalusia.[27] From the very beginning of Spanish-American writing, the merger is evidenced: from Mexico *maís, razo* for *raso, calsas* for *calças, piesas* for *pieças, ortalisa* for *hortaliza, sinquenta* for *cincuenta*, etc. (1525), in Cuba *çurto* for *surto, oçequias* for *obsequias* (1539) (Lapesa 1980, 377), from Colombia *benefisiado* for *beneficiado, averiguasion* for *averiguación, justisia* for *justicia, feneser* for *fenecer, depozito* for *depósito* (Cock 1969, 105; Parodi 1976). Although the confusion may not have been universally found from the very beginning, it soon became established as the norm.

---

[27] In contrast with Alonso (1969), most modern scholars do not believe that it is possible to conceive of parallel but independent developments in Spain and America (e.g., Kiddle 1977). Danesi points out that the one really solid datum for the so-called "andalucismo" of American Spanish is the *seseo*. He even goes so far as to conclude that "neither can it be established, with any degree of certainty, that American *seseo* is due directly to Andalusian influence" (1977, 193). The real question is what is meant by "directly." There can be no question that the merger of ç and s was well under way in Andalusia at the end of the fifteenth century. Danesi questions the statistics on the numbers of Andalusian settlers in the early days of the exploration of America without taking into account that in linguistic evolution the outcome of phonetic development is not determined by some sort of democratic process, with the majority necessarily winning. He is on much more solid ground when he points out that when phonological systems are in contact, mergers are much more likely to occur.

The *seseo* was probably adopted because it seemed more socially acceptable (Lapesa 1956).

The Shift from /š/ to /x/

A further change that is related to the preceding ones is the shift of the palatal hushing fricative to a velar fricative. With the deaffrication of /tˢ/ and /dᶻ/, Castilian had three sibilant phonemes (if we disregard for the moment the voiced sibilants which were disappearing). All of them were articulated in the front region of the mouth. The acoustic quality of the palatal /š/ made it clearly distinct, and yet, because of the articulation of the /ś/ somewhat toward the palate, the latter phoneme often had a slightly palatal quality. As we saw in chapter 4, a number of words containing /ś/ had developed alternate forms with /š/ in Old Spanish, e.g., *xerga, serga* 'serge, coarse cloth' < SĒRICA, *tiseras, tixeras* 'scissors' < TONSŌRIĀS, etc.

In the fifteenth and sixteenth centuries a goodly number of words had alternate forms with /ž/ (spelled J or G + E, I) in place of /z/: *celosía–celogía, frisol–frijol, iglesia–eclegia igleja–igreja* (already in the *Cid*), *quise–quije, resistir–registir, visitar–vigitar, residente–regidente*. The reverse process is also seen, with forms with /ž/ being replaced by ones containing /ź/, although such alternations seem to be rarer and later than those listed above: *relisión–religión, colesio–colegio, disistir–digestir, mesor–mejor, parasismo–parajismo, sanguisuela–sangijuela*. Such shifts of individual words, however, were simply isolated cases of change of one phoneme to another aided by general phonetic similarity, rather than a regular phonetic development (Alonso 1947).[28]

The process of exaggerating the acoustic quality of the ç to make it more clearly distinct from the /ś/ was at work on the palatal /š/ as well. The fact that /ś/ and /š/ had the similarity demonstrated above can be seen to be sufficient stimulus to induce speakers to retract the articulation of /š/ so that it would be even less likely to be confused with /ś/ by becoming a distinct velar fricative /x/. Thus, from a system of three sibilants, all articulated in a rather restricted area in the anterior part of the mouth, the modern system developed by exaggeration of the two extreme members of the group so that they lost their sibilant quality and became clearly distinct from /ś/, which could then remain without any change. Another factor favoring the change was the lack of any velar fricative corresponding to fricatives at other points of articulation (Alarcos 1968, 272).

The period in which this last change became more widely used is toward

---

[28] It is curious to note that when such alternate forms were created, they went quite consistently in the direction of /š ž/ rather than vice versa. In the case of /ś/ > /š/, it may well be, as we saw in chapter 4, that the absence of any inherited Latin words beginning with [š-] induced speakers to fill up this space in the phonological pattern. On the other hand, there were many words beginning with [ž-].

the middle and end of the sixteenth century. It may have started some time before 1550, but so far only a few bits of evidence have been found before 1568. In 1517 Torres Naharro wrote the exclamation commonly spelled *hao*, with the spelling *Jau!* (Canellada 1978), and in 1519 a play published in Valencia has the spelling *hentil* instead of the usual *gentil* (Frago Gracia 1977–78). In 1547 *hermanía* is found in place of *germanía*, although in this example there may be some influence of the word *hermano* (Lapesa 1980, 379). In recently discovered letters written in 1568 and 1569 by a Sevillano residing in America we find spelling errors that indicate that the former /š/ had already become identified with the aspirate derived from /f/. Thus, G is used to spell the /x/ found in modern Spanish, and also the [h] < /f/, e.g., *trugo* 'he brought' < *truxo*, *guntamente* 'together' for *juntamente*, *giso* 'he did' for *hizo*, *garan* 'they will do' for *harán* < *farán*, *gerera* for *Herrera*, *garta* 'full' for *harta* < *farta* (Boyd-Bowman 1975, 2). In the work of Antonio de Torquemada in 1574 the sound represented by x and J are described as being pronounced "con lo último del paladar cerca de la garganta, teniendo la boca abierta, y saliendo la pro- nunciación entre la lengua y el paladar" (Quilis and Rozas 1963, 447). This description seems to be that of the *ich-laut* of German [ç].

The new velar pronunciation alternated for some time with the older palatal, as can be seen in the way that Cervantes' *Don Quixote* was trans- lated, in French as *Don Quichotte* and in Italian as *Don Chisciotte*. Cer- vantes, having been born before the middle of the sixteenth century, very likely maintained the older pronunciation in his own speech. The new pronunciation was originally characteristic of low class persons. Thus, the *Buscón* of Quevedo, whose protagonist received a lesson in how to speak like one of the criminal class of Seville: "Haga vucé cuande hablare de la *g*, *h*, y de la *h*, *g*: y diga conmigo *gerido*, *mogino*, *mohar*" (Lapesa 1980, 379). From 1614 on, most grammarians mention the [x] or [ç] articulation and by the middle of the seventeenth century /x/ had become the norm of the court, and has remained standard until today (Kiddle 1965, 74).

One effect of the new velar fricative was a confusion with the aspiration resulting from the shift of /f-/ to /h-/. Although the aspirate [h] had disappeared in northern Spain, it was still living in the southwest (Anda- lusia, Extremadura and adjoining regions). When the new /x/ became established, it could not be distinguished from the older [h]. This particular merger may account for the fact that the velar is pronounced with less friction than in Castile and with a more pharyngeal quality in many areas, especially in the south and in American Spanish (Menéndez Pidal 1962, 138). Another factor may account for the tendency toward a pharyngeal quality for the Castilian /x/ (which might be represented with a different symbol in order to distinguish it from a slightly more forward [x], for example [X]. Since in the Andalusian and American system the *ceceo-seseo* merger had reduced the system of sibilants to two, with the old alveolar sibilant pronunciation having disappeared altogether, the movement of the /š/ to the posterior part of the mouth did not have to go as far as it did in the northern Castilian system in order for it to be clearly distinguished from the front sibilant. In the regions in which the apico-alveolar sibilant /ś/ still existed, the same degree of movement backward from the sibilant would have taken the /š/ closer to the pharynx (García 1976). It is, however, not especially the position of the posterior fricative that distinguishes Andalusian and American Spanish from Castilian, but the degree of closure, which tends to be much greater in Castilian, producing greater friction. The lesser degree of friction found in Andalusian and American Spanish is undoubtedly due to the identification of the new [x] with the old [h].[29]

The Merger of /l̬/ and /y/: Yeísmo

The difference in the realization of /l̬/ and /y/ is often fairly slight. In the pronunciation of the palatal fricative /y/ the apex of the tongue is not involved directly, except in so far as it tends to point downward and touch the back of the lower teeth, while the blade of the tongue makes no contact at all with the palate (Navarro Tomás 1952, 129). In the articulation of the palatal lateral /l̬/, in contrast, the tongue makes a much wider contact with the palate so that the air may pass through the sides of the mouth or through one side or the other (Navarro Tomás 1952, 133–34).[30] Any degree of relaxation in the articulation of /l̬/ can serve to make it resemble the /y/. In the fifteenth century there is occasional documentary evidence that such a relaxation was occurring sporadically in some areas of Aragon and portions of eastern Castile.

In one manuscript of the *Libro de Alexandre* (P) is found *llago* for *yago* 'I lie down', while in a glossary of El Escorial, dated about 1400 examples such as *llema* for *yema* 'egg yolk', *callado* for *cayado* 'shepherd's crook', *papagallo* for *papagayo* 'parrot'. In other Aragonese sources are *capisayllo* for *capisayo* 'mantelet', *rallo* 'unglazed porous jug', derived from the verb *rayar* 'to run (of water), drip', *bedollo* 'pruning hook' < **vedoyo* (Corominas 1953, 83–84).

Since all instances we know of show that when such sounds are merged, it is the [j] that invariably absorbs the lateral, it is surprising to note that these examples are of what might better be called *lleísmo*, the substitution of /l̬/ for /y/. It is more likely, however, that the examples we see represent cases of hypercorrection, indicating that there must have been a

---

[29] García (1972, 112) believes that the change of /tˢ/ to /θ/ must be later than the shift of /š/ > /x/, but, as we have seen, the beginnings of interdentalization date before the shift to a velar fricative. The latter change, however, was completed before final identification of the older sibilant with a completely interdental sound. In other words, the first shift took much longer to go to completion than the second one so that that both overlapped only partially in time.

[30] A comparison of the palatograms in the pages mentioned in Navarro Tomás (1952) shows clearly much greater contact of the front part of the tongue in the articulation of /l̬/ as opposed to /y/.

strong reaction against the tendency toward merger. There are a few examples of /l̦/ being written Y: in another MS of *Alexandre* is found *yeva* for *lleva* 'he carries' (Corominas 1953, 86), and possibly a close search of sources would bring to light some more. Some of the hypercorrect forms resulting from resistance to the tendency have become part of the standard lexicon of Castilian: *grulla* 'crane' < OSp. *grúa*, *pulla* 'cutting remark, dig' < OSp. *púa, puya, llanta* 'rim of a wheel' < Gascon *yante*.

In those areas which show that the merger existed as a sporadic variant, the reaction against it was evidently sufficiently strong to eliminate the incipient yeísmo, but the same tendency toward merger broke out once again in the sixteenth century. Toward the end of the fifteenth century, one example is found in Toledo: *ayo* for *hallo* 'I find' and the hypercorrect form *sullo(s)* for *suyo(s)* 'his, her' (Lapesa 1980, 383). Numerous examples are found in America written by Spanish colonists: Mexico City, 1527, *contrayen* for *contrallen*; Honduras, 1528, *ayá* for *allá*; Mexico, 1532, *papagallos* for *papagayos*, Mexico City, 1537, *hoyando* for *hollando*; Cuzco, 1549, *cogoio* for *cogollo*; Mexico City, 1574, *allan* for *hayan*; Venezuela, 1575, *papagallos* for *papagayos*, plus several more (Parodi 1977, 243–44). In Puebla, Mexico, letters written by a dyer from Brihuega in Spain in 1581, reveal several cases of evident merger: *vallan, hayarés, salla, alla, valla, yamáis* for *vayan, hallarés, saya, haya, vaya, llamáis* (Guitarte 1971).

As far as it is possible to identify the authors of these examples, there is no one geographical area from which all come, although all those who are identified come from areas that are today *yeístas*, Santander, Valladolid, Seville, Ciudad Real. Nor can it be said that all are clearly examples of a sound change in progress. In several words, it is likely that there have been some lexical influences or confusions; thus the present subjunctive of *haber, haya*, resembles the present tense of *hallar* 'to find', and the adverb *allá* 'there'. In the case of *papagayo* 'parrot', there may have been some confusion with *gallo* 'rooster', and the verb *hollar* 'to tread, trample' may have influenced the spelling of *hoyo* 'hole', and vice versa (Parodi 1977, 245). Nevertheless, there are other examples where such influence is not evident.

Therefore we may conclude that the merger of /l̦/ and /y/ was an incipient variable which would have been supported in some cases by such lexical influence. It probably became an obligatory rule in the speech of the lowest classes, probably first in Andalusia. There is some indication of the change in the representation of the speech of black characters in the sixteenth century dramas, *yeísmo* is constantly found (Chasca 1946, 337).[31] In

---

[31] One may be skeptical of how much reliance can be placed on what are fundamentally formalized representations of the speech of foreigners. Most of the features characteristic of this type of language have little relation to the speech of native speakers of Spanish, e.g., confusion of vowels, liquids, etc. The choice of *yeísmo*, in spite of that, may not unreasonably be considered to be a borrowing from the speech of the uneducated.

the early seventeenth century a story written by a Morisco after the expulsion of the Moriscos in 1609 also constantly mixes the spelling LL and Y.[32]

The spread of the merger in Spain and America is not easy to follow. It was not considered an acceptable form of speech and thus we can only find sporadic traces of it in writing from time to time, traces that have been increasingly discovered in recent years and will undoubtedly be augmented in time. The merger is found in America from the beginnings of the conquest, and although it is clear that it did not find the rapid acceptance that the *seseo* did, it may have become standard in the speech of certain regions long before it was acceptable anywhere outside of the lowest classes in Spain (Parodi 1977, 247). Thus, we find that in Peru toward the end of the seventeenth century, it was characteristic enough of the speech of the inhabitants of Lima that a satiric poet from Jaén, D. Juan del Valle Caviedes, could write several strophes mocking those who pronounce /y/ instead of /ļ/, writing words like *mirayas, miyones, batayas, estreyas*, etc. instead of *mirallas* 'to look at them', *millones* 'millions', *batallas* 'battles', *estrellas* 'stars'. He also makes fund of those who substitute /ļ/ for /y/ with words like *aller, ballo, desmallo, llo* instead of *ayer* 'yesterday', *bayo* 'bay (color)', *desmayo* 'faint, swoon', *yo* 'I', etc. (Alonso 1954, 76–77). In the title of one of the poems, the author speaks of the merger as being characteristic of the native-born inhabitants of the city (Guitarte 1971, 189), while those who wish to avoid this type of pronunciation fall into the opposite error of hypercorrection.

In spite of the spread of the merger to many parts of America, it has not become general in American Spanish, since most conservative areas still maintain the distinction: Paraguay, the regions of Argentina closest to Paraguay, and the Andean areas of Bolivia, Peru (excluding Lima and other coastal areas), Ecuador, and Colombia (Zamora 1966, 76–77; Paufler 1970). Not all areas that maintain the opposition between the two phonemes realize them in the same way. Thus, in Ecuador, in the conservative areas, the /ļ/ is realized as a palatal sibilant [ž] while /y/ is a simple palatal fricative (Alonso 1954, 70). The merger spread to a number of regions in southern Spain, although not all of Andalusia has become *yeísta* even today. In the provinces of Seville, Málaga and Huelva, a number of places still distinguish the two phonemes (ALEA, T. 6, Map 1703).

In the nineteenth century the merger spread to the north and had reached Castile by 1930, although it was still only a variable and had not

---

[32] Guitarte (1971, 182, note 7) is skeptical that the language of this Morisco actually reflects that of the Andalusian dialect: "¿Será posible que el relato revela influencias del árabe en sintaxis, como muestra abundantemente Galmés, y que la fonética, en cambio, esté libre de toda interferencia?" The question of syntactic influence has nothing to do with phonetics in this case, at any rate, since, as Galmés points out, Hispano-Arabic writers never confused /ļ/ and /y/ when they represented Romance words. Their custom was to use either letters for LI (indicating the palatal quality of /ļ/) or a double L (transliterating the Castilian spelling). Even more importantly, the *aljamiado* literature of the Moriscos rarely fails to distinguish the two consonants and even the most uncultivated ones maintained the distinction by pronouncing /ļ/ as [li] (Galmés 1957, 283–84).

yet become the norm in all parts of New Castile at that time (Navarro Tomás 1964). Now that Madrid has become *yeísta* (with rare exceptions), the merger has become the urban norm for the rest of the country so that younger speakers consider the maintenance of the distinction old-fashioned and/or rustic. As one scholar puts it, in the minds of many, it is thought of as "un rasgo rural del que hay que desprenderse como de abarcas o alpargatas" (Lorenzo 1966, 26).[33] In South America also, it is spreading as an urban norm in places which formerly had distinguished the two phonemes, as in Bogotá, for example (Montes Giraldo 1969).

The Structure of the Syllable and Syllable-Final Consonants

The preponderance of open syllables in Spanish from earliest times, and the drive to make all syllables as open as possible had had a continuous effect on syllable-final consonants. A number of consonant groups were simplified in Late Latin (chapter 3), thus producing even more open syllables, and, as we saw in the previous chapter, the last wave of syncope that eliminated all posttonic vowels except for /a/ in earliest Castilian, produced a number of new closed syllables in medieval Spanish. For the most part, those closed syllables which ended in permissible consonants (sibilants, liquids, and nasals) have remained until today (pp. 200–02).

With regard to the nasals, there has been a general assimilation to the point of articulation of the following consonant. Thus, we find that the early forms like *comde, comdessa, limde, semda* all became *conde, condessa, linde, senda*. In the case of the bilabial fricative /b/, there was a further weakening of pronunciation so that by the fourteenth century, the bilabial had become in essence a semivowel: *cabdal, cabdiello, debda, cibdad* were usually *caudal, caudillo, deuda, ciudad*. If the vowel preceding the B was a back vowel, the semivowel was absorbed: *cobdo > codo, dubdar > dudar*. In the case of *bebdo* 'drunk' < BIBITU, there has been a shift of accent with the semiconsonant becoming /o/, *beodo*.[34] The group /-dg-/ has continued as before, although with the establishment of the new interdental fricative the former DG is now spelled ZG, e.g., *juzgar* 'to judge' < *judgar*.

Neutralization of /-l/ and /-r/

Very early there are some signs that syllable-final liquids were being merged. Some examples from Mozarabic documents in the twelfth century

---

[33] Lorenzo speaks of how the tone set by Madrid has spread to other cities: "La conquista casi absoluta de Madrid para el *yeísmo*, del que nos defendemos románticamente escasos representantes, hace posible ... conquistas espectaculares, como la que se advierte en algunos islotes prácticamente sometidos a la influencia masiva de los yeístas, pero rodeados de tierra 'irredenta' ' (1966, 26).

[34] The special development of *beodo* can possibly be explained by the existence of the verb *embebdar* 'to get drunk', in which the sequence *-eud-* would have been incompatible with a pretonic position (Malkiel 1975–76, 486). If this conjecture is acceptable, then the adjective must have developed in close association with the verb.

are *Arbarez* for *Alvarez, Balnegrar* for *Valnegral, menestrare* for *menes-tral, carrascal* for *carrascar, senar* for *senal* (the last two examples from the *Fuero de Madrid,* dated before 1202) (Lapesa 1980, 385). From the thirteenth century we find *arcarde* along with *alcalde* (1246, Ocaña). Given the paucity of examples and the fact that these early examples all involve words in which there are at least two liquids, perhaps what we see is a dissimilation rather than a true neutralization. Something similar is seen in the metathesis of /r/ and /l/ in some semilearned words, *milagro* 'miracle' < OSp. *miraglo* < MĪRACULU, *peligro* 'danger' < OSp. *periglo* < PERĪCULU. Dissimilation is evident in a later example sometimes considered important because associated with a famous poet. The last will and testament of Garcilaso in 1529 specifies that he was to be buried in *San Pedro Martil* for *San Pedro Martir.* Most of the other examples from the fourteenth and fifteenth centuries involve words with at least two liquids.

When, however, we find *solviendo* for *absorbiendo* in 1448, and *comel* for *comer* in a manuscript of 1521, *Aznal* for *Aznar* in 1525, *alçobispo* for *arçobispo* and *silven* for *sirven* in 1576, and especially when the final /-r/ is omitted altogether as in examples like *hazé* for *hazer* (1498, Tenerife), *quexame* for *quexarme* (1568–69, Mexico), *servidó* for *servidor* (1560, Arequipa), *repatimento* for *repartimento* (1560, Quito), *muje* for *mujer* (1586, Quito), etc., plus words ending in a vowel but written with a final -R, it is clear that we are dealing with another phenomenon. The weakening of the pronunciation of /-l/ and /-r/ had reached a point in some areas that they were no longer clearly distinguished in syllable-final position. The resulting articulation may be similar to that of the lateral in other positions. Thus, in modern Andalusia a commonly found realization of the archiphoneme of liquidity is simply an alveolar fricative [ɹ], an alveolar flap [r], more rarely a multiple trill [r:] or an alveolar lateral [l]. Even rarer are a fricative somewhere between a lateral and an alveolar fricative [ɹ̣], a pharyngeal aspirate [h], a semivowel [i], a palatal lateral [l], or a cacuminal lateral [l] (ALEA, T. 6, map 1720). Similar realizations are found in America.

The Aspiration of Syllable-Final /-s/

Related, in part at least, to the preceding phenomenon is the weakening of syllable-final /-s/ into an aspiration which may eventually become so weak that it disappears. The earliest written examples so far are a number of words from the late fifteenth century which omit the final -s of the plurals, e.g., *mandamo* (1467), *juego vedados, todas la otras* (1499) (Frago Gracia 1985, 298). A frequently cited form is from an autograph note by Fernando Colón, the son of the admiral, in which the name *Sophonisba* is written *Sofonifa* (Lapesa 1980, 387). The F written for sв may reflect both the aspiration of the /-s/ > [-h] and its subsequent unvoicing of the voiced bilabial fricative, to [φ]. Increasing evidence of a weakening of the articulation of /-s/ is found in documents from the end of the sixteenth and the beginning of the seventeenth centuries. In 1550 is found *para que vo lo digan* with *vo* for *vos* (Frago Gracia 1985, 298). In 1575 a letter written by a musician from Toledo spells *muestra* twice as *muetra*. Twenty years later another manuscript omits final /-s/ in a number of words: *la puertas, los maestrasgo, la casas*, etc. Letters written by persons from Seville in America show a loss of final /-s/ from the middle of the sixteenth century onward: *los quale* (1556), *soy* for *sois* (1560), *vos enbiaste* (1560) for *vos embiastes, decanso, decisey, quedavadi*, etc. for *descanso, dieciséis*, and *quedábades* (1568–69). Such examples indicate that the weakening and loss of final /-s/ so characteristic today of Andalusia and much of Spanish America, must have been well established at least among the lowest social classes by the end of the sixteenth century.[35] Undoubtedly more examples can be found by further examination of early documents.

The origin and causes of this particular shift have not been extensively studied. It has usually been considered to be an isolated phonetic shift characteristic of Andalusian Spanish, and, by extension, as in the case of the *ceceo-seseo*, to American Spanish (Walsh 1985, 231–32). The increasing amount of evidence that this change is not a late one, but rather can be documented extensively in the sixteenth century, makes us suspect that it is not isolated at all but is intimately connected with the reorganization of the Old Spanish sibilants discussed above. We recall that the palatal sibilant /š/ shifted its point of articulation back farther in the mouth to a velar or pharyngeal articulation, with a consequent merger with the results of the aspiration of /f/. It could be asked then whether there is any connection with the aspiration of syllable-final /-s/. In other words, could it be that syllable-final /-s/ was articulated by some speakers with a palatal realization?

Modern Portuguese has just such an articulation, e.g., *estas portas* is articulated as [éstašpórtaš], and this articulation is attested as early as the thirteenth century in the *Cancioneiro da Ajuda*, e.g., *Lixboa, seix*, and *dex* for *Lisboa, seis*, and *dez* (Walsh 1985, 236, n. 3). Such an articulation existed in some Leonese dialects and is attested in some sixteenth century texts which attempt to represent low-class pronunciation. Thus, Lucas Fernández, from Salamanca, writes *oyxte* for *oíste* and other similar forms, and Bartolomé de Torres Naharro, from Estremadura, puts in the mouth of rural characters forms like *ex habrado* and *caxcos* for *es hablado* and *cascos* (Walsh 1985, 237).

Although Andalusian is definitely a dialect of Castilian, the conquest of Andalusia was a joint enterprise of Castile and Leon, and several features of Leonese dialects are attested in Andalusian. For example, the raising of final /-e/ and /-o/ to /-i/ and /-u/, the sporadic substitution of /r/ for /l/ in onset clusters, e.g., /pr-/ and /br-/ for /pl-/ and /bl-/, and the velarization of word-final /-n/. In other words, the palatal articulation

---

[35] Present day realizations of -s are discussed in Zamora Vicente 1968, 319–21, and can be seen in ALEA, T. 6, maps 1707, 1725–1732.

attested in Leonese would not have been the only phonetic feature to crop up on southern Castilian. A recent study of the origin of the resettlers of Jerez de la Frontera shows that 45 per cent were natives of Leonese- or Galician-Portuguese-speaking areas, and a large contingent of Galicians was among the settlers of Seville after its conquest by Fernando III. A large number of Leonese participated in the settlement of other southern areas too, so that although the dominant dialect was Castilian, it undoubtedly was strongly colored by Leonese features (Walsh 1985, 239–40). This would have been especially true of subphonemic features such as a palatalization of syllable-final /-s/.

If then this palatal articulation was a wide-spread feature of southern Castilian at the time that the Old Spanish sibilant system was being shifted to its modern form, it would be only natural that it would have also been affected in the same way. Speakers with a palatal articulation of final /-s/ would have had no way of knowing that this sound was any different from any other /š/. There is evidence of such a change in other areas remote from Andalusia whose dialect is derived from Leonese, such as Tudanca in Cantabria, and Andiñuela in the Maragatería region of southwestern Leon where it is the oldest speakers who typically aspirate final /-s/ (Walsh 1985, 241–243). The conclusion that aspiration is not an isolated phonetic feature spreading to the north from Andalusia but rather just one more phonetic result of the change from the Old Spanish sibilant system to the modern one is a very reasonable one.

Groups of Consonants in Learned Words

The tendency to weaken syllable-final consonants had an effect on the numerous words that were being added to the Spanish lexicon during the late Middle Ages and the Renaissance from classical sources. Learned words became increasingly frequent beginning in the fourteenth century with the great work of Alfonso X. Those words that contained consonant sequences that were uncommon in popular Spanish tended to be simplified according to the general tendency to vocalize or eliminate syllable-final consonants, especially those other than nasals, liquids, and sibilants. Thus, most of these consonants in such words were simply omitted:

	Full Form		Simplified Form
/-kt-/	*efecto*	/-t-/	*efeto*
	perfecto		*perfeto*
	respecto		*respeto*
	secta		*seta*
/-pt-/	*aceptar*	/-t-/	*acetar*
	baptismo		*bautismo*
	concepto		*conceto*
/-kθ-/	*afección*	/-θ-/	*afición*
	lección		*lición*
	perfección		*perfeción*

	Full Form		Simplified Form
/-gn-/	*dign-o, -ificar*	/-n-/	*din-o, -ificar*
	magnífico		*manífico*
	significar		*sinificar*
/-mn-/	*columna*	/-n-/	*coluna*
	solemnidad		*solenidad*
/-mpt-/	*prompto*	/-nt-/	*pronto*

Of course, we cannot be certain in earlier periods whether the spelling of a learned group meant that its pronunciation was any different from that of words spelled with simplification. Only when the educational system and formal practice required that all consonants be pronounced were the simplified forms generally rejected. The influence of printing and learning and the Academy have tended to work together to impose the forms of words with learned sequences as the ones acceptable in standard literary Spanish. During the Middle Ages and Renaissance and the Golden Age, the reduced forms could be used in literary works as well as in popular speech with no special stigma attaching to them. The reduced forms since then have been relegated to popular and uneducated speech.

In a few cases one of the forms has become associated with a specific meaning of the original word and thus a doublet is created. Thus, *respeto* has continued the meaning of 'respect, esteem', with the learned form is restricted to use in the expression *con respecto a* 'with regard to'. *Afición* has been limited to the meaning 'fondness, taste for something, esp. a game or sport', while *afección* has kept the more general meaning of 'affection'.

Consonant Clusters: /-sk-/ > /-θk-/

In a few words, we see that in a fairly common consonant cluster of Old Spanish, /-sk-/, the /s/ has been replaced in modern Spanish by the interdental fricative /θ/, e.g.

Old Spanish	Modern Spanish
biscocho	*bizcocho* 'biscuit'
esquierdo	*izquierdo* 'left'
mesclar	*mezclar* 'to mix'
mesquino (< Ar.)	*mezquino* 'petty'
	'poor, wretched, miserable'
Viscaya (< Basque)	*Vizcaya*

Such a change could, of course, occur sporadically due to simple chance, but given the number of words showing the change we might not go wrong in seeking some specific cause. In this case, it is conceivable that a specific morphological change, namely the development of an analogical extension of the consonant /θ/ in form 1 of the inchoative verbs in *-esçer* (see p. 355). The existence of a quantity of verbs changing from former /-esko/ in form 1 to modern /-eθko/, could have provided a model for other examples of the cluster such as those shown above (Malkiel 1969–70).

THE MORPHOLOGICAL SYSTEM

The Nominal System

The Demonstratives

The apocopated forms differed somewhat in frequency depending on the individual form. Thus, *est* and *aquest* competed with *este* and *aqueste*. The latter forms were the more authentically native ones since apocopation after consonant groups was encouraged chiefly by Gallic influence. *Es* < *esse*, however, was general in the twelfth century, although undoubtedly in popular usage there was competition with *esse*. *Esse* later came to be the standard form, in spite of the general loss of /-e/ following /-s-/. Probably the reestablishment of *esse* as the only form was due to analogy with *este* and the need to avoid homonymy with the verb *es* (Lapesa 1979, 205–06).[36] The longer forms of the first and second person demonstratives, *aqueste* and *aquesse*, continued to be found in literary works as late as the seventeenth century, but the shorter forms must have predominated in popular usage so that they finally became the standard ones. *Aquel*, of course, was the sole third person form.

Personal Pronouns

The subject pronouns corresponding to verb forms 4 and 5 were used in an emphatic form: *nos-otros, vos-otros*, which, toward the end of the Middle Ages, began to be used as the normal forms even when no special emphasis was intended.

The object pronoun *vos* developed a shorter form for use after the imperative: *os*. In the sixteenth century this form became generalized and eventually displaced *vos*.

The third person indirect object pronoun used before third person direct object pronouns, which had been /že/ *ge* in medieval Spanish, naturally became unvoiced to /še/ when the unvoicing of the voiced sibilants became more common. As it then more closely resembled the reflexive pronoun *se, se* began to be used in place of it and eventually replaced it completely (Schmidely 1979).

---

[36] Lapesa believes that there may have been phonetic support for the retention of -E after /-s-/, and cites in support the fact that non-apocopated forms of past subjunctives like *pudiés* and *amás* for *pudiesse* and *amasse* never managed to become dominant during the twelfth to the fourteenth centuries, at the height of the extreme apocope of -*e*. The -*e* in this case, however, as in form 3 of the present indicative of the -*er* and -*ir* verbs, and the present subjunctive of -*ar* verbs, is a morpheme with a distinct function. This fact alone would have encouraged speakers to retain it even when non-morphemic final -*e* was being dropped extensively in all other instances. It is true that the word *miesse* 'harvest' continues to be found until the end of the sixteenth century, but one wonders whether the same is true of all other words ending in -s.

The function of *le* and *lo* has been subject to considerable fluctuation, but since it is essentially a problem of syntax, discussion will be postponed until the next volume.

Possessive Adjectives

The distinction in the second and third person singular adjectives between the masculine forms *to* and *so* and the feminine forms *tu* and *su* begins to be blurred, with some preferring the feminine forms for both genders, a practice which eventually prevailed. The former distinction remained in use among some groups of speakers as late as the fourteenth century (Menéndez Pidal 1941, 258). The form *mió* gave way to *mío*, probably through analogy with the feminine form *mía* and the other singular masculine forms *tuyo* and *suyo*. Like them, it was limited to use in stressed positions and remains so today.

The Verbal System

The Present Tenses

As we saw in chapter 4, the consonant insert /g/ had become identified with form 1 of the present indicative and all of the present subjunctive of those verbs that in Late Latin had had a palatalized consonant in these form, e.g., *tengo, -a, vengo, -a, pongo, -a*. Being very common verbs, they tended to provide a model on which other verbs could be patterned. Thus, some speakers began to extend the pattern to other verbs in which the verb stem consisted of a single closed syllable, e.g., forms like *duelgo* 'I hurt', *suelgo* 'I am accustomed to', *valgo* 'I am worth', *salgo* 'I leave', etc. Only the last two managed to become popular enough to win acceptance finally in the standard language (Malkiel 1973–74, 326).

The identification of the consonant /g/ with the *-o, -a,* forms of verbs was undoubtedly aided by the pattern of other commonly used verbs such as *digo* 'I say' and *fago* 'I do', and *yago* 'I lie (outstretched)' (not to speak of verbs like *colgar* 'to hang' and *seguir* 'to follow' in which the /g/ characterized all forms of the stem and not just the ones before *-o* and *-a*.

A number of verbs contained an intervocalic /y/ in form 1 of the present indicative and all forms of the present subjunctive. As we recall from chapter 4, the /y/ in some verbs was derived historically from a Latin palatal (/-di-, -gi-/), while in other verbs the /y/ was analogical and in many verbs served to break a vocalic hiatus, e.g., *creyo, trayo, cayo*, etc. The verbs whose stem ended in a front vowel eventually absorbed the palatal, resulting in the modern forms like *creo*. An important structural factor is that the /y/ appeared in the same pattern as the *-go, -ga* verbs, i.e., before /-o/ and /-a/.

Such was the growing strength of the *-go, -ga* pattern that there grew up along with *trayo, cayo*, and *oyo*, alternate forms: *traigo, caigo*, and *oigo*. *Oigo* 'I hear' would have been especially supported by *digo* 'I say'. These forms grew increasingly popular as the pattern became entrenched until by the seventeenth century they almost completely replaced the earlier -*yo*, -*ya* forms. Inevitably the new pattern was extended to other verbs as well; *huigo* 'I flee' came to be used as well as *huyo*, while occasionally there appeared *restituigo* 'I restore' and *destruigo* 'I destroy' for *restituyo* and *destruyo*. The high vowel /u/ was, however, characteristic not only of *huir*, but also of a variety of semilearned verbs in -*uir* such as *atribuir* 'to attribute', *constituir* 'to constitute', *construir* 'to construct', *arguir* 'to argue', and others mostly based on the families of STATUERE 'to set up, erect, establish' and TRIBUERE 'to distribute, bestow, allow' (cf. popular *atrever* 'to dare'). These verbs all used the medial /y/ in the -*o*, -*a* forms, with the /u/ being strengthened by the pattern we have seen before, namely the association of high vowels with -*ir* verbs. Thus, older *foir* and *destroir* were rejected as not fitting the pattern, while *oir* was tolerated out of the need to maintain a difference between it and *huir*, especially once the initial /f-/ > /h-/ had disappeared.[37] These semilearned verbs in -*tribuyo* and -*stituyo* undoubtedly strengthened the position of *huyo* against any tendency to maintain *huigo* (Malkiel 1973–74, 338).

Such was the impact of the -*go*, -*ga* pattern that it began to affect even verb forms in -*ya* that had no counterpart in -*yo* such as *vaya* (← *ir*), *haya* (← *haber*), producing the popular forms *vaiga* and *haiga*. Other verbs whose stem ended in a vowel likewise adopted the /g/ insert in present subjunctive forms: *creiga*, *leiga*, and *reiga* for *crea* (← *creer*), *lea* (← *leer*), and *ría* (← *reír*). These last forms, like *vaiga* and *haiga*, never gained acceptance in the literary language and remain relegated to popular, uneducated speech (Menéndez Pidal 1941, 295). Some other, less commonly used verbs whose stems also ended in a vowel, like *raer* 'to scrape, grate', and *roer* 'to gnaw', and which had form 1 in -*yo*, similarly developed new forms with /g/: *raigo* and *roigo*. In the case of these two verbs, however, both the /g/ and the /y/ forms are still permissible in written Spanish.

During the late Middle Ages, the last holdouts of the original Late Latin -*ir* pattern with the -*esc*- interfix were eliminated in favor of the -*ecer* ending in all forms of the verb. The -*ecer* suffix maintained the original Latin inceptive meaning for the most part so that most verbs containing it still continue to denote the beginning of an action or state, e.g., *adormescer* 'to go to sleep', *anochecer* 'to become night', *enriquecerse* 'to become rich', etc. Thus, the remaining forms that reflect the earlier Romance pattern, i.e., the infinitive and past participle in -*ir* and -*ido*, give way to -*e(s)cer* and -*e(s)cido*. Thus, in the fourteenth century text, *Rimado de Palacio*, both

---

[37] Penny (1972, 352) points out this reason for the maintenance of *oir* in contrast with the general pattern of the -*ir* conjugation. In those areas where some other phonetic feature could suffice to distinguish the two verbs, the descendants of AUDĪRE could adopt a high vowel. Thus, if the medial /-d-/ was preserved there was nothing to prevent the appearance of a form like *udieron* 'they heard' (La Rioja). In Aragon where initial /f-/ was retained in *fuir*, the present of *oir* became 3. *huye*, 6. *huyen* (Penny 1972, 349).

adormido 'asleep' and ***adormescido*** are found. Possibly the latter form has a contrasting meaning, 'demoralized'. The majority of verb forms in this work contain the full suffix, e.g., ***aborrescido*** 'abominable, ***mal agrade-scido*** 'ungrateful', ***endurescido*** 'hardened', etc. We note, however, that one manuscript of the text has ***escarnir*** where another has ***escarnescer*** 'to scorn' (Malkiel 1969–70, 194).

There was also a slight change in the form of these verbs. The previous medieval form in *-o, -a* verb forms was *-sco, -sca*, which reflected the Latin source. Increasing regularization of verb forms led to the adoption of the -ç- from the other forms of these verbs in form 1: *-eçco* (MSp. *-ezco*), a change which may have helped to stimulate a similar change in some non-verbal forms (Malkiel 1969–70)(see p. 351). The existence of a large number of verbs with the *-e(s)cer* suffix attracted other verbs which by chance ended in a similar sequence of phonemes: *luzir* 'to shine' < LŪCĒRE, *plazer* 'to please' < PLACĒRE, *conduzir* 'to lead, conduct', and all other *-duzir* verbs. All of these verbs adopted the same sequence in the *-o -a* forms: *luzco, conduzco, conozco, plazco*, etc.

The Creation of Present Tense Forms in -y

Toward the end of the Middle Ages we find that those verbs whose form 1 in the present indicative was monosyllabic (including *estar* whose initial /e/ is required by a basic rule of Spanish phonetics), that is, *ser, dar, estar,* and *ir,* all develop a new form ending in a palatal semivowel /-i/:

	Earlier Form	Modern Form
se(e)r	*so*	*soy*
estar	*estó*	*estoy*
dar	*do*	*doy*
ir	*vo*	*voy*

Various sources have been posited for this new element, which is un-usual in the Spanish verbal system. Some have thought that it derives from a form ending in /-e/, e.g., *soe*, with subsequent reduction of the hiatus and the formation of a diphthong. This final *-e* may be attributed to hypercorrection, i.e., a false restitution of final *-e* which speakers mista-kenly believed had been dropped during the period of most intense apo-cope of *-e*. Another possibility might be that the *-e* was an analogical extension of the /e/ from the reduced form of *sodes*, i.e., *soes* which was further reduced to *sois* in the sixteenth century. Or possibly it might have been borrowed from form 1 of the other tenses such as the past for future subjunctive forms, *fuesse, fuere*. If either of these hypotheses were correct, we might expect to find many examples of forms like *soe*, the presumed original form (Müller 1963, 240–42). Not only is *soy* earlier than the rare examples of *soe*, however, but no forms like **doe* appear at all. Thus, we must conclude that *soe* was a derivative of *soy* rather than the reverse.

Another suggestion is that the *-y* is analogically derived from *ey*

Latin /aio/ < HABEŌ. Since the change of /ai̯/ > /ei̯/ > /e/ was accomplished at the latest by the beginning of the twelfth century in Castilian, and probably much earlier, this notion is clearly untenable (Müller 1963, 247–48). Another idea is that possibly the preterite of *ser, fui,* is somehow related to the phenomenon (cf. OFr. *sui,* Pope 1934, 360). In the absence of other examples of the influence of the preterite on the present tense, this conjecture also seems unlikely.

One theory is that these forms do not originate in Castilian at all, but rather in a Leonese dialect in which speakers were conscious of the fact that in some more western areas the diphthong /ou/ corresponded to the diphthong /oi/ in other regions. We find that in certain Portuguese words, for example, tonic /ou/ alternates in some words with /oi/, e.g., *cousa - coisa* 'thing' < CAUSA, *ouro - oiro* 'gold' < AURU, *doutor - doitor* (dialectal) (Gorog 1980, 160). According to this view, in some areas of Leon, some speakers may have created alternate forms like *doy, soy,* etc. corresponding to *dou, sou* of standard Portuguese. It is true that the Leonese forms are thus far documented earlier than the Castilian ones, but even so this theory seems highly speculative. No reason is given as to why Castilian should have borrowed just these very common and frequently used forms from Leonese, when it is Castilian that in almost all cases imposes its forms on other dialects.[38]

A more plausible explanation is the one that sees in the newer verb forms a false division occurring after the verb when followed by the pronoun *yo.* It is assumed that when speakers said *do yo, so yo,* etc. they then interpreted the syntactic group [so - yo] as *soy yo,* rather than in its original form. It might be asked then why speakers did not simply create new forms like **soyo* or **doyo,* especially given the existence of forms ending in *-yo,* e.g., *trayo, cayo* (Müller 1963, 249). Also, since the subject pronoun is always stressed, it would be more likely that any new form incorporating the pronoun would have been stressed on the last syllable, e.g., **soyó.* Such a result would have been clearly impossible as the final stressed /-ó/ is characteristic only of form 3 of the preterite. Finally, it would be necessary for speakers to forget that *yo* was a subject pronoun. However, the notion of false division is not impossible, especially because with glide elements, there is a strong phonetic tendency to spread the glide over two syllables when it appears between vowels, e.g., *voy a morir* may be pronounced as [bo-ya-mo-rir] or [boi-ya-mo-rir] (Navarro Tomás 1952, 151).

---

[38] It is true, as de Gorog, says, that verb forms, even very common ones, can be borrowed from other languages. Thus, the English copula form *are* is said to have been borrowed from the Danes who settled in northern England. This example is not exactly parallel to the Spanish since the northern form *we aron* 'we are' had existed previously as opposed to the West Saxon *syndon.* Nevertheless, the extension of *are* to English was undoubtedly due to the added influence of the Danes (Baugh 1957, 121). The Danish influence was, however, most felt at a time when Old English was by no means the standard language of all England. This is not really comparable to the position of Leonese vis-a-vis Castilian at the period in which *soy* was created.

A more probable theory is that the element -*y* represents the ancient adverb *y* < IBI (DCELC IV, 769). It is not unknown in Romance for non-verbal elements to be used so frequently with certain verb forms that eventually they become fused with the verb itself and the original non-verbal meaning is completely lost. Thus, we find that in Provençal the preterite verb form *fon* 'he was' was originally *fo'n* < *fo en* < FUIT INDE 'he was (from there)'. It is interesting to note too that in Rhaeto-Romance a new first person singular ending, -*el*, has come into use since the seventeenth century, derived from the third person masculine object pronoun, e.g., *jeu affel* 'I find' < 'I find it' (Ulleland 1965). In Provençal the verb *vai* 'he goes' derived from *va i* < VADIT IBI 'he goes there' (Müller 1963, 252–53). In Spanish we have the example of *hay* 'there is' < *ha y* < HABET IBI (literally 'it has there'). Y originally had a topical meaning, 'there, in that place' and frequently appeared with forms of *se(e)r* 'to be': *sera y, eran y, fuere y, seremos i, fue i, fu y, hi era, y sera, hi seran*, etc. (Pottier 1968, 212). In the preceding examples the *y* is apparently stressed and thus more or less equivalent to *allí* or *ahí*. The creation of the fused form (*h*)*ay* must be parallel to the similar French construction *il y a*, in which the adverb is atonic. In this particular construction, *y* is no longer anaphoric and does not refer to any specific place as it does when it is stressed. Used atonically, *y* refers rather to the general notion of space in a much vaguer sense.[39] Thus, there grew up along with the anaphoric use of *y*, a construction with (*h*)*a* which designated the general notion of existence, i.e., 'there is . . . , there are . . . '. This special use would explain why it is only form 3 of the present tense that fuses with *y*, and not the other tenses. Since the present tense is really the only tense that does not refer specifically to any given time but can refer to all times in general or no time at all, it is best adapted to the general expressions of existence without further qualifications (Molho 1969, 63). In the thirteenth century the fused form *ay* came to alternate with the simple form *ha* (and occasionally even *y ha*), as well as with the older uses of *y aver* in which the *y* was genuinely anaphoric.

From the last half of the thirteenth century there was increasing use of *ay* alternating with *ha* in which the -*y* was no longer perceived as anything other than a verbal ending. As long as *ha* and *y* were felt to be two separate words, the negative was rarely used with *ay*, the more common construction being *non ha* (in Alfonsine prose, for example). As *ay* became more commonly used, there was less resistance to its use in the negative (Molho 1969, 79). In popular usage, (*h*)*ay* had become predominant at least by the beginning of the fourteenth century.

Next the form *soy* began to be used along with the older *so*, in which the -*y* no longer has the adverbial meaning that it had previously had, as in the examples cited above. Originally the fused forms may have had a vaguer

---

[39] "[I]l ne signifie plus, par rappel anaphorique, un lieu singulier, mais, dans l'en-dessous de cette représentation, celle d'un *avant* de ce lieu, qui n'est autre que l'espace, lieu général contenant de tous les lieux particuliers pensable auxquels il préexiste inévitablement" (Molho 1969, 72).

meaning, 'about that, with regard to that', which may be perceived in expressions like, e.g., ". . . rrecibo estas sousa sobredichas . . . e soi abastado dellas," and "soy pagado" 'I am satisfied *with it*' or '. . . *about it*' (Müller 1963, 262). It is possible too that the increasing popularity of *(h)ay* helped to reinforce the use of *soy*, especially since *ser*, like *aver*, was a verb indicating existence in general.[40] Thus, as *hay* refers to the general notion of existence, *soy* can refer to a specific quality of existence, that of the speaker (Molho 1969, 86–87). *Soy* becomes widely used in the fourteenth century, alternating with *so*, considerably before the *-y* spread to the other monosyllabic verbs. We can assume that in part at least, the extension of *-y* to *dar*, *estar*, and *ir* came from both topical meanings, e.g., *vo y* 'I'm going there', *so y* or *estó y* 'I am there', and metaphorical meanings as in *do y* 'I give (it to someone)', e.g., "do hi comigo quanto que he en Huércanos . . ." (1227, DLE 86:9). In the fifteenth century the *-y* becomes attached to all of the monosyllabic verb forms, alternating with the earlier ones in *-o*.

Several elements probably worked together in the creation of these new forms: the false division with the postverbal use of *yo*, and, more importantly, the fusion of the adverb *y* with the verb. At the same time, there must have been a clinching factor that led to the addition of *-y* to these forms alone rather than to any others. After all, *yo* could also be used after other verbs e.g., *digo yo*, *creo yo*, etc. What distinguished the monosyllabic verbs from all others was precisely their monosyllabic nature which necessarily resulted in their being stressed, unlike all other present tense verbs in form 1 in which the ending *-o* is unstressed. The stressed /-ó/ is identified with the preterite, as mentioned above. Speakers therefore must have felt a certain discomfort in using the same stressed vowel in the present tense in a different person. The addition of the adverb *y*, especially when it had lost most of its adverbial force, would have served to create a new form that was obviously not a preterite and yet would be identified as a present tense form (Montgomery 1979, 235). A negative factor would also have contributed to these new forms, namely the lack of any other monosyllabic words in the lexicon ending in *-oy*, with the sole exception of the adverb *hoy*. As a result, the new forms were distinctive and did not conflict with any preexisting sound pattern.[41]

The Second Person Plural Endings

As we noted earlier in the section on phonology, in the fourteenth century we find the first indications of the merger of medial /-đ-/ and /-d-/. It is then that the older personal ending of form 5 in the present and future tenses, *-des* begins to alternate with forms lacking the *-d-* so that

---

[40] Undoubtedly too the construction *so yo* was more common than the others, especially when we think of the normal answer to the question, *qui es*? or *quien es*?

[41] It is interesting to note than in the Friulian dialect in northern Italy, these same verb forms appear: *sòi, dòi, vòi, stòi* and also form 1 of *ole* 'to want' < *VOLĒRE, *uei* (Gregor 1975, 102–03). It is possible that the regular present tense ending for form 1 had some influence in this dialect: *-i*.

instead of *vayades* (← *ir*), *sodes* (← *seer*), *publiquedes* (← *publicar*), *divulguedes* (← *divulgar*), etc. there appeared *vayaes, soes, publiquees, divulguees*. The ending for *-ir* verbs, *-ides* similarly gave *-íes*. When the result of the loss of *-d-* was /-ee-/, there was a natural tendency to merge the two identical vowels into a single one, much as we find that older *veer* and *seer* tended to reduce to *ver* and *ser*. So forms like *avés* 'you have (pl.)', *podés* 'you are able', *irés* 'you will go', and *darés* 'you will give' replace *avedes, podedes, iredes*, and *daredes*.

The reduction of hiatus was a continuing tendency of Spanish. Thus, the reduction of those new hiatus groups soon followed, aided undoubtedly by the frequency of use of form 5, especially since this form was used as a singular to show respect. Therefore the *-aes* ending soon gave way to the diphthongal monosyllable, *-áis*. The model offered by the ending *-és* probably stimulated the further reduction of *-áes* to *-ás*, and *-íes* to *-ís*. At the same time the model of *-áis* led to the creation of *-éis*. Although the earliest system of reduced forms was *-áis* and *-és*, the *-éis* form eventually became predominant and the monophthongal forms *-ás* and *-és* disappeared in continental Spanish. Probably the chief factor that favored the triumph of *-áis* and *-éis* was the need in the very frequently used monosyllabic verbs *dar, estar, ver*, and *ir* to keep a clear distinction between the singular and the plural of the second person. Adoption of one syllable endings would have made forms like *das-des, estás-estés, ves-veas, vas*, ambiguous. They could refer to a person addressed as *tú* or *vos*.

It was during the sixteenth century that the new system of second person pronouns was coming to replace the medieval system. In earlier times, the plural form was used as a respectful form. Speakers could use *tú* with intimates and social equals or inferiors, and *vos* with superiors. With the increasing use of *vuestra merced* and other constructions requiring the third person, to indicate respect (e.g., *Vuestra Señoría, Vuestra Excelencia*), *vos* was left in an anomalous position between the new pronouns of respect and the old familiar pronoun *tú*. In Spain and in the parts of America most influenced by peninsular usages, i.e., the Caribbean, Mexico, and Peru, *vos* began a descent in social estimation until it eventually disappeared from normal use. In the Spanish of America, on the other hand, *vos* came to be more closely associated with the *tú* form so that eventually they merged in most areas, usually to the benefit of the *vos* forms, except in the areas mentioned above. In those regions of Spanish America that kept the *vos* forms in popular usage, there was no need to maintain the diphthongal form and the monophthongal forms, *-ás, -és, -ís*, became very commonly used, although in some areas diphthongal forms still appear. The form *-ís* in the peninsula was undoubtedly determined originally by the pressure from the imperfect form *-iés* which was still alive in the fourteenth and fifteenth centuries. (For details of the whole process see Lapesa 1970.)

The same need to distinguish between *tú* and *vos* (and at the same time between singular and plural) probably helped to maintain the final *-d* of the plural imperative in peninsular Spanish, which in modern popular usage has been identified with the -*r* of the infinitive. In much of American Spanish it disappeared, leaving the imperative for *vos* as a stressed vowel, -*á*, -*é*, -*í*. Another feature of the plural imperative was the tendency to metathesize the final -*d* and the *l*- of a following object pronoun, producing forms like *daldo*, *poneldo*, *embialdo* (Lapesa 1980, 391). The factor favoring these metathesized forms was the relative frequency of the group /-ld-/ as against the rarity of /-dl-/, but the need to distinguish the separate morphemes overcame phonological ease and the metathesized forms disappeared after the seventeenth century.

Form 5 Endings in the Non-Present Tenses

At the same time as the endings without /d/ were becoming established as the norm in the present tenses, the proparoxytonic endings continued for a long time to preserve the medial consonant and thus contrast more sharply the present from the other tenses: -*ávades*–-*íades*, -*iésedes*–-*ásedes*, -*árades*–-*iérades*, *érades*, *íbades*, etc. In literary usage these medieval endings were almost exclusively used until the seventeenth century. Forms showing loss of medial /d/, as in the present tenses, were not common in literature until then, although they did exist before the seventeenth century and were undoubtedly in widespread popular use by the beginning of the century. They are given as parallel forms in Texeda's grammar of 1619 (Blaylock 1986).

A variety of reasons have been given for the conservation of the -*d*- in these endings. One suggestion is that the influence of the syncopated form of the future subjunctive, e.g., *amardes*, *fuerdes*, etc., in which the *d* would not have been subject to loss, influenced the other tenses in which the *d* did not appear in a tonic syllable. Another reason given is that Spanish speakers were relatively unused to finding diphthongs in atonic syllables, since the diphthongs had originated almost exclusively in tonic syllables. Also they were completely unused to triphthongs. Therefore there would have been some resistance to creating new diphthongs, especially off-gliding ones, in atonic syllables (Malkiel 1949). A more recent suggestion has been that the loss of *d* first in the present tenses is due solely to the greater frequency with which the present tenses are used (Mańczak 1976),[42] since phonetic reductions are far more likely to occur in the most frequently used forms of words. One final reason that may have restrained speakers from dropping the the /-d-/ would have been the fact that in the past subjunc-

---

[42] Mańczak is not quite accurate in stating that Malkiel believes that a Spanish speaker at the end of the Middle Ages was incapable of pronouncing a diphthong in a posttonic position (1976, 186). Malkiel only says that the phonological system of Spanish was unused to having diphthongs in this position. Speakers were perfectly capable of pronouncing diphthongs, but could well have been reluctant to pronounce them in positions in which they had not appeared before. It is clear that capability had nothing to do with the matter, but rather that the earlier structural tradition required more time to be overcome. Mańczak's article is flawed in a variety of other ways as well (Blaylock 1986).

tive, the loss would have created a new form identical with form 2: *amás-sedes*, *comiéssedes* > *amasses*, *comiesses*. The distinction between singular and plural is especially important as we saw above, as long as the plural form was used as a polite singular (Lapesa 1970, 528–29). Probably all these factors worked together to encourage the preservation of *d* in the non-present endings. Eventually, however, the pressure of the reduced present tense endings and the general weakening of medial /-d-/ led to the adoption of the reduced form in all tenses, with the diphthongal form being analogically adopted in the past subjunctive instead of the regular phonetic development to *-es*. When the *-eis* was extended to form 5 of the preterite, *-steis*, the way was open for the extension of the singular ending *-s*, already characteristic of form 2 in all tense forms except the preterite, to be used in the preterite as well, *-stes*. Although very common in popular speech, it is still condemned as incorrect in educated Spanish.

The Imperfect in *-ié*

The imperfect endings for the *-ar* verbs have remained unchanged from their form in Late Latin: /-aba/, spelled *-ava* in medieval Spanish. The modern spelling *-aba* reflects the etymologizing concerns of the eighteenth and nineteenth centuries. The endings for the *-er* and *-ir* verbs are today as they were in early Romance, *-ía*. For a period of several centuries, however, the latter ending was threatened by a new imperfect suffix that became dominant for a while and then receded in favor of *-ía*.

In the literary works of the thirteenth century we find that the dominant conjugational pattern for the *-er*, *-ir* verbs was as follows (using *tener* as a model):

1. *ten-ía*	4. *ten-iemos*
2. *ten-iés*	5. *ten-iedes*
3. *ten-ié*	6. *ten-ién*

For verbs in the *-ir* conjugation, the palatal affected the stem vowel in the same way as in forms 3 and 6 of the preterite, raising the midvowels to high vowels: *cubriés*, *cubrié* (←*cobrir* 'to cover'), *cuntiés*, *cuntié* (*contir* 'to occur, happen'), *durmié*, *durmiemos* (←*dormir* 'to sleep'), *ixiedes*, *ixién* (←*exir* 'to leave'), *sintié*, *sintién* (*sentir* 'to feel, perceive'), etc. The conditional of all verbs, being based on the imperfect of *aver* likewise followed the new pattern: *amarié*, *amariés*, *amarié*, *amariemos*, *amariedes*, *amarién*.

Although dominant, this pattern was not exclusively found anywhere. In the *Cantar de Mio Cid*, for example, in forms 3 and 6 the ending *-ía(n)* appears in several places, and in some other works, there is some competition between *-ía* and *-ié*, in these forms especially (Malkiel 1959, 474), and on very rare occasions a form 1 in *-ié* appears. Sporadic combinations of the two endings resulted in an occasional *-íe*, with apocope of the final *-e*, e.g., *sey* (Cid 2278) 'he was (staying)' < *seíe*.

This new imperfect pattern was dominant in Castile, Aragon, and Leon (excluding the westernmost areas), but never took root in Galician-Portuguese. The literature that has been preserved from the thirteenth century shows very wide usage of the new forms, but then in the fourteenth century the *-ié* endings begin to give way to the older *-ía* so that by the fifteenth century, the *-ía* endings had once again become the most frequent and *-ié* was in full retreat, relegated to lower class and regional usage.

A number of interesting questions are posed by this newcomer to the conjugational system of Spanish, which, for a while, seemed to bid fair to replace altogether the ancestral imperfect forms. First, under what conditions did the new endings arise and temporarily replace the *-ía* endings in most forms? Secondly, why did the *-ié* ending never manage to displace the *-ía* of form 1? Lastly, how and why did the new endings begin to recede?

The conditions of origin have been debated extensively for many years, with those who look for some sort of phonological law as the source of *-ié* < *-ía* tending to be more numerous than those who have preferred to seek some sort of analogical origin.[43] The solution that at present best fits the available facts is the one which sees in the beginning of the use of *-ié* for *-ía* a side effect of the new perfect for the *-er* and *-ir* verbs. That new (or relatively new) perfect is the one whose source is the -DEDI perfect discussed in the previous chapter (pp. 301–03). This perfect, which was itself in competition with the older *-i-* perfect, had in the plural the endings *-iemos*, *-iestes*, *-ieron*. Although the preterite and the imperfect tenses have been kept separate in all the Romance languages, the fact that they share the common feature of 'past' has sufficed in some cases for one tense to have some analogical influence on the form of the other, without there being any general movement to suppress the aspectual distinction between them. In some circumstances, the pronunciation of *-ía* was much less as two separate syllables and much more as a single syllable. As we have seen, the reduction of hiatus through the formation of a diphthong is a constant tendency of the Spanish phonological system. Thus, when a verb appeared in a non-emphatic position in a sentence, as, for example, when the sentence stress was on an element following the verb, speakers would be much more likely to pronounce a word like *vendíamos* (ordinarily /ben-dí-a-mos/) as /ben-dia-mos/, e.g., *Antes vendíamos los huevos, no los pollos* . . . in which the main stress is on the objects sold. Such unstressed usage of the imperfect would be especially common in verbs which normally served as auxiliaries, such as *aver* 'to have', *poder* 'to be able', *querer* 'to want', *seer* 'to be', etc.

In such a position the phonetic result of the elimination of the hiatus

---

[43] Malkiel (1959) gives a detailed analysis of the various approaches to the problem and a final summary of the most likely solutions.

could easily produce a verb form that sounded much like the new preterites, e.g., *vendiemos*, or *pudiemos*, especially since atonic vowels are not as easily distinguished as tonic ones. This sort of pronunciation might have become established first with the auxiliary verbs, which, as just mentioned, tend to be less distinctive in a sentence. Therefore in sentences in which the aspectual distinction between the two tenses was not very important, speakers could interpret *vendiemos* as an imperfect form. It is notable, in this regard, that in form 4 the imperfect ending *-iemos* was found almost without any competition. In the *Cantar de Mio Cid*, for example, there are no examples of *-íamos* (Malkiel 1959, 474–75). From this initial starting point, speakers probably adopted the ending *-iedes* for form 5, always closely associated with form 4. From a strong lodging in these two forms, the *-ié-* then spread to forms 2, 3, and 6. The new imperfect was rapidly adopted by many as a part of the latest vogue and soon became entrenched in the literary language.

The failure of the *-ié* to reach form 1 can probably be attributed to a desire on the part of speakers to maintain a distinction between form 1 and form 3. Of course, the traditional, inherited imperfect forms manage to tolerate the homonymy of these forms without provoking the creation of a new and distinctive form 1. Although tradition can maintain this homonymy, the advent of a new and unusual ending would have afforded speakers the opportunity, which they seized eagerly, to create a useful distinction that ordinarily they could not maintain. There are, in fact, parallels to this sort of a distinction in other Romance dialects. Italian, for example, in its older forms had homonymous forms 1 and 3 of the imperfect of the *-are* verbs, e.g., *-ava*. Modern Italian, in contrast, has adopted the *-o* of the present tense for form 1; *-avo*, now distinguished from *-ava*. In Upper Aragonese there is also found a new form 1 for the *-ar* imperfect: *-abai* (Malkiel 1959, 476).

The new imperfect ending then, in part at least, established itself through the force of novelty, and for a while managed to overcome all traditional forces, except in form 1. It is in the nature of fashions, however, especially those that rise to favor rapidly, to decline as quickly as they bloom. After the *-ié* had ceased to be the "latest thing," its momentum was gone and traditional forces could reassert themselves. It is not clear from the available evidence whether the traditional *-ía* endings had continued to exist as part of the linguistic heritage of a substantial number of speakers or whether the forms in *-ía* that appear in texts in competition with the popular *-ié* simply represent analogical extensions of the *-ía* of form 1. In addition to the importance of the fading of a vogue in the reestablishment of the traditional *-ía* endings, another factor may have been the fact that the *-ié* endings were completely anomalous in the conjugational system. Perhaps both reasons are valid. At any rate, after 1300 the *-ié* imperfect began to recede until finally it was limited to a small number of social and regional dialects. In the early sixteenth century it was a relic of the past. In 1515, Francisco López de Vilalobos, in his *Diálogo sobre las fiebres interpo-*

ladas, remarks in his criticism of Toledans who believe that their language is superior to that of other Castilians that "en Castilla los curiales no dicen *hacién* por *hacían*, ni *comién* por *comían*, y así en todos los verbos que son desta conjugación" (quoted by Lázaro Mora 1978–80, 269). By the seventeenth century the formerly dominant pattern had disappeared completely.

The Arrhizotonic Preterite

As we saw in chapter 4, the regular -*ar* verbs had a preterite formation that reflected to a large extent the regular phonetic development. Form 2 frequently appeared as -*este*, analogically based on form 1, but after the thirteenth century it declined in use, replaced by the traditional -*aste*. It is preserved in relic areas in Asturias. The analogical form -*emos* for form 4 still remains in popular Spanish in Castile.

The older traditional endings for forms 4 and 5 of the -*er*, -*ir* verbs, -*imos*, -*istes*, existed in vigorous competition with the newer endings derived from the -DEDĪ perfects, -*iemos*, -*iestes*, which, as we saw above, were probably the model for the vogue of the -*ié* imperfect. Undoubtedly these perfects were something of the latest thing also for a while, but, after their novelty had passed, the traditional forms reasserted themselves. An important factor in the eventual triumph of -*imos*, -*istes* was probably the model of the singular forms 1 and 2, -*í*, -*iste* which had remained without change. Only in form 6 did -*ieron* replace whatever may have been the earliest form in proto-Castilian and remain until today. In this particular form it may be the deciding factor was the existence in the singular form -*ió* of a palatal on-glide which would have served as a model for the plural.

The creation of a new form 5 in -*steis* has been discussed above.

The Rhizotonic Preterite

A number of the rhizotonic preterites found in older Spanish gave way to the pressure of the regular arrhizotonic pattern. Thus, the sigmatic perfects of the verbs *escrevir* 'to write', *exir* 'to leave', *meter* 'to place (into)', *remanecer* 'to remain' were already in the *Cantar de mio Cid* found with the forms *escriuio*, *yxio*, *metió*, *remaneció*, in place of the earlier *escri(p)so*, *ixo-exo*, *miso*, *remaso* (Menéndez Pidal 1944, 1. 279). For *ceñir* 'to gird on' we find *ciñió* in the *Vida de Santo Domingo* in place of the older *cinxo* found in the *Cid*. *Tañer*, -*ir* 'to play (an instrument)' had the preterite in *tanxo* which was soon replaced by *tañó*, as were *riso* 'he laughed' by *rió*, *destruxo* 'he destroyed' by *destruyó*, *tinxo* 'he dyed' by *tiñó*, *coxo* 'he cooked' by *coció*, *fuxo* 'he fled' by *fuyó*, *priso* 'he took, seized' by *prendió*, and its related forms *apriso* 'he learned' by *aprendió*, *despiso* 'he expended' by *expendió*, and the form *respuso* 'he replied' by *respondió*.

The commonest verbs, *querer* 'to want', and *poner* 'to put' retained the traditional forms, *quiso* and *puso*.

The -*d*- preterites had a certain vogue for a while: *andido* 'he went', *estido* 'he was', and the compromise form that blended *andido* and *anduvo* into *andudo* (possibly supported by *pudo*), gave way to the pattern of *aver* and the forms *estuvo anduvo* became the standard ones. In the case of *ver*, the form that preserved medial /-d-/ from Latin, *vido*, which we recall was probably preserved through paradigmatic pressure, and the analogical form 1 *vide*, were eventually replaced in the standard language by regularized forms, *vi* and *vio*. As late as the sixteenth century *vido* is found in literary texts, and in modern Spanish dialects it appears all over the Spanish-speaking world, with *vide* being somewhat less used (Malkiel 1960, 334–40).

Of the numerous analogical preterites of *traer* which we saw in chapter 4, only two persisted in competition into modern times, *traxe*, the form based on the present stem, and *troxe*, which in its evolved form, *truje*, continues to be found in rural speech in the Iberian peninsula and in popular speech in the New World, where it is now characteristic of uneducated speech (Malkiel 1967–68, 496–98).

The /o/-Stem Verbs

We remember that in Old Spanish there was a class of rhizotonic preterites containing an /o/ in the stem (< Late Lat. /au/, or by analogy):

aver	*ove*
atrever	*atrove*
caber	*cope*
creer, crescer	*crove*
plazer	*plogue*
saber	*sope*
se(e)r	*sove*
tener	*tove*
traer	*troxe*
yazer	*yogue*

Besides these very commonly used verbs there was a smaller group of verbs with /u/ in the stem, resulting from Late Lat. /u/ or /o/ raised by metaphonic influence of final /-i/:

aduzir	*aduxe*
conosçer	*conuve*
destroir	*destruxe*
poner	*puse*
poder	*pude*

Along with these last verbs we may include the analogical preterite of *foír*, *fuxo*, which was soon replaced by the weak preterite *huyó*.

At this point we may mention too those verbs which had /i/ in some forms of the stem, e.g., *dezir - dixe*, *fazer - fize*, *venir - vine*, and others which in the previous chapters were dealt with solely in terms of the consonant which ended the preterite stem. One further group in the class of -*ir* verbs that alternate /o/ and /u/, as does *sobir* 'to go up', whose present indicative had /u/ in forms 1–3 and 6: *subo, subes, sube(n)*, and in the subjunctive and future forms as well.

The most notable characteristic of all of these verbs is that during the fourteenth and fifteenth centuries, all adopted the high vowels /u/ and /i/ consistently in all forms of the preterite, and the forms with /e/ and /o/ were completely eliminated. In the case of the verbs owing the /i/ of form 1 to metaphony, of this form probably led to the extension of the vowel to form 3, e.g., *vino* and form 2, *viniste*. Although this analogical extension began very early, the preservation of stem forms with /e/ continues until quite late, in those forms where the /e/ would have been aided by the general tendency to dissimilate from /i/ before stressed /i/, e.g., *heciste, hecimos*, forms which Nebrija still gives in his grammar (Menéndez Pidal 1941, 320).

The development of the /o/ verbs to uniform preterites with the stem-vowel /u/ may be related to a general movement of sound symbolism. As we saw in chapter 4, the general association of stative verbs with the -*er* class was reflected in the limitation of stem-vowels of the majority of the verbs of this class to /e/ and /o/ (/a/ being neutral in this respect). Verbs of the -*ir* class were, we recall, by and large those with high vowels in at least some of their forms, and most of the verbs of this conjugation are action verbs. Stative verbs, by their basic meaning, are verbs that are predominantly associated with the imperfective aspect, since they refer to continuing processes or states. In the tense system the preterite tense contrasts with the imperfect tense specifically in aspect; it refers to actions or states that are limited in time. Thus, a stative verb, by being used in the preterite, to some extent loses its stative quality. This change is most clearly illustrated by the meaning of verbs like *querer* 'to want' and *tener* 'to have'. In the preterite, the limitation of time implied by the tense requires that they be interpreted not as states but rather as single acts of the basic notion of the verb. Therefore, *quise* is often translated by English 'I tried' (i.e., the wanting was expressed by an effort, limited to a specific time) and *tuve* is often translated by 'I received, got'. One must be wary of such translation equivalents which are, by their very nature, simply a reflection of the lack of exact parallelism of structure between two different languages. However, in the case of *tener* it is clear that the notion conveyed by the preterite cannot be that of durative possession since possession is an indefinite state.

What appears to have happened in the development of modern Spanish out of the medieval system is the association of high vowels with perfective aspect, and, as a consequence, the generalization of the high vowels in the stem of the rhizotonic verbs. There were few words in Spanish with the sound pattern of -*uve* or -*uvo*. *Nube* 'cloud' and *rubo* 'bramble' are the only examples. Even the pattern of stressed /ú/ + consonant+ /e/ or /o/ is very rare except in the case of derived words with the suffixes like -*uco*,

-ucho, -udo, -ufo, -ullo, etc., all of which "convey an impression of emphasis and concreteness" (Montgomery 1979, 231). We can conclude, in accordance with Montgomery 1979, that the small number of clearly distinguished vowels, even in atonic syllables, may have encouraged speakers to exploit the vowel system by developing complementary polarities. In the case of the verb system the distinction between high vowels and lower vowels can, in many verbs, serve to contrast more clearly the difference between the perfective and imperfective aspects in the past.

In part, this tendency was encouraged by the loss of the consonantal ending for form 3 which left only vowels to distinguish this form from others. In the arrhizotonic verbs, the stressed /-ó/ was sufficient to set this form apart, as did the stressed /-é/ and /-í/ of form 1. As we saw previously, the association of stressed /ó/ with form 3 of the preterite may have been an important factor in the fusion of *-y* in the monosyllabic form 1 verbs in the present tense.

The Other Past Tenses

The pluperfect in *-ra* continued to exist as a form but syntactically began to be more and more limited in use to hypothetical constructions as the compound pluperfect with *aver* became more frequent. This limitation of the *-ra* form brought it into increasing competition with the past subjunctive constructions. The forms of these two tenses remained without further change, beyond the development of form 5 mentioned earlier. The stem vowels, as usual, parallel those of the preterite.

The future subjunctive preserved the distinctive form 1 in *-o* as late as the fourteenth century, e.g., *fuero, tomaro, pudiero,* etc. (Menéndez Pidal 1944, l. 277). The pattern of all other subjunctive forms, which had identical endings in forms 1 and 3, led, however, to the analogical creation of a new form 1 in *-re.* Eventually the older forms were dropped entirely. In form 5 the syncopated form was extremely common. As Nebrija remarks in his grammar: "por *amárades, leiéredes, oiéredes* decimos *amardes, leierdes, oierdes*" (Menéndez Pidal 1941, 314). These forms were also replaced by the non-syncopated ones.

The Future and Conditional

The syncopated forms of the future which were fairly common in the Middle Ages were replaced by regularized forms with the full form of the infinitive in almost all instances. Only those verbs whose frequency of use was very high managed to keep the syncopated forms: *caber, decir, hacer, poder, querer, saber, tener, venir, valer,* and *salir.*

The Past Participles: Decline of the *-udo* Ending

As we saw in chapter 4, the *-udo* ending for *-er* verbs had probably never become popular in central and western Ibero-Romance and was tending to be overshadowed by the *-ido* ending. Thus, although participles in -*udo* were found, they were constantly in competition with -*ido*. In literary usage, for example, they seemed to have reached the height of their vogue in Alfonsine prose, though even there they alternated with forms in -*ido*.[44] By the beginning of the fourteenth century there is a noticeable recession of the -*udo* forms, both in prose (Juan Manuel) and poetry (Juan Ruiz), and by the end of the century the form is virtually extinct.[45]

In Portuguese we still find *creçudo* as late as Gil Vicente (Juiz de Beira), and *deteudo* in a seventeenth century text. The more tenacious hold of the pattern in Portuguese is also reflected in the modern word *conteúdo* 'content' vs. Sp. *contenido*.

---

[44] In a single chapter of the *Primera Crónica General* we encounter *uençudos* (322b39), *perdido* (322b51), *uençudo* (325a5), *perdudos* (323a21), *perduda* (323a39), *sabida* (324a3).

[45] One form occurs in MS E of the *Rimado de Palacio: somos tenudos* vs. N, *tenidos*.

REFERENCES

This list contains only those works cited in the main text and the notes of this book. The author's name is given first, followed by the year of publication, and title of the article or book. Articles are followed by the journal or other sources, followed by the volume number, a period, and the pages on which it is found, e.g. 16.304–15 means "Volume 16, pages 304 to 315, inclusive." After a book title, the place of publication and the publisher is given, followed by page numbers if reference is made only to part of a book.

Abbreviations

AGI	Archivio Glottologico Italiano.
AJPh	American Journal of Philology.
ALEA	Alvar, Manuel, con la colaboración de A. Llorente y G. Salvador. Atlas lingüístico y etnográfico de Andalucía. 6 vols. Granada: Universidad de Granada, C.S.I.C., 1961- 1973.
ALLG	Archiv für lateinische Lexicographie und Grammatik.
ArL	Archivum Linguisticum.
BF	Boletim de Filologia.
BDELC	Corominas, Joan. 1967. Breve diccionario etimológico de la lengua castellana. 2nd ed. Madrid: Gredos.
BHS	Bulletin of Hispanic Studies.
BRP	Beiträge zur romanischen Philologie.
BRAE	Boletín de la Real Academia Española.
BSLP	Bulletin de la Société de Linguistique de Paris.
CFS	Cahiers Ferdinand de Saussure.
CIL	Corpus Inscriptionum Latinarum.
CLHM	Cahiers de Linguistique Hispanique Médiévale.
Congr ILPR	Congrès (congreso, congresso, congres) Internationale de Linguistique et Philologie Romanes. (The acts of these congresses are published in different cities and the titles will be in French, Italian, Romanian or Spanish, depending on the place of publication. The number of the congress is identified by a Roman numeral and the volume number by an Arabic numeral.)
DCELC	Corominas, Joan. l954. Diccionario crítico etimológico de la lengua castellana. 4 vols. Berne: Francke.
DLE	Menéndez Pidal, Ramón, ed. 1919. Documentos lingüísticos de España. Vol. 1: Reino de Castilla. Madrid: Junta Para Ampliación de Estudios e Investigaciones Científicas. (Document number and line numbers of words cited are given.)
EMP	Estudios dedicados a Menéndez Pidal. 7 vols. Madrid: C.S.I.C., 1950–62.
ELH	Alvar, Manuel, Antonio Badía, R. de Balbín, and L. F. Lindley Cintra, eds. 1960, 1967. Enciclopedia lingüística hispánica. Tomo 1: Antecedentes, onomástica. Madrid: C.S.I.C.; Tomo 2: Elementos constitutivos, fuentes.
HR	Hispanic Review.
IF	Indogermanische Forschungen.
Lang.	Language.
MLN	Modern Language Notes.
Neoph.	Neophilologus.
NRFH	Nueva Revista de Filología Hispánica.
Orígenes.	Menéndez Pidal, Ramón. 1950. Orígenes del español. Estado lingüístico de la península ibérica hasta el siglo XI. 3a edición muy corregida y adicionada. Madrid: Espasa-Calpe. (References are to section numbers.)
RDTP	Revista de Dialectología y Tradiciones Populares.
RFE	Revista de Filología Española.
RFH	Revista de Filología Hispánica.
RLaR	Revue des Langues Romanes.
RLiR	Revue de Linguistique Romane.
RPh	Romance Philology.
RR	Romanic Review.
RRL	Revue Roumaine de Linguistique.
StL	Studia Linguistica.
Ron.	"Ronshu". Aoyama Gakuin University, Tokyo.

StCL   Studii şi Cercetări Lingvistici.
TLCP   Travaux du Cercle Linguistique de Prague.
TLL   Travaux de Linguistique et de Littérature.
TPS   Transactions of the Philological Society.
UCPL   University of California Publications in Linguistics.
ZRPh   Zeitschrift für romanische Philologie.
ZPAS   Zeitschrift für Phonetik und allgemeine Sprachwissenschaft.

Authors and titles.

Adams, Douglas B. 1975. The distribution of retracted sibilants in medieval Europe. Lang. 51.282–92.
Aebischer, Paul. 1971. Le pluriel -as de la première déclinaison latine et ses résultats dans les langues romanes. ZRPh 87.74–98.
Ahlqvist, Anders, ed. 1982. Papers from the 5th International Conference on Historical Linguistics. (Amsterdam Studies in the Theory and History of Linguistic Science. Series IV: Current Issues in Linguistic Theory.) Amsterdam: John Benjamins Publishing Co.
Alarcos Llorach, Emilio. 1951. Alternancia de f y h en los arabismos. Archivum 1.29–41.
——. 1954. Resultados de Ge, i en la península. Archivum 4.330–42.
——. 1958. Quelques précisions sur la diphtongaison espagnole. Al. Rosetti, ed. Omagiu lui Iorgu Iordan. Bucharest: Academiei Republicii Populare Romîne, 1–4.
——. 1968. Fonología española. 4a edición aumentada y revisada. Madrid: Gredos.
Allen, Andrew. 1977–78. The interfix I/ESC in Catalan and Rumanian. RPh 31.293–311.
Allen, J. H. D., Jr. 1964. Tense/lax in Castilian Spanish. Word 20.295–321.
Allen, W. Sidney. 1978. Vox latina. A guide to the pronunciation of classical Latin. 2nd ed. Cambridge: Cambridge University Press.
——. 1973. Accent and rhythm. Prosodic features of Latin and Greek: A study in theory and reconstruction. Cambridge: Cambridge University Press.
Alonso, Amado. 1947. Trueques de sibilantes en antiguo español. NRFH 1.1–12.
——. 1954. La 'll' y sus alteraciones en España y América. EMP 2.41–89.
——. 1955. 1969. De la pronunciación medieval a la moderna en español. Ultimado y dispuesto para la imprenta por Rafael Lapesa. Madrid: Gredos. Vol. 2: 1969.
Alonso, Dámaso. La fragmentación fonética peninsular. ELH 1. Suplemento. Madrid: C.S.I.C.
Altheim, Franz. 1951. Geschichte der lateinischen Sprache. Frankfurt am Main.
Alvar, Manuel. 1952. Más sobre pérdida de f- inicial. Actas del Primer Congreso Internacional de Estudios Pirenaicos. Zaragoza: C.S.I.C. Instituto de Estudios Pirenaicos. Tomo 7, Seccion 6. Filología, 23–32.
——. 1952a. El imperfecto «iba» en español. Toribio M. Lucero and Alfredo Dornheim, eds. Homenaje a Fritz Krüger. Mendoza, Argentina: Universidad Nacional de Cuyo. I:42–45.
—— and Bernard Pottier. 1983. Morfología histórica del español. (Biblioteca Románica Hispánica. III. Manuales, 57.) Madrid: Gredos.
Andersen, Hennig. 1972. Diphthongization. Lang. 48.11–50.
——. 1973. Abductive and deductive change. Lang. 49.765–93.
——. 1974. Towards a typology of change: Bifurcating changes and binary relations. Anderson and Jones 1974 2.17–60.
Anderson, James M. 1964. Neutralization of phonemic opposition in Vulgar Latin. Romance Notes 6.86–88.
——. 1965. A study of syncope in Vulgar Latin. Word 21.70–85.
——. 1973. Structural aspects of language change. London: Longman.
——, and Jo Ann Creore. 1972. Readings in Romance linguistics. The Hague: Mouton.
——, and Bernard Rochet. 1979. Historical Romance morphology. Ann Arbor, Mich.: University Microfilms International.
Anderson, John M., and Charles Jones, eds. 1974. Historical linguistics. Proceedings of the First International Conference on Historical Linguistics, Edinburgh, 2–7 September 1973. 2 vols. New York: American Elsevier.
Antkowski, Ferdynand. 1956. La chronologie de la monophtongaison des diphtongues dans les langues indo-européenes. Posnan: Pantswowe Wydawn Naukowe.
Anttila, Raimo. 1972. An introduction to historical and comparative linguistics. New York: MacMillan.
——. 1977. Analogy. (Trends in Linguistics. State of the Art Reports, 10.) The Hague: Mouton.

Arlotto, Anthony. 1972. Introduction to historical linguistics. Boston: Houghton-Mifflin.
Árnason, Kristján. 1980. Quantity in historical phonology. Icelandic and related cases. (Cambridge Studies in Linguistics, 30.) Cambridge: Cambridge University Press.

Badía Margarit, Antonio M. 1962. Nuevas precisiones sobre la diptongación española. RLiR 26.1–12.
Bailey, Charles-James N. 1975. Old and new views on language history and language relationships. MS.
Baldi, Philip and Ronald N. Werth, eds. 1978. Readings in historical phonology: Chapters in the theory of sound change. University Park: Pennsylvania State University.
Baldinger, Kurt. 1958. La position du gascon entre la Galloromania et l'Ibéroromania. RLiR 22.241–92.
———. 1972. La formación de los dominios lingüísticos en la península ibérica. 2a edición corregida y muy aumentada. Madrid: Gredos.
Barbarino, Joseph Louis. 1978. The evolution of the Latin /b/-/u/ merger. A quantitive and comparative analysis of the B-V alternation in Latin inscriptions. North Carolina Studies in the Romance Languages and Literatures, No. 203.). Chapel Hill, N. C.: University of North Carolina, Dept. of Romance Languages.
———. 1981. Latin and Romance intervocalic stops. A quantitative and comparative study. (Studia Humanitatis.) Madrid: Porrúa.
Baugh, Albert C. 1957. A history of the English language. 2nd ed. New York: Appleton-Century-Crofts.
Beeler, Madison S. 1952. The relation of Latin and Osco-Umbrian. Lang. 28.435–43.
Belardi, Walter. 1979. Dal latino alle lingue romanze. I: Il vocalismo. Roma: Bulzoni. (Instrumenta Philologiae 2.)
Beveniste, Emil. 1939. Répartition des consonnes et phonologie du mot. TCLP 8.27–35.
Berkhofer, Robert F., Jr. 1969. A behavioral approach to historical analysis. New York: Free Press.
Bertoldi, Vittorio. 1939. I criteri d'indagine storico geografica applicati al latino. Napoli: Stabilimento Tipografico Editoriale.
Bhat, D. N. Shankara. 1968. Is sound change gradual? Linguistics 42.5–18.
———. 1972. Sound change. Poona: Bhasha Prahashan.
———. 1976. Dichotomy in phonological change. Lingua 39.333–51.
Blake, Robert. (forthcoming) Scribal worries and sound changes in medieval Spain. (To appear in Studies in Romance Languages.)
Blansitt, Edward L., Jr., and Richard V. Teschner, eds. 1980. A festschrift for Jacob Ornstein. Studies in general linguistics and sociolinguistics. Rowley, MA: Newbury House Publishers, Inc.
Blaylock, Curtis. 1964–65. The monophthongization of Latin AE in Spanish. RPh 18.16–26.
———. 1964–65a. Hispanic metaphony. RPh 18.253–71.
———. 1975. Los pretéritos fuertes en -sk- del español medieval. Studia hispanica in honorem Rafael Lapesa 3.91–96.
———. 1986. Notes on the chronology of a morphonological change in Golden-Age Spanish: The loss of -D in proparoxytonic forms of the second person plural verbs. HR 54.279–84.
Bloomfield, Leonard. 1933. Language. New York: Holt.
Bolinger, Dwight L. 1958. A theory of pitch accent in English. Word 14.109–49.
Bonfante, Giuliano. 1935. El tratamiento de "bl-" en castellano. RFE 22.189–90.
———. 1941. The Latin and Romance weak perfect. Lang. 17.201–11.
———. 1946. Reply. RR 37.247–51.
Boyd-Bowman, Peter. 1975. A sample of sixteenth century 'Caribbean' Spanish phonology. William G. Milan, John J. Staczek, and Juan C. Zamora, eds. 1974 Colloquium on Spanish and Portuguese Linguistics. Washington: Georgetown University Press, 1–11.
Brandenstein, W. 1951. Kurze Phonologie des Lateinischen. Supplement to Altheim 1951, 491–98.
Brosnahan, L. F. 1961. The sounds of language. An inquiry into the role of genetic factors in the development of sound systems. Cambridge: W. Heffer.
Bruner, Jerome S., and Donald O'Dowd. 1958. A note on the informativeness of parts of words. Language and Speech 1.98- 101.
Bunge, Mario. 1959. Causality: The place of the causal principle in modern science. Cambridge, Mass.: Harvard University Press.
Burger, André. 1955. Phonématique et diachronie à propos de la palatalisation des consonnes romanes. Cahiers Ferdinand de Saussure 13.18–33.

Campbell, Lyle. 1974. On conditions of sound change. Anderson and Jones 1974, 1.89–97.

——. 1976. Language contact and sound change. Christie 1976, 181–94.

Canellada, María Josefa. 1978. Velarización temprana. (Notas para la historia de la fonética.) Estudios ofrecidos a Emilio Alarcos Llorach. Oviedo: Servicio de Publicaciones, Universidad de Oviedo, II.61–64.

Canfield, Delos Lincoln. 1962. La pronunciación del español en América. Ensayo histórico-descriptivo. Bogotá: Instituto Caro y Cuervo.

Caro Baroja, Julio. 1945. Materiales para una historia de la lengua vasca en su relación con la la latina. (Acta Salmanticensia. Filosofía y Letras, Tomo 1, num. 3.) Salamanca.

Carvalho, José G. C. Herculano de. 1956. A evoluçao portuguesa dos grupos -KY- e -TY- intervocálicos. VR 15.259–78.

Castellani, Arrigo. 1965. La diphtongaison des e et o ouverts en Italien. Congr ILPR, X, 3.951–64.

——. 1970. Ancora sul dittongamento italiano e romanzo. Seconda risposta a Friedrich Schürr. Cultura Neolatina 30.117–30.

Castro, Americo. 1966. La realidad histórica de España. 3a edición. México: Porrúa.

Catalán, Diego. 1954. Resultados apico-palatales y dorso- palatales de -LL-, -NN-, y de LL- (<L-), NN- (<N-) RFE 38.1–44.

——. 1955. La escuela lingüística española y su concepción del lenguaje. Madrid: Gredos.

——. 1956. El çeçeo-zezeo al comenzar la expansión atlántica de Castilla. BF 16.306–34.

——. 1956–57. El asturiano occidental. Examen sincrónico y explicación diacrónica de sus fronteras fonológicas. (1). RPh 10.71–92.

——. 1957. The end of the phoneme /z/ in Spanish. Word 13.283–322.

——, ed. 1957a. 1962. Estructuralismo e historia: Miscelánea homenaje a André Martinet. Vol. 1; Vol. 3, 1962. La Laguna: Universidad de La Laguna.

——. 1962a. Dialectología y estructuralismo diacrónico. Catalán 1962, 69–80.

——. 1967–68. La pronunciación [ihante], por /iffante/ en la Rioja del siglo XI. Anotaciones a una observación dialectológica de un historiador árabe. RPh 21.410–35.

——. 1971. En torno a la estructura silábica del español de ayer y del español de mañana. Coseriu and Stempel 1971, 77–110.

——. 1972. Ibero-Romance. Sebeok 1972, 927–1106.

——, and Alvaro Galmés de Fuentes. 1954. La diptongación en leonés. Archivum 4.87–147.

Chasca, Edmund de. 1946. The phonology of the speech of negroes in early Spanish drama. HR 14.322–39.

Chen, Matthew. 1972. The time dimension: Contribution toward a theory of sound change. Foundations of Language 8.457–98.

——. 1976. Relative chronology: Three methods of reconstruction. Journal of Linguistics 12.209–58.

—— and Hsui-i Hsieh. 1971. The time variable in phonological change. Journal of Linguistics 7.1–13.

—— and William S.-Y. Wang. 1975. Sound change: Actuation and implementation. Lang. 51.255–81.

Chevalier, Jean-Claude. 1975. Du latin au roman. (Réflexions sur la destruction de la déclinaison nominale.) Haim Vidal Sephilia, ed. Mélanges offerts à Charles Vincent Aubrun. Paris: Editions Hispaniques, 171–90.

Chomsky, Noam, and Morris Halle. 1968. The sound pattern of English. New York: Harper and Row.

Christie, William M., Jr., ed. 1976. Current progress in historical linguistics. Proceedings of the Second International Conference on Historical Linguistics, Tucson, Arizona, 12–16 January 1976. New York: North-Holland Publishing Co.

Cock Hincapié, Olga. 1969. El seseo en el Nuevo Reino de Granada: 1550–1650. (Publicaciones del Instituto Caro y Cuervo, 26.) Bogotá.

Codoñer, Carmen. 1973. Introducción al estudio de los demostrativos latino. Revista Española de Lingüística 3.81–94.

Cohen, Maurice R. 1942. Causation and its application to history. Journal of the History of Ideas 3.12–29.

Coleman, R. G. G. 1971. The monophthongization of /ae/ and the Vulgar Latin vowel system. TPS, 175–99.

——. 1974. The monophthongization of Latin ae: A reply. TPS, 86- 92.

Collinge, N.E. 1970. Computation and Latin Consonants. Collectanea linguistica: Essays in general and genetic linguistica. (Janua linguarum, Ser. Min. 21.) The Hague: Mouton, 192–218.

Conkin, Paul K. 1974. Causation revisited. History and Theory 13.1–20.

Copceag, Dimistrie. 1970. Une tendance 'roman' a la syllabe ouverte? Cahiers de Linguistique Théorique et Appliqués 7.57–62.

Corbett, Noel L. 1970–71. Reconstructing the diachronic phonology of Romance. RPh 24.273–90.

——. 1976. Corrélations phonologiques, redondance, et changement phonétique: La diphtongaison romane. Congr ILPR XIII, 1.119–33.

Cornu, J. 1884. Mélanges espagnols. Romania 13.285–314.

Corominas, Juan. 1953. Para la fecha del yeísmo y del lleísmo. NRFH 7.81–87.

Corrientes, Federico. 1978. Los fonemas /p/, /č/ y /g/ en árabe hispánico. VR 37.214–18.

Coseriu, Eugenio. 1973. Sincronía, diacronía e historia. El problema del cambio lingüístico. 2a ed. revisada. Madrid: Gredos.

——. 1978. Hervás und das Substrat. StCl 29.523–30.

——, and Wolf-Dieter Stempel, eds. 1971. Sprache und Geschichte. Festschrift für Harri Meier zum 65. Geburtstag. Munich: W. Fink.

Craddock, Jerry R. 1969. Latin legacy versus substratum residue. (UCPL, 53.) Berkeley - Los Angeles: University of California Press.

——. 1970. Review of Lehmann and Malkiel 1968. Lang. 46.688–94.

——. 1980. The contextual varieties of yod: An attempt at systematization. In Blansitt and Teschner 1980, 61–68.

——. 1983. Descending diphthongs and the regular preterite in Hispano-Romance. BHS 60.1–14.

Danesi, Marcel. 1977. The case for andalucismo re-examined. HR 45.181–93.

Dardel, Robert de. 1964. Considérations sur la déclinaison romane à trois cas. CFS 21.7–23.

——. 1976. Une analyse spatio-temporelle du roman commun reconstruit (à propos du genre). Cong IPLR XIV, 2.75–82.

de Graaf, Tjeerd. 1983. Vowel duration and vowel quality. In Hattori-Inoue 1983, 602–05.

Delbouille, M. 1966. Réflexions sur la génèse phonétique des parlers romans. CFS 26.17–31.

Delesalle, Simone. 1980. L'analogie: D'un arbitraire a l'autre. La Linguistique 46.90–111.

Devine, A. M. 1970–71. Ausnahmslosigkeit and Stammbaumtheorie: Questions of method. Lingua 26.348–69.

——, and Laurence D. Stephens. 1977. Two studies in Latin phonology. I: The Latin labiovelars; II: The Latin consonant clusters. (Studia Linguistica et Philologica, Vol. 3.) Saratoga, CA: Anma Libri.

Devoto, Giacomo. 1930. I fondamenti del sistema delle vocali romanzi. Rendiconti del R. Istituto Lombardo di Scienze e Lettere 63.593–605; reprinted as Il sistema protoromanzo delle vocali. Scritti minori. Florence, 1958, 328–37.

——. 1956. La romanisation de L'Italie médiane. Cahiers d'Histoire Mondiale 3.443–62; reprinted in Scritti minori, 287–304.

Di Pietro, Robert J. 1966. Juncture and the preservation of voiceless stops in West Romance. Orbis 15.68–72.

Díaz y Díaz, Manuel C. 1962. Antología del latín vulgar. 2a ed. aumentada y revisada. Madrid: Gredos.

Doman, Mary Gay. 1969. H aspirada y f moderna en el español americano. Thesaurus 24.426–58.

Dray, William. 1957. Laws and explanation in history. London: Oxford University Press.

——. 1964. Philosophy of history. Englewood Cliffs, NJ: Prentice-Hall.

Dressler, Wolfgang. 1965. i-Prothese vor s impurum in Kleinasien (und im Vulgärlatein). Balkansko Ezikonanie 9.93–100.

Dworkin, Steven Norman. 1974. Studies in the history of Latin primary -D- in Hispano-Romance. PhD Dissertation in Romance Philology: University of California, Berkeley.

Dyen, Isidore. 1963. Why phonetic change is regular. Lang. 39.631–37.

Emmet, Dorothy. 1958. Function, purpose and powers. Some concepts in the study of individuals and societies. London: Macmillan.

Enk, P. J. 1953. The Latin accent. Mnemosyne 6.93–109.

Ernout, Alfred. 1909. Les éléments dialectaux du vocabulaire latin. Paris.

Esper, Erwin A. 1973. Analogy and association in linguistics and psychology. Athens: University of Georgia Press.

Espinosa, Aurelio M. 1927. Review of Orígenes del español. Lang. 3.142–50.

Fagan, David S. 1979. On diphthongization in northern Portuguese. Congr ILPR XIV, 3.197–211.

Faria, Ernesto. 1955. Fonética histórica do latím. (Biblioteca Brasileira de Filologia, No. 9.) Rio de Janeiro.

Ferguson, Charles A., and John J. Gumperz, eds. 1960. Linguistic diversity in South Asia: Studies in regional, social and functional variation. (International Journal of American Linguistics 26/3, Part 3.)

Fischer, I. 1968. Remarques sur le traitement de la diphtongue *au* en latin vulgaire. RRL 13.417–20.

——. 1979. Preliminării la o descriere fonologică a consonantismului latin. StCL 30.307–14.

——. 1980. La date de l'assibiliation de lat. y: Un point d'interrogation épigraphique. RRL 25.495–96.

Fisiak, Jacek, ed. 1978. Recent developments in historical phonology. (Trends in Linguistics. Studies and Monographs, 4.) The Hague, Paris: Mouton.

Foley, James. 1970. Phonological distinctive features. Folia Linguistica 4.87–92.

Font Ruis, J. 1957. La sociedad en Asturias, León y Castilla en los primeros siglos medievales. J. Vicens Vives, ed. Historia social y económica de España y America. Tomo I: Coloniza- ciones, feudalismo, América primitiva. Barcelona: Editorial Teide, 253–371.

Fontán, Antonio. 1965. Historia y sistemas de los demostrativos latinos. Emerita 33.71–107.

Fontanella de Weinberg, Maria Beatriz. 1971. Review of Malkiel 1968. Filología 15.318–27.

Foster, David William. 1967–68. Phonemic issues associated with the four yods of Spanish. Filologia Moderna 29–30.151–58.

Fouché, P. 1949. De quelques changements de quantité dans le latin parlé. Mélanges de philologie romane et de littérature médiévale offerts à Ernest Hoepffner. Paris: Les Belles Lettres, 13–28.

Fourquet, Jean. 1962. Pourquoi les lois phonétiques sont sans exceptions. Horace G. Lunt, ed. Proceedings of the Ninth International Congress of Linguists. The Hague: Mouton, 638–44.

Frago Gracia, Juan A. 1977–78. Para la historia de la velarización española. Archivum 27.28.219–26.

——. 1983. El reajuste fonológico del español moderno en su preciso contexto histórico. Sobre la evolución /ŝ ẑ/>/x/. Lázaro Carreter, Vol. 1.219–30.

——. 1985. De los fonemas medievales /ŝ ẑ/ al interdental fricativa /θ/ del español mo- derno. Philologica hispaniensia in honorem Manual Alvar. II: Linguistica. Madrid: Gredos, 205–16.

Francescato, Giuseppe. 1970. Sostrato, contatto linguistico e apprendimento della lingua materna. AGI 55.10–28.

Franceschi, Temistocle. 1976. Sull'evoluzione del vocalismo dal latino repubblicano al neola- tino. Scritti in onore di Giuliano Bonfante. Vol. 1. Breschia: Editrice Paideia, 257- 79.

Gallie, W. B. 1955. Explanations in history and the genetic sciences. Mind 64.160–80.

Galmés de Fuentes, Alvaro. 1956. Influencias sintácticas y estilísticas del árabe en la prosa medieval castellana. BRAE 36.65–131; 255–307.

——. 1957. Lle-yeismo y otras cuestiones lingüísticas en un relato morisco del siglo XVII. EMP 7.273–307.

——. 1961. El arcaismo fonológico de los dialectos del norte portugués y su importancia para la lingüística románica general. BF 20.19–30.

——. 1962. Las sibilantes en la Romania. Madrid: Gredos.

——. 1977. El dialecto mozárabe de Toledo. Al-Andalus 42.183- 206; 249–99.

——. 1983. Dialectología mozárabe. (Biblioteca Románica Hispánica III. Manuales, 58.) Ma- drid: Gredos.

Gamillscheg, Ernst. 1935. Romania germanica. Sprach- und Siedlungsgeschichte der Ger- manen auf dem Boden des alten Römerreiches. Vol. 2. Berlin: Walter de Gruyter.

——. 1968. Zur Geschichte der Assibilierung und der Palatalisierung. Festschrift Walther von Wartburg zum 80. Geburtstag. Tübingen: M. Niemeyer, 1.445–50.

García, Erica. 1976. La jota española: Una explicación acústica. Actas del III Congreso de la Asociacion de Lingüística y Filología de la América Latina. San Juan: Universidad de Puerto Rico, 103–13.

García de Diego, Vicente. 1950. El castellano como complejo dialectal y sus dialectos internos. RFE 34.107–24.

——. 1951. Gramática histórica española. Madrid: Gredos.

García Moreno, Luis A. 1975. El fin del reino visigodo de Toledo. Decadencia y catástrofe. Una contribución a su crítica. Madrid: Universidad Autónoma.

García y Bellido, A. 1967. La latinización de Hispania. Archivo Español de Arqueología 40.3–29.

Gardiner, Patrick. 1952. The nature of historical explanation. London: Oxford University Press.

Gauchat, Louis. 1905. L'unité phonétique dans le patois d'une commune. Halle.

Gavel, Henri. 1936. Remarques sur les substrats ibériques, réels ou supposés, dans la phonétique du gascon et de l'espagnole. RLiR 12.36–43.

——. 1952. Note sur les redoublements de consonne devant semi- voyelle en latin vulgaire. Annales publiées par la Faculté des Lettres de Toulouse. (June), 101–10.

——. 1953. Note sur les glissements d'accent après i ou u devant voyelle dans les mots latins. Annales publiées par la Faculté des Lettres de Toulouse. Pallas. Etudes sur l'antiquité. Feb. 158–66.

Gerola, Berengario. 1950. Il nominativo plurale in -as nel latino e il plurale romanzo. Symbolae Philologicae Gotoburgenses, 327–54.

Gifford, D. J., and F. W. Hodcroft. 1966. Textos lingüísticos del medioevo español. 2a ed. Oxford: Dolphin Book Co.

Godel, Robert. 1953. Les semi-voyelles en latin. StL 7.90–99.

Gonzalez Ollé, P. 1972. Resultados castellanos de 'kw' y 'gw' latinos. Aspectos fonéticos y fonológicos. BRAE 52.285–318.

——. 1977. Precisiones sobre la etimología de *aquel*. Homenaje al Prof. Muñoz Cortés. Murcia: Universidad de Murcia, 863–89.

Gorog, Ralph de. 1980. L'origine des formes espagnoles *doy, estoy, soy, voy*. CLHM 5.157–62.

Gougenheim, Georges. 1960. Review of Dardel 1958. BSLP 55.123–25.

Gradenwitz, Otto. 1904. Laterculi vocum latinarum voces latinas et a fronte et a tergo. Leipzig: Hirzel.

Granda Gutiérrez, Germán de. 1960. Las vocales finales del dialecto leonés. Alvaro Galmés de Fuentes, ed. Trabajos sobre el dominio románico leonés. Tomo 2. Madrid: Gredos, 27–117.

——. 1966. La estructura silábica del dominio ibero-romanico. (RFE Anejo 81.) Madrid: C.S.I.C.

——. 1966a. La velarización de RR en el español de Puerto Rico. RFE 49. 181–227.

——. 1973. Dialectología, historia social y sociología lingüística en Iscuandé (Departmento de Nariño, Colombia). Thesaurus 28.445–70.

Grandgent, Charles H. 1927. From Latin to Italian. Cambridge, Mass.: Harvard University Press.

Gregor, D. B. 1975. Friulan: Language and literature. New York: Oleander Press.

Griffin, David A. 1958. Los mozarabismos del Vocabulista atribuido a Ramon Martí. Al-Andalus 23.251–337; 24.85–124, 330–30; 25.93–169.

Guarducci, Margherita. 1980. La cosidetta fibula Praenestina. Memorie della Classe di Scienze Morali e storiche dell'Accademia dei Lincei. Roma. 24.413–574.

Guitarte, Guillermo. 1955. El ensordecimiento del žeísmo porteño. RFE 39.261–83.

——. Notas para la historia del yeísmo. Coseriu and Stempel 1971, 179–98.

Guiter, Henri. 1966. Atlas linguistique des Pyrenées Orientales. Paris: Centre Nationale de la Recherche Scientifique.

Gulsoy, J. 1969–70. The -i words in the poems of Gonzalo de Berceo. RPh 23.173–87.

Hadlich, Roger L. 1965. The phonological history of Vegliote. (University of North Carolina Studies in the Romance Languages and Literatures, No. 52.) Chapel Hill: University of North Carolina Press.

Hall, Robert A., Jr. 1964. Introductory linguistics. Philadelphia: Chilton Books.

——. 1964a. Initial consonants and syntactic doubling in West Romance. Lang. 40.551–56.

——. 1968. An essay on language. Philadelphia: Chilton Books.

——. 1976. Proto-Romance phonology. New York: American Elsevier.

——. 1980. The gradual decline of case in Romance substantives. Frans van Coetsem and Linda R. Waugh, eds. Contributions to historical linguistics. Issues and materials. Leiden: E. J. Brill.

Harris, James W. 1969. Sound change in Spanish and the theory of markedness. Lang. 45.538–52.

Harris, Martin. 1982. On explaining language change. In Ahlqvist 1982, pp. 1–14.

Harvey, Van A. 1966. The historian and the believer. The morality of historical knowledge and Christian belief. New York: Macmillan.

Hattori, Shiro, and Kazuko Inoue, eds. 1983. Proceedings of the XIIIth International Congress of Linguists, August 29- September 4, 1982, Tokyo. Tokyo.

Haudricourt, André G., and Alphonse Juilland. 1952. Romania orientale et Romania occidentale dans le vocalisme. Cahiers Sextil Puşcariu 1.241–54.

——. 1970. Essai pour une histoire structurale du phonétisme français. 2e ed. revisée. The Hague: Mouton.

Heffner, Roe-Merrill Secrist. 1949. General phonetics. Madison: University of Wisconsin Press.

Herman, Jozsef. 1968. Statistique et diachronie: essai sur l'évolution du vocalisme dans la latinité tardive. Word 24.242–51.

——. 1971. Essai sur la latinité du littoral adriatique à l'époque de l'empire. Coseriu and Stempel 1971, 199–226.

Herslund, Michael. 1974. Phonologie des voyelles du latin vulgaire. RR 9.232–43.

Hiersche, Rolf. 1965. Der Wechsel zwischen anlautenden f and h im Lateinischen. Glotta 43.103–18.

Hill, Archibald A. 1954. Juncture and syllable division in Latin. Lang. 30.439–47.

——. 1958. Introduction to linguistic structures. New York: Harcourt Brace.

Hilty, Gerold. 1969. Zur Diphthongierung im Galloromanischen und im Iberoromanischen. Wolf-Dieter Lange and Heinz Jürgen Wolf, eds. Philologische Studien für Joseph M. Piel. Heidelberg: Winter, 95–107.

——. 1979. Das Schicksal der lateinischen intervokalischen Verschluszlaute -p-, -t-, -k- im Mozarabischen. Höfler, Vernay, Wolf 1979. I.145–60.

Hockett, Charles F. 1954. Two models of grammatical description. Word 10.210–34.

——. 1955. A manual of phonology. Baltimore: Waverly Press.

——. 1958. A course in modern linguistics. New York: MacMillan.

——. 1965. Sound change. Lang. 41.185–204.

——. 1967. The quantification of functional load. Word 23.300–20.

Hoenigswald, Henry M. 1960. Language change and linguistic reconstruction. Chicago: University of Chicago Press.

——. 1964. Graduality, sporadicity, and the minor sound change processes. Phonetics 11.202–15.

——. 1978. The Annus Mirabilis 1876 and posterity. Transactions of the Philological Society, 17–35.

Höfler, Manfred, Henri Vernay, and Lothar Wolf, eds. 1979. Festschrift Kurt Baldinger zum 60. Geburtstag 17 November 1979. 2 vols. Tübingen: Max Niemeyer.

Homeyer, Helen. 1957. Some observations on bilingualism and language shift from the sixth to the third century B.C. Word 13.415–40.

Hospers, J. 1946. On explanation. Journal of Philosophy 43.337–56.

Householder, Fred. 1972. The principal step in linguistic change. Language Sciences No. 20.1–5.

Hsieh, Hsui-i. 1972. Lexical diffusion: Evidence from child language acquisition. Glossa 6.89–102.

Iliescu, Maria. 1969. Stammen die romanischen Substantive lateinischen Ursprungs von der Akkusativform ab? RRL 14.477–79.

Izzo, Herbert J. 1972. Tuscan and Etruscan. The problem of linguistic substratum influence in central Italy. Toronto: University of Toronto Press.

——. 1972a. The layer-cake model in historical linguistics. General Linguistics 12.159–68.

——. 1977. Pre-latin languages and sound changes in Romance: The case of Old Spanish /h-/. Michio Peter Hagiwara, ed. Studies in Romance linguistics. Proceedings of the Fifth Linguistic Symposium on Romance Languages. Rowley, Mass.: Newbury House, 227–53.

Jackson, Gabriel. 1972. The making of medieval Spain. New York: Harcourt, Brace, Jovanovich.

Jakobson, Roman. 1962. The concept of sound law and the teleological criterion. Selected writings. The Hague: Mouton 1.1–2.

——. 1966. Henry Sweet's paths toward phonemics. Charles Ernest Bazell, ed. In memory of J. R. Firth. London: Longmans, 242–54.

Janson, Tore. 1979. Mechanisms of language change in Latin. Stockholm: Almqvist and Wiksell International.
——. 1982. Sound change and perceptual compensation. In Maher et al. 1982, 119–27.
——. 1983. Sound change in perception and production. Lang. 59.18–34.
Janssen, H.H. 1956. *qu* and *gu* en latin. Hommages à Max Niedermann. (Collection Latomus, Vol. 23.) Brussells, 189–90.
Jespersen, Otto. 1922. Language. Its nature, development and origin. New York: Holt.
Joos, Martin. 1952. The medieval sibilants. Lang. 28.222–31.
Joynt, Carey B., and Nicholas Rescher. 1959. On explanation in history. Mind 68.383–88.
Jucquois, G. 1970. Un problème de phonostatistique: Le cas du *m* en latin. Elie Nieuwborg, ed. Mélanges offerts au professeur J. L. Pauwels à l'occasion de son éméritat. (Université de Louvain Recueil de Travaux d'Histoire et de Philologie, 4e série, 46.) Louvain: Bibliothèque de l'Université, 145–68.
Jungemann, Fredrick H. 1955. La teoría del sustrato y los dialectos hispano-romances y gascones. Madrid: Gredos.

Katičić, Rodoslav. 1970. A contribution to the general theory of comparative linguistics. The Hague: Mouton.
Kelly, David H. 1967. Distinctive feature analysis in Latin phonology. AJPh 88.67–77; reprinted in Strunk 1973, 47–58.
Kent, Roland G. 1945. The sounds of Latin. 3rd ed. rev. Baltimore: Linguistic Society of America.
Kerlouegan, F. 1978. Les voyelles longues du latin classique: étude phonologique. Langages 50.32.37.
Kiddle, Lawrence B. 1975. The chronology of the Spanish sound changes: *š* > *x*. Studies in honor of Lloyd A. Kasten. Madison, Wisc.: Hispanic Seminary of Medieval Studies, 73–100.
——. 1977. Sibilant turmoil in Middle Spanish. HR 45.327–36.
King, Robert D. 1967. Functional load and sound change. Lang. 43.831–52.
——. 1969. Historical linguistics and generative grammar. Englewood Cliffs, N.J.: Prentice-Hall.
——. 1969a. Push chains and drag chains. Glossa 3.3–21.
Kiparsky, Paul. 1974. Remarks on analogical change. Anderson and Jones 1974, 257–75.
Kiss, Sandor. 1972. Les transformations de la structure syllabique en latin tardif. (Studia Romanica, Series Linguistica, fasc. 11.) Debretin.
Klausenburger, Jürgen. 1975. Latin vocalic quantity to quality: A pseudo-problem? Mario Saltarelli and Dieter Wanner, eds. Diachronic studies in Romance linguistics. The Hague-Paris: Mouton, 107–17.
——. 1979. Morphologization: Studies in Latin and Romance morphophonology. Tübingen: Niemeyer.
Křepinský, M. 1965. Chronologie de la fusion de U avec U dans les langues romanes. Omagiu Rosetti 1965, 451–56.
Kurath, Hans, ed. 1939–41. Linguistic atlas of New England. Providence, R.I.: Brown University Press.

Labov, William. 1963. The social motivation of a sound change. Word 19.273–409.
——. 1966. The social stratification of English in New York City. Washington: Center for Applied Linguistics.
——. 1968. On the mechanism of linguistic change. O'Brien 1968, 259–82.
——. 1970. The study of language in its social context. Studium Generale 23.30–87.
——. 1972. The internal evolution of linguistic rules. Stockwell and Macaulay 1972, 101–71.
——. 1973. The social setting of linguistic change. Thomas A. Sebeok, ed. Current trends in linguistics, Vol. 11. Diachronic, areal, and typological linguistics. The Hague, Paris: Mouton, 195–251.
——. 1975. On the use of the present to explain the past. Luigi Heilmann, ed. Proceedings of the Eleventh International Congress of Linguists, Aug. 28 - Sept. 2, 1972. Bologna: Società Editrice il Mulino, 2.825–51.
——. 1981. Resolving the Neogrammarian controversy. Lang. 57.267–308.
——. 1982. Building on empirical foundations. In Lehman and Malkiel 1982, 17–92.
——, Malcah Yeager, and Richard Steiner. 1972. A quantitive study of sound change in

378 LLOYD: FROM LATIN TO SPANISH

progress. (Report on National Science Foundation Contract NSF-GS-3287, University of Pennsylvania.) Philadelphia: The U. S. Regional Survey.

Lafon, René. 1960. Evolución de la lengua vasca desde la época de los textos más antiguos. ELH 1.88–91.

Lakovary, N. 1955. Contribution a l'histoire linguistique ancienne de la région balkano-danubienne et à la constitution de la langue roumaine. VR 14.310–46.

Lambert, Charles. 1908. La grammaire latine selon les grammariens latins du IVᵉ et du Vᵉ siècle. (Revue Bourguignonne, publiée par l'Université de Dijon, 18. Nos. 1–2.) Dijon, Paris.

Lantolf, James P. 1974. Linguistic change as a socio-cultural phenomenon: A study of the Old Spanish sibilant devoicing. PhD Dissertation, Pennsylvania State University.

——. 1979. Explaining linguistic change: The loss of voicing in the Old Spanish sibilants. Orbis 28.290–315.

Lapesa, Rafael. 1948. Asturiano y provenzal en el Fuero de Avilés. (Acta Salmanticensia, 11:4.) Salamanca.

——. 1951. La apócope de la vocal en castellano antiguo. Intento de explicación histórica. EMP 2.185–226.

——. 1956. Sobre el ceceo y el seseo en Hispanoamérica. Revista Iberoamericana 21.409–16.

——. 1957. Sobre el ceceo y el seseo andaluces. Catalán 1957b, 67–94.

——. 1970. Las formas verbales de segunda persona y los orígenes del voseo. In Magis 1970, 519–31.

——. 1975. De nuevo sobre la apócope vocálica en castellano medieval. NRFH 24.13–23.

——. 1979. Nominativo o caso oblicuo latinos como origen de demostrativos y artículo castellanos. Höfler, Vernay, Wolf 1979. I.196–207.

——. 1980. Historia de la lengua española. 8a ed. Madrid: Gredos.

Lausberg, Heinrich. 1939. Die Mundarten Südlukaniens. (ZRPh, Beiheft 90.) Halle.

——. 1965. Lingüística románica. Tomo I. Madrid: Gredos. Tomo II, 1966.

Lázaro Carreter, Fernando. 1949. F > h, fenómeno ibérico o romance? Actas de la Primera Reunión de Toponomia Pirenaica. Zaragoza, 165–76.

Lázaro Mora, Fernando A. 1978–80. RL > LL en la lengua literaria. RFE 60.267–83.

Le Coultre, J. 1905. La prononciation du latin sous Charlemagne. Mélanges Nicole. Geneva: W. Kundig, 313–34.

Leed, Richard L. 1970. Distinctive features and analogy. Lingua 26.1–24.

Lehiste, Ilse, Katherine Morton, and M.A.A. Tatham. 1973. An instrumental study of consonant gemination. Journal of Phonetics 1.131–48.

Lehmann, W. P., and Yakov Malkiel, eds. 1968. Directions for historical linguistics. A symposium. Austin and London: University of Texas Press.

——. 1982. Perspectives on historical linguistics. Amsterdam/Philadelphia: John Benjamins Publishing Co.

Lenfest, Donald E. 1978. An explanation of the /G/ in 'tengo', 'vengo', 'pongo', and 'valgo' Hispania 61.894–904.

Leonard, Clifford. 1978. Umlaut in Romance. An essay in linguistic archaeology. (Giessener Beiträge zur Sprachwissenschaft, 12.) Gossen-Linden: Hoffman-Verlag.

Lepscky, G. G. 1962. Il problema dell'accento latino. Rassegna critica di studi sull'accento latino e sullo studio dell'accento. Annali della Scuola Normale Superiore di Pisa 31.199–246.

Leumann, Manu. 1977. Lateinische Laut und Formenlehre. Munich: C. H. Beck.

Levy, John. 1973. Tendential transfer of OSp. HEDO < FOEDU to the family of HEDER < FOETERE. RPh 27.204–10.

Liénard, Edm. 1969. Réflexions sur l'accent latin. Jacqueline Bibauw, ed. Hommages à Marcel Renard. Brussels: Latomus Revue d'Etudes Latines, 1.551–60.

Lindsay, Wallace Martin. 1894. The Latin language. Oxford: Clarendon Press.

Lipski, John M. 1974. The reduction of falling diphthongs: Towards a theory of feature hierarchies. RRL 19.415–35.

Live, Anna. 1959. Prehistory of Latin phonemic structure. PhD Dissertation in Linguistics, University of Pennsylvania.

Llorente Maldonado de Guevara, Antonio. 1958–59. Importancia para la historia del español de la aspiración y otros rasgos fonéticos del salmantino noroccidental. RFE 42.151–65.

Lloyd, Paul M. 1970. The contribution of Menéndez Pidal to linguistic theory. HR 38, No. 5.14–21.

——. 1970a. A note on Latin syllable structure. Classical Philology 65.41–42.

——. 1971. L'action du substrat et la structure linguistique. Congr ILPR XII Bucharest: Editions de l'Académie de la République Socialiste de Roumanie, 2.953–63.
——. 1977. La metafonía vocálica y el sistema verbal románico. Atti XIV Congr ILPR, Napoli, 15–20 aprile 1974. Amsterdam: Benjamins, Vol. IV, 297–311.
Löfstedt, Einar. 1959. Late Latin. Oslo-Cambridge, MA: Harvard University Press.
——. 1961. Studien über die Sprache der langobardische Gesetze. Uppsala: Almqvist and Wiksells.
Loicq, J. 1962. La quantité de la voyelle devant -gn- la nature de la quantité vocalique. Latomus 21.257–78.
López García, Angel. 1977–78. Simetría, asimetría y disimetría en el vocalismo ibero-rrománico. Archivum 27–28.293–334.
Lord, Robert. 1966. Teach yourself comparative linguistics. London: The English Universities Press.
Lorenzo, Emilio. 1966. El español de hoy, lengua en ebullición. Madrid: Gredos.
Louch, A. R. 1969. Explanation and human action. Berkeley, Los Angeles: University of California Press.
Lozovan, Eugène. 1954. Unité et dislocation de la Romania orientale. Orbis 3.123–37.
Lüdtke, Helmut. 1956. Die strukturelle Entwicklung des romanischen Vokalismus. (Romanistische Versuche und Vorarbeiten, 2.). Bonn: Romanisches Seminar an der Universität Bonn.
——. 1957. Zur Entwicklung der Gruppen -KY- und -TY-. VR 16.272–76.
——. 1962. Zur Aussprache von lat. /ā/ und /ā/. Glotta 40.147–50.
——. 1970. Les résultats de /-i/ latin en espagnol ancien et moderne. In Phonétique et linguistique romanes. Mélanges offerts à Georges Straka. Lyon-Strasbourg: Société de Linguistique Romane, 1.52–56.

McClelland, Peter. 1975. Causal explanation and model building in history, economics, and the new economic history. Ithaca: Cornell University Press.
Madrid, Ayuntamiento. 1963. El fuero de Madrid. Madrid: Raycar.
Magis, Carlos H., ed. 1970. Actas del Tercer Congreso Internacional de Hispanistas. México: El Colegio de México.
Maher, J. Peter. 1973. Review of Stockwell and Macaulay 1972. Language Sciences No. 25.47–52.
——, Allan R. Bomhard, and E. F. Konrad Koerner, eds. 1982. Papers from the 3rd International Conference on Historical Linguistics. Amsterdam: John Benjamins B.V.
Malécot, André and Paul M. Lloyd. 1968. The /t/:/d/ distinction in American alveolar flaps. Lingua 19.264–72.
Malkiel, Yakov. 1945. Old Spanish nadi(e), otri(e). HR 13.204–30.
——. 1948. Hispanic algu(i)en and related formations. A study of the stratification of the Romance lexicon in the Iberian Peninsula. UCPL 1.357–442.
——. 1949. The contrast tomáis-tomávades, queréis-queríades in Classical Spanish. HR 17.159–65.
——. 1951. Lexical polarization in Romance. Lang. 27.485–518.
——. 1952. Los derivados hispánicos de TEPIDUS. Romania 74.145–76.
——. 1953–54. Language history and historical linguistics. RPh 7.65–76.
——. 1954. La f inicial adventicia en español antiguo (femencia, finchar, fenchir, fallar, finojo). RLiR 18.61–91.
——. 1959. The Luso-Hispanic descendants of POTIŌ. Frank Pierce, ed. Hispanic studies in honour of Ignacio González-Llubera. Oxford: Dolphin Book Co., 193–210.
——. 1960. Paradigmatic resistance to sound change. Lang. 36.281–346.
——. 1962. Weak phonetic change, spontaneous sound shift, lexical contamination. Lingua 11.263–75.
——. 1962–63. Towards a unified system of classification of Latin-Spanish vowel correspondences. RPh 16.153–69.
——. 1963. The interlocking of narrow sound change, broad phonological pattern, level of transmission, areal configuration, sound symbolism. Diachronic studies in the Hispano-Latin consonant clusters. ArL 15.144–73; 16 (1964) 1–33.
——. 1964. Initial points versus initial segments of linguistic trajectories. Horace G. Lunt, ed. Proceedings of the Ninth International Congress of Linguists. Cambridge, Mass., Aug. 27–31, 1962. The Hague: Mouton, 402–05.

——. 1966. Diphthongization, monophthongization, metaphony. Studies in their interaction in the paradigm of the Old Spanish -IR verbs. Lang. 42.430–72.
——. 1967. Multiple versus simple causation in linguistic change. To honor Roman Jakobson. The Hague: Mouton, 2.1228–46.
——. 1967a. Each word has a history of its own. Glossa 1.137–49.
——. 1967–68. Range of variation as a clue to dating. I. RPh 21.463–501.
——. 1968. The inflectional paradigm as an occasional determinant of sound change. Lehmann and Malkiel 1968, 21–64.
——. 1968a. Deux problèmes de linguistique générale illustrés par le parfait fort de l'ancien hispano-roman. Mélanges offerts à Rita Lejeune. Gembloux: Eds. J. Duculot, 471–83.
——. 1969. Morphological analogy as a stimulus for sound change. Lingua e Stile 4.305–27.
——. 1969–70. Sound changes rooted in morphological conditions: The case of Old Spanish /sk/ changing to /θk/. RPh 23.188–200.
——. 1970. Le nivellement morphologique comme point de depart d'une loi phonétique. La monophtongaison occasionnelle de *ie* et *ue* en ancien espagnol. Mélanges de langue et de littérature du Moyen Age et de la Renaissance offerts a Jean Frappier par ses collegues, ses élèves et ses amis. Geneva: Droz, 2.701–35.
——. 1971–72. Derivational transparency as an occasional co- determinant of sound change: A new causal ingredient in the distribution of -c- and -z- in ancient Hispano-Romance (I). RPh 25.1–52.
——. 1973. Etiological studies in Romance diachronic phonology. Acta Linguistica Hafniensia 14.201–42.
——. 1973–74. New problems in Romance interfixation (1): The velar insert in the present tense (with an excursus on -zer/-zir verbs.) RPh 27.304–55.
——. 1975–76. From falling to rising diphthongs: The case of Old Spanish *io* < *eu* (with excursuses on the weak preterite, on the possessives, and on *judío, sandío*, and *romero*). RPh 29.435–500.
——. 1976. Multi-conditioned sound change and the impact of morphology on phonology. Lang. 52.757–78.
——. 1976a. In search of 'penultimate' causes of language change: Studies in the avoidance of /z/ in Proto-Spanish. Fritz G. Hensey and Marta Luján, eds. Current studies in Romance linguistics. Washington: Georgetown University Press.
——. 1976–77. Contacts between BLASPHEMĀRE and AESTIMĀRE. RPh 30.102–17.
——. 1977. On hierarchizing the components of multiple causation. Studies in Language 1.81–108.
——. 1977–78. Old Spanish FAR, FER, FAZER. RPh 31.257–62.
——. 1980. Etymology as a challenge to phonology: The case of Romance linguistics. Manfred Mayrhofer, Martin Peters, and Oskar E. Pfeiffer, eds. Lautgeschichte und Etymologie. Akten der VI. Fachtagung der Indogermanischen Gesellschaft Wien, 24–29 September 1978. Wiesbaden: Reichert, 260–86.
——. 1980–81. Points of abutment of morphology on phonology: The case of archaic Spanish *esti(e)do* 'stood'. RPh 34.206–09.
——. 1981. Drift, slope, and slant: Background of, and variations upon, a Sapirian theme. Lang. 57.535–70.
——. 1982. Interplay of sounds and forms in the shaping of three Old Spanish medial consonant clusters. HR 50.247–66.
——. 1982a. Between monogenesis and polygenesis. In Maher et al. 1982, 235–72.
——. 1983. Alternatives to the classic dichotomy family tree/wave theory? The Romance evidence. Irmengard Rauch and Gerald F. Carr, eds. Language change. Bloomington: Indiana University Press, 192–256.
——. 1984. Old Spanish resistance to diphthongization? Lang. 60.70–114.
——. 1984a. Spanish diphthongization and accentual structure in diachronic perspective. Diachronica 1.217–41.
——. 1984b. The development of three Late Latin consonant clusters in Old Spanish and Old Portuguese: *ardeō, *perdiō, hordeolu, vir(i)dia; grundiō, irā-, vērēcundia; audiō, gaudiō.* Neuphilologische Mitteilungen 85.7–18.
——. 1985. El desarrollo de PERTICA en español, a la luz de una "ley fonética" desconocida. Revue Romane 20.36–45.
Malmberg, Bertil. 1958. Le passage castillan *f* > *h* —perte d'un trait redondant? Cercetări de lingvistică 3.337–43; also in Phonétique générale et romane. The Hague, Paris: Mouton, 1971, 459–63.

——. 1959. Review of Martinet 1955. StN 31.298–306.
——. 1961. Linguistique ibérique et ibéro-romane. Problèmes et méthodes. StL 15.57–113.
——. 1962. La notion de force et les changements phonétiques. StL 16.38–44; reprinted in Spanish in Malmberg 1965.
——. 1963. Encore une fois le substrat. StL 17.40–46.
——. 1963a. Gémination, force et structure syllabique en latin et en roman. Etudes romanes dédiées à Andreas Blinkenberg à l'occassion [sic] de son soixante-dixième anniversaire. Copenhagen: Munksgaard, 106–12; reprinted in Spanish in Malmberg 1965.
——. 1964. Tradición hispánica e influencia indígena en la fonética hispano-americana. Presente y futuro de la lengua española: Actas de la Asamblea de Filología del I Congreso de Instituciones Hispánicas. Madrid: C.S.I.C., 2.227–43; reprinted in Malmberg 1965.
——. 1965. Estudios de fonética hispánica. Madrid: C.S.I.C.
——. 1967. Structural linguistics and human communication. 2nd ed. revised. Berlin, Heidelberg, New York: Springer.
——. 1971. Note sur l'articulation du [s] et le traitement de l'affriquée [ts] en roman occidental. Phonétique générale et romane. The Hague: Mouton, 349–52.
Mańczak, Witold. 1965. Développement phonétique irrégulier et fréquence d'emploi en français. Congr ILPR X 3.911–23.
——. 1969. Le développement phonétique des langues romanes et la fréquence. (Zeszyty Naukowe Uniwersytetu Jagiellonskiego CCV. Prace Jezykoznawcze, Zeszyt 24.) Krakow: Nakadem Uniwersytetu Jagiellonskiego.
——. 1970. Evolution phonétique et 'rendement fonctionnel.' RRL 15.531–37.
——. 1974. Métaphonie devant U dans les langues romanes. Kwartalnik Neofilologiczny 21.343–53.
——. 1976. Espagnol classique "tomáis, queréis" mais "tomávedes, queríades". Kwartalnik Neofilologiczny 23.181–86.
Maniet, Albert. 1975. La phonétique historique du latin dans le cadre des langues indo-européennes. 5e edition, augmentée et corrigée. Paris: Klincksieck.
Mariner, Sebastián. 1957. Valor fonemático de los diptongos del latín clásico. Helmantica 8.17–30.
——. 1958. Caracterización funcional de los fonemas del latín clásico. Emerita 26.227–33.
Martinet, André. 1950. Some problems of Italic consonantism. Word 6.26–41.
——. 1951. Review of Wartburg 1950. Word 7.73–76.
——. 1951–52. The unvoicing of Old Spanish sibilants. RPh 5.133–56.
——. 1952. Function, structure, and sound change. Word 8.1–32.
——. 1952a. Celtic lenition and western Romance consonants. Lang. 28.192–217; also in Martinet 1955.
——. 1955. Economie des changements phonétiques. Berne: Francke.
——. 1965. Les problèmes de la phonétique évolutive. Proceedings of the Fifth International Congress of Phonetic Sciences. Basel - New York, 82–104.
Martínez Álvarez, Josefina. 1976. Acerca de la palatalización de /s/ en español. Estudios ofrecidos a Emilio Alarcos Llorach (con motivo de sus XXV años de docencia en la Universidad de Oviedo). Oviedo: Servicio de Publicaciones de la Universidad de Oviedo, 1.221–36.
Mattausch, Josef. 1965. Untersuchungen zur Wortstellung in der Prosa des Jungen Goethe. Berlin: Akademie-Verlag.
Matthews, P. H. 1974. Morphology: An introduction to the theory of word structure. Cambridge: Cambridge University Press.
Maurer, F. 1932. Die Sprache Goethes im Rahmen seiner menschlichen und Künstlerischen Entwicklung. Erlangen: Palm und Ecke.
Maurer, Theodoro Henrique, Jr. 1959. Gramática do latim vulgar. Rio de Janeiro: Livraria Academica.
Meadows, Gail Keith. 1948. The development of Latin hiatus groups in the Romance languages. PMLA 63.765–84.
Meier, Harri. 1970–71. La ƒ- etimológica en el español antiguo. ASNS 207.439–46.
Menéndez Pidal, Ramón. 1910. Review of Eric Staaff. Etude sur l'ancien dialecte léonais. Upsala: Almqvist et Wiksel, 1907. Revue de Dialectologie Romane 2.119–30.
——. 1918. Sobre las vocales ibéricas ę y ǫ en los nombres toponímicos. RFE 5.227–55.
——. 1941. Manual de gramática histórica española. 6a edición. Madrid: Espasa-Calpe.
——. 1944. Cantar de mío Cid. Texto, gramática, y vocabulario. 2a ed. Madrid: Espasa-Calpe.
——. 1944a. La unidad del idioma. Madrid: Instituto Nacional del Libro Español.

——. 1950. Modo de obrar el sustrato lingüístico. RFE 34.1–8.

——. 1954. A propósito de *l* y *ll* latinas. Colonización suditálica en España. BRAE 34.165–216.

——. 1960. Repoblación y tradición en la cuenca del Duero. ELH l.xxv–lvii.

——. 1962. Sevilla frente a Madrid. Algunas precisiones sobre el español de América. Catalán 1962, 99–165.

——. 1963. El estado latente en la vida tradicional. Revista de Occidente (2a Epoca). Mayo, 129–52.

Meyer-Lübke, Wilhelm. 1895. Grammaire des langues romanes. Vol. 2: Morphologie. Traduction française par Auguste Doutrepont et Georges Doutrepont. Paris: H. Welter.

——. 1921. La evolución de la *c* latina delante de *e* e *i* en la península ibérica. RFE 8.225–51.

——. 1936. Zur Geschichte von lat. *Ge, Gi* und *J* im Romanischen. VR 1.1–31.

Meyerstein, R. S. 1970. Functional load. Descriptive limitations, alternatives of assessment, and extensions of application. The Hague, Paris: Mouton.

Michel, Louis. 1953. Etude du son "s" en latin et en roman. Des origines aux langues romanes de la phonétique au style. Paris: Presses Universitaires de France.

Michelena, Luis. 1957. Las antiguas consonantes vascas. Catalán 1957b, 113–58.

——. 1964. Románico y circunrománico sobre la suerte de latin 'ae.' Archivum 14.40–60.

——. 1968. Lat. s: el testimonio vasco. Cong ILPR Xl 2.473–89.

——. 1975. Distribución defectiva y evolución fonológica. Studia hispanica in honorem R. Lapesa. Madrid: Gredos, 337–49.

Mignot, Xavier. 1975. Phonologie pragoise et phonologie générative dans la description du latin. BSLP 70.203–31.

——. 1978. Homonymies entre les désinences casuelles du latin. Langages 50.45–50.

Mihăescu, H. 1960. Limba latină in provinciile dunărene ale imperiului roman. Bucharest: Academiei Republicii Populare Romîne.

Mikesell, Marvin W. 1968. Comparative studies in frontier history. Richard Hofstadter and Seymour M. Lipset, eds. Turner and the sociology of the frontier. New York: Basic Books, 152–71.

Molho, Maurice. 1969. Essai dur la sémiologie des verbes d'existence en espagnol. In Linguistiques et langage.Bordeaux: Editions Ducros, 57–99.

Montes, Giraldo, José Joaquín. 1969. ¿Desaparece la *ll* de la pronunciación bogotana? Thesaurus 24.102–04.

Montgomery, Thomas. 1975. La apócope en español antiguo y la *i* final latina. Studia hispanica in honorem R. Lapesa. Madrid: Cátedra- Seminario Menéndez Pidal, 351–61.

——. 1975–76. Complementarity of stem-vowels in the Spanish second and third conjugations. RPh 29.281–96.

——. 1978. Iconicity and lexical retention in Spanish: Stative and dynamic verbs. Lang. 54.907–16.

——. 1979. Sound symbolism and aspect in the Spanish second conjugation. HR 47.219–37.

——. 1983. *(Tú) eres*: A neologism. HR 51.249–54.

Mourin, Louis. 1974. Rejets et analogies dans la structuration des radicaux des parfaits irréguliers romans. RRL 19.191–217.

——. 1976. Restructuration en Latin vulgaire des rapports entre parfaits et participes passés irréguliers. RRL 21.461.67.

Muljačić, Žarko. 1965. Per un analisi binaristica dei fonemi latini. Omagiu Rosetti 1965, 599–605; in Strunk 1973.

Müller, Bodo. 1963. Spanisch *soy, estoy, doy, voy* im Licht der romanischen Endungsbildung mit flexionsfremden Elementen. RF 75.240–63.

Muller, Henri F. 1951. Review of P. Groult, La formation des langues romanes. Tournay, Paris. Word 7.76–79.

Nandriş, Octave. 1952. Les palatalisations romanes (origines, facteurs, problèmes et aspects). Orbis 1.136–45.

——. 1963. Phonétique historique du roumain. (Bibliothèque française et romane. Serie A:5.) Paris: C. Klincksieck.

——. 1965. Le problème de *l* (*ll*) en latin et dans les langues romanes. Congr ILPR X. 3.925–43.

——. 1970. La palatalisation romane et le problème de ses origines. Mélanges de linguistique et de philologie romanes dédiés à la mémoire de Pierre Fouché (1891–1967). Paris: Klincksieck, 1–15.

Narasimhia, A. N. 1941. A grammar of the oldest Kanarese inscriptions. Mysore: University of Mysore.

Naro, Anthony. 1972. On 'f > h' in Castilian and western Romance. ZRPh 88.435–47.

Navarro Tomás, Tomás. 1952. Manual de pronunciación española. 5a edición corregida. New York: Hafner Publishing Co.

——. 1964. Nuevos datos sobre el yeísmo en Espara. Thesaurus 19.1–17; also in Capítulos de geografía lingüística de la península ibérica. (Publicaciones del Instituto Caro y Cuervo, 35.) Bogotá.

——, Aurelio M. Espinosa (hijo), and L. Rodríguez-Castellano. 1933. La frontera del andaluz. RFE 20.225–277.

Nelson, Dana A. 1972–73. The domain of the old Spanish -er and -ir verbs: A clue to the provenience of the Alexandre. RPh 26.265–305.

Nève de Mévergnies, François-Xavier. 1976. Note sur la chronologie des palatalisations romanes. VR 35.12–21.

Nevins, Allan. 1938. The gateway to history. Boston: D. C. Heath.

Niedermann, Max. 1926. Zur Beurteilung der r-Epenthese im Romanischen. Festschrift Louis Gauchat. Aarau: H. R. Sauerländer, 40–51.

——. 1953. Phonétique historique du latin. 3rd ed. Heidelberg: C. Winter.

Nielsen, Niels Age. 1952. La théorie des substrats et la linguistique structurale. Acta Linguistica 7.1–7.

O'Brien, Richard J., ed. 1968. Georgetown University Round Table. Selected Papers on Linguistics 1961–1965. Washington, D. C.: Georgetown University Press.

Olson, David R. 1977. The formalization of linguistic rules. John T. MacNamara, ed. Language learning and thought. New York: Academic Press, 111–16.

Omagiu lui Alexandru Rosetti la 70 de ani. 1965. Bucharest: Editura Academiei Republicii Socialiste Romanie.

Omeltchenko, Stephen W. 1971. A quantitative and comparative study of the vocalism of the Latin inscriptions of North Africa, Britain, Dalmatia, and the Balkans. PhD Dissertation Columbia University.

Orbán, A. P. 1972. Die Frage der akkusativ- oder Nominativ form sing. als Herkunft der romanischen Substantive und die sächlichen Imparisyllaba der dritten Deklination. RRL 17.521–29.

Orr, John. 1936. F > H phenomène ibère ou roman? RLiR 12.10–35.

Otero, Carlos-Peregrín. 1971. Evolución y revolución en romance. Mínima introducción a la fonología. Barcelona: Seix Barral.

Palau Marti, Ferran. 1969. Sur la notion de rendement fonctionnel des oppositions phonologiques. StL 22.15–32.

Palmer, L. R. 1954. The Latin language. London: Faber and Faber.

Pariente Herrejón, Angel. 1969. El problema de la forma eres. Revista de la Universidad de Madrid 18.281–97.

Parodi de Teresa, Claudia. 1976. Para el conocimiento de la fonética castellana en la Nueva España: 1523. Las sibilantes. Actas del III Congreso de la Asociación de Lingüística y Filología de la América Latina. San Juan: Universidad de Puerto Rico, 115–25.

——. 1977. El yeísmo en América durante el siglo XVI. Anuario de Letras 15.241–48.

Pascucci, Giovanni 1966. A proposito di muta cum liquida. Studi Italiani di Filologia Classica 38.41–62.

Passy, Paul. 1892. Etude sur les changements phonétiques et leurs caractères généraux. (Separatabdruck aus dem Literaturblatt für germanische und romanische Philologie, No. 9.)

Paufler, Hans-Dieter. 1970. Die territoriale Ausgliederung des 'yeísmo' in Lateinamerika in deskriptiven Sicht. BRP 9.118–24.

Penny, Ralph J. 1972. Verb-class as a determiner of stem vowel in the historical morphology of Spanish verbs. RLiR 36.343–59.

——. 1972a. The re-emergence of /f/ as a phoneme of Castilian. ZRPh 88.463–82.

——. 1976. The convergence of B, V and -P- in the peninsula: A reappraisal. A.D. Deyermond, ed. Medieval hispanic studies presented to Rita Hamilton. London: Tamesis Books, 149–59.

——. 1979–80. Do Romance nouns descend from the Latin accusative? Preliminaries to a reassessment of the noun-morphology of Romance. RPh 33.501–09.

——. 1983. Secondary consonant groups in Castilian. Journal of Hispanic Philology 7.135–40.

Pensado Ruiz, Carmen. 1984. Cronología relativa del castellano. Salamanca: Ediciones Universidad de Salamanca.

Pérez de Urbel, Fr. Justo. 1969. El condado de Castilla. Los 300 años en que se hizo Castilla. Vol. 1. Madrid: Editorial Siglo Ilustrado.

Perini, Giorgio Bernardi. 1974. Due problemi di fonetica latina. I. Muta cum liquida; II. S finale. Roma: Edizioni dell'Ateneo.

Petrovici, Emil. 1958. Le roumain a-t-il hérité du roman commun la corrélation palatale des consonnes? Revue de Linguistique 3.5–11.

Pighi, Giovanni B. 1951. Les formes du latin dit «vulgaire». Actes du Premier Congrès de la Fédération Internationale des Associations d'Etudes Classiques. Paris: C. Klincksieck, 199–206; in Italian as Il latino così detto volgare. Convivium (1951) No. 1.103–12.

Pisani, Vittorio. 1954. Palatalizzazione osche e latine. AGI 39.112–19.

——. 1981. Il grupo latino ps nelle lingue romanze. Paideia 36.58–60.

Politzer, Robert L. 1952. On b and v in Latin and Romance. Word 8.211–215.

——. 1954. On the development of Latin stops in Aragonese. Word 10.60–65.

——. 1959. A note on the distribution of prothesis in Late Latin. MLN 74.31–36.

Pope, M. K. 1934. From Latin to Modern French with especial consideration of Anglo-Norman. Phonology and Morphology. Manchester: Manchester University Press.

Poppe, Nicholas. 1955. Introduction to Mongolian comparative studies. (Mémoires de la Société Finno-Ougrienne, 110.) Helsinki: Suomalais-Ugrilainen Seura.

Porzio Gernia, Maria Luisa. 1976. Tendenze strutturali della sillaba latina in età arcaica e classica. Scritti in onore di G. Bonfante. Brescia: Paideia Editrice, 757–79.

——. 1978. Per una definizione del latino ae: Grafemi, sistemi, interferenza linguistica. AGI 63.35–77.

Posner, Rebecca. 1961. Consonantal dissimilation in the Romance languages. Oxford: Basil Blackwell.

——. 1961. The imperfect endings in Romance. TPS, 17–55.

——. 1963–64. Phonology and analogy in the formation of the Romance perfect. RPh 17.419–31.

——. 1965. Romance imperfect and conditional endings—a further contribution. StN 37.1–10.

——. 1966–67. Positivism in historical linguistics. RPh 20.321–31; reprinted in Anderson and Creore 1972, 38–51.

——. 1979. Chronologie de la palatalisation romane. Congr ILPR XIV. 3.35–52.

Postal, Paul. 1968. Aspects of phonological theory. New York: Harper and Row.

Posti, Lauri. 1965. Kann Lautwandel durch fremden Einfluss verursacht werden? Studia Fennica 12.74–85.

Pottier, Bernard. 1968. Forma española soy. In Lingüística moderna y filología española. Madrid: Gredos, 211–13.

Prinz, Otto. 1937. Zur Entstehung der Prothese vor s- impurum in Lateinischen. Glotta 26.97–115.

Pulgram, Ernst. 1949. Prehistory and the Italian dialects. Lang. 25.241–52.

——. 1954. Accent and ictus in spoken and written Latin. Zeitschrift für Vergleichende Sprachforschung 71.218–37.

——. 1955. Neogrammarians and sound laws. Orbis 4.61–65.

——. 1957. Linguistic expansion and diversification. Ernst Pulgram, ed. Studies presented to Joshua Whatmough on his sixtieth birthday. The Hague: Mouton.

——. 1965. The accentuation of Greek loans in spoken and written Latin. AJPh 86.138–58.

——. 1970. Syllable, word, nexus, cursus. The Hague: Mouton.

——. 1975. Latin-Romance phonology: Prosodics and metrics. Munich: Wilhelm Fink.

——. 1979. The voiceless bilabial spirant in Indo-European. Bela Brogyanyi, ed. Festschrift for Oswald Szemerényi on the occasion of his 65th birthday. (Amsterdam Studies in the Theory and History of Linguistic Science, IV. Current Issues in Linguistic Theory, Vol. 11.) Amsterdam: John Benjamins, 691–704.

Purczinsky, Julius. 1969–70. A neo-Schuchardtian theory of general Romance diphthongization. RPh 23.J92–528.

Quilis, Antonio, and Juan M. Rozas. 1963. Para la cronología de la fricativa, velar, sorda, /x/, en castellano. RFE 46.445–49.

Reighard, John. 1974. Variable rules in historical linguistics. Anderson and Jones 1974, 1.251–62.

Reinheimer-Rîpeanu, Sanda. 1979. Variante palatale și variante africate de la latină la limbile romanice. StCL 30.73–88.

Richman, Stephen H. 1967. A quantitative analysis of Romance words. StL 20.86–98.

Richter, Elise. 1934. Beiträge zur Geschichte der Romanismen. (ZRPh, Beiheft 82.) Halle.

Risch, Ernst. 1976. Frühe Palatalisation von K ^{e,i} und G ^{e,i} im Lateinischen? VR 35.22–23.

Rivers, Wilga M. 1971. Linguistic and psychological factors in speech perception and their implications for teaching materials. Paul Pimsleur and Terence Quinn, eds. The psychology of second language learning. London: Cambridge University Press, 123–34.

Rix, Helmut. 1966. Die lateinische synkope als historisches und phonologisches Problem. Kratylos 11.156–65; Strunk 1973, 90–102.

Rodríguez Adrados, Francisco. 1969. Fonologia, «ley fonética» y sonantes indoeuropeos. Estudios de lingüística general. Barcelona: Editorial Planeta, 173–206.

Rodríguez de Mora, María del Carmen. 1971. Lorenzo Hervás y Panduro. Su aportación a la filología española. Madrid: Partenón.

Rohlfs, Gerhard. 1955. Vorrömische Lautsubstrate auf der Pyrenäenhalbinsel? ZRPh 71.408–13.

——. 1955a. Oskische Latinität in Spanien? RLiR 71.408–13.

——. 1966. Grammatica storica della lingua italiana e dei suoi dialetti. Traduzione di Salvatore Persichino. I. Fonetica. Torino: Giulio Einaudi.

——. 1970. Le gascon. Etudes de philologie pyrénéene. 2e édition, entièrement refondue. (ZRPh Beiheft 85.) Tübingen: Niemeyer.

Rolfe, J. C. 1913. Suetonius with an English translation. Vol. 1. Cambridge, Mass.: Harvard University Press.

Romeo, Luigi. 1968. The economy of diphthongization in early Romance. The Hague: Mouton.

Rosoff Gary H. 1974. The phonetic framework of the universal sound correlates in Romance vowel diachrony. Linguistics 135.57–71.

Rousselot, Pierre Jean, abbé. 1892. Les modifications phonétiques du langage étudiés dans le patois d'une famille de Cellefrouin. 2e Partie: Modifications historiques de l'ancien fonds du patois. Revue des Patois Gallo-Romans 5.209–380.

Sabatini, Francesco. 1978. Lingua parlata, scripta e coscienza linguistica nelle origini romanze. Congr ILPR XIV. 1.445–53.

Safarewicz, Jan. 1950. La valeur phonologique des diphtongues latines. Eos 44.123–30.

——. 1964. Sur le développement des consonnes occlusives finales en latin. Eos 54.99–106.

——. 1965. Sur l'abrègement des voyelles en syllabes finales en latin. Omagiu Rosetti 1965, 801–03.

Samuels, M. L. 1972. Linguistic evolution. (Cambridge Studies in Linguistics, 5.) London: Cambridge University Press.

Sánchez-Albornoz, Claudio. 1951. El nombre de Castilla. EMP 2.629–41.

——. 1956. Panorama general de la romanización de Hispania. Revista de la Universidad de Buenos Aires. 5a Epoca. 1.37–74.

——. 1966. Despoblación y repoblación del Valle del Duero. Buenos Aires, Universidad de Buenos Aires.

——. 1974. Los vascos y la repoblación. Vascos y navarros en su primera historia. Madrid: Ediciones del Centro, 209–17.

Sánchez Álvarez, Mercedes. 1979. Un testimonio temprano del timbre ciceante de la «z» espanol. Congr ILPR XIV 3.179–86.

Sapir, Edward. 1921. Language. New York: Harcourt Brace.

Scalise, Sergio. 1976. Gradualità versus nongradualità nel mutamento fonetico. Lingua e Stile 11.293–312.

Schmidely, Jack. 1979. De «ge lo» a «se lo». CLHM J.63–70.

Schmidt, Gerhard. 1956. The philosophy of language. Orbis 5.164–68.

Schneider, Gisela. 1973. Zum Begriff des Lautgesetzes in der Sprachwissenschaft seit den Junggrammatiker. (Tübinger Beiträge zur Linguistik, 46.) Tübingen.

Schourup, Lawrence D. 1972. Why sound change is gradual. Working Papers in Linguistics, No. 11. (Ohio State University, Department of Linguistics), 127–35.

Schuchardt, Hugo. 1868. Der Vokalismus des Vulgärlateins. Leipzig: Teubner. Vol. 3.

Schürr, Friedrich. 1951. La diptongación ibero-románica. RDTP 7.379–90.

——. 1956. La diphtongaison romane. RLiR 20.107–44; 161–248.

——. 1959. Efeito de substrato ou selecção fonológica? BF 18.57–66.

——. 1963. La filiación románica de los diptongos iberorrománicos. RLiR 27.345–63.

——. 1964. La inflexión y la diptongación del español en comparación con las otras lenguas románicas. Presente y futuro de la lengua española. Actas de la Asamblea de Filología del I Congreso de Instituciones Hispánicas. Madrid: C.S.I.C.

——. 1969. Epilegomena a la diphtongaison romane en général, roumaine et ibéromomane en particulier. RLiR 33.17–37.

——. 1970. La diphtongaison romane. (Tübinger Beiträge zur Linguistik, 5.) Tübingen.

——. 1975. Caractères et fonctionnement de la métaphonie romane. Débarras de mirages phonétiques. RLiR 39.296–307.

Sebeok, Thomas A. ed. 1972. Linguistics in western Europe. (Current Trends in Linguistics, vol. 9.) The Hague, Paris: Mouton.

Séguy, Jean. 1954. A propos de la diphtongaison de "e" et "o" ouverts. Annales du Midi 66.307–11.

Şiadbei, T. 1958. La prothèse vocalique dans les langues romanes. Revue de Linguistique 3.153–63.

Shevelov, George Y., and John J. Chew, Jr. 1969. Open syllable languages and their evolution: Common Slavic and Japanese. Word 25.252–74.

Silvestri, Domenico. 1978. La teoria del sostrato: metodi e miraggi. Napoli: Gaetano Macchiaroli.

Skårup, Povl. 1966. Filiolum: déplacement d'accent ou synérèse? Revue Romane 1.104–09.

Sletsjøe, Leif. 1959. La prononciation de *l* et *n* en latin. Symbolae Osloenses 35.144–55.

Smelser, Neil. 1963. Theory of collective behavior. New York: Free Press of Glencoe.

Smith, Colin, ed. 1972. Poema de mio Cid. Oxford: Clarendon.

Söll, Ludwig. 1964. Der Zusammenfall von *b* und *v* und die Variation der stimmhaften Verschlusslaute im Iberoromanischen. BRP 3.80-98.

Sommer, Ferdinand. 1977. Handbuch der lateinischen Laut- und Formenlehre. 4 neubearbeitete Auflag. Heidelberg: C. Winter.

Sommerfelt, Alf. 1970. L'élément social dans les changements phonétiques et phonémiques. Mélanges Marcel Cohen. The Hague: Mouton, 137–39.

Sommerstein, Alan H. 1977. Modern phonology. Baltimore: University Park Press.

Spaulding, Robert K., and Beatrice S. Patt. 1948. Data for the chronology of "theta" and "jota". HR 16.50–60.

Spence, N. C. W. 1963. A problem of Romance accentuation. RLiR 27.449–57.

——. 1965. Quantity and quality in the vowel system of vulgar Latin. Word 21.1–18; Anderson and Creore 1972.

——. 1974. A further note on the monophthongization of Latin *ae*. TPS, 81–85.

Spore, Palle. 1972. La diphtongaison romane. Odense, Denmark: Universitets Forlag.

St. John, Jack. 1976. Latin -uit/-vit. ArL 7.60–65.

Stati, Sorin. 1964. Probleme ale consonantismului latin din secolul al II-lea e.n. StCL 15.711–26.

Steiger, Arnald. 1932. Contribución a la fonética del hispano-árabe y de los arabismos en el ibero-románico y el siciliano. (Revista de Filología Española, Anejo 17.) Madrid: Casa Editorial Hernando.

Stephens, Laurence. 1978. Universals of consonant clusters and Latin GN-. IF 83.290–300.

Stockwell, Robert P., and Ronald K. S. Macaulay, eds. 1972. Linguistic change and generative theory. Bloomington-London: Indiana University Press.

Straka, Georges. 1953. Observations sur la chronologie et les dates de quelques modifications phonétiques en roman et en français prélittéraires. RLaR 71.247–307.

——. 1959. Durée et timbre vocaliques. Observations de phonétique générale appliquées à la phonétique historique des langues romanes. ZPAS 12.276–300.

——. 1965. Naissance et disparition des consonnes palatales dans l'évolution du latin au français. TLL 3.117–67.

Strunk, Klaus, ed. 1973. Probleme der lateinischen Grammatik. Darmstadt: Wissenschaftliche Buchgesellschaft.

Sturcken, H. Tracy. 1969. Basque-Cantabrian influence on Alfonsine Spanish. StN 41.298–306.

Sturtevant, Edgar H. 1940. The pronunciation of Greek and Latin. 2nd ed. Philadelphia: Linguistic Society of America.

——. 1947. An introduction to linguistic science. New Haven: Yale University Press.

Sweet, Henry. 1900. The history of language. New York: Macmillan.

Tekavčić, Pavao, 1974. Grammatica storica dell'italiano. Vol. II Fonematica. Bologna: Società editrice il-Mulino.

Terracini, Benvenuto. 1957. Come muore una lingua. Conflitti di lingue e di cultura. Venezia: Neri Pozza Editore, 15–18.

Terry, Robert M, 1980. Open syllabification and diphthongization of /è/ and /ò/ in preliterary Spanish. Word 31.199,215.

Tesch, Gerd. 1978. Linguale Interferenz: Theoretische, terminologische und methodologische Grundfragen ihrer Erforschung. (Tübinger Beiträge zur Linguistik, 105.) Tübingen: TBL-Verlag Narr.

Timpanaro, Sebastiano. 1965. Muta cum liquida in poesia latina e nel latino volgare. Rivista di Cultura Classica e Medioevale 7.1075–1103.

Togeby, Knud. 1959–60. Les explications phonologiques historiques sont-elles possibles? RPh 13.401–13.

——. 1963–64. Qu'est-ce que la dissimilation? RPh 17.642–67.

——. 1966. Le sort du plus-que-parfait latin dans les langues romanes. CFS 23.175–84.

——. 1972–73. L'apophonie des verbes espagnols et portugais en -ir. RPh 26.256–64.

Torreblanca, Máximo. 1974. Estado actual del lleísmo y de la h- aspirada en el noroeste de la provincia de Toledo. RDTP 30.77–89.

——. 1981–82. La S hispanolatina: el testimonio árabe. RPh 35.447–63.

——. 1983–84. La "f" prerromana y la vasca en su relación con el español antiguo. RPh 37.273–81.

——. Forthcoming. Las oclusivas sordas hispanolatinas: El testimonio árabe.

Touratier, Christian. 1971. Statut phonologique de gu et de gu en latin. BSLP 66.229–66.

——. 1972. Morphophonologie du verbe latin. BSLP 67.139–74.

——. 1978. Linguistique et latin. Langages 50.3–16.

Tovar, Antonio. 1948. La sonorización y caída de las intervocálicas y los estratos indoeuropéos en Hispania. BRAE 28.265–80.

——. 1950. Pre-indoeuropeans, Pre-Celts, and Celts in the Hispanic Peninsula. Journal of Celtic Studies. 1.11–23.

——. 1951. La sonorisation et la chute des intervocaliques, phénomène latin occidental. Revue des Etudes Latines 29.102–20.

——. 1952. Sobre la cronología de la sonorización y caída de intervocálicas en la Romania occidental. Toribio M. Lucero and Alfredo Dornheim, eds. Homenaje a Fritz Krüger. Mendoza: Universidad Nacional de Cuyo, I.9–15.

——. 1958. Das keltiberische, ein neuer Zweig des Festlandkeltischen. Kratylos 3.1–14.

——. 1963. Les celtes en Bétique. Etudes Celtiques 10.354–73.

——. 1976. Estado latente en latín vulgar: ¿Cuando se inicia la diptongación de breves? Estudios ofrecidos a Emilio Alarcos Llorach. Oviedo: Servicio de Publicaciones. Universidad de Oviedo, 1.241–46.

Trudgill, Peter. 1972. Sex, covert prestige, and linguistic change in the urban British English of Norwich. Language in Society 1.179–95.

Tuttle, Edward F. 1975. The development of PL, BL, and FL in Italo-Romance: Distinctive features and geolinguistic patterns. RLiR 39.400–31.

Ulleland, Magnus. 1965. L'el ascitizio nella prima singolare del verbo soprasilvano. StN 37.305–15.

Vachek, Josef. 1965. On the internal and external determination of sound-laws. Biuletyn Polskiego Towarzystwa Jesykoscogo 23.49–57.

Väänänen, Veikko. 1966. Le latin vulgaire des inscriptions pompéiennes. 3e édition, augmentée. (Abhandlungen der Deutschen Akademie der Wissenschaften zu Berlin, Klasse für Sprachen, Literatur und Kunst, Jahrgang 1966, No. 3.) Berlin: Akademie-Verlag.

Valdés, Juan de. 1928. Diálogo de la lengua. Edición y notas por José F. Montesinos. Madrid: La Lectura.

Vendryes, J. 1925. Language. A linguistic introduction to history. Tr. by Paul Radin. New York: Knopf.

——. 1925a. Celtique et roman. RLiR 1.262–77.

Vennemann, Theo. 1978. Phonetic analogy and conceptual analogy. Baldi and Werth 1978, 258–74.

——, Terence H. Wilbur. 1972. Schuchardt, the neogrammarians, and the transformational theory of phonological change. Four essays by Hugo Schuchardt, Theo Vennemann, Terence H. Wilbur. (Linguistische Forschungen, 26.) Frankfurt: Athenäum Verlag.

Versteegh, C. H. M. 1982. Structural change and pidginization in the history of the Arabic language. In Ahlqvist 1982, 362–73.

Vidos, B. E. 1963. Manual de lingüística románica. Traducción de la edición italiana por Francisco de B. Moll. Madrid: Aguilar.

Vincent, Nigel. 197J. Analogy reconsidered. Anderson and Jones 1974, 2.427–45.

Viudas Camarasa, Antonio. 1979. Sobre la evolución de PL- a PLL- y CL- a CLL- en aragonés antiguo. Anuario de Estudios Filológicos 2.355–75.

Vogt, Hans. 1954. Contact of languages. Word 10.365–74.

Voronkova, G. V., and Mi. I. Steblin-Kamenskij. 1975. The phoneme—a bundle of DF? Linguistics 146.73–89.

Wagner, Max Leopold. 1941. Historische Lautlehre des Sardischen. Halle: Max Niemeyer.

Walker, Douglas C. 1975. Competing analyses of the Vulgar Latin vowel system. Canadian Journal of Linguistics 20.1–22.

Wallace, W. A. 1972. Causality and scientific explanation. Ann Arbor: University of Michigan Press.

Walsh, Thomas J. 1985. The historical origin of syllable-final aspirated /s/ in dialectal Spanish. Journal of Hispanic Philology 9.231–46.

Wang, William S.-Y. 1969. Competing changes as a cause of residue. Lang. 45.9–25.

Ward, Ralph L. 1944. Afterthoughts on g as n in Latin and Greek. Lang. 20.73–77.

——. 1951. Stop plus liquid and the position of the Latin accent. Lang. 27.477–84.

Wartburg, Walther von. 1950. Die Ausgliederung der romanischen Sprachräume. (Bibliotheca Romanica, Series prima VIII.) Berne: Francke.

Weerenback, B.H.J. 1930. Remarques sur l'ancienne diphthongaison des voyelles latines e et o dans les langues romanes. Neoph. 15.161–78.

Weinreich, Uriel. 1953. Languages in contact. New York: Linguistic Circle of New York.

——, William Labov, and Marvin I. Herzog. 1968. Empirical foundations for a theory of language change. Lehmann and Malkiel 1968, 97–195.

Weinrich, Harald. 1958. Phonologische Studien zur romanischen Sprachgeschichte. (Forschungen zur romanischen Philologie, Heft 6.) Münster Westfalen: Aschendorff.

——. 1959. Phonemkollisionen und phonologisches Bewusztsein. Phonetica 4.45–58.

Wheeler, Benjamin Ide. 1887. Analogy and the scope of its application in language. (Cornell University Studies in Classical Philology. No. 2.) Ithaca. Cornell University Press.

Whitney, William D. 1875/1979. The life and growth of language. New York: Dover.

Wilbur, Terence H, ed. 1977. The Lautgesetz-controversy: A documentation. (Amsterdam Studies in the Theory and History of Linguistic Science, Vol. 9.) Amsterdam: John Benjamins.

Wilkinson, Hugh E. 1967. The Latinity of Ibero-Romance. Ron. 8.1–34.

——. 1969. The Vulgar Latin conjugation system. Ron. 10.81–121.

——. 1971. Vowel alternation in the Spanish -IR verbs. Ron. 12.1–21.

——. 1973. The strong perfects in the Romance languages (Part I). Ron. 16.157–94.

——. 1974. The strong perfects in the Romance languages (Part II). Ron. 15.23–44.

——. 1975. The strong perfects in the Romance languages (Part III). Ron. 16.15–31.

——. 1976. Notes on the development of -KJ- and -TJ- in Spanish and Portuguese. Ron. 17.19–36.

——. 1977. Notes on Spanish -I0 < -EU and the weak preterite ending. Ron. 18.21–34.

——. 1978. Palatal vs. velar in the stem of the Romance present (I). Ron. 19.19–35.

——. 1979. Palatal vs. velar in the stem of the Romance present (II). Ron. 20.19–35.

——. 1980. Palatal vs. velar in the stem of the Romance present (III). Ron. 21.V1–62.

Williams, Edwin B. 1962. From Latin to Portuguese. Historical phonology and morphology of the Portuguese language. 2nd edition. Philadelphia: University of Pennsylvania Press.

Wright, Roger. 1976. Semicultismo. ArL 7.13–28.

——. 1976a. Speaking, reading and writing Late Latin and early Romance. Neoph. 60.178–89.

——. 1976b. Pretonic diphthongs in Old Castilian. VR 35.133–43.

——. 1982. Late Latin and early Romance in Spain and Carolingian France. Liverpool: Francis Cairns.

——. To appear. El concilio de Burgos de 1080 y sus consecuencias lingüísticas. Congr ILPR XVI.

Zamora Vicente, Alonso. 1967. Dialectología española. 2a edicion muy aumentada. Madrid: Gredos.

Zimmerman, A. 1904. Die Personennamen auf *-utus, -utius*. ALLG 13.130–33.

Zipf, George K. 1965. The psychobiology of language: An introduction to dynamic philology. Cambridge, Mass.: M.I.T. Press. (First ed. 1935)

——, and Francis M. Rogers. 1939. Phonemes and variphones in four present-day Romance languages and Classical Latin from the viewpoint of dynamic philology. Archives Néerlandaises de Phonétique Expérimentale 15.109–47.

Zirin, Ronald A. 1970. The phonological basis of Latin prosody. The Hague: Mouton.

WORD AND MORPHEME INDEX

DERECTU, 194
derelinquid, 281
-dero, 319
des, 359
-des, 281, 358
descanso, 349
descend, 315
DESCENDERE, -*DEDĪ, 169, -E, 315
descir, 291
deseo, 196
DĒSIDIA, 196
DĒSIDIU, 196
desmallo, -ayo, 346
(d)esnudo, 233, 235
desnúo, 233, 233
desnuyo, 235
despiciad, 281
despierto, 314
despiso, 305, 364
destroir, 297, 354, 365
DESTRUERE, 297
destruigo, 354
destruxe, 365
DESTRŪXIT, 305
destruxo, 305, 364
destruyo, 297, 354
destruyó, 364
destruyo, -es, -e, -n, 297
DETESTOR, 148
deteudo (Port.), 368
detto (It.), 314
deuant, 212
deuda, 347
deuisa, 238
DEUNX, 84
DEUS, 191, 275
deus (Port.), 192
devo, 161
devono (It.), 161
DEXTER, 64
de-x, -z (Port.), 349
dezir, 257, 258, 267, 270, 283, 286,
    287, 291, 293, 312, 365, -imos,
    -ides, 293
di, -ste(s), etc., 302
día, 191
*DIA, 156
diabaúlus (Goth.), 151
DIABOLUS, 133, 151
Diaç, 267
diçen, 329
DĪCERE, 257, 283, 285, 314
diçie, 329
DĪCŌ, 295, -UNT, 228, 77, 101, 103,
    163, -IS, -IT, 295

DICTU, 314
dicho, 314
DIDACUS, 120
DIDŌ, 36
DIĒBUS, 133
dieciséis, 349
diemos, -stes, -ron 302, 306
Diego, 120
DIĒS, 63, 156, 191
diesen, 329
diestro, 64
diey, 302
digestir, 342
DIGITU, 248
dignificar, 351
digno, 351
digo, 258, 293, 295, 296, 353, 358
digunt, 228
dinificar, 351
dino, 351
DIOMEDIS, 133
DIONISIUS, 133
diós, 192, 275
díos, 320
dirá, 312
DIRECTUS, 194
direito (Port.), 194
DISCĒDERE, 233, 291
disen, 341
disensiones, 341
disistir, 342
DISPENDIT, 305
DITŌ, 36
dive, 58, 59, 60
dívida (Port.), 200
divulgar, 359
divulgue(d)es, 359
dixe, 254, -o, 253, 305, 365
DĪXĪ, 253, -T, 101, 305
diz(e) que, 322
diz, 322, -e, -s, 293, 295
dizer (Port.), 287
dizir, 286,
diziembre, 259
dizimelo, 286
dizque, 322
dizré, 312
do, 298, 355
do(y), 355
DŌ (DARE), 192
doblar, 231
doblegar, 201
doce (Sp., Port.), 183
DŌCĒRE, 98, 103
dodzi, 333

miede, -an, 293
miedo, 1
miel, 317
mieo (Leon.), 279
miércoles, 63, 276
mierlo, 317
miesse, 352
MIHI, MĪ, 92, 107, 157, 278
milagro, 8, 28, 348
millones, 346
MINACIA, 261
MINIM- *-ĀRE, 204
minto (Port.), 163, 292
mío, 193, 279, -a, 353, mió, 192, 279, 353
miona (Leon.), 233
MĪRĀCULU, 7, 348
miraglo, 7, 8, 28, 348
mirallas, 346
mirar, 290
MIRĀRĪ, 290
mirayas, 346
mirl-o, -a, 317
MĪSĪ, -T (MITTERE), 110, 305
miso, 305, 310, 364
*MĪSSĪ, 110
MITTERE, 110, 242, 284
miyones, 346
*MŌ-BILE, 200
moara (Rum.), 123
moarte (Rum.), 123
MOBILE, 316
moço, 250
MODIU, 196
MODŌ, 107
mogino, 343
mohar, 343
moillier (OFr.), 121
MOIROS, 77
moitié (Fr.)
MOLA, 122, 123
moler, -ldrié, 312, -ido, 313
MOLERE, 284
MOLLESCERE, 161
MOLLĪRE, 162
MOLLIS, 161
MOLLITUS EST, 162
MOLŌ, -ERE, 102
MOLUĪ, 102
MOMORDĪ (MORDĒRE), 168
mondo (It.), 29
MONĒTA, 88
Montoto, 25
Moratín, 277
morcillo, -iello, 316

morder, 282
MORDĒRE, 168, 282
MORĪ, -ĪRĪ, 104, 161, 282, 314
morir, 161, 282, 287
*MORIT, 282
moro, 189
morrer (Port.), 287
MORSĪ (MORDĒRE), 101, 168
mort (Fr.), 134
MORT(U)U, 134, 314
MORTE, 122, 123
morte (It.), 122
-mos, 281
mouse, 62
mouyda, 313
mouth (verb; subst.), 40
MOVEŌ, 100
mover, -rá, 311, -uda, 313, -ida, 313
MOVĪ, 100
moyo, 196
mᵘart (Friulian), 123
MUCCU, 72
mucho, 182, 197, 254
MŪCUS (C.L.)
mudo, 1
mudzere (Sardinian), 72
mueble, 200, 316
mueblería, 316
muela, 123
muele (Fr.), 122
muerde, 282
muere, 282
muerte, 123
muerto, 134, 314
mue(s)tra, 349
mugier, 199, 247, 254
muit, 198
muito (Port.), 197
muje, -er, 348
muku (Basque), 72
MULCEŌ, 104
MULIERE, 72, 88, 121, 199, 247
MULSUS (MULCĒRE), 104
MULTU, 182, 197, 198, 254
MUND-ICIEĪ, -ITIEĪ, 133
mundo, 66, 182, 183
MUNDU, 182
MUNEŌ, -ĒRE, 103
muola (It.), 122
muorto (It.), 134
murió, -ieron, 199
murs (OFr., Cat.), 151, 210
muru (Basque), 72
MŪRUS, 72, 77, 151, -ŌS, 210
-MUS, 55

place (Fr.), 261, 268, 333
PLACEŌ, -ĒRE, 82, 268, 294, 354
PLACITU, 205, 228
PLACUĪ, -ISTĪ, etc., 304
plaço (Port.), 294
PLAGA, 225, 226
plago (Leon.), 294
plaisir, 268
PLANCTU, 225
planda (Arag.), 329
plañer, -ir, 227, 285
PLANGERE, 163, 227, 285, 294
PLANTA, 329
PLANTĀGINE, 188
plaser, 341
plassa (Prov.), 261
PLATEA, 138, 227, 261, 268, 333
*PLATTEA, 333
PLAUSTRA, 107
PLAUTIDIUS, 106
playa, 226, 227
plazco, 294, 354
plaz(d)o, 205, 209, 228
plazer, 289, 290, 354, 365
plazo, 205
plegar, 226, 283
pleit, 211
PLĒNUS, 82, 181, 225
PLEO, -ĒRE, 101
PLĒVĪ, 101
PLICĀRE, 225, 226, 283
plogue, -o, 304, 365
plomo, 182, 264
*PLOPPU, 225
PLŌRĀRE, 82, 225, 227
PLOSTRA, 107
PLOTIDIUS, 106
plueia (OProv.), 123
PLUMBUM, 27, 82, 182, 264
PLUTEA, 261
PLUTEU, 225
PLUVIA, 123, 182, 197, 225, 264
pobre, 157
pobreza, 156
pocilca (Arag.), 229
pocilga, 229
poço (Port.), 261
poçón, poçoña, 261
poder, 289, 292, 309, 362, 365, 367,
   -edes, -és, 161, 359, -iero, 311
PODIU, 196, 247
podrir, 285
POENA, 106
poison (Fr.), 261
POLA, 106

poldro (Port.), 115,
poleo, 248
polish, 333
pómez, 276
pon, 315
pon(t) (Cat.)
Ponce, 277
pondré, 312
PŌNE, 315
poneldo, 360
poner, 61, 284, 294, 296, 312, 364, 365
ponga (Prov.), 165
pongo (Sp., It.), 165, 353
ponho, 164
PONIĀMUS, 164
PŌNŌ, -ERE, 61, 98, 102, 140, 164,
   284, 314
ponrrá, 312
pont (Fr.), 210
pon(t) (Cat.), 210
PONTE, 207, 210
pontesuela, 341
PONTIFICĀTUS, 228
PONTIĪ, 277
PONTIVACĀTUS, 228
populu (Basque), 72
PŌPULUS, 71, 72, 201, 231
POPULUS, 71, 225
*POR-, 215
Porma, 215
porrá, 312
portadgo, 205
PORTĀRE HABEŌ
PORTĀTUS FUIT, 103
portillo, 317
PORTŌ, -ASSE, -ĀTU, -ĀTUM,
   -ANS, -NTIS, -ĀTŪRUS, 102, 159,
   160
poseer (Sp., Gal.-Port.), 288, 289
POSIT, 130
POSITUS, 114, 140, 314
poso, 267
POSSE, 95, 161
possed(d)ir (Arag., Cat.), 288
posso, 267
POSTUS, 114, 140
POSUĪ, -T (PONĒRE), 102, 305, 308
*POTĒRE, 161
POTIŌNE, 261
potro, 115
POTUĪ, 7, 308
pousse-, 333, -r (Fr.), 268
poutre (Fr.), 115
poyo, 196, 247
pozo, 270

seme (Basque), 72
SĒMEN, 72
semençera
SĒMENTIA, 255
semient, 211
SĒMINĀRE, 62, 283
SĒMITA, 181, 203
sempnadura, 204
seña, 187
senado, 341
senal, -ar, 348
SENĀTUS, -ŪS, -Ī, 155, 156
senço (OPort.), 163
senda, 181, 203, 347
sendos, 256
SENERE, 161
señero, 255
SENIŌRE, 187, 247
senna, 244
sennale, 212
señor, 187, 247, 338
SENSĪ, 101
SENSU, 72, 243
SENTĪRE, 281, 292, -IŌ, -IAM,
    -IĀMUS, 199, 292, -IĒS, -IAT, *-O,
    -IS, -IT, 281, -ĪMUS, 61, 98, 101,
    162
sentar, 233
sentir, 61, 281, 292, 292, -imos, -ides,
    61
senzi(e)llo, -a, 256, 341
seo, 297
sepa, 163, 189, 264, 297
SEPARŌ, 110
*SEPPARŌ, 110
SĒPIA, 197, 264, 265, 292
sept (Fr.), 122
SEPTEM, 2, 122, 123, 207
SE(P)TEMBRE, 139
SEPTIMĀNA, 113
SEPTIMIŌ, 139
SEPTUM, 106
SEQUOR, -*ĪRE, -*ERE, 231, 291
ser, 289, 320, 358, 359, 365, -á, 357
serba, 319
serga, 265, 342
SĒRICA, 265, 342
SERŌ, -ERE, 102
serondo, 205
seroño, 205
SEROTINU, 205
SERUĪ, 78
servas, 341
SERVĪ, 78
SERV- -IĀMUS, -IĀTIS, 292, -IŌ,
    293, 318

servidó, -or, 348
servilla, 265
servir, 291
SERVĪRE, 291
SERVU, 238
seseo, 339
seso, 243
sessaenta, 248
SESSUS (SEDĒRE), 104
seta, 350
SĒTA, 106
sete (It., Rum.), 2
SETEMBRE, 139
SE(P)TIMIŌ, 139
setmana, 209
seto, 106
sette (It.), 122
SEU, 77, 191
seven, 7
SĒVĪ, 102
sevillano, 338
SEX, 198, 254
SEXAGINTA, 248
SEXTA, 318
sey, 361
seya, 297
seyer, 235
sey- -o, 235, 296, 297, -e, -emos,
    -edes, -n, 299
seyó, 234
sheep, 56
SIBI, 278
sí, 278
SICCUS, 109, 242, 333
sied- -es, -e, 299
si(e)glo, 318
sieguen, 293
siella, 317
siembra, -n, 283
siento, -es, -e, 281,
siervo, 318, -e, -a, -en, 293
siervo, 238
siesta, 318
siete, 2, 123, 207
SIGILLU, 248
siglo, 318
SIGNA, 197, 244
significar, 351
silguero, 265
silven, 348
SI-M, -S, 300
simiença, 255
sinab (Mozar.), 212
SINAPI, 212
SING- -*ELLU, 256
SINGULĀRIU, 255

INDEX